Steel Construction Manual

SCHULITZ

SOBEK

HABERMANN

BIRKHÄUSER – PUBLISHERS FOR ARCHITECTURE
BASEL · BOSTON · BERLIN

EDITION DETAIL
MÜNCHEN

The original German edition of this book was conceived and developed by
DETAIL, Review of Architecture.

Authors:

Helmut C. Schulitz
Prof. Dipl.-Ing., architect
Head of the Institute for Building Structures and Industrial Design, Braunschweig Technical University

Werner Sobek
Prof. Dr.-Ing.
Head of the Institute for Lightweight Structures, Stuttgart University

Karl J. Habermann
Dr.-Ing.
Architect and technical writer

Assistants:
Stefan Schäfer, Dipl.-Ing.; Martin Siffling, Dipl.-Ing.
Thomas Müller, Volker Rohweder, Britta Schmähring, Thies Wachter

Published by:
Institut für internationale Architektur-Dokumentation GmbH, Munich
Editorial services:
Karl J. Habermann, Dr.-Ing.; Christian Schittich, Dipl.-Ing.
Susanne Funk M.A.; Johanna Reichel-Vossen, Dipl.-Ing.
Drawings:
Marion Griese, Dipl.-Ing.

Translators (German/English):
Gerd Söffker, Philip Thrift, Hannover

A CIP catalogue record for this book is available from the Library of Congress,
Washington, D.C., USA

Deutsche Bibliothek – Cataloging-in-Publication Data

Steel construction manual / [publ. by: Institut für Internationale Architektur-Dokumentation GmbH, Munich].
Schulitz ; Sobek ; Habermann. [Transl.(German/Engl.): Gerd Söffker; Philip Thrift]. – Basel ; Boston ; Berlin : Birkhäuser;
München : Ed. Detail, 2000
Einheitsacht.: Stahlbau-Atlas <engl.>
ISBN 3-7643-6181-6

This book is also available in a German language edition.

© 2000 Birkhäuser – Publishers for Architecture, P.O. Box 133, CH-4010 Basel, Switzerland
Printed on acid-free paper produced from chlorine-free pulp. TCF ∞

Printed in Germany

ISBN 3-7643-6181-6

9 8 7 6 5 4 3 2

Contents

Preface

"Iron is the best tool in life and at the same time the worst. It gives us the power to turn the soil, plant trees, cut hedgerows and harvest the grapes; it helps us build dwellings and dress the stones. We need iron for many useful tasks. But also for war, plunder and murder. ... For when we breathe life into iron, we give Death wings."
Pliny the Elder, 1st century AD

Since it became widely available at the beginning of the 19th century, steel has had a fundamental effect on the whole evolution of architecture. Whereas the master-builders of earlier times could only employ – apart from timber – materials capable of being loaded in compression, which restricted spans quite drastically, this new material suddenly opened up a whole new vista of possibilities in terms of length of span and height of buildings.

The old building forms, which had evolved over centuries from the constraints imposed by the constructional options, lost their credibility overnight. For instance, the realization of the basilica form in iron at the turn of the century illustrates the gulf between the traditional forms and the new, as yet unexplored, possibilities. This is well demonstrated by the Notre Dame du Travail Church in Paris.

Construction technology today tempts us to aim for ever greater achievements and new building forms. The reaction to this is the growing regret that obligations which applied in the past are today no longer taken into account, often leading to a certain arbitrariness of building forms determining our urban surroundings. In engineering terms there are almost no limits to what is possible with steel in the construction sector; we can build anything – even the absurd! For architectural design this results in the problem that architects, relying on the fact that anything is feasible, leave it to the structural engineer to make the conception buildable. But the structural engineer is not usually a planner of structures, and only such a planner would work with the architect from the start to devise an intelligent solution.

The authors of this new edition of the *Steel Construction Manual* see it as their task to demonstrate the synthesis between design and construction, to formulate clearly the design obligations which arise from the material and the complete spectrum of its use from production to erection. Our task is not simply to record everything that has become routine in today's structural steelwork and present that as "standard" but rather to describe a selection of constructional forms that appear sound, above all in terms of reducing use of material and construction work to a minimum.

Right from the start of the book, the "History of steel construction", historical developments are not treated according to categories of use, as was typical in the past, but instead – for the first time and parallel with the following chapters covering the fundamentals – according to construction principles, along individual lines of evolution. Another essential aspect of the presentation of the historical sequence of events is the step-by-step approach to the current construction scene. Only in this way does historical knowledge gained from experience remain fresh and useful. A wealth of original quotations underpin the bid to achieve a high degree of authenticity. Sigfried Giedions, in his famous book *Bauen in Frankreich, Bauen in Eisen, Bauen in Eisenbeton*, published in 1928, posed a thesis which may well serve to illustrate this point ideally: "The purpose of iron is: to condense high loadbearing ability to the slimmest of dimensions. ... Iron opens up space. The wall can become a transparent glass skin. ... This leads to new laws of design." Such aspects of the aesthetics of open steelwork have remained a topic of architectural debate to this day.

In the following chapters of this book, the fundamentals of steel construction are linked with the built examples in chapter 6, thereby underlining the claim of an integrated overall review. The chapters on the fundamentals have been completely recast in the form of a textbook on steel construction. For the sake of clarity, terms are introduced which have long since been standard in other sectors of the steel industry. "Built examples" covers projects which have been realized. These cover the whole gamut of structural steelwork, from simple sheds and multistorey buildings to complicated structures and skyscrapers.

The approach chosen – a historical analysis followed by the fundamentals reflecting the current situation and, finally, practical applications of the engineering principles outlined in an extensive collection of examples – has long since become standard for the construction manuals of the Edition *DETAIL* series. This manual represents a comprehensive work of reference on structural steelwork, providing important information on design and construction for practising architects and engineers as well as teachers and students. However, we should point out that both the fundamentals and the examples are not to be seen as ready-made solutions but rather as a basis for designs and details which then have to be developed further.

Only with the help of numerous colleagues at home and overseas was it possible to assemble the wealth of information presented in this book. A special debt of gratitude is owed to Rainer Graefe, Theodor Hugues, Bertrand Lemoine, Werner Lorenz, Ted Ruddock, Christian Schädlich and Eberhard Schunck for their help with the history of steel.
Likewise, we would like to thank Stefan Schäfer for his help with the fundamentals of the material as well as Martin Siffling, Thomas Müller, Volker Rohweder, Britta Schmäring and Thies Wachter for their assistance with the chapter on examples, all of whom showed great commitment towards the production of this book.

The Authors

Part 1 • The history of steel construction

Karl J. Habermann

"La Tour de 300 mètres",
Paris 1889, Gustave Eiffel

**Lines of evolution in building with
iron and steel**

1.1   St Peter's in Rome, peripheral iron tie beam in the
      dome, Michelangelo, after Josef Durm,
      Handbuch der Architektur, 1905
1.2   "Iron houses", *Allgemeine Bauzeitung*, Vienna, 1845

"The first iron dwellings were portable houses produced in England and intended for her colonies. Owing to the strength of the individual parts and the simplicity of their connections, these houses were able to withstand fire and earthquake as well as attack by woodworm, prevalent in hot countries and spreading destruction at an alarming rate. The only trouble with these buildings was that their walls consisted of simple metal sheets; in the heat of the blazing sun, these quickly became so hot that to remain in such houses must have been unbearable."[1]

This quotation from an article in an 1845 issue of *Allgemeine Bauzeitung* – the author is anonymous – provides an interesting insight into the situation in the early days of iron construction. Fascinated by the engineering possibilities of this new material and encouraged by the fact that the material was obviously available in sufficient quantities, a sort of industrial prefabrication for export purposes commenced, albeit rather prematurely. The local climatic conditions were not examined adequately and the building science aspects ignored. This approach is not unusual. Even today, development aid employing European technology is implemented in construction projects with a total disregard for local resources and methods – with disastrous consequences for those affected. The corrugated iron hut persists as a symbol of inappropriate development policies. Only in recent years do we see positive approaches: Glen Murcutt is undertaking building projects for the Australian aborigines which use current methods of production and carefully planned combinations of materials, but not without first analysing in detail the climate and lifestyle of his clients.

The special properties of iron make it a valuable material and thoroughly indispensable in modern construction. Only improper processing and application lead to problems. Iron has always played a dominant role in the course of history, although rather less frequently in its peaceful uses as a raw material for jewellery, tools or farm implements. The technical possibilities of its development have by no means been exhausted.

The history of building throws up a myriad of applications throughout the ages. Here is a brief résumé of the most significant stations en route:

The Greeks were already using iron clamps to secure large square stones in their temples in the 5th century BC, a technique that was later imitated by the Romans.

Iron tie rods were employed during the building of the massive vaults of the Hagia Sophia in Constantinople (532-37).

Whereas the structures of the Romanesque period managed almost completely without iron, the Gothic age included buildings which could not have been built without this material. Windows and tracery were skilfully stabilized with the help of iron bars, the vaults anchored with tie rods of wrought iron. The most prominent domes of the 16th and 17th centuries rely on anchors, indeed even complete peripheral tie beams made of iron (Michelangelo included six such beams in his design for St Peter's in Rome in 1546 – six more had to be added in 1743-48).

The engineer-architects of the Renaissance and Baroque used this valuable material primarily as reinforcement, mainly concealed. In designs employing a combination of iron and stone or iron and timber, the iron components accommodate the tensile forces, to a lesser extent shear forces too, while the stone resists compressive forces. As we can see, the roots of reinforced concrete theory go back an astoundingly long way!

The availability of iron in sufficiently large quantities of adequate quality was a key factor for the emergence of an autonomous construction technology. A style of architecture in which iron played a chief role was only able to establish itself in line with the step-by-step development of correspondingly efficient components (accommodation of compressive and tensile forces) and jointing techniques. The smelting of iron by means of charcoal was constrained for a long time due to the lack of efficiency in the process. Only after lengthy trials in the mid-18th century rendered it possible to smelt iron ore by means of pit coal converted into coke were the signals set for the widespread use of iron as an engineering material in buildings.

1.1

1.2

"One wraps wrought iron with a dough of ash, coals, urine, animal bones, lime, soot, etc., and places this together in an iron capsule and subjects it to fire, whereupon it incandesces without melting and hence within a few hours all iron thus placed will be coated with steel. The longer one leaves it in the fire, the greater is the change. When it has then reached the proper degree after the sampling, the mass is plunged into cold water. This method is used by the armourer, cutler and sword-maker in order to transform their iron into steel."[3]
Johann Georg Krünitz, 1838

Although the history of the application of iron has been more or less fully documented, there still remain a number of gaps in our knowledge when it comes to producing the material itself. But experimental archaeology is hard on the heels of the early production methods for iron and steel. Reproductions of so-called bloomery hearth furnaces are being used to investigate diverse issues, e.g. quality and preparation of the ore to be processed, material and shape of furnace walls, firing with charcoal, introduction of air, etc., and their effects, and to compare the results. Another approach is attempting to revive the knowledge of bygone production methods still extant in Africa; techniques common in Europe in the Middle Ages were still in use here up to the time of colonization. For instance, the ethnologist Hans Peter Hahn is venturing to recreate a traditional blast furnace of clay "pats" with the help of the inhabitants of a village in northern Togo. When fed with charcoal and smaller quantities of iron-ore lumps, the arrangement of the 2.5-m-high furnace and its innovative air feed system provides surprising results: tool steel in a quality better than that produced in Germany around 1900 (i.e. with higher oxygen content).[2] Different designations for iron and steel originate from the manner with which they are produced or subsequently processed. The *Oeconomische Enzyklopädie* of Johann Georg Krünitz (begun in 1785) already differentiated between iron and steel. Processes that are more reminiscent of the methods practised in alchemy, such as the way in which armourers, cutlers and sword-makers harden their blades, are described in detail under the heading "Steel" (recipe No. 5, see above).
The still much-quoted *Geschichte des Eisens* by Otto Johannsen distinguishes between four principal periods. Following prehistory the first important station is the end of the Middle Ages, with the establishment – in both economic and technical terms – of a comprehensive iron technology. Besides details of the extraction of coal and iron ore, preparing the ore and furnace technology, the book contains information on the subsequent processing of the material for different trades, authenticated by numerous contemporary illustrations.
The subsequent periods are entitled "The age of the charcoal furnace" (16th and 17th centuries) and "The age of the pit coal furnace" (18th century to the present day).

The principal designations iron and steel are defined by carbon content. Steel is characterized by a higher tensile strength and superior hardness. However, in everyday usage the distinction between the terms remains diffuse and varied, even today, although the first serious attempt to define the material names dates from the Philadelphia World Exposition of 1876: "All wrought iron compounds of typical composition produced from a doughy mass, by faggoting or by any other method – except smelting – which cannot be noticeably hardened and tempered and which in any way resemble those materials now known as wrought iron shall be called wrought iron. When such compounds can be hardened and tempered by any means and resemble the material presently known as puddled steel, then such materials shall be designated wrought steel. All forgeable iron compounds of typical composition which are obtained by casting from a liquid state and which do not harden appreciably upon heating them to red heat and cooling them in water shall be called cast iron. All such iron compounds which can be hardened by any means shall be designated cast steel."[4]
Frank Werner and Joachim Seidel have verified the phase of intensive efforts to obtain a mathematical approximation of the actual material behaviour by means of a series of stress-strain diagrams for iron and steel between 1889 and 1944.[5]

National and international economic interests as well as rapid developments in materials technology make the efforts to define the terms and standardize procedures particularly difficult.

1.3 Evolution of stress-strain diagrams for iron and steel: approximation of the actual material behaviour

E Modulus of elasticity $E = \dfrac{\delta}{\varepsilon}$

I: σ_P Limit of proportionality
II: σ_E Elastic limit
III: σ_{Fo} Upper yield point
IIIa: Ultimate yield strength
IV: σ_{Fu} Lower yield point
V: Failure

δ Stress at failure
F_o Original cross-sectional area of test specimen
l_o Original length of test specimen
Δl Elongation

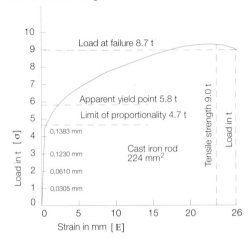

1887 Mehrtens, Georg

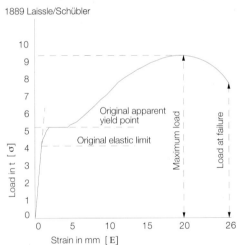

1889 Laissle/Schübler

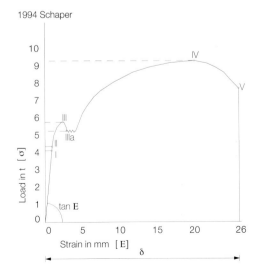

1994 Schaper

Iron: the material of the Industrial Revolution

"Iron and its properties were already known in earliest times. But up until very recently it has not been possible to produce iron at such low prices and in such large quantities and pieces that it could have been considered the equal of stone and timber when it comes to building materials."[6]
Otto Königer, 1902

1.4

Iron played a fundamental role in the Industrial Revolution. Methods of production were raised to the level of subjects worthy of art and reflected the relationships in impressive style. The English painter Julius Caesar Ibbetson (1759-1817) captured a scene from a forge in his work "Cyfarthfa Castle Works", which depicts red-hot lumps of iron being drawn out under the heavy, usually water-powered, hammer.
"Nothing is more magnificent than to see the way in which the human hand tames the ferocious metal. Everywhere one looks one sees attentive hands. Over there the sprightly worker rolls the iron bloom around in the puddling furnace with a mighty lever, watching it through a hole in the wall of the furnace. To stare at the white-hot mass of metal for too long would result in blindness. Then a worker opens the doors of the refining hearth, seizes a monstrous ingot with the tongs and drags it quickly across the floor of cast iron plates and beneath the huge hammer. ... In such workplaces one can really recognize the triumph of the human spirit over the misshapen mass, and here one can best follow its development. This is where one finds the archetypal human body, in which hard work has doubled the muscle power – fitting models for the sculptor."[7] This portrayal of the work of the forges at Fourchambault, published in the *Illustrierte Zeitung* of 1849, idealizes the tough working conditions in heroic form.
The transition from charcoal to pit coal and coke for the firing of the blast furnaces, along with a number of other developments, was the breakthrough which rendered possible the mass production of iron. The consequences that this would have for rural and urban surroundings as well as the environment can be seen in the illustration of the Laura ironworks, at that time one of the most advanced.
The vertical section through a blast furnace is intended to illustrate the main stages in the process. The location on the side of a hill obviates the need for a material hoist to feed the furnace. Coal, ore and additives are tipped in continually from above. The gases produced are able to escape through the opening at the top. The filling subsides as a result of the melting process. Preheated air is blown in from below. The molten metal is run off at regular intervals.

1.5

1.4 "Cyfarthfa Castle Works",
Julius Caesar Ibbetson (1759-1817)
1.5 The blast furnaces of the Laura ironworks
1.6 Section through blast furnace
1.7 Section through puddling furnace
1.8 Bessemer converter
1.9 Detail of a Bessemer steelworks

1.6

1.7

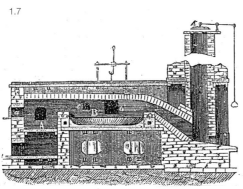

1.8

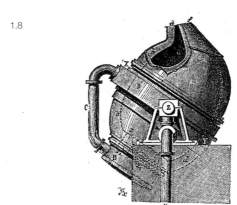

The cast iron produced in great quantities at that time was still plagued by its brittleness and low tensile strength. Variations in the qualities of the raw material led to inconsistent results. Nevertheless, a compressive strength 100 times that of stone meant that it was not long before the building industry became interested in the new material, primarily as a means of saving material and weight. As methods of calculation were non-existent and the metalline properties of cast iron were by no means fully understood, builders had to rely on experiments at a scale of 1:1. The first tentative footsteps were taken with industrial buildings and bridges.

Further processing of the raw iron in the so-called puddling furnace, invented in 1784 by Henry Cort, reduced the carbon content of the iron. The iron was melted, stirred and formed into blooms which were subsequently drawn out by the bloom hammer to form bars about 500 mm long and 70-100 mm in diameter. Rolled out to form flat bars, the complete processing of the puddled iron involved faggoting and welding (flat bars, cut down to 500 mm were placed in groups of four, heated to incandes-cent heat and finish-rolled).

Parallel with the constant refinements in furnace technology and metallurgy, steam power and the railways, important components of industrialization, were also undergoing developments. These benefited from progress in iron technology and were able to employ its latest products directly. While the steam engine took over crucial tasks in the operation of blast furnaces, forges and rolling mills, the railways became indispensable for transporting the raw materials and the semifinished goods. And the development of machine tools (the lathe had been invented in 1810 by Maudslay) also played a key role in the subsequent processing of this new material.

For the next station in the history of iron production we must turn to William Kelly in the USA and Henry Bessemer in Europe.

The invention of the "Bessemer converter" (the initial idea goes back to 1855) rendered possible the direct production of steel from pig iron. A blast of oxygen was introduced in order to remove the carbon from the iron, but the quality was still not adequately guaranteed. Only non-phosphoric ores could be processed. The technique introduced by Sidney Gilchrist Thomas in 1879 remedied this situation.

1.9

1.10

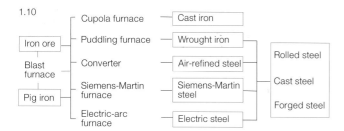

	Cupola furnace	Cast iron
Iron ore	Puddling furnace	Wrought iron
Blast furnace	Converter	Air-refined steel
Pig iron	Siemens-Martin furnace	Siemens-Martin steel
	Electric-arc furnace	Electric steel

Rolled steel

Cast steel

Forged steel

1.11

The Siemens-Martin open-hearth method (principle of regenerative heating) was initially employed for melting down scrap and waste from rolling mills. After overcoming numerous technical hurdles this new "hearth-type furnace" was also suitable for the mass production of steel from ore.

The production of steel using electricity is another stage in the progress outlined here. Its roots go back well into the 19th century. But it has only been in recent times, with the availability of a reliable supply of electricity, that this method has also become economic.

The increase in the quality of material technology over the past 100 years is illustrated by the oft-quoted example of the Eiffel Tower. Whereas when it was built this optimum design in terms of structure and use of material required about 7000 t of steel, these days only 2000 t would be necessary. The visual outcome would certainly be considerably different...

When we take into account that iron has been known to mankind for some 3000 years, the period of its use (and that of steel) as a constructional material is relatively brief (250 years). The use of iron and steel for loadbearing members can be divided into three periods: the cast iron (1780-1850), wrought iron (1850-1900) and steel (1880 to the present day) periods. The transitions are fluid. Cast and wrought iron were for a long time also used in combination, depending on requirements. While the early iron loadbearing structures still necessitated extensive trials, the period 1850-70 witnessed a change in the method of design. Simple structures could now be verified mathematically in most cases. Thanks to William Rankine's extensive and practical theory of elasticity (*Manual of Civil Engineering*, 1859), a well-developed graphical method for determining forces (based on previous experience with timber buildings), and defined rivet strengths, the engineer was now in the position to determine his structures on the drawing board. The change from wrought iron to steel (around 1880-1900) allowed the use of higher permissible stresses and larger rolled sections, but it was not until the 1930s that the next major development took place. The introduction of welding gave rise to a fundamental change in manufacturing. Conception and design had to harmonize. Stability provided by rigid corners rather than diagonal bracing led to the princi-

1.12

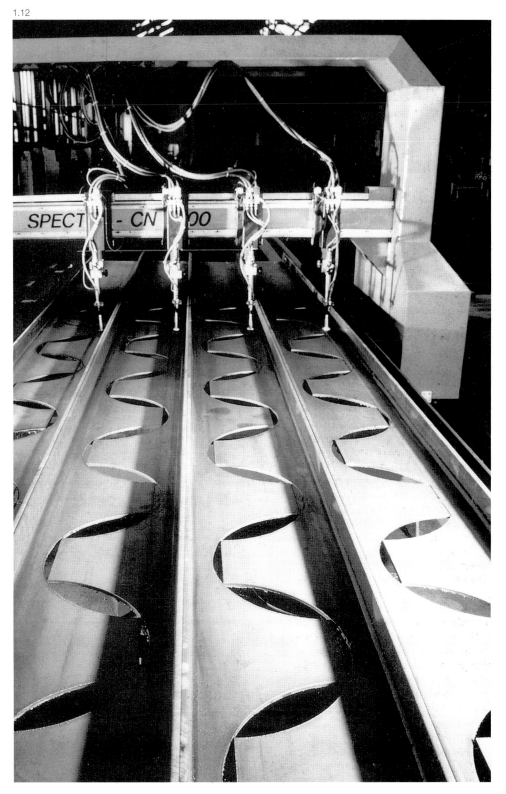

ple of the portal frame, a structural form that
had a not inconsiderable impact on later structures – architecture too. In terms of design
methods, the elastic theory was joined by the
plastic theory. Today, the computer enables us
to carry out a highly refined mathematical optimization of a structure by analysing the construction as a whole, e.g. by including the influences of all secondary components such as
facades, cladding and partitions.

The development of semifinished goods with
ever greater dimensional accuracy ("near net
shape casting") with precisely defined material
properties and machining by means of CNC
cutting and welding techniques will continue to
make building with steel a highly noteworthy
issue. The aspect of its reusability, the recyclability of the material, also plays a not inconsiderable role in the construction industry in a
climate of enhanced ecological values; and
recycling does not always mean just mixing
scrap with the raw materials! The material's
ability to adapt to the most diverse situations,
complying with demands for conversion, dismantling and re-erection, cannot be matched
by any other material.

Educating for iron

One important source when tracing the technical progress of iron to its intrinsic place in the constructions of today is Jean-Baptiste Rondelet's five-volume *Traité théorique et pratique de l'art de bâtir* (Paris, 1802-17). Sixteen further editions were published between 1810 and 1881, thus contributing to technology transfer in all areas of construction for very nearly a century. Therefore, Rondelet's work occupies a key position between the classic architectural treatises of Vitruvius, Alberto and Palladio, right up to Blondel, the 18th century as the Age of Enlightenment and the period of the first encyclopaedias (Diderot and d'Alembert: *Encyclopédie ou dictionnaire raisonné des Sciences*, Paris, 1750-80), and the building technology textbooks of the 19th and 20th centuries. The chapter entitled "Fitter's work" deals with anchors, fixings and roof trusses. The technology of cast iron components is treated in as much depth as the spectacular use of iron in bridge-building. Impressive illustrations show the bridge at Coalbrookdale, the Pont des Arts in Paris and typical details of a chain bridge. Precise elevational views are complemented with details of supports and jointing. The rapid engineering developments led to a constant differentiation and specialization in the literature. Considering "educating for iron architecture"[9] by means of individual publications of the most diverse nature helps not only to forge important relationships but also to bring to light and reappraise fundamental sources little heeded up to now.

Trade journals for the building industry

The trade journals founded in France, England, Austria and Germany from 1830 onwards played an important role by reporting on new developments in all areas of construction. *Annales des Ponts et Chaussées* (Paris, 1831-1934) concentrated primarily on engineering. Christian Friedrich Ludwig Förster´s *Allgemeine Bauzeitung* (Vienna, 1836-1916) had a broader basis from the beginning and was intended to appeal equally to (as the title expresses it) "architects, engineers, decorators, building specialists, economists, contractors and all who are involved in the developments and accomplishments of recent times in architecture and its associated branches". The English journal *The Builder* (1842-1966) also signals its universal appeal with the sub-title: "An illustrated weekly magazine for the

architect, engineer, archaeologist, constructor, sanitary-reformer and art-lover".

One important aspect in the dissemination of new technological developments was the fact that the reports on outstanding structures not only explained functions and aesthetics by way of scale drawings in special illustrations, but that additional detail drawings – obviously specially produced for the publication – provided insights into systems of construction and jointing. Brief descriptions accompanied the visual material. Even structural calculations were included. This enabled the interested architect to broaden his mind with engineering aspects and the engineer to consider the latest arguments on architectural aesthetics. One extensive theme stretching over decades was the rapid growth of the railways and all the associated facets such as the routeing of lines, optimization of track beds, project planning for stations of all sizes right up to design and construction of locomotives and rolling stock. The contents of these articles quickly found their way into textbooks on building or were incorporated in specialist compendiums produced by the same publishers. One good example of this is the two-volume *Baukunde des Architekten*, edited by the publishers of the *Deutsche Bauzeitung* (3rd ed., Berlin, 1893).

Only around the turn of the 20th century did the prevalence of this common information medium begin to dwindle; the individual disciplines started to publish their own specialist literature more and more. Indeed, a sort of language barrier gradually appeared, which became entrenched. The surmounting of this barrier has only recently been dared in the training establishments for architects and engineers – with differing degrees of success – (e.g. "Dortmund Construction Model", with common lectures and projects for both disciplines).

Building textbooks for iron

"There is no difference between the principle of constructing with solid members made of wood or those made of iron or any other metal. The only difference lies in the proportions and dimensions of the parts, corresponding to the physical differences between the two materials, of which it is assumed you are aware. Further, it should be remembered that the metal does not suffer, or only to a small degree, from some of the shortcomings of wood as a tectonic material: i.e. it is not hygrometric, does not warp, does not contract or expand unevenly. But compared to wood, linear metal members have the disadvantage of greater pliancy and elasticity, cast metal greater brittleness. From this comparison we can see that construction with linear metal members lies infinitely further from great art than does timber construction, and that the absolute stability relationships here contradict to an even greater extent those relationships which correspond with the mechanical work of the parts than is the case with wood."[11]

This opinion expressed by Gottfried Semper in his book *Der Stil* (vol. II, 1863) is by no means an isolated example, but instead reflects the underlying mood of the architects of the day. The reputation of being unsuitable for prestige architectural projects was to dog iron for a long time to come. It was understandable that early textbooks should retract on their claims in their very titles. *Die Eisenkonstruktionen für Brücken und Dachstühle* ("Iron constructions for bridges and roof trusses") by J. Langer kept to the range of applications already prescribed by Rondelet and highlighted the focus for the future of the new material.

In the preface to his *Lehrbuch der Eisenkonstruktionen* (1876) E. Brandt remarked: "It was first necessary to screen the over-ornate and constantly progressing material, to dispense with older forms of construction and replace them by newer and more elegant associations."[12] The division of the book into material properties, the joining of primary elements (beams of cast and wrought iron) and the design of elements such as floors, roofs, stairs, oriels and balconies is a legitimate and pragmatic succession. There was a chapter on calculations for iron roofs for engineers, and the book is full of detail drawings. The attempt to include prominent structures such as Baltard's market halls, the Gare du Nord by Hittorf or the cast iron stairs in the palace of Prince Carl in Berlin by Schinkel is proof of the efforts to make the material, and above all its architecture, socially acceptable.

Rudolph Gottgetreu employed a similar approach in his *Lehrbuch der Hochbaukonstruktionen, 3. Teil Eisenkonstruktionen* (1885). As an architect and also professor at Munich Technical University, he took the opportunity to record local examples. His chapter on jointing is particularly impressive. The first two illustrations of his manual present an easy-to-read catalogue of cast and wrought iron connections as well as riveted connections for rolled sections. The emphasis is on the design of long-span roofs. References to the successful use of cast iron elements by renowned colleagues such as Schinkel, Hesse, Knoblauch, Stüler, Hitzig, Neureuther and Adler can be found in his engaging "Concluding words on the styling of iron". The following passage is also worthy of study for the evaluation of our present-day planning and building climate: "The architectural, properly styled design of our ever more self-assured iron constructions is a task of our age which has not yet been started, whose solution can only be expected through the joint efforts of all those involved; in this respect, the demand for stricter separation of the faculties – building and engineering – cannot be justified in the interests of the art."[13]

A significant standard work of reference for the building profession is the four-volume *Allgemeine Baukonstruktionslehre* by G. A. Breymann (from 1853). One whole volume, *Die Konstruktionen in Eisen* (1st ed. 1853, but then titled *Die Konstruktionen in Metall*) is dedicated to the material which was now gradually apparently becoming accepted as the equal of stone (masonry) and timber. In the preface to the first edition Breymann remarks: "Owing to the plan of my book, which was to teach the individual constructions independently of their incorporation in whole buildings, I was unable to include entire structures of iron, e.g. iron houses already produced in Belgium and England for their overseas colonies, and the latest wonder of our age, the 'Crystal palace' housing the Great Exhibition in London."[15] But aesthetic reservations were the more likely cause for excluding these examples from a textbook on architecture. The work was revised several times in the following years or thoroughly over-

1.13

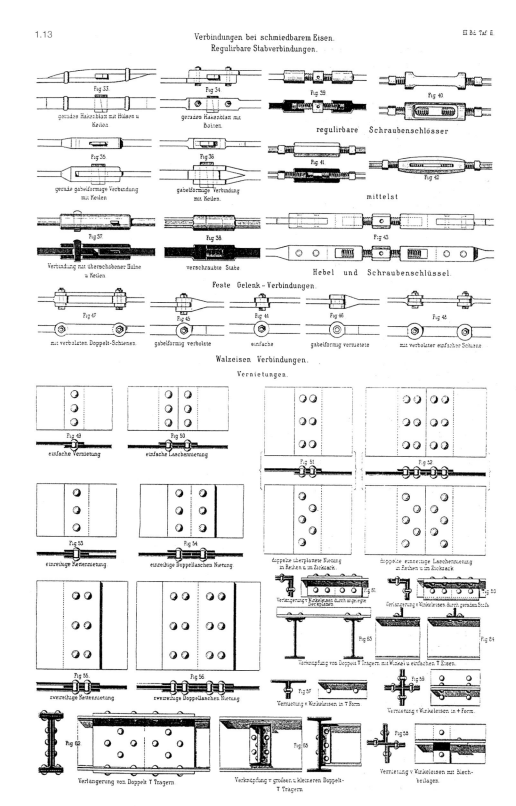

"Most of the iron roof constructions actually built are pure utilitarian structures in which a particular architectural order does not even apply. ... In any case, the architectural appearance is strictly derived from the purpose, construction and material; in no way can the characteristic shape be eradicated nor can an ornamental form be employed which is foreign to iron and was borrowed from arrangements in stone and timber..."[14]
Max Foerster, 1909

hauled, e.g. by H. Lang in 1877. Kutruff, an engineer, became responsible for the mathematical part. A further 57 illustrations were added to the chapter of examples, a significant indication of the rapid developments in building with iron during the second half of the 19th century.

Otto Königer revised the 5th (1890) and 6th (1910) editions. In his introduction to the latter he comments, almost resignedly: "Externally, iron will thus remain hidden from view in all our grand buildings to the same extent as timber was excluded in the past. Therefore, for such buildings the artistic treatment of iron can only be considered in the layout of the interior. ... Without going into the difficult question of the architectural form of iron constructions more deeply at this point, we should only note that ambitions in this respect will only be crowned with success when the architect himself learns to conceive such arrangements more than in the past and hence gains an understanding of the essence of every single element in the construction, without which artistic glory cannot be achieved. However, the acquisition of the necessary wisdom is associated with more effort than is the case with masonry and timber constructions."[16]

In the following years it proved impossible to unite architectural and engineering knowledge in one work. The field of construction dealing with a particular material was increasingly relegated to an overall portrayal in one book or a series of books. It was not long before the multi-volume Handbook of Architecture was matched by an equally extensive Handbook of Engineering. Aspects of building with iron were dealt with in many subsections related to components or uses (stations, market halls, etc.) as in the Handbook of Architecture, or classified under shed-type buildings, skeleton construction or bridge-building as in the engineering literature. It became more and more laborious for engineers and architects interested in structural steelwork to keep abreast of the respective specialist knowledge. Despite numerous new findings in methods of analysis, in metallurgy and manufacturing, the aesthetics level stagnated. It even began to steadily

decline. The priority awarded to design is clear from the above quotation of Foerster. The extremely comprehensive and highly detailed supplementary volume to the multi-volume Handbook of Engineering records the most important structures of the time. The volume of illustrations contains drawings of, among others: Alexanderplatz station in Berlin, Frankfurt am Main station, the central stations in Cologne, Hamburg and Dresden, the dome over the Reichstag in Berlin, the spectacular dome over the cigarette factory in Dresden. Iron played a dominant role in large-span structures and the budding skyscraper revolution of the coming decade led to further constructional opportunities.

The slump in both architectural and engineering development in Central Europe during two world wars cannot be overlooked. Other applications for iron were more pressing...

In American skyscraper architecture, the steel skeleton – albeit well shielded and wrapped in fire protection envelopes of various materials – fulfilled the demanding specification for flexible assembly in confined spaces and sheer unlimited stability. In 1926 Edmund Schüler organized an exhibition in Munich entitled "New American Architecture". The evaluation of the American scene from the European standpoint by Thomas E. Tallmadye in the catalogue is coloured by, on the one hand, a certain arrogance but, on the other, by awe as he writes in his essay Forwards in architecture: "In the eighties there were few trained architects in the United States. ... In terms of style we experienced a period of the purest eclecticism. ... America's most individual contributions here are the insides (the steel skeleton), the construction from which the walls are suspended, no longer built up, reinforced concrete (a new element in architecture), plus the fast elevator and other, more functional things."[17]

As structural steelwork gradually presented itself as a technically well-developed building medium, it found itself increasingly in competition with reinforced concrete. Notable in this context is Fritz Schumacher's call for "material honesty", also dating from 1926: "A building

material can be applied to the most diverse functions in construction terms and must remain genuine in a way which does it justice. Layering and fixing of masonry, mortising and scarfing of timber, elastic cubic growth of reinforced concrete, riveting and bracing of iron, must, where exposed, really be appropriate to the constructional function it serves. ... In particular, with the static, purposeful designs of iron, the most ambitious attempts have been made to combine the iron with artistic, decorative forms. The two world expositions in Paris and numerous significant engineering structures of the turn of the century provide examples of this. The attempt proved to be hopeless."[18]

Today, this statement must be looked at critically in many ways. The dream, as described here, of a construction that justifies the material, which throws up no unanswered questions for the casual observer, can today no longer be upheld in the same manner as a maxim for planners and designers given our complex demands regarding thermal insulation, acoustics, corrosion protection, recyclability, etc. The pronounced aesthetic valuation opposing the ornamentation in the architecture of history is easy to understand today in terms of the history of building. The criteria have long since changed again, especially in assessing the accomplishments of early iron architecture.

In 1931 Alfred Hawranek presented the first book on steel skeleton construction. It was a first attempt to gain ground on the equally young but, in Europe, astoundingly successful reinforced concrete. It was aimed at both architects and engineers. The author treated the known fundamentals of the time systematically and backed them up with up-to-date examples. The extensions to the Deutsches Museum in Munich by German Bestelmeyer (no-one would suspect a carefully integrated steel skeleton here), Hans Poelzig's IG-Farben office block in Frankfurt am Main and the multi-storey Allgemeine Bankvereinigung building in Antwerp (at 87 m then the tallest steel building in Europe) are all covered. "The codes for the

1.14 Swiss National Exhibition in Lausanne: temporary station by Pierre Zoelly. Extracts from the project documentation by Konrad Gatz and Frank Hart in: *Stahlkonstruktionen im Hochbau*, 1966.

design of steel buildings are on the whole less strenuous in America than they are in Europe,"[19] was the conclusion of the author and he closed his book with the Empire State Building.

After the war it took some time before new developments in engineering and architecture found their way again into textbooks and handbooks on steelwork. Not before 1966 did Konrad Gatz and Franz Hart present an inaugural résumé in their book *Stahlkonstruktionen im Hochbau*. Franz Hart's fact-packed introductory chapter traces the progress from the Industrial Revolution to Egon Eiermann's German embassy in Washington (1964). The highly detailed chapter of examples contains works by Kurt Ackermann, Max Bill, Fritz Haller, Walter Henn, Ludwig Mies van der Rohe, Joachim Schürmann, Heinz Wilke, Pierre Zoelly and many others. The *Stahlbauatlas* by Franz Hart, Walter Henn and Hansjürgen Sontag (1974), albeit confined to multistorey buildings, followed the concept of a fundamental work for steel structures. The revised and enlarged edition of 1982 – translated into seven languages – remained a standard work of reference for many years and so was a tough act to follow for later books with similar ambitions. The answer to just how successful was the original idea of stimulating multistorey structural steelwork in Europe can be found in the chapter of examples (pp. 224-387) in the present book. In 1987 Alan Ogg inaugurated a series of interesting new books on steel with his *Architecture in Steel – The Australian Context*. The careful and succinct treatment of historical developments in Europe and the USA quite naturally integrates the local construction scene and provides a wealth of detailed information. *Construire en Acier* (1993) forms the French counterpart. Although not as strict and distinct in its arrangement, it provides plenty of up-to-date basic information.
The British view is represented in *Architecture and Construction in Steel* (1993), a reference work skilfully put together from a mass of interesting contributions by renowned authors. Norway too provided an important addition to this theme with a book published in 1996.

1.14

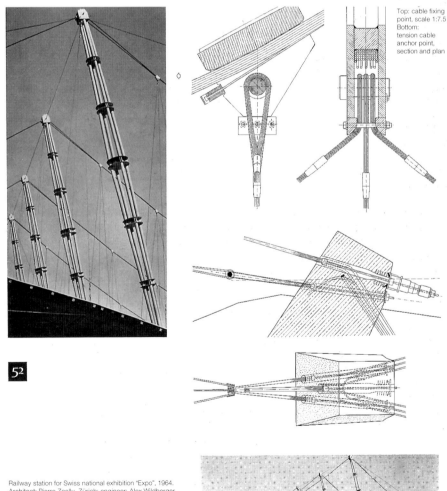

52

Top: cable fixing point, scale 1:7.5
Bottom: tension cable anchor point, section and plan

Railway station for Swiss national exhibition "Expo", 1964. Architect: Pierre Zoelly, Zürich; engineer: Alex Wildberger, Schaffhausen. The brief called for a temporary railway station for the heavy volume of rail traffic expected during the exhibition. There were two 300 m platforms for each pair of tracks, and a roof with enough space underneath for approx. 6000 people. It was decided to have a totally suspended structure with a thin roof covering of corrugated asbestos-cement sheeting. The asymmetric roof arrangement is suspended from four pylons. On the lake side the roof measured 34 x 70 m and covered open waiting zone, ticket counters, kiosks and toilets. On the mountain side the roof measures 20 x 70 m; this is where the "presorting" of passengers took place. Area covered: 3600 m²

1.15

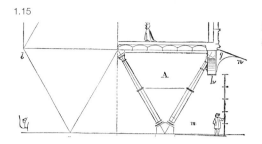

200 years of jointing and styling with iron and steel

1.15   Section through a market hall with inclined cast iron columns, Viollet-le-Duc, *Entretiens sur l'architecture*, Paris, 1872
1.16   Kitchen in the Royal Pavilion, Brighton, 1815, John Nash, design with slender columns of cast iron
1.17   ibid., column heads decorated with palm motifs after completion

The detail on the facing page of the Ecole du Sacré-Cœur by Hector Guimard is symptomatic of many aspects in the evolution of the joint in cast iron, wrought iron and steel. It represents almost 100 years of technical and aesthetic development. The form of the detail, conceived by master-builder and theoretician Viollet-le-Duc in a sketch and magnificently produced perspectives, was realized decades later by Hector Guimard, at a time when Art Nouveau was beginning to establish itself. Then already a technical anachronism, cast iron columns – inclined in this example – support a riveted beam of wrought iron, which in turn carries a grid of rolled sections partly encased in concrete. Brickwork vaulting completes the fire-resistant floor construction. The interaction of the individual elements was not artistically masked, as was usual, but instead left exposed. Hence, in the light of the coming developments, this building was considerably ahead of its time.

The following cross-section through the evolution of jointing and styling with iron and steel is not merely a strict chronological sequence and history-of-art appraisal of the major structures, imposing bridges, stations, exhibition halls and skyscrapers of the past 200 years. The emphasis is on details, with particular lines of development and cross-references being shown. This method was chosen in order to make it easier to relate this particular chapter on the history of building to today's construction industry.
The early attempts to use the new material – cast iron – in architecture were characterized by the property of its high compressive strength coupled with relatively slender dimensions. The first steps involved replacing existing masonry and timber constructions with substitutes made from the new material. The column and the arch – the archetypal forms – were the first elements to be treated in this way, with the early pioneers gradually expanding applications to new areas. However, the primary mission of the protagonists was to introduce and establish a new aesthetic.

The example of the Royal Pavilion in Brighton by John Nash illustrates very well the design problems encountered in using the new technical possibilities. The first drawing of the interior of the kitchen depicts a group of four amazingly slender columns and plain column heads. The unexpected outcome obviously presented the architect with a design headache until he hit upon the idea of concealing, alienating the loadbearing action by attaching metal palm leaves. Therefore, the real structural effect recedes into the background. The palm motif performs its distracting manoeuvre very well. The tops of the slender cast iron columns in the other rooms of the building were also provided with a variety of botanical ornamentation. In the end, the harmony, both inside and outside, of this picturesque architecture with its prevailing Indian and Chinese influences was retained. John Nash was presumably hardly interested in innovative technical and constructional details.

1.16

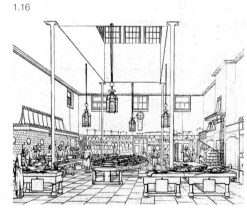

1.17

Ecole du Sacré-Cœur,
Paris 1895,
Hector Guimard

**Cast iron elements
Columns, beams, arches**

Owing to its properties, the use of cast iron in arched form was almost self-evident. Amazing feats were accomplished in bridge-building, where the material was employed from the very beginning of its development and where the constructional opportunities offered by the material were tested. The experience gained here was also put to good use in the buildings of later periods. One outstanding example is the bridge over the River Severn at Coalbrookdale, still standing today, which has prompted a multitude of historical studies concerning design and construction with iron. Five cast iron arched trusses span approx. 30.5 m with a rise of 13 m. The structural basis for the design was still that of the conventional building methods using masonry and timber. Each truss consists of two 6 t half-arches cast in an open sand bed. The connections were borrowed from timber construction: bolts and wedges and scarf joints. A cast iron bearing plate distributes the point loads from the ribs over the foundation. The bridge is still used today for pedestrian traffic.

The Pont des Arts in Paris was the oldest iron bridge in France until 1980. However, it was subjected to a wholescale "reconstruction with identical character" by L. Arretche in 1982-83. In doing so the number of trestles was reduced from eight to seven. This structure too was an important prototype for cast iron bridge-building technology. J. B. Rondelet included both bridges in his standard work *Traité théorique et pratique de l'art de bâtir*.

The comparison between the bridge at Coalbrookdale and the roof structure to the Dianabad in Vienna substantiates the theory that building design benefited directly from the new bridge-building technology, albeit with a slight delay, and was influenced by its results. As during this period the results were not categorized according to architecture or engineering (architects were confronted with details of locomotives and engineers were given insights into proportion and classical design), the reasons for the similarity in structural design were plain to see. The roof trusses consisted of separate cast members, suitably designed for joining together by means of bolts. The use of a cast iron loadbearing structure left exposed over the full 16 m span in a public building initiated a gradual shift in notions of aesthetic value.

1.18

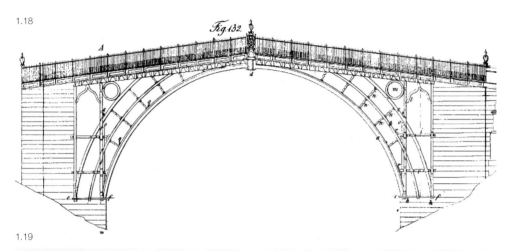

1.19

1.20

1.21

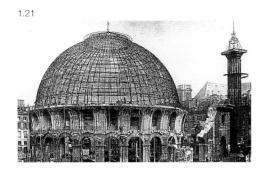

1.22

One of the most amazing accomplishments of the pioneering years of the cast iron period from 1790 to 1870 is the 40-m-span cast iron dome over a Parisian grain silo. This, the Halle au Blé, became the Bourse de Commerce in 1888. The original timber dome had burned down in 1802 and with the help of the new material it was possible to erect an extremely delicate network of iron ribs and ring purlins. To make this possible, the architect, François-Joseph Bélanger, had probably also obtained engineering advice from England.

The country at the heart of the Industrial Revolution had quickly adopted the idea of reducing the high fire risk in textile mills by employing the new, non-combustible material. The first step was to replace the timber columns by cast iron ones; later, the timber floor beams were replaced by heavy rail sections, until the introduction of specially formed beam sections to carry the vaulted brickwork directly, and finally the completely "fireproof floors". Stanley Mill in Stonehouse is a splendid example of how a near-Gothic-style loadbearing structure led to a particular constructional solution. The circles remind the observer of Coalbrookdale.

From time to time the Gothicizing elements were joined by the basilica principle in shed-type structures. The structure of the foundry shop of the Sayner Works not only seems to pay homage to the new technology, but at the same time demonstrates to potential customers the spectrum of the company's engineering abilities. The architect, Karl Ludwig Althans, changed an initial draft for a massive structure in the "Greek style" to the delicate solution in a "Gothic mantle" which was actually built. In doing so he was guided by Schinkel's *Collection of architectural designs*. It is suspected that the new Gothic cast iron tracery windows of the nearby palace were manufactured at the works. So we have come full circle.

1.23

1.24

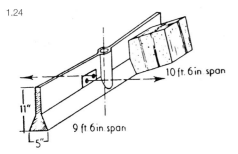

This next section deals with the preliminary steps towards iron skeleton frames. The elements required, such as beams and columns, had already been developed in cast iron. However, the fully fledged skeleton frame first became possible with the introduction of riveted frames of wrought iron.

Charles Bage had developed a floor beam for Shrewsbury Mill which was shaped to accept column connections as well as the intermediate masonry floor vaulting. Solid masonry outer walls were still necessary to guarantee the stability of the building. The spans achievable were limited by the brittle iron which could hardly accommodate any bending stresses.

Many years later, James Bogardus built one of the first cast iron facade frames for his own factory building in New York. In the following years numerous other facades were completed. However, the architectural style still clung to the stone language of the past. The project was proudly advertised on the cover of the magazine *The Iron Age*. It is suspected that the remaining structure consisted of masonry walls and timber floors, like the Edgar Laing Stores, which until its demolition in 1971 was a worthy example of this highly developed facade technique. The 1966 survey and the careful documentation of the elements (during demolition) carried out by students led by James Marston Fitch provide a good picture of the quality of the detailing and accuracy of fit. U-shaped edge sections of cast iron provide a good bearing for the timber floor beams, with pier elements being attached via pins or bolts. Shaped spandrel panels and fascia elements reinforced the horizontal associations. The rapid growth of American cities has only left us with a few examples from this period.

The conventional masonry external walls of Cooper Union, a school funded by a powerful railway company, concealed an internal cast iron skeleton frame which is as imaginative as it is effective in the way it is integrated. In the hall on the upper floor, which extends partly over two storeys, the advantages and the potential of the new system are exposed for all to see. The building was constantly adapted in subsequent years to suit changing needs.

1.25

1.26

1.27

1.28

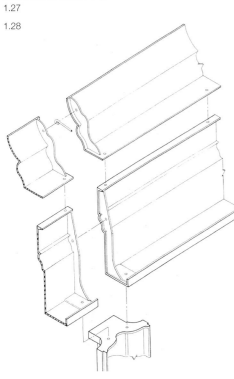

1.24 Shrewsbury Mill, 1797, Charles Bage,
     cast iron floor beam
1.25 ibid., interior view
1.26 Edgar Laing Stores, New York 1849,
     James Bogardus
1.27 Bogardus Factory, New York 1848,
     James Bogardus

1.28 Edgar Laing Stores, New York 1849,
     James Bogardus, cast elements of fascia
1.29 ibid., facade elements
1.30–1.32 ibid., parts removed during demolition
1.33 Cooper Union, New York 1853–59,
     F. A. Peterson, sketch of interior
1.34 ibid., detail of loadbearing structure

1.30

1.31

1.32

1.29

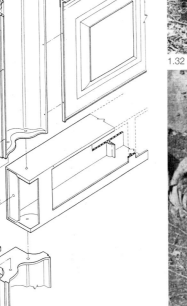

1.33

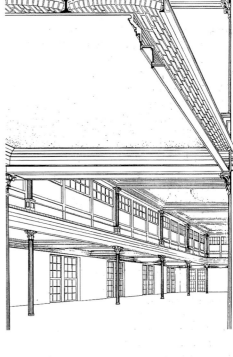

1.34

"It will take a long time before iron, indeed any metal which has rediscovered its rights as a building material, is understood so comprehensively in technical terms that it can claim its place of honour alongside stone, brick and timber as an artistic element in beautiful architecture," wrote Gottfried Semper in an essay in 1849. He continued: "One conspicuous example is the new Sainte-Geneviève library in Paris, a building that offers much of interest and can be regarded as the most important edifice of the last republican era. However, the architect, Mr Labrouste, has unsuccessfully incorporated an exposed iron roof truss and seen fit to paint it dark green, thus depriving users of the building, which also serves as the reading room, of the sedate introspective ambience so necessary for serious study. It is difficult to exit the building in a contented frame of mind."[20]

This opinion shows how arduous it was to overcome centuries of criteria laid down for the design of public "monuments". With his reading room, Labrouste dared to ignore the generally acknowledged aesthetic conventions by trying to target new aesthetic solutions with the new material. He placed slim, perforated cast arches on top of his slender cast iron columns. The barrel vault roof consists of plastered wire netting. The two "naves" of the building gave it an almost church-like appearance. The skilful ornamentation of the loadbearing elements dissolves their character. The connections seem to have been incorporated at random but they did correspond with the latest ideas in structural analysis and casting methods at that time. And externally the building conforms with all the expected architectural conventions. Labrouste's friendship with Cesar Daly, publisher of the important architectural journal *Revue général de l'Architecture et des Travaux Publics*, enabled him to publish details of his ideas and projects, but his architectural opinions made him a loner.

1.35

1.36

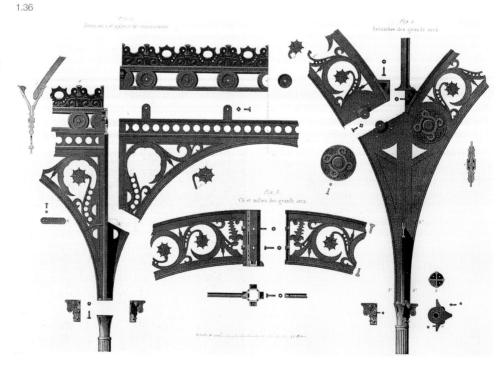

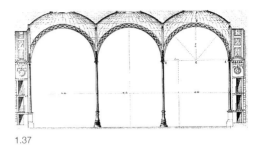

1.37

The energetic Gothic revival movement of the same period had important adherents in the UK, notably Augustus W. N. Pugin and John Ruskin. Although the latter was known for his hefty criticism of new iron architecture, principally stations, he played a not inconsiderable part in advising Deane and Woodward on their new museum in Oxford. The Gothic style is here realized in iron and, clad in glass "scales", led to a new and surprising experience of the interior. The coloured pointed arches are made from riveted wrought iron. The columns had initially been conceived in wrought iron but this was changed to cast iron on the advice of the experienced engineer and iron expert William Fairbairn. The slender columns are skilfully grouped to give the effect of conventional, solid stone columns. However, John Ruskin's maxim on the correct use of iron contradicts this: "This rule is, I think, that metals may be used as a cement, but not as a support. ... But the moment that the iron in the least degree takes the place of the stone, and acts by its resistance to crushing, and bears superincumbent weight, or if it acts by its own weight as a counterpoise, and so supersedes the use of pinnacles or buttresses in resisting a lateral thrust, or if, in the form of a rod or girder, it is used to do what wooden beams would have done as well, that instant the building ceases, so far as such applications of metal extend, to be true architecture."[21]

Henri Labrouste was given a chance to further experiment with exposed, innovative iron load-bearing elements in another public building with the addition of the national library to the Palais Mazarin. Nine domed vaults with glass rooflights created a completely new interior impression. The infills between the iron frame consist of light-coloured, satin-finish faiences manufactured in Sèvre. They reflect the light from above and scatter it across the room. The iron construction stands out from the solid envelope of the building. However, the protruding masonry piers are a response to the slender (300 mm diameter, 10 m high) cast iron columns placed immediately in front of them. The result is not without its effect.

1.38

1.39

1.40

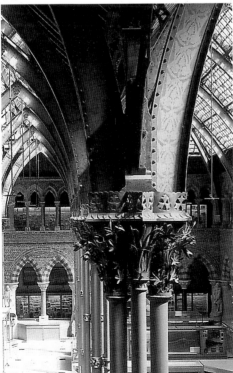

1.41 Ca d'Oro, Glasgow,1872,
      John Honeyman
1.42 Drinking Fountain, Newport on Tay, 1882
1.43 Metro entrance, Porte Dauphine, Paris,
      1898–1901, Hector Guimard

1.43

1.41

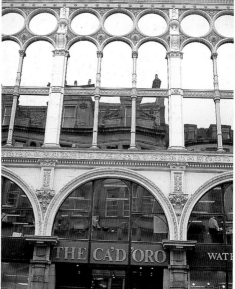

1.42

"Iron constructions are only considered for new structures for economic reasons, whereas with grand objects, where the artistic side prevails, these as yet unlovely iron constructions are avoided. However, if such do come to fruition, then only a genius can discover the right way to achieve a stylish result."[22] Theophil Hansen was in good company when he uttered this opinion in 1860. Even 10 years later Schwatlo was still writing: "In any case, we must first develop a taste for any new form. Just like a Gothic cathedral cannot be judged according to classical standards, so we must not expect antique relationships from, for example, iron columns."[23] Although the aesthetic prejudices had by no means been eradicated by the end of the century (resentment still exists today), the volume of cast iron components – for facades and display windows, or street furniture (pavilions of all kinds, stairs, fountains, grids, balustrades, lampposts) – grew steadily. The material was extremely adaptable.
In Glasgow, Gardener's Building by John Baird (1863) and the Ca d'Oro by John Honeyman (1872) introduced a series of filigree cast iron facades which seem to anticipate the grid facades of steel skeleton structures which were to appear many years later. The building erected at Göggingen near Augsburg in 1886 appeared as an anachronism of building technology: the administrative centre of a spa town in lavishly ornamented and colourfully painted cast iron, assembled from a manufacturer's catalogue, albeit packaged in a stone mantle. The material experienced a transient final boom during the Art Nouveau period, with Hector Guimard using it magnificently for his entrances to the Paris Metro.

Suspension bridge,
Dumfries, Scotland, 1875

Suspended constructions
Chains, rods, cables, nets

An early drawing of an iron chain bridge in Faustus Verantius' *Machinae novae* signalled a new engineering possibility in bridge-building. That was in 1617. Around 1800, following failed attempts with cast iron arched bridges, experiments began with suspended constructions of wrought iron chain links and cables for spanning larger distances. However, a sufficient quantity of wrought iron was essential for design and realization. In 1801 James Finlay obtained the first patent for a suspension bridge employing iron chains. Samuel Brown's first large suspension bridge in England already spanned 132 m across the River Tweed. The chains of this bridge were composed of flat iron plates joined with bolts, an arrangement which was to be employed in all subsequent chain bridges. Thomas Telford's chain bridge across the Menai Strait, sketched by Karl Friedrich Schinkel, also generated great interest. The centre span was 175 m. It was opened in 1826 and had to be strengthened immediately because the oscillations which occurred in the horizontal plane were too large. While Telford was still relying mainly on his engineering instinct and constant materials tests, the French engineer Louis Navier was working out the first methods of calculation for suspension bridges. His work signalled the start of scientifically based bridge-building. Navier was not favoured with luck in his practical efforts. The early days of the suspension bridge were dogged by high risks and a multitude of as yet unsolved technical problems. Nevertheless, the basis of our modern technology was in place at the beginning of the 19th century.

With a span of 237 m the Saane Bridge near Fribourg surpassed Telford's masterpiece. Continuous wire ropes were used instead of chains. Built in 1834, the bridge was described in detail by its designer, Joseph Chaley, in 1839. The suspension cables were draped over cast iron rollers on the masonry piers. One peculiarity in this group is the Britannia Bridge by Robert Stephenson and William Fairbairn. Originally conceived as a suspension bridge, the deck beam became a hollow box girder and, owing to its inherent stiffness, no longer required the planned suspension system. Extensive tests on models preceded the actual construction. A steam-driven riveting machine was used. The box girders were prefabricated to their full length, floated into posi-

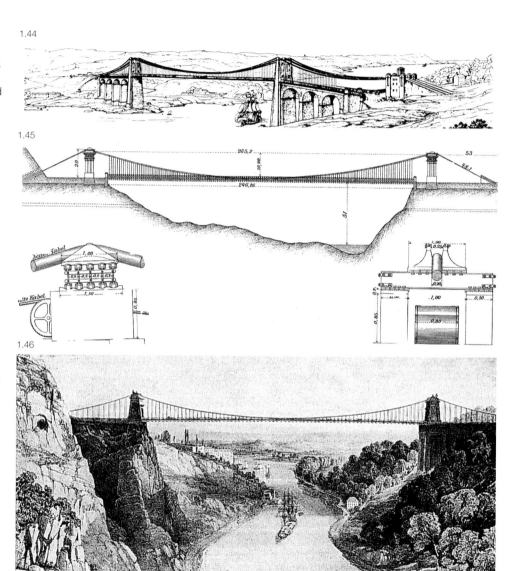

1.44

1.45

1.46

1.47

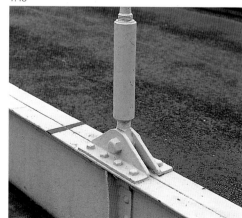

1.48

1.49

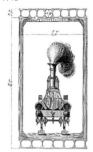

1.50

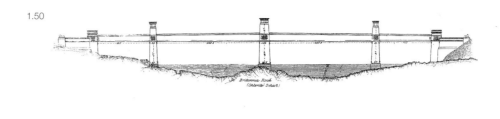

1.51

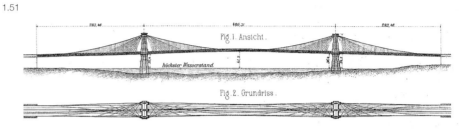

1.52

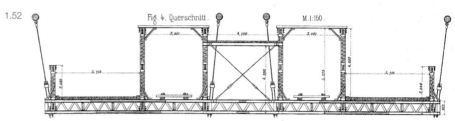

tion beneath the piers and raised to their final positions by means of hydraulic jacks. Isambard Kingdom Brunel's project for the well-known Clifton Suspension Bridge over the River Avon stemmed from a tedious procedure involving two competitions, with Thomas Telford as one of his rivals. The span is approx. 214 m. Brunel was able to use the double chain he had used for his Hungerford Bridge in London, which had to make way for a new railway bridge. All that was needed was to add a third chain at the new location – an early and impressive example of reusing established iron components in a new construction project. Brunel achieved a sag ratio of 1:10 for his main chain, which still corresponds to modern engineering requirements. The bridge is still open to motor traffic today. However, the bridge requires scrupulous maintenance, in particular constant inspections for signs of corrosion.

Like many of his colleagues, Brunel was characterized by great versatility. Railways formed the focus of his work, including planning of routes as well as design of tunnels, bridges and stations. But he was also successful in shipbuilding, with great iron ships like the *Great Western* and the *Great Britain* to his credit.

With its overall length of 1054 m, a centre span of 486 m, road width of 26 m and a 41.14 m clearance, the Brooklyn Bridge in New York marked another milestone in the history of the suspension bridge. The pylons rise to 107 m. Johann August Roebling was responsible for the planning, his son, Washington August Roebling, for the construction. Building work commenced officially on 2 January 1870. The material used was cast steel. New developments were necessary in spinning the cables and in the caisson foundations for the piers. The reserves of strength built into the design rendered possible several conversions and a considerable increase in permissible loads in the years following its construction.

1.53

It took a long time before the principle of suspended construction – with rods, cables and
nets – was tried out in building structures.
However, archetypal early tent forms can be
traced back to prehistoric times. Ropes made
of plant fibres were used for tents as well as for
early suspension bridges, but had to be constantly replaced owing to their limited lifespan.
After early designs for suspended roofs with
spans of up to 100 m, by de Mondésir and
Lehaitre, were published in the *Gazette des
architectes* (1864) and the *Allgemeine Bauzeitung* (1866), the Russian engineer Vladimir
Grigorevič Šuchov set a milestone in the evolution of new structural systems employing
cables and nets with his patent application for
a "net-like system" for roofing over buildings
(1895). The patent drawing shows two structural forms. Over a circular plan, Šuchov combined a suspended roof, with a surface curved
in two planes, and a central lattice dome, with
arched compression elements. While the mesh
of the suspended roof changes towards the
outside, the dome is made up of identical elements intersecting at right-angles. Following
the successful trial of the concept on a workshop for a boiler manufacturer in Moscow in
1894, another impressive demonstration of this
new construction technique was witnessed at
the 1896 All-Russian Exhibition at Niznij Novgorod, a showcase for hand-made goods and
industrial production in tsarist Russia. The exhibition guide described it as follows: "The rotun-
da and the adjoining rectangular buildings can
rightly claim to be exhibits in themselves. They
are built of iron by the engineer Bary according
to the system of mechanical engineer Šuchov.
What is new about these buildings is that their
roofs are built without rafters and form a tightly
stretched, suspended net covered with iron
plates. As a result of this system, the roof takes
on the shape of a catenary curve."[24] The roof
covering to the net, made up of riveted flat iron
strips, consisted of galvanized iron sheeting. In
a detailed analysis, Rainer Graefe suspects
that the sheeting formed rigid areas which
counteracted deformations in the case of
unevenly distributed loads or wind suction.
Šuchov's development was not taken up again
for many decades. In the meantime, Le Cor-
busier had amazed the world with his Pavillon
des Temps Nouveaux at the 1937 World Exposition in Paris. He hung a cable net between
delicate pylons and attached tent material to

1.54

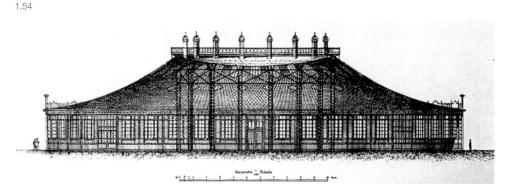

1.55

1.56

1.57

1.58

1.59

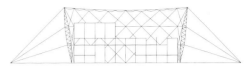

1.60

1.61

this to create an airy, ephemeral exhibition space.

The next climax in the story of suspended construction was certainly the tent-like structure designed by Rolf Gutbrod and Frei Otto for the German Pavilion at the 1967 World Exposition in Montreal. Comprehensive and fundamental research work on tension structures, described by Frei Otto in a two-volume work, preceded the project itself. The actual construction required numerous technical trials, particularly for the erection of the complicated and broad expanse of the tent medium.

A new technology had to be developed from scratch: methods for shaping and exact three-dimensional appraisal, the provision of certain cable and membrane qualities, the design of suitable connections and the drawing-up of detailed erection instructions.

The idea of a tent landscape underwent, besides technical, a fundamental functional and aesthetic enhancement with the structures for the 1972 Munich Olympics: the combination of tent structure (Behnisch & Partner, Frei Otto, Leonhardt + Andrä) and landscape design (Bernhard Grzimek). The prime technical difference between Montreal and Munich is that the latter is designed to be permanent. It has to be attributed to the stamina of all those involved that the complex retained the light, ephemeral character of its conception right through to the end. The stadium roof is formed by a succession of nine saddle-shaped nets with edge cables. This roof is suspended from eight tall masts and anchored directly to the ground. In the peripheral ring, the forces are balanced via common or coupled nodes. The prestressed cable net carries the loads of wind, snow and self-weight from the roof covering and transfers these to the edge cables. The roof is a square mesh with nodes at a constant spacing of 750 mm. For assembly, the cables were woven from flexible wires with minimum cross-section; strands of 19 wires (2.3-3.4 mm dia., heavily galvanized) are intended to keep corrosion at bay. The sealed edge cables are 81 mm in diameter and have a permissible load-carrying capacity of 3000 kN (factor of safety = 2 after considering all capacity-reducing influences). The nodes were manufactured from cast steel, following the necessary geometry. The ends of the prestressed cables were sealed with a newly developed compound. The roof covering of prestressed acrylic glass has now been

1.62, 1.63, 1.67, 1.68   Roof to Olympic Stadium,
    Munich, 1972, Behnisch & Partner, Frei Otto, Leon-
    hardt + Andrä, details and sectional elevation
1.69   ibid., underside of stadium roof
1.64, 1.70   Warehouse, Swindon, 1984, Norman Foster,
    Ove Arup Partnership, section and photo
1.65, 1.71   Research building, Princeton, 1986,
    Richard Rogers, F. J. Samuely & Partner,
    section and photo
1.66, 1.72   Research building, Cambridge, 1984,
    M. Hopkins, A. Hunt, Ove Arup Partnership,
    section and photo

1.62

1.63

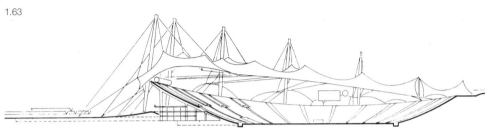

1.64

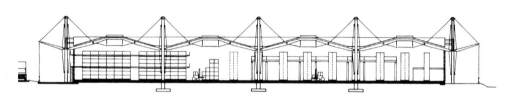

replaced after an astonishingly long time of
26 years and should guarantee the unimpeded
functioning of this worldwide unique roof construction for the next quarter of a century.

A modular grid of 16 m pylons forms the basis
of the building for an automobile manufacturer
in Swindon. This design, by Norman Foster,
accommodates offices and showrooms as well
as storage space for spare parts, and is capable of extension. Double-cranked and trussed
steel beams are suspended from prestressed
circular steel columns. Prestressing the
columns increases the stiffness and reduces
the size. The geometry of the cable stays and
trusses in the roof structure matches the bending moment diagram of the main beams.
"Shape and size of main loadbearing members
make the structural system crystal clear:
columns under compression, beams subjected
to bending, rods as tension elements,"[25] is how
Kurt Ackermann analyses the building in his
book *Industriebau*. Helmut C. Schulitz, in his
essay *Industriebau – Zukunft der Tradition*,
establishes analogies in the history of building.
Design proposals by Heinrich Hübsch (1825)
and the suspension system of Lehaitre and
Mondésir (1866) mentioned above are con-
strued as early, similar forerunners to Foster's
design. Comparing these produces amazing
results.

Rooflights have been incorporated in the ani-
mated roof structure in such a way that there is
always adequate daylight in the interior. The
rooflights at the centre of each bay serve as
both ventilation openings and smoke vents.
The evolution of the research and administration building in Princeton (Richard Rogers) is

1.65

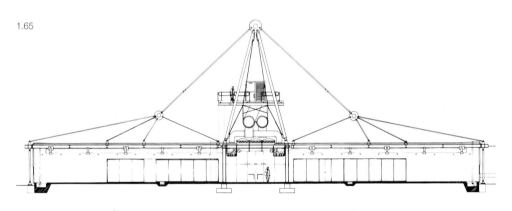

1.66

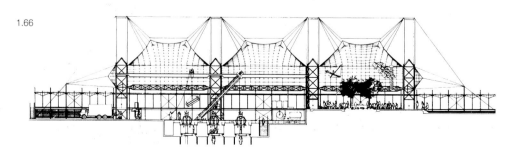

1.67

1.68

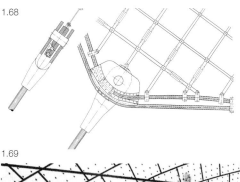

1.69

clearly recognizable. The backbone of the complex is formed by an 8 x 80 m glass-roofed arcade in which most of the utility services are incorporated. Clear spans of 22.8 m on both sides of the arcade guarantee maximum flexibility in terms of usage. The requirements of the client's specification were able to be realized through the use of a tall suspended construction of standardized components.

The constructional core of the research building in Cambridge by Michael Hopkins is formed by two steel frames made up of steel girders at different levels with differing spans and depths. Two single-storey parallel research blocks running north-south enclose a zone characterized by three 24-m-wide areas of varying height which serve common functions, e.g. central test laboratory, conservatory restaurant, and are roofed over with a translucent membrane. Pylons rise from the edges of the central large modules and are stressed by means of cable stays. The prestressed envelope of PTFE-coated glass-fibre textile is suspended from the tops of the pylons.

When combined with textile membranes in particular, suspended constructions are ideal for the most diverse applications, both temporary and permanent. The spectrum of possibilities appears to be inexhaustible and developments by no means over. Membranes offer protection against the weather, both precipitation and excessive solar radiation. Flexible roof arrangements are also being increasingly requested and realized. Elements from mechanical engineering are appearing more and more alongside conventional steelwork, cable and textile technology.

1.70

1.71

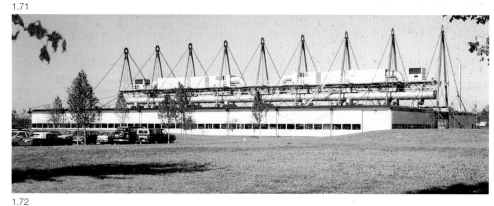

1.72

1.73   Factory, Lessay, 1992,
       Alluin & Mauduit, Groupe Arcora
1.74   Distribution centre, Roissy, 1992,
       Bianchi, Groupe Arcora

1.73

1.74

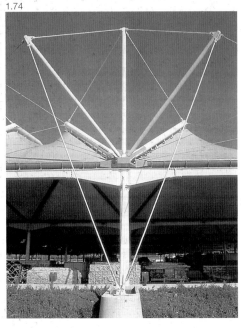

The membrane roof construction of the factory
in Lessay lends the linear form of the complex
not only an unusual appearance but also
ensures pleasant daylighting effects in the circulation zone. The modular roof structure of
steel and polyester textile over the distribution
centre in Roissy fulfils a different function.
Here, a large area has to be protected against
the elements with economic means.

Victoria Station,
London, 1862, John Fowler

The principle of the truss
Wrought iron as a prerequisite

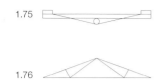

1.75

1.76

1.75   Sketch of principle of trussed beam
1.76   Sketch of principle of Polonceau truss
1.77   Rudolph Gottgetreu, *Lehrbuch der Hochbau-konstruktion*, 1885, Part 3, Iron constructions, roof structures of timber and iron
1.78   E. Brandt, *Lehrbuch der Eisenkonstruktionen*, 1876, trussed beam

1.77

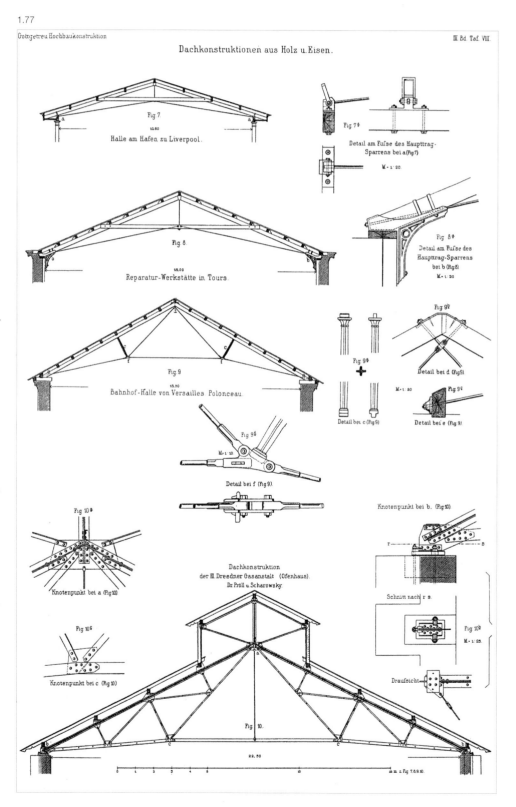

Combining horizontal or cambered cast iron beams with wrought iron tie rods results in improved loadbearing properties and hence an increase in the spans which can be achieved for floors and roofs. This idea was taken up by Friedrich August Stüler for an exhibition room on the upper floor of the Neues Museum in Berlin. He employed a cambered cast iron beam appropriately shaped at each end to accept two circular rods of wrought iron as prestressing tendons. The resulting structural unit was covered with ornamental attachments of cast zinc. T-shaped sections were laid at right-angles to this and the bays filled in with masonry vaulting. Only in the anteroom were the beams left, as Werner Lorenz assumes, deliberately exposed. The standard arrangement of trussed horizontal beam with stub compression member placed centrally (see Fig. 1.78) was still to be found in the 1876 edition of E. Brandt's *Lehrbuch der Eisenkonstruktionen*.

The adjacent illustration taken from Gottgetreu's *Lehrbuch der Hochbaukonstruktion* shows the development from timber roof trusses, suitably modified step by step to attain greater spans – from post truss to complete cast iron and wrought iron structures, as the engineers Wiegmann and Polonceau invented independently in 1836 and 1839 respectively. Only ductile wrought iron is suitable for members subjected to tension. The so-called Polonceau truss was used in a number of important structures in the following years.

For example, in the buildings for the 1867 World Exposition in Paris. These were conceived by Frédéric Le Play and detailed design work was carried out by the architect Léopold Hardy and the engineer Jean-Baptiste Krantz. The building is in the shape of an enormous oval measuring 490 x 386 m. The structure was written about in great detail by all the leading building journals. Carefully documented working drawings verify the rapid progress in construction technology thanks to the new materials iron, glass and corrugated metal sheeting. One part of the building made use of the trusses developed by Camille Polonceau. This skilfully orchestrated structural medium, in which tensile and compressive forces are easily distinguished, was also used for station roofs. St Lazare Station in Paris, rebuilt in 1852-54 by

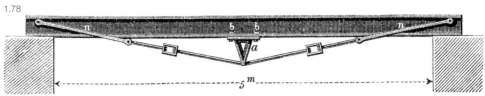

1.79 World Exposition, Paris, 1867, Léopold Hardy,
      Jean-Baptiste Krantz, section through halls
1.80 ibid., structural details of intermediate bays
1.81 Gare d'Austerlitz, Paris, 1869,
      Pierre L. Renaud, Louis Sévène
1.82 Bradbury Building, Los Angeles,1893,
      George Herbert Wyman,
      atrium with glass roof

the architect Alfred Armand and the engineer
Eugène Flachat, included Polonceau trusses
spanning 40 m. The great roof over the Gare
d'Austerlitz in Paris, built in 1869, used the
same principle, but in this case the span was
even longer – 52.55 m. The top chords of the
trusses were in themselves lattice girders. The
trusses were spaced at 10 m intervals and
firmly braced in the longitudinal direction by
purlin-type girders. The train shed was 22 m
high and 280 m long. The engineer was Louis
Sévène and the architect Pierre-Louis Renaud.
Their endeavours to use a minimum of material
while simultaneously increasing span and
load-carrying capacity are clearly recognizable
here. The different treatment of cast and
wrought iron enabled the two materials to be
easily distinguished: the cast, decorated columns, the rolled sections of the riveted girders
and beams, the drawn truss rods. The language of the connecting elements – restricted
to an economic minimum – can easily match
any of today's components.
The Polonceau truss was introduced in many
other stations and market halls, not only in
France. The atrium of the office and business
block designed by George Herbert Wyman for
Louis Bradbury in Los Angeles (completed in
1893) captivates the observer owing to the
high level of daylight which enters through the
high, pitched glass roof with its particularly
delicate Polonceau trusses. Iron is a dominant
feature throughout the atrium – in the exposed
loadbearing frames of the peripheral galleries
as well as the staircases and open lift shafts.
However, the building envelope remains a conventional mixture of masonry and sandstone.

Nevertheless, many years were to pass before
this type of trussed structure was rediscovered
in our own age.

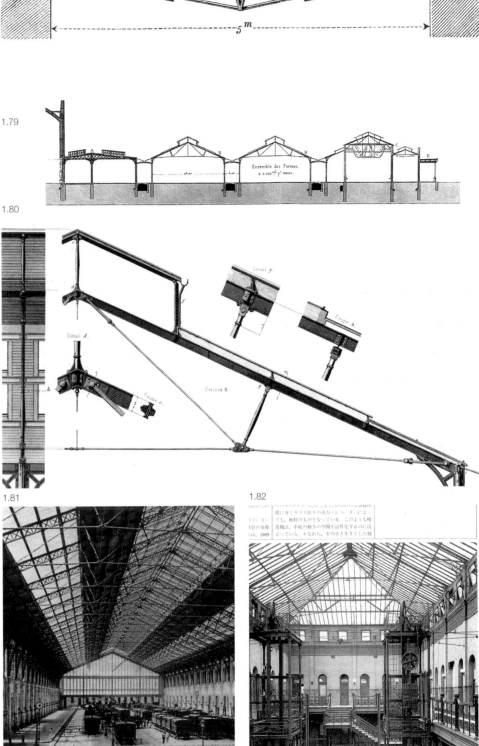

1.83

1.84

1.85

The principle of trussing can be particularly effectively employed with arched structures. The horizontal thrusts acting on the enclosing walls can be easily accommodated by inserting a tie (rod or cable) between the ends of the arch.

Paddington Station, London, (1851) designed by the architect Matthew Digby Wyatt together with that all-round-talent Isambard Kingdom Brunel as engineer, originally consisted of a central section (span 31 m, length 213 m) and two side spans each of 21 m. The slender cast iron arch sections are trussed with tie rods. The wide glazed section employs the "ridge and furrow" system designed by Paxton. One special feature is the two transverse roof sections, which are important for the longitudinal bracing of the structure. Fox & Henderson, the iron specialists who had been so successful with the Crystal Palace (also in 1851), were also responsible for Paddington Station.
At about the same time, Richard Turner designed a roof for Lime Street Station in Liverpool, using crescent-shaped trusses of wrought iron. The span in this case was 47 m. The trussed lattice-beam arches over Victoria Station in London (1860-62) were the work of John Fowler. The horizontal tension members of wrought iron chain links were prevented from sagging by a radial arrangement of sag rods.

The profound creations of the Russian engineer V. G. Šuchov went unnoticed for a long time. However, he was the first person to undertake a systematic investigation of the constructional possibilities of arched arrangements with non-rigid ties. Murat M. Gappoev describes these efforts in great detail in a contribution to Rainer Graefe's review of Šuchov. The starting point for his investigations is formed by the simplest case of an arch with three tension members, i.e. with two inclined members in addition to the customary horizontal tie. As only tensile forces can be accommodated, these members are redundant when compressive forces are acting. Šuchov drew up detailed calculation and design guidelines for these new systems.
The great machine hall of the All-Russian Exhibition in Niznij Novgorod by A. N. Pomerancev was one of the first trial applications for

1.86
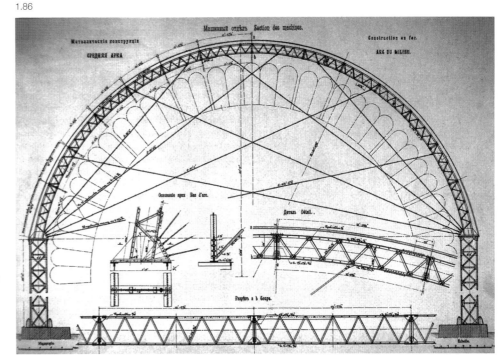

this new theory; a long-span lattice girder was stabilized by eight inclined tension members. The famous roofs to the arcades of the GUM department store in Moscow employed the same principle. The turnbuckles normally included to combat sag are missing here. As the very comprehensive information on details and erection have not supplied any adequate explanation, Gappoev has assumed, in his analysis, that Šuchov prestressed all inclined tension members in this case. The fine network of tension rods is hardly perceptible from a distance and produces an exceedingly delicate result. The amount of material was reduced to a minimum.

The logical conclusion of the extension of this arrangement to form a complete circle is the spoked wheel. World Expositions have always been proving grounds for experimental constructions. For instance, the US Pavilion at the 1958 Exposition in Brussels was quite astonishing in that it generated a greater response in engineering publications than in contemporary architectural journals. The unclad loadbearing structure was far more interesting than the finished building decorated in the fashion of the day. A multi-bay lattice girder rests on two rings of 72 steel stanchions. From here, 36 descending and 72 ascending cable stays span out radially to an upper and a lower ring beam in the centre of the building. Perpendicular props keep the two ring beams apart and diagonal cross-bracing stabilizes the resulting cylinder. The multiple-shear connections of the cable stays at the inner ring beam employed wide steel flats and high-strength bolts, and were tested at Karlsruhe Technical University prior to construction. The locked loadbearing cables consist of round and wedge wires internally and profiled wires externally. The ends of the cables are cast in. Levels and angles were constantly measured from a central platform during construction. The radial spacings were checked using steel wires running over pulleys and tensioned by counterweights.

1.87
1.88
1.89
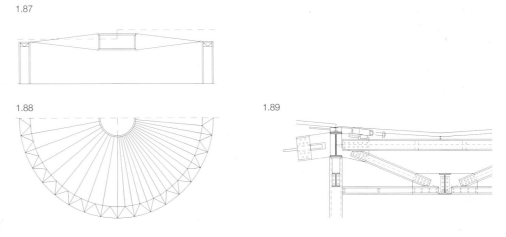

1.90

1.91 Thames Reach housing, London, 1987,
      Richard Rogers
1.92 Centre Commercial St Herblain, Nantes, 1987,
      Richard Rogers
1.93 Channel 4 headquarters, London, 1994,
      Richard Rogers

1.91

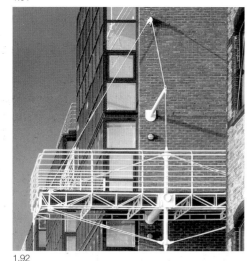

1.92

1.93

Details which, following the principle of trussing, lead to delicate loadbearing structures
with minimum use of materials characterize
numerous works by Richard Rogers and his
team. The main members of diverse items,
such as balconies, walkways, bridges, can be
made slimmer and the effects of tension and
compression rendered visible, thus leading to
a very special, new aesthetic quality.

Thames Reach residential development, situated alongside the River Thames, is dominated
by the generously sized balconies. These
appear to float like decks between the individual apartment blocks and, with their horizontal
balustrading, awaken associations with ship
superstructures.

The terrain at the St Herblain commercial complex near Nantes renders possible an imposing, bridge-like entrance arrangement. Further
accents and distinguishing elements are
superfluous.

The excitingly staged entrance foyer to the
Channel 4 television studios in London is also
accessed via a sort of walkway with printed
glass flooring. The exposed structure gives the
space below a special significance, even
though it lies in the basement.

Karl Scheffler:
"He (Endell) has retained
the profane basic forms
that have simply come
about, but has placed
them in a rhythmic order
so spiritualized, so
grouped that one can for
the first time speak of a
specific race course architecture. In his hands the
hideous iron and timber
frames have become inge-
nious, ruggedly graceful
engineering
architecture..."[26]

Trotting course grand-
stand, Berlin-Mariendorf,
1912, August Endell

The truss as a beam
Trusses in multistorey construction

1.94

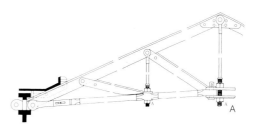

"A truss is any system of linear members whose ends are connected together in an articulated manner."[27]
Otto Königer, 1890
"Trusses are systems of linear members which can accommodate the loads of the entire construction by means of axial forces."[28]
ESDEP, 1996

1.95

The classic truss of the mid-19th century was made of iron. Countless preceding stages, variations and spinoffs, many in timber or a mixture of timber and iron, make any attempt at classification virtually impossible. The Polonceau truss dealt with in the preceding section can also be included under this heading of pin-jointed frames or the forerunners thereof. While the early forms of truss evolved via empirical methods, the publication of the first general theory of trusses by J. W. Schwedler in 1851 enabled methods of calculation to be used for their design. Wilhelm Ritter and Karl Culmann were involved in refining the theory, as was Luigi Cremona, whose "Cremona Plan" provided a graphic aid. In Russia too, similar developments took place, but only later did the West learn of these. As knowledge of these new methods of design and calculation spread, so the variety of forms diminished drastically. Only with the advent of the computer did engineers overcome this problem. It is interesting that the evolution of the iron truss can be traced by way of a few significant examples. The roof structure to Euston Station in London exhibited the typical truss geometry at an early date. The design of the elements as well as the articulated arrangement of the nodes was remarkable. Victoria Station in Manchester employed a very similar design over a greater span.

In the *Allgemeine Bauzeitung* of 1835 the engineer Karl Etzel described his impression of the new Marché de la Madeleine in Paris: "The dainty roof structure resembling a spider's web and beneath it the elegant tables, cabinets, scales and other market paraphernalia, and the wares displayed with French flirtatiousness made a very satisfying picture."[29] The drawings are reproduced in separate illustrations. However, the poor transverse bracing led to the building collapsing soon after (in 1842). Karl Muffat took up the idea of the delicate roof construction of the Marché de la Madeleine in his design for Maximilian's grain market in Munich; he ensured long-term stability by introducing additional anchors to resist tension. "All iron parts were subjected to compressive or tensile tests depending on their function in the construction,"[30] confirmed L. Wind in a lengthy report in the *Allgemeine Bauzeitung* of 1856. While a cross-section through the building exhibits similarities with the Polonceau truss, the elevation reveals a surprise: the raised roof

1.96

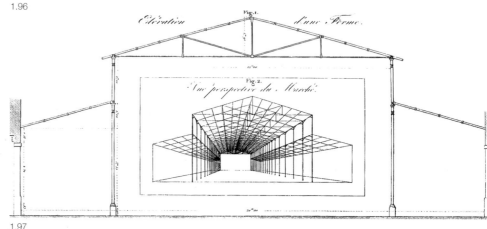

1.97

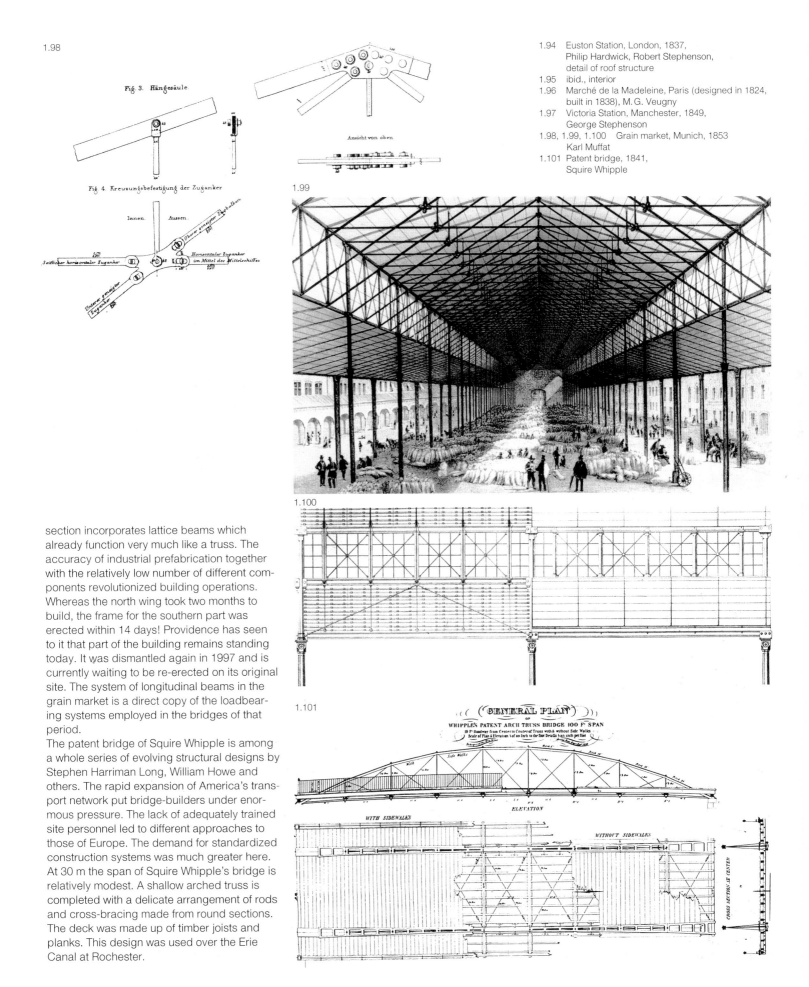

1.98

Fig. 3. Hängesäule
Ansicht von oben
Fig. 4. Kreuzungsbefestigung der Zuganker
Innen.
Aussen.
Oberer geneigter Zugbalken
Horizontaler Zuganker
im Mittel des Mittelschiffes
Seitlicher horizontaler Zuganker
Unterer geneigter Zuganker

1.94 Euston Station, London, 1837, Philip Hardwick, Robert Stephenson, detail of roof structure
1.95 ibid., interior
1.96 Marché de la Madeleine, Paris (designed in 1824, built in 1838), M. G. Veugny
1.97 Victoria Station, Manchester, 1849, George Stephenson
1.98, 1.99, 1.100 Grain market, Munich, 1853 Karl Muffat
1.101 Patent bridge, 1841, Squire Whipple

1.99

1.100

section incorporates lattice beams which already function very much like a truss. The accuracy of industrial prefabrication together with the relatively low number of different components revolutionized building operations. Whereas the north wing took two months to build, the frame for the southern part was erected within 14 days! Providence has seen to it that part of the building remains standing today. It was dismantled again in 1997 and is currently waiting to be re-erected on its original site. The system of longitudinal beams in the grain market is a direct copy of the loadbearing systems employed in the bridges of that period.

The patent bridge of Squire Whipple is among a whole series of evolving structural designs by Stephen Harriman Long, William Howe and others. The rapid expansion of America's transport network put bridge-builders under enormous pressure. The lack of adequately trained site personnel led to different approaches to those of Europe. The demand for standardized construction systems was much greater here. At 30 m the span of Squire Whipple's bridge is relatively modest. A shallow arched truss is completed with a delicate arrangement of rods and cross-bracing made from round sections. The deck was made up of timber joists and planks. This design was used over the Erie Canal at Rochester.

1.101

GENERAL PLAN
OF
WHIPPLE'S PATENT ARCH TRUSS BRIDGE 100 Ft SPAN
ELEVATION
WITH SIDEWALKS
WITHOUT SIDEWALKS
CROSS SECTION AT CENTER

1.102

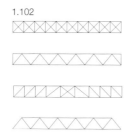

A compact arrangement of iron halls fulfilled the function of the "belly" of Paris for more than 100 years. The architect Victor Baltard visited relevant structures in England, Belgium, the Netherlands and Germany before embarking on his project. The first draft – solid masonry with only the roofs of iron – triggered bitter criticism. Following a competition which attracted more than 40 entries, Baltard, together with his colleague Félix Emmanuel Callet, drew up the design which was realized in several stages between 1854 and 1857, and 1860 and 1878. On the instruction of Prefect Baron Haussmann – a political intervention similar to what had happened with the grain market in Munich – an exclusively iron structure was favoured. Joly, a contractor with experience in similar structures (Gare de l'Est) was brought in to help with the work. In contrast to later projects in other European cities, the facades were also characterized by the new iron technology. The comprehensive building documentation prepared by the architects themselves included all important detail drawings as well as the customary plans, sections and elevations. A framework of cast iron columns and lattice girders, riveted together from rolled sections, formed the basis. Infills were glass and masonry, later also metal sheeting. Despite a high degree of differentiation between the individual pavilions, the underlying pattern meant that the number of different components could be kept relatively low. All connections between columns and beams, panels and frame, were drawn in great detail. And the technical precautions for maintaining better hygiene conditions for foodstuffs (cooling apparatus etc.) had already been well developed. "The new central halls of Paris can be regarded as models of such facilities, although they have been erected at more expense and with greater luxury than would have been strictly necessary,"[31] wrote one reporter in the *Allgemeine Bauzeitung* of 1859. Despite a number of efforts to preserve them, the last of the famous halls of Paris was demolished in 1971. (Only one pavilion was rebuilt in Nogent in 1976.)

Hardly any work dealing with the history of building can fail to include the chocolate factory in Noisiel by Jules Saulnier. The building was a direct translation of the hitherto common

1.103

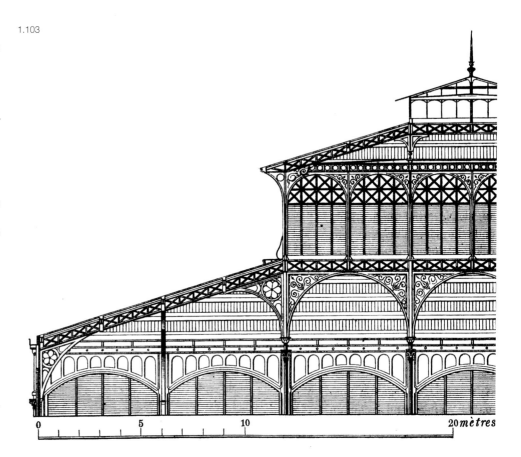

1.104

1.105

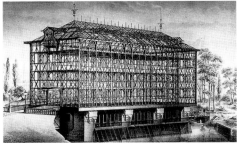

timber frames into the new material iron. In engineering terms, the visible diagonal wind bracing, the columns and floor beams all function together to form a vast three-dimensional pin-jointed frame for the entire building, completely made of iron. In typological terms, the factory can be classed as a multistorey bridge structure. The drawing of the iron skeleton shown above is proof of this. In the magazine *Encyclopédie d'Architecture* (1874 issue), the architect himself describes the evolution and construction of the project: "I suggested to Mr Menier that everything be demolished and presented him with my plan for a building made entirely of iron and clay bricks, whereby the walls of the facade should act as beams themselves, like the beams of a bridge of iron trusses. ... This building was, in terms of location, size and function, the most important of his factories; he was not put off by the high cost and resolved to design it in a most comely manner in a way that is hardly typical of industrial plants."[32] In terms of its aesthetic quality, the factory could certainly be described as an early example of the implementation of a corporate identity. The high cost of building the double-leaf infills of facing brickwork was certainly one of the main reasons for the rather cool reception to this highly publicized building.

During the recent refurbishment work, the high quality of the engineering input was able to be analysed in detail. Only the availability of highly accurate rolled sections of high loadbearing capacity made from puddled iron made it possible to construct this extraordinary design. As this large metal framework expands/contracts by up to 50 mm in the longitudinal direction as a result of normal temperature fluctuations, the joints between brick infills and iron sections have to be filled with a highly elastic mortar in order to prevent possible cracks and hence damage to the fabric of the building. Even the original colour scheme could be verified and reproduced.

1.106

1.107

1.108

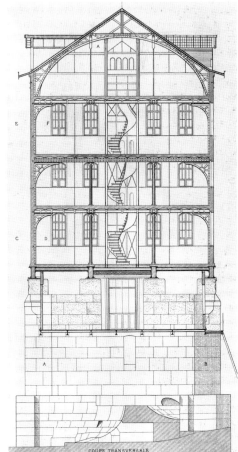

1.109

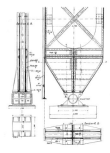

1.110

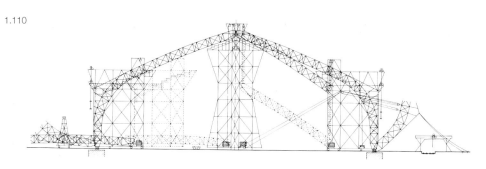

1.111

The structures here represent highlights in the history of pin-jointed iron frames. On the Garabit Viaduct, Gustave Eiffel had already developed and tested numerous details which were to prove beneficial in the construction of the "Tour des 300 Mètres". His assistants, Emile Nouguier and Maurice Koechlin, had, in the run-up to the preparations for the World Exposition of 1889, already made drawings of a tower to act as a symbol and landmark. Stephen Sauvestre, the team's architect, added detail to the concept. As the chance to realize the tower became real, Eiffel bought the design from his own colleagues, portrayed it as his own idea and did everything in his power to make sure the tower was built. Design, tonnages, costs and erection schedule were all finalized within a short time. This gave Eiffel a head start over his competitors that was finally to bring success in the 1886 outline design competition. Dutert, Eiffel/Sauvestre and Formigé were awarded the three first prizes. Eiffel's contract with the government, the local authority and the city included his personal liability for the building of the tower and its use for 20 years. Massive protests by the artistic establishment, encouraged and supported by the influential architecture journal *La Construction Moderne* were answered by Eiffel in a highly business-like manner. Although undisputed as a feat of engineering, the tower was not acknowledged as an architectural accomplishment to the same degree for many years. The project was covered in the architectural press merely by way of brief reports on the state of progress on site. In the end, Eiffel recorded all the details of the project himself in a large-format work entitled *La Tour des 300 Mètres*. One of the limited print run of just 500 copies was presented to the Deutsches Museum in Munich with a personal dedication. The immense planning achievement of Eiffel and his assistants is still evident today through the scrupulously detailed working drawings. The precise specification and strict quality control – defective parts were immediately returned to the factory – rendered possible a construction period of just 26 months. While the lower section required extensive timber scaffolding, the upper sections made use of a climbing crane developed by the team.

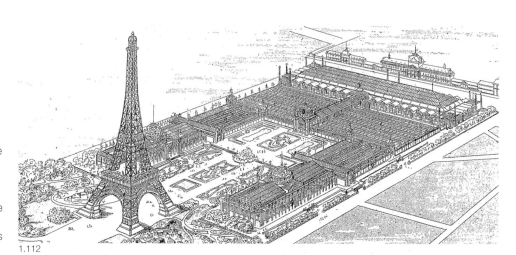

1.112

1.113

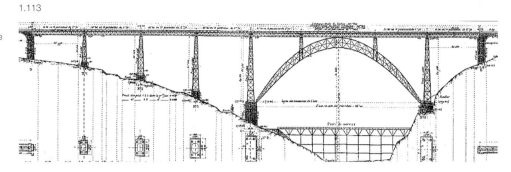

The technical details of the Palais des
Machines by Ferdinand Dutert and Victor Cont-
amin (420 m long x 115 m wide x 43.5 m high)
were described in great detail in architectural
journals. Particularly interesting is the fact that
the two contractors involved used different
methods of erection. Conventional assembly
by means of extensive scaffolding was pitted
against the joining of larger prefabricated truss
elements involving substantially less scaffolding. This latter method placed tougher
demands on the accuracy of the fabrication.
The efficiency of the three-pin arch, which had
been developed step by step for bridges, was
demonstrated here on a building in impressive
fashion. However, the contrast with notions of
aesthetics prevalent up until then could hardly
have been greater. The customary wide,
confidence-inspiring base was missing; the
lightness of the hinges, like the delicacy of the
arched beams, provoked protest. The hinged
base finally chosen was the result of a lengthy
design process, proof of the careful, gradual
optimization of this critical detail. This building
was a prominent feature at the next World
Exposition, in 1900, but in 1909 it was demolished for want of a suitable use. In terms of
both its language and its engineering, this
structure acted as a model for the great railway
stations of later years.
The design of the bridge spanning the Firth of
Forth was characterized by a raised aware-
ness of safety shown by the client and his
designers; the Tay Bridge to the north had col-
lapsed shortly before. The more elegant suspension bridge design was immediately rejected.
The principle of cantilevering trusses with intermediate trussed girders (H. G. Gerber) led to a
unique sculptural style. Steel was used for the
first time. The combination of riveted tubes of
steel plate (compression) with lattice beams of
rolled sections (tension) is also remarkable. In
contrast to the high degree of prefabrication
used for some parts of the Eiffel Tower, sections and plates were connected in situ here. A
hydraulic riveting machine and a plate bending
machine were developed for the project. The
Forth Rail Bridge has been recorded in great
detail in words and pictures.

1.114

1.115

1.116

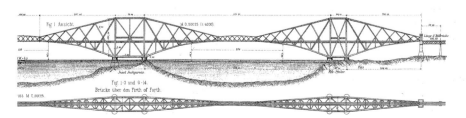

1.117

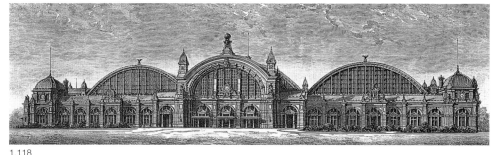

1.118

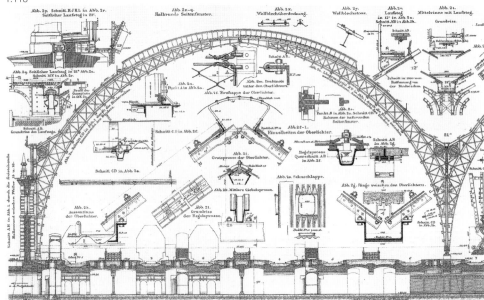

1.119

Besides their use in bridge-building, trusses were employed in large-span roofs over major railway stations. In 1866 St Pancras Station in London achieved a height of 31 m, a length of 210 m and a span of 73 m, thus preempting the spatial effect of the Galerie des Machines. The engineers W. Barlow and R. Ordish designed a pointed arch divided into segments and without a hinge at the crown but with a tie below floor level. This was partly masked afterwards by G. Scott's hotel and terminus building in New Gothic style. The critics of the day praised the harmony of the two structures. The arduous and complicated history of Frankfurt am Main central station has been thoroughly recorded. Responsible for the draft design were the Senior Building Officer Schwedler and the State Master-Builder Frantz. For reasons of cost, Schwedler considerably modified the shed solution in the course of the competition: "Owing to the shape of the ironwork and the junction with the masonry construction, it is prescribed that all manner of artistry must be avoided..."[33] The platforms and tracks were spanned with three arches. A three-pin arch was used in each case. The three-pin arch over the Galerie des Machines was the logical next step after the roofs at St Pancras and Frankfurt. The exhibition-style architecture underscores the continuing aesthetic emancipation of exposed iron roof structures. Railway stations devoid of ornamentation but built using delicate and unobtrusive iron structures became standard throughout Europe, indeed the world. However, the adjoining terminus buildings generally adhered to the requirements placed on public buildings, i.e. solidity, massiveness, and were clad accordingly in natural stone. The stations in Hamburg and Leipzig sustained the new trend.

Far less troublesome in terms of aesthetics was the use of exposed iron structures for industrial buildings. It was already rather unusual to devote too much attention to the architectural treatment of such facilities, as the chocolate factory by Saulnier shows. In the case of the Zollern II colliery machine shop it was possible for the architect Bruno Möhring to lend the commanding iron frame a special charm by carefully introduced Art Nouveau elements. From today's viewpoint we would

1.120

1.121

probably also attribute an almost sacred appeal to the interior. Advocates of Art Nouveau like Hector Guimard and Victor Horta were successful in evolving new language traits with the new material (see p. 28). The Maison du Peuple in Brussels by Victor Horta generated disparate feelings among his contemporaries. The naked iron frame was felt to be an affront to style: "Disregarding the failure to create an overall artistic impression, the grappling with the form is nevertheless very interesting on a small scale,"[36] was the damning judgement of Alfred Gotthold Meyer. The manifold technical and architectural opportunities presented by the new material were not recognized. Even by 1964 the merit of the building had still not attained a high enough level to prevent it from being demolished.
"Of the many building materials which industry invents daily in order to achieve ever better results in the building sector, the discovery of iron, i.e. the fabrication of iron beams and trusses, was without doubt the most important in both constructional and stylistic terms. For iron could now become, alongside stone and wood, the third major building material and hence inaugurate a new age of architecture. However, we can say today that iron, although immensely significant as such, has not delivered what it promised at the beginning, and that the so-called 'iron style', i.e. a style in a narrower sense, as a material style, is non-existent. Furthermore, it seems unlikely that any movement in this direction can be expected in the future."[37] This resigned opinion was expressed by Henrik Berlage, the designer of the Amsterdam Stock Exchange, in 1905. The great care with which he detailed the transition from iron trusses to adjoining masonry is still clearly recognizable today. In 1905 Berlage himself drew attention to the fact that more stringent fire protection regulations would in the future prevent the erection of buildings like his Stock Exchange of 1903.

1.122

1.123   Flender bridge-builders, production building for
        two airships, Friedrichshafen, 1909, section
1.124   ibid., shed under construction
1.125   Aircraft hangar, Oberwiesenfeld, 1929,
        K. J. Moßner
1.126   ibid., interior view

1.123

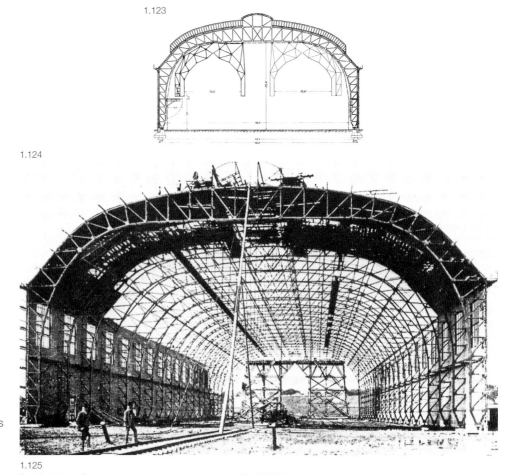

1.124

We might well be surprised upon first hearing that the roof covering to the first iron airship production facility employed an 80-mm-deep layer of reinforced concrete and a bituminous finish, and the iron frames to the side walls were provided with two leaves of masonry having an air cavity and rendering on the outside. However, the reason for this was the need to maintain a constant internal temperature and prevent unnecessary heating-up of the interior, which is also the reason why large rooflights were not used. The clear inside dimensions are fascinating: 43 m wide, 20 m high, 178 m long. Likewise the delicate structure, visible in the section drawing and the photo of the building under construction. Travelling cradles permitted access to all sides of the airship's hull. After 20 years the building had served its purpose and was demolished. A total of 28 airships had been built here, but the growing size of airships made it necessary to construct larger facilities. Oberwiesenfeld, today the site of the Olympics complex, was once the home of Munich's airport. Completed in 1929, the character of the terminal building proclaimed new monumentalist tendencies but the aircraft hangar was surprising in that the geometry of its loadbearing structure remained clearly discernible. The lattice girders appear purposeful and unobtrusive, far removed from Ludwig Mies van der Rohe's aesthetically overstated Convention Hall of the 1950s. "The purpose of iron is: to condense high loadbearing ability to the slimmest of dimensions. If comparisons are admissible, then the iron of a building is both muscles and skeleton. Iron opens up the interior. The wall can become a transparent glass skin. The wall as a loadbearing element becomes an untenable farce. This leads to new laws of design."[38] These are the words of Sigfried Giedion, taken from his programmatic work *Bauen in Frankreich, Bauen in Eisen, Bauen in Eisenbeton* (1928). This notion is reflected in the aircraft hangar at Oberwiesenfeld.

It is also interesting to compare such shed-like structures with the construction of the aircraft of the period. Here too we discover trussed frames. While thin steel sheet had been used for many early aeroplanes, the introduction of the new material aluminium was a major step forward in terms of weight reduction. The build-

1.125

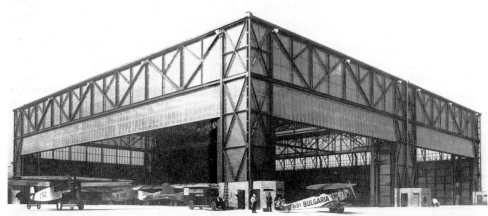

1.126

1.127

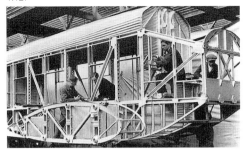

1.128

ing industry in turn benefited from the progress made in the aircraft and automotive industries using this construction principle. Issue 23/1929 of the magazine *Die Form – Zeitschrift für gestaltende Arbeit* contains an interesting mixture of contributions. The architect Fritz Block records details of ships in order to subject them to a "technical analysis of form". Otto Haesler writes about braced steel frames: "The braced steel frame overcomes the constraints imposed on the human race by stone construction for thousands of years. ... The clad and enveloped braced steel frame usual up to now does not represent a consummate unity. Therefore, steel sections must undergo modifications and improvements until the mutual conformity of the steel frame and the infilling produces a constructional and aesthetic permanent whole."[39] To conclude, Roger Ginsburger analyses the latest trends in railway rolling stock and cars, without forgetting one or other cross-reference to the aircraft industry. The political upheavals of the following years resulted in a pause for thought in Europe until the emergence of Renzo Piano, Norman Foster, Peter Rice and others.

In the USA Albert Kahn became the dominant figure in industrial architecture. Besides car plants he designed enormous buildings for the aircraft industry. Skilfully incorporated strips of rooflights guaranteed even illumination of work surfaces with adequate levels of daylight. The structure shown here (Fig. 1.128) with an unobstructed floor area of 100 x 150 m was used five years later by Mies van der Rohe as the background for a photo collage. "Levitating" walls and ceilings were intended to emphasize the concept of a modern concert hall.

Craig Ellwood latched onto Mies van der Rohe's train of thought. In his production building for an electronics firm, the language of structure and details were intensified, but not always wholly logically and consistently in terms of engineering and building science.

In the Sainsbury Centre for the Visual Arts, Norman Foster reintroduced the lattice girder – long reserved for industrial buildings – into a prestige object. This was combined with innovative details in the envelope.

1.129

1.130

1.131 Sabolovka radio mast, Moscow, 1922,
       V. G. Šuchov
1.132 John Hancock Tower, Chicago, 1969,
       Skidmore, Owings & Merrill, Fazlur Khan

1.131

1.132

A brief look at the role of trusses in towers and skyscrapers will complement this line of development and pave the way for a look into the future.

V. G. Šuchov was an outstanding personality at the turn of the last century. The well-known lattice towers represent just one facet of his accomplishments. The 150 m Sabolovka radio mast in Moscow, although much shorter than originally planned (350 m), was nevertheless a masterpiece of engineering expertise and use of material – a huge cone comprising several sections formed by hyperboloids, the diameter of the connecting rings gradually decreasing with the height. Further rings were evenly spaced between these. The precision of the resulting network was amazing considering the plant available at the time. The mast was erected using the telescope principle; the individual sections were lifted through the middle in succession. The diameter of the base of each section was reduced with tie rods.

The John Hancock Tower in Chicago follows the principle of a tapering square tube. The group of outer columns is joined horizontally at regular intervals and further stabilized by means of cross-bracing. This is what the engineers call a "trussed tube", a highly efficient structural system. The tower's 100 storeys reach a height of 332 m. The success of the building is primarily due to its special blend of parking decks, offices, service zones and apartments. Optimum vertical transportation by means of express and local lifts is of course indispensable in such a building.

Norman Foster's 1000 m Millennium Tower project for Tokyo represents, for the time being, the final step in this evolutionary chain. The principle of diagonal bracing on the outside features again here, but this time the tapering structure is conical. Both Šuchov and Fazlur Khan, the structural engineer for the John Hancock Tower, are evidently the godparents.

860–880 Lake Shore Drive apartment blocks
Chicago, 1948–51,
Ludwig Mies van der Rohe

Beams in bending
Rigid frame, braced frame, "tube"

1.133

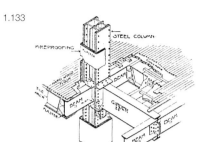

1.133 Fair Store, Chicago, 1891,
       William le Baron Jenney, column detail
1.134 Old Colony Building, Chicago, 1894,
       Holabird & Roche
1.135 ibid., section
1.136 ibid., storey-height frame
1.137 ibid., beam-column connection

1.134

1.136

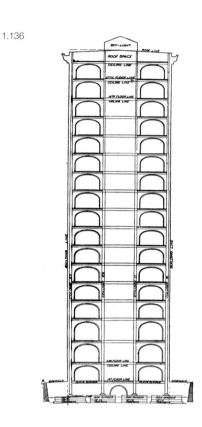

The steps preceding the braced iron frame have been dealt with in the section on cast iron (pp. 22-28). The individual components here consist of cast iron, a material that can accommodate compressive forces without any problems but can only be used to a limited extent for members subject to bending owing to its brittleness. The complete braced iron frame only became possible and expedient after the introduction of riveted frame structures of wrought iron. One early example of a complete braced iron frame is the chocolate factory in Noisiel by Jules Saulnier (1872) (see p. 46). However, this must be regarded as a timber frame interpreted in iron. Although complete framed structures were developed in France thanks to Eiffel, e.g. the well-known Bon Marché department store in Paris (1876), we must look to the USA for the successful continuation of the development of the iron multi-storey building. Our focus of attention here is the upwardly mobile commercial and industrial metropolis Chicago. After the devastating fire of 1871, new solutions in building technology became essential. Unemployed railway engineers – the railways were now all linked – saw their chance in buildings. Heavy industry was experiencing a major boom. Iron was the obvious choice. The enormous pressure on economic expansion was to have undreamed-of consequences for the density of urban development.

Besides the purely constructional problems, however, there was still the question of the vertical transportation of people to be answered, as well as other building services such as electric lighting, telecommunications, mechanical ventilation and sanitary facilities. Elisha Graves Otis was the inventor of the safety elevator, first demonstrated at the 1853 World Exposition in New York. Otis quickly equipped hotels and department stores with steam-driven systems whose speed was constantly increased. His sons carried on his work and played a major part in the development of the first generation of skyscrapers (First Chicago School).

Braced frames in iron and steel evolved in leaps and bounds. Besides the constant improvements in material quality, further developments in jointing and construction technology played a great role.

The First Leiter Building designed by William le Baron Jenney originally had five storeys before two more were added in 1888. It employed

1.135

1.137

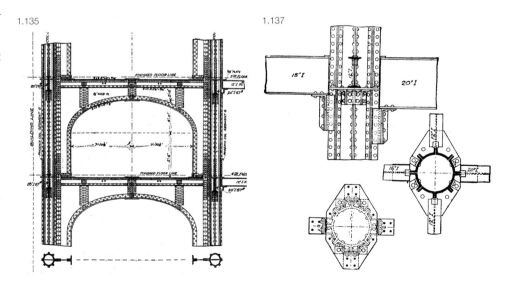

1.138   First Leiter Building, Chicago ,1879,
        William Le Baron Jenney
1.139   Tacoma Building, Chicago, 1887,
        Holabird & Roche
1.140   Reliance Building, Chicago, 1894,
        Charles Atwood
1.141   McClurg Building, Chicago, 1900,
        Holabird & Roche

cast iron columns, wrought iron beams and timber joists transversely as well as masonry-clad facade columns. With its open-plan interior and modestly ornamented but uncompromisingly displayed framework form externally, the language of this building was way ahead of its time. The 10-storey Home Insurance Building by the same architect completed six years later is universally accepted as the first multistorey building employing a complete iron frame. In addition, the first steel sections were used above the sixth floor. All connections are bolted. Fig. 1.133 shows a column-beam connection used on Fair Store, a detail which was typical of the period. The rigidity attainable with this connection was limited though, and the fireproofing made from prefabricated terracotta pieces could be described as tailor-made.

The Tacoma Building by Holabird & Roche (13 storeys) was the first multistorey building of any significance to employ riveted connections. The oriel-style relief of the facades was intended to increase the amount of daylight reaching the interior. The facade of Charles B. Atwood's Reliance Building was even more delicate. The frame is of steel and the oriels are supported on corbels on the outer columns. Terracotta elements were used for the spandrel panels and cladding to the posts. The high proportion of glazing anticipates the step to the technique of the curtain wall.

The Old Colony Building built at the same time has an external appearance which tends to hark back to bygone days. However, the interior is remarkable: on two transverse axes, stacks of portal frames assembled from riveted flat sections. These ensure the necessary strength to resist wind loads. In his book *Skeleton Construction in Buildings*, William H. Birkmire proclaimed this to be the most perfect steel frame of the period.

The facade of the McClurg Building by Holabird & Roche, in contrast to other buildings of the period, is an attest to maximum topicality in terms of proportions and the differentiation of its components.

1.138

1.139

1.140

1.141

1.142

1.143

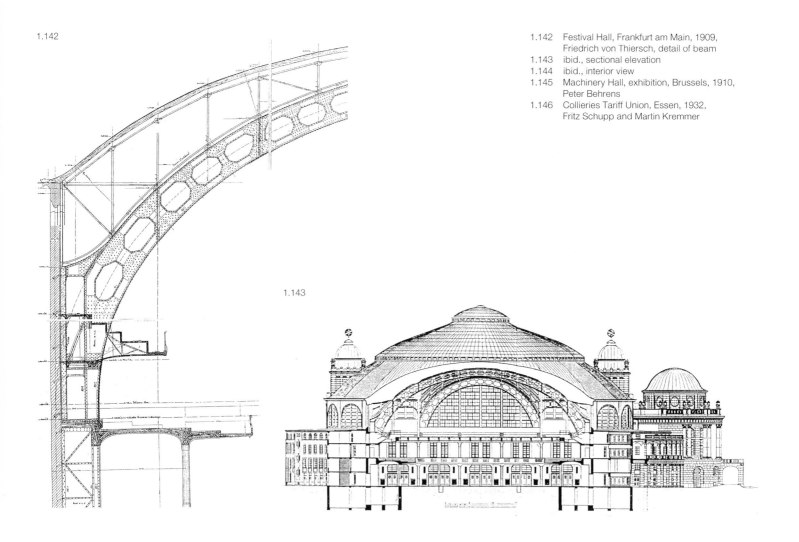

1.144

The Festival Hall, Frankfurt am Main, by Friedrich von Thiersch (completed in 1909) has a roofscape of elliptical dome and circular barrel-vault elements. The loadbearing structure consists of curved Vierendeel girders. In the commemorative publication marking the opening of the hall, the decision to adopt an exposed iron construction is explained in detail. What we today might regard as architectural language, was in no way the outcome of a brief burst of creativity but rather an arduous chain of individual considerations often burdened with scruples. "Only at the third attempt did the author achieve the complete exposure of the actual iron construction – insofar as it rises above the two galleries as a supporting structure – and arrange it in such a way that it contributes to the formation of the interior space as a universally comprehensible and pleasing, primary factor."[40] The theses of one Gottfried Semper, according to whom iron

would not be suitable for creating a "monumental architecture", were still having their effect. It is remarkable that alongside the "modern beam design", the foundations and galleries make use of reinforced concrete, a material at that time in its infancy but which was soon to take precedence over the only recently established material iron – for long spans as well. This is verified by the example of the Breslau Jahrhunderthalle by Berg (1911-13). Besides its advantages in terms of building science, reinforced concrete seemed to offer the long-standing optical qualities of monumentalism and solidity still being asked for.

Further developments in structural steelwork in the following years were mainly in the realm of industrial buildings. The solid, welded frame increasingly replaced the delicate, riveted truss. The German Mechanical Engineering Pavilion designed by Peter Behrens for the 1910 World Exposition in Brussels presented a successful stepped internal arrangement. The transition to the Modern Age was already discernible. While a phase of restorative Neo-Classicism propelled monumentalist building more and more into the foreground, structural steelwork enjoyed a straight-line upward progression in industrial architecture. Architects such as Fritz Schupp and Martin Kremmer set significant accents with complexes like the Collieries Tariff Union in Essen (1928-32). The entire complex is now protected by a preservation order and the boiler house has been converted into a regional design centre by Norman Foster. Exhibitions are held beneath the full-height portal frames of the former central workshop, conscientiously renovated by Heinrich Böll and Hans Krabel. During the refurbishment work great care has been exercised to retain as much as possible of the original steel post-and-rail framing with its infills of facing brickwork.

In industrial structures and special tasks in buildings, steel remained irreplaceable. While steelwork for industrial buildings was left exposed, it was generally still kept hidden behind intentionally massive cladding in other types of buildings during the following decades. This was for reasons of fire protection and building science as well as aesthetics.

1.145

1.146

1.147 PSFS Building, Philadelphia, 1932,
       George Howe, William Lescaze
1.148 ibid., under construction
1.149 Seagram Building, New York, 1957,
       Ludwig Mies van der Rohe, Philip Johnson,
       horizontal section through corner of building
1.150 ibid., completed building
1.151 ibid., under construction

1.149

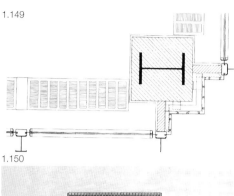

1.147

1.150

"Only during construction do skyscrapers reveal the bold constructional ideas, only then do we gain the overpowering impression of the ascending steel skeleton. Filling the facade with masonry destroys this sensation entirely, obliterates the constructional concept, the necessary principle of the artistic design, and enshrouds it with a (frequently) inappropriate and trivial fashionable pretext."[41] This is how Ludwig Mies van der Rohe expressed his dissatisfaction in 1922 and drew attention to his design for a glass skyscraper for the Friedrichstrasse Station in Berlin. As New York became the focal point for business instead of Chicago, so the American skyscraper scene also shifted its emphasis. A zoning plan was introduced to overcome the problems of light in densely developed urban areas. This led to a skyline with pyramid-shaped, stepped buildings. All shades of eclecticism celebrated their triumphs. The famous stainless-steel clad topmost storeys of the Chrysler Building by William van Allen (1930) may well suffice as an example. The Philadelphia Saving Fund Society Building by George Howe and William Lescaze completed a couple of years later is today acknowledged as the linguistic dawn of the Modern Age. It was to this building that Henry Russel Hitchcock and Philip Johnson attached the label "International Style". Huge transfer structures rendered possible the spacious three-storey banking hall above the entrance level. This usage is visible externally like elsewhere on this building. The service core, in this case placed to the side, is clearly demarcated from the volume of the actual office zones. This skyscraper has a steel frame. On the longitudinal facades the columns protrude and hence emphasize the verticality. Therefore, the now legible frame structure preempts the later ideas and buildings of Mies van der Rohe and his colleagues. Mies van der Rohe's famous Lake Shore Drive apartment blocks in Chicago were erected in 1948-51. The photograph taken during construction (see plate facing p. 54) illustrates the unambiguous nature of the structure. To maintain the uniformity of the whole, the architect insisted on identical off-white curtains for all apartments! But as the columns and edge beams to the floors were unprotected, considerable building science problems arose after-

1.148

1.151

1.152

1.152 Sears Tower, Chicago, 1974,
Skidmore, Owings & Merril (SOM), Fazlur Khan,
storey-height frame
1.153 Thyssen Building, Düsseldorf, 1959,
Helmut Hentrich, Hubert Petschnigg
1.154 ibid., under construction
1.155 Sears Tower, Chicago, 1974,
Skidmore, Owings & Merril (SOM), Fazlur Khan
1.156 ibid., under construction

1.153

1.155

wards; these difficulties were avoided in subsequent projects by hanging a continuous glass skin in front of the columns. The construction was thus protected against temperature fluctuations and the resulting movements. The ducts for heating and air-conditioning were placed in the cavity between columns and facade. The principle of the curtain wall was complete. The stylistic climax to this doctrine was achieved by Mies van der Rohe in his Seagram Building in New York (1958). "The Seagram Building, together with its plaza, represents probably the most classical building that Mies designed,"[42] was the verdict of Franz Schulze in his 1986 biography of the architect. He searched successfully for inconsistencies and artistic flair but still concluded: "The treatment of every detail discloses the care for which Mies was famous." Details, elevation and structure speak for themselves.

Of Germany's steel skyscrapers, the so-called Dreischeiben-Hochhaus (Thyssen Building) in Düsseldorf by the architects Hentrich and Petschnigg, completed in 1960, is worthy of mention. The frame with four rows of hinged hollow columns and hinged longitudinal beams has wind bracing in the front faces of the three slab-like blocks.

The further evolution of the steel skyscraper mainly took place in the USA. New construction techniques became necessary as buildings rose higher and higher. The principle of the hollow box with additional horizontal bracing led to the "framed tube" (e.g. World Trade Center, New York, 110 storeys). The "tube-in-tube" system was an alternative. This structural form with internal and external tubes of steel is economic up to 80 storeys.

Sears Tower in Chicago, completed in 1974, was, at 442 m, for a long time the world's tallest building. It is based on the bundled tubes concept. At the top of each tube, a space truss joins the tubes in the horizontal plane. The (diagonal) trussed tube with horizontal bracing levels has already been dealt with on p. 54.

1.154

1.156

1.157 Office block, Berlin, 1930,
      Emil Fahrenkamp
1.158 Office block, Illinois 1963,
      Eero Saarinen
1.159 German Embassy, Washington 1964,
      Egon Eiermann
1.160 Technical university, Brugg-Windisch, 1966,
      Fritz Haller

1.157

1.158

1.159

1.160

The architectural language that allowed so little of the steel frame to be seen from the outside and was constrained by an obligation to traditional models of monumentalism in the sense of Gottfried Semper, the language that Mies van der Rohe so bemoaned during the 1920s, was only cast aside in isolated instances. Names like Hans Luckhardt, Erich Mendelsohn and Emil Fahrenkamp represent the unadorned experimentation of the Modern Age. Fahrenkamp's well-known office building adjacent the Landwehr Canal in Berlin demonstrates the opportunities that emerge with a delicate steel frame. Even today, the corrugated travertine facade – an early example of a veneer-type stone skin – is probably still a source of stimulation. In the following years, political turmoil checked the development of construction technology in Europe for a long time.

Eero Saarinen used the newly invented weatherproof steel for his office building in Illinois. The layer of rust which prevents further corrosion allowed for unusual stylistic effects to be achieved. Unfortunately, the ambitious claims uttered for this interesting material were not able to be matched in the long run.

The idea of lending a grid facade a visual depth by incorporating functions like sunshading, weather protection, maintenance, thermal and sound insulation, daylighting and screens for privacy in separate layers was brilliantly implemented by Egon Eiermann at the German Embassy in Washington.

In the 1960s and 1970s the Swiss architect Fritz Haller revived the inheritance of Mies and took it a step further. The steel frame of the technical university in Brugg-Windisch, coated as it were with a layer of stainless steel and glass, is a good example of the many possibilities for harmonizing the use of steel and glass.

Biosphere,
Montreal, 1967,
Richard Buckminster Fuller

Building systems
from Paxton to Fuller

"But nevertheless we are still convinced that it is not architecture; it is engineering – of the highest merit and value – but not architecture. The building is completely devoid of any form, the concept of stability and solidity is missing."[43]

Ecclesiologist, 1851

1.161

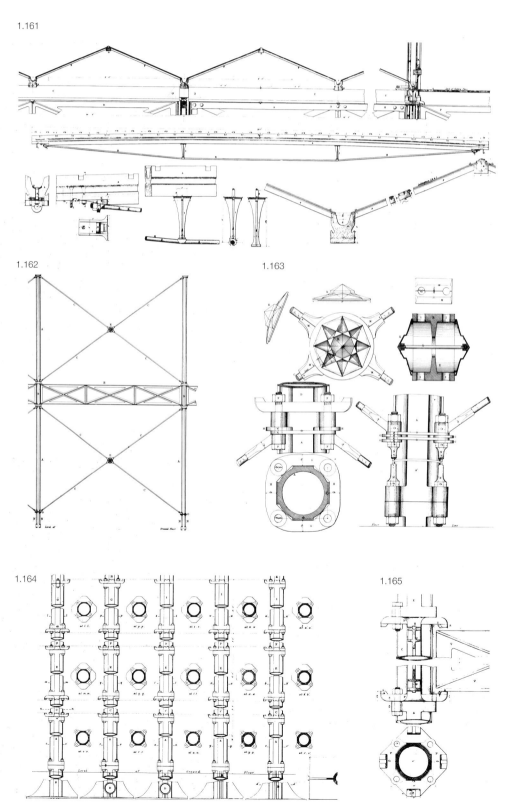

1.162

1.163

1.164

1.165

Despite the brief, which called for a merely temporary structure, the building to house the Great Exhibition in London in 1851 became an icon in the history of modern architecture. And the use of the new materials cast and wrought iron in a prefabricated system for a building subject to extreme expansion played an intrinsic part. A major international design competition attracted 233 entries before the deadline; among these works were a large number of interesting solutions and indeed two prizes were awarded – to Hector Horeau and Richard Turner. However, in no way could either of the two prize-winning entries have been erected within the time and price constraints. The Exhibition Committee put forward its own, less than convincing, proposal for a conventional building; the response was mediocre. In a process filled with obstacles, the greenhouse specialist Joseph Paxton and his backers managed to present Paxton's own idea for an attractive but at the same time "inexpensive" exhibition building to the Committee and the public. The drawings and calculations of the engineer Charles Fox made a very valuable contribution to Paxton's success.

Paxton's by then patented ridge-and-furrow roof system for greenhouses as well as numerous other innovations make the Crystal Palace, even today, a treasure chest of details. New machines for the accurate fabrication of individual components were invented or existing ones improved. Nevertheless, most of the building was erected using human muscle power, with only the large beams over the main hall being installed with the help of horses. During construction, organized site visits satiated the public's thirst for knowledge of progress.

Travelling covered cradles were used for installing the vast areas of glazing to the roof. Protected against wind and rain, 80 glaziers were thus able to fit 18,000 panes of glass each week. And where the engineering requirements and economic considerations made it worthwhile, timber was also used, e.g. for the large curved ribs over the transverse section. The great building was completed in just six months. Today, the 360-page exhibition catalogue reveals a somewhat conflicting pic-

1.166

ture of building and contents. Although the building, even today, is interesting in many ways, the contents exhibited therein under the title of "The Industry of all Nations" would more likely be labelled bric-a-brac!

By 1854 the building had been transferred to Sydenham and undergone certain modifications. Two further transverse sections had been inserted and the barrel-vault roofs were now of iron. The building continued to be used, converted and modernized – proof of the flexibility of the architectural concept – until it was destroyed by fire in 1936.

Another "glass palace", this time the one in Munich by August von Voit, was conceived as a temporary building for an industrial exhibition. Built in 1854, it remained a cultural focus until it fell victim to an arson attack in 1931. Many ideas were copied from the London original: the use of glass and iron as the main materials, a clear grid system, standardized components. And like in London, powerful building contractors were able to ensure that the building was completed on schedule. The differentiated structure of the Munich building emphasized the thesis of technical progress. In contrast to Paxton, von Voit was able to arrange that the loadbearing structure be visible externally as well. And here too, the hollow cast iron columns doubled as rainwater downpipes; but the roof guttering managed without any wood in this case. Leaks appeared like with the London original.

The extracts from the working drawings of the Crystal Palace reproduced here reveal the immense innovative thrust that building with glass and iron underwent. The ridge-and-furrow roof glazing had already been tried out and developed on various greenhouses. Trussed beams ensured the necessary rise at the middle of each bay. The gutters, still made of wood in this project, had extra channels internally for condensation, but bring with them a danger of leaks due to the material itself and its processing. Diagonal, prestressed rods end at high-precision cast iron nodes and stabilize the whole structure. Some 140 years later these details inspired the likes of engineer Anthony Hunt and architects Norman Foster and Richard Rogers.

1.167

1.168

1.169 House of corrugated metal sheeting "for dispatch
to uncultivated places overseas"
1.170 Various forms of corrugated metal sheeting
1.171 Steel house, Dessau, 1926, Georg Muche

Galvanized corrugated metal sheeting was
invented around 1840. The shallow or deep
corrugations, depending on the loads to be
carried, proved suitable for a wide range of
applications. In housebuilding the new semifinished product was used immediately for
walls and roofs as well as floors. Sheets cambered along the corrugations were able to
span great distances without intermediate supports. Manufacturers' catalogues contained not
only many different types of houses, large and
small, but also complete iron churches! One
important aspect was that the structures, in
separate pieces, were easy to transport to the
place where they were required for assembly
by unskilled labour. In the *Buch der Erfindungen, Gewerbe und Industrien*, published in
1906, the advantages of the house pictured
adjacent were described as follows: "The
house destined for Africa is encircled by wide,
shaded verandas and, further, is ideal for tropical regions because the material of its construction is highly conductive to heat and so
after sunset always cools down rapidly to provide pleasantly tempered rooms at night. On
the other hand, these houses exhibit the
advantage in any region that they are highly
resistant to crude violence and wild animals
and at no point offer easy access to vermin."[44]
This one-sided description of the qualities of
these new export iron goods did nothing to
change the fact that local climatic conditions
and the needs of the inhabitants were
researched wholly inadequately (see the introductory remarks on p. 10). The corrugated
metal hut was to become a synonym for slums
and ghettos worldwide.
Only after World War 1 did industry rediscover
the possibilities which steel would or could
offer the building industry. The architect Hans
Spiegel became an advocate of the new construction. Under the heading of "The ways to
rational housing production" in his book *Der
Stahlhausbau* he analysed the traditional,
labour-intensive methods, which, in his opinion, were no longer in the position to cope economically with the rising demand for living
accommodation. He saw the solution in the
industrialization and standardization of housebuilding and declared, without any beating
about the bush: "The slackness in sales following the demise of the armaments industry
occasioned the steel processing industry to
look for new sales opportunities."[45]

1.169

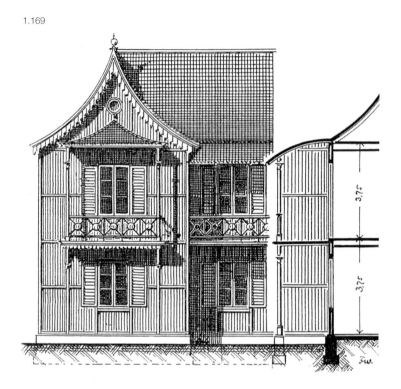

1.170

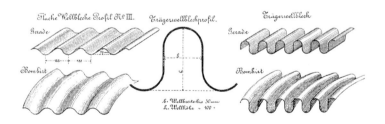

1.171

1.172   1.173

1.174

With references to the Crystal Palace in London and the impressive braced steel frames of America, Spiegel made use of the historical triumphs of iron and steel. He presented the latest examples from England, France and Germany in order to deal systematically with steel slat construction, steel panel construction, braced steel frames and rigid steel frames in words and pictures. Each type of house was complemented by a photo of the naked structure and the completed house. It is interesting to note that the prime aim was to make the final product resemble a conventional masonry building, a phenomenon that is still fashionable today.

On the other hand, it is no surprise to learn that revered names from the circle of the so-called classical modernists (e.g. J. P. Oud, Gerrit Rietveld, Adolf Rading, Georg Muche, Walter Gropius, Ludwig Mies van der Rohe), also participated in this phase of innovative experimentation. The building exhibitions in Stuttgart (Werkbund Exhibition, 1927), Dresden ("The Technical City", 1928) and Breslau ("Home and Work Exhibition", 1929) were conceived to help establish these new ideas.

Walter Gropius remarked on his trial house in Stuttgart: "...the fabrication of such houses cannot take place on site but rather in fixed workshops. By employing high-quality, industrially processed materials the loads and mass of the construction are to be decreased but its stability and insulation increased so that it becomes possible to transport a detached family home in dismantled form on a few lorries from the factory to any building site and to assemble it within a very short time regardless of season and weather."[46] The loadbearing structure of the house consisted of rolled sections. Cork sheets provided the insulation, asbestos sheeting the external cladding. The internal walls made use of cane fibre, silicate-bound wood fibre or asbestos cement sheets depending on requirements. The U-value of the outer walls was equal to that of a clay brick wall 160 mm thick and built "with a normal careful standard of workmanship". In his description, Hans Spiegel pointed out the weak point where the insulation was interrupted at the butt joints between the sheets in front of the steel sections. The demonstration house of Walter Gropius was developed on a strict grid which enabled standardized production but also room for variation.

1.175

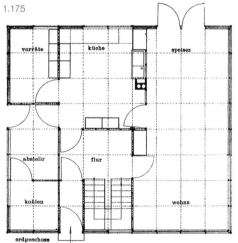

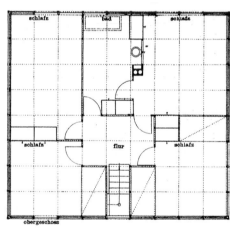

1.176

1.177

1.178

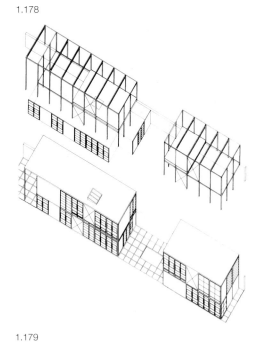

1.179

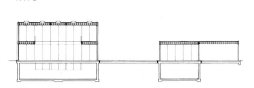

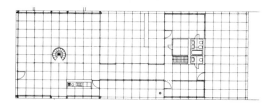

1.180

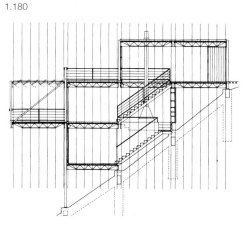

1.181

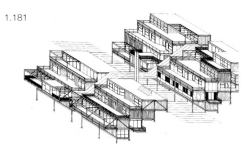

In a second volume (1930) Hans Spiegel laid down fundamentals for building with steel. All the important technical data known at that time was collected and presented in this compendium. He also included experiences with braced steel frames in other countries. The first steps in the direction of lightweight steelwork are also discernible. Here was another statement with interesting analogies with other branches of industry: "Like a car assembled from individual components designed and using materials to suit the various tasks, like in an automotive plant where vehicle types with different trim levels are assembled from different types of components according to schedule and for differing production costs according to budget, like a medicine composed of separate ingredients whose nature and quantity are determined by the intended more or less intense effect of the medicine, so the braced frame presents the new age of building with a scientifically exact, systematic framework derived from the task and geared to the scale of the requirements."[47]

The first master and pioneer of lightweight steelwork was Jean Prouvé. The history of building places him in the same class as Telford, Paxton, Bogardus and others who were equally successful as engineers, innovative designers and contractors. Trained as an artistic metalworker, in 1929 Prouvé procured a gas welding apparatus, electric drills, punching presses and the first powered folding press in order to experiment with these new technical possibilities. In 1931 he was granted a patent for a modular demountable partitioning system using steel sheeting. His first building in lightweight steelwork was the clubhouse for the aerodrome at Buc. On his new bending press he fabricated the loadbearing frame, floors, stairs, sanitary cabins and framework for the glass walls. With his Colonial House of 1949 and his so-called Sahara Houses he was the first person to develop a system of sensible, well-thought-out, portable steel buildings after the hardly satisfying early exports made from cast iron and corrugated metal sheeting; at last a system matched to the respective local climatic conditions. Almost all the renowned architects and engineers who thereafter devoted

time to system-building in steel were indebted to the work of Jean Prouvé.

The designers Ray and Charles Eames played a similar pioneer role. In 1945 the publishers of the magazine *Arts & Architecture* initiated an ambitious experiment in housebuilding. Eight architectural practices were asked to take part. World War 2 had only just ended. Building materials were still scarce. Now architects could take up the products and technologies of prefabrication developed during the war and put them to use for peaceful purposes. The new materials included plastics, bonding agents, aircraft adhesives and synthetic resins. The resulting designs for the "Case Study Houses" Nos. 8 and 9 by Charles Eames and Eero Saarinen were published at the end of 1945 in *Arts & Architecture*. Eames later completely revised the design for his house (No. 8) because the prefabricated steel components had already been delivered to the site. The finished house was presented to the world in 1949. Although it became a symbol for the whole programme, a closer inspection from today's viewpoint reveals that it can hardly be taken as a paragon of industrial prefabrication. To make all the pieces fit perfectly, many hours of painstaking manual work were required. And mention must also be made of the huge cost of maintenance. The former office worker Richard Donges visited the house two or three times every week from the early 1960s to 1979 in order to carry out repairs both large and small. Despite all its limitations the Eames house cannot be ranked highly enough in terms of its exemplary aesthetic role in the development of modular steel construction.

At the other end of the scale from the Eames team stands Fritz Haller. Whereas the subtly assembled semifinished products which make up the Eames house can only be preserved through expensive, tedious, constant maintenance, Fritz Haller has developed his buildings right from the outset using functional, well-thought-out and well-tested components with a high requirement profile. Added to their quality in terms of serviceability we have aspects like easy adaptability. The necessity of adaptable buildings is explained by Fritz Haller himself: "Buildings are erected to house particular

1.182

1.177 Clubhouse, Buc, 1936, Jean Prouvé, roof structure
1.178 Private house near Los Angeles, 1949, Ray and Charles Eames, isometric projection
1.179 Private house, Solothurn, 1977, Fritz Haller, section and plan
1.180 Housing development in modular system, Beverly Hills, California, 1976, Helmut C. Schulitz, section

1.181 ibid., perspective view
1.182 as 1.179, roof structure
1.183, 1.184 as 1.178, external views
1.185 as 1.179, external view
1.186 as 1.180, part-elevation

1.183

1.184

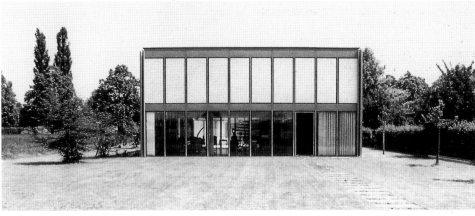
1.185

1.186

functions – homes, schools, offices, factories – and as a rule to meet the specific conceptions of client and architect. In reality most of these buildings are used for their defined purpose for only a brief period. This relatively short initial usage is followed by many other uses not envisaged at the planning stage and so not allowed for. In recent decades this fact has come to light owing to the ever faster economic and technological development, particularly in buildings for the manufacturing and service sectors. This fact should actually encourage building designers to conceive their buildings along more general lines."[48]

Therefore, Haller developed modular systems with the possibility of non-destructive conversion and extension as well as integrated and adaptable building services. The loadbearing structure of the Cantonal School in Baden was built using prefabricated elements. The "Midi" system for multistorey structures and the "Maxi" version for single-storey sheds were further developed in the years thereafter and have since been used for numerous projects. Furthermore, the "Mini" system can also supply solutions for the residential market. As we can see from the pictures of the private house in Solothurn, individual expression clearly takes a back seat. By comparison, the well-known house of Helmut C. Schulitz in Los Angeles appears much more interesting. On the one hand, the climatic conditions permit greater design freedom. On the other, the modular system used is designed as a so-called open system. When Schulitz arrived in California in 1966, Ezra Ehrenkrantz had already completed the prototype for his SCSD (School Construction Systems Development). Norman Foster and Richard Rogers were to be inspired by this in later years. Schulitz recognized the advantage of a certain compatibility with other competing systems and saw this as the excuse to set about designing a new but open system. The study group T.E.S.T. (Team for Experimental Systems-building Techniques) was formed at the university in 1971 to examine the compatibility of the components already on the market. New developments could concentrate on the missing components for this system of standard components. His own home, built

1.187

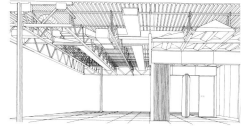

1.188

1.188

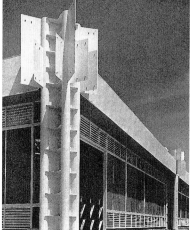

1.191

using this idea, was intended to prove that great variety could be achieved in this way and hence certainly avoid the threatening monotony in industrial building which comes as result of mass production.

In the late 1960s and early 1970s the development of megastructures for expanding and renewing the urban environment were another focus of interest. The call for adaptability and flexibility could at that time it seemed only be met by large-scale systems and structures. People dreamed of realizing urban visions by way of flexible structural steelwork concepts. The VE 66 steelwork system developed by a group of Swiss architects and engineers was publicized in the magazine *DETAIL* in 1976. Looked at from our present viewpoint it is exaggerated and hence possesses only limited suitability for fundamental changes to technical conditions (e.g. those required by quality standards) and is not readily compatible with other products on the market.

In his factory building pictured here, Noriaki Kurokawa signalled the all-round extendability of his prefabricated structure by way of the special column design. Lattice girders of tubular sections span the 17 x 17 m bays diagonally. The ancillary rooms placed on the periphery were designed to be demountable.

The new hospital services wing of the regional medical centre in Schongau (1989) was built using a composite steel and reinforced concrete system in order to save volume.

The detailing of the structure comprising extendable and stackable tables is ideal for

1.193

1.194

1.193 Hospital extension, Schongau, 1986, Karl J.
Habermann, Hackl + Amon and Sepp Rottmayr,
structural design, erection
1.194 ibid., interior view of structural carcass
1.195 ibid., part-elevation
1.196 T.E.S.T. open system, 1974, Helmut C. Schulitz

1.196

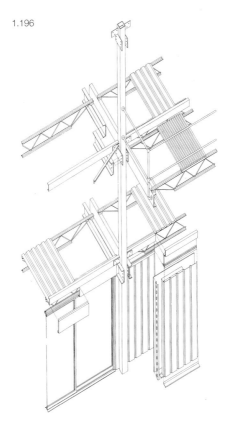

1.189

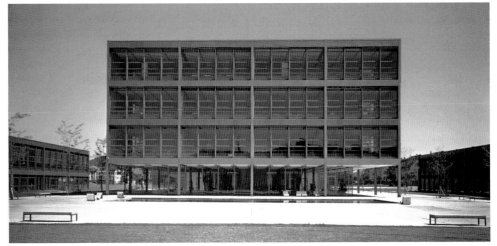

1.192

1.195

accommodating service penetrations. Prefab panels with reinforcing ribs of steel sections with hexagonal cutouts are employed as auxiliary beams. There is space for continuous service ducts along the main beams, vertical service ducts on the sides of the columns with no incoming beams. The vertical permeability of the floor system can be further increased by providing trimmers to the auxiliary beams. The combination of reinforced concrete prefab and steelwork components fuses benefits in terms of fire protection with the greater precision of steelwork. The necessary adaptation during the planning and building phases – which can never be ruled out, especially in hospitals – as well as the option of extensions to all sides were taken into account here. Fast, quiet and dust-free assembly is also an important consideration for the execution of construction projects directly adjacent ongoing operations.

Helmut C. Schulitz generalizes the current claims placed on the increasing industrialization in building and states: "System theory, rules of combination, permutation and variation reaffirm our vision of architecture as a process and not a finite object."[49]

1.197   Aircraft hangar project, 1951,
        Konrad Wachsmann
1.198   ibid., wedged node points
1.199   US Pavilion, 1967 World Exposition, Montreal
        (now the "Biosphere"), Buckminster Fuller
1.200   ibid., welded node points
1.201   Church, Oer-Erkenschwick, 1972,
        Joachim Schürmann
1.202   ibid., screwed node points

1.203   Climatroffice, 1971, Norman Foster,
        Buckminster Fuller
1.204   Hammersmith Centre 1979, Norman Foster

"The Crystal Palace has now, in fact, become apparent as the real turning point at which the whole evolution of building took up a new compass heading. What is fascinating here is that the whole consists of simple, small parts; there are no overwhelming, colossal sections. There is nothing which cannot be immediately understood right down to the tiniest detail."[50]

This is how Konrad Wachsmann generates the link to the historical roots of building systems in his programmatic book *Wendepunkt im Bauen* (1959), which was published in English two years later under the title *The Turning Point of Building: Structure and Design*. Besides the accomplishments of Paxton, Eiffel and Roebling, he honours Alexander Graham Bell, who at the turn of the century experimented with building systems based on the geometry of the tetrahedron. Using this concept, Bell built aerodyne flying machines as well as a surprisingly delicate viewing tower. After pointing out the constructional finesse of airships as well as the form of a bicycle frame, long since accepted, the author concludes his analytical review before expounding his own ideas. After a general introduction to industrial machining methods and a digression via modular principles Wachsmann quickly comes to the crux of his idea – the intelligent jointing of standardized elements to form larger constructions. From 1951 onwards, carefully organized teamwork resulted in a large-scale study of the feasibility of giant aircraft hangars. Besides the development of a lightweight, three-dimensional modular structure of steel tubes, it was vital to invent a node detail which would permit the articulated connection of any arrangement of up to 20 tubes. With the help of three wedges, every node was ultimately fixed. These projects were not realized.

Wachsmann was always of the opinion that industrialization in no way inevitably means the onset of monotony in architecture. The development of essentially open systems owes much to his work. For this, he formulated what he considered were the resulting aesthetic notions: "The open space will primarily influence all planning. The great spans will lead to new definitions of space, the like of which could never have been conceived before. ... Definitions of mass, facade and monumentalism, merely unrelated optical effects, will cancel each other out..."[52]

In addition to Wachsmann, Buckminster Fuller

1.197

1.199

1.201

1.203

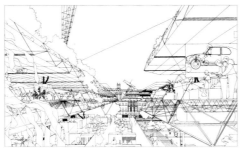

1.204

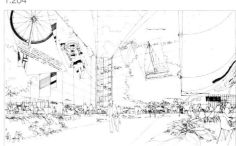

"In the case of architectural structures, dynamic responsive systems, acting much like flexing muscles in a body, will reduce mass to minimum by shifting loads and forces with the aid of an electronic nervous system which will sense environmental changes and register indivdual needs."[51]
Richard Rogers

1.198

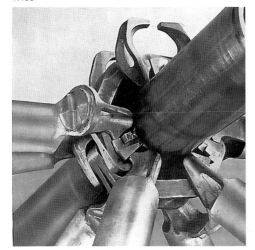

1.200

1.202

and Max Mengeringhausen also developed universal node joints for long-span lightweight space frames. The latter started in 1937 with the development of modular systems. The first space frames with what are now well-known nodes first appeared in 1942. By 1962 a number of existing applications were ready for publication in *Komposition im Raum*. Both eminent and lesser-known architects now had access to this product. The book featured shed-like structures for industry, also those for cultural events and exhibitions, and sacred buildings, the sector with the highest aesthetic demands. However, the most convincing solutions are in the realm of temporary structures because here the supporting structure generally remains unclad and so its ephemeral effect is not impaired. One example of this is the grandstand to the hockey stadium for the 1972 Olympic Games in Munich (Karg & Schraud). Today, alongside Wachsmann and others, Buckminster Fuller is regarded as a visionary of high-tech architecture. He was also involved with that key product of industrial production – the motor car. Aspects of aerodynamics served him in the development of his "Dymaxion Car", not as an end in itself, as a design gesture, but in trying to optimize design, function and form. As long ago as 1927 he had conceived housing using prefabricated lightweight steelwork and aluminium components which would be delivered to site by means of airships. The aspect of minimal material but maximum performance played a key role in, above all, his geodesic domes. Fuller's pavilion represented the USA at the 1967 World Exposition in Montreal. The cultural achievements and technology of the space travel nation were demonstrated inside the dome. The effect of the object itself, even after a fire during renovation work destroyed the plastic covering in 1976, is imposing enough in itself. The now open three-dimensional framework embraces the space as before and reinforces the vision of a geodesic dome as Fuller himself had envisaged for hostile environments such as desert and arctic regions. Even whole city centres could be enveloped in such a dome with a controlled climate. The famous aerial view of Manhatten covered in a giant soap bubble is integral to any work on building in the latter half of the 20th century.

These proposals were refined in 1971 on a smaller scale; for example, in collaboration with Norman Foster – the "Climatroffice" project. Beneath an oval envelope, designed like the dome in Montreal, there would be a vertically and horizontally unconstrained office landscape, flexible in terms of use and layout and without the customary visual barrier to the outside world. With the minimum of necessary surface, Foster and Fuller wanted to enclose a maximum of usable space in an energy-saving design. This idea was expanded in 1977-79 in the project for the Hammersmith Centre in London. The interior of an urban block, with skilfully integrated bus/rail transport terminal, was to be transformed into a climate buffer by means of a cable-net membrane roof. This year-round weather protection would offer a wide palette of functions including offices, retail outlets, exhibition halls, cinemas, restaurants and ice rink. Unfortunately, the project was not realized owing to the diverse interests of the investors, although public opinion was surprisingly favourable.

Albert G. H. Dietz held a much-heeded lecture in 1970 on the subject of "Large enclosures and solar energy". Although the visions of Wachsmann, Fuller and Mengeringhausen still remain to be fulfilled on a large scale, their ideas are none the less topical, especially in light of the current focus on solar energy and other ecological concepts in building. On a smaller scale, the plethora of atria which have sprung up makes it easy to recognize the trend towards urban spaces with a controlled climate. The technique of delicate cable-net membrane with monitored, controllable properties needs to be continually developed to meet this need.

Year	Material, semifinished product	Means of jointing	Loadbearing system
2000	"TM" steels		
	(for seamless, rolled hollow sections)		
1990			Cable-net domes
	Non-corroding structural steels, Z 30.1-44		
1980	Weathering steels, DASt 007	CNC production	
	Close-grained steels, DASt 011		
1970	Cast steel	HSFG bolts, DASt 010	Large tent structures
1960		Electric-arc welding of shear studs	Lightweight plane frames
1950			
1940	Grade St 60	High-strength bolts	Lightweight trusses
1930	Grade St 52		Storey-height frames
1920	Grades St 48, St 37	Welding	
1910	Higher-strength steels		
1900	Wide-flange beams		Cranked trusses
1890			
1880			
1870	Cast iron		Hinged girders, frames
1860			
1850			Lattice girders
1840	Rolled sections	Rivets	Braced frames
1830	Round iron bars, chains		Truss-type systems
1820	Wrought iron	Wedges, clamps, straps	Trussed beams
1810	Cast beams, columns & arches		
1800	Cast iron	Bolts	Columns, arches, beams

Structural theory	Project	Architects, engineers	Year
			2000
			1990
DIN 18800 (Nov 1990)		Foster	
	Centre Pompidou, Paris	Piano + Rogers, Arup	1980
	Sears Tower, Chicago	SOM	
	Olympic Stadium, Munich	Behnisch et al.	1970
	John Hancock Tower, Chicago	SOM	
Steel composite beams, DIN 4239	US Pavilion, Brussels	Stone	1960
	Seagram Building, Chicago	Mies v. d. Rohe	
Finite element method	Apartments, Chicago	Mies v. d. Rohe	1950
	Eames House, Los Angeles	Eames	
			1940
Load-factor design method	Maison de Verre, Paris	Chareau	1930
Bleich	House, Dessau	Muche	
			1920
	Trotting course grandstand, Berlin	Endell	
	Turbine factory, Berlin	Behrens	1910
	Festival Hall, Frankfurt	von Thiersch	
	Stock Exchange, Amsterdam	Berlage	1900
	Maison du Peuple, Brussels	Horta	
Graphical methods of calculation	Galerie des Machines, Paris	Dutert & Contamin	1890
Müller-Breslau, Cremona	Garabit viaduct	Eiffel	
	First Leiter Building, Chicago	William Le Baron Jenny	1880
	National Library, Paris	Labrouste	
	Chocolate factory, Noisiel	Saulnier	1870
	St Pancras station, London	Scott	
Rivet calculations, Schwedler	Les Halles, Paris	Baltard & Callet	1860
	Maximilian's grain market, Munich	Muffat	
Truss analysis,	Crystal Palace, London	Paxton	1850
Schwedler, Wiegmann	Bogardus Factory, New York	Bogardus	
	Dianabad, Vienna	Etzel	1840
	Euston station, London	Hardwick	
	Sayner Works, Bendorf	Althans	1830
	Menai Bridge	Telford	
Basics of structural analysis, Navier	Royal Pavilion, Brighton	Nash	1820
	Stanley Mill, Stonehouse	Strutt	
	Halle au Blé, Paris	Bélanger	1810
	Pont des Arts, Paris	Cessart	
Basics of mechanics	Shrewsbury Mill	Bage	1800
Newton, Euler, Bernoulli, Hooke			

Footnotes

1 Allgemeine Bauzeitung, Vienna 1845, p. 110
2 Roland Knauer, Qualitätsstahl aus dem Lehmofen,
  in: Die Zeit No. 39, 22 September 1995, p. 52
3 Johann Georg Krünitz, Oeconomische Enzyclopädie,
  keyword "Stahl" 1838, "Rezept Nr. 5", p. 609
4 Definition from Philadelphia 1876
5 Frank Werner, Joachim Seidel, Der Eisenbau. Vom
  Werdegang einer Bauweise, Berlin 1992, p. 38f.
6 Otto Königer, Allgemeine Baukonstruktionslehre.
  Die Konstruktionen in Eisen, Leipzig 1902, p. 1
7 Illustrierte Zeitung, Leipzig 1849, p. 55ff.
8 as 5, p. 41
9 Heinrich Pudor, Erziehung zur Eisen-Architektur,
  in: Süddeutsche Bauzeitung, No. 37 1903, p. 294ff.
10 Ruskin, John, The Seven Lamps of Architecture,
   The complete works of John Ruskin, London, 1903,
   Vol. VIII, p. 66
11 Gottfried Semper, Der Stil, vol. II, Munich 1863,
   p. 263
12 E. Brandt, Lehrbuch der Eisenkonstruktionen, Berlin
   1876, Preface p. VII
13 Rudolph Gottgetreu, Lehrbuch der Hochbaukonstruktionen, Part 3 Eisenkonstruktionen, Berlin 1885,
   p. 398
14 Max Foerster, Die Eisenkonstruktionen der Ingenieur-
   Hochbauten, Leipzig p. 724
15 G. A. Breymann, Allgemeine Baukonstruktionslehre.
   Die Konstruktionen in Metall, Preface 1st ed.,
   Leipzig 1902
16 as 6, Preface 6th ed., p. 2
17 Thomas E. Tallmadey, Vorwärts in der Architektur, in:
   Edmund Schüler, Neue Amerikanische Baukunst,
   Munich 1926, p. 18ff.
18 Fritz Schumacher, Das bauliche Gestalten, Hamburg
   1926
19 Alfred Hawranek, Der Stahlskelettbau, Berlin/Vienna
   1931, p. 276
20 Gottfried Semper, Der Wintergarten zu Paris, in:
   Zeitschrift für praktische Baukunst 1849, p. 516ff.
21 as 10, p. 68
22 Walter Rieger, Eisenarchitektur im Wiener Histo-
   rismus, ICOMOS, Munich 1979, p. 127
23 C. Schwatlo, in: Zeitschrift für praktische Baukunst,
   1870, col. 18ff.
24 V. G. Šuchov 1853–1939, Kunst der Konstruktion,
   exhibtion catalogue pub. by Rainer Graefe et al.,
   Stuttgart 1990, p. 30
25 Kurt Ackermann, Industriebau, Hannover 1986, p. 40
26 August Endell, Vom Sehen, Texte 1896–1925, pub.
   by David Helge, Basel/Boston, p. 110
27 as 6, p. 118
28 ESDEP CD-ROM, Lektion 7.12 Fachwerke, p. 2
29 Karl Etzel, Allgemeine Bauzeitung, Vienna 1835,
   p. 33ff.
30 L. Wind, Allgemeine Bauzeitung, Vienna 1856, p. 14
31 Allgemeine Bauzeitung, Vienna 1859, p. 240
32 Jules Saulnier, Encyclopédie d'Architecture, Paris
   1874, p. 118
33 H. Wegele, Die Hauptbahnhofsanlagen in
   Frankfurt a. M., Berlin 1892, p. 71
34 as 13, p. 398
35 as 13, p. 404
36 A. G. Meyer, Eisenbauten. Ihre Geschichte und
   Ästhetik, Esslingen 1907, p. 171

37 H.P. Berlage, Über die wahrscheinliche Entwicklung
   der Architektur, in: Über Architektur und Stil –
   Aufsätze und Vorträge 1894–1928, Basel/Boston
   1991, p. 88
38 Sigfried Giedion, Bauen in Frankreich. Bauen in
   Eisen, Bauen in Eisenbeton, Leipzig/Berlin 1928,
   p. 17
39 Die Form, issue 23/1929, p. 365
40 Friedrich v. Thiersch, Die Ausstellungs- und Festhalle
   zu Frankfurt am Main, Frankfurt 1909, p. 20
41 Frühlicht, Summer 1922 (pub. by Bruno Taut)
42 Franz Schulze, Mies van der Rohe Leben und Werk,
   p. 288ff.
43 Ecclesiologist 1851, p. 28
44 J. Faulwasser, Technik des Bauwesens, in: Das Buch
   der Erfindungen Gewerbe und Industrien, Leipzig
   1896, p. 386ff.
45 Hans Spiegel, Der Stahlhausbau 1, Leipzig 1928, p. 5
46 as 41, p. 131
47 Hans Spiegel, Der Stahlhausbau 2, Berlin 1930, p. 62
48 Werk, Bauen + Wohnen 7/8 1992, p. 9
49 Helmut C. Schulitz, Schulitz & Partner, Buildings and
   Projects, Berlin 1996, p. 23
50 Konrad Wachsmann, The Turning Point of Building:
   Structure and Design, New York 1961, p. 14
   Original edition:
   Konrad Wachsmann, Wendepunkt im Bauen, 1959
51 From: Chris Wilkinson, Supersheds, Oxford 1991,
   p. 111
52 as 50, p. 231

Part 2 • The material steel

Werner Sobek
with Stefan Schäfer

The material and its manufacture

Raw materials

Steel is the name given to alloys of iron (Fe), carbon (C) and other tramp and alloying elements smelted from ore.

The tramp elements include:
- phosphorus (P)
- sulphur (S)
- nitrogen (N)

The alloying elements include:
- manganese (Mn)
- silicon (Si)
- chromium (Cr)
- nickel (Ni)
- molybdenum (Mo) and others

Every type of steel contains small quantities of additives which, depending on the composition, influence its quality. For instance, silicon, chromium or manganese could be added to the melt to increase the strength. The carbon content has a very fundamental effect on the properties of the various steels. As carbon content rises, so hardness and tensile strength increase but at the same time fracture toughness and ductility decrease. Suitability for welding improves as the carbon content drops.

The carbon content is used to distinguish between different steels:

- unalloyed steel, C < 0.2%
- low-alloy steel, C > 0.2% and total amount of alloying elements < 5%
- high-alloy steel, with total amount of alloying elements > 5%

Corresponding metering of the chemical composition and specific heat treatment enable the material properties of the steel to be finely tuned to suit the intended purpose.

For example, a distinction is made between:
- structural steel
- reinforcing steel
- prestressing steel
- stainless steel (corrosion-resistant)
- creep-resistant steel
- tool steel

2.1

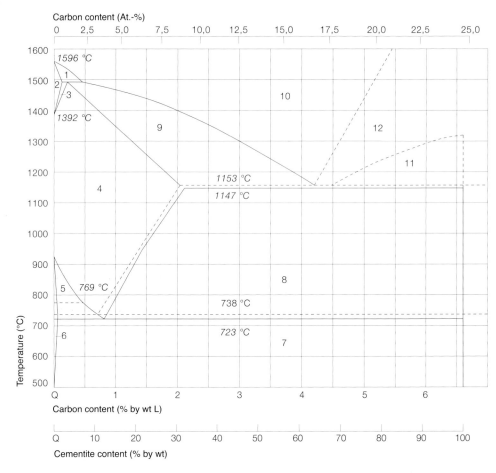

The figures in the above diagram designate fields

1	melt + δ mixed crystals	5	γ + α mixed crystals	9	melt + γ mixed crystals
2	δ mixed crystals	6	α mixed crystals (ferrite)	10	melt
3	δ + γ mixed crystals	7	α mixed crystals + Fe_3C	11	melt + Fe_3C
4	γ mixed crystals (austenite)	8	γ mixed crystals + Fe_3C	12	Fe_3C (cementite)

2.2

Cast steel grade Abbreviation	Material number	Mass proportions % C	Si ≤	Mn	P ≤	S ≤	Cr ≤	Mo	Ni	Others
GS-16 Mn 5	1.1131	0.15–0.20	0.60	1.00–1.50	0.020	0.015	0.30	≤ 0.15	≤ 0.40	–
GS-20 Mn 5	1.1120	0.17–0.23								
GS-8 Mn 7	1.5015	0.06–0.10	0.60	1.50–1.80	0.020	0.015	0.20	–	–	Nb ≤ 0.05 V ≤ 0.10 N ≤ 0.02
GS-8 MnMo 7 4	1.5430	0.06–0.10	0.60	1.50–1.80	0.020	0.015	0.20	0.30–0.40	–	Nb ≤ 0.05 V ≤ 0.10 N ≤ 0.02
GS-13 MnNi 6 4	1.6221	0. 08–0.15	0.60	1.00–1.70	0.020	0.010	0.30	≤ 0.20	0.80–1.20	Nb ≤ 0.05 V ≤ 0.10 N ≤ 0.02

2.1 The constitution diagram (equilibrium phase diagram) for iron-carbon (after Report 180 of the VDEh Material Committee, 4th ed., 1961). The dotted lines refer to the iron-graphite stable system, the solid lines and the designations of the phase fields to the iron-cementite metastable system. [384]
2.2 Chemical composition of cast steel grades according to melt analysis to DIN 17182
2.3 Chemical composition of general structural steels to DIN 17100 suitable for steel construction
2.4 Chemical composition of StE 460 and StE 690 steels [440]

2.3

Grade Abbrev.	Material number	Type of deoxidation[1]	Chemical composition (mass content in %) C for product thickness (mm) ≤16	>16 ≤40	>40 ≤100	>100 max.	P	S	N[2]	Additional nitrogen setting agents[3]
St. 37-2	1.0037	—[4]	0.17	0.20	0.20	as agreed	0.050	0.050	0.009	—
USt. 37-2	1.0036	U	0.17	0.20	0.20		0.050	0.050	0.007	—
RSt. 37-2	1.0038	R	0.17	0.17	0.20		0.050	0.050	0.009	—
St. 37-3	1.0116	RR	0.17	0.17	0.17		0.040	0.040	—	yes
St. 44-2	1.0044	R	0.21	0.21	0.22		0.050	0.050	0.009	—
St. 44-3	1.0144	RR	0.20	0.20	0.20		0.040	0.040	—	yes
St. 52-3[5]	1.0570	RR	0.20	0.22	0.22		0.040	0.040	—	yes

1) U = unkilled
   R = killed (inc. semikilled)
   RR = specially killed
2) The max. value given may be exceeded when a phosphorus content of 0.005% P below the given max. value is maintained per 0.001% N. However, the nitrogen content may not exceed 0.012%.
3) e.g. at least 0.020% Al_{total}
4) not specified
5) Silicon and manganese contents may not exceed 0.55% and 1.60% respectively.
6) max. 0.20% C for thickness 16-30 mm

2.4

Grade	Type	%C	%Si	%Mn	%P	%S	%N	%Cr	%Cu	%Nb	%Ni	%Ti	%V	%Mo	%Zr	%B
StE 460	Ni-V	≤0.20	0.10/0.50	1.1/1.7	≤0.035	≤0.030	≤0.020	—	—	—	0.15/0.80	—	0.10/0.20	—	—	—
	Cu-Ni-V	≤0.18	0.10/0.55	1.1/1.5	≤0.035	≤0.030	≤0.020	—	0.30/0.70	≤0.03	0.40/0.70	—	0.08/0.20	—	—	—
	Ni-Ti	≤0.20	0.10/0.60	1.1/1.6	≤0.035	≤0.030	≤0.007	—	—	—	0.50/0.80	0.10/0.20	—	—	—	—
StE 690	Ni-Cr-Mo-B	≤0.20	0.15/0.35	0.60/1.0	≤0.025	≤0.025	≤0.015	0.40/0.65	0.15/0.50	—	0.70/1.0	—	0.03/0.08	0.40/0.60	—	0.002/0.006
	Cr-Mo-Zr	≤0.20	0.50/0.90	0.70/1.1	≤0.025	≤0.025	≤0.015	0.60/1.0	—	—	—	—	—	0.20/0.60	0.06/0.12	—

1) All steels must be close-grain smelted and may, in addition to the elements in the table, contain traces of aluminium.

For the building industry, the "general structural steels" according to the definition in DIN 17100 are of particular interest as well as stainless steels and a number of steels for fasteners.

The so-called corrosion-resistant steels are produced from alloyed steels with min. 12% chromium content. A higher chromium content or the addition of nickel or molybdenum improves corrosion resistance. It should be pointed out here that, generally, there is no such thing as a rustproof steel; there are only steels which do not corrode under certain ambient conditions. When using stainless steel it should always be ensured that the right steel is chosen for each application. The corrosion-resistant steels which may be used for load-bearing components in Germany are not covered by a DIN (Deutsches Institut für Normung, i.e. German Standards Institute) standard but instead by building authority certification.

Close-grained steels are produced from low-alloy, high-strength structural steels. These steels possess a comparatively low carbon content, which results in such steels being particularly suitable for welding. The yield strengths lie around 880 N/mm². In Germany the high-strength steels StE 460 and StE 690 are approved for loadbearing components in structural steelwork. The letter E in the material designation indicates that the following number refers to the yield strength.

Weatherproof steels (e.g. Cor-Ten steel) form a thin layer of rust on their surfaces after erection as a result of atmospheric influences. This layer acts as passive protection for the body of the underlying material and prevents further corrosion. The use of such steels has proved disadvantageous in some cases because the layer of rust has been washed off by rain. Light-coloured components, e.g. concrete, underneath the weatherproof steel have thus suffered unsightly discoloration.

Production

In the smelting of steel, the elements entrapped in pig iron – phosphorus, manganese, silicon – must be removed or reduced by a combustion/gasification process. These impurities are burned off by the introduction of oxygen, the so-called blowing process. Parallel

2.5

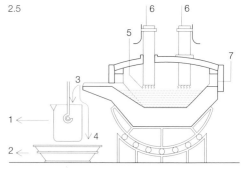

1	To casting pit	5	Electric arc
2	To slag tip	6	Carbon electrodes
3	Crude steel	7	Furnace door
4	Slag		

2.6

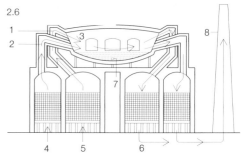

1	Hot air	6	Colder gas to chimney
2	Hot gas	7	Dross
3	Combustion	8	Chimney
4	Cold gas		
5	Cold air		

2.7

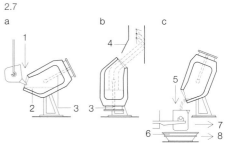

a	Filling position	4	Chimney
b	Blowing position	5	Crude steel
c	Discharging position	6	Thomas slag
1	Lime	7	To casting pit
2	Pig iron	8	To mill
3	Compressed air entry		

**Turning the material into
semifinished products**

with this, the desired chemical composition of the steel is achieved through refining (= addition of lime slag for bonding the phosphorus) and deoxidation (= removal of oxygen). The multitude of (sometimes) highly disparate methods of crude steel production can be differentiated principally by the manner in which the oxygen is introduced and by the temperature gradient. The processes used these days are the Thomas method (converter with oxygen fan) and the LD method (converter with oxygen jet), the LDAC method (addition of oxygen and lime) and the Siemens-Martin method (addition of steel scrap and extra, external heating). Common to all the smelting apparatus is their large surface area in comparison to the depth of the bath.

To avoid segregation (i.e. fine bubbles of carbon and oxygen residue entrapped in the material that can occur upon casting the molten steel into ingots) quantities of Si, Mn, Ca or Al are added to the melt. The steels killed in this way are not susceptible to ageing and are highly suitable for welding.

A distinction is made between teeming methods for steel:
• unkilled (U)
• killed (R)
• specially killed (RR)

Using various heat treatments, differing treatment states are achieved with respect to graininess, embrittlement and fracture toughness. Therefore, the following letters are added to the steel designations:
• as rolled (U)
• normalized (N)
• hardened and tempered (V)

The molten steel in the melt can be converted to a solid state in several ways:

• Teeming into ingot moulds as vertical (or gravity) casting (= casting in individual, so-called chill moulds) or the "concast" method (= continuous casting guided by a system of rollers) with subsequent hot-forming to produce flat products, hollow sections, bars and structural sections.
  In the secondary processing industry, further hot- and/or cold-forming processes may also be carried out.
• Teeming into final moulds with different casting methods using patterns. Some of the products can be further processed, also without additional metal-cutting processes. Casting usually involves sand moulds into which the desired product shape is pressed with the help of a 1:1 model.

• In the Shaw method, which is very popular for producing castings with complicated geometrical shapes, a model of the casting is first made in plastic or hard wax. This can also be formed via a second cast method. The complete model is assembled and then enclosed in a ceramic or sand mould. The plastic is then gasified or the wax melted (lost-wax process). In this process the void created is filled with molten steel. After the steel has hardened the jacket is destroyed. The surface quality thereby obtained is very good and the tolerances are low.

• Sintering of compressed steel powder. In this process loose steel powder is pressed into the final shape and subsequently baked by sintering. This method is employed for mass production of intricate small parts.

In general terms we always distinguish between:
• raw products
• semifinished products (shaped raw products, e.g. forged)
• finished products (ready for use)

2.8 Relationship between minimum wall thickness of unalloyed cast steel and largest dimension of casting dependent on method of casting [303]
2.9 Examples of cross-section arrangements for cast parts [303]

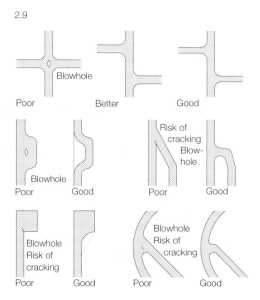

2.8

1 Chilled casting
2 Sand moulding (inc. shell moulding)
3 Lost-wax casting

Casting

The importance of casting techniques for the metalworking industry can be attributed to the great degree of freedom possible in the design of cast items. A small number of successive operations and great leeway in the process have led to a wide range of applications.

In terms of material, cast steel is distinguished from cast iron alloys by reserving the former term for materials with a carbon content < 2% and the latter for those with higher carbon contents. Both are so-called multi-component alloys with the main constituents being iron, carbon, silicon and graphite; the latter is a principal component in cast iron.

Liquid cast iron materials solidify by forming very diverse crystalline structures, the particular form depending on the composition of the alloy and heat treatment state. The crystals are assigned various names depending on their configuration and determine the properties of the metal to a considerable degree. One example is ferrite (mixed crystal with cubic body-centred crystal lattice). Apart from the crystal matrix, the mechanical properties of iron-carbon casting materials are determined by the form and quantity of the graphite inclusions. Spherical graphite (spheroidal graphite iron) leads to a behaviour which is preferred for building materials, characterized by high strength and, sometimes, very high ductility. In contrast, lamellar graphite inclusions, which act like internal notches, are responsible for the well-known and less esteemed properties of classic cast iron.

Compared to cast iron, cast steel exhibits improved behaviour at elevated temperatures and has better fracture toughness; loadbearing welded seams can be readily accomplished. However, the greater tendency to form blowholes during casting as well as inferior teeming characteristics give rise to higher manufacturing costs as well as larger minimum wall thicknesses and corner radii. A distinction is made between unalloyed, low-alloy and high-alloy cast steel, depending on the percentages of the alloying agents.

Under certain conditions – above all in vertical (or gravity) casting – voids, so-called blow-

2.9

holes, can become trapped inside the blank. Similar negative phenomena arise through embedded deoxidation products – tramp elements like silicon and alumina – prevented from escaping as the steel solidified in the mould. Such defects are normally found inside the products and only manifest themselves during the course of subsequent processing or through appropriate quality control measures. The most diverse test methods have been developed for checking the quality of steel workpieces. These include ultrasound, radiography and metallographic examination (involving destruction of the test specimen) such as sulphur prints, microetching and macrophotographs or microphotography. Steel castings may be welded for structural, manufacturing or repair purposes. Structural welds in particular (i.e. joining cast pieces or joining castings to other formed parts) are subject to more rigorous requirements. The workpieces to be joined must be preheated or heat-treated prior to welding depending on their composition, size/volume and the welding technique to be employed.

Rolling

Rolling is a secondary process carried out on a raw product formed by casting. For rolling, the semifinished product is heated to approx. 1250°C before being shaped by pressure applied directly to the casting, normally by rolls, in the temperature range 800-1200°C. As a result of this hot-working, the material properties are improved, the microstructure compacted. The cross-section of the, typically, long products is consistent along the whole length, the surfaces usually smooth (as-rolled finish) or profiled.
At the end of the rolling operation the semifinished product is still hot and must be cooled in air or along a controlled cooling line.
The tools employed are the so-called roll stands which accommodate the various rolls. Stands in series, used as break-down and finishing stands, form a tandem arrangement. The greater the intended deformation of the raw product, the greater the number of roll stands required. If more than five successive roll stands are required, then we speak of a mill train. There are section and wire trains for individual sections and rods/wires.

We distinguish between the following rolled steel products depending on shape, dimensions, production method and surface quality:
· hot-rolled long products
· wire rod
· reinforcement for concrete
· rails
· sheet piling sections
· finished flat products

Forging

Forging, like rolling, is a hot-working process. Shaping is in essence carried out by compressive forces which are applied directly to the material by the forging tools. Forging techniques are:
· upsetting
· drop-forging
· hammer-forging
· precision-forging
Hammers, presses and forging rolls are employed. Drive power is provided by steam, air and spring pressure for lighter forging work, screw and crank presses for heavy jobs.

The way in which the force is applied acts directly on the flow of material during the shaping process. With hammer-forging the steel fills the die in the opposite direction to the action of the hammer; with pressing this action is reversed.

The microstructure of the material is altered during forging: the open-grained structure of the casting is transformed into a close-grained one. Depending on the forming temperature, existing voids are welded and inclusions stretched, which results in a considerable increase in strength. A perfect microstructure presupposes thorough heating and shaping of the entire workpiece.

2.10

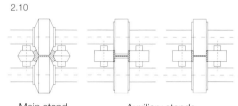

Main stand   Auxiliary stands

2.11

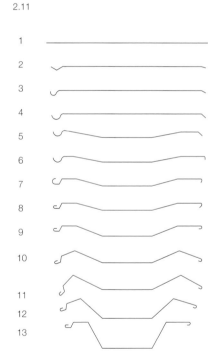

2.12

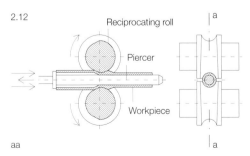

Normally, a cylindrical piercer is used when rolling after preheating, a conical one when rolling at room temperature.

2.13

Further hot-working processes are:
- punching
- extruding
- tube-drawing
- dishing
- beading
- deep-drawing
- bending

Hardening and tempering

When cooling down from high temperatures, the rate of cooling influences the recrystallization. With extensive temperature retardation, the carbon in the crystal lattice remains disrupted; we obtain a very hard type of microstructure with, however, only average fracture toughness values, known as martensite and bainite. The process of raising the temperature into the austenitic range followed by rapid cooling (quenching) is called hardening.

Repeatedly increasing the temperature to just below the lower transition point (phase transition) and maintaining it there (tempering) causes the carbon contained as a constrained solution in the iron lattice to separate out in the form of finely distributed carbides, and the high density to be partly reduced. Thus yield strength and tensile strength drop while elongation at rupture and other toughness characteristics increase. The scope of the influence on the properties can be controlled through temperature and duration of tempering.

We speak of water or oil quenching depending on the liquid used for quenching. Some steels used for nuts and bolts in structural steelwork are subjected to oil quenching; high-strength close-grained structural steel is supplied water-quenched.

Upsetting 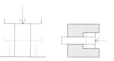		Reduces the depth, width or length of a workpiece between simple, flat tools (upsetting dies).
Stretch-forming 		Reduces the cross-section of a workpiece by a succession of upsetting forces applied transverse to the longitudinal axis by pressing dies, whereby the material moves essentially in the longitudinal direction.
Flattening 		Widens the material by a succession of upsetting forces applied with curved pressing dies.
Die-forging 		Manufacturing by means of pressure, bending and shearing actions with forming tools which surround the part completely or at least to a large extent, in conjunction with other methods of cutting and jointing.
Precision-forging 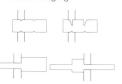		Manufacturing by means of shaping, cutting and jointing on a workpiece with simple tools which match the shape of the workpiece only partly or not at all.
Rolling 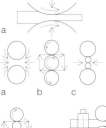		Stretching of the workpiece and forming the cross-section by means of the compressive and stretching action of rotating rolls. a) Two-high reversing stand b) Three-high stand c) Four-high stand d) Lauth-type three-high stand e) Universal slab ingot stand

2.14

Flat products (sheet, strip), width 600 mm

Light plate	0.35-3.0 mm thick	DIN 1541	As rolled = black plate or with surface finishing, e.g. aluminized; hot-dip galvanized; hot-dip galvanized + plastic-coated = coil-coated
Medium plate	3.0-4.75 mm thick	DIN 1542	Floor plates, 3-20 mm (chequer flooring etc.)
Heavy plate	> 4.75 mm thick	DIN 1543	
Wide flat steel	width 150-1250 mm, ≥ 4 mm thick (hot-rolled all 4 sides), DIN 59200, EURONORM 91		

Steel bar Designation	Abbreviation	Typewriter	Dims (mm) Depth	Width	Remarks, standards
T-section	T	T	20-140	20-140	Deep web or wide flange, rounded corners DIN 1024; sharp corners DIN 59051
Channel	[	[	30-65	15-42	Tapered flanges, rounded corners DIN 1026, EURONORM 24-62
Z-section	Z	Z	30-160	38-70	Parallel flanges, rounded corners DIN 1027
Angle	L	L	20-200	20-100	Equal angles DIN 1028, EURONORM 56-65; unequal angles DIN 1029, EURONORM 57-65, rounded corners; sharp corners DIN 1022

Steel bars include all round [1], square [2], hexagonal and special sections. 1) DIN 1013, EURONORM 60   2) DIN 1014, EURONORM 59

Section Designation	Abbreviation	Typewriter	Dims (mm) Depth	Width	Remarks, standards
Channel	[	[	80-400	45-110	Tapered flanges, rounded corners DIN 1026, EURONORM 24-62
Narrow beam	I	I	80-600	42-215	Tapered flanges, rounded corners DIN 1025 Sht 1
Medium beam	IPE	IPE	80-600	46-228	Parallel flanges, sharp corners DIN 1025 Sht 5, EURONORM 19-57 • Special sections IPE a, o, v to works standards
Wide beam	HE (IPB)	HE	96-1008	100-402	Parallel flanges, rounded corners. Several versions: special light: works standard HEAA light: DIN 1025 Sht 3, EURONORM 53-62; HE-A (IPBl) normal: DIN 1025 Sht 2, EURONORM 53-62; HE-B (IPB) strengthened: DIN 1025 Sht 4, EURONORM 53-62; HE-M (IPBV) Further series to works standards: HD, HL, IPBS

In the HE-B series depth and width are equal from 100 to 300 mm, thereafter the width remains constant at 300 mm. Similar for series HE-A and HE-M.

2.15

Hollow sec. Designation	Abbreviation	Typewriter	Dims (mm)	Wall thickness, s	Remarks, standards
Tube	○	CHS	Diameter D 51-1016	2.6 -10	Seamless tubes DIN 2448; welded tubes DIN 2458
Hollow section	□	SHS	Side length 40-260	2.9-17.5	Hot worked DIN 59410, cold worked DIN 59411
Hollow section	▭	RHS	50 × 30 to 260 × 180	2.9-14.2	

Cold-worked sections   Sections of flat-rolled steel with almost identical wall thickness. Shaped by rolls (> 0.4 to 8.0 mm thick) and folded (up to 20 mm thick). DIN 59413 as well as works standards. Large selection of shapes and sizes.

Trapezoidal profiles   Sheets with high loadbearing capacity rolled from thin plate. Width 500-1050 mm, depth 10-200 mm, thickness 0.65-1.5 mm, length up to 22 m.

Wires, ropes, bundles   Twisting or grouping many thin wires (generally 0.15-0.35 mm dia.) produces cables of high strength and pliability. These serve to transfer tensile forces, e.g. in bridges, suspended roofs and cable stays to masts, aerials, chimneys, etc.; DIN 3051 Sht 496.

2.16   Cross-sections and parameters of various
         sections from the series 200 [438]

2.16

Designation of seamless steel tube, St 35 material, 168.3 mm O.D., 4.5 mm wall thickness: tube DIN 2448 – St 35 – 168.3 x 4.5

Seamless tubes to DIN 2448

| O.D. D | Dims | | Area of section | Weight | | | | |
| | Std wall thk s | Clear I.D. d | F | G | J | W | i |
mm	mm	mm	cm²	kg/m	cm⁴	cm³	cm
219.1	6.3	207.3	42.1	33.1	2386	218	7.53

Designation of square hollow section with side length a = 80 mm and wall thickness s = 4.5 mm, S 235 JRG 2 material to DIN EN 10025: hollow section 80 x 80 x 4.5 DIN 59410 S 235 JRG 2

Hot-rolled square steel tubes to DIN 59 410

Nom. dim. a	Wall thk s	Area of section F	Weight G	Surface area U	Properties				
					for the axis of bending x-x = y-y			for the torsional constants	
					J_x	W_x	i_x	J_t	W_t
		cm²	kg/m	m²/m	cm⁴	cm³	cm	cm⁴	cm³
200	6.3	47.8	37.5	0.778	2960	296	7.86	4660	472
	8.0	59.8	46.9	0.773	3620	362	7.78	5780	588
	10.0	73.4	57.6	0.766	4340	434	7.69	7020	718

Designation of rectangular hollow section with side lengths a = 100 mm and b = 60 mm and wall thickness s = 5.6 mm, S 235 JRG 2 material to DIN EN 10025: hollow section 100 x 60 x 5.6 DIN 59410 S 235 JRG 2

Hot-rolled rectangular steel tubes to DIN 59 410

Nom. dim. a	Wall thk s	Area of section F	Weight G	Surface area U	Properties								
					for the axis of bending						for the torsional constants	
					x-x			y-y				
					J_x	W_x	i_x	J_y	W_y	i_y	J_t	W_t
		cm²	kg/m	m²/m	cm⁴	cm³	cm	cm⁴	cm³	cm	cm⁴	cm³
200	6.3	37.7	29.6	0.618	2010	201	7.30	910	152	4.91	2030	277
x	8.0	47.0	36.9	0.613	2440	244	7.21	1100	183	4.84	2490	342
120	10.0	57.4	45.1	0.606	2890	289	7.10	1290	216	4.75	2990	414

Designation of channel with depth h = 300 mm, S 325 J material to DIN EN 10025: channel 300 DIN 1026 S 235 J

Hot-rolled channel sections with rounded corners to DIN 1026

Abbr.	Dims (mm) for						Nom. area of section	Weight[1]	Surface area	For the axis of bending						Eccentr. of axis	
										x-x			y-y				
U	h	b	s	t	r_1	r_2	F	G	U	J_x	W_x	i_x	J_y	W_y	i_y	e_y	X_M
							cm³	kg/m	m²/m	cm⁴	cm³	cm	cm⁴	cm³	cm	cm	cm
200	200	75	8.5	11.5	11.5	6	32.2	25.3	0.661	1910	191	7.70	148	27.0	2.14	2.01	3.94

1) 7.85 kg/dm³

Designation of equal angle with leg length a = 80 mm and leg thickness s = 10 mm, S 235 J material to DIN EN 10025: angle 80 x 10 DIN 1028 S 235 J

Hot-rolled equal angles with rounded corners to DIN 1028

Dim (mm)			Nom. area of section	Weight[1]	Surface area	Eccentricity of axes				For the axis of bending								
										x-x = y-y			ξ–ξ		η–η		
Abbr. L	r_1	r_2	F	G	U	e	w	v_1	v_2	J_x	W_x	i_x	J_ξ	i_ξ	J_η	W_η	i_η
			cm²	kg/m	m²/m	cm	cm	cm	cm	cm⁴	cm³	cm	cm⁴	cm	cm⁴	cm³	cm
200 x 16	18	9	61.8	48.5	0.785	5.52	14.1	7.80	7.09	2340	162	6.15	3740	7.78	943	121	3.91
20[2]			76.4	59.9		5.68		8.04	7.15	2850	199	6.11	4540	7.72	1160	144	3.89
24			90.6	71.1		5.84		8.26	7.21	3330	235	6.06	5280	7.64	1380	167	3.90

1) 7.85 kg/dm³   2) Preferred sizes as recommended by DSTV

Hot-rolled medium I-sections (IPE series) to DIN 1025

Abbreviations	Dims (mm)					Nom. area of section	Weight[1]	Surface area	For the axis of bending					
									x-x			y-y		
IPE	h	b	s	t	r	F	G	U	J_x	W_x	i_x	J_y	W_y	i_y
						cm²	kg/m	m²/m	cm⁴	cm³	cm	cm⁴	cm³	cm
IPE a 200	197	100	4.5	7.0	12	23.5	18.4	0.764	1590	162	8.23	117	23.4	2.23
IPE 200	200	100	5.6	8.5	12	28.5	22.4	0.768	1940	194	8.26	142	28.5	2.24
IPE o 200	202	102	6.2	9.5	12	32.0	25.1	0.779	2210	219	8.32	169	33.1	2.30

1) 7.85 kg/dm³

Non-standardized sections IPEa, IPE o, IPE v. IPE a from ARBED rolling programme. IPE o, IPE v from Thyssen Stahl AG and Preussag/ Peine rolling programmes.

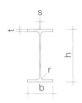

Hot-rolled wide-flange I-sections (HEA series, light version) to DIN 1025

Abbreviations	Dims (mm)					Nom. area of section	Weight[1]	Surface area	For the axis of bending					
									x-x			y-y		
HE-A (IPB$_l$)	h	b	s	t	r	F	G	U	J_x	W_x	i_x	J_y	W_y	i_y
						cm²	kg/m	m²/m	cm⁴	cm³	cm	cm⁴	cm³	cm
200	190	200	6.5	10	18	53.8	42.3	1.14	3690	389	8.28	1340	134	4.98

1) 7.85 kg/dm³

Designation of wide-flange I-section with parallel flanges, light series (HEA), with depth h = 350 mm, S 235 J material to DIN EN 10025: HE 360 A EURONORM 53–62 S 235 J (IPBl 360 DIN 1025 S 235 J)

Hot-rolled wide-flange I-sections (HEB series) to DIN 1025

Abbreviations	Dims (mm)					Nom. area of section	Weight[1]	Surface area	For the axis of bending					
									x-x			y-y		
HE-B (IPB)	h	b	s	t	r	F	G	U	J_x	W_x	i_x	J_y	W_y	i_y
						cm²	kg/m	m²/m	cm⁴	cm³	cm	cm⁴	cm³	cm
200	200	200	9	15	18	78.1	61.3	1.15	5700	570	8.54	2000	200	5.07

1) 7.85 kg/dm³

Designation of wide-flange I-section with parallel flanges (HEB), with depth h = 360 mm, S 235 J material to DIN EN 10025: HE 360 B EURONORM 53–62 S 235 J (IPB 360 DIN 1025 S 235 J)

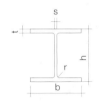

Hot-rolled wide-flange I-sections (HEM series)

Abbreviations	Dims (mm)					Nom. area of section	Weight[1]	Surface area	For the axis of bending					
									x-x			y-y		
HE-M (IPBv)	h	b	s	t	r	F	G	U	J_x	W_x	i_x	J_y	W_y	i_y
						cm²	kg/m	m²/m	cm⁴	cm³	cm	cm⁴	cm³	cm
200	220	206	15	25	18	131	103	1.20	10640	967	9.00	3650	354	5.27

1) 7.85 kg/dm³

Designation of wide-flange I-section with parallel flanges, strengthened series (HEM), with depth h = 395 mm, S 235 J material to DIN EN 10025: HE 360 M EURONORM 53–62 S 235 J (IPBv 360 DIN 1025 S 235 J)

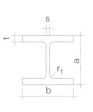

Hot-rolled unequal angles with rounded corners (preferred sizes) to DIN 1029

Dims (mm)			Area of section	Weight[1]	Surface area	Eccentricity of axes							Pos. of axis	For the axis of bending										
													η-η	x-x			y-y			ξ-ξ		η-η		
Abbr. L 200×100×	r_1	r_2	F	G	U	e_x	e_y	w_1	w_2	v_1	v_2	v_3	tan α	J_x	W_x	i_x	J_y	W_y	i_y	J_ξ	i_ξ	J_η	i_η
			cm²	kg/m	m²/m	cm	cm	cm	cm	cm	cm	cm		cm⁴	cm³	cm	cm⁴	cm³	cm	cm⁴	cm	cm⁴	cm
10	15	7.5	29.2	23.0	0.587	6.93	2.01	13.2	8.76	3.75	5.98	2.22	0.266	1220	93.2	6.46	210	26.3	2.68	1300	6.66	133	2.14
12			34.8	27.3		7.03	2.10	13.1	8.82	3.84	5.95	2.26	0.264	1440	111	6.43	247	31.3	2.67	1530	6.63	158	2.13
14			40.3	31.6		7.12	2.18	13.0	8.88	3.93	5.92	2.32	0.262	1650	128	6.41	282	36.1	2.65	1760	6.60	181	2.12

1) 7.85 kg/dm³

Designation of un-equal angle with leg lengths a = 100 mm and b = 50 mm and leg thickness s = 10 mm, S 325 J material to DIN EN 10025: angle 100 × 50 × 10 DIN 1029 S 235 J

The subsequent processing and machining of the semifinished products

Forming

Forming is defined in DIN 8580 as the manufacture by way of plastic deformation of a solid body while retaining its mass and material composition. Hence, forming does not belong to the group of metal-cutting manufacturing methods, e.g. milling, drilling, grinding.

There are more than 200 different forming techniques distinguished by way of their principal features. However, these may be further combined to produce countless variations.

The methods fall into one of five groups depending on the forces exerted on the material:

Compressive forming
· Single or multiple axis compression, e.g. rolling, free-, die- and indentation-forming, extrusion.

Tenso-compressive forming
· Combined tension and compression, e.g. stripping-plate moulding, deep-drawing, collar-forming, acute-angle bulging.

Tensile forming:
· Single or multiple axis tension, e.g. stretch-reducing, bulge- and stretch-forming.

Forming by bending:
· Bending loads, e.g. bending, die-bending, edge-rolling, form-bending by sliding-action drawing, bulging, roll-bending, folding, circular-bending, etc.

Shear-forming:
· Shear loads, e.g. displacement by shear parallel to adjacent surface, twisting with rotary tool movement, crossing.

Taking into account tool movements, tool and workpiece geometries, etc., further sub-categories can be derived. Methods may be further differentiated as follows:
· forming without altering strength
· forming with temporary change in strength
· forming with permanent change in strength.

In industrial production merely two principal groups are distinguished: massive forming and pressing. The distinguishing features are, on the one hand, the force and hence energy required, and on the other, the geometry of the

2.17
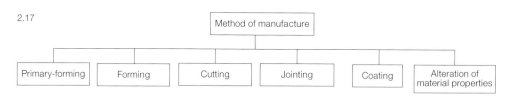

2.18
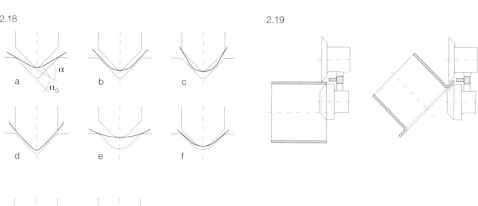

2.19
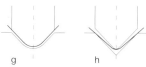

Small die radius
a   Air bending
b   End of air bending operation
c   End of overbending
d   End of reverse bending

Large die radius
e   Air bending
f   Further bending upon 2-point bearing on die radius
g   Onset of finishing stress
h   Finishing stress in half-open die

2.20

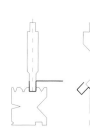
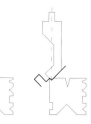

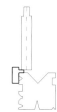

workpiece (in three dimensions) and its wall thicknesses.

Metal-cutting technologies

Cutting processes involve the use of tools to alter the shape or surface of a workpiece by removing layers or chips of material. If no chips or irregularly shaped pieces occur, then we speak of division. Apart from sawing, grinding or filing, metal-cutting activities are primarily carried out by machines. A distinction is made depending on the tools used:

- Metal-cutting defined geometrically, numerically and with respect to the workpiece: e.g. turning, drilling, milling, planing, sawing, rasping, etc.
- Metal-cutting not defined geometrically, numerically and with respect to the workpiece: e.g. grinding, abrasive-blasting, barrel-polishing, etc.

Polishing is not regarded as an independent method of manufacture because, as a rule, it is only used in conjunction with other processes.

Turning

Turning is cutting by way of complete, usually circular cutting movements combined with any feed rates at right-angles to the direction of cut.

The whole operation consists of roughing, with maximum possible material removal, and finishing, in which the necessary surface quality as well as shape and dimensional tolerances are achieved.

A distinction is made between:
- turning
- facing
- threading
- rolling
- contouring

Drilling

Drilling is a cutting operation using tools with single or multiple (usually two) cutting edges for the forming of through-holes and blind holes. All the cutting edges of the tool are in contact with the metal and generally perform rotational and feed movements.
According to DIN 8589, drilling countersinking and reaming are subdivided thus:

- spot-facing
- tapping
- profile-drilling
- contour-boring
- drilling by hand

Milling

In milling the tool performs the rotary cutting movements and the feed movement is carried out by the workpiece at right-angles to the axis of rotation. The constant interruptions to the cutting process lead to "comma"-shaped chips. Milling is among the cutting techniques using multiple cutting edges and geometrically defined cutters. There are many variations.

Milling can be divided into:
- face-milling
- peripheral-milling
- internal cylindrical milling
- end-milling
- gear-milling

Broaching

Broaching tools comprise a series of successively larger cutters. The feed rate per tooth corresponds to the rate of rise of the teeth. The cutting movement is normally linear. Both internal and external surfaces may be broached.

DIN 8589 defines broaching according to method and cutting conditions:
- flat-broaching
- round-broaching
- helical-broaching
- form-broaching
- non-linear broaching
- turn-broaching

Grinding

Grinding is one of those cutting operations with geometrically undefined cutters. It is used to finish components where high demands are placed on accuracy.

A distinction is made between:
- external cylindrical grinding
- internal cylindrical grinding
- surface grinding
- centreless grinding
- abrasive cutting
- belt-grinding
- special grinding operations

2.21

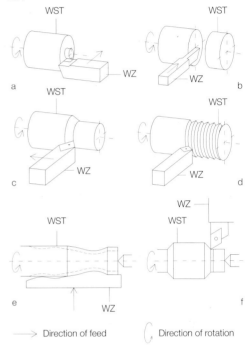

→ Direction of feed   ↻ Direction of rotation

WST = workpiece, WZ = tool,
a = facing, b = parting-off, c = turning,
d = threading, e = contouring (WST shape is cut by special tool), f = contouring

2.22

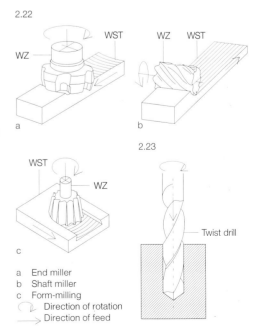

2.23

a End miller
b Shaft miller
c Form-milling
↻ Direction of rotation
→ Direction of feed

Cutting

Cutting is performed by:

- shearing
- sawing
- oxygen arc
- water jet
- laser
- underwater cutting

Shearing always results in slight crushing of the material along the edges of the cut, a problem that can be avoided by sawing. Oxygen arc, water jet and laser cutting techniques permit multiple as well as curved and three-dimensional cuts.

New technologies

Outsert method

- Using injection-moulding methods, plastic parts are added to metal articles normally produced by means of punching, bending and deep-drawing. A bond of high quality is developed between the materials.

Insert method

- Metallic components are embedded in a plastic body.

Shot-peen forming

- This is a substitute for bending intended to avoid the so-called plastic hinges. Accelerated balls impact with the material to be shaped in such a way that the surface is stretched on one side and leads to a controlled strain deformation.

Piston forming

- This is a variation on shot-peen forming. It is especially suitable for planar shaping of thick-walled components. Here, the balls are replaced by a single pressure piston.

2.26

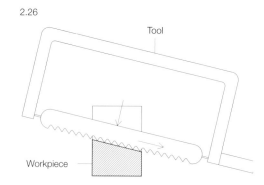

Tool

Workpiece

2.24

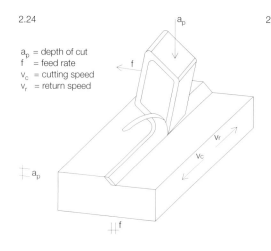

a_p = depth of cut
f   = feed rate
v_c = cutting speed
v_r = return speed

2.27

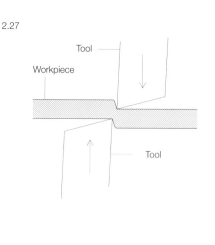

Tool

Workpiece

Tool

2.25

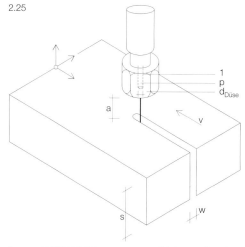

2.28

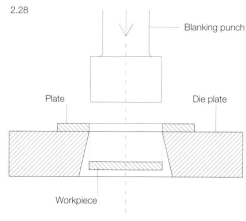

Blanking punch

Plate

Die plate

Workpiece

1   = cutting nozzle   s   = thickness of work-
p   = pump pressure   piece
$d_{Düse}$ = nozzle diameter   w   = width of cut
a   = nozzle-workpiece   v   = feed rate
        clearance

2.29

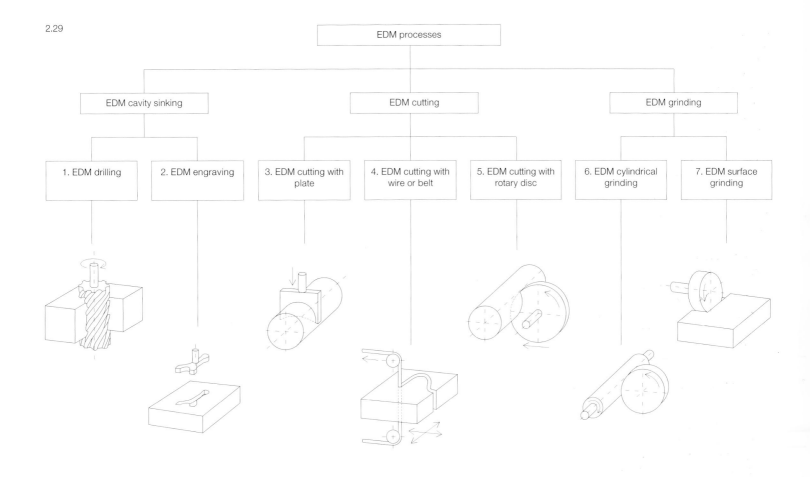

The properties of steel

The technical possibilities available to us enable the properties profile of a steel product to be preset precisely. When selecting the required characteristics, we have to take into account how the material is to be processed and used as well as the desired strength.

It is the mechanical properties in particular that are of interest when the steel is to be used as a loadbearing element in a structure. Frequently, such properties can only be defined by characteristic values determined in standardized laboratory tests. The results are recorded in tables or diagrams. The most important tests for determining the mechanical properties of steel are:

- tensile test
- creep rupture test
- fatigue test
- notched bar impact bending test
- hardness test

One test often reveals several properties of a test specimen. On the other hand, for testing just the hardness of steel there are four different methods:

- Rockwell C hardness – penetration depth of diamond cone
- Brinell hardness – area of indentation of hard metal ball
- Vickers hardness – size of impression of diamond pyramid
- Shore hardness – rebound height of impacting test body for very hard steels

When performing, assessing and interpreting tests it must be remembered that a steel component does not usually possess isotropic qualities. For example, sulphidic and oxidic impurities lead to the formation of deposits which, depending on the degree of deformation in the manufacturing process (e.g. rolling), become aligned and so have an unfavourable effect in that direction (risk of lamellar tearing when loaded perpendicular to the direction of rolling). Inherent hardening during manufacture (e.g. by cold-working) is also directional.

The most important properties of steel are strength, fracture toughness, suitability for welding, plasticity and resistance to corrosion. These can be defined by means of measurable characteristic values as given below.

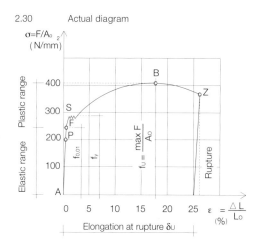

2.30   Actual diagram

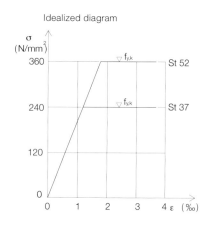

Idealized diagram

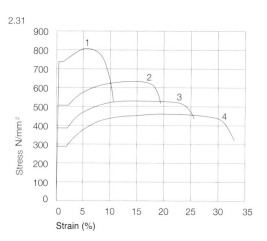

2.31

Test specimen: round tensile specimen B 8 x 80
(test length = 100 mm), test temperature = room temp.
1   St E 690
2   St E 460
3   St 52-3
4   St 37-3

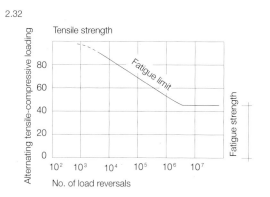

2.32

Properties important for material processing

· Castability
· Cold-workability
· Weldability
· Yield strength
· Elongation at rupture
· Bending angle
· Forgeability
· Plasticity

Properties which have an effect on strength

· Fatigue strength
· Hardness
· Notched bar impact work
· Yield strength
· Resistance to wear
· Fracture toughness
· Uniform elongation
· Elongation at rupture
· Tensile strength

Properties important for the use of the material

· Chemical resistance
· Corrosion resistance
· Magnetic properties
· Thermal fatigue resistance

Stress-strain behaviour

Rupture tests provide information on the tensile or compressive strength of a material. Stress-strain tests also provide details of elongation and reduction in area ("necking") at rupture as well as uniformity of elongation and modulus of elasticity.

The strength and plasticity properties of steel depend on the temperature and rate of load application. At higher temperatures we see a significant decrease in ultimate strength with simultaneous increase in elongation at rupture; at low temperatures the reverse occurs, but this is less critical. As the rate of load application or rate of deformation increases, so the ultimate strength rises but at the same time the elongation at rupture falls.

Fracture toughness

The fracture toughness is significant for the brittle fracture and plasticity characteristics of the steel. The notched bar impact work, also an important value for the fracture toughness, is determined by way of the notched bar impact bending test. The value obtained is influenced by the temperature, rate of load application, dimensions of test piece and notch geometry.

Suitability for welding

A type of steel is considered to be weldable when it is possible to produce loadbearing welded connections economically using conventional apparatus. There is no formula that allows for all influencing variables, but material composition, grain size and degree of purity all play a crucial role. The structural steels in common use are all weldable. Problems occur during welding due to:
· formation of cracks
· changes in material properties
· embrittlement
· loss of hardening-and-tempering properties in the heat affected zone (HAZ)

The tendency to crack is an assessment criterion for weldability. The suitability for welding can be controlled by altering the chemical composition of the basic material and the welding conditions. High-strength steels with a large quantity of alloying elements are more troublesome to weld. A weld can be tested by:
· Tekken test (root welds)
· CTS test (throat welds)
· implant test

Non-destructive testing is achieved by:
· dye penetration test
· magnetic particle inspection
· ultrasound or X-rays
· eddy current test

Plasticity

Methods for shaping steel components are divided into hot-working and cold-working. The latter involves forming below the recrystallization temperature and alters material properties depending on degree of deformation. This strain hardening is subject to a time-related ageing process and leads to increased embrittlement which impairs, above all, a product's suitability for welding. These disadvantages can be compensated for by subsequent processing such as annealing or hardening and tempering.

Hot-working capacity can be defined by the behaviour of the steel upon forging and rolling. A guide as to the deformability upon heating is provided by hot-heading and hot-twisting tests,

2.33
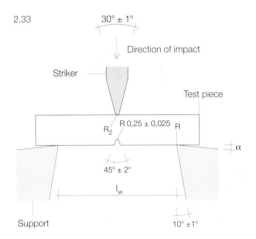

2.34
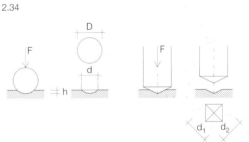

taking into account heat and rate of change of shape, as well as forging and rolling tests, with measurements of the compressive forces required.

The forgeability and rollability depend, in the first instance, on the chemical composition. Low-carbon steels alloyed with nickel or manganese exhibit better deformability. Similarly, materials which already exhibit good deformability at room temperatures are usually easily forged and rolled. A large reduction in area at rupture and high fracture toughness also point to good forging and rolling properties.

Corrosion resistance
Corrosion is the measurable chemical, electro-chemical or metallophysical reaction shown by a metal material to surroundings which have a detrimental effect on it. Relevant influencing factors for corrosion are supplied by the composition of the surrounding atmosphere and its pollutants which, together with water, form aggressive acids. The oxygen content of the medium surrounding the metal forms a protective oxide skin as the concentration rises; this delays the chemical reactions. Various circumstances lead to the breakdown of this protective layer either at isolated positions or across the entire surface, thereby allowing the material underneath to be attacked. The formation of protective oxide or hydroxide layers is reinforced by the addition of:
· chromium
· phosphorus
· copper

Appropriately high percentages of these tramp or alloying elements produces weatherproof steels. These form a protective (passive) coating. Only continual wetting and drying guarantees a homogeneously formed coating which can react very sensitively to local climatic conditions.
The rate of corrosion is influenced by:
· chemical composition of atmosphere
· chemical composition of steel and alloying elements
· exposure to weather and climatic attack
· local temperature fluctuations
· coverings

Dynamic loading ability
In structural steelwork the superimposition of dynamic and static loads can lead to failure of the material below the maximum permissible stresses for static loading. Therefore, the fatigue limit of steel under alternating loads is tested (Wöhler fatigue test), with 2×10^6 E load cycles.

Notches have a decisive, negative influence on the fatigue limit of a component. Therefore, they should always be avoided.

Hardness
The hardness of steel can be determined non-destructively and very simply (see above). From this value, conclusions can be drawn as to the consistency of the material, its tensile strength and, possibly, its resistance to wear.

Resistance to brittle fracture
The properties mentioned up to now are not suitable for completely describing the behaviour of the material as a building component. Therefore, particularly for very complicated components, tests are carried out reproducing the actual loading conditions. The influencing variables include temperature, rate of deformation, state of stresses and geometrical dimensions. A series of test rigs are available for such tests.
These include:
· wide-plate test
· notch-tensile and notch-bend tests
· weld bead bend test
· crack arrest test
· drop weight test

Grades of steel in building
· General structural steels
· Weatherproof steels
· High-strength close-grained structural steels
· Steels for nuts, bolts and rivets
· Steels for wire ropes

2.35

Steel grade	Tensile strength ≥3[3] ≤100 N/mm²	>100	Upper yield point ≤16	>16 ≤40	>40 ≤63	>63 ≤80	>80 ≤100	>100	Elong. Piece orientation	≥3 ≤40	>40 ≤63	>63 ≤100	>100	Bending Piece orientation Mandrel diameter[4]	≥3 ≤63	>63 ≤100	>100	Impact Treatment state[3]	Test temp.	≥10 ≤16	>16 ≤63	>63 ≤100	>100
			N/mm² min.						% min.					Mandrel diameter[4]						J min.			
St 37-2	340	as agreed	235	225	215	205	195	as agreed	longit.	26	25	24	as agreed	longit.	1a	1.5 a	as agreed	U, N	+ 20	27	—	—	as agreed
USt 37-2	to													transv.	2 a	2.5 a		U, N	+ 20	27	—	—	
RSt 37-2	470		235	225	215	215	215		transv.	24	23	22						U,N	+ 20	27	27	—	
St 37-3														longit.	1 a	1.5 a		U	± 0	27	27	23	
														transv.	1.5 a	2 a		N	− 20	27	27	23	
St 44-2	410								longit.	22	21	20		longit.	2.5 a	3 a		U, N	+ 20	27	27	—	
	to		275	265	255	245	235											U	± 0	27	27	23	
St 44-3	540								transv.	20	19	18		transv.	3 a	3.5 a		N	− 20	27	27	23	
St 52-3	490		355	345	335	325	315		longit.	22	21	20		longit.	2.5 a	3 a		U	± 0	27	27	23	
	to 630								transv.	20	19	18		transv.	3 a	3.5 a		N	− 20	27	27	23	

1) The values from tensile and folding tests are valid for longitudinal specimens apart from flat products ≥600 mm wide, from which transverse specimens must be taken.
2) The average of three tests is taken as the test result.
   The min. average value of 23 or 27 J may only be exceeded by a single value, and then only by max. 30%.
3) U = hot-worked, untreated; N = normalized.
4) a = thickness of specimen.

2.36

Steel grade	Form of product	Treatment state	Yield strength for thickness (mm)[2] ≤12	>12 ≤16	>16 ≤35	>35 ≤50	>50 ≤60	Tensile strength for thickn. (mm)[2] ≤50	>50 ≤60	Elongation at rupture (L₀=5 d₀) % min	Test piece Type	Orientation	Notched bar impact work[3] at -60°C	-40°C	-20°C	0°C	+20°C	Mandrel dia. in folding test[4][5][6][7] longitudinal	transverse
			N/mm²[2] min.					N/mm²[2] min.		% min.			J min.						
St E 460	Sheet, section, welded. hollow sect. (tube)	N	460	460	450	440	430	560 - 730		17	ISO-V	longit.			39	43	51	3a	4a
	Seamless hollow sect. (tube)		460	450	440	420	—	530 - 730			ISO-V	transv.			31	31			
St E 690	Sheet, section, welded. hollow sect. (tube)	V	690	690	690	690	—	790 - 940		16	ISO-V	longit.	30	40	50	60		3a	4a
												transv.	27	31	35	40			

1) N = normalized; V = water-quenched and tempered.
2) Appropriate values are to be agreed for thicker products.
3) The average of three tests is relevant. The required min. value may only be exceeded by a single value, and then only by max. 30%.
4) Required angle of bending 180° in each case.
5) a = thickness of specimen.
6) Longitudinal or transverse test pieces are to be agreed when placing an order.
7) Not for hollow sections (tubes).

2.37

Abbreviation	Material No.	Tensile strength at room temperature N/mm²	Upper yield point at room temperature for wall thickness (mm) ≤16	>16 ≤40	>40 ≤65[2]	Elongation at rupture at room temperature (L₀=5 d₀) longitud.	transv.	Notched bar impact work[1] (ISO longitudinal test piece) Test temp. °C	J min.
			N/mm² min.			% min.			
USt. 37-2[3]	1.0036	340 - 470	235	—	—	26	24	+ 20	27
RSt. 37-2	1.0038	340 - 470	235	225	215	26	24	+ 20	27
St. 37-3	1.0116	340 - 470	235	225	215	26	24	− 20	27
St. 44-2	1.0044	410 - 540	275	265	255	22	20	+ 20	27
St. 44-3	1.0144	410 - 540	275	265	255	22	20	− 20	27
St. 52-3	1.0570	490 - 630	355	345	335	22	20	− 20	27

1) The average of three tests shall be taken. The specified min. value may only be exceeded by a single value, and then only by max. 30%.
2) This range of thicknesses is possible for seamless tubes.
3) Only for welded tubes with wall thickness ≤ 16 mm.

2.38 Steel grades for fasteners classified according to steel groups in DIN EN 3506
2.39 Mechanical properties of cast steel grades [DIN 17182]
2.40 Yield and tensile strengths of stainless steel fasteners
2.41 Characteristic values of selected materials (stainless steels)

2.38

No.	Steel grade Abbreviation	Material No.	Steel group	Designation for bolts with heads to DIN EN ISO 3506 Pt 1 Strength grade 50	70	80	Designation for threaded bars, studs, nuts and washers to DIN EN ISO 3506 Pt1 & 2 Strength grade 50	70	80
3	X5CrNi18-10	1.4301	A2	≤ M 39	≤ M 24	≤ M 20	≤ M 64	≤ M 45	–
4	X6CrNiTi18-10	1.4541	A3	≤ M 39	≤ M 20	≤ M 16	≤ M 64	≤ M 30	–
6	X3CrNiCu18-9-4	1.4567	A2L	≤ M 16	–	–	≤ M 24	≤ M 16	–
7	X5CrNiMo17-12-2	1.4401	A4	≤ M 39	≤ M 24	≤ M 20	≤ M 64	≤ M 45	–
8	X2CrNiMo17-12-2	1.4404	A4L	≤ M 39	≤ M 24	≤ M 20	≤ M 64	≤ M 45	≤ M 16
9	X6CrNiMoTi17-12-2	1.4571	A5	≤ M 39	≤ M 24	≤ M 20	≤ M 64	≤ M 45	≤ M 16
10	X1NiCrMoCu25-20-5	1.4539	AK [1]	≤ M 39	≤ M 24	≤ M 20	≤ M 64	≤ M 45	≤ M 16
11	X2CrNiMoN22-5-3	1.4462	FA [1]	–	≤ M 20	≤ M 20	–	≤ M 64	≤ M 16
12	X2CrNiMoNi17-13-5	1.4439	AK [1]	≤ M 20	–	–	≤ M 64	–	–
13	X2CrNiMnMoNbN25-18-5-4	1.4565	KK [1]	–	≤ M 20	≤ M 20	–	≤ M 64	≤ M 20
14	X1NiCrMoCuN-25-20-7	1.4529	KK [1]	≤ M 39	≤ M 20	≤ M 20	≤ M 64	≤ M 45	≤ M 20

1) The designation for steels to Appendix D of DIN EN ISO 3506 Parts 1 & 2 is regulated by certification because these are not covered by any standards at present.

2.39

Cast steel grade Abbreviation	Material No.	Treatment state	Wall thickness mm	Yield strength [2][3] R_eH N/mm² min	Tensile strength [2] R_m N/mm²	Elongation at rupture A_s % min	Notched bar impact work [2][4][5] A_v J min.
GS-16 Mn 5	1.1131	normalized (N)	≦ 50	260	430 - 600	25	65
			50 - 100	230	430 - 600	25	45
GS-20 Mn 5	1.1120	normalized (N)	≦ 50	300	500 - 650	22	55
			50 - 100	280	500 - 650	22	40
			100 - 160	260	480 - 630	20	35
			> 160	240	450 - 600		
GS-20 Mn 5	1.1120	hard. & temp. (V)	≦ 50	360	500 - 650	24	70
			50 - 100	300	500 - 650	24	50
			100 - 160	280	500 - 650	22	40
GS-8 Mn 7	1.5015	hard. & temp. (V)	≦ 60	350	500 - 650	22	80
GS-8 MnMo 7 4	1.5430	hard. & temp. (V)	≦ 300	350	500 - 650	22	80
GS-13 MnNi 6 4	1.6221	hard. & temp. (V I)	≦ 500	300	460 - 610	22	80
		hard. & temp. (V II)	≦ 200	340	480 - 630	20	80

1) Values apply to specimens taken from test pieces cast integrally or separately.
2) Values also apply to specimens taken from the casting.
3) If no yield point is discernible, use the values for the 0.2% proof stress.
4) Average of three values.
5) ISO V-notch test pieces.

2.40

	1 Strength class	2 Yield strength $f_{y,b,k}$ N/mm²	3 Tensile strength $f_{y,b,k}$ N/mm²
1	50	210	500
2	70	450	700
3	80	600	800

Notes to table on facing page:
(1) Section 3.3.81 must be observed for stability analyses.
(2) The yield strengths are to be verified within the scope of the certification for filler materials. For connections between different materials, the max. design values are listed in tables 5-7.
(3) If compressive stresses are present, then $f_{y,k} = 355$ N/mm²
(4) If compressive stresses are present, then $f_{y,k} = 355$ N/mm², unless a higher figure has been verified.

2.41

Strength class	Material No.	$f_{y,k}$ Components Cold-rolled strip (N/mm²)	$f_{y,k}$ Components Other (N/mm²)	$f_{y,k}$ Welded connections[2] Cold-rolled strip (N/mm²)	$f_{y,k}$ Welded connections[2] Other (N/mm²)	Tensile strength $f_{y,k}$ (N/mm²)	Resistances, deformations E / G (N/mm²)	enforced cutting variables E / G (N/mm²)	simplified E (N/mm²)	with secant modulus $E_{sec,y}$ (N/mm²)	Coef. of thermal expansion ($10^{-6} \times k^{-1}$)	Density (kg/dm³)
235	1.4587	–	175	–	–	450	170 000	200 000	–	–	16	7.9
	1.4301	220	190	220	190	500	65 400	76 800	170 000	60 800		7.9
	1.4541											
	1.4401	240	200	240	200					63 000		8.0
	1.4404											
	1.4571											
	1.4539	240	220	240	220					68 800		
	1.4003	240	–	240	–	450				70 300	10	7.7
	1.4016	–	240	–	–	400			–	–		
275	1.4003	200	275	280	275	650	170 000	200 000	170 000	76 000	10	7.7
	1.4301	275		275	275		65 400	76 900		60 900	18	7.9
	1.4541	–		–	–							
	1.4507	275		275	275				–	–		
	1.4401								170 000	63 000		8.0
	1.4404											
	1.4571											
	1.4539									66 800		
	1.4439	290		290	275					76 000		
	1.4529	300	300	300	300					79 700		7.7
355	1.4318	350	330	350	300	800	170 000	200 000	170 000	83 700	18	7.9
	1.4301	355	355	355	355		65 400	78 900		60 000	18	
	1.4541											
	1.4507	–		–	–				–	–		
	1.4401	355		355	355				170 000	63 000		8.0
	1.4404											
	1.4571											
	1.4539	–		–	320					66 800		
	1.4529	355		355	355					79 700		7.7
460	1.4565	460	420	350	350	600	170 000	200 000	170 000	93 900	16	8.0
	1.4003	–	460	–	320		65 400	76 900		70 300	1	7.7
	1.4301	460		355	355					60 900	16	8.0
	1.4541											
	1.4567	–		–	–				–	–		7.9
	1.4401	460		355	355				170 000	63 000		8.0
	1.4404											
	1.4539	–		–	320					66 800		
	1.4571	460		355	355					63 000		
	1.4529	–		–	420					79 700		7.7
	1.4402[3]	480		–	450					86 800	13	7.6
690	1.4567		690	–	–	800	170 000	200 000	–	–	16	7.9
	1.4539			–	320		65 400	78 900	170 000	66 800		8.0
	1.4529				420					79 700		7.7
	1.4565			–	350					93 900		8.0
	1.4404			–	355					63 000	16	8.0
	1.4571			–								
	1.4462[4]			–	450					88 800	13	7.8

Part 3 · Steel construction technology

Werner Sobek
with Stefan Schäfer

Surface treatments
Surface preparation
Mechanical treatments
Thermal treatments
Chemical surface treatments
   which do not form a coating
Chemical surface treatments
   which do form a coating
Quality control
Construction to suit the surface treatment
Coating wear

Anti-corrosion measures
Corrosion and anti-corrosion measures
Types of corrosion
Corrosion classes
Corrosion problems with stainless steel
Steels which form a protective layer
Anti-corrosion systems
Metallic coatings: galvanizing
The process of galvanizing
Coating systems
Duplex system

Fire protection
Principles
Structural fire protection
Composite construction designed to provide fire
   protection

Thermal insulation
Thermal insulation
Steel and insulation

Sound insulation in steelwork
General
Sources of noise and sound insulation requirements
Sound insulation measures

Erection and dismantling
Planning documents
Dimensional and modular coordination, tolerances
Special aspects of erection and dismantling

Recycling

Surface treatments

This section is devoted to non-protective surface treatments. Preservative or protective treatments will be dealt with separately in a later section.

Surfaces and layers immediately below the surface are usually the areas of the material most at risk of damage or attack, having to withstand a wide range of different circumstances. The requirements profile includes such properties as surface roughness and smoothness, hardness, lubricant adhesion, corrosion protection, etc.

Surface treatments usually involve several operations. These can be divided into two main groups: removal of material and organic/metallic coating of the material. The latter creates a new composite whose basic stability is as a rule determined by the substrate, while the properties profile is determined by the coating.

Surface preparation

The primary requirement in preparing the surface is to clean it. We distinguish between:
• cleaning
• rinsing
• removal of coatings

Impurities may bind with a parent material in two ways: by chemical bonding forces or by absorption forces. Accordingly, the cleaning process is a two-track operation. Either the chemical bonds are broken down using lye, solvent, etc., or an absorber product is used which creates a stronger bond with the surface than the actual contaminating particles. The choice of surface preparation is influenced by the size of the workpiece, its weight, accessibility of the surfaces, and the material's sensitivity to chemical or thermal treatments. In the metal-processing industry, cleaning operations are mostly automated and carried out with the help of "washing lines".

Rinsing is generally reserved as a post-treatment and is especially important for the success of the surface treatment. Generally, it is only through rinsing that all those processes that have already commenced can be halted.

Mechanical treatments

These are mechanical processes which alter the topography of the surface in some way. Exceptions are those measures undertaken primarily to improve the dimensional accuracy of the workpiece.

Mechanical surface treatments result in elastic and, in particular, plastic deformation of the boundary layers of the material. This involves processes aimed at hardening in these layers, which depends on the creation, breakdown or rearrangement of lattice imperfections in the microstructure.

The following methods are in use:
• sand-blasting
• shot-blasting
• high-pressure water-jetting
• brushing
• grinding
• polishing
• deep-rolling
• special techniques

In sand-blasting, grains of sand are fired at the surface at high speed using a jet of compressed air. This is similar to shot-blasting, in which granules of varying size are fired at the surface, and where the high kinetic energy of the impacting particles has a metal-cutting effect. The effectiveness of blasting depends, in part, on the ratio of the size of the grains/particles to the surface roughness.

In grinding, a metal-cutting effect is achieved by the friction between a multitude of hard crystals of varying size (abrasive grain) and the surface of the workpiece. The coarser the abrasive grain, the deeper the scratches on the surface. The high temperatures (> 1000°C) produced by the friction can be reduced by using a liquid coolant. On the other hand, polishing does not remove material but merely has the effect of forcing the protruding burrs into the adjacent microrecesses of the surface. Quartz, pumice, corundum, diamond, chalk, slate and some synthetic materials are suitable as grinding/polishing media.

Thermal treatments

The most important of the thermal treatments for surfaces are:
• flame-cleaning
• annealing

Chemical surface treatments which do not form a coating

Various preparatory measures are necessary for chemical treatments, some of which are very involved and costly. The nature of the required method of treatment depends on both the parent and the coating material. The most important processes are:
• cleaning
• chemical deburring
• etching
• pickling
• burnishing

Pickling is employed to remove rust and other oxidation products. Furthermore, it is used to improve the adhesion of subsequent coatings.

Highly oxidizing solutions applied to burnish iron materials produce a dense film on the surface. This method involves cleaning, rinsing, burnishing, rinsing and finally applying a coating of oil. The high melting temperatures of the salts used may lead to distortion of the workpiece.

Chemical surface treatments which do form a coating

The choice of coating always depends on the functions required of it when in use, e.g. decorative, corrosion protection, wear resistance, etc. Organic, metallic and non-metallic coating substances are used in different thicknesses. These are applied by immersion, spraying, rolling and pouring, although the latter two are less significant.
• Chromalizing
• Phosphatizing
• Metal-spraying
• Hard-facing
• Plating
• Hot-dip galvanizing
• Thin-film technologies
• Hot-dipping
• Anodizing
• Oxidizing
• Enamelling
• Chemical and electroplating

3.1 Terms for describing a rough surface [332]
   1 Depth of ripple
   2 Directionality of surface roughness
   3 Peak-to-valley height
   4 Spacing of ripples
   5 Groove spacing

3.1

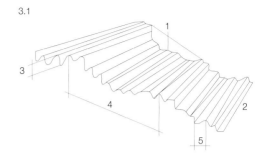

- Diffusion-coating
- Galvanizing
- Painting
- Laminating
- Printing

The formation of chromate layers is generally only used for aluminium and zinc. Yellow, green, blue, black and transparent chromalizing is possible. The chromic acids applied form an amorphous chromate coating which hardens upon drying and creates reflections on the metallic surface through interference phenomena.

Phosphatizing creates a vapour barrier which, in terms of organic coatings, leads to a far superior form of corrosion protection compared to conventional non-watertight painting systems.

Surfaces subject to mechanical damage or severe conditions can be protected by applying generous metal coatings (up to several millimetres thick). In addition to very hard alloys which may be employed in metallized form, layers can be applied by means of welding or spraying.

A great amount of steelwork is hot-dip galvanized, primarily to provide corrosion protection. This is carried out either as a continuous process or by immersing separate components/assemblies (batch galvanizing).

Particularly thin coatings with special properties can be achieved in two different ways: by way of a chemical coating-forming reaction taking place local to the surface (CVD = chemical vapour deposition), or by selective coating deposition by way of physical processes such as vapourizing or condensing (PVD = physical vapour deposition).

Aluminium materials can be protected against corrosion by an artificial layer of oxide. Coloured finishes without the use of paints are also possible and are achieved either chemically or electrochemically. The colouring is due to organic or inorganic dye ions. Multicoloured effects can also be obtained through the use of certain drying procedures.

With enamelling, the vitreous, non-crystalline enamel applied to the steel in molten form creates a new composite material at the junction of coating and steel. Besides acid resistance and thermal and corrosion protection, enamelling provides a number of other qualities which can be controlled via the chemical composition of the enamel. Application of one or more layers can be carried out by way of immersion, brushing or spraying.

Plating is the covering of a cheap parent material, which forms the bulk of the component, with an expensive metal finish to improve mechanical or other properties. Various methods of application are employed, e.g. chemical, electrical, sprayed, welded, molten. Aluminium, chromium, cobalt, nickel, copper, brass, bronze, zinc, silver, cadmium, tin and lead can all be used as plating metals.

Paints, lacquers and similar products consist of organic or inorganic polymers and may contain binders, pigments, additives, fillers, solvents and water in varying concentrations which are processed in intensive mixing and grinding operations. Unlike many surface treatments, painting etc. rarely has an influence on the underlying material (substrate).

Printing methods which can be employed in the metalworking industry are silk-screen and intaglio printing. However, only a small amount of steel is treated in this way.

Quality control
In the majority of cases a processed surface is not measured by machine but rather assessed by way of a visual inspection or by comparing the finish with samples. The measurement of surface quality only plays a minor role in the construction industry. The main methods of quality control are:
- visual inspection
- feel and touch comparisons
- comparison with samples
- preparation of a surface profile with a contact stylus instrument
- measurement of layer thickness
- magnetic measuring techniques
- X-ray measuring techniques

Construction to suit the surface treatment
To achieve the desired properties for a component, certain construction principles have to be adhered to depending on the type of surface treatment. The following chief considerations should be allowed for:
- The surface must be cleaned beforehand in a way that is compatible with the intended surface treatment. This includes the removal of grease, rust and layers of oxides and other foreign matter as well as roughening or sealing the surface.
- Gaseous, liquid and solid treatment media must be able to reach and leave the surface unhindered.
- Prevention of air bubble formation during the treatment process as a result of recesses, projections or grooves.
- Sharp edges must exhibit small, minimal radii.
- Drainage openings must be incorporated at awkward returns.
- Preventing an accumulation of coating material adjacent holes and edges.

Coating wear
Disintegration or wearing of an applied coating or treated surface can arise due to:
- abrasion
- corrosion
- erosion
- adhesion
- fatigue

Anti-corrosion measures

Corrosion and anti-corrosion measures

The steels used by the building industry are freed from undesirable tramp elements and are in an optimum chemical state for their purpose. In this condition the steels are particularly vulnerable to corrosion when the air humidity rises above 65%. Only above this humidity level does oxygen react with iron at the surface of the steel.

Corrosion phenomena on loadbearing components are frequently associated with a considerable decrease in their loadbearing capacity, particularly in lightweight steel construction. In structural steelwork corrosion protection is therefore an essential safety feature. Furthermore, prudent anti-corrosion measures have both an economic and ecological significance.

Modern anti-corrosion systems and methods can provide permanent corrosion protection for steel components, even in onerous conditions. In addition, anti-corrosion measures can also assist with design intentions regarding, for example, surface finish and colour.

Types of corrosion

Surface corrosion, particularly atmospheric corrosion

Surface corrosion is a form of corrosion in which electrochemical processes disintegrate the metal. This can take place in the open air, underground or underwater. Apart from ports, bridges, offshore and similar steel structures, atmospheric corrosion which takes place in the open air is probably most important.

Atmospheric corrosion is oxidic corrosion in an environment alternating between wet and dry. In atmospheric corrosion, tiny corrosive elements form on the surface of the metal. Each of these consists of an anodic and a cathodic part. The iron starts to break down at the anode, where the metal dissolves in the form of an ion by liberating two electrons. At the cathode the electrons migrating from the anode react with water and oxygen to form hydroxyl ions (OH). As hydroxyl ions create an alkaline, protective environment, the cathode is protected against corrosion. So the rust forms at a third point, i.e. at the place where the ferrous ions encounter the hydroxyl ions and can oxidize to a higher valency with oxygen from

3.2

Location	Rate of corrosion (mm/year)
Moderately populated areas	0.02-0.05
Residential districts in urban areas	0.05-0.10
Large industrial centres	0.08-0.15
Coastal regions	0.06-0.17
Freshwater	0.05-0.10
Saltwater, aggressive water	0.15-0.20

3.3

1	2	3
Type of building	Exposure to corrosive attack	Corrosion protection class
Surfaces in enclosed buildings	exposed	I
	not exposed	II
	chemical attack internally [1]	III
Surfaces in open buildings	exposed	I, II, III [2]
	not exposed	II, III [3]
	chemical attack internally [1]	III

1) This includes elevated sulphur dioxide or chloride content, acid fumes, etc., also in conjunction with increased occurrence of condensation.
2) Depending on the external air.
3) Class II is only permitted if the corrosive attack on non-exposed steel surfaces corresponds approximately to that of an internal area.

3.4

Type of atmosphere [1]	Accessibility [2]	Corrosion protection class [3]
L (rural)	accessible	I
	inaccessible	II
S (urban)	accessible	II
	inaccessible	III
I (industrial)	accessible	III
	inaccessible	III
M (marine)	accessible	III
	inaccessible	III
Special situations	accessible	III [4]

1) See DIN 55928 Part 1, Nov 1976 edition, sections 3.1 and 4.
2) Steel components are classed as accessible if they can be reached without significant constructional modifications so that the necessary anti-corrosion measures can be applied, inspected and maintained; see DIN 55928 Part 2, Oct 1979 edition, section 3.2.1.
3) The classes are as follows:
   I For a comparatively low degree of corrosive attack or short period of protection.
   II For a moderate degree of corrosive attack or long period of protection.
   III For particularly aggressive corrosive attack or particularly long period of protection.
4) The systems graded class III in tables 3.3 and 3.4 are not generally suitable for all types of chemical or other non-standard forms of attack. Therefore, a system must be chosen relevant to the particular circumstances.

the electrolyte. In dry periods the layers of oxide formed during wet periods are compacted and the process of corrosion often comes to a halt, while in wet periods the mechanisms continue in the sense of oxidic corrosion.

When the extent of the surface corrosion varies locally, we speak of wide-pitting, when small holes are formed, then pitting. Crevice corrosion is a localized worsening of corrosion in joints and gaps.

The rust formed by the corrosion process has a greater volume than the iron itself. This can lead to an expansive effect, especially in joints. Therefore, crevices, slits and joints must be very well sealed to prevent corrosion.

Bimetallic corrosion
So-called bimetallic (or galvanic) corrosion occurs when two different metals are joined in a conductive sense and are located in the same electrolyte. Here too the – at least occasional – presence of an electrolyte is necessary for corrosion to take place. In bimetallic corrosion the less noble metal, i.e. the one lower down the electrochemical series, corrodes. The possibility of bimetallic corrosion in steelwork often occurs at fixings for cladding and roofing made from other metals, e.g. aluminium.

Corrosion classes
Various categories have been designated depending on the risk of corrosion and accessibility for maintenance and inspection of the components requiring protection.

Corrosion problems with stainless steel
The use of stainless steel does reduce the problems outlined above but in no way entirely. Even stainless steels can corrode, given certain critical ambient conditions. Therefore, a specialist consultant should always be brought in when planning to use stainless steel in, for example, marine environments or where chlorinated splashing water or corresponding condensation is expected. Owing to their high Cr and Ni additions, stainless steels are expensive and hence only normally used in the form of thin sheets or as fasteners. But it is precisely these parts that are especially sensitive to a corrosion-related reduction in the loadbearing capacity.

One interesting variation is to plate normal steel with a thin layer of stainless steel (Platinox). However, special attention must be given to the corner and edge details of such composite sheets.

Steels which form a protective layer
Among the group of low-alloy structural steels there are, for example, steels where surface corrosion initially progresses rapidly but almost ceases in the long term. The corroded surface forms a protective layer for the steel underneath. This mechanism functions reliably provided the construction can al-ways dry out again. Constant moisture causes the corrosion process to continue unabated. Therefore, structures incorporating such steels must be designed accordingly.

Anti-corrosion systems
A distinction is made between the following systems:
· metallic coatings, e.g. hot-dip galvanizing
· coating systems consisting of 1-4 layers
· combinations of metallic and organic coatings, so-called duplex systems

Metallic coatings consist of a layer of metal applied to the surface of the steel. The most common method used in structural steelwork is hot-dip galvanizing, carried out by immersing the components in a bath filled with molten zinc.

Coating systems consist of several successively applied thin layers of mostly organic polymers usually blended with additional fillers. Coatings are available in a wide range of colours and with gloss, satin or matt finishes depending on the product.

The duplex systems exploit the advantageous combination of the anti-corrosion properties of both metallic and organic coatings. A metallic coating, usually galvanizing, is applied first followed by covering with an appropriately coordinated system.

Subjected to normal atmospheric conditions, modern anti-corrosion systems have a life expectancy of 15-20 years. After this time has expired, renewal and/or repairs are necessary.

3.5

Metal		Standard electrode potential (V)
gold	Au	+ 1.50
mercury	Hg	+ 0.85
silver	Ag	+ 0.80
copper	Cu	+ 0.35
hydrogen	H	0
lead	Pb	– 0.12
tin	Sn	– 0.14
nickel	Ni	– 0.23
cadmium	Cd	– 0.40
irom	Fe	– 0.44
chromium	Cr	– 0.56
zinc	Zn	– 0.76
manganese	Mn	– 1.05
aluminium	Al	– 1.68
magnesium	Mg	– 2.34
potassium	K	– 2.92

3.6

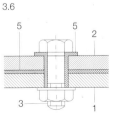 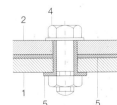

1 Steel part
2 Aluminium part
3 Steel bolt
4 Aluminium bolt
5 Isolating gaskets

3.7

1 South Bend (USA), rural atmosphere, facing south,
   inclined at 30°
2 Olpe, rural atmosphere, facing south, inclined at 45°
3 Cuxhaven, urban/rural atmosphere, facing south,
   inclined at 45°
4 Mülheim/Ruhr, industrial atmosphere, facing south,
   inclined at 45°
5/6 Oberhausen, industrial atmosphere, facing north,
   vertical
7 Curve derived from test results

▨ direct exposure in severely polluted industrial areas
— measured
-- extrapolated

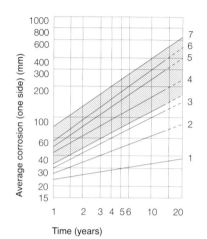

3.8

Components in indoor pool atmosphere without regular
cleaning

Water complying with drinking water statute [1]	Water rich in chloride salt [2]
Materials 10 and 12	Materials 13 and 14

(1) Cl ≤ 250 mg/l
(2) e.g. brine water

3.9

No.	Steel grade		Micro-struct. [1]	Strength class S [2] and form of product [3]					Corrosion resistance class/ requirement	Typical applications for components and fixings
	Abbreviation	Material No.		235	275	355	460	690		
1	X2CrNi12	1.4003	F	B, Ba, gH, P	B, Ba, D, gH, S, W,		D, S,		I/low	Interiors with no chloride present
2	X6Cr17	1,4016	F	D, S, W	D, S					
3	X5CrNi18-10	1.4301	A	B, Ba, D, gH, P, S, W	B, Ba, D, gH, P, S	B, Ba, D, gH, S	Ba, D, S		II/moderate	Accessible constructions
4	X6CrNiTi18-10	1.4541	A	B, Ba, D, gH, P, S, W	B, Ba, D, gH, P, S	Ba, D, gH, S	Ba, D, S			
5	X2CrNiN18-7	1.4318	A		B, Ba, D, P, S					
6	X3CrNiCu18-9-4	1.4567	A	D, S, W	D, S	D, S	D, S	D, S		
7	X5CrNiMo17-12-2	1.4401	A	B, Ba, D, gH, P, S, W	B, Ba, D, gH, P, S	Ba, D, gH, S	Ba, D, S		III/medium	Inaccessible constructions
8	X2CrNiMo17-12-2	1.4404	A	B, Ba, D, gH, P, S, W	B, Ba, D, gH, P, S	Ba, D, gH, S	Ba, D, S	D, S		
9	X6CrNiMoTi17-12-2	1.4571	A	B, Ba, D, gH, P, S, W	B, Ba, D, gH, P, S	Ba, D, gH, S	Ba, D, S	D, S		
10	X1NiCrMoCu25-20-5	1.4539	A	B, Ba, D, gH, P, S, W	B, Ba, D, S	D, P, S	D, S	D, S	IV/high	Constructions with high corrosion loads due to chlorides and/or chlorine
11	X2CrNiMoN22-5-3	1.4462	FA				B, Ba, D, gH, P, S, W	D, S		
12	X2CrNiMoNi17-13-5	1.4439	A		B, Ba, D, gH, S, W					
13	X2CrNiMnMoNbN25-18-5	1.4565	A				B, Ba, D, gH, P, S, D, P, S	D, S		
14	X1NiCrMoCuN-25-20-7	1.4529	A		B, D, S, W	B, D, gH, P, S		D, S		

1) Microstructure: A = austenite, F = ferrite, FA = ferrite-austenite
2) The lowest stress classes in each case are achieved by strain-hardening through cold-working
3) B = sheet, Ba = strip, D = drawn wire, gH = welded hollow section, P = section, S = bar, W = rolled wire

Metallic coatings: galvanizing

There are various methods for galvanizing steel components. Hot-dip galvanizing is the most commonly used method of applying a metallic coating to structural steel components. This represents a high-quality means of corrosion protection. The principle of protection is founded on applying a watertight barrier to the surface of the steel.

All structural steels in general use can be hot-dip galvanized. However, high-strength steels require special quality control procedures. Galvanized high-strength bolts up to grade 10.9 may only be used as complete sets (nut, bolt, washers) from one manufacturer.

It must be remembered that the sizes of items to be galvanized are limited by the galvanizing baths available, and hence maximum sizes must be agreed at the design stage. Furthermore, consistency in the thickness of individual parts throughout the construction is also important. The thicknesses of the steel parts should be more or less consistent throughout the construction. When this is not the case, the zinc layer will be inconsistent and – more importantly – differences in thickness may lead to different cooling rates which can result in component distortion. The zinc tends to accumulate along edges and at corners – an advantageous phenomenon as these areas are difficult to protect by other means.

Fully enclosed voids must include suitably positioned vent holes; otherwise the temperature-related expansion of the trapped air can cause the components literally to explode upon immersion in the bath! Further, the zinc that flows into such voids must be able to drain away quickly enough when the component is lifted out of the bath. These factors determine the sizes and positions of drain and vent holes, all of which will be visible on the finished component and so galvanizing considerations must be harmonized with architectural aspects.

A layer of zinc will always become thinner over the years as a result of corrosive attack. In the long term this leads to the loss of the corrosion protection. As the duration of protection is essentially determined by the thickness of the coating, this must be specified at the design stage.

The process of galvanizing

Surface preparation

Unlike polymer coatings, galvanizing does not exhibit a self-cleaning effect. Therefore, the surface must be finished to a high quality prior to galvanizing. In the case of hot-dip galvanizing, the workpiece is cleaned in an acid bath; for zinc spraying, Sa 3 quality is required. Firstly, rust, millscale and general contamination are removed from the steel parts in an acid bath before being rinsed with water and finally wetted in another tank filled with flux.

Applying the protection by hot-dip galvanizing

After the flux has dried, the component is immersed in a bath filled with molten zinc. This operation is connected with severe temperature changes in the component and the release of gases. After a short holding time (a few minutes at most), the component is lifted out of the bath and rotated in such a way that all excess zinc drains off. If necessary, cooling of the component is accelerated in a water tank (caution: quenching effect!). The zinc coating can be subsequently worked.

This procedure provides the steel with a firmly adhering, dense layer consisting of iron-zinc alloys of various compositions right up to pure zinc. The thickness of the adhering layer of zinc is chiefly dependent on the thickness of the steel component, the steel grade and the immersion time. The zinc is relatively thick on silicon-killed and weathering steels; it also rises with increasing component thickness and immersion time. Normally, the thickness of the zinc fluctuates between 50 and 100 µm, the most frequent value being around 75 µm. The surface finish of the zinc varies from a metallic sheen to a dark grey matt, but this does not have any relevance for the quality of corrosion protection. Ductile pure zinc layers have a metallic sheen, iron-zinc alloys a dark grey matt appearance.

Zinc-spraying

Batch galvanizing presupposes that the maximum length of any item to be protected is twice the length of the galvanizing bath (immersed twice). This constraint does not apply to zinc-spraying. Therefore, this method is used to provide high-quality corrosion protection for components which cannot be dis-

3.10	
Surface finish quality	Principal features of prepared steel surface
Sa 1	Merely the removal of loose millscale, rust and other coatings.
Sa 2	Removal of virtually all millscale, rust and other coatings, i.e. any millscale, rust and other coatings residue still adhering to the surface (not a congruent layer) must be such that the overall impression corresponds to the photo of the reference samples.
Sa 2.5	Removal of millscale, rust and other coatings to such an extent that any residue on the steel surface merely appears as insubstantial nuances of colour as a result of the colouring of pores.
Sa 3	Complete removal of millscale, rust and other coatings (viewed without enlargement).

3.11					
Method	Designation	Intensities			
Blasting	Sa	1	2	2.5	3
Partial-blasting	PSa	–	–	2.5	–
Hand-held machine cleaning	St	–	2	–	3
Flame-cleaning	Fl	–	–	–	–
Pickling	Be	–	–	–	–

3.12

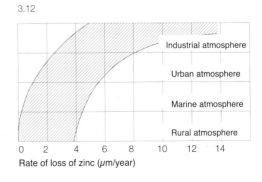

Rate of loss of zinc (µm/year)

mantled or where that would be impracticable. However, owing to its high cost, zinc-spraying is less common than hot-dip galvanizing.

Applying the protection by zinc-spraying
The spraying of zinc involves heating zinc, in the form of powder or wire, in a spray-gun until it melts. Using compressed air the molten zinc is then sprayed onto the steel surface previously cleaned to Sa 3 quality. However, the layer of zinc which builds up on the steel is uneven and porous and therefore must always be subsequently sealed with a polymer coating. The thickness of the zinc layer is related to the number of passes of the spray-gun and can be varied at will. One advantage of zinc-spraying is that there is no risk of distortion of the components due to changes of temperature.

Electrogalvanizing
This involves applying a layer of zinc just a few microns thick in the wet-dip process while applying an electric current (DC). Electrogalvanizing serves as temporary corrosion protection. It is mainly used to protect small items such as screws, nails and other fasteners.

Sherardizing
This is the application of a polymer-bound zinc dust. Therefore, this is actually an organic and not a metallic coating. Its uses include making good defects and weld seams on components made from hot-dip galvanized semifinished products, but mainly as a primer for subsequent polymer coatings.

Coating systems
Multilayer coating systems based on organic polymers represent the most common method for protecting against corrosion.

The main properties of polymer coatings are:
· easily adapted to suit differing corrosive situations
· easily adapted to suit different processing techniques
· economic compared to alternatives
· the wide range of finishes and colours present many design options
· the protective coating is relatively thin

Polymer coatings comprise binders (normally organic polymers), pigments, fillers, solvents or dispersants and additives.

3.13

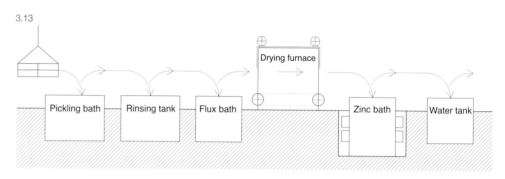

3.14			Atmosphere	
External environment	rural	urban	marine	industrial
DIN 50960 (supplement) old	1.0–3.4	1.0–6.0	2.4–15.0	3.8–19.0
DIN 50959 (1977 draft)			2.0–4.0	9.0–13.0
Baumann	1.9–2.2	2.8–5.6	2.4–3.6	5.6–11.0
Evaluation from publications	1.0–2.0	2.0–4.0	2.0–6.0	6.0–12.0
Average values	1.3–2.5	1.9–5.2	2.2–7.2	6.4–13.8
Average	1.9	3.5	4.7	10.1
Internal environment			average value 1.5	

(All values in μm/year)

3.15

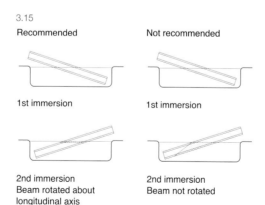

Recommended   Not recommended

1st immersion   1st immersion

2nd immersion
Beam rotated about
longitudinal axis

2nd immersion
Beam not rotated

3.16

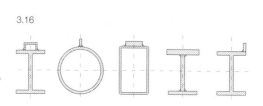

Organic polymers
· Very large molecules, mostly in a linear arrangement, made up of carbon chains with attached hydrogen atoms and many reactive groups in which oxygen, nitrogen, chlorine, etc. can appear.
· Natural organic polymers (natural resins, dry oils, rubber, bitumen) were used in the past; today, we use synthetic polymers (plastics). The chemical precursors of polymers, which are initially liquid but are then transformed into polymers upon hardening, are being increasingly used as binders (epoxides, polyurethane).

Pigments
· Particles of the order of magnitude of 1 μm which give the coating its colour, protect the binder against fading and help the chemical corrosion protection afforded by the coating.
· Coloured pigments are primarily used in the finish layer. Anti-corrosive pigments are only used in underlying layers (red lead).

Fillers
· Solid particles of the order of magnitude of 10 μm which, above all, ensure adhesion to the substrate, improve mechanical resistance, lower the cost of materials, contribute to the fading resistance of pigments and create a favourable rheological behaviour for the processing of the coating materials.

Life expectancy of polymer coatings
The UV portion of light slowly breaks down the binder (organic substance) on the surface (rate of degradation approx. 0.5-5 μm/year). Apart from that, the ageing process of the polymer binder brings about an increase in hardness, a decrease in strength, a rise in inherent stresses and increased permeability. The corrosion protection pigments react with aggressive substances diffusing into the coating.

As a rule, polymer coatings consist of several separate layers (primer and finishing coats). Combinations of various coating systems are common because within each steel structure the corrosive loads can vary considerably.

The primer coat is frequently provided with so-called active pigments which create a chemical environment which either prevents or considerably slows the corrosion process. Red

lead, chlorides and sulphates bind other substances chemically and hence render these corrosion stimulators harmless, regardless of whether these permeate the coating from the outside or are present in the steel surface as a consequence of inadequate cleaning. Red lead as a pigment is also particularly important when corrosion products cannot be fully removed from the surface of the steel prior to coating.

Polymer coatings can be produced with the most diverse finishes and colours.

Coating, application, surface preparation
The surface quality required for applying the surface coating depends on the self-cleaning effect of the primer coat. Coating systems may only be applied to suitably cleaned and pre-treated steel parts. The recommendations of the coating manufacturer should always be adhered to with regard to the surface quality required.

It is impossible to achieve a metal surface that is perfectly clean at the time of coating and, likewise, a coating that is completely free from electrolyte-forming substances. Therefore, the primer coat must include active pigments. The surface of the metal must be sufficiently wetted with the coating material so that anode and cathode are prevented from forming a corrosion element.

Applying the protection
Coating materials can be applied with rollers and brushes, but application via compressed-air or airless spraying is more usual. Airless spraying permits much larger areas to be covered than compressed-air spraying. Electrostatic spraying, immersion, flooding, whirl-sintering, etc. are reserved for factory application.

The separate coating layers should be of different colours in order to distinguish them and each layer should be dry before the next layer is applied. However, the time between applying the layers should not be too long or the bonding of the individual layers cannot be guaranteed. The different colours of the various layers ensures that the coverage of each successive layer is easy to identify by way of visual inspection.

3.17

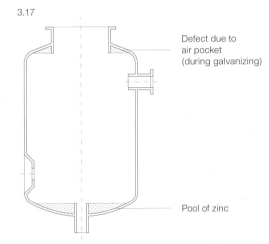

Defect due to air pocket (during galvanizing)

Pool of zinc

Shop primers are applied in order to protect components during production itself. These do not provide durable protection and are not adequate for use as primer coats. If a shop primer is to be used as part of the priming coat, it should be cleaned and repaired beforehand. The typical thickness of a shop primer is 15-25 µm.

One or two primer coats, total thickness 40 µm for standard coating systems, 80 µm for high-build systems, are applied over the shop primer.

One, two or three finish coats, total thickness 40 µm for standard coating systems, 80 µm for high-build systems, are then applied over the primer coat(s).

Duplex system

A duplex system is an anti-corrosion system which consists of a metallic coating (normally hot-dip galvanizing) and a coating applied over it.

Coloured coatings over galvanizing are usually chosen for aesthetic reasons or to achieve a required proclamatory effect. The use of a duplex system enables such requirements to be met while at the same time substantially improving the corrosion protection. A duplex

system offers long-term protection which, owing to the synergy effect, is considerably longer than the sum of the lifetimes of the individual layers – in fact some 1.2 to 2.5 times this figure.

With hot-dip galvanized steel, the coating materials have to be selected very carefully in order to achieve the necessary adhesion of the coating, particularly with freshly galvanized steel. Suitable materials are, for example, those based on vinyl resin, epoxy resin, acrylic resin, epoxy resin tar, coal tar and bitumen-oil combinations. By contrast, sprayed zinc tolerates a wider range of coating materials. However, in this case the thickness of the first coat is critical because the porous sprayed metal layer also soaks up coating material.

In duplex systems the thickness of the metallic coating is 50-85 µm. The subsequent one or two finish coats total 40 µm for standard coating systems, 80 µm for high-build systems.

Fire protection

3.18 Idealized stress-strain curves for St 37 steel in
relation to temperature [440]
3.19 Fire resistance classes [438]
3.20 Building materials classes [440]

3.18

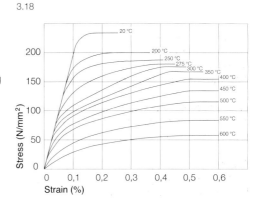

Principles

Steel does not burn and does not propagate fire. However, a fire-related temperature rise alters the mechanical properties of the steel, properties such as tensile strength, yield strength and Young's modulus as well as, under certain circumstances, the metallic microstructure of the material. Therefore, during a fire we can assume that the loadbearing capacity of the construction is reduced. After a fire, the material must be carefully analysed to establish whether any permanent change has taken place in its microstructure and hence in its ability to carry loads.

The length of time taken for a component or structure to fail in a fire situation is termed its period of fire resistance.

The loadbearing capacity of the construction is reduced commensurate with the course and duration of a fire. In calculating this (diminished) loadbearing capacity, the strengths actually available at elevated temperatures can be assumed.

Structural fire protection

The task of structural fire protection is to prevent or at least delay the heating-up of steel components such that their failure temperature is not reached before the desired period of fire resistance expires.

The measures employed to achieve structural fire protection fall into three categories: insulating, shielding and heat-dissipating. They act directly (as casing, coating or filling) or indirectly (by shielding).

Casings

Cement-bound sprayed plasters and concretes, cast in-situ concretes or claddings of mineral fibres. All these systems are forms of fire protection applied on site and can be used for columns, beams and other members.

Most of the sprayed plasters used these days adhere directly to the surface of the steel without the need for any form of metal lathing for support. But it is important to ensure that the applied fire protection is compatible with the existing corrosion protection.

Concrete, which is an ideal means of achieving structural fire protection, is either applied in sprayed form or the steel members are fully encased in concrete.

Claddings

Prefabricated boxes or shaped pieces are the most usual form. Boards cut to suit on site and joined by mechanical fasteners enable all shapes and sizes of steel members to be protected.

Intumescent coatings

These thermally insulating coatings are regarded as particularly suitable for steelwork. They are applied as paints or foils and, when exposed to fire, exfoliate and so form a thick, protective layer. This exfoliation begins in the range 200-300°C. This layer, which can reach a thickness of several centimetres, delays the heating-up of the steel underneath and prevents flames coming into contact with the steel. As exposure to the fire continues, the degree of protection normally decreases as the coating is gradually consumed and cracks start to form.

In the so-called passive state such intumescent coatings are hardly noticeable to the layperson. However, they are easily recognized by experts as the surface appears unusually crude for a paint finish, with brush marks often being readily visible. Intumescent coatings are available in different colours and also provide good corrosion protection.

The following build-up is typical of an intumescent coating system:
• Primer as corrosion protection. It must be compatible with the subsequent coats and must not run under the effects of heat.
• Intumescent coating. Normally applied in several separate layers. The thickness depends on the members to be protected and the desired degree of protection.
• Finish coat. This protects all the layers underneath against the effects of moisture and other environmental influences. It must not hinder the exfoliation process in any way.

3.19

Fire resistance class	Period of fire resistance (min)	Requirement to be satisfied
F 30	≥ 30	fire-retardant
F 60	≥ 60	
F 90	≥ 90	fire-resistant
F 120	≥ 120	
F 180	≥ 180	

3.20

Building materials class	Building authority designation
A	incombustible materials
A$_1$	
A$_2$	
B	combustible materials
B$_1$	not readily flammable materials
B$_2$	flammable materials
B$_3$	highly flammable materials

Intumescent coatings are available with organic (carbon foam structure) and inorganic (ceramic foam structure) compositions. According to current building authority codes, intumescent coatings must achieve fire resistance class F 60.

Shieldings
In this case unprotected steel components are shielded against the direct effects of flames and heat by floor, ceiling or wall systems.

Water-filled hollow sections
Water inside a hollow section absorbs the thermal energy acting on the member. The following systems are feasible:
- Non-replenishable filling of water or an aqueous solution. This delays the rise in temperature of the hollow section in a fire situation but does not prevent it altogether. The vapour pressure which builds up inside the hollow section must be allowed to escape via valves or similar measures because otherwise the hollow section can literally explode!
- Replenishable filling of water or an aqueous solution. This method can dissipate virtually any amount of heat, even in a prolonged fire.

Water-filled systems are extremely good. However, a number of factors must be taken into account if such a system is to be used:
- Since water expands when it freezes, antifreeze should be added to the water filling in external components.
- With tall columns it should not be forgotten that the ensuing internal hydrostatic pressure can cause a considerable, perhaps even enormous, load on the material. Therefore, tall buildings typically use separate systems of limited height.
- Systems employing flowing water must incorporate measures to prevent steam from developing in the system during a fire as this can cause failure of the pumps.
- Corrosion within the system must be avoided. Therefore, air should be excluded from the system or the filling must contain suitable additives.

It is also possible to flood hollow sections only upon the outbreak of a fire. However, in this case it must be guaranteed that any fire is detected quickly and that the necessary quantity of water can be introduced quickly enough. Sprinkler systems are another method of protecting steelwork from the effects of fire.

Composite construction designed to provide fire protection
In a fire the loadbearing capacity of the steel/reinforced concrete combination is made up of the capacities of the two materials. Owing to its lower thermal conductivity and higher heat storage capacity, the concrete protects the steel. The steel must be designed such that in the event of a fire (despite the omission of other means of protection) an adequate factor of safety remains for the duration of the required fire resistance, even if there are exposed steel surfaces within the composite construction.

Feasible floor constructions
The examples illustrate profiled steel sheeting with conventional fire protection by means of sprayed plaster or a suspended ceiling. In example 1 very good adhesion is essential.

The other examples show unprotected floors. These employ trapezoidal profile sheeting with a concrete topping, i.e. the steel sheeting is merely used as permanent formwork; this does not qualify as composite construction. The reinforcement in example 3 consists of welded mesh and that in example 4 longitudinal bars in the ribs. These floors are designed for the standard and fire cases according to DIN 1045 and DIN 4102 (Parts 2 and 4) respectively. The concrete protects the steel in the event of a fire while the steel sheeting prevents concrete from spalling off from the underside.

"True" composite floors are illustrated in examples 5 and 6. In example 5 the fire resistance is achieved by way of additional reinforcement. In example 6 the narrow, dovetail-shaped ribs prevent the steel within the rib from heating-up too intensely and so it continues to function as tension reinforcement. For continuous floor slabs, the upper reinforcement for the fire case is designed to DIN 4102 as for reinforced concrete floors.

3.21

Min. thickness for claddings (mm)
(manufacturers' figures)

A = Profile claddings of sprayed vermiculite and sprayed mineral fibre (figures in brackets) for fully loaded beams

B = Box claddings for columns (prefabricated fibre-reinforced silicate boards)

U = Perimeter of section			A = Area of section		
U/A [1/m]	F 60		F 90		F 120	
	A	B	A	B	A	B
up to 70	10		15	15	20	
71- 90	(10)	10	(20)		(30)	20
91-120	10 (15)		20 (25)	20	30 (35)	
121-145	15	12	25		35	25
146-175	(20)	15	(30)		(40)	
176-200						30
201-215				25		
216-235		20				35
236-245	20		30		40	
246-265	(25)		(35)	30	(50)	40
266-275						
276-290				35		
291-300		25		40		

Partially encased steel beams
Steel beams with a concrete filling between the flanges secured by way of shear studs welded to the web or shear links welded to or penetrating the web and held in place by longitudinal bars. In a fire, the loadbearing capacity of the unprotected flange decreases as a result of the rise in temperature. The web, protected by the concrete, heats up considerably slower and together with the web/flange junctions is directly responsible for maintaining the beam's loadbearing capacity.

Fully and partially encased steel columns
The loadbearing capacity of steel/concrete columns depends to a large extent on whether filled hollow sections or encased rolled sections are being used.

In the concrete-filled hollow-section column the steel heats up relatively quickly, partly because the thermal energy is only taken up slowly by the concrete core. The strength of the steel diminishes correspondingly quickly. In addition, the outer tube expands with respect to the inner core, and with thin-walled sections this can cause local buckling of the steel. The loadbearing capacity of this type of column in the fire case mainly relies on the strength of the concrete core. This can be improved by adding longitudinal reinforcing bars. As the loadbearing capacity of the steel is severely reduced, suitable details must be used to ensure that the loads from beams attached to the column are not transferred exclusively to the hollow section but instead to the entire cross-section.

With steel column sections fully encased in concrete the casing prevents the steel within from heating up too rapidly. Virtually all rolled, special and solid sections are suitable for encasing in concrete. Prolonged exposure to flames causes an increasingly uneven temperature distribution within the cross-section which gives rise to restraint forces. Failure is accompanied by buckling of the web or flanges; therefore, heavier, thick-walled sections should be used. The concrete cover should be at least 50 mm thick.

The concrete of fully encased steel sections has to be reinforced with welded mesh or else it can become detached from the flanges.

Partially encased steel sections (e.g. an I- or H-section with concrete filling between the flanges) heat up in a fire like a similarly constructed beam subjected to bending. Upon exposure to flames the outer, exposed parts of the steel lose almost all of their loadbearing capacity. However, the web and the concrete filling are still available to carry the load. As, in contrast to beams, columns tend to be axially loaded with little need for bending strength, this change in the loadbearing capacity is therefore less critical. Such columns exhibit a good fire resistance.

3.22

3.23

1   2   3

4   5   6

Thermal insulation

Sound insulation in steelwork

Thermal insulation

The individual components of a building must conform to the thermal insulation requirements of DIN 4108 as well as the provisions of the Thermal Insulation Act (minimization of energy use).

Correct thermal insulation will:
- lower the energy required for heating and cooling
- protect against saturation by condensation
- prevent inadmissible expansion of components
- protect against general damage

The thermal insulation properties of building materials are influenced by:
- ratio of air to voids (insulating capacity)
- relative density (storage capacity)
- thickness (internal surface resistance)
- layers of air at the boundaries of the component (external surface resistance)
- areas of glass (solar heat gain)

Steel and insulation

Steel has a high thermal conductivity and so easily forms an undesirable thermal bridge. This leads to, on the one hand, thermal losses and, on the other, the accumulation of condensation on the cold steel surfaces. At all places where steel components penetrate the building envelope special care should be taken to ensure adequate ventilation in order to prevent condensation. If this is not possible, then the component should be heated. Only in exceptional circumstances is the build-up of condensation and the subsequent formation of ice acceptable. On no account should steel components be simply "wrapped" in mineral wool etc. where condensation is expected.

General

Adequate sound insulation is one of the chief necessities for healthy living, working and leisure conditions. A distinction is made between insulating against external noise and insulating against internal noise. The sound insulation of the outer components must be arranged in such a way that the external local noise levels are reduced by the outer components to a prescribed recommended level based on medical studies. The same is true for internal noise levels, which have to be screened by the inner components. The acceptable sound levels depend on the purpose of the building and the type of activity within the building. In purely commercial situations the allowable noise level is considerably higher than in residential developments or hospitals, health resorts and nursing homes.

DIN 4109 and E 1984 stipulate the minimum requirements for sound insulation measures; standard values and suggestions on how to achieve better insulation are also included. The minimum values for the sound insulation index and maximum values for the standard impact sound level are stated. Furthermore, the sound pressure level generated by building services is also limited.

VDI 2058 contains supplementary information, e.g. regarding acceptable sound levels.

Sources of noise and sound insulation requirements

Examples of sources of noise are:
- traffic, up to 85 dB(A)
- loud conversation, up to 70 dB(A)
- offices, up to 70 dB(A)
- workshops, over 100 dB(A)
- restaurants, up to 90 dB(A)

Owing to the logarithmic measurement of sound intensity, an increase of 10 dB(A) is perceived as a doubling of the volume.

The sound insulation requirements placed on building components are regulated by both E 1984 and DIN 4109. These contain minimum insulation figures with which buildings or components thereof have to comply. The upper limits for incoming noise are:

- rest rooms, up to 30 dB(A)
- patient accommodation in hospitals, up to 30 dB(A)
- classrooms, up to 35 dB(A)
- meeting rooms, up to 35 dB(A)
- offices, up to 40 dB(A)

In some cases higher values are permissible during the day.

Sound insulation measures

The degree of insulation against airborne sound is improved by
- increasing the mass of the component(s) (high weight per surface area of building envelope)
- increasing the number of layers of components (avoidance of acoustic paths)
- avoiding double-skin resonance with multi-skin construction
- ensuring adequate airtightness at joints (possible loss of up to 20 dB(A) in insulating value)
- minimizing flanking path transmissions

The degree of insulation against impact sound is improved by
- ensuring a high weight per surface area of the loadbearing floor slab
- using soft or resilient floor coverings
- using non-rigid soffits
- laying floating screeds
- avoiding acoustic paths
- employing homogeneous components and multi-skin construction

The aforementioned standards or relevant specialist publications should be consulted for more detailed information.

Erection and dismantling

Building with steel means building with prefabricated elements to a very large degree. The individual members such as columns, beams, connecting plates or even steel castings are prepared ready for erection at the steel fabrication works and subsequently provided with an anti-corrosion system. Galvanizing is carried out in galvanizing shops and coatings are applied either in the fabrication plant itself or in factories specializing in such work, although the final coat is often applied on site after erection. In the case of composite construction, the finished steel parts are usually sent to a concrete plant to enable the reinforced concrete to be added. This – sometimes costly – situation is the outcome of a tradition based on many decades of firms each handling only one material.

Steel fabrication yards are often set up on site for very large construction projects. But here too, the members which leave the yard are always ready for erection.

Ideally, components delivered to site should be lifted by crane directly from the transport vehicle to the point at which they are required for immediate installation. This avoids intermediate storage on site, which is always costly and carries with it the inherent risk of damage to the components.

On site, subsequent modifications to the parts awaiting erection are only possible to a limited extent and always involve high costs. Therefore, with structural steelwork in particular, careful planning and manufacture is vital. This also involves taking into account the tolerances of the steelwork and harmonizing these with the tolerances of other materials such as reinforced concrete, the favourite material for foundations. Again and again, on the building site the welcome precision with which steel components can and are made comes up against considerably less precise reinforced concrete or timber components. Therefore, dimensional inaccuracies and tolerances must be compensated for at the interfaces between steelwork and other trades. Detailing these junctions between different materials requires care and skill in order to provide a detail that is compatible with both materials and the constraints of the building site. The competence of the skilled designer is demonstrated at these interfaces between factory-made items and in-situ finishing, or between diverse building materials.

Planning documents

The planning documents necessary for structural steelwork include the architect's layout drawings and the working drawings of the structural engineer. These are complemented by the stipulations of the tender, special engineering provisions and the structural calculations. The workshop drawings, without which production cannot begin, are prepared on the basis of these documents.

In preparing the fabrication of the steel, the stipulations of the architect and/or structural engineer are adapted to suit the needs of production. Such modifications can lead to considerable changes in the architectural appearance or loadbearing behaviour of the construction. Therefore, alterations at this stage necessitate close coordination between fabricator and design office; workshop drawings must be checked and approved by the design office. This checking and approval of workshop drawings is therefore a vital link in the quality control chain which is, unfortunately, overlooked all too often.

The workshop drawings form the basis for the steel fabricator's production. However, one further set of drawings is still required – the erection drawings. These include details of:
- erection sequence
- requirements for dimensions, weights and tolerances
- requirements for temporary works and other equipment
- safety
- means of ascent

Dimensional and modular coordination, tolerances
Dimensional coordination
The SI (Système Internationale) stipulations apply to units of measurement. The unit of length used in steelwork is the millimetre (mm).

Standardized figures for construction are nominal measurements and the individual, structural and finished dimensions derived from these.

Nominal measurements form the theoretical framework for the coordinating sizes. These are the dimensions of components including their joints.

Reference (target) sizes are the measurements which a component should exhibit. These are given on the drawings.

The actual, measurable sizes may deviate from the reference sizes stated on the drawings by up to a certain amount – the permissible deviation.

The tolerance is the deviation between target (desired) and actual (measured) size. The figures given in Tab. 3.24 are the permissible tolerances for length, width, height/depth, diagonals and cross-sectional dimensions of prefabricated steelwork. The upper and lower limits represent the maximum amounts by which the actual size may be larger or smaller than the reference size.

The permissible deviation is the agreed maximum difference between the actual and the target size. The deviation above the reference size does not necessarily have to be identical to the deviation below.

The dimensional tolerance expresses the permissible upper and lower deviations.

Tolerances
No structure and no component can be produced and assembled to match the specified quality and dimensions exactly. It is therefore imperative to consider the tolerable divergences (= tolerances) from the outset and to plan accordingly, especially with regard to the details. Furthermore, there must be an unambiguous written agreement between client, designers, fabricator and contractor specifying the tolerances to which all must work. Tolerances are normally specified in the tender documentation. If this is not the case, the values given in the relevant standards automatically apply.

In order to avoid having to provide an exhaustive list of required tolerances for every single structure, references may be made to standards or other regulations. In Germany DIN 18201, DIN 18202 and DIN 18203 specify tolerances for a great number of situations. These standards also distinguish between different classes of accuracy. A tender may contain references to a standard and class of accuracy in order to cover tolerance requirements. Generally speaking, it can be said that a lower tolerance, i.e. higher degree of accuracy, is coupled with higher production costs. Therefore, every project must be looked at in terms of what degree of accuracy is desirable and reasonable. In some instances it may be necessary to exceed the requirements of DIN or other standards. Where this is deemed necessary, the feasibility of maintaining such a high standard of accuracy must be discussed in advance with the steelwork fabricator.

Specifying and working with tolerances demands an understanding of a number of special expressions and contexts. The most important of these are explained below.

Dimensional tolerances are the permissible upper and lower limits to dimensions.

Building tolerances are the permissible deviations from the target sizes of the finished construction as specified on the drawings.

Component tolerances are the permissible deviations from the target sizes specified on the drawings which can be measured on the component as delivered and before it is incorporated in the construction. Manufactured sizes and hence conformity to component tolerances are measured in the unloaded condition at a temperature of 15°C.

Rolling margins are the permissible deviations of the cross-sectional sizes of rolled steel sections from their reference sizes. Manufacturers specify their rolling margins in their technical terms of supply.

During the design stage careful consideration should be given to ensuring that the various tolerances can be sensibly integrated. In particular, the fact that tolerances can add up must not be ignored. A group of components

3.24

Structure and parts of structure	Limits of size (mm) for reference sizes up to				
	3 m	6 m	15 m	30 m	>30 m
1 Lengths, widths, grid lines and grids on plan	± 12	± 16	± 20	± 24	± 30
2 Heights/Depths on the structure, e.g. storey heights, platform heights	± 16	± 16	± 20	± 30	± 30
3 Clear dimensions between components on plan	± 16	± 20	±24	± 30	–
4 Clear heights/depths, also beneath beams and joists	± 20	± 20	± 30	–	–
5 Structural openings for windows, doors, integrated items	± 12	± 16	–	–	–
6 Openings as for 5 but with finishes to sills, heads and jambs	± 10	± 12	–	–	–

3.25

2000	4000	8000	12 000	16 000	>16 000
± 1	± 2	± 3	± 4	± 5	± 6

DIN 18 203 Part 2

3.26

	Road transport not requiring a special permit				Heavy and special transports	
	2-axle vehicle	with > 2 axles	articulated vehicle	road train	with annual permit	with individual permit
Length	12.00 m	12.00 m	15.50 m [1]	18.00 m	25.00 m	>25.00 m
Width	2.50 m	2.50 m	2.50 m	2.50 m	3.00 m	> 3.00 m
Height	4.00 m	4.00 m	4.00 m	4.00 m	4.00 m	> 4.00 m
Total weight	16.00 t	22.00 t	40.00 t	40.00 t	40.00 t [2]	>40.00 t

1) 16.50 m according to Euronorm
2) 42.00 t for indivisible loads

may be supplied where the actual size of each one is just within its upper limit of size. But the addition of all these maximum deviations can lead to considerable problems. For example, DIN 18203 Part 2 specifies a tolerance of ±1 mm for a component with a reference size of 1000 mm, and ±4 mm for a component with a reference size of 12 000 mm. If the 12 m long component is replaced, for whatever reason, by 12 components each 1 m long, the sum of the permissible deviations is 12 mm.

Modular coordination
A module is a unit of measure used as a basic dimension or incremental unit. Modular coordination, which for the building industry is covered by DIN 18800, is intended to improve standardization and rationalization without impinging on architectural or constructional diversity.

Dimensional stipulations:
The basic module according to DIN 18800 is M = 100 mm. Multimodules are preferred multiples of the basic module:

$$3\,M = 300\ \text{mm}$$
$$6\,M = 600\ \text{mm}$$
$$12\,M = 1200\ \text{mm}$$

The preferred figures are the limited multiples of multimodules:

$$1,2,3, \ldots 30 \times\ \ M$$
$$1,2,3, \ldots 30 \times\ \ 3M$$
$$1,2,3, \ldots 30 \times\ \ 6M$$
$$1,2,3, \ldots 30 \times 12M$$
etc.

When possible, the preferred sizes of the 12M multiple should be used. This leads to the sizes very common in construction: 1.20 m, 2.40 m, 3.60 m, ... 7.20 m, etc. Submodular sizes are smaller than the basic module. These are, for example, 25 mm, 50 mm and 75 mm, and are always made up to M.

Geometrical stipulations:
The system of Cartesian coordinates is employed as a reference system. The units of measurement of the axes of the reference system are the so-called controlling sizes, which correspond to multimodules or multiples thereof.

Coordinating spaces with different references are assigned to the reference system. These references are distinguished as follows:
• axial control – the axes of a component coincide with the coordinating plane
• facial control – the component is placed between two coordinating planes

The grids established within a reference system can be arranged offset. This allows the structural grid to be completely detached or matched with the finishes grid.

Special aspects of erection and dismantling
Connections
The general tolerances specified allow dimensional discrepancies to be integrated in the construction. Hence, costly and time-consuming modifications on site can be avoided. The cheapest type of on-site connection is the bolt; it requires very little in the way of preparations and is already preadjusted by the accurate predrilled holes. At the same time, any corrosion protection already applied is not disturbed in any way. It is best if only one size and type of bolt is used per connection. The number of bolts can be determined precisely by prior calculation. The provision of access holes at the appropriate points eases the insertion of bolts in awkward positions.

By contrast, welded connections demand precise adjustment of the parts, which can result in delays and the need for scaffolding. In addition, unsightly support brackets are sometimes needed. If in-situ welding is necessary, then the equipment and methods are best agreed upon with the contractor, particularly in the case of large welds and complicated geometries. Wherever possible, welding should be carried out at the fabricator's works.

Columns
If a column can remain standing alone in the erection condition by complying with suitable precautions, then encumbering guy ropes can be avoided. Normally, the column is levelled by inserting steel packings between underside of steel and top of foundation or floor slab, adding an expanding grout to make a solid joint. The anchorage lengths must take into account the maximum permissible tolerance. Aids to alignment can be permanently marked

3.27

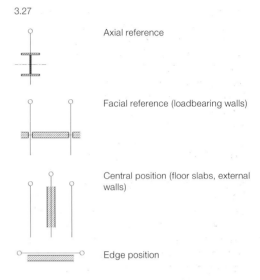

Axial reference

Facial reference (loadbearing walls)

Central position (floor slabs, external walls)

Edge position

3.28

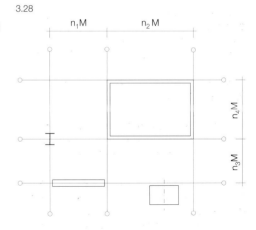

on the head or base plates. The intended
orientation/position must be legible (e.g.
marking of main grid lines).

Beams
If possible, all obstructing bracing layers
should be added after erecting the beam. By
determining the direction of assembly, self-
imposed hindrances can be avoided. If a continuous action must be achieved, then the
effect as a single-span beam is to be secured
by providing (temporary) additional fixings in
the erection condition.

See the section on recycling for further information.

3.29

adjustable

3.30

3.31

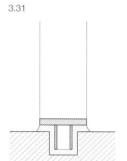

3.32

Recycling

The average life expectancy of a conventional building is 20-50 years, depending on the level of industrialization. Consequently, this same chronological cycle applies to the conversion to scrap of the many millions of tonnes of steel produced annually throughout the world for buildings, bridges and other structures.

The growing need for sustainable resource management will assign an increasingly important role to recycling our built environment in the future. The logistical and technical framework for widespread steel recycling is already in place and industrialized countries have been collecting scrap on a large scale for some time. It is 100% recyclable and constitutes approx. 50% of the raw material for the production of crude steel worldwide.

The recycling of steel is very much simplified by its magnetic properties. This guarantees fast sorting of building debris. There are no known problems with the smelting of steel covered in, for example, paint.

Iron is a natural element with no detrimental effects on water, air or soil. Steel and iron products that are disposed of in landfill sites decompose to oxidation products without harming the environment.

Part 4 • Shaping and connecting semi-finished products to form primary components

Werner Sobek
with Stefan Schäfer

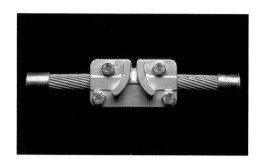

4.1 A component fabricated in differential construction
4.2 Integral construction: two mating pieces milled from solid material
4.3 Integrating construction: sections connected by welding to form a monolithic whole
4.4 Integrating construction: adhesive joints [424]

4.1

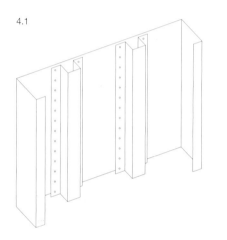

4.2

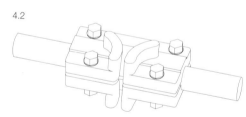

4.3

4.4

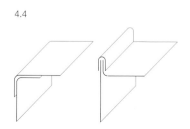

Shaping and connecting semifinished products to form primary components

Fundamentals

In structural steelwork, designing is synonymous with building. Good-quality building is only possible when the designer is not only aware of the mechanical properties of the material but the diverse options for shaping and forming it as well as the wide range of connection techniques.

The reason why the information contained in this section far exceeds the content of all previous textbooks on steelwork design is simple: the scope for working the material has expanded dramatically in recent years. The building industry too must recognize this fact. Moreover, the steelworking trades outside the building industry have continued to perfect established jointing techniques and to develop new ones which the building industry has yet to exploit.

Both aspects present the industry with great opportunities. In addition, it is now accepted that shaping and connecting should no longer be regarded merely as "building", in the sense of assembling, but rather should include recycling, disassembly and "disconnection" as fundamental aspects of the planning and design process.

The term "type of construction" which is introduced in the next section permits an analysis of shaping and connecting which is independent of the material. Also included are explanations and discussions of these types of construction in relation to steel construction.

Jointing and connecting: the different types of construction

"Type of construction" denotes the manner in which individual materials are shaped and joined together to form components.

The term "type of construction", which has been employed in the aircraft and automotive industries for many years, is introduced here because it serves as a foundation for design and building irrespective of material. Consequently, this represents a radical new approach to building with steel. Dividing steel construction into
• differential construction
• integral construction
• integrating construction
• composite construction
makes it possible to quickly evaluate the structural/constructional properties of a component and to draft a basic appraisal of the recyclability of the construction. Therefore, by assigning a component to a type of construction category it is possible, with one expression, to define its assembly, behaviour within the structure, behaviour upon disassembly and recycling options.

Differential construction

A component fabricated in differential construction consists of two or more relatively simple parts. These individual parts, which may be made from different materials, are joined together by means of discrete fixings to form a component. The forces in the individual parts are transferred via these discrete fixings, which may be, for example:
• pins
• rivets
• bolts/screws
• nails
• spot welds
• stitches

The transfer of forces into or out of a part via the discrete fixings is generally linked with stress concentrations near the fixing points. The normally uniform flow of forces within the part becomes concentrated adjacent the fixings. If the cross-sectional area remains constant, a concentration of forces always implies an increase in stress. It is typical for a design based on differential construction that the cross-sectional area of a part is determined by the high local stress concentrations near the fixings. Furthermore, as many types of discrete

4.5

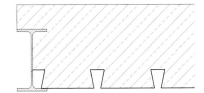

4.5 Composite construction: trapezoidal profile steel sheeting with concrete topping
4.6 Discrete fixing: pinned joint
4.7 Detail of pin: cover plate fixed with countersunk-head screw
4.8 Pinned joint in double shear [440]
4.9 Composite construction: sandwich panels comprising metal sheeting and polyurethane core

4.10 Elastic tensile stress peaks adjacent holes: 1, 2 – without rivet, 3 – with force transfer by rivet. Influence of hole spacing and edge distance. [486]
4.11 Elastic stress peaks in eye bars: increase with constricted neck, decrease with relieving gap. [486]

fixings (e.g. bolts, rivets) require a hole to be drilled in the part, this too gives rise to stress concentrations. The order of magnitude of these increased stress levels around holes is quite remarkable.

Differential construction permits the simple jointing of parts made from different materials to form one component. It enables a component to be ideally matched to the requirements profile, to the respective function. In steelwork, bolts and rivets are the traditional fasteners of differential construction. A more detailed analysis of the most important jointing techniques in differential construction for steelwork is given below.

Rivets
Riveting is the permanent joining of parts by means of an upset fastener (rivet). The necessary pressure is applied by a riveting hammer, riveting press or automatic riveting machine.

The classic rivet has become a rarity in modern steel construction. The reasons for this are the high noise levels which accompany riveting as well as the time-consuming and demanding work necessary when handling hot rivets. However, traditional (solid) rivets are still used on buildings subject to preservation orders or in repairs to riveted structures.

Besides the classic rivets there are a number of newer developments which have become particularly significant in light-plate work. Rivets made from steel or age-hardening AlCuMg 0.5 are the most common types.

The most important types of rivets used in building are:
• Solid or normal rivets – the classic form. Each white/red-hot rivet is removed from the rivet furnace with riveting tongs and then descaled with a wire brush. The rivet is then inserted in the hole and the projecting cylindrical part formed into a head with a riveting set. This axial upsetting process causes the rivet to fill the hole entirely. As it cools down, the rivet contracts and so pulls the connected parts tightly together.
• Blind rivets – for places where access is only possible from one side, the snap-head side, without any brace from behind. These rivets are used on pipes, hollow sections, tanks and other hollow constructions. The use of

4.6

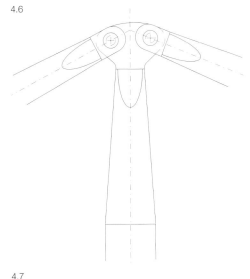

4.7

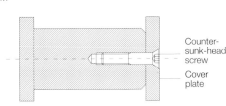

Counter-sunk-head screw

Cover plate

4.8

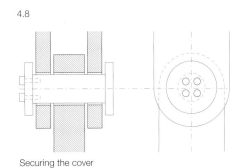

Securing the cover

4.9

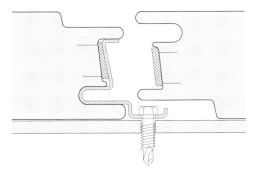

4.10

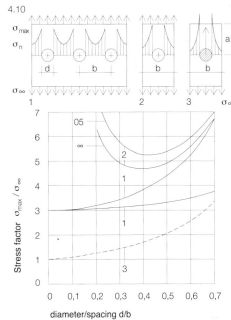

1 Without rivet
2 Force transfer by rivet
3 $\dfrac{\sigma_n}{\sigma_\infty} = \dfrac{1}{1 - d/b}$

4.11

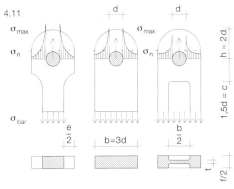

1 Edge of hole
2 Area of bar
3 Reduction in area

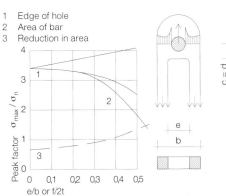

4.12

4.13

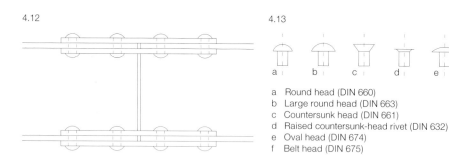

a Round head (DIN 660)
b Large round head (DIN 663)
c Countersunk head (DIN 661)
d Raised countersunk-head rivet (DIN 632)
e Oval head (DIN 674)
f Belt head (DIN 675)

blind rivets, sometimes for high-strength or watertight connections, has opened the way for new methods, chiefly in the automotive industry.

· Pop rivets – applied from one side with the help of an integral mandrel with predetermined break point. The tubular body of the rivet is pulled towards the mounting side using a special tool. The mandrel snaps off when the head meets the workpiece.

In addition, there are also:
· explosive rivets (pressure applied by means of an exploding cartridge)
· Chobert rivets
· self-drilling rivets (no pilot hole necessary)
· special rivets (shear-tension rivet)

Bolts and screws
Bolted or screwed connections are among the most important non-permanent joints. The great advantages of these connections are:
· easy availability of the fasteners
· no special training necessary for operatives
· no special ambient conditions necessary while making bolted connections (hence bolts/screws are predestined for on-site connections)
· easily removed and so an important requirement for consistent recyclability of components and materials

4.14

Tensioning unit (schematic) and tensioning procedure

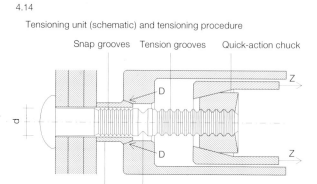

Snap grooves   Tension grooves   Quick-action chuck

Snap collar   Predetermined break point

4.15

Snap-collar pin, completed connection

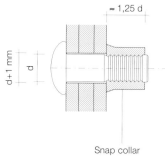

≈ 1,25 d

Snap collar

Bolts and screws can be employed to carry axial tension or transverse shear or a combination of both simultaneously. Sizes are selected according to relevant codes of practice. It must be remembered that certain edge distances (distance between centre of bolt/screw and edge of part) must be adhered to; these depend on diameter of fixing, loads to be carried and thicknesses of parts to be joined. Bolts and screws are suited to many applications. For example, heavy plates and rolled sections are joined by a nut-and-bolt combination; specially shaped washers are added in the case of lighter plates, with self-punching or rivet-type receptor inserts if necessary. Predrilled light plates are often joined by means of self-tapping screws which automatically cut the female (= nut) thread themselves. And the use of self-drilling screws obviates the need for drilling pilot holes first – a costly process. Self-tapping and self-drilling screws require no nuts.

4.16   4.17

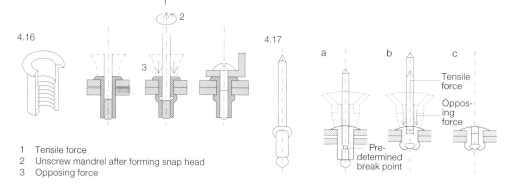

1 Tensile force
2 Unscrew mandrel after forming snap head
3 Opposing force

4.18 Stages in the formation of a hexagon-head bolt
4.19 DIN 7968 hexagon-head close-tolerance bolt for steelwork
4.20 Flush connection with machine screw
4.21 Washers to DIN 7989
4.22 Washers to DIN 6916
4.23 Taper washers
4.24 Countersunk-head screw with hexagon socket

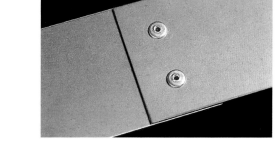

The resolve to rationalize, improve productivity and simplify the procurement of components makes the use of standardized bolts, screws, nuts and washers highly advisable. The fabrication of special fasteners to architects' or engineers' drawings, although possible, only makes economic sense when large quantities are involved. There are a great many types of screw and bolt fixings on the market in a variety of materials. The only types of threaded fixings approved for structural steelwork are hexagon-head turned or close-tolerance bolts and hexagon-socket countersunk bolts/screws; the approved materials are grades 3.6, 4.6, 5.6, 8.8 and 10.9. Screws and bolts made from other materials or with different forms may only be used as loadbearing connectors after obtaining appropriate certification ("Building Authority General Certificate" or "Specific Project Certificate").

The abbreviated designation for a bolt/screw includes, in this order:
· bolt/screw type (e.g. close-tolerance bolt)
· type of thread (M = metric thread)
· diameter of thread (mm)
· material of bolt/screw (see below)

The material of the bolt or screw is designated by two numbers separated by a dot. The number before the dot is 1/100th of the ultimate tensile strength (N/mm²), the number after the dot designates the quotient of yield stress to fracture stress. For example, a bolt made from "5.6" material has an ultimate tensile strength of 500 N/mm² and a yield stress of 500 x 0.6 = 360 N/mm².

Accordingly, the abbreviation for a high-strength close-tolerance bolt with a 20 mm diameter metric thread made from 10.9 material is: high-strength close-tolerance bolt M20 grade 10.9.

All bolt/screw dimensions, as well as those of associated nuts and washers, are standardized. In structural steelwork, a washer must be placed under every nut; for high-strength bolts a washer is required under the head of the bolt as well. This latter washer is necessary because on a high-strength bolt the transition from head to shank is radiused in order to avoid stress peaks. If the washer was omitted, then this rounded transition would prevent the

4.18
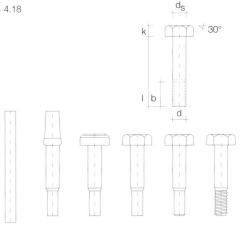

4.19
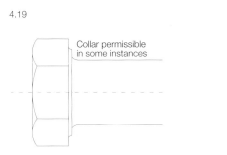

4.20
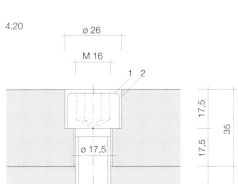
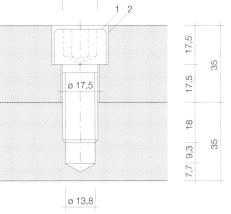

1 Machine screw with hexagon socket to DIN 912, M16 x 35, grade 8.8
2 Recess for machine screw to DIN 74, type K

4.21
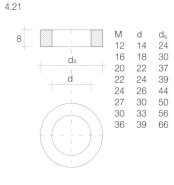

4.22
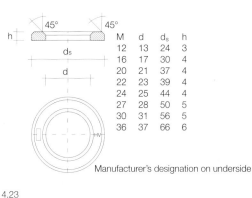

Manufacturer's designation on underside

4.23

DIN 6917 for I-sections 14% taper
DIN 6918 for channels 5-8% taper

4.24
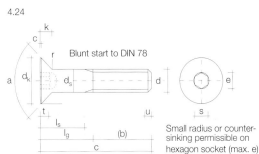

ds only for screws with shank
u = max. 2P incomplete thread

4.25   Dimensions of typical bolts

4.25

Hexagon-head bolts to DIN 7990, standard strength, grades 4.6, 5.6

Designation		M 12	M 16	M 20	M 22	M 24	M 27	M 30	M 36
Diameter of thread	d=ds	12	16	20	22	24	27	30	36
Length of thread	b	17.75	21	23.5	25.5	26	29	30.5	
Pitch	P	1.75	2	2.5	2.5	3	3	3.5	4
Distance across corners	min $_e$	19.85/20.88	26.17	32.95	37.29/35.03	39.55	45.20	50.85	
Depth of head	k	8	10	13	14	15	17	19	
Depth of nut	m	10	13	16	18	19	22	24	29
Distance across flats	s	18/19	24	30	34/32	36	41	46	55

Hexagon-head bolts to DIN 7968, standard strength close-tolerance, grade 5.6

Designation		M 12	M 16	M 20	M 22	M 24	M 27	M 30	M 36
Diameter of thread	d	12	16	20	22	24	27	30	36
Diameter of shank	d_s	13	17	21	23	25	28	31	
Length of thread	b	17.12	20.5	23.75	25.75	26.5	29.5	31.25	
Pitch	P	1.75	2	2.5	2.5	3	3	3.5	4
Distance across corners	min $_e$	19.85/20.88	26.17	32.95	37.29/35.03	39.55	45.20	50.85	
Depth of head	k	8	10	13	14	15	17	19	
Depth of nut	m	10	13	16	18	19	22	24	29
Distance across flats	s	18/19	24	30	34/32	36	41	46	55

Hexagon-head bolts to DIN 6914, high strength, grades 8.8, 10.9

Designation		M 12	M 16	M 20	M 22	M 24	M 27	M 30	M 36
Diameter of thread	d=ds	12	16	20	22	24	27	30	36
Length of thread	b	21/23	26/28	31/33	32/34	34/37	37/39	40/42	48/50
Pitch	P	1.75	2	2.5	2.5	3	3	3.5	4
	d_w	20	25	30	34	39	43.5	47.5	57
	c	0.4 : 0.6	0.4 : 0.6	0.4 : 0.8	0.4 : 0.8	0.4 : 0.8	0.4 : 0.8	0.4 : 0.8	0.4 : 0.8
Distance across corners	min $_e$	23.91	29.56	35.03	39.55	45.20	50.85	55.37	66.44
Depth of head	k	8	10	13	14	15	17	19	23
Depth of nut	m	10	13	16	18	19	22	24	29
Distance across flats	s	22	27	32	36	41	46	50	60

Hexagon-head bolts to DIN 7999, high-strength close-tolerance, grade 10.9

Designation		M 12	M 16	M 20	M 22	M 24	M 27	M 30	M 36
Diameter of thread	d_1	12	16	20	22	24	27	30	36
Diameter of shank	d_2	13	17	21	23	25	28 .	31	37
Length of thread	b/y	18.5/6.5	22/7.5	26/8.5	28/8.5	29.5/10	32.5/10	35/11.5	
	d_w	19	25	32	34	39	43.5	47.5	57
	c	0.4 : 0.6	0.4 : 0.6	0.4 : 0.8	0.4 : 0.8	0.4 : 0.8	0.4 : 0.8	0.4 : 0.8	0.4 : 0.8
Distance across corners	min $_e$	22.78	29.59	37.29	39.55	45.20	50.85	55.37	66.44
Depth of head	k	8	10	13	14	15	17	19	23

4.26 Mechanical properties of bolts/screws according to grade

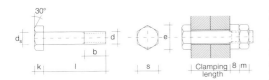

Hexagon-head bolt to
DIN 7990
(standard strength)
grades 4.6, 5.6

Washer to DIN 7989, 434
or 435
Nut to DIN 555 or
ISO-DIN 4034

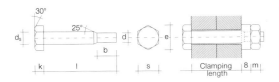

Hexagon-head bolt to
DIN 7968
(standard strength close-
tolerance)
grade 5.6

Washer to DIN 7989, 434
or 435
Nut to DIN 555 or
ISO-DIN 4034

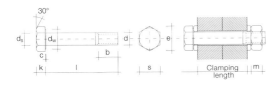

Hexagon-head bolt to
DIN 6914
(high strength)
grades 8.8, 10.9

Washer to DIN 6916, 6917
or 6918
Nut to DIN 6915

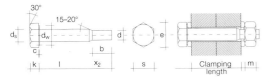

Hexagon-head bolt to
DIN 7999
(high strength close-
tolerance), grade 10.9

Washer to DIN 6916
Nut to DIN 6915

4.26		Grade									
		3.6	4.6	4.8	5.6	5.8	6.8	8.8	8.8	10.9	12.9
Ultimate tensile strength βz N/mm^2	nom	300	400	400	500	500	600	800	800	1000	1200
	min	330	400	420	500	520	600	800	830	1040	1220
Yield stress β_s N/mm^2	nom	180	240	320	300	400	480	—	—	—	—
0.2 % proof stress $\beta_{0.2}$ N/mm^2	min	—	—	—	—	—	—	640	660	900	1100
Elongation at rupture δ_5	nom	25	22	14	20	10	8	12	12	9	8
Vickers hardness HV	min	95	120	130	155	160	190	230	255	310	372
	nom	220	220	220	220	220	250	300	336	382	434
Brinell hardness HB	min	90	114	124	147	152	181	219	242	295	353
	nom	209	209	209	209	209	238	285	319	363	412
Notched bar impact work (J)	min	—	—	—	25	—	—	30	30	20	15
Former designation		4A	4S	4S	5D	5S	6S	8G	8G	10K	12K
								≤M16	>M16		

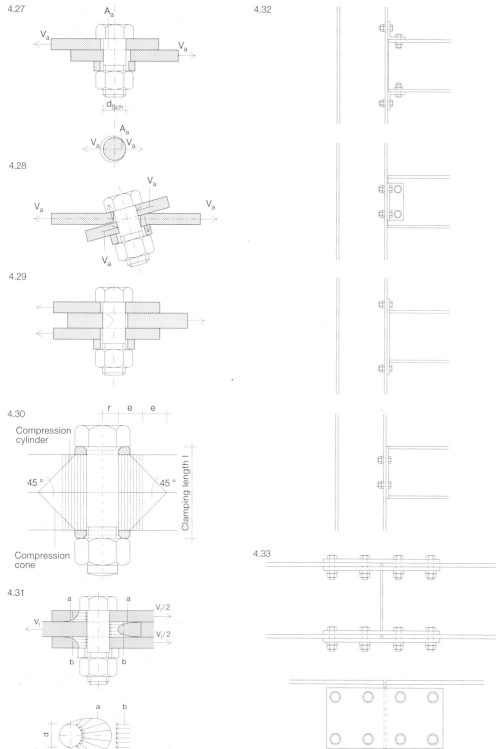

4.27

4.28

4.29

4.30
Compression cylinder
45°   45°
Clamping length l
Compression cone

4.31

4.32

4.33

head of the bolt from resting squarely on the parts to be joined.

For I-beams with tapered flanges, matching taper washers are available for bolts/screws which pass through such flanges.

Again and again we encounter bolts or screws which, for constructional or architectural reasons, are screwed into a threaded blind hole. A nut is not required in such cases. However, minimum insertion depths must be observed, primarily dependent on the strength of the fastener and the material being joined. In most cases this minimum insertion depth is equal to 0.8-1.4 times the fastener diameter. Details can be found in the relevant codes of practice. Further, bolts/screws that are inserted into blind holes must be secured with adhesive or pretensioned in order to ensure they remain in place.

Connections in sheet metal, e.g. steel trapezoidal sheeting, vehicle bodywork, frequently
make use of screws which drill their own hole
and subsequently cut their own thread (self-
drilling screws) or those which cut their own
thread in a predrilled pilot hole (self-tapping
screws). Neither of these types requires a nut.
The forces carried by such screwed connections are usually comparatively low, which is
why these screws are normally used in groups.

Self-drilling and self-tapping screws fall into
the group of self-drive screws. These are
described below:
• Self-tapping screws cut the required pitches
  upon being screwed into a predrilled pilot
  hole. Compared with a conventional screwed
  joint, this eliminates the need for a thread to
  be cut after the hole has been drilled.
• Thread-forming screws create a thread without having one themselves. The material into
  which the screw is being screwed must possess sufficient fracture toughness to permit
  this non-cutting form of processing. This procedure leads to clamping forces along the
  length of the thread which help to prevent
  the screw from working loose.
• The "Flow Drill" screw makes use of the heat
  generated by friction to soften the plates to
  be joined and so allow the thread to be
  formed. These screws are fitted from one
  side and do not require nuts.
• Self-drilling screws form their own hole upon
  being inserted and at the same time cut their
  own thread. This precludes the need to drill
  pilot holes beforehand – necessary, of
  course, for self-tapping and thread-forming
  screws.

4.38

4.39

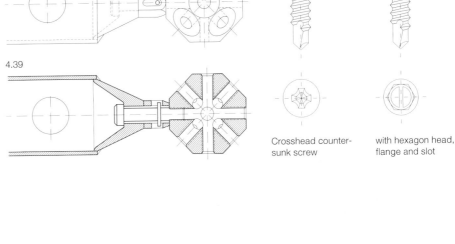

4.42

Crosshead counter-   with hexagon head,
sunk screw   flange and slot

4.40

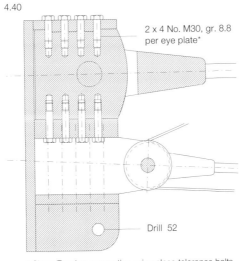

2 x 4 No. M30, gr. 8.8
per eye plate*

Drill 52

* Shear/Bearing connection using close-tolerance bolts

4.43

1. Nominal length and diameter

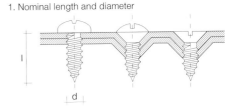

2. Screw head variations for self-tapping screws

DIN 6901   DIN 7971   DIN 7972   Din 7973

DIN 7976   DIN 7981   DIN 7982   Din 7983

3. Screw tip variations for self-tapping screws

Type B   Type BZ   with drill bit point

4.41

4.44 Inclined pin joint resisting shear in
      one direction [440]
4.45 "Dumb-bell" pin connection [440]
4.46 Retrofitting by means of flange clamps [440]

4.44

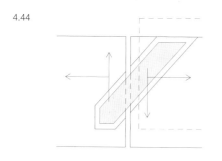

4.45

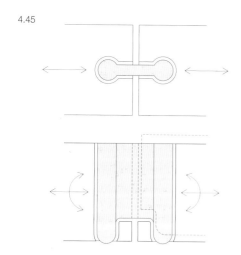

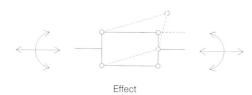

Effect

4.46

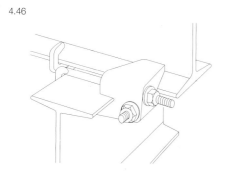

Pins

Pinned connections are used comparatively rarely in steel buildings and bridges. However, this method is mentioned here because it can be a very good solution where high loads occur in combination with limited space. Pinning involves driving cylindrical pins into corresponding holes in solid steel parts or castings; both pin and hole are precision-made to ensure an accurate fit. Accordingly, the pins carry forces only via the cylindrical joint faces by way of friction or bearing. They are therefore ideal for compact shear connections.

Wedges

In this form of joint, the two pieces to be joined are pressed together by self-locking wedges. The shape of the wedges allows forces to be transmitted to a limited extent by way of combined friction and bearing.

As can be seen from the above summary of the main jointing techniques belonging to differential construction, this method of construction permits simple assembly and disassembly of components, also on site. This is a decisive aid to the recyclability of structures. To ease dismantling, all connections should be readily accessible and exhibit a high degree of standardization, i.e. employ identical fasteners wherever possible.

Integral construction

A component fabricated in integral construction is made in one piece; it consists of one material. Very complex shapes can be created using the appropriate technology. Geometry and changes in thickness are adjusted to suit the flow of forces in the component, thereby achieving a very homogeneous utilization of the material while avoiding any concentrations of stress. Compared to differential construction, this reduces the overall weight of the component.

The best-known methods of fabrication in integral construction are:
- casting (steel, aluminium, etc.)
- rolling
- extruding
- forging
- machining

As a component fabricated in integral construction always consists of just one material, it is generally ideal for recycling.

Components in integral construction are fabricated by machining or forming semifinished products. The technologies and processes for this have been described in detail in "The material and its manufacture". Therefore, only the chief aspects of these methods will be repeated here.

Casting

Casting permits the production of complicated shapes. Distinctions are made between different methods of casting and different materials for casting. The method and material chosen essentially depend on the shape of the component, the required surface quality, the weldability and the mechanical loads on the component.

What all cast parts have in common is the relatively high cost of the initial model (plastic, wood or metal). Therefore, casting is only employed when
- the required geometry cannot be obtained by any other method,
- a large number of parts are required/feasible.

Well-known examples of cast parts are the "spiders" (usually cast by means of the lost-wax method) used to hold the discrete bolted fixings for glass panes, or the junctions (normally cast in a sand bed) of so-called tree columns. The reintroduction of steel castings into building was considerably helped by the structures for the Munich Olympic Games of 1972 and the Centre Georges Pompidou in 1976. In the former project, cast steel components were mainly used for multi-cable couplings and for cable saddles at the tops of masts, for example.

Rolling

Rolling permits the production of long components of constant cross-section made from a single material. This is the most common method of forming steel for construction purposes. The rolling of steel is described in detail in "The material and its manufacture". The most important feature of rolled products is their

constant cross-section over the full length of
the component. Rolled products for structural
steelwork include round or Z-section cables, I-
and H-beams, angles, channels, Z- and T-sections as well as round bars, plates and sheets.

Extruding
Extruding involves forcing red-hot steel at high
pressure through a suitably shaped die. This
method, rarely used for building components,
enables the production of cross-sections with
several internal chambers or awkward re-
entrant corners, which are not possible with
standard rolling methods.

Both of these techniques, rolling and extruding, produce long components with constant
cross-section. However, such items are only
suitable as tension members and, in the case
of suitably designed hollow sections, for torsion loads. Compression and bending ideally
require a cross-section which varies over the
length, as is possible with, for example, casting, forging or machining.

Forging
Compared to casting or machining a blank,
forging is even more limited in terms of size
and weight of component. These constraints
are due to the forging process itself. Please
refer to "The material and its manufacture" for
further details. In steelwork, forged items are
mainly used for the end fittings to cables or
cable clamps.

Machining
Machining (metal-cutting) is used on nearly all
steel components, regardless of type of construction. The metal-cutting methods employed
are described in detail in "The material and its
manufacture". For integral construction, the
entire component is manufactured from one
blank by means of machining. Thus the material thickness can be matched to the loads and
lowly stressed sections can be removed. Fabrication, even complex shapes, is no longer a
problem thanks to computer-controlled
machining. For example, whole series of edge
cable clamps can be produced by milling from
solid material quicker and cheaper than by
casting.

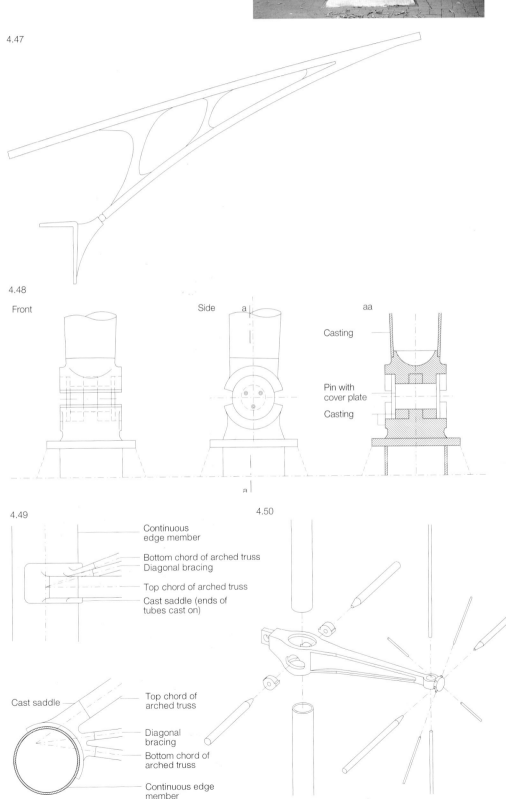

4.47

4.48

Front

Side

aa

Casting

Pin with
cover plate

Casting

a

4.49

4.50

Continuous
edge member

Bottom chord of arched truss

Diagonal bracing

Top chord of arched truss

Cast saddle (ends of
tubes cast on)

Cast saddle

Top chord of
arched truss

Diagonal
bracing

Bottom chord of
arched truss

Continuous edge
member

4.51 Extruded steel section
4.52 Cast end piece to hollow section steel column
4.53 Cable saddle made from cast steel [259]
4.54 Forged edge cable clamp

4.51

4.52

Pin with cover plate
and countersunk-
head bolt   Cast end piece

Circular
hollow section
steel column

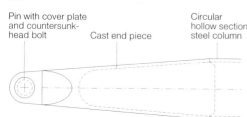

4.53

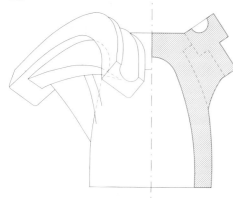

4.54

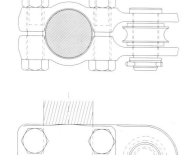

All of the above methods – casting, rolling, extruding, forging, machining – involve constraints on the size and weight of the workpiece. This is where the advantages of integral construction – seamless, single-material components with thicknesses matched to stresses – meet their limits.

Integrating construction
This type of construction involves joining together several pieces of the same material to form a quasi-homogeneous component. The aim of this is to amalgamate the advantages of differential construction, i.e. simple fabrication of complex components by joining several easily produced pieces, with those of integral construction, i.e. the homogeneous flow of forces within the complete component.

The best-known jointing techniques in this type of construction are:
· gluing
· welding

Gluing
Gluing is the joining of two components by way of a combination of adhesion and cohesion, utilizing a (usually) organic adhesive. Adhesive joints offer a number of advantages over the classic jointing methods, e.g. welding:
· Different materials may be joined
· Contact across the entire interface, so the transmission of forces can be influenced.
· As the joint faces do not have to be pre-heated, there is no alteration in the micro-structure.
· Sealed joint faces
· Excellent adhesion, sealing and electrical isolation of the connection, hence no risk of corrosion caused by flux or welding electrode residue or electrochemical processes.

The disadvantages are:
· The negligible high-temperature stability compared to steel. At temperatures > 100°C the strength of the adhesive declines rapidly; cannot withstand temperatures > 250°C.
· Some adhesives are not resistant to moisture or certain chemicals.
· Some adhesives deteriorate with age, which is linked to a loss of strength.
· High strength and durable, secure joints are only possible with careful, involved preparation of the joint faces, e.g. by degreasing, pickling, etc.
· Very sensitive to peeling forces.

Adhesive joints presuppose conscientious workmanship under controlled ambient conditions. As that is difficult to achieve on the building site, loadbearing adhesive joints are best made under controlled factory conditions (e.g. in the aircraft industry since 1935). In the meantime in the aircraft industry, 70% of all joints to the passenger cabin are glued. Newer production technologies for ultralight and load-bearing composites would be inconceivable without adhesives. Therefore, alongside welding and screwing, gluing is one of the most important jointing techniques in industrial production.

Like welding, soldering and riveting, adhesive joints are permanent and cannot be disassembled without damaging the components.

4.55 Examples of glued joints [424]
4.56 Effective and less effective glued joints [424]
4.57 Stress distribution in glued joints
4.58 Loads applied to glued joints

When planning adhesive joints, the following points must be observed:

· Joints may only be loaded in compression and/or shear.
· The joint faces must be sufficiently large and rough.
· Larger gaps can only be bridged with fillers (fibrous or powdery additives).
· Combined connections must be used where peeling forces occur on simple overlaps.
· The adhesive must be applied in a thin, even coat.
· Large or curved joint faces can often only be properly mated by the application of pressure.
· Stress concentrations must be avoided; likewise abrupt changes in cross-section at the joint faces and the thickness of the adhesive layer.
· The shape of the joint should match the transfer of forces in order to achieve – as far as possible – a uniform stress condition within the joint.

The adhesives used are:

· One-part adhesives – curing is by way of pressure and heat.
· Two-part adhesives – the constituents are mixed immediately prior to use; the curing time can be considerably reduced by the application of heat.

The application and mechanical properties of the adhesives can be adjusted across a wide range, e.g. by adding solvents, softeners, fillers.

With glued forms of construction a two-component material results upon dismantling, particularly if the adhesive has been liberally applied.

Adhesives are only used in a few instances for loadbearing steel elements because the adhesives currently available do not have adequate short- and long-term strength at elevated

F = tension
M_i = bending moment
s = plate thickness
$l_ü$ = overlap
d_i = inside diameter
d_a = outside diameter

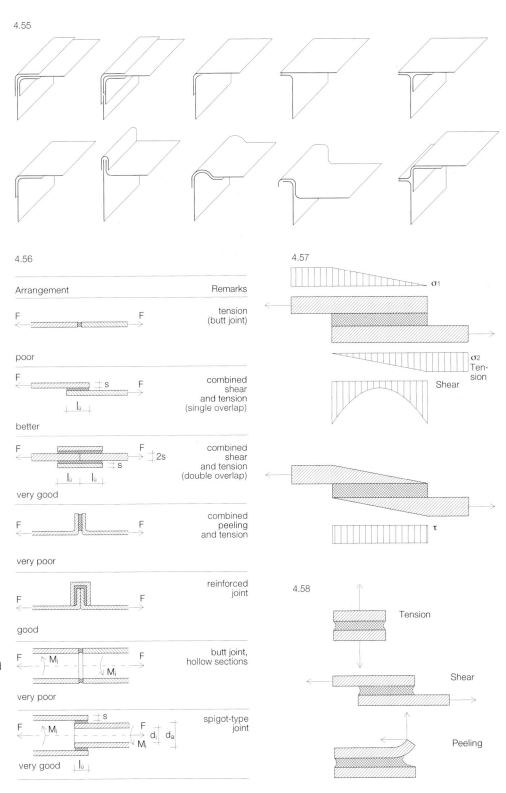

4.55

4.56

Arrangement	Remarks
F ⟷ F	tension (butt joint)
poor	
F ⟷ F	combined shear and tension (single overlap)
better	
F ⟷ F	combined shear and tension (double overlap)
very good	
F ⟷ F	combined peeling and tension
very poor	
F ⟷ F	reinforced joint
good	
F ⟷ F	butt joint, hollow sections
very poor	
F ⟷ F	spigot-type joint
very good	

4.57

4.58

133

temperatures, e.g. in a fire situation. However, when it can be assured that the joint will not be subjected to fire, adhesives represent an interesting alternative.

Welding
Today, welding can be considered as a standard means of jointing in steel construction, alongside bolting and screwing. It is an ideal method of producing components in integrating construction – i.e. virtually devoid of any stress concentrations – in any size in the workshop or on site. In terms of recycling, welding is ideal because the single-material welded components are easy to cut and re-smelt.

In welding, identical or at least similar steels are fused together by melting or plastic deformation of the joint area. This can be accomplished with or without adding a further material. While welding, the weld pool must be protected against the ingress of oxygen (in the air) or other substances which could lead to impurities in the finished weld. Therefore, the weld pool is shielded during the welding process by setting up a local, artificial atmosphere. The different welding techniques are distinguished by the way they create this protective atmosphere.

Soldering, unlike welding, involves only the melting of the additional material, the solder.

In the discussion about whether a connection can or cannot be welded, we often hear the rather imprecise term "weldability". To simplify the analysis of this problem let us replace this term by the following, more specific, expressions:
• suitability for welding (of the material)
• reliability of welding (of the construction)
• feasibility of welding (in production)

A material's suitability for welding increases as the specific properties of the material become less and less critical during welding and as the risk of welding altering the properties of the material decreases.

The essential properties which a steel must exhibit in order to be suitable for welding are:
• no cracking in the heat affected zone (HAZ)
• low tendency to form a brittle microstructure susceptible to cracking

The reliability of welding increases as the factors affecting the choice of material for a certain welded construction become less and less critical. The feasibility of welding exists when the planned welding work on a construction can be performed within the given framework conditions.

The welding techniques available can be sorted according to the most diverse criteria. The techniques suitable for the building industry can be categorized as follows:
• Fusion welding
  Local, limited flow of molten material without the application of pressure, with or without flux. Most methods employ an electric arc as the energy source. Gas, electrical resistance and laser or electron beams are used as heat transfer media.
• Pressure welding
  Employs the application of pressure, with or without filler material. This technique includes methods in which the joint is made by moving the parts (e.g. friction welding) or by heating up the joint faces.

Owing to its great importance for steelwork, the most significant welding processes are discussed below.

Fusion welding
Electric-arc welding:
In this method an electric arc is produced between the electrode and the component by applying a high voltage. The heat generated by this melts the electrode (wire).

In manual welding, the wire electrodes used are coated in a flux. As the wire melts and this molten metal drops onto the joint between the two components, the flux ensures the local,

oxygen-free atmosphere protecting against impurities. Some of the flux turns to gas but the rest floats on the weld pool and has to be removed before the application of a further weld run. Overhead, vertical and horizontal welds are possible.

Shielded metal-arc inert gas (MIG) welding uses a bare wire electrode melted by an electric arc. In this case the weld pool is protected by a gas fed right to the weld. Inert gases are usually employed. The electrodes used are either consumable wires coated with flux or non-coated continuous wires. Depending on the type of electrode, protective gas and electric arc, we distinguish between a number of shielded MIG welding techniques: atomic-hydrogen welding, inert gas tungsten-arc welding and gas-shielded metal-arc welding. Overhead, vertical and horizontal welds are possible.

Flash-butt welding involves igniting an electric arc between the two components to be joined. The weld is achieved without the addition of a weld deposit. The protective atmosphere is created by a gas, a separate flux or shielding. This method is mainly used for welding small items, e.g. welding on shear studs. When welding on shear studs, a ceramic collar normally protects the weld against the ingress of oxygen and impurities.

4.59 Classification of fusion welding techniques to
DIN 1910 Part 2
4.60 Electric-arc welding [307]
4.61 Schematic diagram of gas-shielded metal-arc
welding [282]
4.62 Producing a butt weld with the aid of run-on/run-off
tabs [307]

4.59

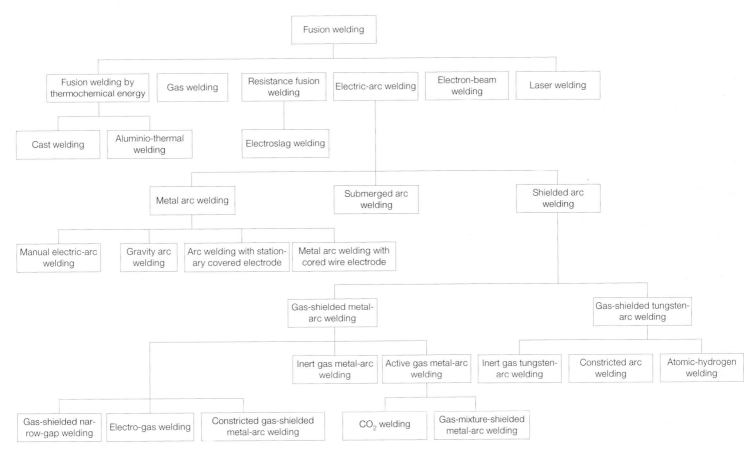

4.60   4.61   4.62

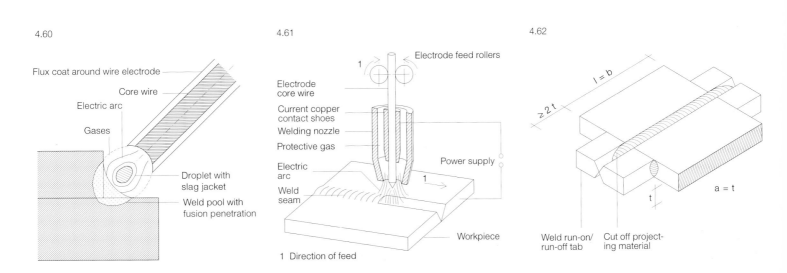

1 Direction of feed

4.63 Types of welded joints, shapes and dimensions to DIN 18800 Part 1 [307]

4.63

		Symbol	Type of weld [1]	Diagram	Calculated throat thickness 'a'
1	Non-full-penetration welds		Butt	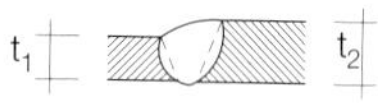t1 t2	$a = t_1$ if $t_1 \le t_2$
2			Twin single-bevel butt	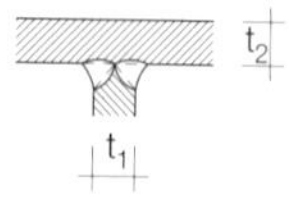t2 t1	$a = t_1$
3			Single-bevel butt — Sealing run behind	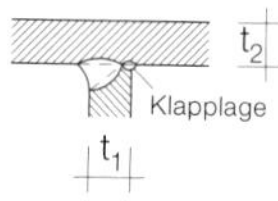t2 Klapplage t1	
4			Single-bevel butt — Full penetration	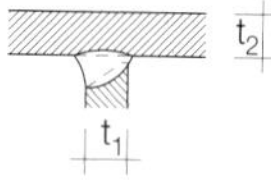t2 t1	
5	Full-penetration welds or those with sealing run		Single-bevel T-butt with fillet [2 3]	possible sealing run 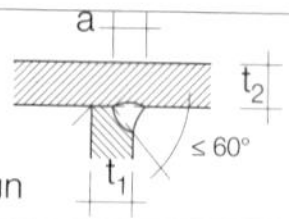a t2 ≤ 60° t1	The throat thickness 'a' is equal to the distance from theoretical root to surface of weld.
6			Single-bevel T-butt [2 3]	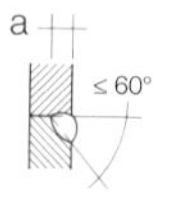a ≤ 60°	
7			Twin single-bevel butt with twin fillet [2]	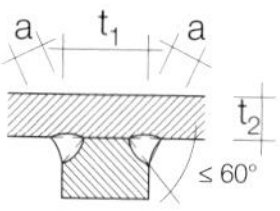a t1 a t2 ≤ 60°	
8			Twin single-bevel T-butt [2]	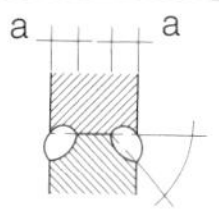a a	
9			Twin square butt without joint preparation (fully mechanized weld)	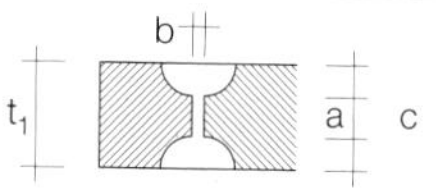b t1 a c	Determine throat thickness 'a' via test. Gap 'b' depends on method (submerged arc b = 0)
10	Fillet welds		Fillet [3]	Theoretical root 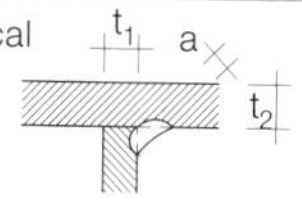t1 a t2	Throat thickness is equal to height of inscribed equilateral triangle measured to theoretical root.
11		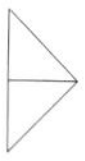	Twin fillet	Theoretical roots 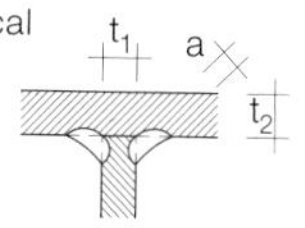t1 a t2	Recommended max. value for 'a': $a > 2$ mm; $\ge \sqrt{\max t} - 0.5$; $a \le 0.7 \times \min t$ (a, t in mm) $t \geqq 3$ mm

Continued on next page

Gas welding:
In this method metallic materials are welded together with the help of a high-temperature flame generated by a combustible gas and air or oxygen mixture. The flux and the heat source are fed in separately. This leads to good mouldability of the weld pool, good gap-bridging and a direct preheating option. The welding speed is usually quite low and the risk of distortion of the components is greater than with most other methods.

Electron-beam welding:
Accelerated negatively charged particles are fired accurately onto the surface of the workpiece with the help of a radiation source. The high kinetic energy of the particles is converted into heat energy upon impact and the metal melted at the focal point of the beam. This method is only used in a vacuum; protective gases and fluxes are unnecessary. Further advantages are the extremely high power density, small HAZ and good controllability of the welding parameters. Electron-beam welding is not terribly significant for the building industry.

Laser welding:
In this method a laser beam (monochromatic, coherent beam of parallel light rays) generates an enormous power flux density at the point of impact (focal point) which is roughly three times the intensity of an electric arc. Laser beam weld seams are characterized by a very large depth-to-width ratio of up to 10:1. This results in high welding rates, high speeds and a low heat requirement, which in turn means less distortion of the components. This method is used in electrical engineering, on vehicle bodywork and tanks (thin plate welding), and also in shipbuilding and the aircraft industry. In the building industry it is currently being introduced for the welding of high-quality delicate facade constructions. Overhead, vertical and horizontal welds are possible.

Submerged arc welding:
In this process a wire electrode is fed to the joint mechanically in a bed of granulated flux. The electric arc burns under cover of this flux, excluding the surrounding air. The electrodes

4.63   Sections through weld seams [307]
4.64   Sections through fillet welds
4.65   Butt welds at changes of plate thickness [307]

used are identical or at least similar to the parent metal, with granular, mineral fluxes. Only horizontal welds can be made with this method.

Pressure welding
Friction welding:
This method typically involves the high-speed rotation of one of the parts to be joined. When the two parts are subsequently mated, the rotating part is braked by the friction and the friction faces are heated and plasticized. It is not necessary to reach the melting temperature in order to form the joint. The simultaneous application of pressure allows good-quality joints to be achieved, even between disparate materials. On production lines the brief welding times permit high outputs. The machines used resemble large lathes and the welded workpieces are primarily rotationally symmetric. But the process is only suitable for small components. In the building industry, friction welding is used for producing cable end fittings, for example.

Ultrasonic welding:
This process is similar to friction welding. The necessary heat is generated by ultrasonic frequencies in the range 15-60 kHz with the simultaneous application of pressure (optional). The joint is made as a spot or seam weld without the need for any flux. The welding procedure takes between 0.1 and 0.3 s. Surface preparation is not necessary, even painted (but not greasy) parts can be joined in this way. This method is especially prevalent in the electrical engineering and precision-engineering industries where materials with different melting points have to be connected without generating great amounts of heat.

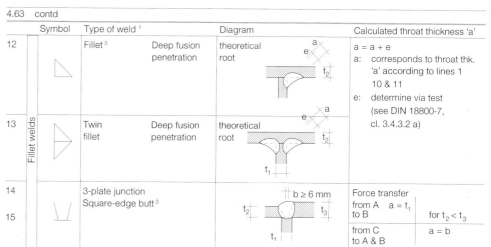

4.63   contd

	Symbol	Type of weld [1]		Diagram		Calculated throat thickness 'a'
12	(Fillet welds)	Fillet [3]	Deep fusion penetration	theoretical root		$a = a + e$ a: corresponds to throat thk. 'a' according to lines 1 10 & 11 e: determine via test (see DIN 18800-7, cl. 3.4.3.2 a)
13		Twin fillet	Deep fusion penetration	theoretical root		
14		3-plate junction Square-edge butt [3]		$b \geq 6$ mm		Force transfer from A $a = t_1$ to B / from C to A & B
15						for $t_2 < t_3$ / $a = b$

1) To DIN 18800-7, cl. 3.4.3
2) For welds according to lines 5-8 with an angle of aperture < 45°, the calculated 'a' dimension is to be reduced by 2 mm or determined by test. Exceptions are welds in gravity and horizontal positions carried out using shielded arc welding.
3) If the sectional sizes are determined according to the elastic-plastic method of analysis with redistribution of moments or the plastic-plastic method, these weld seams may not be used in the vicinity of plastic hinges when subjected to $\sigma_\perp$ or $\tau_\perp$ stresses. This also applies to welds according to line 4 if these welds cannot be tested, unless the possible deficit is compensated for by appropriate reinforcement (fillet weld).

4.64

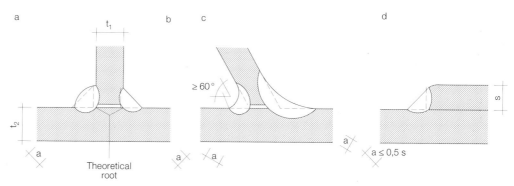

a) Convex fillet weld
b) Flat fillet weld
c) Concave fillet weld, min. size of throat angle
d) Recommended max. throat thickness at rounded section edges

4.65

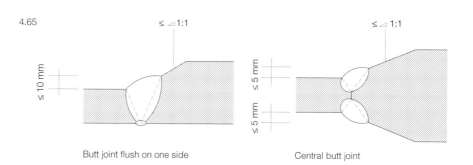

Butt joint flush on one side   Central butt joint

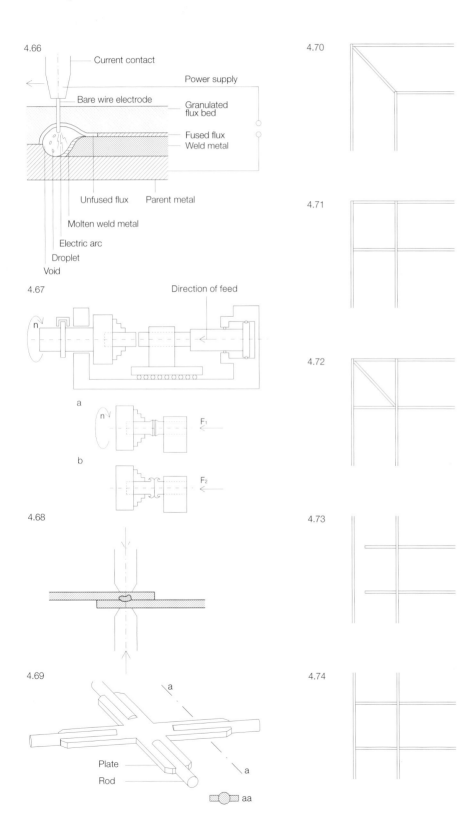

4.66

Current contact

Power supply

Bare wire electrode

Granulated flux bed

Fused flux
Weld metal

Unfused flux   Parent metal

Molten weld metal

Electric arc

Droplet

Void

4.67

Direction of feed

n

a

n

F₁

b

F₂

4.68

4.69

a

Plate

Rod

a

aa

4.70

4.71

4.72

4.73

4.74

Resistance welding:
The necessary heat is generated by an alternating current flowing through the contact-resistance at the joint to be welded. Welding can be carried out with and without the application of pressure. Only overlapping and butt welds are possible. The weld is completed in a few seconds, flux and subsequent treatment are unnecessary. Linear (seam) welds and discrete (spot) welds can be produced. This method is often used when building with sheet metal.

Stud welding:
A brief electric arc heats up the joint faces of the workpieces which are subsequently pressed together, usually without the need for flux. One well-known method is pressure welding with an electric arc moved by a magnet.

Design of welded connections
The shape and function of the parts to be joined in a welded construction determine the type and form of weld seam. The choice of weld seam is also influenced by other factors such as:
· thickness of workpiece
· nature of loading
· flow of forces
· method of welding
· number of pieces
· costs

The geometry and cross-section of the joint are to be chosen such that reliable full penetration and complete fusion of the joint faces are possible with the method of welding to be used.

The material, the method of welding, the nature of the loading and the construction itself are the determining factors for the failure of a welded connection. The strength of a weld is mainly influenced by:
· the local heating-up and the subsequent contractions and residual stresses upon cooling
· notches
· imperfections in the weld

Inspecting weld seams

Loadbearing welds may only be carried out by suitably qualified welders. All work must be supervised by competent welding specialists. To ensure good quality welds, appropriate procedures should be agreed beforehand.

Besides the metallurgical and destructive test methods, there are a number of inspection techniques which, in particular, ascertain the serviceability of welded components. Such tests must include all areas of the material affected directly and indirectly by the welding process in order to be able to reach conclusions about the fracture toughness, strength, deformability and also defects in the parent material.

The atomic structure in the region of the weld often provides a key to the quality. The most popular testing procedures make use of:
• X-rays
• ultrasound

Welding work on components already subjected to loads is normally only permitted in exceptional circumstances. In such instances the structural engineer and the welding specialist should ascertain whether or not the sudden heating and the subsequent cooling could lead to an unacceptable redistribution of stresses within the component. It is not at all difficult to cause a highly loaded component to collapse as a result of the excessive local heat produced in the course of welding work.

Composite construction

In contrast to integral construction, composite construction combines two or more materials in one component. The selection and arrangement of these materials within the component is carried out according to their properties profiles. Consequently, composite construction enables materials with selected properties to be positioned exactly within a component in such a way that their properties are especially well exploited or fully utilized.

Composite construction can be divided into the following groups:
• general composite construction
• fibre-reinforced and hybrid construction
• sandwich construction

General composite construction includes, for example:
• steel-concrete composites
• steel-reinforced concrete composites.
Reinforced concrete itself, i.e. a multitude of reinforcing bars passing through a concrete matrix, is actually a fibre-reinforced construction. Also belonging to this group are the
• fibre-reinforced plastics

If different fibres are used within a fibre-reinforced plastic component, then we speak of hybrid construction.

Sandwich construction generally involves three layers: a central core with a facing top and bottom. These three layers are normally glued together. If a polyurethane core is used, then no further adhesive is necessary in order to attach the facings.

Examples:
• blockboard
• sandwich panels comprising metal sheeting and polyurethane
• wood-wool lightweight panels
• aluminium-honeycomb systems

An optimum bond between the materials makes composite construction very efficient. The force transfer lengths are hence short, while the anchorage lengths consuming material and hindering compact detailing can be reduced to a minimum. However, an optimum bond, desirable from the point of view of load-carrying ability within the component, leads to considerable problems when the component has to be disassembled, because separating the multi-material mixture is almost impossible. Therefore, the totally unsatisfactory bond between concrete and steel reinforcement can

4.75 Steel-reinforced concrete combinations:
    a Steel trapezoidal profile sheeting with concrete topping
    b Steel trapezoidal profile sheeting with concrete topping
    c Reinforced concrete floor slab on permanent formwork supported by steel beam
    d Reinforced concrete floor slab supported by composite beam
    e Reinforced concrete floor slab supported by steel girder

    f Steel circular hollow section with reinforced concrete filling
    g Steel column encased in concrete
    h Composite column comprising steel I-section with concrete infill between the flanges
    i Composite column comprising various steel sections
4.76 Composite column, Commerzbank, Frankfurt a. M. (see p. 380)
4.77 Composite column, Commerzbank, Frankfurt a. M. (see p. 380)

4.75

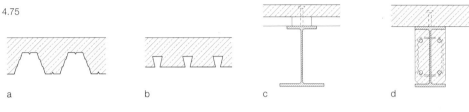

a   b   c   d

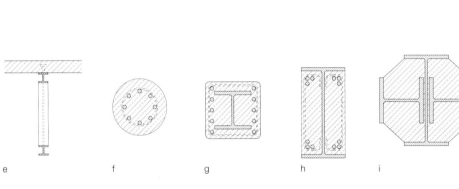

e   f   g   h   i

4.76

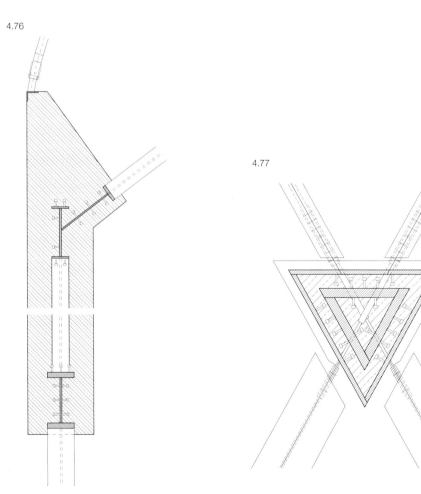

4.77

be regarded as very beneficial to recycling because it is this fact that makes this composite material ideal for recycling.

Up to now, composite construction in steelwork has always been used, rather imprecisely, to refer to steel-(reinforced) concrete combinations. The use of steel in sandwich construction was also referred to, similarly imprecisely, as composite construction.

If we look at the group of general composite construction methods, we realize that steel-reinforced concrete combinations have grown in significance in recent years. The reason for this is that steel, compared to concrete, is relatively expensive when it comes to carrying compression. Therefore, it seems obvious to construct compression members wholly or partly of concrete. The same applies to components subjected to bending, where the compression zone is made of concrete, the tension zone of steel. In both cases it is the joint load-carrying capacities of concrete and steel within the component or component cross-section that have to be guaranteed. So an appropriate bond between the materials must be assured, a requirement which can often only be fulfilled with difficulty and at a certain cost. This is also true for creep and shrinkage, to which concrete is particularly prone. Steel does not suffer from shrinkage and the creep of steel is negligible for building purposes.

Fundamental to steel-(reinforced) concrete combinations in terms of their applicability is the fact that the coefficient of expansion of each material is virtually identical. This is pure coincidence – but without this the worldwide popularity of reinforced concrete would not have been possible.

Another feature of this combination is the fact that the concrete cover protects the steel from corrosion. This means that, provided the thickness of concrete cover is adequate, the surfaces of the embedded steel bars or sections require no anti-corrosive treatment.

4.78 Classic arrangement of composite floor slab
       supported on steel beams
4.79 Composite construction: floors, beams and
       columns made from steel-reinforced concrete
       combination, CIM Institute, Braunschweig
       (see p. 284)

4.78

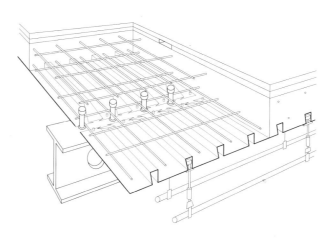

Finally, we should mention the shielding and
retarding effect that concrete cover has on
temperature changes to steel components.
The period of fire resistance of a steel column
encased in concrete or an I-section with concrete infill between the flanges can be substantially increased compared to an unprotected steel member. Together with corrosion protection and the fact that the concrete carries
compression at lower cost, this is a major argu-
ment in favour of the use of composite construction employing steel and (reinforced) concrete.

As (reinforced) concrete does not adhere well
enough to the comparatively smooth steel surfaces, appropriate measures must be taken to
establish a bond between the two materials.
This is normally achieved by way of shear connectors or studs welded on.

4.79

Steel trapezoidal profile sheeting with suitable
cross-section and/or profiling of the surfaces in
conjunction with in-situ reinforced concrete
topping has been employed with great success in recent years as a flooring system
("composite flooring"). The trapezoidal profile
sheeting serves as permanent formwork and,
depending on the system, can be considered
as "external" reinforcement, contributing to the
floor's load-carrying capacity. All trapezoidal
profiles which are considered to carry part of
the load must have appropriate building
authority certification.

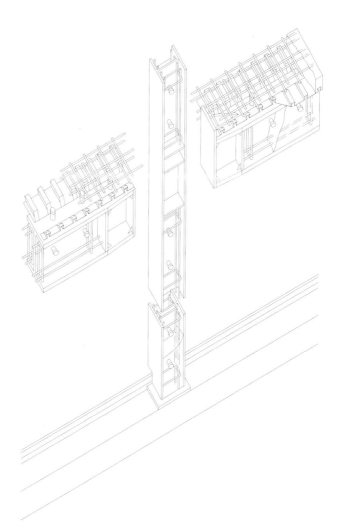

The steel trapezoidal profile sheeting usually
has to be supported temporarily until the concrete has reached its full strength. The inter-
lock between sheeting and steel beams is
normally accomplished by means of shear
studs welded through the sheeting.

Another very successful group of composite
constructions is the sandwich panels – thin,
possibly profiled steel sheeting as facings and
a core of polyurethane foam. The elements,
which are used – primarily in industrial buildings – as walls or roofing panels, combine the
high loadbearing capacity of polyurethane-

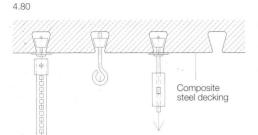

4.80

Composite
steel decking

Continuous dovetail-shaped channels
every 150 mm serve to support all
manner of suspended loads.

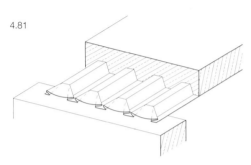

4.81

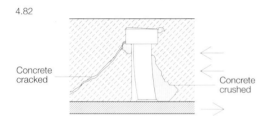

4.82

Concrete
cracked

Concrete
crushed

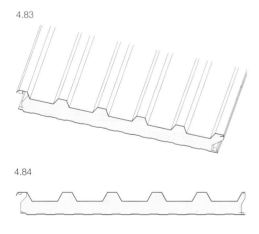

4.83

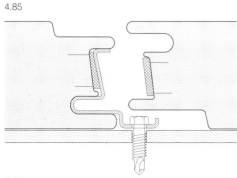

4.84

4.85

4.80   Feasible suspension arrangements beneath a
       composite floor [440]
4.81   Deformed steel decking for shear connection
       [440]
4.82   Interaction between shear stud and concrete –
       failure condition [440]
4.83   Sandwich panel comprising steel sheeting with
       polyurethane core [440]
4.84   Sandwich panel comprising steel sheeting with
       polyurethane core, section [440]
4.85   Fixing of and joint between sandwich panels

core sandwich construction with the building
science advantages of thick insulation. These
very lightweight and completely prefabricated
components can be very quickly and easily
fixed to a steel supporting structure. Sealed
joints are achieved by way of stepped joints
and extra gaskets.

In a fire the loadbearing effect of the core fails.
The residual loadbearing capacity is then
guaranteed by the facings. Severe deformations are acceptable. Owing to their loss of
load-carrying ability in a fire, sandwich elements with foam cores are only approved as
primary loadbearing members in exceptional
circumstances.

Elementary stresses and strains:
linear members

Linear components subjected to tension

A component that is intended to transfer a tensile force from point A to point B should exhibit
a straight system axis and a constant cross-
section. The straight axis ensures that the component, if we ignore self-weight, is not subjected to bending. As will be shown in the section
"Linear components subjected to bending",
bending is always coupled with an ineffective
utilization of the material. Therefore, a constant
cross-section for tension members is advisable
because the magnitude of the force does not
change along the axis of the component. Since
straight members subjected to tension do not
suffer from stability problems, they are ideal for
transmitting forces over long distances.

Holes, openings and the like bring about local
reductions in the cross-section, resulting in the
so-called net loadbearing area. This net area is
crucial for the structural analysis. These holes
and openings have the effect of creating an
inhomogeneous stress condition within the net
area frequently characterized by stress peaks.
In every case, therefore, the criteria with which
the component is to be assessed in the region
of the net area must be ascertained. Materials
which possess sufficient plasticity prevent the
stress peaks from occurring in the first place
thanks to their (local) plastic behaviour. We frequently speak – incorrectly – of the "reduction
in stresses due to plastic behaviour". Actually,
the local plasticizing of the material evens out
the stress distribution in the region of the net
area. For example, bolted connections in structural steel grades St 37 or St 52 can be designed with sufficient accuracy by assuming a
homogeneous, constant stress distribution
across the net area, provided the edge distances are maintained. However, in reality the
stress distribution is not uniform. With materials
which do not possess sufficient plasticity, and
all high-strength materials can be included in
this group, it is quite wrong to assume an even
stress distribution across the net area.

All non-vertical tension members – in addition
to axial tensile forces – are also subjected to
non-axial force components due to the self-

4.86 Axial tension
4.87 Wire rope: core and six strands
4.88 Spiral cable
4.89 Spiral cable
4.90 Fully locked cable

4.91 Cable end fittings:
a   Cast closed conical socket
b   Cast open conical socket, narrow version
c   Pressed open conical socket
d   Cylindrical cast socket
e   Cylindrical cast socket with internal and external threads

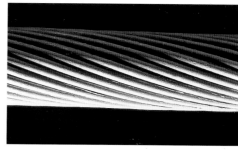

weight of the member. This uniformly distributed linear load leads to deflection of the tie – usually visible to the observer. Further, this deflection reduces the available strain rigidity in real terms with respect to the axial strain stiffness of the member: as the axial tensile force increases, so the deflection of the member decreases initially. However, this results in additional displacements of the support points of the member. The stiffness of the component is hence markedly reduced, which is why an attempt should always be made to limit such deflection, e.g. by means of additional supports, hangers or other types of pretensioning.

Basically, all components with straight axes and constant net area can be employed as tension members (ties). In trusses, for example, ties can be made from angles, I-beams or hollow sections. But if we wish to render visible the way in which the loads are carried, i.e. the tasks of individual members within the construction, then we should use round bars or cables for such members.
Tie bars are normally cheaper to fabricate than cables and, when provided with left-hand/right-hand threads at the ends and screwed end fittings, have the advantage that their length can be easily adjusted on site. This allows construction tolerances to be accommodated more readily. Ties with forged eye bars do not offer this option.

Cables have higher usable strengths than standard tie bars, enabling them to carry higher loads for the same cross-section. However, the modulus of elasticity of cables, $E = 155\,000$ to $165\,000$ N/mm^2, is much lower than that of bars ($E = 210\,000$ N/mm^2). Therefore, ties which need to be particularly rigid and also slender, are better designed as bars or rods.

One great advantage of cables is their flexibility, facilitating the erection of long tension members. If, however, very long solid bars are chosen, for whatever reason, then special measures, e.g. temporary cross-bars, are often necessary.

4.86

F $\longleftarrow$ $\longrightarrow$ F

4.87

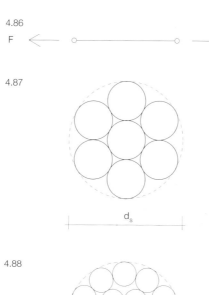

d_s

4.88

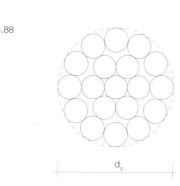

d_s

4.89

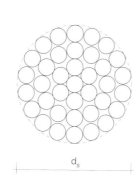

d_s

4.90

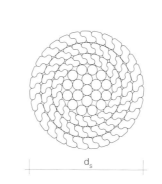

d_s

4.91

a

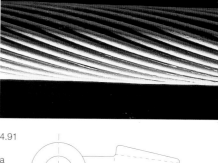

b

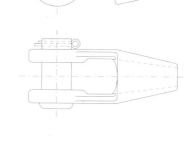

c

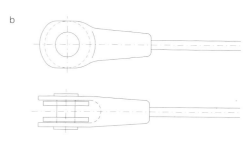

d

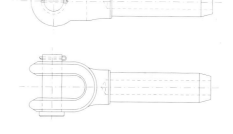

e

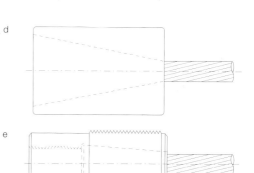

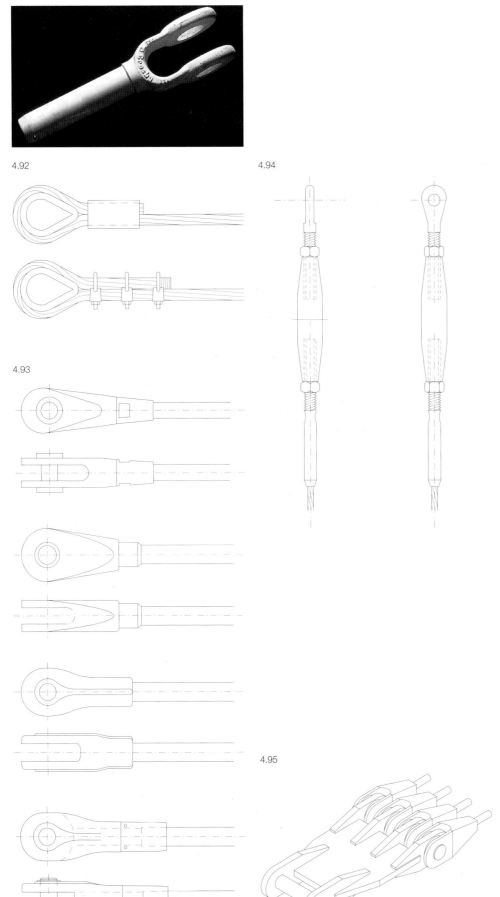

4.92

4.93

4.94

4.95

4.96

Linear components subjected to compression

A component that is intended to transfer a compressive force from point A to point B should exhibit a straight member axis but not a constant cross-section. The straight axis prevents bending stresses building up in the member as a result of the eccentricity of the line of the action of the force with respect to the member axis. Problems of component stability are taken into account by providing a varying cross-section. Non-vertical compression members are also subjected to bending stresses due to the self-weight of the member.

In contrast to members subjected to tensile forces, those designed for compression always suffer from stability problems. This can be a global stability issue, e.g. buckling, twisting, or a local one, e.g. buckling of a web or flange. Several of these stability problems can arise simultaneously within a member; it is up to the structural engineer to decide which of these is relevant or critical for the design.

In terms of global stability failure of a linear member, we distinguish between buckling and twisting of the member axis.

The nature of the buckling of the member axis is very much dependent on the support conditions at the ends of the member. According to Leonard Euler, who explained the eigenvalue problem which he solved using the example of a slender column, there are four cases to be considered. These four Euler cases cover a wide range of the (global) buckling stability problems which occur in practice. In more complex situations, e.g. elastic supports or buckling problems with continuous columns having regularly spaced lateral restraints, the engineer must refer to the literature on this subject or solve the buckling problem with the aid of non-linear calculations assuming a geometric imperfection in the construction. The stability problem is hereby transformed into a stress problem. The selection of the "imperfect" geometry is of course of vital significance. The eigenshape of the member is normally used as a starting point. An experienced engineer can estimate the shape of such critical buckling

modes sufficiently accurately for preliminary design purposes. It should be noted that the buckling mode shapes and oscillating dynamic eigenforms of a member are only identical in exceptional cases.

It is easy to recognize that a member under axial compression with an inherent geometrical imperfection is also subjected to bending stresses which vary over the length of the member. A constant cross-section leads to a very uneconomic use of material. It is far better to vary the cross-section of the strut in line with the bending moment diagram. This can result in an open cross-section made up of more than one element joined by plates. Latticed or battened stanchions are also possible, with the main compressive members linked by cables or ties.

The design of a strut should always take account of the fact that, normally, buckling is possible in all planes. Accordingly, a circular hollow section is particularly appropriate as a one-piece strut. If buckling is prevented in one plane, then the strut can be analysed as a singly symmetric section, e.g. elliptical tube, rectangular hollow section, I-section. Composite sections whose geometry conforms to these considerations are of course also feasible.

With standard rolled sections there is no local buckling or wrinkling of the web (also no buckling of the wall in the case of hollow sections). But the situation is different in the case of composite sections, especially if thin or very thin plates are employed. In such instances very careful analyses are necessary with respect to possible local stability failures caused by buckling or wrinkling.

For many sections, e.g. I-beams, used as struts, buckling of the member is accompanied by simultaneous twisting of the section; we speak of torsional-flexural buckling. This phenomenon can also occur when the ends of a member are restrained to prevent twisting about the axis of the member. Twist without simultaneous buckling is also possible under

4.97

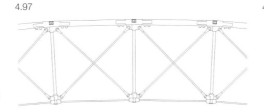

4.98

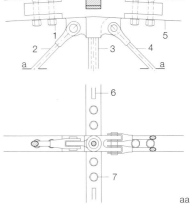

1   M 20 countersunk-head bolts with domed nuts
2   Diagonal tie, 1 No. 20 mm dia.
3   Strut, 38 mm dia x 10 mm thk, grade St 52
4   Diagonal tie, 2 No. 16 mm dia.
5   Top chord, Bl 80 x 60, grade St 52
6   Longitudinal member, BL 60 x 50, grade St 52
7   Splice joint in longitudinal member, M16 countersunk-head bolts with domed nuts

4.99

Asymmetric section	Singly symmetric section		Doubly symmetric section		

MP = centre of gravity
SP = shear centre

P_{kr} | P_{kz} | P_{kr} | P_{kz} | P_{ky} | P_{kt}

Torsional-flexural buckling | Flexural buckling about z-axis (in y-direction) | Torsional-flexural buckling (in z-direction and about MP) | Flexural buckling about z-axis (in y-direction) | Flexural buckling about y-axis (in z-direction) | Torsional buckling

aa

4.100 Pylon subjected to compression; cross-section
matched to buckling form of Euler case 2
4.101 Section
4.102 Buckling forms and effective buckling lengths of
the so-called Euler cases [440]

4.100

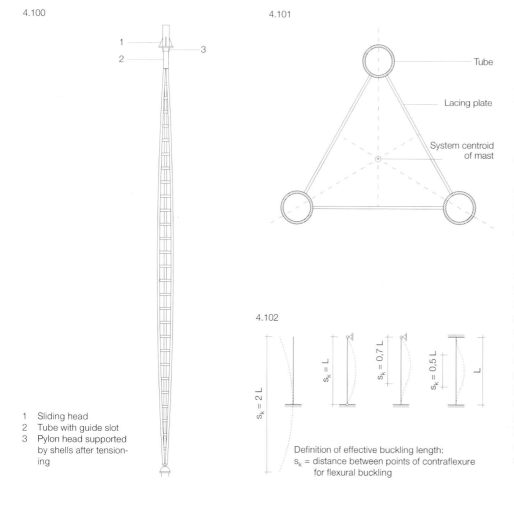

1 Sliding head
2 Tube with guide slot
3 Pylon head supported
by shells after tension-
ing

4.101

Tube

Lacing plate

System centroid
of mast

4.102

Definition of effective buckling length:
s_k = distance between points of contraflexure
for flexural buckling

compressive forces, even when the ends of the
member are restrained to prevent twisting
about its axis. In both cases the components
must be analysed to verify stability against this
mode of failure. The inclusion of stiffeners, a
form of construction which is virtually obsolete
today, can diminish the problem of twist in
struts.

Preventing stability failures is always coupled
with the provision of more material, and hence
increased costs. As a strut becomes more
slender, so the amount of extra material
increases and costs rise disproportionately. So
in lightweight construction compressive forces
are always only transmitted via short members.

Holes, openings and the like bring about local
reductions in the cross-section and this must
be just as carefully analysed as for tension
members. The stress concentrations present
around the edges of such holes and openings
are normally critical for the design. Unsupported edges of webs or flanges subjected to
compression frequently require stiffening or
similar measures to prevent buckling. Holes
placed eccentric to the axis of the member
should never be included without some form of
local strengthening because otherwise they
lead to a displacement of the component's
centroidal axis, and hence give rise to bending
stresses.

4.103 Articulated junction in edge cable of membrane
      roof, car showroom, Frankfurt a. M.
4.104 Articulated butt joint
4.105 Strut adjustable for length, arrangement of end
      fitting
4.106 Cable-stayed struts, schematic drawings of
      various arrangements
4.107 Hinged column base, suitable for transmitting
      tensile and compressive forces
4.108 Column splices, welded and bolted versions
      [440]

4.103

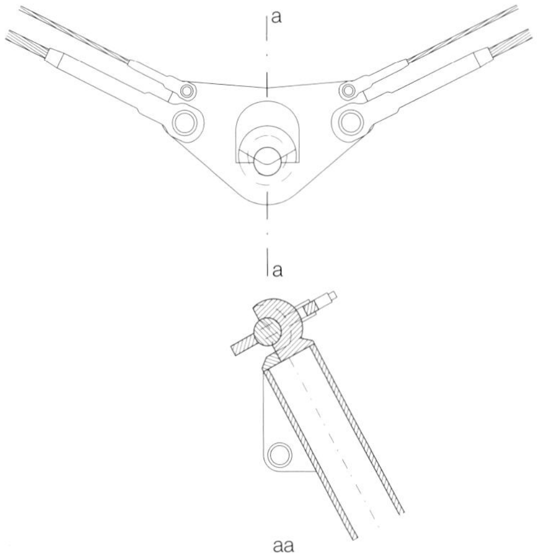

a

a

aa

4.104

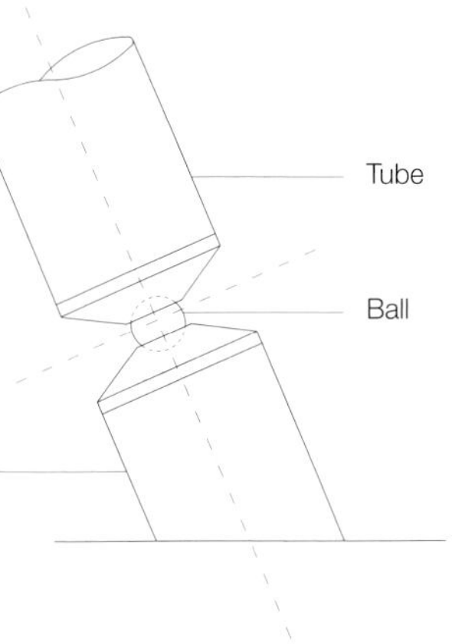

Tube

Ball

Tube

4.105

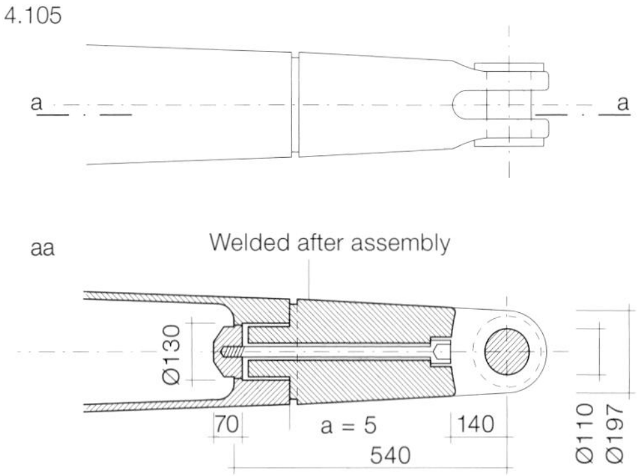

a ———— a

aa

Welded after assembly

Ø130

70   a = 5   140

540

Ø110
Ø197

4.106

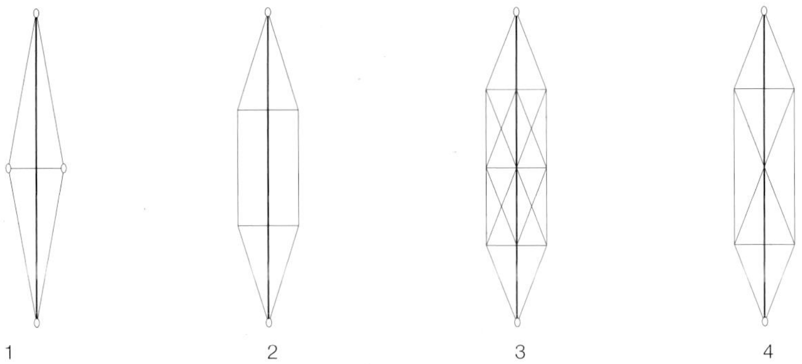

1   2   3   4

4.108

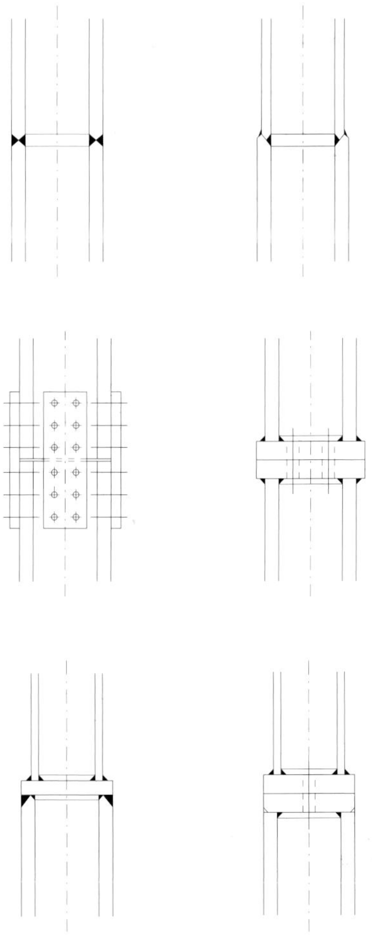

4.107

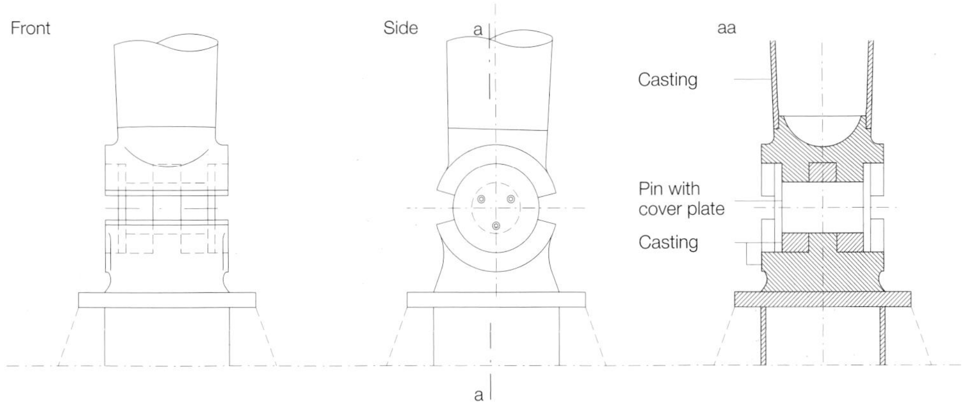

Front   Side   a   aa

Casting

Pin with
cover plate

Casting

a

147

4.109   Bending
4.110   Stress distributions in rectangular and I-sections
        subjected to uniaxial bending

4.109

4.110

Linear components subjected to bending

All members subjected to force components perpendicular to their axes, or corresponding couples (moments), undergo bending. The magnitude and distribution of this bending action is typically described by the so-called moment diagram.

All non-vertical members are subjected to bending purely as a result of their own weight. Together with the vertical imposed loads, which usually have to be carried at the same time, this leads to uniaxial bending. If horizontal forces acting transverse to the direction of the member are added to these, the result is biaxial bending.

On a member of constant cross-section subjected to uniaxial bending as a result of its own weight we find that this bending action always leads to a very inhomogeneous stress distribution within the member, indeed within the cross-section. Consequently, the utilization of the material is correspondingly inconsistent: there are highly and lowly stressed regions of both tension and compression. As steel is a highly efficient but comparatively expensive building material, bending members should be designed with their cross-section and form arranged in a manner that ensures optimum uniformity and material utilization. However, two further aspects have to be considered. In comparison to masonry or concrete structures, structural steelwork is a relatively lightweight form of construction in which the stresses caused by dead loads frequently lie below those brought about by external loads. As the direction and magnitude of external loads often changes, we must determine which loading case is to be the overriding criterion. Further, the work involved in adjusting the cross-section for such a situation can be considerable; again and again, a compromise has to be made between the structurally desirable and the economically viable form.

In trying to find an answer to the optimization of the cross-section of a member subjected to bending, we should first investigate the region of maximum bending moment and negligible shear force. The maximum stresses occur in the outermost "fibres" of the section; so the material should be concentrated there. Near the axis of the member, the bending stresses

4.111   Matching the shape of the beam to the bending
        moment diagram: footbridge made from steel
        plates
4.112   Single-span beams with cantilevers, pin-jointed
        frame construction
4.113   Lifting bridge consisting of three single-span
        beams

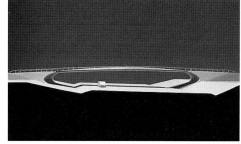

4.111

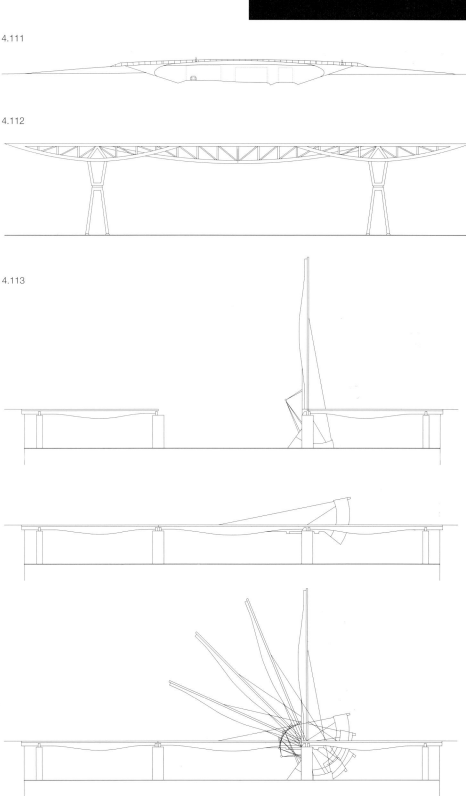

4.112

4.113

are very low. Therefore, an I-beam with a web whose thickness decreases towards the axis of the member represents an ideal cross-section for this part of the member. A hollow box section with appropriately designed side walls is the equivalent in structural terms. Indeed, I-beams are preferred as bending members in structural steelwork, albeit with webs of constant thickness. This is, however, not due to limitations in the rolling process but rather, on the one hand, to simplify the connection of other components to the web and, on the other, to take account of the load-carrying behaviour of the member in the region of higher and high shear. In such regions, e.g. at positions of local force transfer or, what basically amounts to the same thing, adjacent supports, the web is subjected to extremely high stresses. So a change of section would be worthwhile at such positions. However, due to economic considerations, this problem is overcome in steelwork by the addition of ribs, stiffeners, etc.

The bending moment does not normally remain constant along a member subjected to bending. With an I-beam, this fact could be taken account of by varying the flange thickness. Wherever flange plates attached above or below a beam do not create any constructional problems, then this is an ideal means of improving the utilization of the material. This is easy to accomplish with welded box sections as the thicknesses of the flange plates can be matched to the stress distribution or supplementary plates welded inside as required.

Instead of countering the inhomogeneous stress distribution in a member subjected to bending by adjusting the cross-section while maintaining the depth, we can of course adapt the depth to suit the stresses – haunched beams. If the type of utilization permits, then both upper and lower flanges can be haunched. The form and size of the haunches should follow the bending moment diagram exactly. However, on small members this often results in very acute intersections which are very unsatisfactory, both from the point of view of fabrication and aesthetics. In such instances it is possible to deviate from the above requirement and provide parallel flanges locally. Openings are permissible in such beams at places where the stresses in the webs are low.

4.114 Asymmetric beam connection, compression flange fixed
4.115 Symmetric beam connection
4.116 Castellated beam, with and without intermediate plates
4.117 Rigid beam-column connection: acceptable openings in beam
4.118 Articulated beam-column connection: acceptable openings in beam

4.119 Stability failure due to lateral buckling
4.120 I-beam with fork bearing
4.121 Lateral buckling prevented by linking auxiliary beams

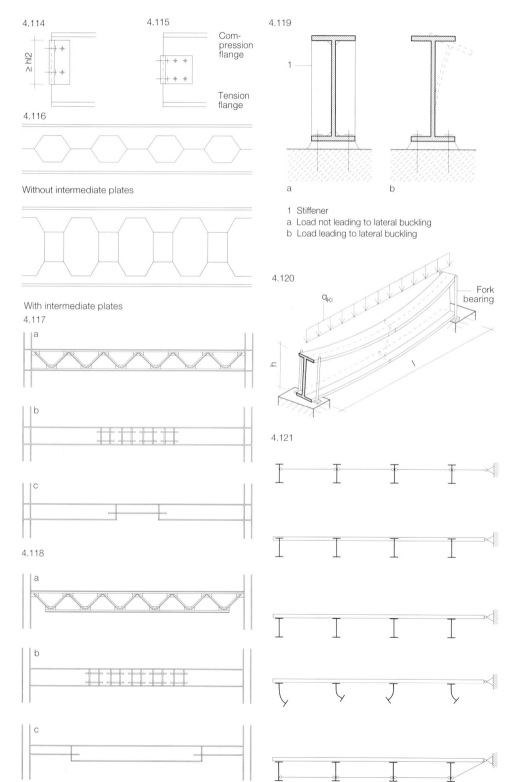

4.114

$\geq h/2$

4.115

Compression flange

Tension flange

4.116

Without intermediate plates

With intermediate plates

4.117

a

b

c

4.118

a

b

c

4.119

1

a

b

1 Stiffener
a Load not leading to lateral buckling
b Load leading to lateral buckling

4.120

q_{Kl}

Fork bearing

h

4.121

If such openings are so large that only thin members remain, then the member would be better designed as an open section, a pin-jointed frame or a Vierendeel girder (see chapter 5).

Openings in the webs of members subjected to bending should only be provided in areas of low shear. In a single-span beam this is in the middle of the span. Circular or square/rectangular holes are allowed but the latter must have radiused corners in order to preclude unnecessary stress peaks. Web openings near supports usually require the web or the perimeter of the hole to be strengthened, or additional stiffeners. Such solutions are acceptable but point to a less-than-masterly handling of the problem. It is much better to strive for openings (usually required for building services) only at suitable places in the beam.

Beams with perforated webs or castellated beams have webs weakened along their full length. High shear forces can prove critical with such beams and if this is the case then local strengthening (e.g. stiffeners) may be needed at supports or under heavy loads.

Components subjected to biaxial bending should be designed keeping the above principles in mind. The use of I-beams results in a composite, cruciform cross-section. However, square or rectangular hollow sections are far more appropriate for biaxial bending. Hollow sections are much easier to deal with, especially in terms of corrosion protection. Furthermore, in most cases connections with other components are far simpler.

Without continuous lateral restraint, all members subjected to bending suffer from a stability problem: lateral buckling of the web. This is a stability failure which involves the section twisting upon its own axis. Such twisting need not occur along the whole length of the member axis; for example, it may not happen at all at supports, at fork bearings or at junctions with other components. But once the twisting action has commenced, it is accompanied by a reduction in the structural depth and hence an increase in the stresses within the member as well as what is now an eccentric application of the external, typically conservative loads. The member then becomes overstressed and

4.122

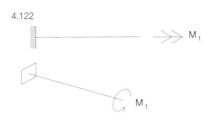

4.122 Torsion
4.123 Optimum positioning of stiffeners to prevent twist
4.124 Cantilever beam fixed to torsion tube

fails, often taking adjacent components with it as a result of the deformation.

The risk of lateral buckling is particularly high with deep, slender bending members, e.g. channels, I-, L- or Z-sections, trusses or Vierendeel girders. Lateral buckling is avoided by selecting a section not at risk, by sizing the bending member accordingly or by stabilizing upper and lower flanges by connecting them to other elements such as floor slabs, or by providing strutting or bracing.

Linear components subjected to torsion
A torsional stress is brought about through the application of a torsional moment and/or forces whose lines of action do not coincide with the axis of the member. The latter is the case with all incoming loads, i.e. from other components supported directly or via brackets on the member, that are not applied centrally. Although it is relatively simple to design an optimum cross-section for members subjected to torsion, dealing with a torsional moment at the supports can nevertheless lead to complicated details. Therefore, like with all components, a torsion load should only be allowed when the overall constructional concept permits suitable detailing of the supports.

Linear members subjected to torsion should have a straight axis.

A torsional moment, like all moments, can be resolved as a couple. Accordingly, a member subjected to torsion could be replaced by two beams (subjected to bending) which then deform in opposing directions. This might lead to simpler details at the supports. Four beams would also be conceivable. However, in the case of long members, carrying a torsion load with pairs of beams leads to massive or large sections. Therefore, from a structural, economic and ecological viewpoint it is more reasonable to carry torsion loads by means of suitably designed cross-sections.

Considering the stress distribution in a solid, cylindrical component subjected to torsion shows immediately that the stresses decrease from the outer edge to the centre. According to one of the principles of lightweight construction, lowly stressed material is removed until the designer is left with the optimum tubular

section for carrying the torsion. All other cross-sections with identical overall dimensions and weight per metre are less effective. The fact that square or rectangular hollow sections are often used as torsion members can be attributed exclusively to their simpler connections with other elements, i.e. this is a purely economic decision.

The optimum tubular sections for carrying torsion, likewise square, rectangular or polygonal hollow sections, all exhibit a characteristic, identifiable, spiral distribution of opposing tensile or compressive trajectories. This type of stress distribution is the prerequisite for the high efficiency of these members. Any openings in such components interrupt these stress patterns and lead to redistribution of the stresses coupled with (sometimes) a dramatic loss in efficiency as well as excessive twisting of the member. In particular, long slits transform the closed into an, at least partly, open section and reduce the torsional strength almost to zero. Of course, even open sections, e.g. channels, I-beams, can accommodate torsion loads. However, their load-carrying behaviour is less than satisfactory for such uses. The designer pays for this wrong choice of section by way of large and heavy sections as well as larger deformations.

4.123

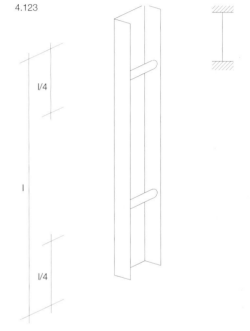

4.124

**Elementary stresses and strains:
planar members**

4.125

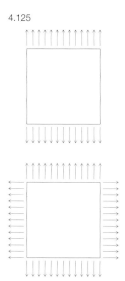

When an external loading is not present in the form of an individual force but rather as a uniformly distributed linear load, or is transported by a member in such a form, then planar members made from steel plates represent a good option. Planar members are large in two directions and comparatively small in the third direction (thickness).

The uniformly distributed linear load acting in or on a member can exhibit differing lines of action. The only requirement for an optimum loadbearing behaviour within the planar member is that the lines of action of the loads all lie in the middle plane of the member. If this is not the case, then the material is subjected to bending and is utilized ineffectively.

Planar members subjected to tension
All uniformly distributed forces acting in the middle plane of the member cause an exclusively tensile stress. Stability problems are non-existent. Depending on the direction of the forces, the member can be subjected to uniaxial or biaxial tension. The magnitudes of the stresses can vary within the member, in which case optimum sizing of the component will lead to a member with varying thickness, provided there is a loading case which quite clearly governs the design.

Applications for planar members subjected exclusively to tension include the thin metal membranes of solar reflectors, the tension flanges of box girders subjected to bending (in bridges as well) and thin web plates interrupted by posts and acting purely as tension elements in slender beams or box girders.

Thin loadbearing plates stiffened by frames and stringers and which can only accept tensile forces are intrinsic to aircraft design. In the building industry, this stressed-skin type of construction has been used by the author in a prize-winning competition entry for the MCC car showroom.

Planar members subjected to compression
Here, the uniformly distributed forces acting in the middle plane of the member cause an exclusively compressive stress. This acts uniaxially or biaxially depending on the direction of the forces. Stability problems now occur. Although in planar compression members

these can be compensated for by increasing the thickness, this solution is only resorted to in the case of small members because the aim is to reduce the amount of steel used. Normally, the members are usually stiffened in one or both directions e.g. compression flanges of box girders for bridges, walls of large pylons.

The loadbearing outer skin of an aeroplane fuselage, stiffened by frames and stringers, is a planar member subjected to biaxial stresses. Buckling in the compression zones is prevented by adding ribs.

Instead of stiffening a planar compression member by way of ribs, the geometry of the member itself can be improved. To do this, flat plates at risk of buckling are replaced by corrugated or trapezoidal profile sheeting. Both are ideal for reducing the stability problem inherent with flat plates, but of course only when the folds or corrugations lie parallel with the direction of the compressive forces.

For thin plates carrying comparatively little load but utilized to the full, the plates at risk of buckling and wrinkling can be stabilized using sandwich techniques, like filling thin-walled tubes under compression with plastics such as polyurethane. This is similar to filling thin-walled hollow sections with concrete or providing a concrete casing to open sections having thin flanges and webs.

Planar members subjected to bending
As soon as the lines of action of individual forces acting on the member no longer lie in the middle plane of the planar member itself, it is subjected to bending. A uniform cross-section is a very inefficient, and therefore expensive, method of carrying the loads. This is only acceptable for small members. Similarly to the solutions mentioned for linear members subjected to bending, the answer here is to try to open up the cross-section of the member, match the depth, or rather thickness, to the bending moment diagram and/or concentrate the material at the top or bottom of the member. This leads to sandwich-type components with an internal grid of steel sections and a covering of steel plates, or plates with ribs on one side, or folded plates (e.g. trapezoidal profile sheeting), or plastic-filled sandwich panels.

4.126

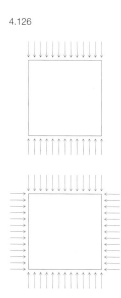

4.127

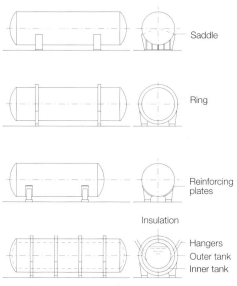

Saddle

Ring

Reinforcing plates

Insulation

Hangers
Outer tank
Inner tank

4.128

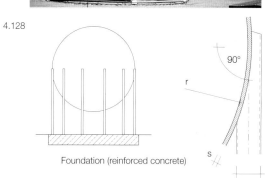

90°

r

s

Foundation (reinforced concrete)

Column O.D.

4.129

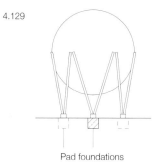

Pad foundations

4.130

4.131

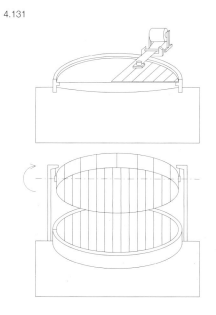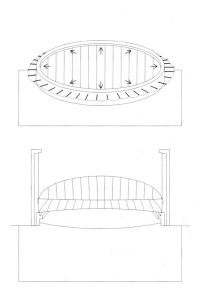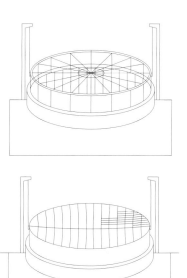

4.132 Buckling of a plate supported on two sides and
       subjected to compression
4.133 Buckling of a plate supported on three sides
4.134 Buckling of a plate supported on four sides
4.135 Bending forces acting on a planar member
4.136 Types of orthotropic plates [440]
4.137 Orthotropic plates, feasible rib profiles
4.138 Sandwich panel

4.139 Machining of I-beams:
    a Straight and oblique cuts
    b Mitre cut
    c Flange notch, one and both sides
    d Flange cut-outs
    e Oblique beam notches, top and bottom
    f Beam notch, top only or top and bottom
4140 Deformation states of facing to sandwich panel
      under compression

4.132

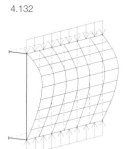

4.135

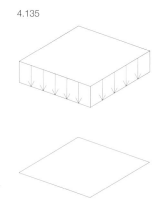

4.136

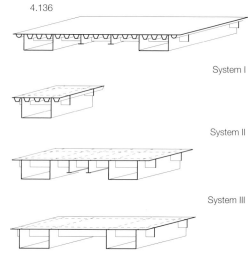

System I

System II

System III

System IV

4.133

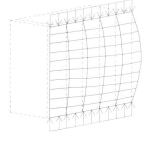

To carry a uniaxial bending stress, a plate's bending strength can be very simply improved by way of appropriate folding or attaching (by various means) profiled ribs. Biaxial bending stresses, for example, those present in steel bridge decks, require two loadbearing ribs which lead not only to complicated constructional solutions but usually to a weakened cross-section at the many intersections as well. Nevertheless, such forms of construction result in purposeful and also economic solutions. The orthotropic plates popular in steel bridge-building are a good example of this.

Again and again, steel buildings employ beam grids coupled with loadbearing floor plates.

Corrugated or trapezoidal profile sheets are very efficient components used extensively as planar members in bending situations. Trapezoidal profile sheeting in particular has become highly significant as a loadbearing roof covering and facade cladding.

Corrugated and trapezoidal profile sheets exhibit an extremely uniaxial load-carrying

behaviour. They can only carry bending stresses parallel to the folds/corrugations. This fact must not be forgotten at their supports. It should also be mentioned that corrugated and trapezoidal profile sheets, owing to their folds, are less suitable as bracing elements than flat plates. Although trapezoidal profile sheeting in particular is being increasingly used as a roof membrane, an analysis of the forces at a fold quickly reveals just how ineffective this sheeting is for this type of load-carrying task.

4.134

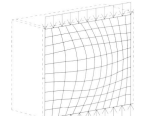

The detailing of openings and the transfer of forces

Holes and openings in a component subjected to external forces always mean disruptions to the stress distribution within the component, which has hopefully been designed so as to provide a near homogeneous distribution. Inhomogeneities in the stress distribution and stress concentrations are the result. Such concentrations of stress occur around the edges of drilled holes. They can assume quite remarkable magnitudes and lead to a very uneven use of the material.

Most designers are unaware of just how high the stress peaks are at the edges of, for example, drilled holes because during the design process the actual stress relationships are masked by the fact that, for a tension connection, the net area is used, and, for a compression connection, the gross area. The reality – that this process is only permissible for sufficiently ductile steels – is all too easily overlooked. Only in steels with sufficient plasticity can stress peaks adjacent holes be lessened by local plastic behaviour. This aspect should not be forgotten when using high-strength and hence less ductile materials; in such cases the real stresses must be allowed for.

If holes are positioned in very highly stressed regions of a component, then the stress concentrations which occur at the edges of such holes govern the size of the total cross-section. Therefore, holes should be reserved for lowly stressed regions of the member or, since in optimized lightweight construction there are no such regions, the position, size and shape of holes must be chosen to reduce the stress concentrations. If necessary, the hole can be "neutralized" by reinforcing the edges.

Even a plate subjected to uniaxial tension and made from a linearly elastic material, and which in comparison to the hole radius is infinitely wide and long, exhibits stresses at the edges of the hole which are three times the underlying stress further from the hole. Only in materials with sufficient plasticity are these stress peaks prevented by means of premature local plastic behaviour. If the material is not sufficiently ductile, as is the case with high-strength steels and high-strength steel castings, then these stress peaks can only be reduced by way of local reinforcement.

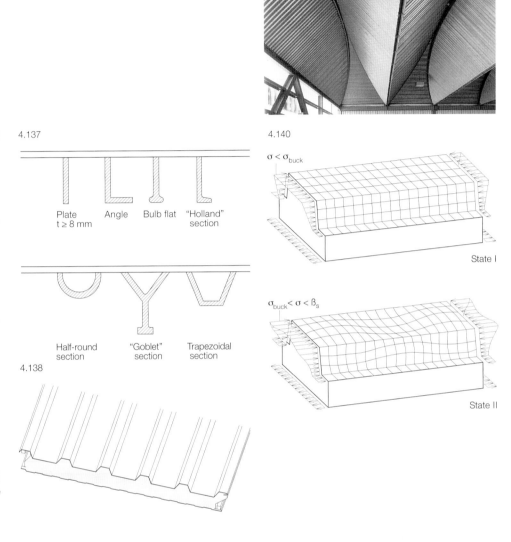

4.137

Plate t ≥ 8 mm | Angle | Bulb flat | "Holland" section

Half-round section | "Goblet" section | Trapezoidal section

4.138

4.140

$\sigma < \sigma_{buck}$

State I

$\sigma_{buck} < \sigma < \beta_s$

State II

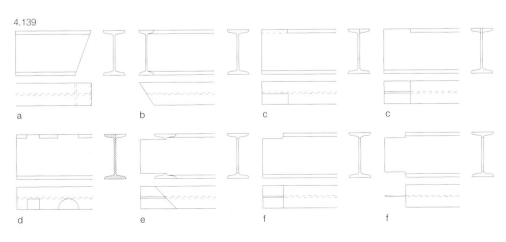

4.139

a   b   c   c

d   e   f   f

4.141   Plate subjected to uniaxial tension: inhomoge-
        neous stress distribution due to drilled hole [485]
4.142   Neutral openings

4.141

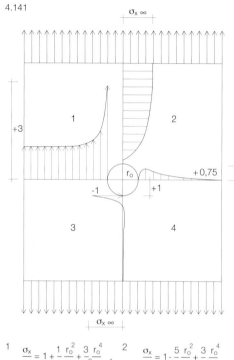

$$1 \quad \frac{\sigma_x}{\sigma_{x\,\infty}} = 1 + \frac{1}{2}\frac{r_o^2}{y^2} + \frac{3}{2}\frac{r_o^4}{y^4}$$

$$2 \quad \frac{\sigma_x}{\sigma_{x\,\infty}} = 1 - \frac{5}{2}\frac{r_o^2}{x^2} + \frac{3}{2}\frac{r_o^4}{x^4}$$

$$3 \quad \frac{\sigma_y}{\sigma_{x\,\infty}} = \frac{1}{2}\frac{r_o^2}{x^2} - \frac{3}{2}\frac{r_o^4}{x^4}$$

$$4 \quad \frac{\sigma_y}{\sigma_{x\,\infty}} = \frac{3}{2}\left(\frac{r_o^2}{y^2} - \frac{r_o^4}{y^4}\right)$$

4.142

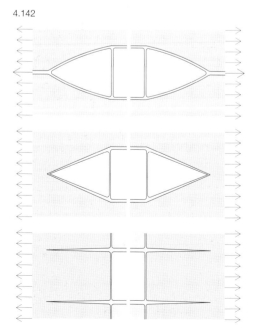

Larger holes, e.g. for building services, can be shaped to allow for the stress condition governing the design. In a plate subjected to uniaxial tension, which of course can also be interpreted as one part of a composite section, the stress peaks can be reduced to twice the underlying stress by using an elliptical hole aligned in the direction of the stress. However, that exhausts the possibilities given by the geometry of the hole. Positioning the hole in a region of relatively low stress avoids the need to design the entire member according to the stress peaks caused by the hole. But strengthening the edges of the hole is unavoidable in the case of large holes and holes in thin-walled sections subjected to compression. In ultralightweight constructions such reinforcement may be incorporated such that a "neutral" opening is the result, i.e. an elementary, undisturbed stress state is maintained in the plane of the plate without any non-uniform stress distributions. The detailing of neutral holes in steel castings does not present any difficulties, but with welded plates or sections leads to complicated fabrication. Neutral holes are rare in the building industry but are a standard technique in the aircraft industry.

Much simpler in terms of fabrication, and hence very common in the building industry, is the strengthening of the perimeter of a hole by means of flat plates, so-called stiffeners.

The transfer of forces

In steelwork the individual components in virtually all cases consist of separate parts which are large in two directions and small in the third, i.e. the thickness. This way of thinking covers open rolled sections, hollow sections and composite sections just as well as flat and folded plates.

The transfer of forces into a component usually signifies the introduction of forces into the individual parts of that component, into its cross-section. Consequently, almost all force transfer problems in steelwork can be simplified to the consideration of the transfer of forces into one individual part which is connected to other parts of the component, or cross-section. Only non-planar cast, forged or similar items have to be considered differently. Therefore, these will be investigated at the end of this discussion.

However, there is no fundamental difference between planar and non-planar elements in terms of force transfer.

When a force acts in the system plane of a component that is large in two directions and small in the third, then we call that component a plate. When a force acts perpendicular to the system plane, then that same component is designated a slab. Forces which act at any angle to the system plane can always be resolved into one vector component in the system plane and one perpendicular to it.

Transferring a point load acting in the plane of the plate (force acting on the edge)
An individual, quasi point load applied at the unsupported edge of a plate leads to extreme stress peaks and corresponding deformations at the point of transfer of the force. Therefore, the obvious answer is to distribute the force over a longer length or larger area while it is being transferred into the plate. The simplest solution is a straight flange arranged parallel to the plate. Its area and length are determined by the size of force to be transferred, the strength and thickness of the plate, and the type of connection between flange and plate.

A welded flange represents the standard solution in steelwork. It transfers the point load into the body of the plate. As it does so, the force in the flange decreases along its length, while the force in the plate steadily increases. This is another reason why the sectional area of the flange should diminish towards the end of the flange. At the same time, a flange represents a local stiffening of the plate, which leads to a sudden change in area at the start and end of the flange. Under load, stress peaks occur here in the plate; these can be regarded as a notch effect. Therefore, in regions which can be assessed as critical in dynamic terms, as well as in structures subject to extreme stresses, the start and end of the flange should be as gradual as possible.

Transferring a point load acting in the plane of the plate (force acting in the area)
The above considerations apply similarly when a force acts in the middle of the area of a plate.

4.143 Plate with sudden change in thickness in direction of tension: influence of transition radius on stress peaks [485]
4.144 Transferring a point load acting in the plane
4.145 Transferring a point load acting perpendicular to the plane

Transferring a point load acting perpendicular to the plane of the plate
The transfer of a point load acting perpendicular to the system plane causes bending in the component, which now acts as a slab. The stress condition in the slab will vary depending on its supports, i.e. how it is joined to other components. In principle, bending should always be avoided because it represents a particularly ineffective way of carrying the load. Therefore, the following examples do not represent recommended solutions but instead answers to situations which cannot be dealt with in any other way.

Suspending two point loads from the bottom flange of an I-beam causes the two halves of the flange to act like cantilever slabs. The loads transferred via points bring about a ripple-like deflection of the two halves of the flange. The load transfer spreads out towards the web, where the forces are "carried" by the web and from there distributed throughout the entire cross-section. Consequently, the web functions as a continuous (linear) support. If the flanges cannot withstand the bending stresses induced in them, then the nature and/or position of the load transfer must be changed, or the flanges stiffened. The latter is best achieved by adding two further linear supports to the "cantilever flange slab" in order to support the slab on three sides in the region of the force transfer. In constructional terms this means the inclusion of two stiffeners; these transmit part of the force directly into the web.

A comparable example is the transfer of a point load into the web of an I-beam. Here too, the load leads to a sort of buckling of the web, linked with bending of the (normally) thin web. In this example the web carries the load as a strip of slab supported along its two longitudinal edges. The bending in the web is now reduced by including two stiffeners, which turn the strip of slab supported on two sides into a strip supported locally on four sides. The primary load-carrying direction is now from stiffener to stiffener and hence considerably shorter than the previous primary load-carrying direction, which spanned from flange to flange. The stiffeners transfer the forces into the loadbearing flanges; these are subjected to bending in their system planes.

An alternative to the principle described above is to suspend the point load from a single stiffener and in this way relieve the beam web completely.

Transferring a point load acting in the plane of the plate (force acting in the area)
The force transfer is very simple and is best achieved in double shear via a bolted, welded or pinned connection. The double shear arrangement ensures that no bending moments are transferred into the plane of the plate. With welded connections we should ensure that the plates are able to carry the anticipated transverse tension. With thicker plates and high loads in particular, the local microstructure of the material can be investigated using X-rays or similar methods.

Pinned joints usually benefit from the addition of local reinforcing rings (boss plates) to raise their loadbearing capacity.

Asymmetric force transfer details, e.g. employing angles or splice plates, always cause bending in the plate. If this leads to unacceptably high bending stresses, then the plate must be strengthened locally by means of stiffeners or similar measures. This has the effect of transferring the bending into the plate via a greater lever arm and hence lowering the bending stresses.

Transferring a uniformly distributed linear load acting in the plane of the plate (force acting on the edge)
Transferring a uniformly distributed linear load on the edge of a plate represents the ideal constructional solution. Stress peaks in the plate can then only occur at the start or end of the distributed load (if at all). Otherwise, the force transfer is ideal and even, with a correspondingly homogeneous stress distribution in the plate.

Transferring a uniformly distributed linear load acting in the plane of the plate (force acting in the area)
The above considerations apply similarly when a uniformly distributed linear load is transferred in the area of a plate.

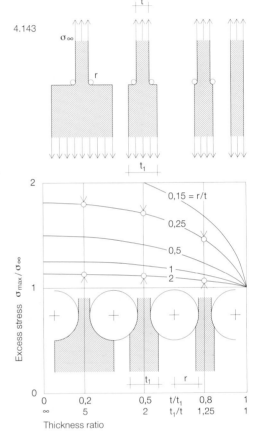

4.143

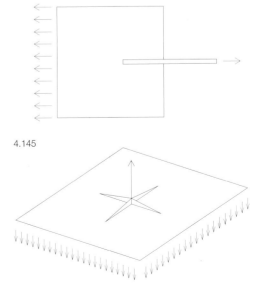

4.144

4.145

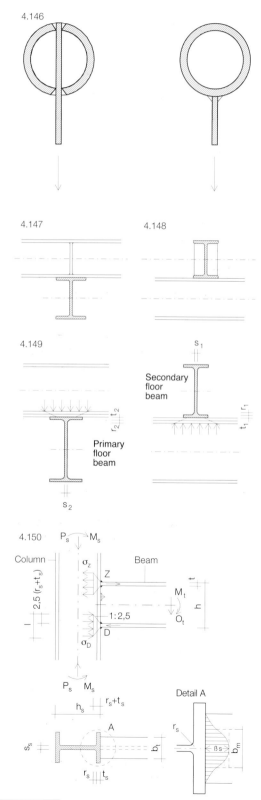

4.146

4.147   4.148

Secondary
floor
beam

4.149

Primary
floor
beam

4.150

Column   Beam

Detail A

Transferring a uniformly distributed linear load acting perpendicular to the plane of the plate
A uniformly distributed linear load acting perpendicular to the system plane causes bending in the plate. Once again we must watch out for possible stress peaks at the start and end of the load. Otherwise, however, the ineffective way in which the load is carried, i.e. through bending, again leads to a marked reduction in the possible spans. Local thickening, local load-distributing strengthening or rigid flanges (stiffeners), which reduce the spans of the thin plate and serve as intermediate supports, are possible remedies.

Uniformly distributed linear loads applied perpendicular to the system plane are very common in structural steelwork. The classic example is suspending a plate subjected to tension from the bottom flange of a hollow section (circular or square/rectangular). The suspended plate transfers a uniformly distributed linear load into the hollow section which can then only carry the load by way of bending. Owing to the low bending strength of the (normally) thin-walls, a local bending problem ensues which can lead to a local stability predicament due to the hollow section's position higher up the loadbearing chain. Apart from the case of a minor loading, we must always ensure that the suspended plate spreads the load as it is transferred to the hollow section, and without stress peaks. One way of achieving this is to cut open the hollow section and weld in the plate like a bulkhead. The plate can also transfer the load to the hollow section via a flanged ring; in this case the section does not need to be cut open.

Another, already classic, example, is the frame corner formed by two I-sections. In the beam loaded in bending and in the column, the forces are essentially concentrated in the flanges. If the beam is butt-welded to the inner flange of the column, then the uniformly distributed linear loads acting in the beam flanges cannot be transferred into the column flange perpendicular to the system plane – its bending strength is much too low in relation to the load to be carried. Welding two plates between the column flanges, practically as extensions to the beam flanges, places the outer flange of the column under load too, perpendicular to its system plane. Splitting the load in a beam flange between two column flanges does help

the problem but does not overcome it. Only by welding a diagonal stiffener into the frame corner can we guarantee that all flange forces are carried as in-plane forces. This diagonal stiffener should be positioned so that it is loaded in tension, i.e. does not suffer from stability problems and so can be kept slender.

Sometimes these diagonal stiffeners are undesirable for architectural reasons. Mies van der Rohe in particular employed the non-diagonally stiffened corner with brilliant success. When such architectural considerations are imperative, or when the bending moment at the corner is only minor, diagonal stiffeners can be omitted. The beam flange forces must then be transferred into the column web via plates welded between the column flanges and from the web back into the column flange – a dramatic loss in efficiency which again and again leads to the column web having to be doubled.

Transferring forces in non-planar components
Many of the aforementioned problems can be avoided when transferring forces in non-planar components. When transferring point loads into a component it is therefore recommended to transfer the forces into a non-planar element first and from there into the thin-walled adjoining components – to avoid these adjoining components suffering from uneven stress distributions. The non-planar force-transfer components are usually relatively small, made from machined thick plates, steel castings or, in the simplest case, from one plate. Numerous different details are feasible depending on architectural demands, the nature of the loads and type of construction. When transferring point loads by way of a sphere, the Hertzian stress in the non-planar element and the sphere as well as the axial stresses in the "equatorial plane" have to be verified. When using a pinned joint the eye bars must be checked for bending as well as bearing, the pins for shear and bending. As the actual stress distributions in a pinned joint are extremely complex and the design task correspondingly difficult and always very involved, the relevant standards normally contain design equations based on an extreme simplification of the actual situation. Accordingly, applying these equations results in joints which err very much on the safe side, i.e. the joints are overdesigned.

The subsoil as part of the construction: foundations for steel structures

The subsoil is the bottommost part of a structure. It forms part of the construction and is hence a fundamental element in the design.

The subsoil accepts forces from the foundation and transmits these further into the ground by way of three-dimensional loadbearing behaviour. Like every loadbearing component, the subsoil also undergoes deformation in doing so. Subsoil deformation, typically settlement, in turn causes deformation of the structure and its components. These deformations, which occur during the building of a structure owing to the constant increase in dead loads, and after completion as a result of varying imposed loads, wind or earthquakes, may not exceed certain limits as otherwise the loadbearing construction and/or the finishes will be damaged.

Deformation in the subsoil, and hence in the structure, can also occur when another structure is erected in the vicinity of an existing structure, or if the characteristics of the subsoil alter, e.g. as a result of the ground drying out following a lowering of the water table.

The most common material for foundations is reinforced concrete. Steel is still used sometimes but these days masonry and timber have all but disappeared from the foundation scene.

Therefore, foundations for steel components or whole steel structures are characterized by the fact that the slender steel elements, with a comparatively small cross-section, transfer large forces into a reinforced concrete base. Here too, like in all cases where a high-strength component is joined to one of low strength, this sudden change of section, which in this case also means a change of material and the interface between factory-fabricated and in-situ works, has to be suitably detailed.

Types of foundations

There are many different types of foundations, classified according to method of production, materials used, way in which forces are transmitted into the subsoil, etc. The following presents a brief review of the most significant types of foundations. A distinction is made between shallow, deep and floating foundations.

Shallow foundations
• Pad
• Strip
• Grillage
• Raft
• Raft with basement (box foundation)

Deep foundations
• Ground anchors
• Piles
• Driven piles
• Bored piles
• Pad
• Pier
• Box caisson
• Pneumatic caisson

Floating foundations

These various types are outlined below.

Shallow foundations
Shallow foundations are recommended for subsoils with good loadbearing capacity and where the foundations carry primarily vertical loads. However, shallow foundations must be founded at least 800 mm below ground level in order to prevent frost heave. Reinforced concrete is used almost without exception for such foundations.

Pad foundations are particularly suitable for carrying vertical point loads, e.g. from steel columns. Strip footings are typically used for supporting masonry or reinforced concrete walls. In steelwork they are used in conjunction with closely spaced steel columns or where pad foundations under a row of steel columns become so large that they converge and so form one long member. The same applies to grillages, which could be regarded as intersecting strip footings; the columns are always placed at the intersections. Raft foundations tend to be employed for constructing basements because such slabs are of course not very suitable for spreading the high point loads of steel columns over a wider area. To do this, it is better to place pad foundations below the raft itself. However, a raft foundation combined with a basement (box foundation) produces a very rigid loadbearing structure.
Steel columns or inclined members should always be founded on those walls which guarantee an appropriate distribution of the load.

4.151   Raft foundations
        a Plain slab
        b Beam and slab (upstand beams)
        c Beam and slab (downstand beams)
        d Local thickening to cope with high point loads
4.152   Rock anchors
4.153   Injection anchor
4.154   Box caisson foundation to a bridge pier [154]

4.151

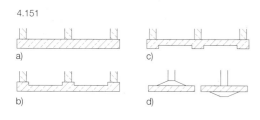

a)

b)

c)

d)

4.152

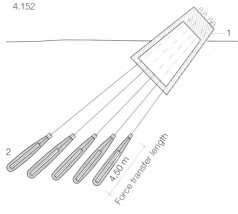

1   Anchorage, foundation
2   Grouted zone

4.153

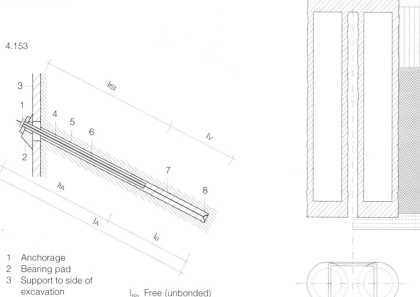

1   Anchorage
2   Bearing pad
3   Support to side of
    excavation
4   Protective pocket
5   Bored hole
6   Steel tendon
7   Grout
8   Base of anchor

l_{fSt} Free (unbonded)
        length
l_V Fixed (bonded) length
l_{fA} Elastic length
l_o Anchorage length
l_A Length of anchor

Deep foundations
Ground anchors can only be used to transfer axial tension loads into the subsoil. A distinction is made between rock anchors, which are used mainly for temporary structures and relatively low tensile forces, and injection anchors, which have been employed with great success for both temporary and permanent applications. Permanent injection anchors are normally anchored in a reinforced concrete element, which renders possible the connection of structural steelwork.

Piled foundations are used when the soil strata near ground level do not possess adequate loadbearing capacity or this cannot be obtained through ground improvement measures. The piles extend down to and are secured in a stratum that is capable of carrying the loads. If rock is present, then the piles can be "stood" on this. Piled foundations make use of driven piles; prefabricated steel or concrete or in-situ concrete or composite versions are possible. These latter two types normally make use of a steel tube which is driven into the ground and then removed before the concrete is poured or even remains in place to form a composite section with the in-situ concrete. The majority of bored piles come in the form of steel piles, composite piles subsequently filled with concrete, or casings extracted prior to or during pouring of the concrete. A pile should always be loaded axially, and is ideal for carrying tensile and/or compressive loads. Non-vertical forces are carried by inclined piles. The forces in a pile are transferred to the subsoil either by friction on the pile shaft or by end bearing. Some types of piles include a specially formed base to the pile in order to improve the end-bearing characteristics.

When very high loads have to be anchored, deep foundations can also be designed as pad foundations. Piers with deep-lying pad foundations are constructed in an open excavation. Box caissons are open at the top but closed at the bottom. Pneumatic caissons have a pressurized working chamber.

Floating foundations
In the presence of very deep strata of soft subsoil, the piles can no longer be driven to a loadbearing stratum – for both engineering and economic reasons. Therefore, the toes of the piles terminate in the region of soft subsoil and end-bearing pressure cannot be established. If the piles are long enough and the soil suitable, then the loads can be carried exclusively by way of skin friction. The entire piled foundation "floats", so to speak, in the ground which, although soft, possesses adequate loadbearing capacity. The deformations in the foundation are of course greater than with a piled foundation "standing" on rock.

Combinations of pad foundations with basements and piles having a composite loadbearing behaviour, and acting as floating foundations, have proved very successful solutions in a number of cases.

4.154

1   Talus deposits
2   Upper shell limestone
3   Middle shell limestone
4   Lower shell limestone

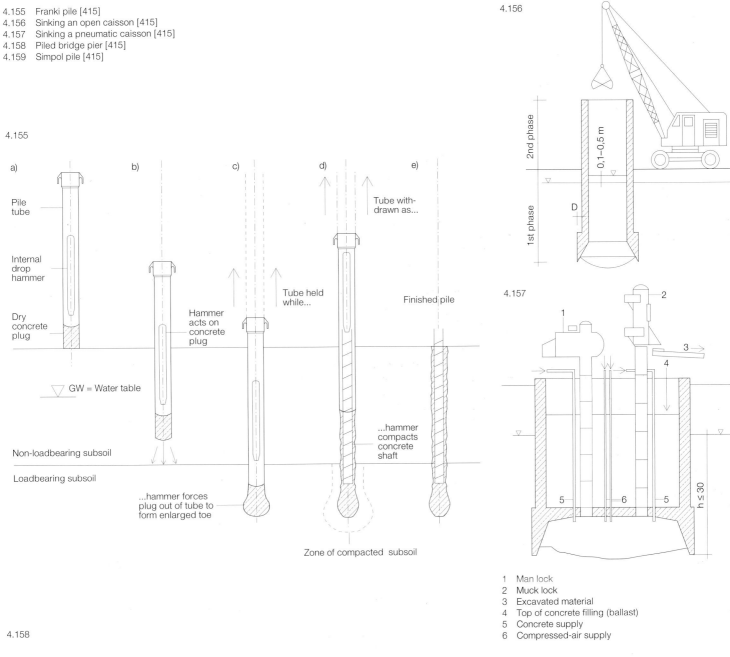

4.155

a)

Pile tube

Internal drop hammer

Dry concrete plug

▽ GW = Water table

Non-loadbearing subsoil

Loadbearing subsoil

b)

Hammer acts on concrete plug

...hammer forces plug out of tube to form enlarged toe

c)

d)

Tube held while...

...hammer compacts concrete shaft

Zone of compacted subsoil

e)

Tube with-drawn as...

Finished pile

4.156

2nd phase

1st phase

0,1–0,5 m

D

4.157

1

2

3

4

5   6   5

h ≤ 30

1   Man lock
2   Muck lock
3   Excavated material
4   Top of concrete filling (ballast)
5   Concrete supply
6   Compressed-air supply

4.158

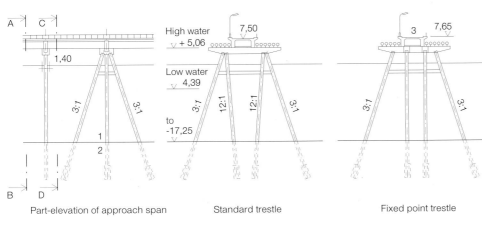

A C

1,40

3:1   3:1

1

2

B D

Part-elevation of approach span

High water
▽ + 5,06

7,50

Low water
▽ 4,39

to
-17,25

3:1   12:1   12:1   3:1

Standard trestle

3   7,65

3:1   3:1

Fixed point trestle

1   Steel tube piles, 546 mm dia., t = 13.5-15.5 mm
2   Gravel and sand
3   Precast concrete parts

4.159

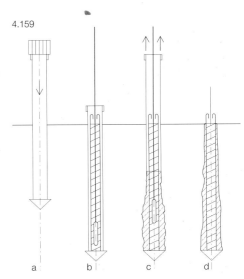

a   b   c   d

4.160   Founding different structures on a common raft
         [415]
4.161   Structures separated by a movement joint [415]
4.162   Structures joined by articulated slabs (schematic
         view) [415]

4.160

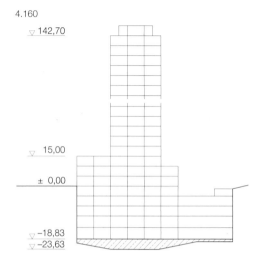

4.161

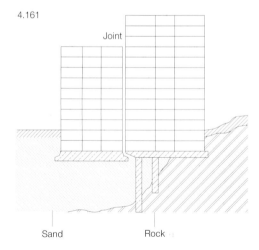

4.162

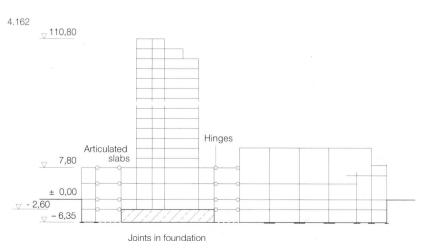

Joints in foundation

**Anchoring structural steelwork to reinforced concrete
foundations**
In principle
· compressive forces
· tensile forces
· shear forces
· moments
or combinations thereof can all be transferred
from steel to concrete components. The detail
chosen is always very much dependent on the
nature and magnitude of the forces to be transferred. Therefore, considering the constructional principles from this point of view is to be recommended.

Transferring a compressive force
Even high-strength concretes are not capable
of accepting stresses transferred from a steel
component by direct contact. Therefore, the
forces in a steel component must be introduced into the concrete in a spread or distributed form. This is best achieved by means of a
base plate, more rarely by embedding the
steel member in the concrete and providing
expanding bolts or similar fixings to transfer
the forces.

When using a base plate it must be ensured
that it is thick enough. A base plate which is
too thin will distort, e.g. by lifting of the corners,
and hence redistribute the stresses. This can
lead to stress concentrations and overstressing of the concrete where concrete and steel
are still in contact.

The edges of thick steel base plates may be
machined to improve their appearance.

Cast steel base plates are normally only used
in conjunction with a hinged column base.

Instead of using thick plates, thinner ones may
be used to which ribs or gusset plates have
been welded – stiffeners between component
and base plate. These transfer some of the
load directly from the component to the base
plate and also stiffen the plate, but this does
lead to additional shear stresses in the component. Thin-walled components, e.g. some
hollow sections, must be analysed to check
their adequacy.

In the case of extremely large base plates, e.g.
when several columns are to be fixed to one
plate, it is recommended to use a thinner plate
stiffened by ribs instead of a very thick plate.
Ideally, the ribs are positioned on the underside to avoid creating water and dirt traps. Of
course, with ribs underneath it must be ensured that the grout can be placed properly.

There should always be a joint of 20-40 mm,
depending on the size of the base plate, between underside of plate and top of foundation. This joint serves to compensate for building tolerances. During erection steel packings
to adjust the height are placed under the base
plate before the grout is injected. The packings
must be positioned well inside the limits of the
base plate so that there is an adequate covering of grout around the edge.

Expanding grout increases in volume as it
cures. Therefore, it presses against the concrete foundation and the steel base plate and
in this way creates a permanent seal between
itself and the steel plate – a great advantage in
terms of corrosion protection. This prevents
ingress of water and (in winter) its subsequent

4.163   Pocket foundation for subsequent filling with
        concrete. The cross-member is only required
        for erection and is later cut off. [440]
4.164   Screwed column base with recessed screws
4.165   Detail of screw
4.166   Column bases.
        Left: I-sections
        Right: square/rectangular hollow sections

a   Transmitting axial compression and transverse
    shear
b   Transmitting axial tension or compression plus
    a small moment
c   Transmitting a large moment
d   Transmitting axial force, transverse shear and
    moment
4.167   Protecting the exposed end of a threaded bar
        with a domed nut

freezing, which would otherwise cause spalling of the edges of the grout bed. This advantage is not present with beds of normal mortar or – often recommended – concrete because these materials shrink upon curing. Therefore, mortar and concrete no longer correspond with the state of the art.

The plan dimensions of a base plate are determined by the permissible bearing pressure of the concrete or grout below the plate.

If it is necessary to secure the position of the steel member, particularly during construction, then this can be accomplished by using cast-in threaded bars or bolts screwed into cast-in sockets. Threaded bars should always be cast in with the help of templates carefully fitted to the formwork to ensure correct, accurate positioning, possibly set out by a site engineer. After the grout has hardened, the excess length (to allow for tolerances) of the cast-in bolts is cut off and the bare ends treated to prevent corrosion. Ideally, a domed nut should be added (in addition to the fixing nut) or the end covered with a plastic cap.

Cast-in steel members allow compression to be comparatively easily transferred into the concrete. Of course, the permissible bearing stresses in the concrete at the contact face may not be exceeded. If this is not possible, then the area of contact must be increased or additional lateral cleats included.

Transferring a shear force
Base plates without any bolts can only carry a shear force equal to the friction between grout bed and base plate induced by the compression. Pretensioning the bolts or threaded bars allows the friction between grout bed and base plate to be increased substantially.

On no account should shear forces be transferred into the concrete by threaded bars. This is because the bars cannot be assumed to carry the load in pure shear; it tends to be a very complex combination of shear and bending, also influenced by the elasticity of the grout. The compact cross-section of the threaded bars is highly unsuited to this type of loading. This detail in particular is repeatedly

4.163
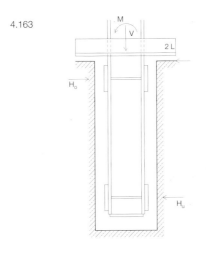

4.164
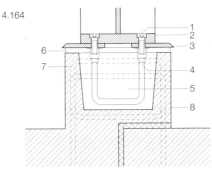

1   Machine screw with
    hexagon-socket head,
    M22 x 50, grade 10.9,
    to DIN 912
2   Base plate, 280 x 280
    x 35 mm
3   Steel plate, 420 x 420
    x 12 mm
4   Reinforcing bar with
    screw socket, e.g.
    Halfen HBS 20 dia.
5   Subsequent filling of
    grade B25 concrete
6   Expanding grout
7   Reinforcement
8   Pocket foundation

4.165
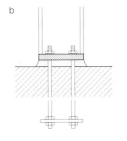

1   Machine screw with hexagon-socket head, M22 x 50,
    grade 10.9, to DIN 912
2   Recess for machine screw, DIN 74, type K

4.166
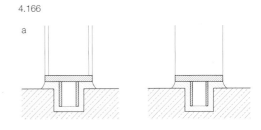

a

b

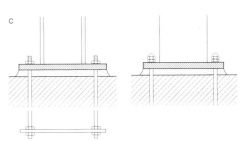

c

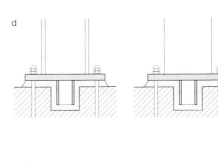

d

4.167
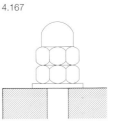

4.168   Circular hollow section column with peripheral gussets
4.169   Circular hollow section column with through-gussets
4.170   Transferring a large tensile force (uplift) into a reinforced concrete slab via an anchor plate
4.171   Transferring a large tensile force (uplift) into a reinforced concrete ground slab via an I-beam

4.168   4.169

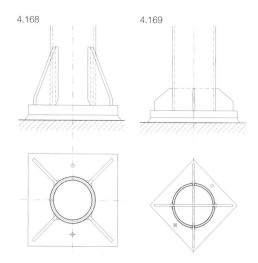

4.170

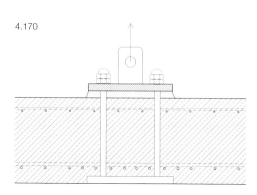

4.171

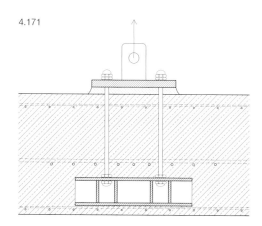

the subject of extensive calculations designed to prove its adequacy. However, the maxim here should be: "Better workmanship and fewer calculations are preferable to shoddy workmanship and subsequent validation."

Larger shear forces are best catered for via one or more shear connectors made from solid or I-sections welded on. These lead to a distributed and hence low-stress transfer of the shear into the concrete. Corresponding pockets need to be provided in the foundation; the grouting follows the principles outlined for compression.

Transferring a tensile force
Transferring a tensile (uplift) force into a reinforced concrete foundation demands special care in terms of design and fabrication because this tensile force has to be transferred "deep" into the concrete in order to be anchored among the reinforcement with its force distribution mechanisms. This is particularly simple with cast-in steel members, although the part of the member to be cast in must be suitably detailed, possibly with ribs or shear studs welded on. The force is then transferred into the suitably reinforced concrete by way of bearing, i.e. compressive, stresses. As the position of the steel member cannot be adjusted after casting in, it must be carefully positioned beforehand and firmly held in place while the concrete is being poured.

Pocket foundations of reinforced concrete with subsequently installed steel columns can accommodate relatively large tolerances. This can be regarded as an advantage, although on the whole the aim should be to strive for higher precision in the building industry, also in the dimensions of concrete elements. A steel column in a pocket can be relatively easily adjusted, but the transfer of tensile forces from the steel to the infill concrete to the foundation itself requires careful detailing and a good standard of workmanship when placing and compacting the concrete in the pocket.

The surface of the pocket concrete must be sufficiently rough. A recess or a void must be avoided when casting the concrete, which is why a generously sized pocket is recommended.

The fixing of steel columns with cast-in angles in conjunction with hooked threaded bars, or T-head bolts and two channels as anchor blocks, are both methods that have no place in modern structural steelwork.

If the steel member subjected to tension is not cast into the concrete foundation, then it is recommended that it be fixed via a base plate (welded on) and cast-in threaded bars. Again, as for the compression case, an adequately dimensioned expanding grout joint must be provided. The threaded bars are carefully set out and fixed to the formwork prior to pouring the concrete. The lower ends of these so-called holding-down (HD) bolts are fixed to an anchor plate which transfers the tension from the bars into the surrounding, suitably reinforced concrete by way of bearing pressure. The length of the cast-in bars is selected such that the cone of compression induced in the concrete by the anchor plate is ideally positioned within the cage of reinforcement. After the grout has reached its full strength, the threaded bars should be pretensioned with the help of the fixing nuts. This closes the joint between base plate and grout permanently and reduces the dynamic load on the bars. Finally, the excess length (to allow for tolerances) of the cast-in bars is cut off and the bare ends treated to prevent corrosion. Ideally, a domed nut should be added (in addition to the fixing nut) or the end covered with a plastic cap.

Like with the anchoring of a compressive force, the tension condition can also lead to a complex stress distribution in the base plate, characterized by bending and, sometimes, considerable shear forces. Here too, choosing a base plate that is not too thin is to be recom-

4.172

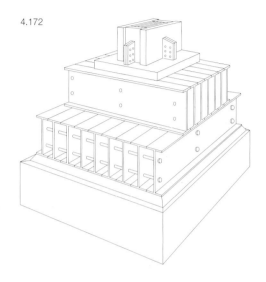

mended, besides performing the necessary, none-too-easy structural analysis. The base plate can be stiffened by ribs placed on the underside to avoid creating water and dirt traps but positioned to avoid causing an unacceptably high stress in the steel member itself.

Transferring a moment
Every moment can be resolved as one tensile and one compressive force component. Therefore, many of the above considerations also apply to the design of a reinforced concrete foundation to accommodate a moment.

If the moment is resolved as a vertical couple, then a base plate with cast-in threaded bars is recommended. The bars on the tension side carry the tension, the grout joint resists the compression. The distance of the threaded bars from the system axis determines the internal lever arm and hence the play of forces. The forces in the bars can only be reduced by enlarging the base plate. The base plate may require stiffening by means of ribs.

If the moment is resolved as a horizontal couple, then this can be accommodated very effectively by embedding the steel member or subsequently casting it into a pocket in a reinforced concrete foundation. Like with the cast-in components subjected to shear, care should be exercised to ensure that the considerable shear stresses induced by this type of foundation are not unacceptably high, especially in the case of thin-walled components.

Fixing steel members to steel foundations
Steel foundations usually take the form of piles beneath circular tubes or, less widespread, I-sections or special sections. The piles are driven by drop or vibratory hammers. They transfer axial tensile or compressive forces into the subsoil. Shear forces are resisted by raking piles, moments by pairs of piles. Piles subjected to bending are structurally inefficient and hence best avoided.

The connection of piles to other steel components, normally above the ground/water, follows the normal rules which apply to connections in steelwork generally and does not need any further clarification at this point. However, it is worth mentioning that piles can exhibit large positional tolerances and so connections must be detailed accordingly.

Part 5 • The formation of structures by assembling primary components

Werner Sobek
with Stefan Schäfer

The formation of structures by assembling primary components

The loadbearing structure as part of the whole construction

Fundamental initial considerations

In the chapter entitled "Shaping and connecting semifinished products to form primary components", we introduced and discussed the fundamental properties of primary components suitable for carrying tension, compression, bending or torsion. The jointing and connecting techniques available were explained in the same chapter in the section on different types of construction. Therefore, we now have the basic building blocks at our disposal in order to design loadbearing steelwork. How this is done and how such loadbearing steelwork interacts with the other systems in a structure and contributes to the overall architectural statement is outlined in this chapter. In doing so, the relationships are again established and clarified from the point of view of structural engineering. The reason behind this approach is a purely didactic one. It is not the intention that the loadbearing construction should always be seen as the main focus of attention in a structure, even one made from steel. Indeed, the loadbearing structure can sometimes be quite insignificant in architectural terms. However, this does not imply that ingenuity and thoroughness should be absent from the construction, even when the components themselves are no longer directly visible. This is not only a question of attitude. During erection, dismantling and recycling, if not sooner, such an approach will be seen to have been legitimate and indispensable.

Structure and loadbearing structure

The loadbearing structure is the outcome of the materialization of a structural system. Together with the materialized systems of
- building envelope,
- building services, and
- interior fitting-out,
it forms the structure.

Within this conglomerate of systems, the task of the loadbearing structure is to transmit to the subsoil all the forces acting on and in the structure. Consequently, the loadbearing structure is an indispensable part of any construction.

Depending on the overall architectural concept, the loadbearing structure may have a very demonstrative effect on the appearance of the construction or it may be completely masked by other architectural elements. Notwithstanding, a loadbearing structure must always be carefully designed and built in a way which is suited to the materials used and method of assembly as well as the desire for recycling.

Owing to the manifold interactions between the individual systems, these should be designed simultaneously within the planning process, interweaving them to the full. As these are usually highly detailed systems, cooperation between architect, structural engineer and the other specialist design teams involved, perhaps even the contractors, is imperative at the design stage. But initial good intentions to cooperate fully all too often fall by the wayside, leading to the all-too-familiar "sequential design". As we all know, this results in only partly optimized solutions and hence can never attain the status of an "art of building".

Primary and secondary loadbearing structures

Every component within a structure has to carry loads and transfer forces and is as such a loadbearing element and, at the same time, part of an overall loadbearing system. A lightweight partition carries its own weight and possibly light impact loads, a window pane transfers wind loads to its frame. Together, all these interlinked individual loadbearing structures form a highly complex system. To render this complex system more comprehensible and

easier to analyse, a complete structure is broken down into a hierarchy of subsystems. The primary structure comprises all those parts required to carry all the forces acting on a construction, including its own weight. Failure of the primary structure is associated with collapse of the entire construction. A number of secondary structures are integrated in or attached to the primary structure. Failure of one of these only results in local collapse, the structure as a whole remains stable. Larger or more complex buildings can even include tertiary structures in the hierarchy.
A strict and deliberate hierarchical analysis of the overall loadbearing system forms the basis for good structural design.
The hierarchy of individual loadbearing systems is explained below taking a high-rise building as an example:

Primary structure:
Loadbearing core, all columns, walls, floors and bracing required to carry horizontal and vertical loads.

Secondary structures:
Floors which are not part of the primary system; built-in items, partitions, roof structures and annexes; facade elements.

Tertiary structures:
All constructions which are part of the secondary structures and whose stability is not critical to the stability of those secondary structures, e.g. a window within a facade element.

The junctions between individual hierarchical levels within a whole structure usually coincide with a change of material or change of trades.

Designing the load-carrying paths

The forces in a loadbearing structure are carried in the way that the design engineer has intended.

There are no "intelligent" loadbearing systems or building materials. Those who speak about or speculate on such matters usually mean the unseen reserves of load-carrying capacity in a construction. But guessing and supposing does not belong to the process of designing, analysing and dimensioning a loadbearing

5.1 Megastructure: further constructions incorporated within a primary structure
5.2 Individual storeys suspended or supported on a catenary member (in tension)
5.3 Lack of residual stability: the loss of one component destroyed by an exploding gas cooker has caused the progressive collapse of a whole section of the building.

5.4 Statically determinate structure: failure of one member leads to collapse. Statically indeterminate structure: in certain circumstances the possibility of redistribution of forces prevents collapse if individual members fail.
5.5 Primary structure, Hong Kong & Shanghai Bank, Hong Kong (see p. 384)

5.6 The glass fin transmits the load and keeps deformations small; upon failure, the aluminium section guarantees residual stability.
5.7 A transfer structure transmits the loads from many columns to a few main columns.

construction; for the failure of a structure is always linked with a risk to people's lives and livelihoods. Therefore, although a good engineer will of course plan the transmission of forces within a structure based on a certain engineering instinct, the subsequent analysis and calculation of the members is carried out on an exclusively rational level, proving that the construction functions in a certain manner.

In statically determinate structures the forces in the individual components can only be controlled by altering the structural system or the geometry. For example, if the wind-induced moments at the base of the core of a high-rise block are too large, then the core can only be relieved by adding a second core, by bracing it or by linking the outer columns to it.

The repertoire of possible solutions is large: members subjected to high bending stresses may be considerably relieved by incorporating a hinge, closing hinges in regions subjected to low bending stresses attracts forces. Long diagonals which when subjected to compression would become unnecessarily massive due to the risk of buckling, can be designed as thin cables or ties. However, these only carry tension and are redundant in the compression case; the forces must then be carried by other members within the structure. The way in which the individual components are connected or separated allows the designer to control the load-carrying paths within the construction.

In the case of statically indeterminate structures, the range of design solutions is even broader: the paths of the forces can now also be influenced by the strain rigidity and flexural rigidity of individual elements. Stiff members normally attract forces and hence relieve less rigid parts. Consequently, by incorporating non-rigid or rigid zones the engineer can control the load-carrying paths in such a way that the loadbearing structure is optimized under the conditions of the overall construction.

5.1
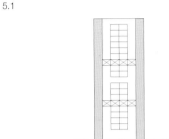

5.5
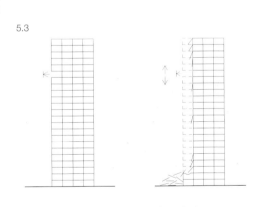

5.2
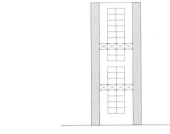

5.6

5.3
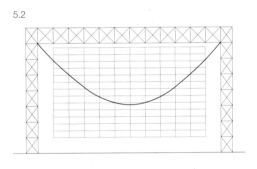

5.4
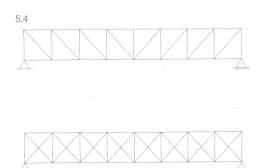

5.7

5.8   Designing load-carrying paths
5.9   Bundled tubes of varying heights: extremely stiff
      (pin-jointed) intermediate floors guarantee uniform
      compression of the individual columns [453]
5.10 Transfer structure: certainly lacking in rigidity
5.11 Transfer structure: usually 1-2 storeys high
5.12 Erection completed: concrete core compressed
      more than outer columns due to service loads and
      creep (schematic diagram)

5.13 Reverse situation: high axial compression of
      columns anticipated under load (schematic
      diagram)
5.14 Optimum pin-jointed frame after Maxwell for one
      point load and two point-like supports [486]
5.15 High-rise braced frame building with core
5.16 Storeys suspended from above
5.17 Storeys supported from below

5.18 Transfer structure supported on minimal ground-
      floor columns
5.19 Wind load resisted by off-centre core
5.20 Wind load resisted by central core
5.21 Pin-jointed frame: diagonals loaded in
      compression with wind in this direction
5.22 Diagonals loaded in tension

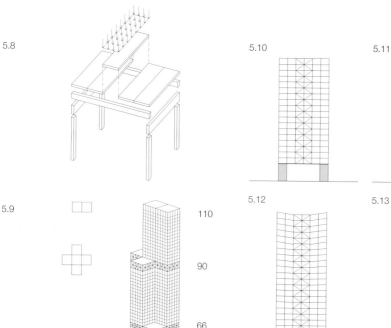

5.8

5.9

110

90

66

50

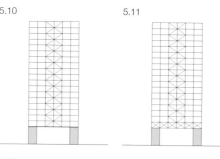

5.10   5.11

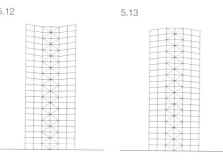

5.12   5.13

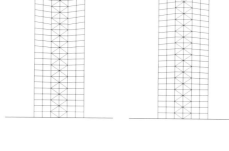

5.14

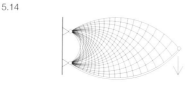

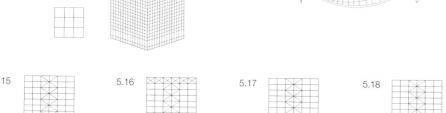

5.15   5.16   5.17   5.18

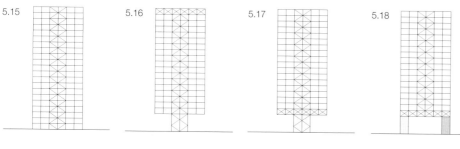

5.19   5.20   5.21   5.22

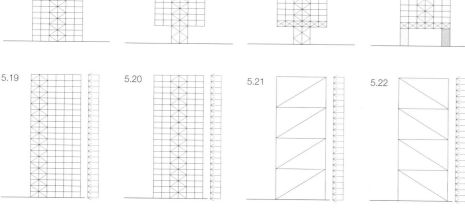

The design procedure itself is a reiterative process whose individual loops check a synthesis for a loadbearing system taking into account the needs of the whole structure by way of successive, strictly rational analyses (calculations) backed up by instinct and experience. If the outcome of the analysis does not satisfy the requirements profile (dimensions of cross-section, appearance, weight, cost, etc.), then a revised synthesis is propounded with broadened or modified boundary conditions.

Supporting vertical loads, three-dimensional bracing and overall stability

All the forces acting on and in a loadbearing structure can be resolved as components in such a way that they are applied in the x, y and z axes, i.e. two horizontal and one vertical direction. Considering the loadbearing system by way of such a grouping of the forces is very easy to follow.

Supporting the vertical forces is accomplished in a steel structure by means of steel or steel-concrete composite columns. Only rarely are reinforced concrete shear walls called upon to assist, although reinforced concrete cores are frequently used.

If the vertical loadbearing members are arranged in a vertical line throughout the height of the building, then carrying the loads presents no difficulties. Problems occur when columns are offset (something to avoid if possible!) or some perhaps omitted altogether (a common occurrence at ground floor level). Transfer structures are then required in order to pick up the loads and transmit them to another pair of columns. Such structures are always subjected to bending; they deflect and naturally cause the columns they carry to sink as well. This can lead to serious problems – in the facade construction too. Therefore, the aim with all such transfer structures is to make them as rigid as possible. Under heavy loads that can mean girders which are the depth of a storey and which lend themselves to being designed as pin-jointed frames.

With tall buildings in particular, the cross-sectional areas of the columns used to carry vertical forces should be chosen so that all

5.23 Relationship between quantity of steel and height
of building, increase due to dead loads and wind
[453]
5.24 Various options for bracing a steel frame
5.25 Possible arrangement of shear walls (plan)
5.26 Core for resisting horizontal wind loads
5.27 Typical deflected forms for braced and rigid
frames subjected to wind loads. The diagram
illustrates the enormous increase in stiffness
when the two systems are coupled. [453]

columns are subjected to a more or less equal
stress condition. The compression in the
columns is in this case approximately the
same, meaning that there are no problems
caused by differing deformations. When steel
or steel-concrete composite columns are combined with reinforced columns or cores, special attention should be given to the issue of
varying compression. Here, the time-related
compression of the concrete components due
to shrinkage and creep must be considered in
addition to equating the elastic compression.
In constructing high-rise blocks this sometimes
leads to the floors having to be built at an
angle in order to take up a horizontal position
after the culmination of all deformations.

To withstand horizontal loads, each horizontal
segment of a loadbearing system must include
at least three shear walls whose system planes
do not intersect at one point. Sometimes these
shear walls are also designated shear frames.
Such shear walls can include openings, which
may become so large that the walls become
rigid or braced frames, or triangulated column-
and-beam systems. In any case, however, the
ability to carry forces in the plane of the shear
wall must always be guaranteed. The transfer
of loads into and out of the shear walls is normally achieved via roof and floor plates. Once
again, these too may be open frames.

The vertical shear walls do not need to be
placed one above the other within a building,
they may be offset. In such a case, however,
the walls must be adequately supported by
columns. These then carry the vertical components of the load transmitted by a wall. The
horizontal components must be carried by
other elements, normally the floor plates, to
which the loadbearing shear walls are connected.

On plan the vertical shear walls should always
be arranged in such a way that they form sufficiently large lever arms with respect to each
other under the various horizontal loading
cases. This guarantees that the individual walls
are not unnecessarily highly loaded, which in
turn reduces their weight and the deformations.

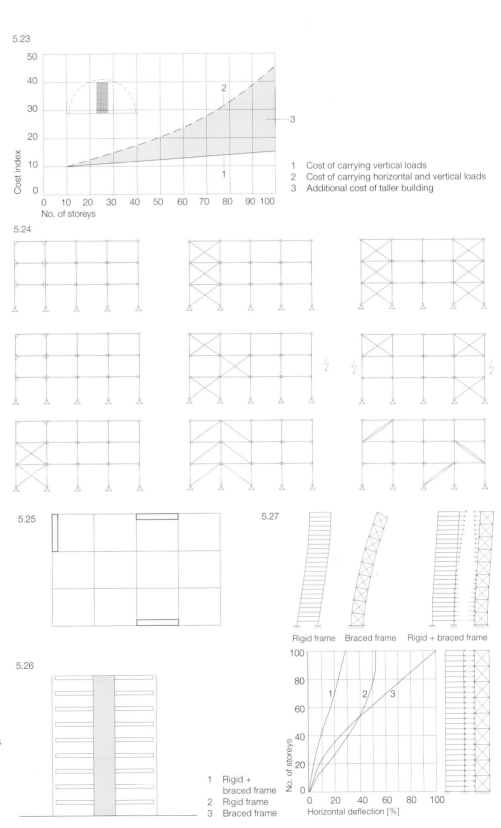

5.23

1 Cost of carrying vertical loads
2 Cost of carrying horizontal and vertical loads
3 Additional cost of taller building

5.24

5.25

5.26

5.27

Rigid frame Braced frame Rigid + braced frame

1 Rigid +
braced frame
2 Rigid frame
3 Braced frame

5.28 High-rise buildings: relationship between No. of storeys and suitability of type of structural system [440]

5.29 Bridges: relationship between span and suitability of type of structural system [453]

5.28

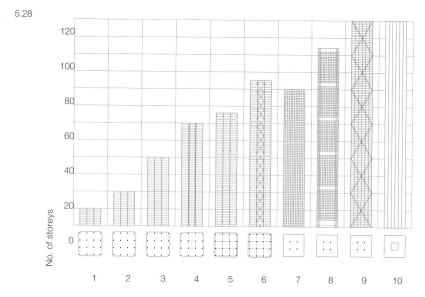

No. of storeys

1	2	3	4	5	6	7	8	9	10

1 Light frame
2 Rigid frame
3 Portal frame
4 Braced frame

5 Pin-jointed frame
6 Braced frame + pin-jointed frame
7 Tube

8 Framed tube
9 Diagonalized tube
10 Tube in tube

5.29

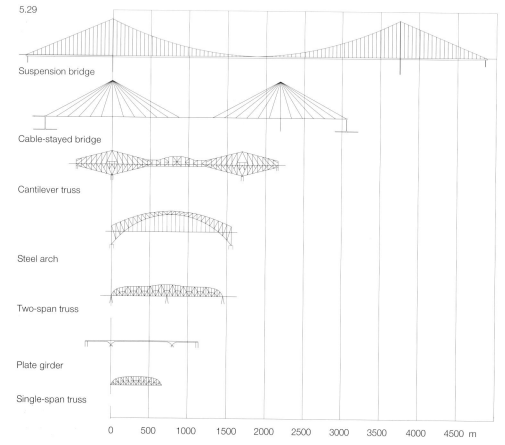

Suspension bridge

Cable-stayed bridge

Cantilever truss

Steel arch

Two-span truss

Plate girder

Single-span truss

0   500   1000   1500   2000   2500   3000   3500   4000   4500 m

When positioning the vertical shear walls within the plan, care should be exercised to ensure that longitudinal movement of the building, e.g. due to shrinkage of concrete floors but especially due to heating and cooling of the construction, is not hindered. These considerations govern the arrangement of the vertical shear walls in buildings with large plan dimensions and those where the loadbearing structure is placed externally.

A core can be considered as a system of four interlinked shear walls which together form a vertical hollow-section beam restrained at the base (subsoil or box foundation). The spacing between the walls is small, the internal lever arm of the construction correspondingly unfavourable. This leads to high forces, which are increased even further by the necessary access openings, e.g. for the lifts. In most situations reinforced concrete is specified for the core in order to satisfy fire protection requirements. A core for lifts and stairs is an ideal element for resisting horizontal loads on low- and medium-rise buildings. But in very tall buildings the deformations of the non-rigid, slender core are extreme. While this may be acceptable for television towers, in office or residential blocks the core must be relieved by including other elements, or its plan size enlarged as far as the external facade of the building.

Horizontal loads, which act on the building at all levels, always lead to additional vertical force components which have to be carried by the columns. These can be dealt with at foundation level if not before, also in the form of moments.

If we regard an entire loadbearing system, including its foundation, as a rigid and stable construction in itself, then the final question we must address is the overall stability of this unyielding edifice. Under the action of horizontal forces this rigid body can, under certain conditions, slide along the soil-structure interface or overturn in its entirety. Both of these effects, sliding and overturning, have to be prevented by suitable design of the structure and its foundation. In addition, a lightweight structure could experience uplift under the action of the wind.

Loads and forces

Introductory remarks

The actions of loads and forces on loadbearing systems are the causes of the reactions of and deformations to those systems. These loads and forces include:
- dead loads (including self-weight)
- imposed loads
- wind
- snow
- earthquakes
- ground settlements
- temperature fluctuations
- impact
- pretensioning

Loads and forces may be static or dynamic. The nature of the loads and forces acting on a component or structure are normally known but, apart from dead loads, when they might occur and the level of their intensity (magnitude) are – to a certain extent – unpredictable.

The greater the number of possible loads and forces, the smaller is the chance that their effects will occur simultaneously, or that their extreme values will coincide. Therefore, the loads and forces expected to occur – and which are to be used in the verification of stability and serviceability – are based on collective experience and statistical analysis. Plausibility considerations lead to the formulation of so-called loading cases in which probable simultaneous loads and forces are combined. Within these loading cases, so-called combination factors and, if applicable, special factors specific to the application (e.g. reduction in vertical imposed loads for multistorey buildings) are used to reduce – in line with statistical criteria – the maximum values of the loads and forces prescribed in standards and similar regulations.

Stresses and strains

The actions of loads and forces give rise to stresses and strains in the materials. These may be static or dynamic, depending on the nature of the actions.

The stresses and strains are countered by the properties of the materials, the components and the fasteners. These properties are not single values but instead are dependent on the

5.30

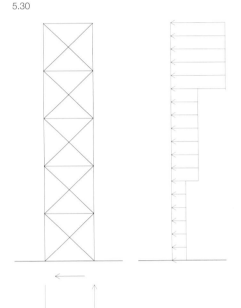

5.31

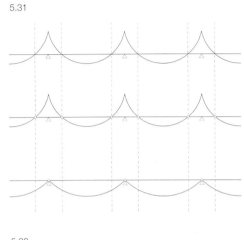

5.32

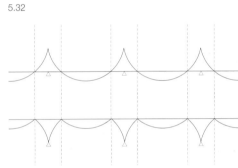

5.33

Sliding

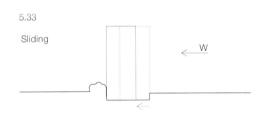

Overturning

Uplift

5.34

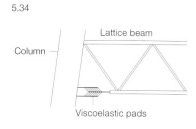

Column

Lattice beam

Viscoelastic pads

Viscoelastic pads

nature of the loads and forces, the material and the type of construction. Each material is assigned a series of characteristic mechanical values; however, these values, e.g. yield strength, vary, for example, within the cross-section of a rolled section, are highly dependent on the plate thicknesses of rolled products and, furthermore, are a function of the temperature of the component.

Yield stresses or ultimate strengths are determined at a standard temperature in quasi static tests. If in reality the rate of load application is very fast or the loads act dynamically, then these values are no longer applicable. Accordingly, permissible stresses and strains must be carefully assessed, taking into account all influencing variables. An important distinction is made between structures subjected to "primarily static loads" and those subjected to "primarily non-static loads". The former can be analysed based on a quasi static approach, ignoring fatigue effects due to dynamic loading. And if the structure is used in a normal temperature range, then this simplifies the design considerably.

At component level, permissible stresses and strains are once again determined not only by the material properties but, for example, by local or global stability issues. The influence of the connections, i.e. the type of construction, is also relevant.

Loads and forces in detail
Dead loads (including self-weight)
The dead loads carried by a steel construction can be established relatively easily and accurately. However, computer-assisted weight calculations for steel constructions in particular often forget to include the weights of fasteners, gusset plates and cleats as well as base plates and stiffeners. Depending on the type of construction, these components can account for 15-20% of the total weight and hence should not be ignored.

Imposed loads
These vary depending on the use of the structure and can include
- interior fittings and furniture
- people
- machines
- stored goods
- moving or parked vehicles

The values of the imposed loads to be used in a structural analysis are normally prescribed by standards. In special instances though they may be specified jointly by the engineer, the client and the supervising authority or institution.

It should be pointed out that some imposed loads can cause horizontal forces in addition to vertical ones. For example, bulk goods stored in silos exert considerable horizontal pressure on the walls; braking vehicles, especially heavy ones, exert a horizontal braking load on the construction.

Moving imposed loads
Imposed loads which do not necessarily remain in one fixed location give rise to varying deformations in the structure over time. If these time-related varying deformations occur at regular intervals, then they are perceived as vibrations.
Such vibrations can lead to
- compromised user satisfaction,
- disruptions to mechanized production,
- noise,
- damage to building components.

Owing to their low weight and low inherent damping, steel structures are particularly susceptible to such movement-induced excitation. Therefore, a careful check must be made in every case to ascertain whether people, groups of people or vehicles could generate vibrations in a structure. If vibrations do arise, then their frequency and amplitude will determine whether or not they are acceptable. Peo-

ple react very sensitively to certain frequency ranges and amplitudes; however, there are other ranges, e.g. production facilities for microtechnology or in microscopic surgery, in which far lower acceptance thresholds are common (see "Structures: stability, serviceability and design").

If the predicted or actual vibrations are unacceptable in terms of frequency and/or amplitude, then either the cause, i.e. the exciter, must be manipulated or, if that is not possible, the construction itself. Altering mass, stiffness or inherent damping can modify the vibration response. Further, by incorporating active or passive dampers it is possible to bring about a permanent change in the vibration response.

When the frequency induced by the moving imposed load coincides with one of the natural frequencies of the construction, total collapse is the inevitable result. If such a danger is recognized, then either the exciting frequency or the natural frequency must be altered. One example of changing an exciting frequency is the rule that soldiers should "break step", i.e. not march, when crossing bridges. Modifying the natural frequency is achieved by changing the mass or stiffness of the structure, or the distribution of that mass or stiffness. Manipulating the damping does not lead to a change in the natural frequency.

Oscillating imposed loads
Machines, bells and skipping/jumping machinery represent a special case. These can cause vibration of the whole structure, depending on their mass and oscillating or movement frequency. The exciting frequencies and the natural frequencies of the structure must be selected with a sufficiently large margin between them. If it is not possible to adjust the exciting frequency, then the natural frequency of the steel construction must be modified by altering the mass or stiffness. Dampers can also be incorporated.

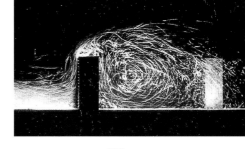

Compared to reinforced concrete structures, steel structures possess only very low inherent damping, so they are particularly sensitive to oscillating imposed loads, e.g. machines.

Wind

The stresses and strains in a construction that arise due to the action of wind loads are very complex and hence difficult to appraise accurately. On the other hand, it seems pointless to expend a great deal of time and effort on optimizing the weight of a structure and in the same breath be satisfied with extremely rough approximations with regard to the governing forces and loads. As wind loading represents, for most cases, the critical horizontal design load, a careful evaluation of the effects of wind loads is advisable for every single structure. In doing so it should not be forgotten that the such effects are largely dependent on the form and location of the structure. So the effects of wind can be influenced by the designer to a great extent!

Only at high altitudes can the wind be assumed to be an approximately laminar flow. At the levels at which the laminar flow interacts with the structured surface of the Earth, the flow becomes turbulent, i.e. eddies varying in magnitude and with differing energy densities are formed. Hence, the speed of the flow near the surface is not constant in terms of time and place. Every measurement of wind speed indicates this typical fluctuating progression characterized by turbulence. If these turbulence-related velocity fluctuations have a high periodicity and sufficient energy density, then this can lead to excitation of the structure; we speak of gust-induced vibration. Of course, the designer must ensure that the exciting frequency of the wind does not coincide with the natural frequency of the building. Turbulence-related velocity fluctuations with high periodicity, in the form of so-called wake buffeting, can arise as the wind passes neighbouring buildings.

5.35

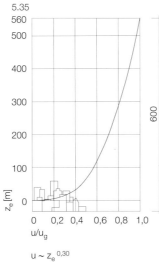

$u \sim z_e^{0,30}$

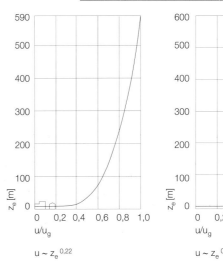

$u \sim z_e^{0,22}$

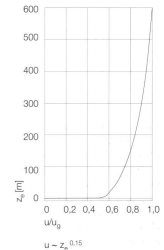

$u \sim z_e^{0,15}$

5.36

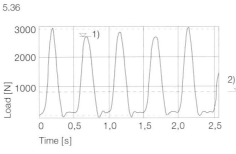

1 F_{p}, max
2 $G = 810$ N

5.37

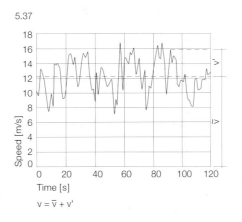

$v = \bar{v} + v'$

5.38

Scale No.	Speed m/s			General effects
0	Dead calm	to	0.2	Smoke rises vertically
1	0.3	to	1.5	Shown by smoke
2	1.6	to	3.3	Breeze felt on face, leaves rustle
3	3.4	to	5.4	Leaves and small twigs in motion
4	5.5	to	7.9	Small branches move, dust and paper rise
5	8.0	to	10.7	Small trees in leaf sway
6	10.8	to	13.8	Large branches in motion, telegraph wires whistle
7	13.9	to	17.1	Whole trees in motion, walking inconvenient
8	17.2	to	20.7	Twigs break off, walking impeded
9	20.8	to	24.4	Slight structural damage
10	24.5	to	28.4	Trees uprooted, structural damage
11	28.5	to	32.6	Widespread damage
12	32.7	to	36.9	Very rare inland, very severe damage
13	37.0	to	41.0	Only at sea and on the coast, widespread devastation
14	41.1	to	46.0	
15	46.1	to	50.9	
16	51.0	to	56.0	
17	>		56.0	

5.39

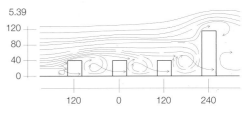

5.40 Wind flows past a building [420]
5.41 Distribution of wind pressure on the surface of a
     building for a certain wind direction [420]
5.42 Von Karmann vortex street: formed, for example,
     by the periodic shedding of vortices as air flows
     past a smooth cylindrical body. [414]
5.43 Wind deflectors on steel chimneys to avoid
     periodic shedding of vortices in windy situations
     [440]

5.40

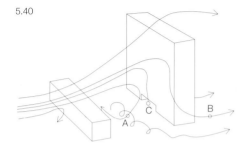

5.41

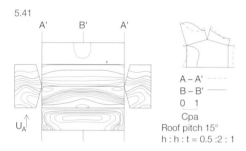

A – A' -----
B – B' ——
0   1
Cpa
Roof pitch 15°
h : h : t = 0.5 : 2 : 1

5.42

5.43

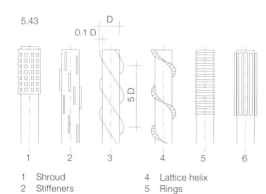

1   Shroud
2   Stiffeners
3   Scruton helix
4   Lattice helix
5   Rings
6   Vertical plates

To ease the design process, a mean wind speed is calculated from the measured and very complex wind speed profile. Basically, it is assumed that the mean wind speed decreases towards ground level. The progression of the mean wind speed with respect to height depends on the roughness – and hence the density of the built environment – of the Earth's surface.

As the flow passes the structure the individual air molecules are deflected from their original trajectories and diverted around the structure. Such trajectories are called streamlines and the space occupied by several streamlines a flow tube. As the flow passes a structure, zones of both higher and lower velocities build up, indeed even wakes can ensue. A laminar flow is disrupted upon passing a building; the turbulence structure of the natural (turbulent) wind is altered correspondingly upon passing a building. Measurements of wind speed at the surface of a building reveal different wind speed profiles at every point on the surface, and hence varying mean wind speeds.

In flowing up to an obstacle the velocity of some streamlines is braked to zero at the so-called stagnation point. If we use the Bernoulli equation to assess the velocity of the streamline and the atmospheric pressure well ahead of the obstacle in relation to the circumstances at the stagnation point, then we obtain an increase in pressure (compared to the atmospheric pressure). This pressure rise is called the dynamic pressure q.

In flowing past an object there are some regions in which the flow tubes are constricted. The velocity of the flow increases in such regions and a negative pressure (compared to atmospheric pressure) builds up. Likewise, as the flow passes the object there are other areas in which the flow tubes widen. The velocity of the flow increases in such areas and an over-

pressure (compared to atmospheric pressure) builds up. These negative and positive pressures p are placed in an equation with the dynamic pressure q:

$$p = c\,q$$

where c = local pressure/suction coefficient.

The coefficient c is normally measured at certain points on a structure in wind tunnel tests. Computer-assisted, mathematical/numerical calculations for determining the local pressure/ suction coefficients are still the exception, even with the simplest of buildings, owing to the complexity of the flow.

The pressure/suction coefficient related to a surface unit of a structure is designated c_p. This coefficient, dependent on form of structure and wind direction, is either obtained from tables or measured in wind tunnel tests. Therefore, the local wind load acting per surface unit is

$$w = c_p\,q$$

Of course, the value c_p is subjected to severe fluctuations along the edges, corners and surfaces of a building. In the tabular method this fact is normally covered by using a primary, uniform value for the surface and secondary, higher values for edges, recesses, etc. This is only a safe approximation of the actual situation. Owing to the multitude of possible structural forms, the relevant codes of practice make use of a small range of standard cases. Just like the need for a particularly lean design, geometries which deviate from these or particularly complex shapes should be a signal to call in an expert to assess the wind effects and/or carry out wind tunnel tests. In the majority of cases a wind tunnel test pays for itself in terms of savings in building materials, fasteners or the foundation.

5.44 Standard snow loads [475]
5.45 Snow load reduction factors for roof pitch [475]
5.46 Snow load zones for Germany [475]

5.44

Standard snow load s_0 in kN/m²

Snow load zone (see 5.46)[1]	Altitude of site [2] above mean sea level (m)									
	≤ 200	300	400	500	600	700	800	900	1000	>1000[3]
I	0.75	0.75	0.75	0.75	0.85	1.05	1.25			
II	0.75	0.75	0.75	0.90	1.15	1.50	1.85	2.30		
III	0.75	0.75	1.00	1.25	1.60	2.00	2.55	3.10	3.80	
IV	1.00	1.15	1.55	2.10	2.60	3.25	3.90	4.65	5.50	

[1] For sites on the boundary between two snow load zones, s_0 may be taken as the arithmetic mean of the two snow loads. Otherwise, the higher of the two s_0 values should be used. In Berlin standard snow load s_0 = 0,75 kN/m².
[2] For altitudes which lie between the given figures, the s_0 value may be interpolated from a straight line between two adjacent values. Otherwise, the s_0 value for the next higher attitude should be used.
[3] Determined by the authority responsible in consultation with the Central Office of the German Meteorological Service in Offenbach.

The integral of the pressure/suction coefficients over the building surface corresponds to the global pressure/suction coefficient, called the shape coefficient c_f. Accordingly, the total wind load acting on a structure is

$$W = c_f\, q\, A$$

where A = projected building surface perpendicular to direction of flow.

In considering the action of the wind on a building it should not be forgotten that negative pressure or overpressure could ensue inside a building as a result of the wind flow. Open doors, windows, etc. can permit a corresponding pressure/suction to build up inside the building. This internal effect is usually uniformly distributed over a large area and is superimposed on the external pressure/suction. This can lead to roofs being torn off or whole buildings being lifted.

The danger of gust-excited vibrations brought about by cyclic gusting of the wind acting on the structure and a corresponding sensitivity of the structure has already been discussed. Another way of causing excitations is through so-called "vortex-induced vibrations", sometimes known as "self-induced vibrations". These vibrations are caused by vortices being shed from the building itself. Smooth cylindrical structures are particularly at risk. This regular shedding of vortices, in the form of a Von Karmann vortex street (or trail), has been observed many times on chimneys, radio masts and cooling towers. The vortices shed from alternating sides lead to an oscillation transverse to the wind direction; in some instances the structure collapses as a result. Preventing the regularity of the shedding, e.g. by roughening the surface with the help of helices or other devices welded on, helps to reduce the danger of vortex-induced vibrations.

5.45

α	0°	1°	2°	3°	4°	5°	6°	7°	8°	9°
0-30°										
30°	1.00	0.97	0.95	0.92	0.90	0.87	0.85	0.82	0.80	0.77
40°	0.75	0.72	0.70	0.67	0.65	0.62	0.60	0.57	0.55	0.52
50°	0.50	0.47	0.45	0.42	0.40	0.37	0.35	0.32	0.30	0.27
60°	0.25	0.22	0.20	0.17	0.15	0.12	0.10	0.07	0.05	0.02
70-90°	0									

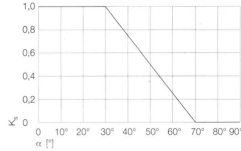

Snow
Snow of medium density has a mass of approx. 1.0 kN/m³, particularly wet snow can reach 2.0-2.5 kN/m³ at any time.

The (standard) snow load s_0 which may come to rest on a horizontal surface is determined on the basis of meteorological data and experience. It varies from region to region and of course with the altitude of the location of the structure. The snow load s_0 to be used in the structural calculations is normally found from snow load zone maps and the relevant standards.

The standards normally permit the snow load on a pitched roof to be reduced with respect to a horizontal surface, the reduction depending on the angle of slope. This takes into account the fact that snow lying on a pitched roof will

5.46

Zones I, II   Zone III   Zone IV

—··— Snow load zone boundary between zones I and II
——— Snow load zone boundary between zones II, III and IV

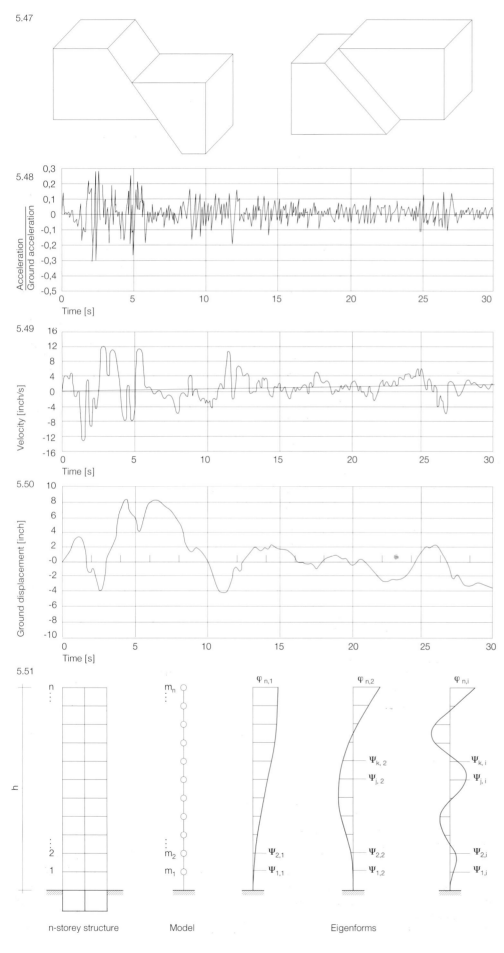

5.47

5.48

5.49

5.50

5.51

n-storey structure   Model   Eigenforms

5.47 Horizontal and vertical displacement of the subsoil as a result of earthquakes
5.48 Earthquake: chronological progression of ground acceleration [453]
5.49 Earthquake: chronological progression of ground velocity [453]
5.50 Earthquake: chronological progression of ground displacement [453]
5.51 Eigenforms of a high-rise building of storey-height frames [331]

tend to slide off and so the total load on the roof will be less than that on a horizontal surface. However, irrespective of the geometry of the roof, corresponding accumulations of snow, caused by slippage or drifting, must be allowed for in the form of additional snow loading. Such piles of snow may at any time give rise to a load many times that of the standard snow load.

With complicated roof forms, long-span constructions and whenever the external influences need to be appraised as accurately as possible without hidden safety margins, it is recommended that a snow report be drawn up by an expert. This normally makes use of detailed meteorological evaluations coupled with extensive knowledge of the local snow conditions and, if necessary, tests in wind tunnels which can simulate the effects of drifting snow.

Earthquakes
Earthquakes are caused by a number of geophysical factors. One of their effects is irregular horizontal and vertical movement of the subsoil over a period of time. The strength of these ground movements varies depending on the seismic region in which the structure is located. In many regions at risk of earthquakes the vertical movement of the subsoil can be neglected when designing the loadbearing system for seismic loading.

Only movements of the subsoil varying over a period of time, i.e. ground accelerations, exert forces on the structure. The nature and magnitude of these forces depend on the distribution of mass and stiffness within the structure as well as the ground accelerations themselves. These facts give rise to a number of considerations concerning the design of a structure in an earthquake zone:

On plan:
• Stiffness centroid and mass centroid should be as close as possible to each other in order to avoid rotational movements.
• Symmetrical arrangement of components transmitting horizontal loads
• Regular plan layout
• Uniform foundations

5.52 "Straightening" an unevenly loaded ground
slab by adding ballast to voids in the cores
5.53 Damage to existing building caused by
new structure
5.54 Damage to existing building caused by
new structure

In section:
• Foundations projecting well beyond the
structure in order to be able to accommodate overturning moments.
• Stiffness remaining constant with the height,
never being allowed to increase.
• No sudden changes of stiffness.
• Heavy loads placed on the lower floors,
ideally in the basement.

Design is carried out with the help of:
• equivalent forces method
• response spectra analysis
• time-history method (dynamic analysis with
effects varying over time)

The directions and magnitudes of ground
accelerations during earthquakes are not constant. This causes load reversals and a changing intensity of loading on the structure. If the
alternation of the ground acceleration exhibits
a sufficiently high periodicity, then the structure
or parts thereof can start to oscillate. Damage
to the structure depends on the magnitude of
these vibrations, which in turn depend on the
distribution of mass and stiffness and well as
the damping. When the frequency of the
ground movement coincides with the structure's natural frequency, collapse of the structure is inevitable.

Ground settlements
Foundations settle after completion of a structure due to deformation of the subsoil. There
are various reasons for this:
• A marked alteration in the imposed loads
• Drying out of the subsoil as a result of a
lowering of the water table
• Unforeseen inhomogeneities in the subsoil,
e.g. lens-shaped inclusions of comparatively
soft ground or even cavities in the ground.
• Incorrectly computed settlement calculations
• Erection or demolition of a neighbouring
structure

Apart from high-rise blocks, where an incorrectly assessed subsoil can lead to unacceptable even settlement of the building as a result
of the high loads, incorrect forecasts in terms
of even foundation settlements are generally
less critical. However, uneven subsoil deformations frequently lead to unacceptable deform-

ation of the structure itself and, depending on
the loadbearing system, sometimes to dramatic redistributions of forces within a loadbearing system. Such redistributions can mean that
some components become overstressed and
may even fail. Therefore, a careful evaluation of
the subsoil, i.e. the bottommost part of a structure, is always essential. The construction of a
building, its loadbearing structure in particular,
has to be matched to the subsoil conditions.

Uneven subsoil deformations normally manifest
themselves as uneven vertical deformations,
only rarely as horizontal effects. If uneven vertical deformations are expected or, at least,
cannot be ruled out, then structures very stiff in
themselves require supports which are statically
determinate. Such supports require a hinged/
non-sliding as well as a hinged/sliding bearing
for two-dimensional loadbearing systems.
In the case of three-dimensional systems, statically determinate supports require one hinged/
non-sliding as well as two hinged/ sliding bearings, although one of these latter two should
only have one axis of movement, which, however, must pass through the non-sliding bearing. So a statically determinate support to a
three-dimensional loadbearing system stiff in
itself may not have more than three supports.
("A three-legged stool doesn't wobble.") If a
loadbearing system is to have more than three
supports, then it should be designed with
appropriate hinges in the system – without en-
dangering the overall stability. This can be
accomplished in diverse ways. In two-dimensional loadbearing systems comprising linear
members, the hinged girder is probably the
best known type of system; with arches the
two-pin form is suitable for accommodating
vertical subsoil deformations free from restraint
stresses.

With three-dimensional systems the braced
frames with hinged connections between
columns and trusses as well as trusses and
core exhibit similar properties.

If uneven horizontal subsoil deformations are
also to be expected or, at least, cannot be
ruled out, then the designer should proceed
similarly to the above but now arrange all
movements in the horizontal plane. Conse-

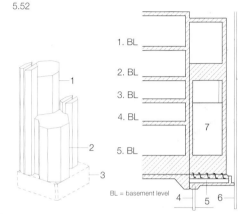

5.52

1. BL
2. BL
3. BL
4. BL
5. BL

7

BL = basement level

4 5 6

1	23 storeys (thereof 10 tower storeys)	4	Sheet piling
2	13 storeys (full storeys)	5	Void
3	5 basement levels	6	Support to side of excavation
		7	Ballast

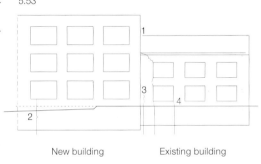

5.53

1
3
4
2

New building   Existing building

1 Joint
2 Settlement caused by new building
3 New building causing settlement of gable on existing building
4 Cracks in masonry to outer and inner leaves

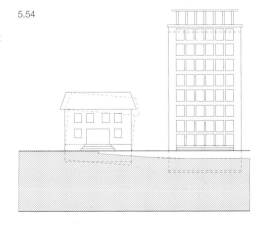

5.54

5.55 Deformation due to heating on one side can
assume an enormous order of magnitude
(schematic)

5.56 Deformation due to + ΔT related to bracing position. In some circumstances buckling of the
beams can only be prevented by incorporating
axial force hinges.

5.55

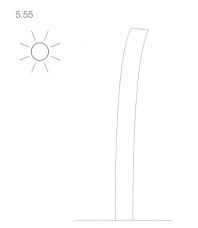

5.56

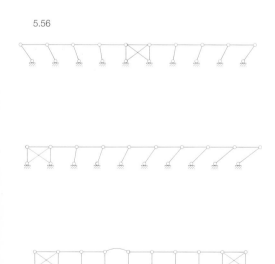

quently, a hinged girder is also given freedom
of movement at the Gerber hinge (longitudinal
force hinge); an arched structure is provided
with a third hinge for accommodating horizontal and vertical subsoil deformations free from
restraint stresses.

Temperature fluctuations
Changes of temperature within a component or
a structure may have a number of causes. The
most frequent of these are:
* heating or cooling of the atmosphere (day-
night, summer-winter,...)
* heating-up due to solar radiation
* heating or cooling inside the building
* fire
* liberation of heat of hydration during curing
of cementitious components

Steel components expand upon heating and
contract upon cooling.

In doing so, the following applies:
$\varepsilon_T = \alpha_T \triangle_T$

where
ε_T = expansion due to temperature change
α_T = coefficient of thermal expansion
   ($\alpha_T = 12 \times 10^{-6}$ for steel)
$\triangle_T$ = temperature change in K

Temperature-related changes in the length of a
component or a structure can assume huge
orders of magnitude. For instance, the length
of a 1000 m suspension bridge changes by
480 mm as a result of a summer-winter temperature difference of 40 K.

If temperature-related changes in the length of
a component are hindered, e.g. by certain
means of support or by combining them with
unheated components, then restraint forces
build up in the component; their magnitude
can be calculated as follows:

$\sigma = E \, \varepsilon_T$
$\sigma = E \, \alpha_T \triangle_T$

Therefore, a rise in temperature of 30 K in a
member prevented from expanding gives rise
to an additional stress of 75.6 N/mm². From this
we can see that restrictions placed on expan-

sion should not be ignored in the case of a fire
or for loadbearing systems subjected to atmospheric temperature changes or solar radiation. Forms of construction which prevent the
occurrence of such restraint forces, or at least
minimize them, are recommended.

Completely enclosed loadbearing structures
undergo their largest temperature fluctuations
during construction. The temperature of the
components rises by up to 40-60 K, depending
on their colour. The expansion of the components is, initially, not critical. However, at
places where expansion is prevented, corresponding restraint forces build up. Expansion is
often hindered by fixing the components to the
foundation or other items whose expansion is
zero or only minimal. In these cases appropriate hinges and/or expansion joints are to be
provided.

So-called mixed structures – structures whose
loadbearing systems consist of different materials – require special attention in terms of temperature fluctuations. On the one hand, different materials have differing coefficients of thermal expansion (e.g. glass and steel) and, on
the other, the components heat up at dissimilar
rates owing to their different colours, cross-
sections and thermal inertias.

In high-rise blocks with exposed columns,
there is a temperature difference between the
south-west side, receiving maximum solar radiation, and the north and east sides, which are
shaded in the afternoon. If we assume a temperature difference of just 20 K, then the south-
west side of a 400-m-high building would
become approx. 96 mm taller than the north
and east sides – without doubt an unacceptable situation. Therefore, in high-rise buildings
with exposed columns the structure must either
be
* thermally insulated and cased (e.g. John
Hancock Tower, Chicago),
* tempered with the exhaust air of the air-
conditioning plant (e.g. Hong Kong &
Shanghai Bank, Hong Kong), or
* made thermally inert, e.g. by filling hollow
columns with water (e.g. US Steel Building,
Pittsburg).

Pretensioned structures exposed to atmospheric temperature changes or solar radiation retain their pretensioned state upon heating or cooling only when the system of forces is a closed one. This includes, for example, spoked wheels on floating bearings or cable-stayed columns with statically determinate bearings. In all other cases, e.g. Jawerth trusses or cable nets pretensioned against the foundation, the pretension changes by 2.5 N/mm^2 per 1 K of heating or cooling. If the loadbearing system is to retain a sufficiently large (residual) pretension under the appropriate loading conditions, then the pretension must be increased by an amount equal to the expected loss of pretension upon heating. When the system cools down, a further increase in the pretension occurs due to the contraction being restricted.

The inclusion of springs or active force-control systems can overcome the need to increase the pretension to avoid the effects caused by heating and cooling.

Impact
Near roads and railways, loadbearing structures must be designed to cope with the potential impact of vehicles and trains. Furthermore, the impact of vehicles and their loads whose height exceeds local restrictions is also possible. Bridges with piers in navigation channels must also reckon with the impact of a boat or ship.

In all these cases, impact is best prevented by suitable defensive measures, e.g. deflectors, barriers, derailment protection, etc. If this is not possible or not desirable, then calculations are required to verify that an impact does not lead to loss of stability. Equivalent static loads are usually employed for such calculations; incidentally, impact in the direction of travel and at right-angles to it must be considered. So the dynamic is translated into a quasi static problem in order to simplify the analysis. The relevant standards prescribe the equivalent loads to be used.

Pretensioning
Whether pretensioning forces should be counted among the loads and forces acting on a structure is disputed in engineering circles. Never-

theless, pretensioning has been deliberately included here because it should be regarded as an intentional manipulation of the internal force condition of a construction.

Pretensioning gives rise to stresses and strains. Sometimes the aim of this is to increase the permissible stresses and strains, sometimes merely to limit the deformations.

A pretensioning force can be introduced into a construction in a variety of ways. The method chosen depends on whether its magnitude is to remain constant or change over time. This in turn has an effect on the way the system is analysed and its safety appraised.

The pretension can change over time when it is influenced by
• creep and shrinkage
• temperature changes
• load variations

This is the case in most types of construction. Pretensioning with ballast, springs or other force-controlling measures enables the pretensioning force to be kept constant.

Applying the customary design safety factors to the pretensioning system is generally incorrect because the pretensioning force is specifically introduced, monitored and documented; its value is not subject to the usual scatter. At the same time, however, it is reasonable to vary the underlying degree of pretension by ±10% in the design in order to take into account possible excess or deficient tensioning.

5.57

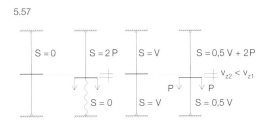

5.58

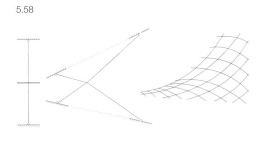

5.59

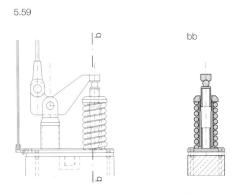

Structures:
stability, serviceability and design

The principles of modern safety concepts

The key function of any loadbearing construction is to carry the forces acting on it while, at the same time, keeping the deformations within acceptable limits. Both of these aspects must be verified by the engineer. This verification process is normally performed before actual construction begins, so the engineer's work is really a prognosis concerning the behaviour of a (usually) comparatively complex construction subjected to the effects of comparatively complex loads.

The verification process has to examine two conditions:

Firstly, in the so-called ultimate condition the aim is to prove that the structure as a whole and its individual components remain stable under the action of the anticipated loads and forces, i.e. that the construction will not fail. The effects of both static and dynamic loads and forces must be taken into account.

Secondly, in the so-called service condition the aim is to prove that the deformation and vibration behaviour of the structure as a whole and its individual components remain within certain defined, acceptable limits under the action of the anticipated loads and forces. Here too, both static and dynamic effects must be taken into account.

Basically, verification of load-carrying capacity and serviceability indicate that a loadbearing system possesses adequate reliability. The verification process should demonstrate that the probability of a loadbearing system reaching its ultimate limit states (e.g. collapse) or serviceability limit states (e.g. unacceptable deformation) remains within acceptable (low) limits. Any forecast of ultimate stability or serviceability is therefore a statement on the reliability of a construction, based on probability appraisals. We can deduce from this that 100% reliability is unattainable.

The magnitudes of all loads and forces can only be appraised in terms of what is likely to occur with a high degree of probability. For example, the snow loads on a roof during one winter vary considerably; comparing individual winters reveals further considerable scatter in the maximum snow loads measured. So it is vital to decide which snow load is to be used as the basis for a design: the load with a probability that it only occurs once every 50 years, or the one with a probability of occurring every 100 years? The latter is much heavier and so leads to larger components and hence to greater consumption of material and energy. This fact is not without its consequences for the economy and the environment.

On the other hand, once a low snow load is chosen, is there a high probability that this will be exceeded during the lifetime of the structure? Damage and even collapse are the likely outcomes. Therefore, the engineer always has to try to apply plausible loads whose likelihood of being exceeded is as low as possible. This has repercussions on the cost of a structure. High quality in construction, coupled with a low probability of damage occurring, is therefore de facto also an expression of a society's prosperity, its ability to fund such structures.

A loadbearing system has to carry, to resist the loads and forces exerted on it. The magnitude of this resistance depends on, for example, the materials used, the dimensions of the components and the means of connection. But these too are subjected to a certain scatter with respect to their properties. For example, the ultimate strength of a material is not constant but rather distributed about a mean value. So the resistance of a construction, like the loads and forces acting on it, is not a constant value.

Therefore, the individual influencing variables determining the reliability of the construction are multiplied by various safety factors in order to take account of the varying probabilities of occurrence and distributions of the various loads and forces as well as resistances. Variables which can be relatively accurately collated, e.g. self-weight of a component, are given lower safety factors, while those variables which are more difficult to measure are given higher ones.

The method used to provide the individual influencing variables with differing safety factors is called the "method of partial safety factors" (part of the limit state design method).

If we call the number j of stresses and strains occurring S_j and the acceptable stresses and strains of the construction R, then the verification equation (inequality) to be satisfied is:

$$v_1 S_1 + v_2 S_2 + v_3 S_3 \ldots \leq R/v_R$$

where v_j = individual safety factor.

The verification analysis has to be carried out separately for each loading case. If several groups of loads occur simultaneously, then supplementary combination factors are introduced. These are based on statistical evaluations and permit the magnitudes of the loads and forces, or rather the partial safety factors, to be reduced.

Using a simple example, let us look at how a component is sized according to the method of partial safety factors.
Single-span beam carrying dead loads only, design for bending:
- Partial safety factor for dead load
  $v_{dead} = 1.35$
- Partial safety factor for grade St 37 steel
  $v_{steel} = 1.1$

The maximum bending moment caused by the dead loads multiplied by the factor 1.35 results in a maximum stress. This stress may not exceed the acceptable (yield) strength of the steel divided by 1.1.

Until a few years ago verifying the ultimate stability of a construction was carried out using the "method of permissible stresses". In this method a stress caused by a load or force (not multiplied by a partial safety factor) was compared with a "permissible", i.e. acceptable, stress for the material which had been reduced by a safety factor.

Analyses using the permissible stress approach were quicker to perform than those employing the method of partial safety factors, which is why the former method enjoyed a certain popularity for a long time. Apart from the fact that, in many countries, this method of analysis is no longer approved, the method of partial safety factors has a number of advantages over permissible stress design:
- The individual influencing variables are dealt with separately and on the same high level of safety.
- This raises the overall level of safety.

5.60 Sandwich panel of steel facings and polyurethane core: buckling of compression zone as a result of overstressing

5.61 Sliding, overturning and uplift

- The method permits more economical construction.
- In the case of a non-linear correlation between an increase in the load or force and the associated increase in the stresses and strains in a member, the method of permissible stresses could lead to a reduced factor of safety.

The disadvantages of the method of partial safety factors are:
- The method is less convenient in its application.
- Not all national standards and statutory instruments have been converted to this newer method. This still leads to problems in loadbearing systems comprising a mixture of materials, for example. However, the use of Eurocodes overcomes this problem.

Neither the method of partial safety factors nor the method of permissible stresses takes into account the significance of a component. Considering the effect of the failure of a single loadbearing element should, however, be second nature. At the design stage, every good engineer must be aware of when and how his/her design will fail. This leads to the recognition that individual components within a structural system have differing degrees of significance for its ultimate stability; the degree of safety against failure can be chosen accordingly. Using the example of a suspension bridge it is immediately obvious that failure of the main cables equates to failure of the entire bridge, whereas the failure of one vertical suspension cable merely means limited serviceability. Aeronautical engineers have such a system at their disposal; they make a distinction between "safe-life", i.e. maximum priority component which must be maintained to preserve stability, and "fail-safe", i.e. acceptance of a localized failure but overall stability still guaranteed. Fortunately, Eurocode 1 provides for the introduction of component classes 1-3, the first step to a similar way of thinking in the building industry.

Eurocode 1 classifies the construction or the elements thereof in three classes which are allocated different safety provisions according to the aim of the protection:

Class 1: primary loadbearing systems, including the foundations, damage to which results in collapse of the entire structure.

Class 2: secondary loadbearing elements which carry forces locally and transfer these to the primary loadbearing system; failure of a secondary loadbearing element does not result in impairment of or damage to the primary loadbearing system.

Class 3: tertiary loadbearing elements, e.g. for roof, interior fitting-out, facade, which transfer forces to primary or secondary systems and whose impairment or failure does not lead to more extensive damage.

Verification of ultimate stability
This involves proving that the ultimate load-carrying capacity of a component or a structure will not be reached – and with an adequate factor of safety. To simplify the verification analyses, a distinction is made between two main groups:
- limit state for load-carrying capacity under primarily static loads
- limit state for load-carrying capacity under primarily dynamic loads

5.60

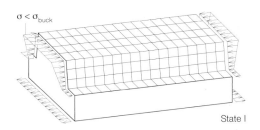

$\sigma < \sigma_{buck}$

State I

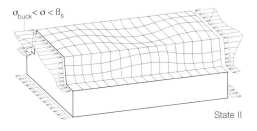

$\sigma_{buck} < \sigma < \beta_s$

State II

5.61

Sliding

W

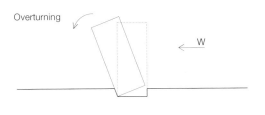

Overturning

W

Uplift

W

5.62 Ground displacements: degree of perception
plotted against frequency [14]
5.63 Ground accelerations: degree of perception
plotted against frequency [14]
5.64 Guiding values for the effects of vibrations on
people [14]

5.62

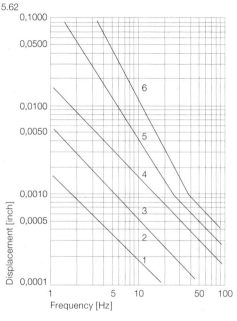

1 imperceptible   4 very perceptible
2 perceptible   5 disturbing
3 easily perceptible   6 very disturbing

5.63

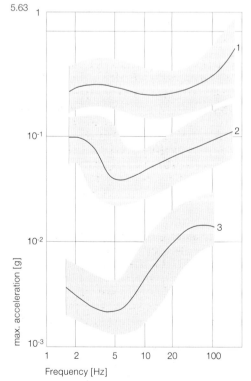

Frequency [Hz]

1 unacceptable
2 unpleasant
3 threshold of perceptibility

5.64

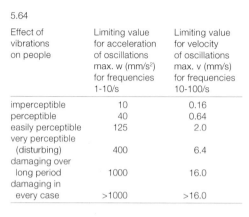

Effect of vibrations on people	Limiting value for acceleration of oscillations max. w (mm/s²) for frequencies 1-10/s	Limiting value for velocity of oscillations max. v (mm/s) for frequencies 10-100/s
imperceptible	10	0.16
perceptible	40	0.64
easily perceptible	125	2.0
very perceptible (disturbing)	400	6.4
damaging over long period	1000	16.0
damaging in every case	>1000	>16.0

These two main groups can be further sub-divided.

Limit state for load-carrying capacity under primarily static loads
Primarily static loads give rise to primarily static stresses and strains. Although this group does include low-level dynamic effects, these only cause minor dynamic stresses and strains which are in no way relevant for the ultimate stability.

In this group we distinguish between:

Strength limit states
These include verification of the elastic-plastic strength of components and their connectors.

Stability limit states
These include all elastic-plastic analyses for
· global component stability (buckling, twist, overturning),
· Local component stability (wrinkling).

Rigid body stability limit states
These include analyses of components and the entire structure with respect to
· sliding,
· overturning,
· uplift.

Limit state for load-carrying capacity under primarily dynamic loads
Dynamic stresses and strains which may arise as a result of, for example, machines, traffic or wind, are countered by the dynamic strength, i.e. the fatigue strength, of the material or the component. The fatigue strength is very much dependent on the number of load cycles and amplitude of oscillation; it is lower than the usable strength of the material under static loading.

The methods of verifying the limit states for load-carrying capacity under primarily dynamic loads are relatively complex and require the reader to have a comprehensive knowledge of engineering. An in-depth discussion would exceed the scope of this book and so the interested reader is referred to the specialist literature on the subject.

Verification of serviceability
Verifying the serviceability of a construction shows that the so-called serviceability limit states are not reached or exceeded. In most instances this concerns deformation and vibration calculations for the construction subjected to the loads and forces actually anticipated or occurring, without the application of partial safety factors. These loads and forces include

external loading, thermal influences, creep, shrinkage and ground deformations.

Serviceability limit states have been reached when:
- unacceptable or intolerable deformations occur. For buildings in general there are no generally and consistently applicable stipulations regarding the permissible deformations of a construction; the tendency is to use practical considerations as a basis. For example, excessive deformations lead to unattractive building outlines, especially with horizontal components; occupants are frequently troubled by such phenomena. Moreover, deformations to the loadbearing structure also influence the facades and interior finishes; damage to non-loadbearing partitions, cracks in floor coverings and considerable sealing problems in the facade are the result. Therefore, it is absolutely essential that the whole design team agrees on the magnitudes of permissible deformations at an early stage of the planning process. Lightweight construction brings about a saving in materials but, as a rule, also larger deformations. In many cases minimizing the weight of the construction is curbed by the maximum permissible deformations, prescribed by the finishes and facades. Comparatively precise stipulations regarding permissible deformations exist for crane rails, traffic installations and similar facilities.
- unacceptable or intolerable vibrations occur. With lightweight, long-span and dynamically loaded components or structures, vibrations can occur which are intolerable. Owing to the low inherent damping of steel (compared to timber or concrete), designers are again and again confronted with unacceptable vibrations. Tolerance levels are highly subjective. Steel footbridges are a case in point: some persons exhibit marked concern upon the occurrence of mild vibrations, while others cross the bridge totally unperturbed. Another example is office blocks which, owing to their height and type of construction, are excited and start to oscillate under high wind loads. A number of tests in which chairs and desks were mounted on vibratory tables and then vibrated with various frequencies and amplitudes revealed a marked subjectivity in workers' responses to vibration. However, clear maximum values above

which the majority of workers experienced discomfort were also established. Therefore, it is absolutely essential that the whole design team agrees on the magnitudes of permissible vibrations at an early stage of the planning process. The relevant standards and scientific findings should of course be taken into account. Vibrations whose (exciting) frequency lies close to the natural frequency of the construction must be avoided since these could lead to collapse. Building or component vibrations can be influenced and reduced by active or passive dampers. The active damper systems measure vibrations continuously. An active, movable mass, e.g. hydraulically operated ballast, is moved in such a way – aligned with the component oscillations – that it causes an oscillation contrary to that of the building and hence reduces the original building oscillation. Passive damper systems usually function according to the principle of energy absorption or the principle of "detuning" the oscillations. Oscillation dampers comprising a mass and spring and/or damping elements have been employed with great success.

Design
The term design in this context means the process of determining (calculating) the dimensions of components, connectors and the total structure.

The engineering design procedure includes verifying the ultimate stability and serviceability of a preliminary design which has already been analysed for its behaviour under the individual loading cases. Written records should be kept, which then form part of the planning documentation. Calculations to establish the sizes of members, like details of loading assumptions and the structural analyses, are checked and approved by the building authorities, normally represented by an independent, experienced engineer.

Two-dimensional loadbearing systems are made up of the members introduced in the section "Elementary stresses and strains: linear members":
- linear components subjected to tension
- linear components subjected to compression
- linear components subjected to bending
- linear components subjected to torsion

An almost infinite number of loadbearing systems can be created by combining these components. It is difficult to place these systems in clear categories. On the other hand, it is possible to develop sensible steel structures using our fundamental understanding of the loadbearing behaviour of the components and the types of construction without needing to be aware of any form of classification for loadbearing systems. Therefore, this section contains principles as well as suggestions for designing loadbearing constructions. A number of "traditional" solutions are also discussed. The author has intentionally refrained from using the classifications prevalent in the literature hitherto because it is has been shown that such classifications are principally incomplete and also hamper the development of new ideas.

Two-dimensional systems subjected to tension
The simplest structures in this group is the cable (or rope) suspended between two supports or, equivalent in terms of geometry and loadbearing behaviour, a chain suspended between two supports. Both exhibit the efficient load-carrying ability discussed in "Elementary stresses and strains: linear members", characterized by the absence of stability problems and uniform stress distribution across the whole cross-section.

A suspended cable responds to a non-linear change in the loading with a comparatively major change to its deflected shape. Therefore, there is a rope geometry to match every loading diagram. Under dead loads alone, the cable takes up the form of a catenary curve. In this case the force in the cable is not constant along the (curved) axis. Applying a uniformly distributed linear load causes the cable to assume the shape of a quadratic parabola, and again, the force in the cable is not constant along the axis. Only in the special case of a constant load with varying direction but

5.64 Two-dimensional system subjected to tension
5.65 The suspended cable
    a Deflection of a suspended cable subjected to a
       uniformly distributed linear load as a result of an
       additional linear load
    b Change to the deflected shape of a cable as a
       result of changing the position of the load
    c Tying a cable to the ground
    d Tying a cable to a second (tensioning) cable by
       means of vertical ties
    e Tying a cable to a second (tensioning) cable by
       means of diagonal ties

5.66 Gravity suspended roof, section and detail
5.67 Cables tensioned against each other: deflections
      caused by non-linear load changes can be
      reduced by including crossing diagonals in the
      centre bay or by converging loadbearing and ten-
      sioning cables; diagonal tie arrangements are the
      most effective.

5.64

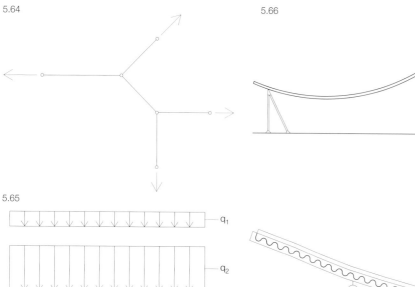

5.65

5.66

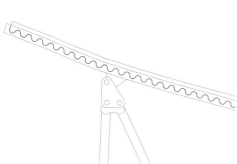

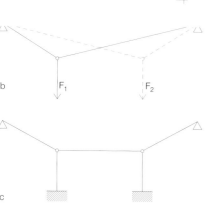

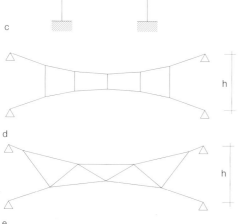

5.67

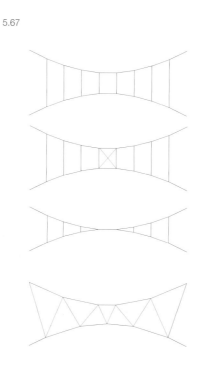

always perpendicular to the cable axis does the cable exhibit a constant force along its axis; the cable is then the shape of a circular arc.

A linear change in the cable loading merely leads to comparatively small deformations based exclusively on the elastic change in length of the cable.

The change in the deflected shape which accompanies the typically non-linear change in the loading on a cable is only acceptable in practice in a very few cases. Therefore, the answer is to reduce the relative magnitude of the non-linear load changes by adding ballast or tensioning the suspended cable against the ground or other components.

Adding ballast to a roof structure of suspended cables creates a gravity suspended roof. Outstanding examples of such roofs have been built but in every case the question must be asked as to whether the lightness of the cable arrangement is counteracted by the ballast and so dilutes the original architectural intention.

Tying the structure to the ground between the suspension points can be a good solution for shorter spans. Such systems are pretensioned so that they continue to function under all loading cases; the degree of pretension depends on system and loads and is normally selected such that no cables become slack and hence "redundant" under any load. It should not be forgotten that the degree of pretension changes with temperature and therefore should not be made too small if heating/ cooling is anticipated.

Tensioning against other components – stiff, quasi immovable parts of a structure are particularly effective – is the method most widely used to reduce deformations in suspended cables as a result of non-linear load changes. In doing so it should be remembered that these parts of the structure can be subjected to considerable additional stresses introduced by the prestressing forces.

If two cables are tensioned against each other by means of cable ties, then we call this a cable truss. The loadbearing behaviour of such

5.68   Two-dimensional cable-net construction for sup-
       porting a glass facade [386]
5.69   Jawerth truss with two upper chords: footbridge in
       Stuttgart [259]
5.70   All the systems illustrated here have the same
       mass regardless of arrangement of members
       (Maxwell principle) [486]
5.71   Pretension achieved by pairs of springs [386]
5.72   Spring system for permanent prestressing of
       cables

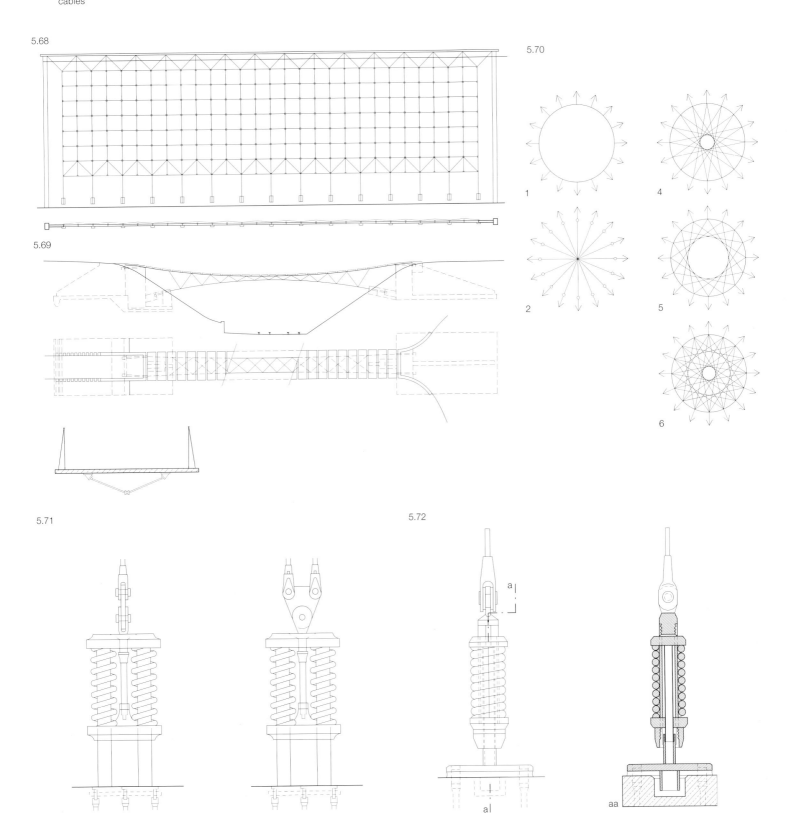

5.68

5.69

5.70

1

2

4

5

6

5.71

5.72

a

aa

a

5.73 Buckled form of multistorey column
5.74 The cross-section of this column is matched to the
     buckled form

5.73

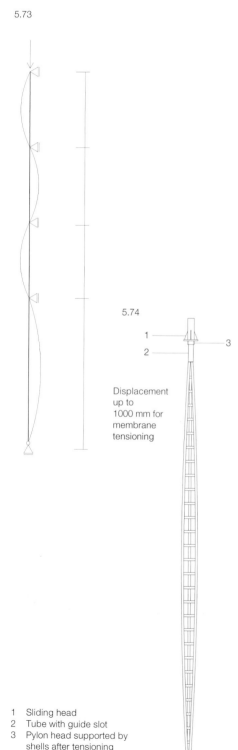

5.74

1
2
                    3

Displacement
up to
1000 mm for
membrane
tensioning

1 Sliding head
2 Tube with guide slot
3 Pylon head supported by
   shells after tensioning

cable trusses is governed by the arrangement
of the cable ties. Parallel ties exhibit the lowest
stiffening effect. If both cables converge at a
point and are joined such that transfer of all
forces is possible, then this brings about a
substantial reduction in the deformations
caused by changing loads. The most effective
solution is the use of diagonal ties; such cable
systems are called Jawerth trusses.

Point loads randomly distributed in a plane,
which together are in a state of equilibrium,
can then be joined with members loaded
exclusively in tension when the lines of action
of these forces intersect at a point and when
the directions of the forces always act outwards from that point. According to the
Maxwell principle the amount of material
required for such a loadbearing system is not
dependent on the arrangement of the members when the line joining the points of application of the loads is always convex. All conceivable structures are in this case minimal
constructions, i.e. of minimum weight.

Two-dimensional systems subjected to compression
The simple strut
The loadbearing behaviour of a member subjected to compression has already been discussed in detail in "Elementary stresses and
strains: linear members". In particular, attention
was drawn to the stability problems and the
increase in mass that this brings about (compared to tension members).

Laterally restrained compression members
continuous over several spans exhibit essentially the same problems as the single-span
member. If such a strut is given a constant
cross-section, then the span with the longest
buckling length governs the design.

The extra mass required (compared to tension
members) to overcome the problem of buckling in a strut can be minimized by applying
various measures:
• matching the cross-section
• opening up the cross-section
• introducing a pretension

Matching the cross-section
This is best done by determining the buckling
form. Note that the strut can buckle in several
directions. The strut will buckle first in the
plane with the lowest radius of gyration; therefore, isolated struts should have a point-
symmetric cross-section, i.e. circular. The
shape of the strut matched to the buckled form
follows the moment diagram of the geometrically imperfect or buckled strut. The internal
lever arm of the strut is thus variable, but the
quotient M/h or M/W and hence the magnitude
of the maximum stresses are constant. The
degree to which a member "bows" along its
longitudinal axis merely affects the magnitude
of the maximum stresses.

Opening up the cross-section
Replacing the strut with several interconnected
individual members also enlarges the internal
lever arm. It must be remembered that the individual cross-sections can buckle between the
system nodes.

Cable-stayed struts
Adding stays to a strut is a particularly elegant
way of matching the buckled form, or a very
attractive way of opening up the cross-section.
With stayed struts the object is usually to
express the delicacy of the construction, which
is why the cross-section of the central compression member is kept compact and the
stays comprise cables or ties with minimal
cross-sections. To do this, props subjected to
compression are required in order to create a
sufficiently large internal lever arm. However, if
the props are made too long, then they have to
be made unnecessarily thick in order to
counter their own stability problem. The extra
weight here often offsets the weight reduction
brought about by the small-section stays.

The stays are pretensioned. As they are normally anchored back to the strut itself, this is
automatically precompressed. This precom-
pression is superimposed on the compressive
forces to be carried by the strut.

5.75 Cable-stayed column: British Pavilion,
World Exposition, Seville, 1992 (see p. 278)
5.76 Cable-stayed column (vertical beam): facade,
Cologne-Bonn Airport, elevation and details

5.75

5.76

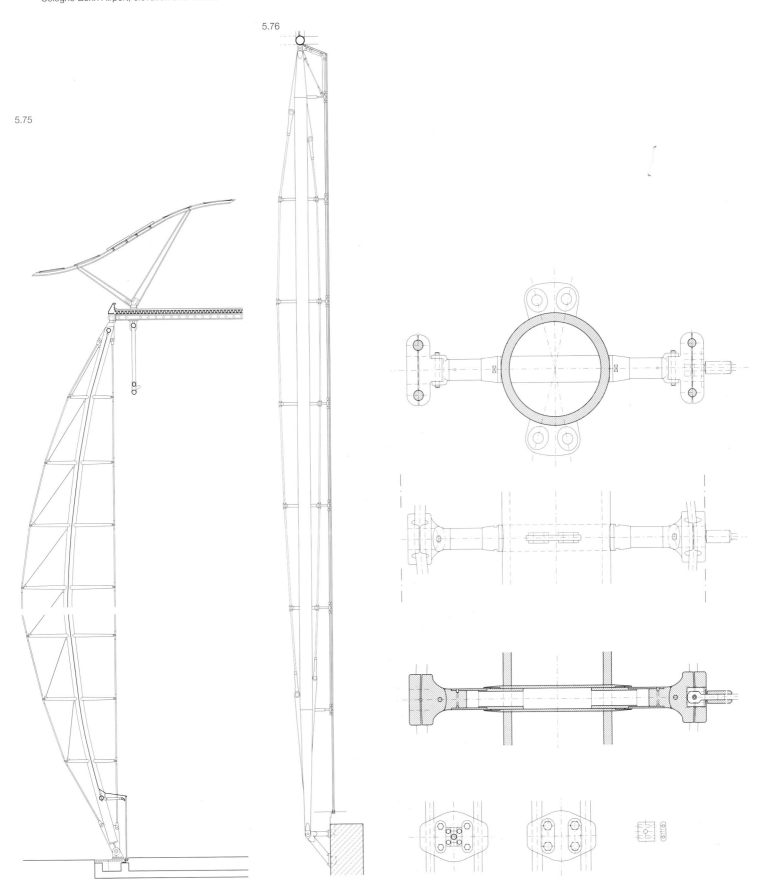

5.77

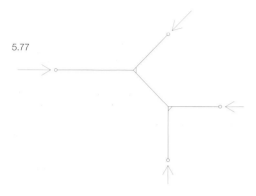

5.77   Polygonal system subjected to compression
5.78   Columns with different "branch" arrangements.
        The outer (upper) ends of the members must
        be held horizontally or restrained with a ten-
        sion ring.

5.78

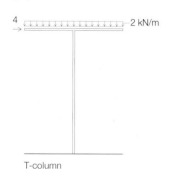

T-column

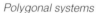

The precise application of the pretensioning in the stays is not always easy and demands careful consideration of the erection procedure. When tie bars with left-hand/right-hand threads are used, the typically unattractive turnbuckles can be omitted. The end fittings can then be designed as delicate and compact items. When cable stays are used, either swaged, threaded fittings and matching end fittings are used or the pretension introduced by lengthening the props.

Between the props the strut still suffers from a stability problem, but with a considerably shorter buckling length.

Polygonal systems
Like with the loadbearing systems subjected to tension, point loads randomly distributed in a plane, which together are in a state of equilibrium, can be joined with members loaded exclusively in compression This is possible when the lines of action of these forces or the resultants thereof intersect at a point and when the directions of the forces always act towards that point. In contrast to the exclusively tensile version, every single component of the structure suffers from a stability problem and so the amount of material required for such a loadbearing system is now dependent on the arrangement of the components.

Umbel columns
An interesting special variation of the polygonal system subjected to compression is the so-called "tree" column, although strictly speaking we should not call it that as it has absolutely nothing in common with the loadbearing behaviour of a tree; the term "umbel column" is much more apt. The fundamental thinking behind this structural system is to direct a group of distributed point loads to one point and from there transmit the total load via a single member to a support point, the point of application of the reaction force providing total equilibrium. In doing so, all members must be loaded exclusively in compression.

As mentioned above, this is only possible when the lines of action of all forces intersect at one point. However, this is not typical of the majority of umbel columns, e.g. for supporting long-span roofs or heavy floors. This makes it necessary to introduce additional tension and/or compression members. The example of umbel columns supporting a roof structure reveals that considerable tensile and compressive forces have to be accommodated at roof level in order to achieve overall equilibrium.

The geometry, or rather the arrangement of members, for umbel columns is determined by using models, assisted by computer or handdrawn graphics. With two-dimensional loadbearing systems, determining the geometry using graphical methods leads to a detailed understanding of the relationships between arrangement of members and forces therein.

It should be pointed out that the structure is composed of members loaded exclusively in compression for one loading case, i.e. the one determining the form. For all other loading cases, the bending strengths of the members, and especially the nodes, must be used.

The members of steel umbel columns are best made from steel tubes, the nodes from cast steel. Cast steel nodes are the easiest way of achieving the often complex geometry of such junctions. Cast nodes allow the flow of forces to be organized very effectively. The members are welded to the nodes. Gusset plates are cheaper but the quality of design is far inferior to that of cast nodes. Tubes welded directly together are conceivable with two-dimensional umbel columns, provided the diameters are carefully coordinated. However, such connections are difficult to achieve in (three-dimensional) practice and a great deal of effort is required to prove their stability.

5.79 Design sketches of umbel columns by Frei Otto
      [342]
5.80 Node arrangements for umbel systems
5.81 Umbel columns, Stuttgart Airport (see p. 326)
5.82 a Suspended model for determining the form of
        an umbel system
      b The model reversed with members loaded
        exclusively in compression with the loading
        case determining the design
5.83 Cast steel node piece for umbel columns

5.79

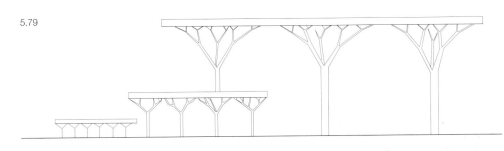

5.82

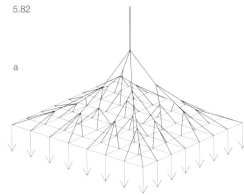

a

5.80

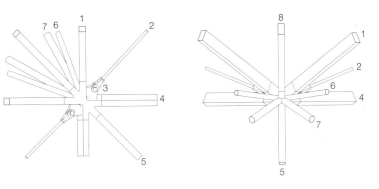

1 Upper chord of arch
2 Diagonal wind
   bracing
3 Cast node piece
4 Longitudinal beam
5 Connecting post
6 Diagonal arch
7 Post of arch
8 Rib

b

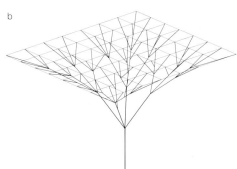

5.81

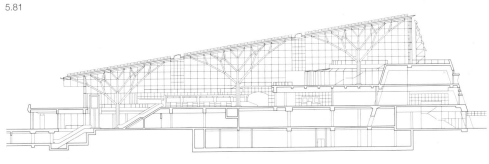

5.83

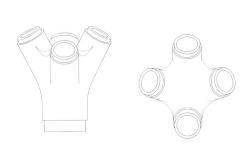

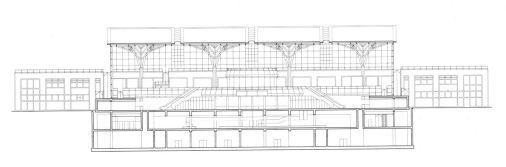

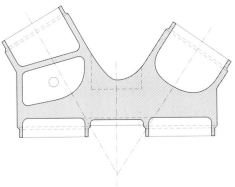

5.84 Cranked beam
5.85 Polygon arch subjected to compression
5.86 Loading case determining form of catenary version subjected exclusively to tension
5.87 Reversed version of 5.86, subjected exclusively to compression
5.88 In a polygon arch bridge the compression members between the post seatings are usually straight, although they could justifiably be lightly curved to take account of self-weight.

5.89 Polygon arch bridge: junction between post and arch member, solution using I-sections
5.90 Solution using hollow sections
5.91 Solution using tubes with cast nodes

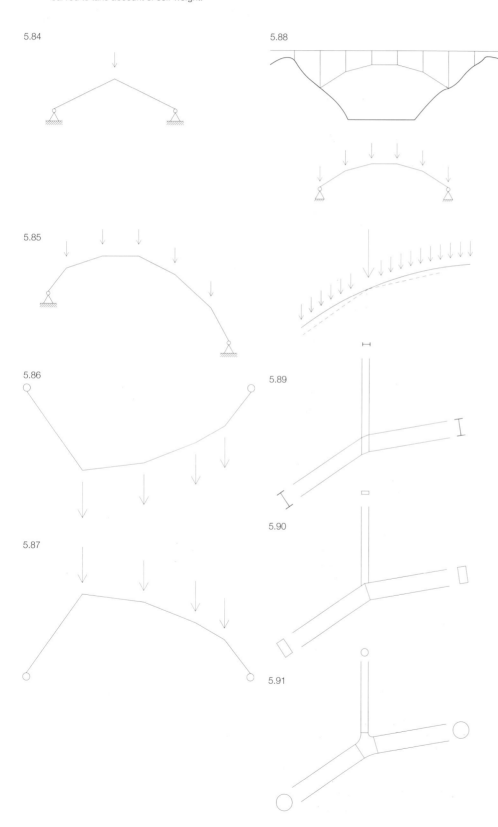

5.84

5.85

5.86

5.87

5.88

5.89

5.90

5.91

Polygon arch structures

Another special variation of the polygonal system is the polygon arch. With a polygon arch, several point loads can be transmitted via a chain of exclusively compression members to two supports. This technique allows forces to be carried over long distances. The two supports must always be rigid. The shape of the polygon arch is determined by:

- the positions of the supports
- the magnitudes and directions of forces to be carried
- the desired camber of the arch

The shape can be determined graphically, mathematically or by using so-called reversed models. These models are used initially to establish the geometry of a catenary spanned between two supports and loaded with the given loads; the shape of this exclusively tensile structure and the exclusively compressive polygon arch are identical – merely reversed. The suspended catenary becomes an "upright" arch!

If the self-weight of the polygon arch is ignored, i.e. is negligible compared to other loads, then the members between the load application points are straight. Once the self-weight can no longer be ignored, the members become curved between the load application points. Only in very few instances does this result in a continuously curved form, e.g. a semicircular or parabolic arch.

Therefore, the geometry of polygon arches must always be developed taking into account the loads governing the design. If, for architectural or constructional reasons, a continuous curve is desired, i.e. a traditional arch, then in most cases considerable bending stresses in the arch must be reckoned with. This leads to a less slender structure.

Only under the action of the loading case governing the design are the members of the polygon arch subjected exclusively to compression. In theory, all the members could be interconnected via hinges for this loading case. However, all the other loading cases give rise to bending in the arch. For this reason, and

5.92 Arch, two-hinged arch and three-hinged arch
5.93 Spoked wheel, horizontal, with open hub
5.94 Cable-stayed arch with cables anchored at the
two springing points [386]
5.95 Cable-stayed arch with cable "spokes" indirectly
anchored via two cable stays [386]

5.92

because a polygon arch can never be fabricated with a perfect geometry, the individual
members of all polygon arches are rigidly connected with each other.

Most polygon arches generate enormous horizontal reactions at the supports, often several
times the sum of the vertical loads. This "arch
thrust" must be taken into account in the
design and the foundations or adjoining components sized accordingly.

Polygon arches may be completely rigid, i.e.
with restrained supports, or they can be provided with one, two or three hinges (single-,
two- and three-hinged arches respectively).
The deformation behaviour as well as magnitude and distribution of bending moments is
controlled by the number and positioning of
these hinges. If uneven vertical settlement is
expected, then a two-hinged arch should be
used; but if uneven vertical and horizontal
(due to arch thrust) subsoil deformation could
occur, then the three-hinged arch is the better
choice.

Like all compression structures, arches and
polygon arches suffer from local and global
stability problems. The former affects the individual members and is relatively easy to deal
with. But the global stability problem affects
the whole arch member and is considerably
more difficult to overcome and normally
requires calculations according to the theory of
large deflections using a geometric imperfection based on the eigenform.

Steel polygon arches are best fabricated from
hollow sections. The nodes can be
· cast fittings,
· gusset plates, or
· directly welded.

Cast nodes are the least conspicuous and are
the best method for preserving the lines of the
design. They are also better than gusset plates
when it comes to transferring large forces into
the arch. Gusset plates represent a simple and
hence in most cases a less expensive form of
construction, and with a little effort they can be
shaped in such a way that they hardly disturb

the lines of the design. If they are not trimmed
to size or, indeed, left square, then the character of the construction is altered accordingly.
With the fabrication techniques available these
days, direct welding of the hollow sections is
possible even for the most complex geometries. The resulting forms are very stream-
lined. It must be ensured that overall sizes and
wall thicknesses are carefully matched in order
to avoid force transfer problems and the associated buckling of thin-walled sections.

When the dead loads determine the form, i.e.
the imposed loads are comparatively small or
are very uniformly distributed, an arch with a
continuous curve may be designed. Circular or
square/rectangular hollow sections are again
ideal as they can be easily bent to the correct
curvature.

Arches stabilized by beams
A good way of stabilizing an arch, or rather
damping the moments caused by a range of
loading cases, is to combine the arch with a
rigid beam. The connection between arch and
beam is achieved by way of ties and/or struts.
A very stiff beam allows the polygon arch to be
correspondingly slender. As the rigidity of the
beam decreases, so the rigidity of the arch
must increase.

Prestressed polygon arches
A very elegant slender arch suitable for
extreme variations in loading can be achieved
by prestressing the arch by means of ties.
These ties enhance the global flexural stiffness
and at the same time serve to stabilize the arch
against buckling.

There are a number of ways in which arches
can be prestressed – in the plane of the arch
and/or in three dimensions. The latter also prevents lateral buckling of the arch.

Probably the best known type of arch stabilized through prestressing is the spoked wheel.
The peripheral – for a bicycle of course circular
– (compression) rim is precompressed by the
pretensioned radial arrangement of spokes
and hence stabilized. If the spokes lie in the
plane of the rim, then they only stabilize the rim

5.93

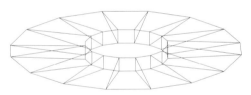

5.94

5.95

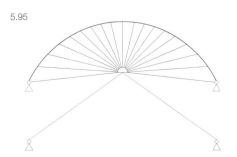

5.96 Detail of connection between hub post, ring cable and spoke cables
5.97 Hub of a cable-stayed arch, Hamburg City History Museum [259]
5.98 Section through a horizontal spoked-wheel, roof over Center Court at Rothenbaum, Hamburg (see p. 368)
5.99 Hub post

5.96

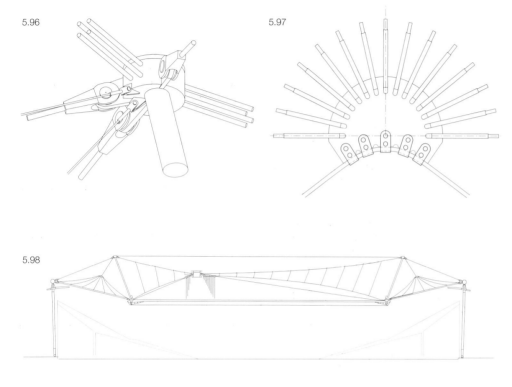

5.97

5.98

5.99

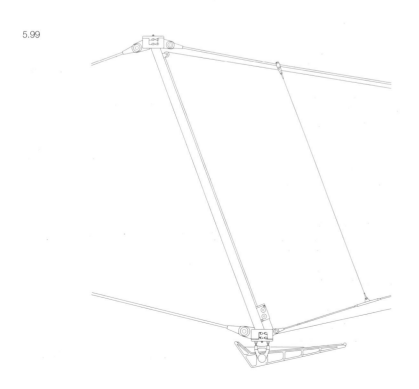

in that plane; two groups of spokes, held apart by a hub member loaded in compression, are required for three-dimensional stability.

The self-contained polygon arch stabilized by spokes is one of the most efficient forms of construction. Consequently, it is also suitable for use as a loadbearing system for lightweight and long-span structures. Examples of its application are correspondingly diverse, ranging from the bicycle wheel to stiffening bulkheads in airships to the, in some cases, the over 100 m spans of horizontal spoked-wheel roofs, e.g. the arena in Zaragoza and the Rothenbaum tennis stadium in Hamburg.

Expanding the hub to form a ring of tension members allows the ensuing opening to be used for other purposes. It should be remembered that the loadbearing behaviour of a spoked wheel with radial spokes is fundamentally changed by the introduction of a hollow hub because the structural system comprising three-hinged subsystems is transformed into one of four-hinged subsystems. This can only reach a reasonable loadbearing capacity by introducing a very high prestress and/or a rigid polygon arch. If these two options are undesirable, then the arrangement of the spokes can be altered accordingly, e.g. so that they form a triangulated truss.

The basic principle of the spoked wheel may be varied at will. For example, one interesting form of construction is the "reversed spoked wheel".

Of course, the polygon arch does not always have to appear in a self-contained form in order to benefit from the spoked-wheel principle. Parts of the arch or some of the spokes may be replaced by corresponding support conditions. This gives rise to the slender arches stabilized by spokes and used as stiffening "bulkheads", e.g. to the roof over the inner courtyard at the Hamburg City History Museum.

5.100   Fabricating a Cellform castellated beam from an
         I-section
5.101   Fabricating a standard castellated beam from an
         I-section, with extra web plates inserted
5.102   Flange plates for strengthening an I-section

5.100

A Cellform castellated beam is an I-section whose depth
has been increased by a simple, patented method.

5.101

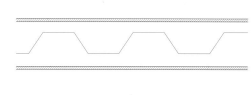

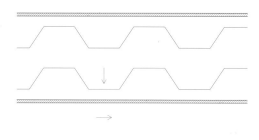

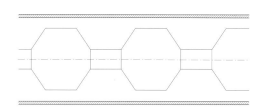

Instead of a radial arrangement of spokes, it is
also possible to place them in a chordal pattern. This solution has the advantage of less
interruption to the space below the arch. This
same advantage is offered by tying the stays
back to the springing points of the arch, as
originated by Šuchov.

The stays of all cable-stayed polygon arches
are pretensioned. The advice concerning introducing the prestressing and detailing of the
system as given in the section "Cable-stayed
struts" also applies here.

Planar beams (in bending)
The beam subjected to uniaxial bending and
shear is among the most common elements
used in construction. Therefore, and because
beams in bending exhibit a very inhomogeneous and hence also very ineffective internal
stress condition, a detailed discussion of this
element is essential.

The shear and moment distributions present
under the various loading cases for single-
span and continuous beams are well known or
at least can be obtained from tables or computer-assisted calculations. It is important to
realize that the maximum moment in a beam is
always equal to the product of a system-
dependent coefficient k, a factor q or P determined by the loading, and the square of the
span. If the beam is subjected to a uniformly
distributed load, then

$$M_{max} = k \, q \, l^2$$

For a single-span beam carrying a uniformly
distributed load we know that k = 1/8.

For continuous beams with different arrangements of uniformly distributed loads, k normally
lies between 1/8 and 1/12, depending on the
span ratios and support conditions. So, changing the structural system enables us to mani-
pulate the maximum moments by up to 50%. In
contrast, changing the span has a exponential

effect: doubling the span brings about a four-
fold increase in the maximum moment, halving
the span reduces the maximum moment to
25% of its original value. Therefore, the necessity of long, uninterrupted spans should always
be questioned.

A linear member subjected to uniaxial bending
displays the characteristic linear stress distribution between the two maximum values at the
extremities of the cross-section. The edge
zones are particularly highly stressed, which is
why the middle of the section may, indeed with
an expensive material such as steel, should,
be lighter. This lightening of the section is
achieved by using an I-section or a hollow section or by removing material. This leads to trusses, Vierendeel girders and their derivatives.

Solid-web beams
Owing to their structurally beneficial cross-
section, their ease of rolling and simple connections, I-sections are very widely used in
structural steelwork. There is a large range of
sections standardized throughout Europe with
various depths and widths as well as different
flange and web thicknesses, enabling a suitable section to be found for almost every situation. The rolling of special sections is also
possible, provided the quantity required justifies the expense.

Rolled I-sections possess a constant cross-
section along their entire length, so the only
way to match the moments which normally vary
considerably along a beam is to join pieces of
different sections. However, going to such
lengths is hardly economic for standard applications and beams of moderate spans of up to
8-10 m. But larger spans and large quantities
could make such a solution justifiable.

Instead of joining different sections, the flanges
can be strengthened in the regions of high
moments by welding on plates of various thicknesses.

5.102

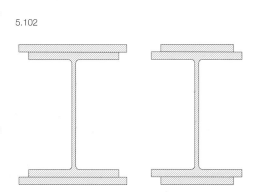

5.103

5.104   5.105

5.106

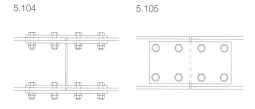

5.107   5.108

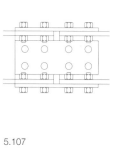

5.109

5.110

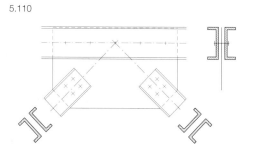

For large spans and/or large quantities, the fabrication of custom-made sections made up of welded plates is recommended. Adjusting the depth to suit the moment distribution and/or grading the plate thicknesses lead to a beam system which is matched exactly to the stresses and strains actually present. In lightweight construction this approach is obligatory. In addition, such an approach gives even the untrained observer an insight into the properties of the construction and therefore an understanding of our built environment.

I-sections may be joined by welding or bolting. If flanges and web are fully welded (not always necessary), then the full load-carrying capacity of the section is maintained right across the joint. Bolting is normally accomplished by adding web splice plates, which allow shear forces but not moments to be transmitted across the joint, or flange splice plates, which then enable the moment to be carried. Instead of flange splice plates, end plates may be welded to the I-section and subsequently bolted together. Most effective here are end plates in which the bolts are located beyond the flanges to increase the internal lever arm. However, this detail is not terribly elegant, so, whenever possible, end-plate splices should always be restricted to regions of low moments; the necessary lever arm for the bolts is then shorter, the bolts can be placed between the flanges and the plates finished flush top and bottom.

An I-section can also be conceived as two channels back to back. The structural properties remain the same but in some cases there are certain advantages when connecting them to other components.

For carrying bending moments, square/rectangular hollow sections have similar advantages to I-sections or channels back to back. However, the two webs of square/rectangular rolled hollow sections are too thick compared to the flanges. In contrast, made-up hollow sections enable the plate thicknesses to be coordinated exactly, both within the cross-section and along the length of the beam. Adjusting the beam depth to suit the moment diagram is also

possible. Joining square/rectangular rolled hollow sections by means of welding is also relatively straightforward, but bolting should be avoided owing to the difficulty in providing access to the nuts and/or bolts.

A planar beam in bending can also be cranked if required for any reason, e.g. to follow an awkward contour. A crank in a beam necessitates an axial tensile or compressive force in at least one of the two parts of the beam; this force must be in equilibrium with the shear forces at the crank. In pitched roofs the ridge is often designed as rigid. Cranked beams are often referred to as frames or half-frames.

Some of the structural and constructional features of beams with axial tensile or compressive forces, as occur in cranked beams, is investigated below. Basically, at every crank in a beam it must be ensured that axial and shear forces as well as the bending moment can be properly transmitted via the crank in practice. This is not always easy. In the case of I-sections, channels back to back and square/rectangular hollow sections it should be remembered that the major part of the moment is resisted by the tensile and compressive forces in the flanges. The direction of these forces can only be reversed by introducing a further force. These additional forces usually cancel out at the crank, but like any force they also need to "materialize". This is normally achieved by way of plates in the form of stiffeners. Incorporating a thicker web plate at the crank or reinforcing existing web plates is possible but does not really solve the constructional problem. In rare instances with extremely high loads, the use of a cast junction is recommended.

The principles outlined in the section "The detailing of openings and the transfer of forces" apply to connections as well as force transfer points in beams subjected to bending. Attention is drawn to the fact that the loadbearing capacities of the webs of the very popular I-sections or channels back to back are often exceeded when transferring point loads into or out of such beams. On the other hand, it is only

5.111   Made-up box section. Inset web plates render possible simple fillet welds; flush web plates require the welded joints to be prepared.
5.112   Cranked beams made from I-sections
5.113   Illustrating the flow of forces at the corner of a frame. A diagonal plate is the most effective solution.
5.114   Partly ineffective and hence superfluous stiffeners (flange)
5.115   The moment in this case is for the most part carried (very ineffectively) via the web plate at the junction.

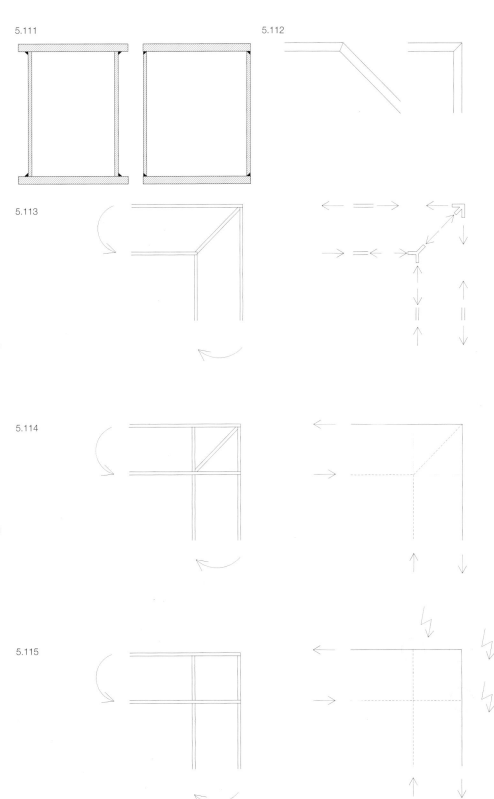

5.111

5.112

5.113

5.114

5.115

the webs that can be employed for transferring such forces as the flanges would suffer severe deformations owing to their poor local bending capacity and so redistribute the stresses. So the webs must be appropriately reinforced near local force transfer positions. Stiffeners to both sides of the webs of I-sections or channels back to back are the simplest solution. The length of the stiffeners is determined by the shear strength of the web.

The force transfer plates are welded to the inside or outside of both webs of hollow sections. Other sections are treated similarly.

The positions and forms of web openings have been dealt with in the sections "Elementary stresses and strains: linear members" and "The detailing of openings and the transfer of forces". The principles outlined in those sections apply similarly to constructions subjected to bending.

If we ask the question of how a beam subjected to bending with initially unknown geometry needs to be designed such that its total weight is a minimum for the loading case governing the form, then the answer is a complicated shape consisting only of individual tension and compression members. The forms of such beams for a few special cases have been determined by Mitchell by analytical means; these are designated Mitchell beams. Generally, appropriate optimization programs would be used. A very skilled engineer is able to estimate these structures to within 20-30% "manually" if he first places a component with continuous material in the support conditions and then draws the main stress trajectories on this beam. If all lowly stressed regions of the component (or those between individual groups of trajectories) are subsequently cut out, then we obtain structures that, in terms of weight, come relatively close to the corresponding minimal structure. Cutting away zones of low stress is an old engineering method for optimizing the weight of a structure. In reverse, this method can of course also be successfully employed for the design of loadbearing systems.

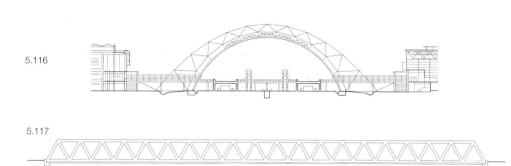

5.116

5.117

5.118

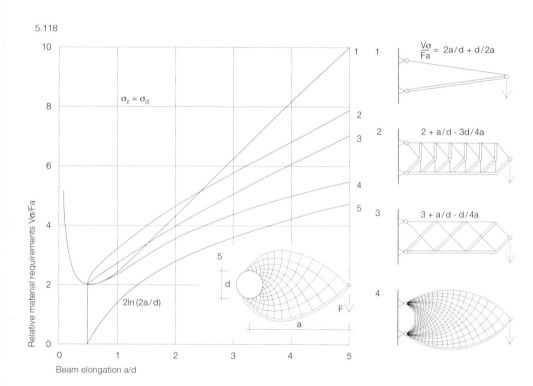

$$\frac{V\sigma}{Fa} = 2a/d + d/2a$$

1

$$2 + a/d - 3d/4a$$

2

$$3 + a/d - d/4a$$

3

4

$\sigma_z = \sigma_d$

$2\ln(2a/d)$

Relative material requirements $V\sigma/Fa$

Beam elongation a/d

5.119

5.120

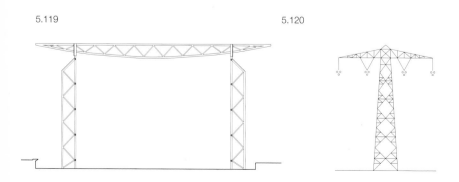

5.121 Gusset plate in bolted truss: influence of angle of
      diagonals on size of plate
5.122 Truss: loading, flow of forces and sections
5.123 1st and 2nd laws of truss design

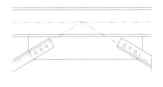

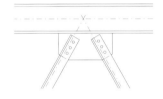

Mitchell and comparable minimal structures all exhibit a quadratic mesh arrangement of their tension and compression elements. Indeed, for the loading case governing the design, even articulated joints between the individual elements are feasible, presupposing a geometrically perfect construction. As in practice this supposition is normally impossible, and as other loading cases occur apart from the one governing the form, the nodes must be rigid. The resulting bending stresses in the individual members make the structure ineffective. This problem is only overcome by using a triangular mesh of pin-jointed tension and compression members. These triangulated systems are known as trusses.

Trusses
Trusses are frames which consist of pin-jointed tension and compression members. Trusses can be constructed as two-dimensional two-chord systems or as three-dimensional systems with (usually) three or four chords. The planar (i.e. two-dimensional) two-chord version is discussed in the following. However, the remarks here can also be applied to three-dimensional (space) frames.

The shape of the bottom chord, the arrangement of the (vertical) posts and the diagonals of a truss are based on the
• ambient conditions arising from the utilization,
• ease of erection/fabrication,
• architectural and stylistic considerations, and
• consideration of the flow of forces and are designed accordingly.

Basically, the following rules must be observed when designing trusses:
• Member axes always intersect at a (node) point.
• Members are considered to be hinged at the nodes.
• Curved members must be avoided owing to their bending stresses.
• Compression members within a truss should be as short as possible in order to avoid stability problems.

• Members should not meet at very acute angles because this leads to long, unattractive gusset plates, or welding problems in the case of a welded truss.
• Loads should only be carried at nodes as otherwise the members are loaded transversely and hence subjected to bending.

Bearing these principles in mind, trusses with the most diverse geometries may be designed. In doing so it must be ensured that the frame is stable both in itself and as part of a larger structure. A system conforming to the 1st and 2nd laws of truss design will always produce a usable frame which is in itself statically determinate.

1st law of truss design
Starting with a (statically determinate) primary member (which can be the ground), every new node is joined via two members. The two members attaching the new node may not lead in the same direction.

2nd law of truss design
Two trusses each constructed according to the 1st law of truss design are connected to each other with three members. The axes of these three members may not pass through a common point, but they should also not be parallel (point of intersection at infinity).

Adding members to trusses designed according to these two laws leads to systems statically indeterminate in themselves. Whether a truss is outwardly statically determinate or indeterminate depends on the number and arrangement of the supports.

The laws of truss design only concern the way in which the individual members are joined, not the geometry as a whole. This is established by considering the flow of forces, the fabrication, the architectural appearance and the utilization.

Trusses with parallel chords (lattice beams/girders) are very common. The forces in the top and bottom chords of such lattice beams are not normally constant. Therefore, the cross-

5.122

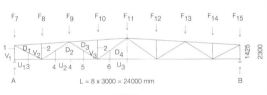

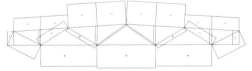

1 HEA 160
2 L 70/7
3 1/2 IPE 220
4 1/2 IPE 270
5 L 60/6
6 L 80/8

5.123

5.124 Plane frames with non-parallel or curved chords:
  a Shallow-pitched upper chord and falling
    diagonals
  b Hog-backed girder (parabolic upper chord)
  c Fish-belly girder (parabolic bottom chord)
  d Inverted bow-and-chain girder
  e Crescent truss
  f Schwedler truss

5.125 Typical trusses for pitched roofs:
  a Swiss truss
  b German truss
  c Belgian truss
  d Polonceau truss
  e Raised-chord Polonceau truss
  f Polonceau truss

5.126 Plane frames with parallel chords:
  a Pratt or N-truss (diagonals falling towards
    centre)
  b Pratt or N-truss with diagonals reversed
    (rising towards centre)
  c Girder statically indeterminate in itself
  d Diamond girder (no posts)
  e Diamond girder requiring centre post for
    stability
  f Mesh
  g Lattice girder with K-bracing
  h Warren girder (no posts)

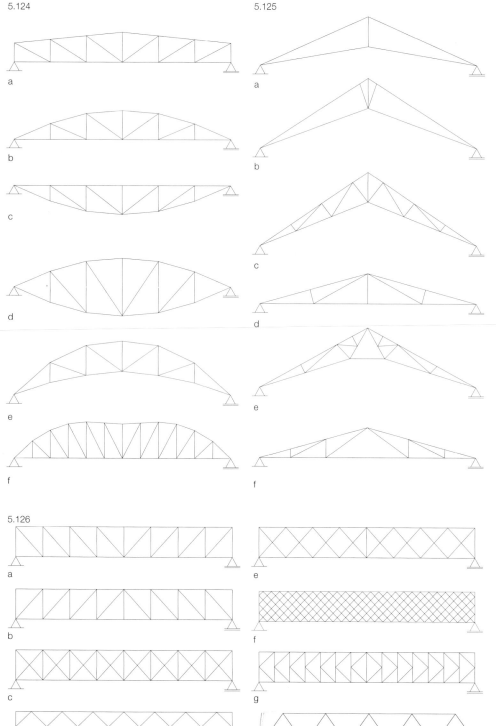

5.124

a

b

c

d

e

f

5.126

a

b

c

d

5.125

a

b

c

d

e

f

g

h

section should change from member to member in order to reduce the weight.

When loaded with point loads acting at the nodes as a substitute for a uniformly distributed vertical or related load,

trusses with vertical posts and cross-bracing have
• posts in compression
• diagonals in tension and compression (watch for ties or cables redundant in compression!)

trusses with vertical posts and "falling" diagonals have
• posts in compressionn
• diagonals in tension

Forces in posts and diagonals increase towards the supports; the section sizes should be adjusted accordingly.

The diagonals of Schwedler trusses always have diagonals loaded exclusively in tension, even with alternating vertical loads.

Hog-backed girders have a top chord with parabolic form. They exhibit a constant force in the chord when subjected to a uniformly distributed vertical load. If instead the bottom chord follows a parabolic curve, then we call this a fish-belly girder. A truss in which both chords are curved is known as an inverted bow-and-chain girder.

When pin-jointed frames are used as roof trusses, the upper chord follows the shape of the roof. Swiss, Belgian and Polonceau trusses are popular solutions for pitched roofs. The latter type can be very simply constructed from two separate trusses joined at the ridge and via a tie at the bottom chord.

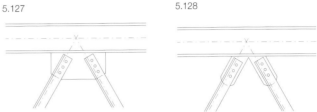

5.127

5.128

Crescent trusses have upper and lower chords both curving in the same direction. These are attractive structures which act, principally, as arches but still possess adequate stability to withstand asymmetric loads. In addition, the risk of lateral buckling of the bottom chord – a problem that has to be addressed in all trusses and girders – can be avoided in a crescent-shaped truss by pretensioning the bottom chord. This obviates the need for – often unsightly – lateral stabilizing elements to the bottom chord.

Optimum geometries for loading cases other than those discussed so far are best designed with the help of models or suitable programs. Trusses with minimum weight are really only possible with the aid of computers. It must be remembered that these optimized trusses are only "optimum", i.e. exhibit minimum weight, for one loading case. Therefore, they are really ideal for heavy, constant dead loads. In light-weight construction there is usually no such dominating load case, which is why other considerations are more significant for such structures.

When designing trusses and girders it should be remembered that the assumption of complete articulation at the joints is of course actually realized only in the rarest of cases. Joints in such frames are normally bolted or welded. Bolting in particular makes use of gusset plates to transfer the forces between the individual members being connected. Obviously, such joints are not hinges in any shape or form. Indeed, bending stresses are induced here – "ancillary stresses" – which are not considered further, neither in structural nor constructional terms. However, such an approach is only permissible when the members of the frame are sufficiently slender. In extremely "stocky" frames and/or those in which unskilful

5.129

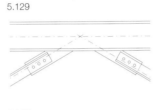

5.130

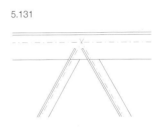

5.131

5.132

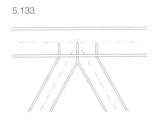

5.133

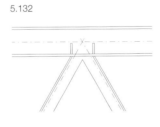

5.134

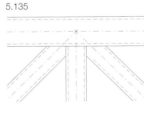

5.135

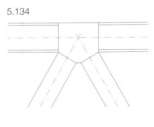

5.136

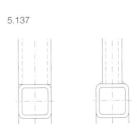

5.137

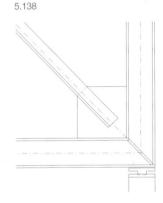

5.138

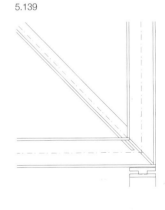

5.139

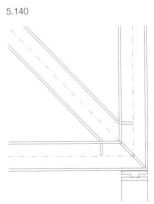

5.140

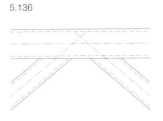

5.147

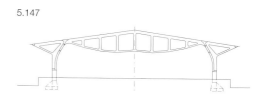

5.141

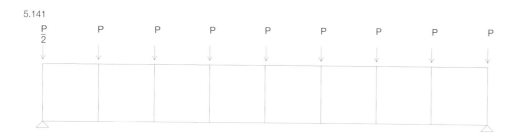

5.142

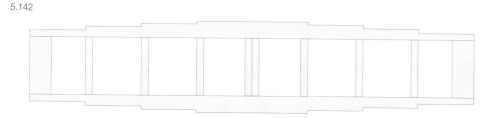

5.143

5.144

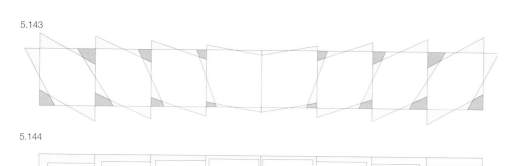

detailing has led to large gusset plates and hence severe bending in the adjoining members, it is not wise to assume hinged joints.

The choice of sections in trusses and girders is very much dependent on the connections to be used. Channels back to back are very popular for bolted constructions with gusset plates, although posts and diagonals can also make use of angles. Bolted frames without gusset plates employ T-sections for the main chords and angles as posts and/or diagonals connected directly to the webs of the T-sections.

Welded trusses and girders are fabricated from I-sections or circular or square/rectangular hollow sections. I-sections are relatively easy to fabricate and weld; circular hollow sections must be profile-shaped or saddled to fit – state of the art now but smaller fabricators often lack the necessary facilities for doing such work themselves. The members of hollow section frames are sealed by welding so only external corrosion protection is necessary.

Vierendeel girders
Named after the Belgian engineer Arthur Vierendeel, this frame is an open, planar system without diagonals. A Vierendeel girder normally has parallel top and bottom chords and posts perpendicular to the chords.

As there are no diagonals, all the nodes of a Vierendeel girder must be rigid. The bending moments in the posts and chords as well as the nodes are in some instances quite high and so play a governing role in the sizing of the sections. Therefore, compared to a pin-jointed frame of equal span and equal depth, a Vierendeel girder is always markedly heavier. On the other hand, Vierendeel girders possess

5.145   5.146

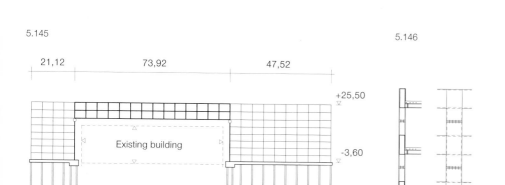

5.148 The main columns of the Hong Kong & Shanghai Bank, Hong Kong, consist of Vierendeel girders (see p. 384)
5.149 Single-span beam subjected to uniformly distributed load and derived beam forms. Left: main loadbearing elements in tension. Right: main loadbearing elements in compression.

5.148

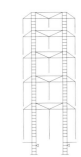

very serene lines and high design quality. Vierendeel girders and their related forms should be constructed of sections which have a high bending strength in the plane of the girder. I-sections and channels back to back are especially suitable because the flanges of these sections can be easily joined by welded plates to achieve a high bending strength at the nodes. The highly stressed flanges (due to local bending moments) of square/rectangular hollow sections are harder to join. The chord can be made continuous of course, but the connection of posts with high bending stresses always presents problems. Plates welded to the outside of each web are one answer, but less than ideal. The best solution is to incorporate cast nodes.

Circular hollow sections are less suitable for Vierendeel girders.

Of course, the loadbearing principle of the Vierendeel girder can be employed in a different form. Girders with parallel top and bottom chords and cutouts are just as conceivable as girders with haunched top and bottom chords. These types of girders are best constructed using two parallel, large web plates, in which the openings have already been cut, and flange plates welded into these openings. This guarantees the bending strength of the individual sections and prevents buckling of the web plates, which in some regions must withstand considerable compressive forces. With triangular cutouts and inclined posts the loadbearing behaviour approaches that of a truss; the inclined posts now act as diagonals and their bending stresses are diminished. Taken to its logical conclusion, appropriate positioning of the openings and correspondingly slender, non-rigid elements produces a truss.

5.149

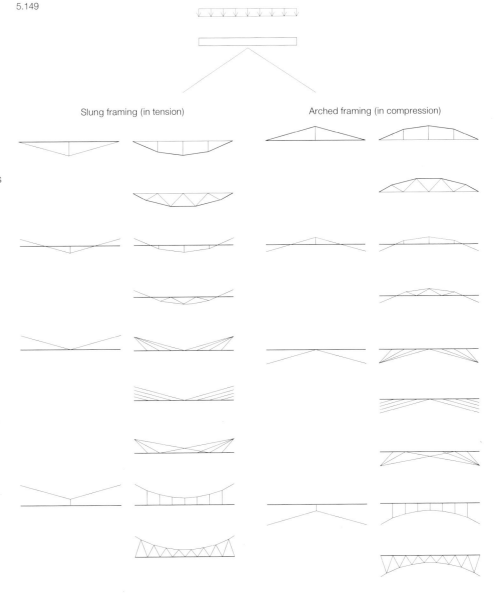

Slung framing (in tension)   Arched framing (in compression)

5.150 The stayed column whose base sits at the same level, on a plinth or in a recess is a good analogy for the stability problem of the trussed beam: imperfect
5.151 Unstable
5.152 Stable
5.153 Deflection of a beam with single-post underslung framing under symmetric and asymmetric loading

5.154 Deflection of a beam with two-post underslung framing under symmetric and asymmetric loading
5.155 Underslung beams
 - Fink truss
 - every post tied to supports
 - Bollmann truss
5.156 Single- and multiple-post underslung beams

5.150

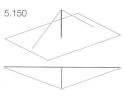

5.155

5.151

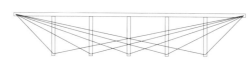

Beams in bending subjected to axial tension and compression
The superimposition of axial tensile or compressive stresses alters the distribution of stresses in all the components of a beam in bending. Moreover, axial compression leads to a global stability problem for which the construction has to be designed.

5.152

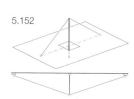

Beams with slung and arched framing
It is frequently the case that a beam is required to be so slender that it is actually no longer suitable for the intended span. If increasing the depth is not desirable, then intermediate supports are the only answer. Extra columns could be added but that is not the intention of this exercise, namely, to span a large distance with a beam which is "too slender". Therefore, indirect intermediate supports are the only way of overcoming this problem.

One or more indirect supports to the beam are provided by adding hangers or posts, in tension or compression respectively, which in turn are held in place by a subsystem subjected to tension or compression. This subsystem can be anchored back to the beam itself or to another part of the structure.

This loadbearing principle renders possible a wide range of structural systems. These include:

5.153

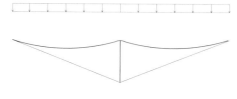

5.156

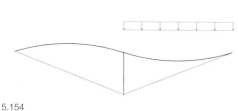

Hangers (tension) and arched framing (tension)
· suspension bridge, self-anchored
· suspension bridge, anchored to the ground
· cable-stayed bridge

5.154

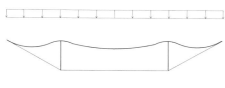

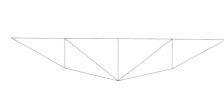

Posts (compression) and slung framing (tension)
· beam with single post
· beam with multiple posts
· beam with multiple-post Fink truss
· beam with multiple-post Le Ricolais truss

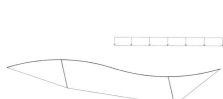

5.157 Arch over Waterloo Station, London (see p. 360):
       framing partly above, partly below
5.158 Detail
5.159 Church at Nürnberg-Langwasser (see p. 240):
       underslung beam
5.160 Detail
5.161 Two-post underslung beam, sports hall, Lorch
       (see p. 300)
5.162 Detail of support
5.163 Detail of framing

5.157
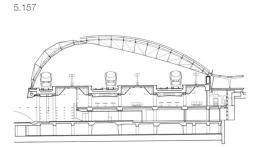

5.158
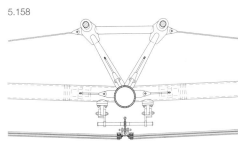

Hangers (tension) and polygon arch system
(compression)
• arch bridge with hangers

Posts (compression) and polygon arch system
(compression)
• polygon arch stabilized by beam
• beam stabilized by polygon arch

5.159
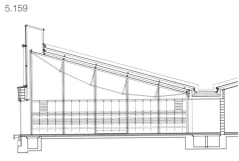

5.160
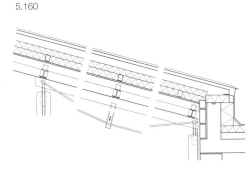

Hangers (tension) and arched framing (tension)
The beam is suspended from a number of
hangers (loaded exclusively in tension)
attached to a cable spanning between two
supports. The hangers represent intermediate
supports for the beam, although the tendency
of the cable to change its deflected shape
under different loading conditions means that
these supports yield somewhat. If dead loading is the dominant case, onto which other
loads of much smaller magnitude are superimposed, then this change in the deflected
shape is minor and the stiffness of the hanger
supports correspondingly high.

5.161
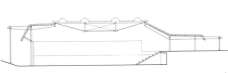

In the ground- or structure-anchored systems,
the tension in the cable is transferred into the
ground/structure via pylons. In this case the
beam is not subjected to axial loads, and is
thus easier to erect. In the self-anchored variation part of the cable force is redirected into
the beam and cancelled out by the force from
the support at the other end. The beam is precompressed by this system.

5.163
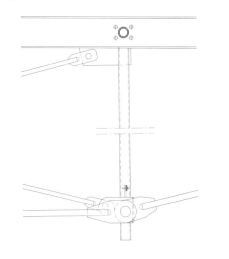

5.162
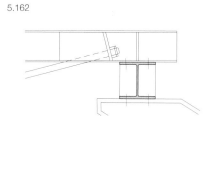

In cable-stayed bridges and comparable systems for buildings, hangers and arches coincide to form a series of inclined hangers.
Depending on the geometry of the inclined
cables, we distinguish between radial, fan,
harp and star arrangements. The cables are
normally anchored to pylons; bending in the
pylons is avoided by incorporating backstays.
An inclined, counterbalanced pylon avoids
bending only in the dead loading case.

5.165 Rigid frames as well as those with one, two and three hinges
5.166 Half-frame appended to main frame and articulated column-beam system
5.167 Storey-height frames
5.168 Bracing planar column-beam systems: with diagonals for tension and compression or cross-bracing with diagonals loaded only in tension
5.169 Braced frame construction with cross-bracing having diagonals loaded only in tension or diagonals for tension and compression
5.170 Pretensioned diagonals lead to a considerable decrease in deflection under horizontal loads

5.165

5.166

5.167   5.168   5.169

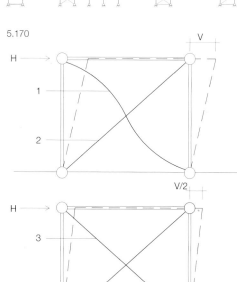

5.170

1 Diagonal redundant
2 Tension
3 Tensile force smaller than in pretensioned condition
4 Tensile force greater than in pretensioned condition

The hangers exclusively in tension form yielding, elastic supports for the beam. At the same time, they cause an axial compressive force in the beam, apart from at the centre, where there is a short section normally free from axial forces.

Posts (compression) and slung framing (tension)
Similar to the arched systems, slung framing increases the depth of the beam. But now the loadbearing cable is placed below the beam and the intermediate elastic supports formed by posts in compression. Anchoring the framing to the beam causes an axial compression in the beam which is superimposed on the bending stresses present all the time.

Underslung beams, like all planar systems subjected to bending, are prone to lateral buckling. The position of the fixing for the truss relative to the axis of the beam determines whether stable, imperfect or unstable behaviour is present. Stability can be assured by way of torsion-resistant encastré beam supports or – much more effective – by placing the ends of the truss below the beam axis.

A number of variations on the basic principle of slung framing, e.g. Fink or Le Ricolais trusses, can be distinguished depending on the arrangement.

Hangers (tension) and polygon arch system (compression)
This is the principle of the arched bridge with suspended road deck, but can be transferred to buildings at any time. The hangers transfer the vertical loads from the beam to the arch above, which is subjected exclusively to compression (ideal situation). If great variations in loading are expected, then either arch or beam must be provided with sufficiently high bending strength. Diagonal hangers attenuate the bending stresses in the arch caused by local loads by spreading these further afield in the arch and, in addition, stiffen the system by way of a truss effect.

Posts (compression) and polygon arch system (compression)
This group includes the polygon arch stabilized by a beam and the beam stabilized by a polygon arch, and all variations, all of which have already been discussed in this chapter.

Two-dimensional column-beam systems
Single-storey sheds, multistorey buildings or general structures for residential, industrial and transportation purposes in most cases consist of a three-dimensional combination of various beams and columns. These systems adhere to the principles outlined in "The loadbearing structure as part of the whole construction" regarding the conception of load-carrying paths or the attainment of overall stability as well as the principles of forming the components and their connections. Therefore, the groundwork for such systems has already been laid. Owing to their widespread use and hence the importance of these constructions, they are looked at in detail in the following. Knowledge gained about two-dimensional systems can be correspondingly applied to the three-dimensional ones.

The simplest way of roofing-over a space is to use frames consisting of columns and beams. Many variations are feasible: fixed column bases, one-, two- or three-hinged frames. As the number of hinges increases, so the deformation of the frame under a given load increases, but that due to restraint forces such as foundation settlement or temperature-related restraint stresses decreases. If possible, the hinges should be used as erection joints. If not, then joints should be incorporated in zones of low bending moment in order to keep the connection details simple.

Further half-frames or pairs of columns and beams with hinged joints may be appended to a main frame. The possible combinations are virtually limitless, although stability of the system must always be borne in mind. Placing erection joints at hinges or in zones of low bending should be regarded as a dictum. Restraint stresses caused by foundation settlement or temperature fluctuations should be kept as small as possible by positioning hinges carefully.

Stacking individual frames on top of each other renders possible multistorey buildings and high-rise towers. As such systems can be simply analysed without the need for computers, in the light of a lack of alternatives they formed the standard solution for high-rise buildings until well into the 1950s. The bases of the columns in such buildings normally incorporate hinges which aid erection. At the same time, the upper corners, subjected to bending, are strengthened. This arrangement is known as a portal frame. Skyscrapers with up to 102 storeys were built using portal frames, including the Chrysler Building, Empire State Building and the Chase Manhattan Bank, all in New York.

Of course, as they carry their loads by way of bending, rigid frames are structurally inefficient constructions. Therefore, only limited spans and heights can be justified economically. Extended horizontal arrangements fare better with inclined or diagonal members to transfer the horizontal loads to the foundation. The best known case is the cross-bracing between two pin-jointed columns linked by a beam or other member. If the diagonals are designed to be loaded exclusively in tension, then they can be very slender as they do not suffer from stability problems. If they are pretensioned, then both always contribute to resisting horizontal loads; no pretensioning means that one diagonal takes all the wind load while the other remains inactive, resulting in greater horizontal deflection of the system. If the diagonals are designed to accommodate compression as well, then under horizontal loading one diagonal is in tension, the other in compression.

A cross-braced column-beam system can also be interpreted as a plate. Like with a rigid frame, virtually any number of half-frames or pairs of columns and beams may be appended to both sides of such a "plate". Again, when designing such systems, the overall stability must be guaranteed, restraint stresses must be avoided and hinges incorporated at erection joints whenever possible.

The stacking of cross-braced column-beam systems leads to tower-like constructions suitable for bridge piers, high-bay racking or multistorey buildings. These systems can also be interpreted as vertical plates. Owing to the absence of bending stresses in the members, these (trussed!) plates are far superior to rigid frames. The amount of material required for these plates is much lower, the connections normally simpler and the horizontal deflections substantially smaller. Of course, diagonal members can be undesirable for some types of use. Therefore, they are placed on the facade, in permanent walls or, for multistorey buildings, in the core.

5.171
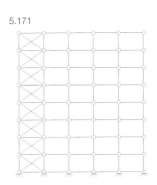

5.172
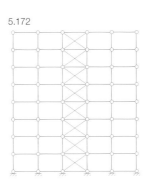

5.173
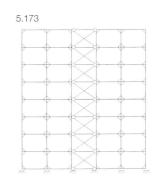

5.174
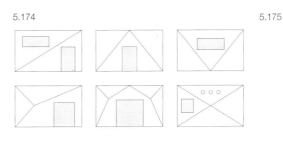

5.175
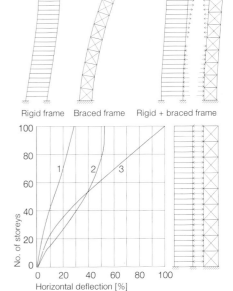

Rigid frame   Braced frame   Rigid + braced frame

5.176
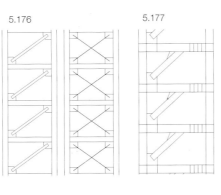

5.177
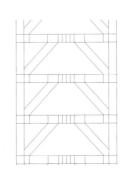
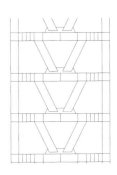

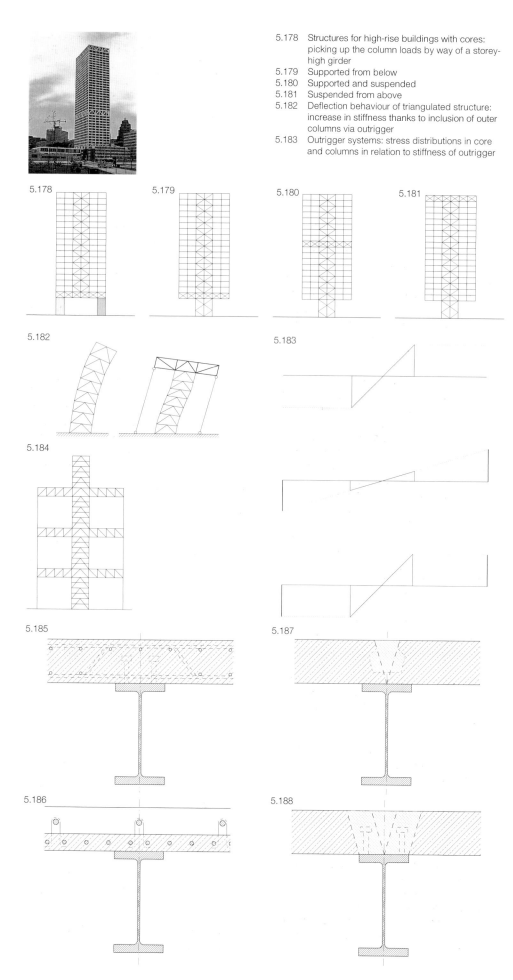

5.178 Structures for high-rise buildings with cores: picking up the column loads by way of a storey-high girder
5.179 Supported from below
5.180 Supported and suspended
5.181 Suspended from above
5.182 Deflection behaviour of triangulated structure: increase in stiffness thanks to inclusion of outer columns via outrigger
5.183 Outrigger systems: stress distributions in core and columns in relation to stiffness of outrigger

5.184 Structure employing several outriggers
5.185 Reinforced concrete floor slab supported on I-sections: in-situ concrete [440]
5.186 Precast concrete planks with later in-situ topping
5.187 Precast concrete planks joined later with grout infill [440]
5.188 Precast concrete planks joined above beam flange by means of shear studs [440]

5.178

5.179

5.180

5.181

5.182

5.183

5.184

5.185

5.187

5.186

5.188

Once again, various column-beam systems can be appended to a trussed plate. The very economical column-in-compression/beam-in-bending systems with hinged joints or hinged connections at the plate are customary. In this case the plate resists all the horizontal and part of the vertical loading. If the deflections under horizontal loads are too large, then the trussed plate should be widened, at least towards the base of the building. Alternatively, or perhaps combined with this, the appended systems could be designed as part-rigid. But compared to enlarging the internal lever arm by widening the plate, this solution consumes considerably more material.

Transfer structures enable the column spacing to be changed. Such structures are frequently necessary in, for example, high-rise buildings, in order to achieve a more spacious layout at ground floor level. With heavy loads and/or a specification calling for minimum deflection, this structure can be constructed as a lattice girder – up to one storey high if necessary.

A transfer structure can also pick up all the other columns of a high-rise block if necessary. We speak of a building on stilts or a point-block. The advantage of such a construction is that the base of the building remains to a large extent free from loadbearing elements.

Providing a sufficiently stiff transfer structure at the top of the vertical plate enables the individual columns to be suspended from above. We get a suspended structure where, once again, the base is virtually unencumbered by loadbearing members. The columns in such buildings, because they are in tension, are noticeably slimmer than in buildings with columns loaded in compression. However, it should be pointed out that the suspended columns, part of the primary structure, require appropriate fire protection. Non-loadbearing fire casings, or structurally significant concrete casings with pretensioned encased columns, bring about a considerable increase in the size of the column over that required for structural purposes.

A stiff transfer structure at the top of the verti-cal plate can also be connected to the col-

Three-dimensional frames and continua

5.189   Various forms of mesh for cable nets; quadri-
        lateral nets are the most common variety [42]
5.190   Cable net clamps:
        a Swaged – no rotation, for low loads
        b Bolted – no rotation and fixed angle
        c Bolted, for twin cables – no rotation and fixed
           angle
        d Swaged and bolted – rotation possible

umns supported by the foundation, particularly the outer columns, by way of hinges. This creates a so-called outrigger system in which the columns, otherwise only used to carry vertical loads, are called upon to carry horizontal loads as well. Owing to the large lever arm of these (outer) columns, an efficient loadbearing system is created, representing a worthwhile solution for high-rise buildings up to 50 storeys or other structures of similar height. Important here, and very interesting from an engineering viewpoint, is the coordination of the stiffening of the transfer structure(s). This enables the forces due to horizontal loads to be distributed precisely to the trussed plate or columns. It is possible to arrange several outriggers one above the other. The load on the trussed plate is reduced accordingly.

For office blocks, residential developments and other fields it is necessary to provide adequate fire protection to lifts and escape stairs. In Europe this requirement is usually fulfilled by providing a core of reinforced concrete. Given adequate loadbearing capacity and a suitable position within the building, this core can take over the functions of the vertical trussed plate providing resistance to horizontal loads. Therefore, the above considerations relating to a "vertical trussed plate" apply equally to a reinforced concrete core.

Three-dimensional frames loaded in tension
Polygonal tie systems
Like with the two-dimensional polygonal tie systems, forces distributed in three dimensions can also be interconnected via a system of linear members subjected exclusively to tension when the lines of action of all forces, or the lines of action of their resultants, intersect at one point and when their lines of action point outwards from this point.

Three-dimensional polygonal tie systems are used for suspended beam systems on pylons, for the trussing of lattice shells, for the three-dimensional tensioning of facades, and similar applications. It has to be ensured that the ties or cables always remain under tensile forces in all loading cases. This prevents slack, sagging cables and also the decrease in stiffness when some members are redundant in certain loading cases, which in turn would lead to greater deformations. If the system of ties is not stabilized by loads which are permanently active, i.e. pretensioned, then pretension is introduced in the form of ballast, tension springs on individual members or by incorporating members which are "too short". Like with all pretensioned systems employing members which are "too short", the pretension is affected by yield at the anchorages (displacement of the supports) and by temperature fluctuations.

As the members in three-dimensional tie systems do not usually meet at right-angles, detailing of the nodes demands special care. The "classic" solutions here are:
· cast steel nodes
· eye bars or plates welded to circular hollow sections or round bars
· eye bars or plates welded to solid steel spheres

Ties can be either high-strength round bars with screwed end fittings or cables with swaged or cast end fittings.
The use of turnbuckles should be avoided unless these can be made sufficiently aesthetically pleasing. Tolerances can usually be accommodated, also at the supports; the pretension is normally best applied by displacing the support(s) or by hydraulic jacks which pull the member(s) towards the support(s).

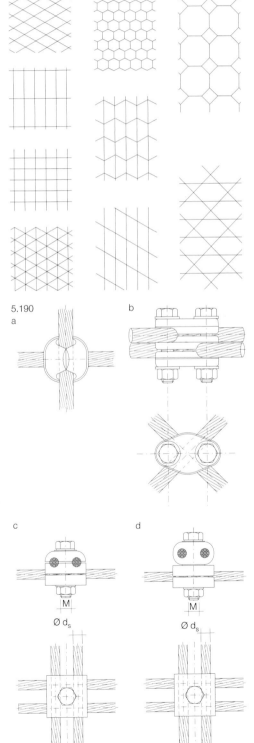

5.189

5.190

5.191 Arrangement of net cables at spandrel: cables running right into the corner should be avoided

5.192 A net cable practically coinciding with an edge cable should be interrupted because the short distances between the two cables are extremely difficult to deal with in practice.

5.193 Single edge cable and festoon cable attached to edge cable

5.194 Typical edge cable clamp for twin cable [259]

5.195 With customary cable clamps there is a kink in the line of action of the force, which results in the edge cable being subjected to bending [259]

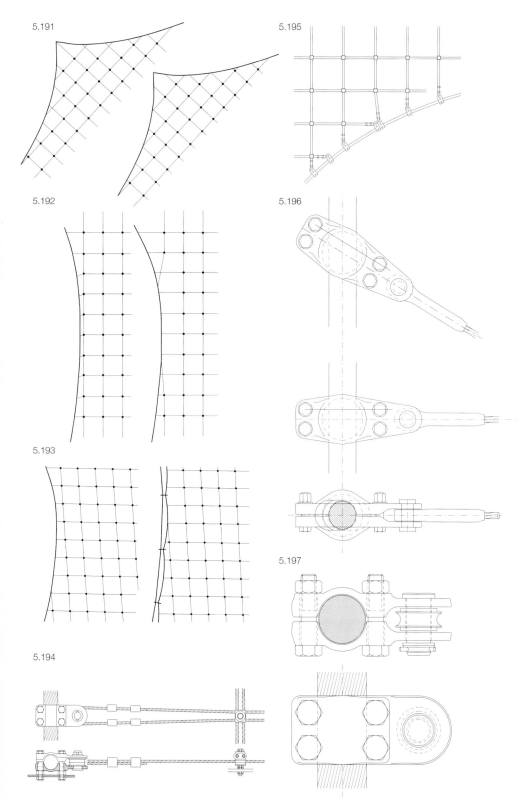

5.191

5.192

5.193

5.194

5.195

5.196

5.197

Cable nets

A cable spanned in one plane exhibits major changes in its deflected shape as the loading case changes. In the three-dimensional situation, a (loadbearing) cable can be stabilized by one or more (tensioning) cables positioned at right-angles to the cable axis. A structure consisting of several loadbearing cables and several tensioning cables is called a cable net. The individual cables of a net are interconnected via so-called cable nodes.

The arrangement of the individual cables results in regular or irregular meshes. Regular forms, e.g. triangular, quadrilateral or pentagonal meshes, are preferred for production reasons. The most popular design is the quadrilateral mesh with equidistant nodes. The reasons for this are, on the one hand, the comparative ease of fabrication and, on the other, the fact that almost any plan shape can be formed with – when pretensioned – normally adequate stiffness. Triangular-mesh nets with equidistant nodes only permit plan shapes with infinitesimal Gaussian curvature to be formed, i.e. plane or single-curvature nets. Double-curvature of the net requires differing node spacings, and that leads to an exceedingly complex fabrication exercise. Cable nets with pentagonal meshes are barely feasible with continuous cables because the cables have to be cranked at the nodes, leading to – with the 8-12 mm dia. cables commonly in use – large nodes because of the minimum bending radii which have to be maintained. Furthermore, cable nets with pentagonal meshes, in comparison to quadrilateral meshes, are much less stiff.

Generally, tension cable nets curved in two directions do not lend themselves to manual design methods. Therefore, so-called form-finding techniques are employed, whereby the use of experimental methods are recommended from the start right through to conclusion of the design. Thereafter, the precise but less graphic mathematical/numerical methods are used to establish the detailed form and geometry.

5.198

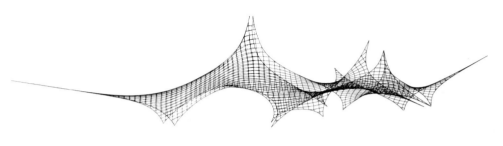

Cable nets are pretensioned in order to reduce the deformations caused by fluctuating external loads. This pretensioning is achieved by raising masts or by prestressing the cable stays. Turnbuckles within the net itself are no longer necessary because nowadays the net cables can be cut to size with sufficient accuracy.

Compared to plane nets, those curved in two directions exhibit less deformation and lower forces in the net cables. However, it must be ensured that the net cables run approximately in the planes of the principal radii of curvature. The further these cables stray from these planes, the less stiff the net becomes. If the net cables eventually approach the asymptote, then the loadbearing behaviour of the double-curvature net is transformed into that of a plane net.

Plane nets according to the "tennis racket" principle are very interesting for loadbearing systems. Such nets are bounded by a compression ring and given a very high prestress so that deflections under loads perpendicular to the net remain sufficiently small. Net and ring form a complete system of forces; foundations or adjoining components remain unaffected by the high prestressing forces. The surface of the net is glazed or covered by some other material; very filigree roofs or facades are thus possible.

Small nets up to 500 m² can be fabricated in the works; when complete they are rolled up ready for transporting to the site by road. Larger nets are assembled in situ and then lifted into position. In both cases the net cables are individually kinked and pulse-loaded prior to joining. Afterwards – still in the pretensioned condition – the positions of the clamps are marked on the cables. The regular quadrilateral meshes favoured these days normally employ twin cables because then the nodes can be connected with a single screw/bolt but still permit any mesh angle through rotation of the individual node levels relative to each

5.199

5.200

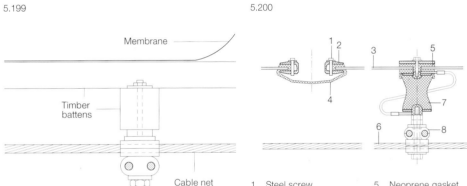

Membrane

Timber
battens

Cable net

1	Steel screw	5	Neoprene gasket
2	Clamping bar	6	Net cable
3	4 mm Plexiglas sheet	7	Neoprene shock-absorber
4	Neoprene seal	8	Net cable clamp

5.201

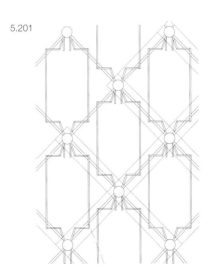

5.202

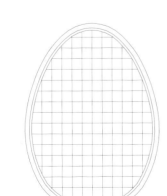

5.203 Solar reflector made from shaped metal
        membranes [259]
5.204 Spherical gas holders [441]
5.205 Horizontal cylindrical tanks [441]
5.206 Umbel column (in compression)

5.207 Lattice dome shaped like a truncated
        sphere [259]
5.208 Details: plan, without glazing [386]
5.209 Section, with glazing [386]
5.210 Stuttgart Airport: joint between umbel
        column and roof grid (see p. 326)

5.203

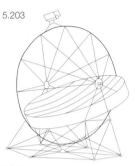

5.204

Foundation (reinforced concrete

Pad foundations

5.205

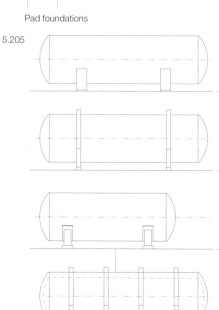

other. Ideal nodes are those made from swaged H-clamps; forged, cast or milled nodes are also possible. The standard clamps used for the joints between net and edge cables lead to bending being introduced in the edge cables. The use of a rotating edge cable clamp overcomes this unfavourable situation.

Cable nets always need to be covered in order to form an enclosing envelope. However, the often complex geometry of such nets means that this task is not always a simple one. Apart from that, such a covering should only be fixed to the nodes, which too creates additional constructional difficulties. Transparent coverings of PMMA or polycarbonate panels or glass shingles are currently popular. The joints between plastic panels are sealed with synthetic rubber gaskets; the panels are attached to the net nodes via individual fixings. But every plastic panel is different. Glass shingles can be used to form roofs which, although not completely weather-tight, do allow the use of a single pane size when a special stirrup fitting is employed. Such roofs are ideal for simple applications, especially in the leisure industry.

Metal membranes
Thin (approx. 0.2 mm) stainless steel plates, joined by means of a special welding process to form large panels, can be shaped to form highly precise double-curvature surfaces. The loading case determining the shape is usually applied by way of negative pressure or overpressure generated by air or water. Special safety measures must be taken when employing air overpressure in order to prevent escape of the compressed air coupled with a sudden relaxation (pressure wave, explosion loading).

Steam boilers, fluid and pressurized-gas holders
These vessels are one area of structural steelwork. They are fabricated by welding together plates cut to size and bent beforehand.

Three-dimensional frames loaded in compression
Polygonal strut systems
Like with the two-dimensional polygonal strut systems (see "Two-dimensional systems subjected to compression"), a system of linear members loaded exclusively in compression can be created in three dimensions when the lines of action of all external as well as reaction forces (or the resultants thereof) intersect at a point and the lines of action of all forces point towards this intersection. In contrast to the plane case where such systems of forces can be easily designed manually, the three-dimensional case normally requires the use of experimental or mathematical/numerical form-finding techniques.

Ideally, the struts are made from tubes, with haunched ends added if necessary. When it can be assured that a member is loaded exclusively in axial compression, forces can be transferred at the nodes via direct contact, if necessary with a retainer for the erection condition. Such connections can be very compact. The transmission of tensile forces must be guaranteed in all other cases, e.g. by a suitably designed bolted, screwed, pinned or welded connection.

Umbel columns
The principles for designing and constructing three-dimensional umbel columns are similar to those for the two-dimensional case (see "Two-dimensional systems subjected to compression"). Owing to the geometrical complexity of three-dimensional systems, experimental or mathematical/numerical form-finding techniques are required for their design.

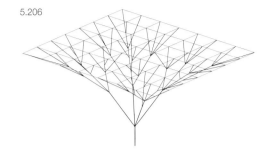

5.206

5.210

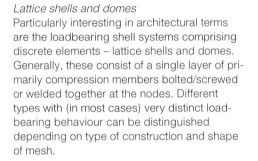

5.207

Lattice shells and domes

Particularly interesting in architectural terms are the loadbearing shell systems comprising discrete elements – lattice shells and domes. Generally, these consist of a single layer of primarily compression members bolted/screwed or welded together at the nodes. Different types with (in most cases) very distinct loadbearing behaviour can be distinguished depending on type of construction and shape of mesh.

Quadrilateral mesh systems with continuous members, bolted/screwed or welded together at the nodes, are known as lattice shells. The great advantage of the lattice shell is its ease of fabrication. Owing to the rotation about the member axis which a non-circular section – always placed tangentially to the surface of a plane in double curvature – undergoes, tubes are best for lattice shells. The great weakness of the lattice shell lies in its low shear strength – attributable to the lack of diagonals. As only low flexural rigidity can be realized at the nodes, the possible spans for this type of loadbearing system are severely limited. One remedy is to add diagonal members to the mesh. Rotationally symmetric systems with diagonals loaded exclusively in tension are designated Schwedler domes. So-called lattice domes are made from identical individual members joined via a special screwed node and braced by pairs of diagonal pretensioned cables. These lattice domes present no difficulties for fabrication. Moreover, they possess an excellent loadbearing behaviour – attributable to the inclusion of diagonals. Owing to the low "shell thickness" and the associated buckling risk, adequate curvature should be ensured; shallow-curved and/or very long-span lattice domes normally require additional bracing, e.g. with cables.

5.208

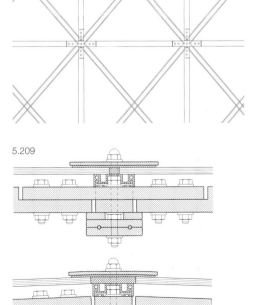

5.209

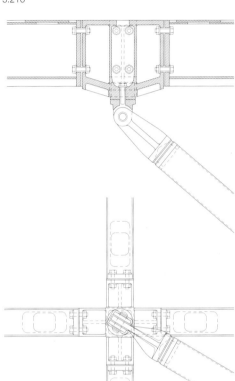

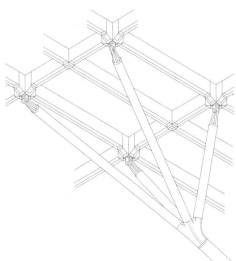

5.211
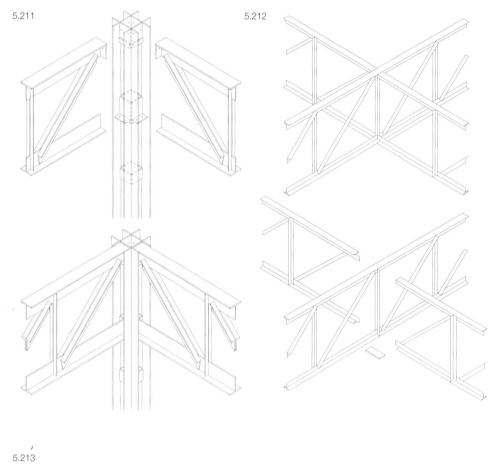

5.212

5.213
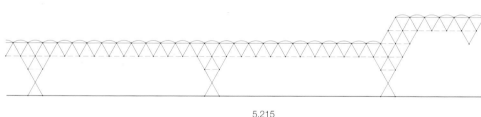

5.214
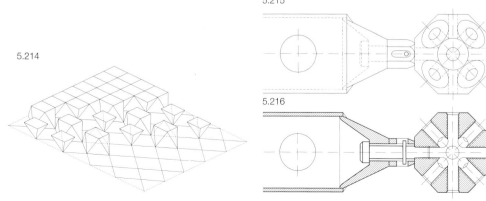

5.215

5.216

Shells and folded plates

Shells and folded plates
Shells curved in two planes and subjected exclusively to compression are comparatively rare in structural steelwork. The reasons for this can be found in the complicated fabrication processes for components curved in two directions (compare shipbuilding, for example) and, above all, the fact that although shells can be designed with thin walls owing to the high strength of the material, the buckling problem normally calls for thicker walls. Hence, this expensive material is not fully exploited and so loses its competitiveness.

Instead of increasing the thickness of the walls, the buckling problem can be countered by introducing stiffening ribs or similar components. Such measures are easily incorporated, particularly for shells with infinitesimal Gaussian curvature, e.g. cylindrical shells. The applications are manifold: steel chimneys, steel caissons, large-diameter pylons, etc.

If folded plates are employed as compression members, then the line of action of the forces must be in the direction of the folds. The folded plate is in this case regarded as a plate stiffened against buckling by its folds. Such components are correspondingly efficient.

Folded plates spanning open spaces are usually subjected to tensile as well as compressive forces. Corrugated or trapezoidal profile sheeting is very effective over short spans and hence very popular for such applications. For longer spans it is necessary to add stiffening ribs or similar to prevent buckling of the thin-walled folded plates in those regions under compression. Details of such stiffening measures are given below in "Orthotropic plates".

Space frames, single-layer grids, orthotropic plates
Space frames
The great structural efficiency of the plane frame and its simple connections led to this form of construction becoming one important domain of structural steelwork. It was thus only a small step to fabricating three-dimensional trusses as well from steel components. But while for the members of a truss nothing changed in the transition from two- to three-dimensional applications in terms of choice and size of section, the detailing of the joints (nodes) for the space frame became a major

trouble-spot. Connecting circular tubes by
way of welding is generally acceptable for
most cases but other hollow sections as well
as I-beams, channels and similar sections
require complicated gusset plates or special,
e.g. cast, nodes. Both methods are expensive,
and the use of gusset plates is highly unlikely
to prove aesthetically sound. In the light of this
problem it is not surprising to discover that
over the years many engineers and architects
have tried to develop the "ideal" node for
space frames. In most instances their ideas
concerning the nodes of space frames were
coupled with concepts for the standardization
and modularization of structural steelwork as
well as the simple in-situ erection of small
units.

The complexity of the jointing problem led to a
wide range of diverse solutions; each development had its own advantages and disadvantages. Generally speaking, the systems pro-
posed only permit members to be joined at
certain angles and positions, thus restricting
the range of geometries possible.

Without doubt the best known design is that of
Max Mengeringhausen (Mero system). The
many other comparable solutions differ only in
terms of the method of attaching the members
and the production of the node itself.

Single-layer grids
These are loadbearing systems consisting of
intersecting beams, normally at right-angles.
Intersections at other angles are possible but
are very much more complicated to fabricate
and hence expensive; they are only rarely
used. The same applies to triangular grids.

Single-layer grids carry loads which act perpendicular to the plane of the system, i.e. the
loads are carried in bending. The load distribution among the beams depends on the
ratios of their stiffnesses and their spans.
Orthogonal single-layer grids with a span ratio
of up to 1:1.5 can normally be assumed to
span in two directions. Higher span ratios lead
to the shorter span being favoured for carrying
the load and so the beams in the other direction play only a minor loadbearing role, indeed
become almost superfluous.

5.217
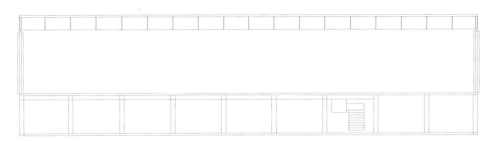

5.218
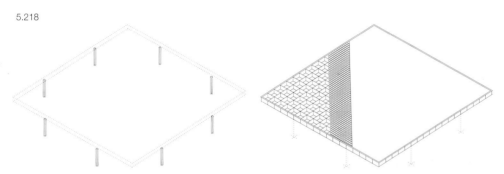

5.219
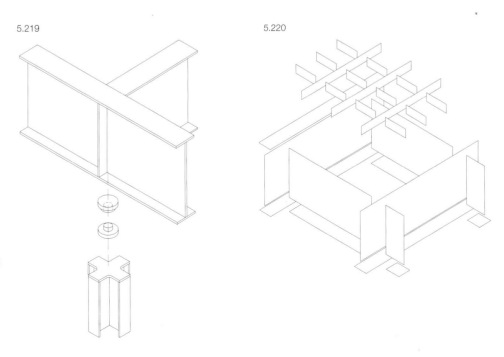

5.220

5.221

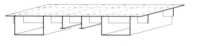

System I

System II

System III

System IV

5.222

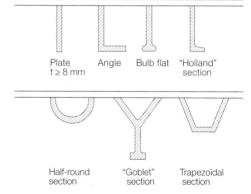

Plate
t ≥ 8 mm

Angle

Bulb flat

"Holland"
section

Half-round
section

"Goblet"
section

Trapezoidal
section

5.223

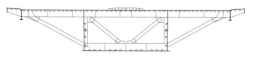

5.221 Orthotropic plates [440]
5.222 Ribs for orthotropic plates [440]
5.223 Section through steel bridge with deck formed
       by orthotropic plates [441]
5.224 Junctions between steel beams and in-situ
       reinforced concrete floor slabs:
       a Slab on I-beams
       b Bolted beam-beam shear connection,
          upper flanges flush
       c Welded beam-beam shear connection,
          upper flanges flush

d Overlapped beam-beam connection, bolted,
   only suitable for minor vertical loads
e Overlapped arrangement
f Beams provided with stiffeners for transferring
   larger vertical loads
5.225 Junctions between steel beams and composite
       floor slabs:
       a Slab on I-beams
       b Bolted beam-beam shear connection,
          upper flanges flush
       c Welded beam-beam shear connection,
          upper flanges flush

The bending capacity, or flexural stiffness, of single-layer grids can be considerably improved by adding framing below the individual beams. Therefore, the rigidity of the beams, now acting as the top chords, can be reduced accordingly. The slung framing arrangements discussed in the section "Beams with slung and arched framing" apply here too. The span ratio should not exceed 1:1.5 in order to ensure adequate two-way spanning, assuming the same depth of framing and identical sections.

Orthotropic plates
These are flat plates stiffened in two directions at right-angles. The plate itself is subjected to (limited) local bending as well as global tension or compression. (Some authors also speak of the shear stiffening effect of the plate. However, shear stiffening merely leads to a combination of tension and compression. The loadbearing behaviour is better understood when the term "shear stiffening" is used only occasionally.)

Most of the load in an orthotropic plate is carried by the system of reinforcing ribs, which are available with various profiles. It is important to ensure simple connections at the intersections and between stiffeners and plate.

Orthotropic plates are frequently encountered in steel bridge-building. Along the length of the bridge the stiffening is normally provided by trapezoidal or L-shaped rolled sections. At right-angles to these, welded T- or I-sections are very popular. Longitudinal and transverse stiffeners are welded to the deck plate in the factory to form large units. The dynamic loads to which bridges are subjected mean that special attention must be given to the detailing of the nodes and the design of the welds.

The orthotropic plate concept common in bridge-building can of course be employed in a similar format for buildings too. Moreover, constructions with rib arrangements, e.g. I-beams in both directions, are also feasible. Incidentally, the shipbuilding industry also makes use of the principle of the orthotropic plate in the construction of hulls and decks; likewise aircraft manufacture – for fuselages and wings.

Three-dimensional column-and-beam systems
Braced frames
These are loadbearing systems comprising columns, flat floor slabs and bracing elements. In the majority of cases the columns are designed as exclusively axially loaded (usually in compression only). In structural steelwork the floors are usually one-way spanning systems utilizing
• composite (trapezoidal profile sheeting with concrete topping),
• precast concrete, or
• in-situ reinforced concrete construction.

Composite and precast/in-situ concrete floors (or roofs) have to be connected to the steel beams such that shear can be transferred across the joint. A floor carries loads perpendicular to its system plane by way of local bending; these vertical loads are in turn carried by the steel beams to the columns. Horizontal loads, e.g. wind on the facade, braking forces, are carried by the plate effect of the floors and transferred to the bracing elements – normally solid wall plates or trussed arrangements, cores or a combination of these. The three-dimensional arrangements of the bracing elements discussed in the section "The loadbearing structure as part of the whole construction" apply here too.

d Overlapped beam-beam connection, bolted, only suitable for minor vertical loads
e Beams provided with stiffeners for transferring larger vertical loads
5.226 Beam supported in pocket
5.227 Beam supported on cleat
5.228 Web bolted to provide shear connection
5.229 Beam supported on cleat, web secured to prevent overturning (web can be designed to accept full shear force if required)
5.230 Moment connection (beam welded to cast-in end plate)

5.231 Bolted column-beam connection: shear carried by end plate, low moment capacity
5.232 Shear carried by angles
5.233 Moment carried by end plate
5.234 Moment carried by angles
5.235 Welded column-beam moment connection
5.236 With stiffeners over full depth of column
5.237 In-situ reinforced concrete floor slab with perimeter angle
5.238 Composite floor slab with perimeter channel
5.239 Precast concrete floor slab
5.240 Frame corner: with diagonal stiffeners

5.241 With continuous flanges
5.242 With continuous flanges and diagonal stiffeners (poor solution)

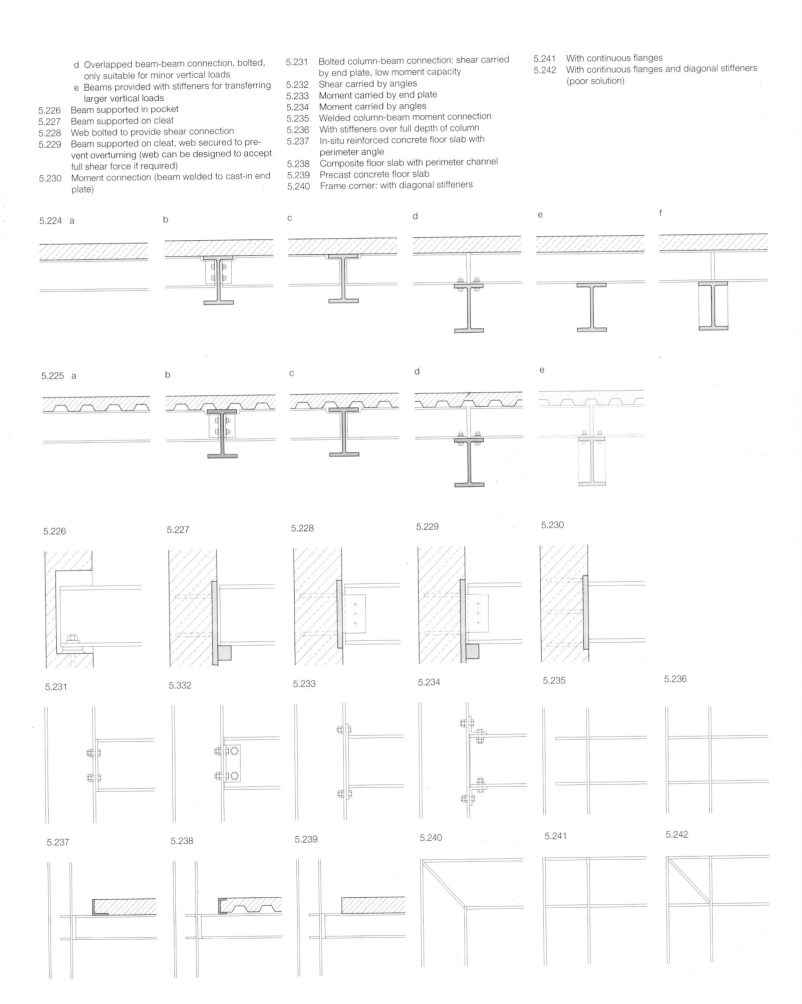

5.224 a   b   c   d   e   f

5.225 a   b   c   d   e

5.226   5.227   5.228   5.229   5.230

5.231   5.332   5.233   5.234   5.235   5.236

5.237   5.238   5.239   5.240   5.241   5.242

5.243   Positioning the core within the plan of a building.
        An eccentric arrangement will mean torsion is
        induced in the core under wind loads.
5.244   Steel collar for connecting steel column directly
        to reinforced concrete slab
5.245   Creating a plate effect by way of horizontal
        girders. Always necessary when a plate effect
        cannot be realized by way of concrete floors etc.

5.243

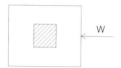

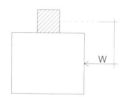

5.244

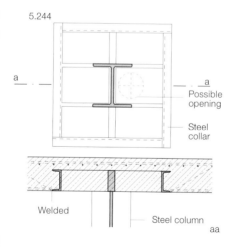

5.245

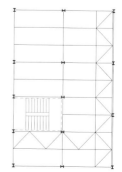

Rigid frames
In a rigid frame, e.g. a building with frames in
both directions, all the vertical loads carried by
the floor structure are transferred either into the
beams linking the columns or directly into the
columns. Horizontal loads are transferred from
the facade to the floors and then into the
beams. The beams and columns, rigidly connected with each other, accommodate the horizontal loads by way of axial, bending and
shear forces.

The columns and beams of a frame system
must be arranged and sized in such a way that
adequate stiffness is achieved to resist horizontal loads. In particular, the maximum permissible horizontal deflections caused by horizontal loads must not be exceeded. The horizontal displacement of a multistorey rigid
frame subjected to horizontal loads is primarily
caused by the bending deformation of the
columns and beams. Therefore, curtailing the
lateral displacement means increasing the
rigidity of the columns and beams. This is usually achieved by enlarging the sections,
changing the spans and enhancing the flexural
stiffness of the column-beam connections.

Loadbearing core systems
Cores, typically used in multistorey buildings
for enclosing (escape) stair shafts, lift shafts,
etc., can also be designed to contribute to the
loadbearing system. For reasons of fire protection, such cores are normally produced in reinforced concrete, although many structural steel
cores have been built, especially in the USA.
The latter are usually trussed constructions
with suitable fire-resistant cladding. A core can
be conceived as a vertical tube restrained in
the basement or the subsoil. So a core is suitable for carrying both vertical and horizontal
loads. Owing to its relatively short internal lever
arm, the stiffness of a core in relation to horizontal loads is comparatively low. Therefore,
pure core systems are very rare for very tall
buildings. When a core forms the only loadbearing element for vertical and horizontal
loads in a building, then the sensible, economic limit is about 30 storeys.

The core should be positioned centrally within
the plan of the building whenever possible in
order to minimize the torsion on the core
brought about by horizontal loads. In addition,
the centre of gravity of each floor slab should
lie in the vertical axis of the core.

One advantage of a pure core system is the
open-plan entrance zone – made feasible
thanks to fewer columns.

Typical loadbearing systems for pure core
arrangements are:
· core with cantilevered floors
· suspended building
· core with transfer structure

Core with cantilevered floors
This arrangement has only been employed for
a few applications because the cantilevering
floors require a considerable depth for the
spans required in offices, and this of course
increases the storey heights.

Suspended building
In this arrangement the columns are formed as
ties (or hangers) suspended from a structure at
the top of the building. This structure carries
the loads in bending and transfers them to the
core, which is then loaded in compression.

The great advantage of the suspended building is the complete freedom from columns at
ground floor. However, as with the pure core
system, the buildable heights are limited owing
to the comparatively low bending strength of
the core.

As the columns are loaded exclusively in tension, they do not suffer from buckling problems
and can be made very slender. However, the
actual column cross-section usually has to be
considerably enlarged to comply with fire protection requirements; thus the advantage of
columns in tension and the associated size
reduction is to a certain extent nullified by the
fire protection measures.

Core with transfer structure

This solution avoids columns at ground floor level by supporting the columns to the upper floors on an elevated structure which transfers the considerable column loads to the core. The high loads on this transfer structure, and the need for deflections to be kept very low and also be evenly distributed around the perimeter, mean that this transfer structure must be very rigid. Therefore, such structures, usually space frames, often have a depth of one, even two, storeys.

Outrigger systems

The outrigger arrangement is a loadbearing system in which the core is linked to the outer columns via a stiff girder at the top of the build-ing (outrigger). Horizontal loads, which would normally induce bending in the core, are in this case partly taken by tensile and compressive forces in the outer columns. The efficiency of the system can be influenced to a consider-able degree by apportioning the stiffnesses of core, girder and columns.

Tubes

Maximum efficiency with respect to wind and seismic loads acting on a slender structure cantilevering from the ground can be achieved when the building is designed as a hollow box of maximum size with additional, internal, hori-zontal stiffeners. This approach leads to the principle of the tube, in which the loadbearing system responsible for carrying horizontal loads is incorporated in the plane of the fa-cade. The internal lever arm of the "expanded core" – and a tube can be regarded as such – is a maximum in this case.

The need to include service and window open-ings in the solid-walled tube led to the devel-opment of the perforated tube. Extrapolating this idea to the limit – large, quadrilateral, regu-lar openings – results in the framed tube. This latter system was developed in the early 1950s and first used for the 43-storey Chestnut-De Witt apartment block in Chicago (arch./eng.: Skidmore, Owings & Merrill, 1963). However, this example is in reinforced concrete.

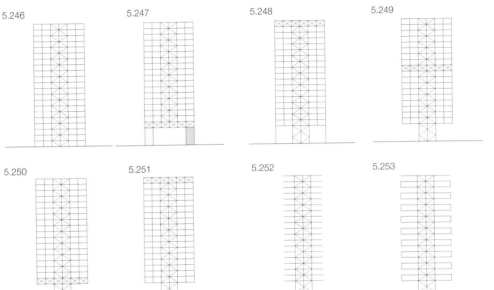

5.246   5.247   5.248   5.249

5.250   5.251   5.252   5.253

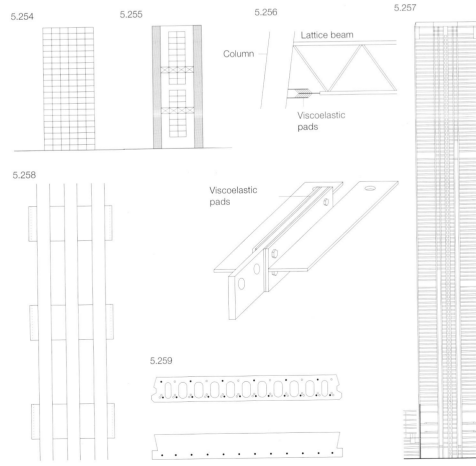

5.254   5.255   5.256   5.257

Column

Lattice beam

Viscoelastic
pads

5.258

Viscoelastic
pads

5.259

5.260

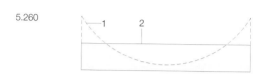

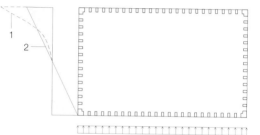

1   Stress distribution in columns as a result of shear lag
2   Stress distribution according to traditional bending
     theory

5.261

5.262

5.263

5.264

The principle of the tube in all its variations is at present the only method available for the economically justifiable construction of buildings exceeding 200 m in height.

Framed tubes

The framed tube system can be regarded as a tubular structure consisting of an extremely close mesh of frames. Horizontal loads are primarily carried by bending in the columns and beams. The beams of such tubes are in the form of spandrel beams. Limiting the building deflections requires highly rigid joints between columns and spandrel beams as well as a relatively close column spacing (1.2-3.5 m) and relatively deep beams (600-1200 mm). So framed tubes do not permit storey-high glazing to the facade.

The twin 110-storey towers of the World Trade Center, New York, (arch.: Yamasaki & Assoc.; eng.: Skilling, Helle, Christiansen & Robertson, 1966-73) are the tallest buildings in the world hitherto erected as single-cell framed tubes. The centre-to-centre spacing of the outer columns is 1.02 m. With its height/base length ratio of 7:1, the World Trade Center has reached the limit of slenderness for high-rise construction. In order to prevent possibly unpleasant oscillations of the building as a result of dynamic wind loads, about 10 000 viscoelastic dampers (working as friction dampers) were incorporated in each of the two towers. These dampers consist of two visco-elastic pads, each 100 x 250 x 1.3 mm, placed between steel plates.

The efficiency of framed tubes diminishes notably above 50 storeys for reinforced concrete and 80 storeys for structural steelwork owing to the so-called "shear lag effect": under horizontal loading each part of the tube parallel to the plane of the load acts as a frame. The columns at and near the corners attract more load than those in the middle of each side. Hence, the former are more highly loaded than should be the case according to traditional bending theory. The bending moments in the

columns and the beams in the end bays therefore become the governing design features in such structures.

The shear lag phenomenon leads to a very inhomogeneous load distribution among the individual columns. The consequence of this is that the columns must be of different sizes, which in turn leads to problems of standardization and detailing for the facade and the interior fitting-out. One answer is to use hollow sections with the same outside dimensions but varying wall thicknesses; however, this still means that the individual joint details vary slightly at each connection.

Tube-in-tube

The efficiency of the single-cell framed tube can be increased by incorporating the lift shaft as a loadbearing element. With slender high-rise office blocks in particular, the plan size of the lift shaft is normally large enough to allow the shaft itself to be designed as an efficient tube. The resulting structural system – an outer and an additional inner tube – is called a "tube-in-tube" system.

The floor structure links the two tubes together, allowing them to react to lateral loads as one unit. This structural interlinking raises the load-carrying capacity quite noticeably. The tube-in-tube system appears to be economic in steel up to about 80 storeys. One of the principal advantages of this type of loadbearing system is the marked reduction in the shear lag effect in the outer tube. Another benefit is the open-plan office spaces uninterrupted by any columns, since all vertical loads are carried by the floors to the outer and inner tubes. The clear span, i.e. the distance between the two tubes, is 10-12 m as a rule.

When designing a tube-in-tube structure it should be ensured that the inner tube is positioned at the centre of gravity of the outer tube. This reduces the wind-induced torsion effect on the core.

5.265

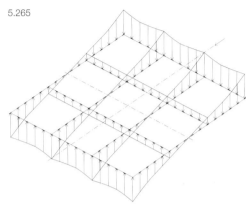

Bundled tube

Besides the tube-in-tube principle, the arrangement of a vertical diaphragm is a good way of improving the efficiency of the tube system even further. An additional diaphragm, normally in the form of a grid of columns and beams, can cut the shear lag effect quite significantly. At the same time, the stiffness in the horizontal plane is enhanced. Structures designed according to this concept looked like a bundle of tubes, hence their name "bundled tubes".

The stress distribution in a twin-cell tube subjected to wind load reveals quite clearly that the supplementary diaphragm parallel to the wind direction transfers the forces to the region of the junction between diaphragm and orthogonal outer wall (side) and in doing so brings about a reduction in the peak stresses along this plane. In comparison to the stress distribution in a single-cell framed tube it is easy to recognize how the additional diaphragm minimizes the shear lag effect in the outer tube and, in addition, how it leads to greater bending strength.

5.266

5.267

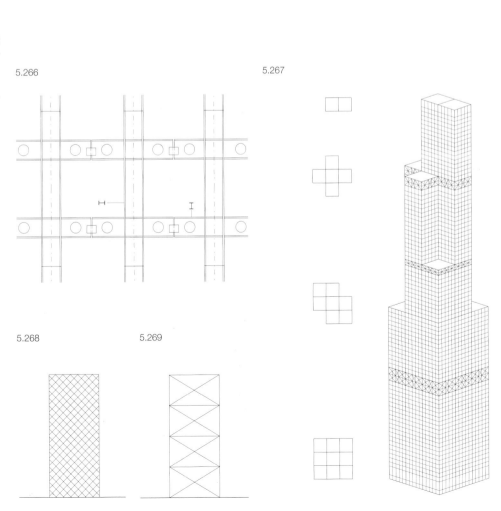

5.268

5.269

5.270

5.271

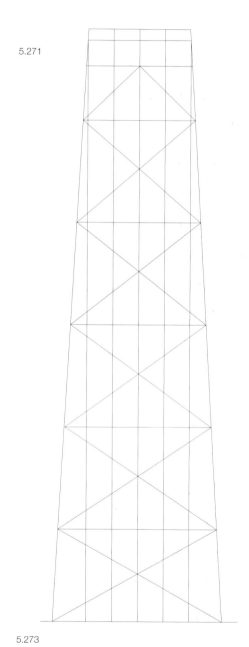

5.272

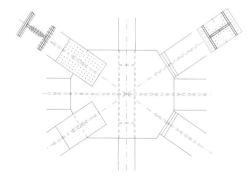

5.273

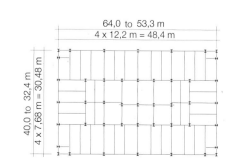

64,0 to 53,3 m

4 x 12,2 m = 48,4 m

40,0 to 32,4 m

4 x 7,68 m = 30,48 m

The bundled tube principle permits economic construction up to about 110 storeys. To obtain the best structural efficiency, the column spacing should not exceed 4.5 m. Furthermore, a certain ratio between the stiffnesses of columns and spandrel beams is necessary.

Sears Tower, Chicago, (arch./eng.: Skidmore, Owings & Merrill, 1974) was the first high-rise building to employ the bundled tube concept, and was the world's tallest building for many years. It is a good example of the efficiency of the bundled tube principle. The 442-m-high tower has 109 storeys and a total floor area of 409 000 m^2. To match internal space requirements, the plan form comprises nine single tubes of differing heights: 50, 66, 90 or 109 storeys. Each tube is made up of columns at a 4.58 m spacing and deep spandrel beams. Columns and beams together act like a framed tube. All column-beam connections are fully welded. The floor bays are formed by parallel girders at 4.58 m spacing and spanning 22.86 m. Each end of these girders is joined directly to a column. The direction of the span of the floor alternates every six floors in order to distribute the vertical loads evenly over the columns. The floor girders are 1.02 m deep.

Trussed tube
It seems that the maximum efficiency of a structure subjected to vertical and horizontal loads can be attained when the loadbearing components are arranged along the trajectories of the correspondingly loaded tubes, or the window openings in a solid-walled tube positioned so that the remaining material reflects the course of the trajectories. The first step in trying to implement this realization in a high-rise building was the trussed tube, consisting only of diagonal members.

Reducing the number of diagonals in the facade and adding vertical columns to carry the vertical loads, results in a so-called diagonalized tube structure. Normally in such a case, only a few sturdy diagonals are used; this reduces the number of oblique penetration points in the primary structure and limits the number of non-standard elements in the facade.

In contrast to a framed tube, which represents a construction with a high bending strength, the members of a diagonalized tube are essentially all axially loaded, leading to considerably better efficiency in terms of use of material. This method, developed for use in high-rise construction by Myron Goldsmith in 1953, was very skilfully employed in the 100-storey John Hancock Center, Chicago, (arch./eng.: Skidmore, Owings & Merrill, 1970). The inner columns of this building are only designed to carry dead loads. The outer columns, the diagonals and the primary and secondary ties form the diagonalized tube.

The shear lag problem is non-existent in diagonalized tubes. There is also no need for deep spandrel beams, which is why this system is ideally suited to storey-high glazing. Spandrel beams not required as horizontal ties merely need to be designed for local floor loads.

Megaframes
This term covers structural systems for high-rise buildings in which the primary structure is formed by a few very large members and the secondary structure then suspended from or supported on this. Typical examples of megaframes (or superframes) are designs in which services and access are concentrated in tower-like shafts coupled together by way of large diagonals or transverse elements.

5.274

5.275

Part 6 • Built examples in detail

Helmut C. Schulitz
with Martin Siffling

The first *Steel Construction Manual* by Hart, Henn and Sontag published in 1974 (2nd edition 1982) confined itself to multistorey structures. Before we embarked on this new edition of the *Manual*, we discussed whether it was sensible and feasible to produce a single book covering both multistorey and shed-type structures.

The authors of this new edition quickly agreed that two separate books, one for multistorey structures, the other for shed-type structures, would be inadvisable because the fundamentals of the material itself, its manufacture and processing, as well as the principles of its fabrication and jointing, are identical for both types of structure.

In the final analysis, a multistorey structure can also be considered as a stack of shed-type structures, and even more complex constructions, such as the Gerber system, can be applied to both multistorey and shed-type structures, as the Centre Pompidou in Paris has shown.

So the only part which remained as a potential candidate for being split into multistorey and shed-type structures was this section on built examples. But here too there were problems in classifying structures because many of those covered here are not clearly one or the other. For example, the design offices in Gundelfingen (No. 27), the circular hall in Berlin (No. 25) or the CIM Institute in Braunschweig (No. 21), all of which are a combination of multistorey and shed-type construction.

Therefore, we decided to take a different approach, as can be seen in the previous chapters: exposing individual construction principles irrespective of type of structure. The function of the structure plays no part in the aim of this approach. So a production plant may well surface alongside a residential development and this in turn rub shoulders with an office block. The arrangement is more of a progression from the simple to the complex; the final examples include ambitious cable-stayed and high-rise projects.

We have tried to assemble examples from all fields of structural steelwork in order to present the most diverse and exemplary construction principles of a more general nature. The emphasis was on recording examples which have managed to minimize consumption of material and erection works by way of careful, intelligent design.

The selection was made according to architectural criteria. As the drawings and documentation of some projects were not made available to us, not all of the structures originally envisaged were able to be included in this selection.

The examples shown here come from a number of countries and are subject to different conditions in terms of climate, standards of building and regulations. Despite the limitations of space, an attempt has been made to place the steelwork in the context of the whole design by means of drawings and photographs. The authors do not regard the object of this exercise as being to highlight particular examples without reference to their location and overall concept in order to transfer these thoughtlessly to other building tasks. Instead, the aim should be to reanalyse, interpret and adapt these to new circumstances; in other words, these examples are intended to serve as inspiration for new creations.

No.	Page	Architects	Structural engineers	Project	Features of the steelwork
1	228	Schaudt Architekten, Constance	Ingenieurbüro Leisering, Constance	Terraced house, Constance	Simple column-and-beam system
2	230	CEPEZED B.V., Delft	ECCS, Hoofdorp	Semi-detached houses, Delft, Netherlands	Simple column-and-beam system
3	232	Schulitz + Partner, Braunschweig	Michael Sprysch, Vechelde	Detached house, Rotenburg/Wümme	Trussed beams, lattice beams
4	236	Schuster Architekten, Düsseldorf	Müller Marl, Marl	Offices, Nordkirchen	Trussed beams
5	240	Eberhard Schunck, Dieter Ullrich, Munich	Fritz Sailer and Kurt Stepan, Munich	Protestant church, Nürnberg-Langwasser	Trussed beams
6	242	Frank Geiser, Bern	Duppenthaler + Wälchli, Langenthal	Local authority offices, Langenthal, Switzerland	Simple column-and-beam system, columns exposed externally
7	246	Jean Nouvel, Paris	Ove Arup & Partners, London	Exhibition hall and offices, Paris	Simple column-and-beam system, storey-height frames longitudinally
8	248	Herbert Schaudt, Constance	Karl Fischer, Constance	Bookshop, conversion and extension, Constance	Simple column-and-beam system, loadbearing balustrades to stairs
9	252	Wilhelm Kücker, Munich	Martinka + Grad , Eichstätt	Library, Ingolstadt	Addition to existing structure, minimization of construction depth by way of made-up section
10	254	Foster and Partners, London	Anthony Hunt Associates, London	Museum, refurbishment and conversion, London	Addition to existing structure, restraint provided by floors
11	258	Gullichsen, Kairamo, Vormala, Helsinki	Raimo Sormunen, Helsinki	Fire station, Espoo, Finland	Diagonal bracing to steel tower
12	260	Ingo Bucher-Beholz, Gaienhofen	Helmut Fischer, Bad Endorf	Houses, Gaienhofen-Horn	Two-hinged frames transverse to building
13	262	Glenn Murcutt and Associates, Mosman	James Taylor and Associates, Mosman	Detached house, Northern Territory, Australia	Rigid frame
14	264	Waro Kishi and K. Associates, Kyoto	Urban Design Institute, Osaka	House, Osaka, Japan	Storey-height frame
15	266	Schulitz + Partner, Braunschweig	Michael Sprysch, Vechelde	Service building, Magdeburg	Frame with girders
16	268	Fritz Haller, Solothurn	Emch and Berger, Bern	Production plant, Münsingen, Switzerland	Frame system with girders
17	270	Benthem Crouwel, Amsterdam	Ingenieurbüro Starmans, Cees van Eden, Groningen	Industrial building, Opmeer, Netherlands	Triangular girder frames with fixed bases
18	274	Finn Geipel, Nicholas Michelin, LAB FAC, Paris	Werner Sobek Ingenieure, Stuttgart with Andrew Sedgwick, Ove Arup & Partners, Cetec Limoges	School of Art, Limoges, France	Vierendeel secondary girders, lattice beams
19	278	Nicholas Grimshaw and Partners, London	Ove Arup & Partners, London	British Pavilion, EXPO 92, Seville, Spain	Fixed-base lattice columns, lateral buckling protection to deep girders
20	282	von Gerkan · Marg + Partner, Hamburg	Schlaich, Bergermann + Partner, Stuttgart	Trade fair hall, Hannover	Fish-belly girders
21	284	Schulitz + Partner, Braunschweig	Motzkus & Völker, Wolfenbüttel Michael Sprysch, Vechelde	CIM Institute, Braunschweig	Composite construction with infill concrete (fire protection)
22	288	Schneider + Schumacher, Frankfurt am Main	Bollinger + Grohmann, Frankfurt am Main	Information centre, Berlin	Composite construction with infill concrete (fire protection)
23	290	Gerhard Spangenberg, Berlin	GSE-Ingenieurgesellschaft, Berlin	Editorial offices, Berlin	Composite construction with infill concrete (fire protection)
24	292	Michael Hopkins and Partners, London	Buro Happold, Bath	Office buildings, Bedfont Lakes, UK	Column sizes corresponding to loads
25	294	Gerd Fesel, Peter Bayerer, Hans-Dieter Hecker, Roland Ostertag, Berlin	Stephan Polónyi, Herbert Fink, Peter Koch, Berlin	Circular hall, Berlin	3-dimensional frame nodes for radial connections
26	296	Renzo Piano Building Workshop, Paris	Ove Arup & Partners, London	Production plant, Saint-Quentin-en-Yvelines, France	3-dimensional girders
27	298	Kurt Ackermann and Partner,	Behringer and Müller, Munich Jürgen Feit, Munich	Design offices, Gundelfingen	Trussed beams on cantilever frame construction
28	300	Behnisch & Partner, Stuttgart	Julius Natterer, Munich	Sports hall, Lorch a. d. Rems	Gerber system girders on cantilever frame construction

No.	Page	Architects	Structural engineers	Project	Features of the steelwork
29	302	Renzo Piano, Richard Rogers, London	Ove Arup & Partners, Paris	"Georges Pompidou" arts centre, Paris	Gerber system with cast steel Gerberettes
30	306	Cox, Richardson, Taylor + Partners, Sydney	Ove Arup & Partners, London	Exhibition centre, Sydney, Australia	3-dimensional stayed construction
31	308	Richard Rogers Partnership, London	Anthony Hunt Associates, London	Factory, Newport, UK	Stayed construction
32	312	Richard Rogers Partnership, London	Ove Arup & Partners, London	Factory, Quimper, France	3-dimensional stayed construction, stability via struts/ties
33	316	Nicholas Grimshaw and Partners, London	Whitby + Bird, London	Production building & offices, Cologne	3-dimensional suspended construction
34	318	Behnisch & Partner, Stuttgart	Schlaich, Bergermann + Partner, Stuttgart	Plenary chamber & presidential annex, German Bundestag, Bonn	Suspended roof construction
35	320	Peter Kulka, Dresden	Varwik-Horz-Ladewig, Cologne	Regional parliament building, Dresden	Beam grid
36	322	Schomers, Schürmann, Stridde, Bremen	Sobek and Rieger, Stuttgart	Bus terminal, Delmenhorst	Beams subjected to torsion
37	326	von Gerkan · Marg + Partner, Hamburg	Weidleplan Consulting, Stuttgart	Airport terminal, Stuttgart	Umbel columns
38	330	Kaag + Schwarz, Stuttgart	Schlumbohm, Stuttgart	Access pavilion to underground car park, Biberach	Free-standing open flared-head column construction
39	332	Foster and Partners, London	Ove Arup & Partners, London	Airport terminal, Stansted, UK	Open flared-head column structures
40	336	Schulitz + Partner, Braunschweig	RFR, Paris	Pedestrian walkway, trade fair grounds, Hannover	Suspended, discrete system
41	340	Renzo Piano Building Workshop, Genoa	L. Mascia, D. Mascia, Genoa	Station for light rail network, Genoa, Italy	2-hinged arch
42	343	Herzog + Partner, Munich	Sailer and Stepan, Munich	Exhibition & congress centre, Linz, Austria	2-hinged arch
43	346	Richard Brosi + Partner, Chur Robert Obrist + Partner, St Moritz	Ove Arup & Partners, London with Peter Rice, Alastair Hughes	Rail and bus terminal, Chur, Switzerland	Arch with internal bracing
44	348	von Gerkan · Marg + Partner, Hamburg	Polónyi + Partner, Cologne Schlaich, Bergermann + Partner, Stuttgart	Central entrance hall, new trade fair grounds, Leipzig	Lattice barrel vault shell with external bracing
45	352	von Gerkan · Marg + Partner, Hamburg	Weber, Poll + Kockjoy, Hamburg	Airport terminal, Hamburg	Triangular lattice girders on raking columns
46	356	Renzo Piano Building Workshop, Paris	Ove Arup & Partners, London	Airport terminal, Osaka, Japan	Triangular lattice girders on raking columns
47	360	Nicholas Grimshaw and Partners, London	Anthony Hunt Associates, Cirencester	Waterloo International Rail Terminal, London	3-hinged arch
48	364	Michael Hopkins and Partners, London	Ove Arup & Partners, London	Multi-purpose hall, Nottingham, UK	Stayed membrane construction
49	368	Schweger + Partner, Hamburg	Sobek + Rieger, Stuttgart	Tennis stadium, Hamburg	Cable construction with opening membrane roof
50	372	Foster and Partners, London	Ove Arup & Partners, London Julio Martinez Calzon	Telecommunications tower, Barcelona, Spain	Stayed mast in multistorey construction
51	374	Murphy/Jahn, Lester B. Knight & Associates, Chicago	Murphy/Jahn	State of Illinois Center, Chicago, USA	Space frame
52	378	Richard Rogers Partnership, London, Architect 5 Partnership	Umezawa Design Office, Tokyo	Business premises, Tokyo, Japan	Storey-height frames with concrete casing, earthquake-resistant design
53	380	Foster and Partners, London	Ove Arup & Partners, London	Bank headquarters, Frankfurt a. M.	High-rise building employing composite construction
54	384	Foster and Partners, London	Ove Arup & Partners, London	Bank headquarters, Hong Kong	High-rise building employing work suspended steelwork

Example 1

Terraced house, Constance

1993

Architects: Schaudt Architects, Constance
Project Architect: Martin Cleffmann
Project team: M. Münzenmaier, J. Dreher
Structural engineers:
Ingenieurbüro Leisering, Constance

This row of eight housing units is the result of a steel design competition. One of the houses was purchased by the architects themselves and built along the lines of open-plan living according to their own drawings. In the other houses, solid masonry walls, reinforced concrete floors and fixed internal partitions were erected instead of the planned open, braced steel frame structure.

The structural steelwork offers excellent flexibility internally and a high degree of transparency thanks to the inclusion of large areas of glass in the facades. The individual floor layouts can be easily rearranged by subsequent owners if desired; this is helped by the lightweight floors made from larch boards. The ground floor can be used separately from the rest of the house.

The entire structure consists of hot-dip galvanized steel. Even some of the floor coverings, furniture and external components make use of galvanized steel.

All the diagonal wind bracing has been left exposed, reinforcing the impression of the bold lightness of the house.

References: [145], [158], [433]

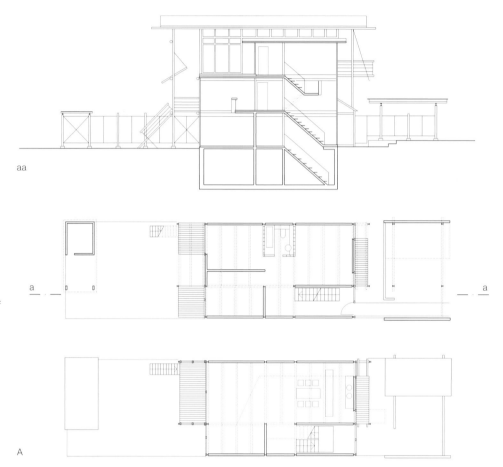

A   Section · plans of ground and
    1st floors, scale 1:250
B   Horizontal section through
    facade, scale 1:20
C   Roof beam, elevation and
    plan, scale 1:75
D   Elevation showing bracing
E   Detail of bracing: elevation
    and horizontal section,
    scale 1:10
F   Vertical section through
    facade, scale 1:20

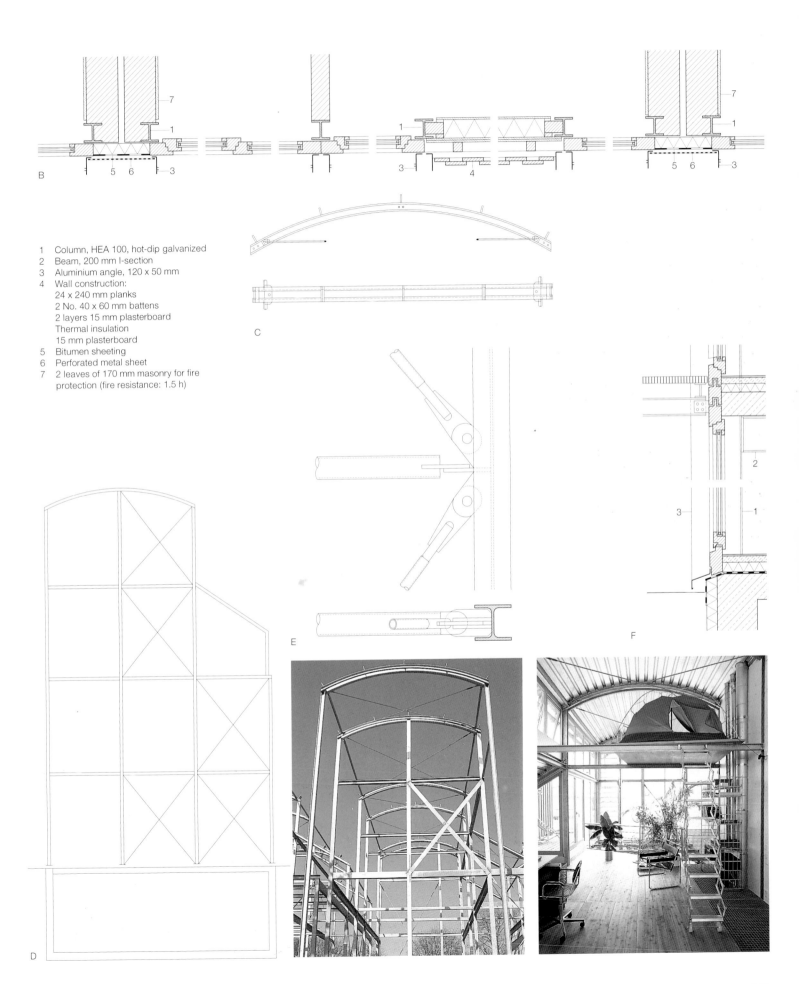

B

1   Column, HEA 100, hot-dip galvanized
2   Beam, 200 mm I-section
3   Aluminium angle, 120 x 50 mm
4   Wall construction:
    24 x 240 mm planks
    2 No. 40 x 60 mm battens
    2 layers 15 mm plasterboard
    Thermal insulation
    15 mm plasterboard
5   Bitumen sheeting
6   Perforated metal sheet
7   2 leaves of 170 mm masonry for fire
    protection (fire resistance: 1.5 h)

C

D

E

F

Example 2

Semi-detached houses, Delft, Netherlands

1990

Architects:
CEPEZED B.V., Delft
J. Pesman
Structural engineers:
ECCS, Hoofdorp

In 1989 the City of Delft, in conjunction with a local designers' group, sponsored a competition for the design of a series of semi-detached houses for a new housing development. From the 50 designs submitted, eight were chosen for the project. The unit described here makes use of a braced steel frame and represents a simple and economic solution.

The steel frames of the two halves of the building are structurally independent. The eight tubular columns (139.7 mm dia.) of each half are placed at 3.77 m centres longitudinally and 6.53 m transversely. At storey height the columns are linked diagonally with IPE 300 beam sections. The core, containing ancillary rooms and services, extends the full height of the building and runs diagonally through the centre of each half. The connections of the steel frame were designed to facilitate quick and simple erection on site, including the prefabricated metal facade elements. Apart from the concrete ground slab and the masonry party wall, steel and aluminium were used throughout so that the building appears as a consistent metal construction.

Reference: [143]

A   Isometric view, not to scale
B   Plans of ground and 1st floors
C   Arrangement of beams, plan of 2nd floor
Scale 1:200
D   Isometric detail of column/beam/facade junction

E   Vertical sections through roof and floor junctions
F   Horizontal section through column/beam/facade junction
G   Horizontal section through corner of facade
Scale 1:10

A

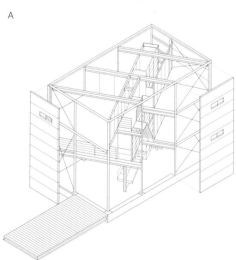

B

C

1 Column, 139.7 dia. x 5 mm circular
  hollow section
2 Beam, IPE 300
3 Wind bracing, 24 mm dia. round section

4 Metal facade sheeting with 100 mm insulation
5 Double glazing in aluminium frame with EPDM
  cover strip
6 Variable sunshading of aluminium louvres

D
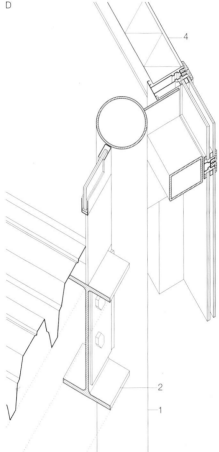

E
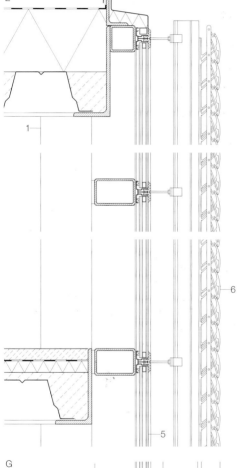

F

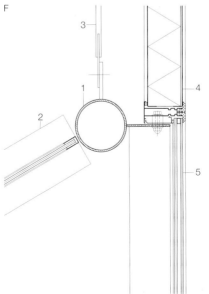

G
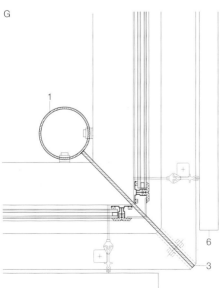

Example 3

Detached house, Rotenburg/Wümme

1995

Architects:
Schulitz + Partner, Braunschweig
H.C. Schulitz, M. Rätzel, J. König
Structural engineer:
Michael Sprysch, Vechelde

The design was based on the theme "Living with Nature" and the house was built in a forest clearing. In contrast to the customary detached family homes of this community, which require artificial lighting indoors even during the daytime owing to the shade from the trees, the transparency of this building allows the changing times of day and changing seasons to be experienced in the interior. The modular plan layout meant that no trees worth preserving had to be felled.

The building is comprised of two blocks either side of a central link whose monopitch glass roof ensures adequate lighting in the interior. The solar heat gain through the glass contributes to heating the house on sunny winter days.

The non-glazed parts of the facade employ a sandwich construction consisting of plasterboard internally and a ventilated weatherproof skin of coated aluminium corrugated sheeting. The loadbearing structure is formed by a frame of hollow sections on a basic grid of 1.8 x 1.8 m. Trussed beams span the individual rooms. The soffit of the roof consists of trapezoidal profile sheeting laid directly on the beams. Internal steel components are finished with a coat of paint to prevent corrosion; the external parts are hot-dip galvanized.

References: [55], [174]

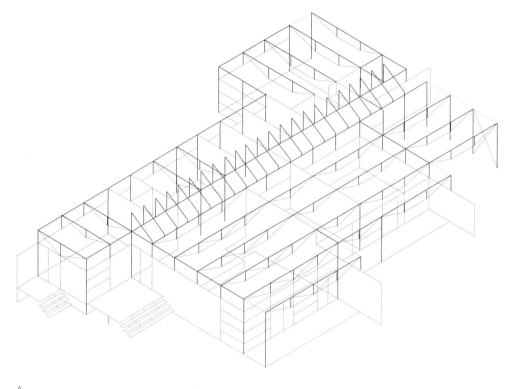

A

A Isometric view of frame, not
  to scale
B Elevation and plan,
  scale 1:200

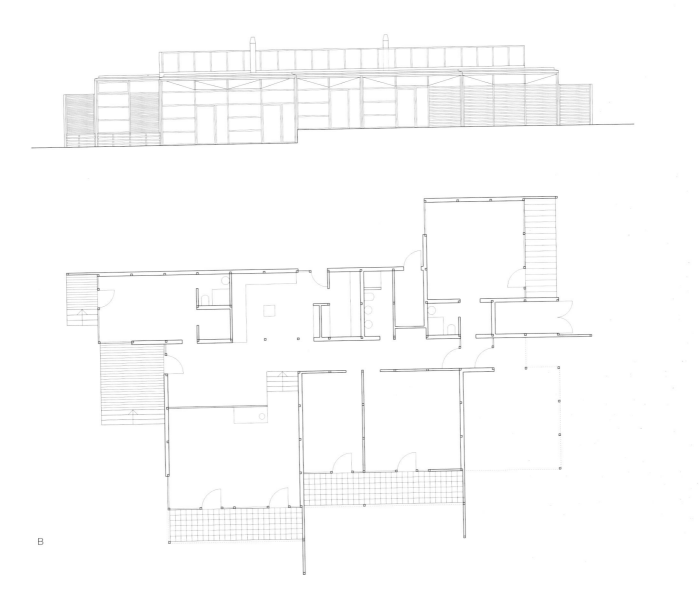

B

Example 3

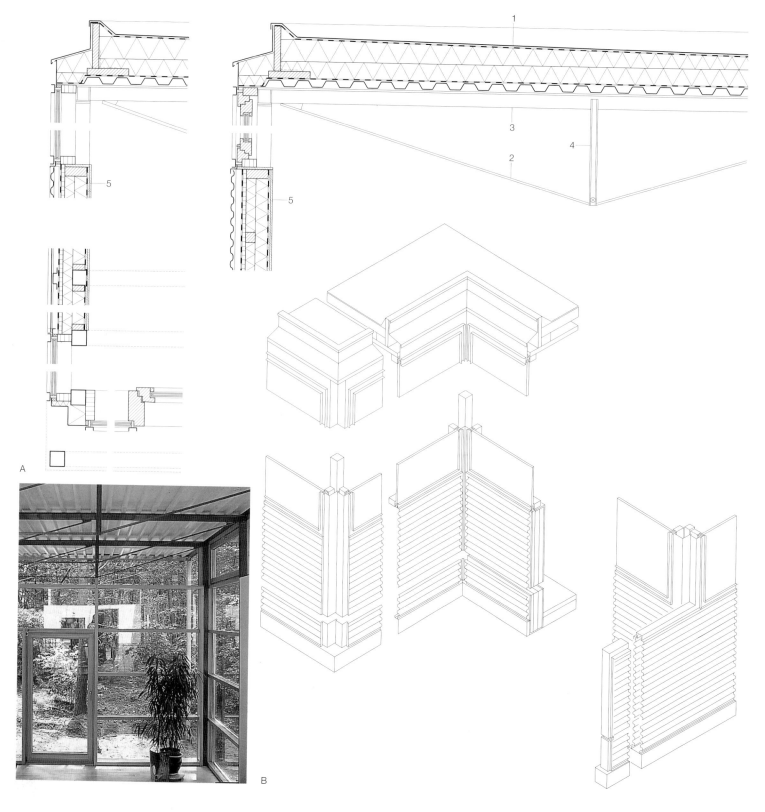

A

B

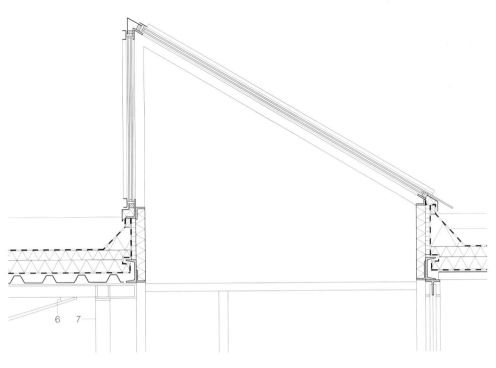

6 7

A   Details of facade: vertical section, horizontal section, rooflight
Scale 1:20
B   Isometric view of facade construction
C   Isometric view of steel to rooflight

1   Roof construction:
    Welded elastomer-bitumen sheeting
    80 mm insulation (supplied in rolls) with
    vapour pressure equalization
    Wedge-shaped layer of insulation (to provide fall),
    min. thk 80 mm
    Vapour barrier
    E40 steel trapezoidal profile sheeting
2   18 mm dia. tie
3   Top chord, 80 x 80 x 9 T-section
4   2 No. 40 x 20 channels
5   Wall construction:
    2 layers 12.5 mm plasterboard
    Vapour barrier
    70 mm mineral-fibre insulation
    Battens with 50 mm mineral-fibre insulation between
    19 mm chipboard
    Foil seal against wind and rain
    Battens with cavity between, 45 mm
    Aluminium corrugated profile panels, 18 x 76 mm
6   9 mm gusset plate
7   80 x 80 mm glulam columns

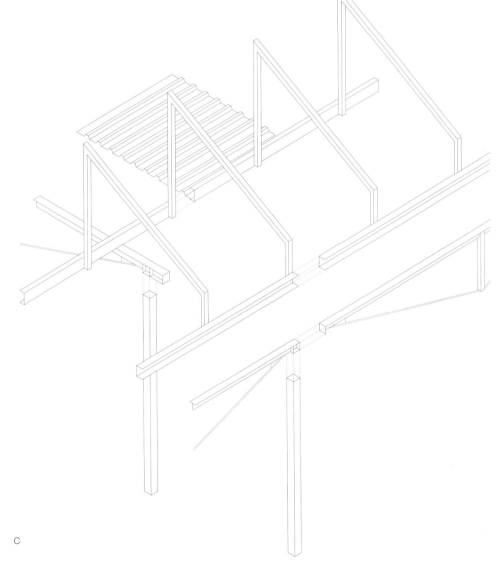

C

Example 4

Offices, Nordkirchen

1994

Architects: Schuster Architects, Düsseldorf
Project Manager: Sabine Koeth
Project team: K. Legner, A. Löf, M. Uhl
Structural engineer:
Müller Marl, Marl

Three cubic blocks clad in aluminium interlinked by transparent halls.
The multipurpose offices in reinforced concrete
present a sharp contrast to the lightweight,
transparent, glass-and-steel constructions of
the halls between, housing entrance zone and
cafeteria.
Hinged columns support the roof construction
of trussed steel sections on which the trapezoidal profile sheeting is laid and left exposed
internally. Horizontal forces are directed via
bearings to the adjoining components. Deli-
cately detailed eaves emphasize the buoyant
character of the roofs over the halls and the
glass curtain walls held by individual fixings
present a homogeneous, transparent skin
spanning between the office blocks. The
double-glazed panes are fixed to the Vierendeel posts via specially developed joints.
Movable glass louvres for ventilation (and acting as smoke vents) are located at the ends
where the halls overlap the offices. Steel, concrete and glass each retain their natural character and are used in a way which suits their
material properties. Thus, the exposed fair-
face concrete contrasts with the precise lines
of the steelwork, while the warm colours of the
maple-wood treads offset the intricate engineering details of the steel stair.

References: [142], [171]

1	Main beam	5	Light fittings
2	Secondary beam	6	Trapezoidal profile
3	Tubular column		sheeting
4	I-section column	7	Sunshading

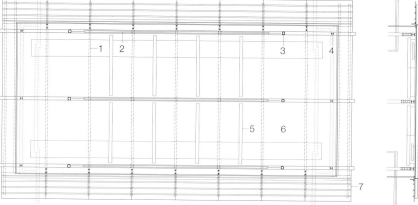
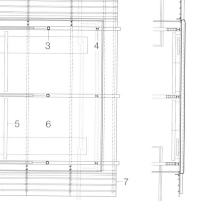

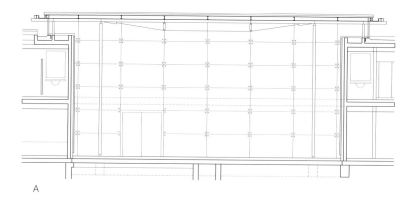

A

A   Entrance zone, underside of
    roof, sections through hall and
    roof, scale 1:200

B   South-east elevation, plan,
    scale 1:500

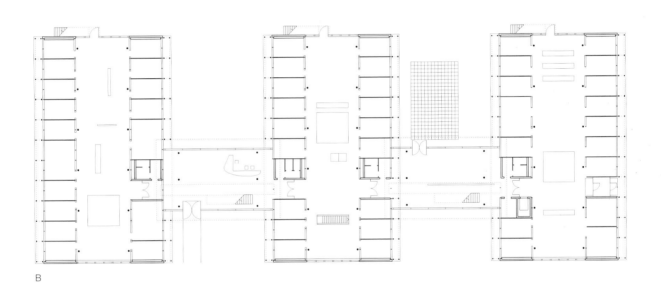

B

Example 4

A   Roof structure over hall,
    junction with office wing,
    scale 1:20

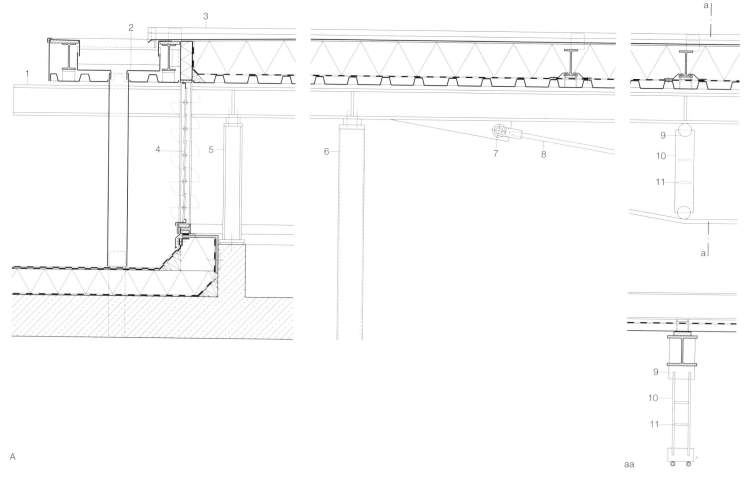

A

B Glazing system,
vertical section through
facade,
scale 1:20

C Horizontal section through standard fixing and junction with door,
scale 1:5

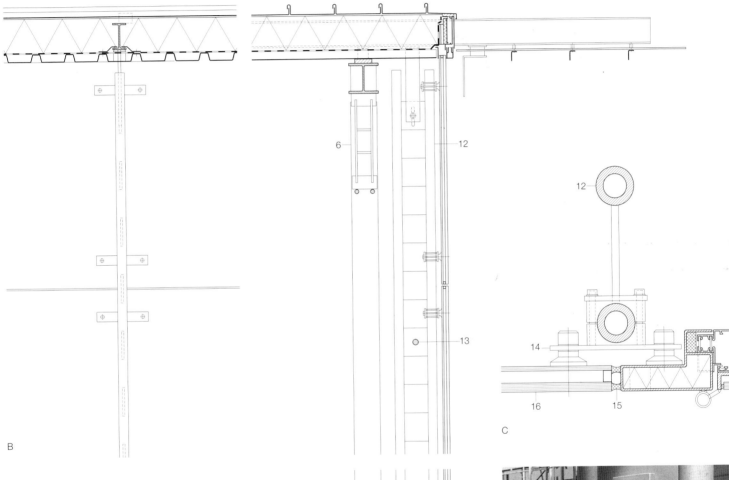

B

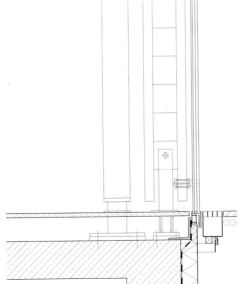

C

1 Beam, IPB 160
2 450 x 90 mm box gutter
3 Aluminium profile panels on
   200 mm thermal insulation
   Aluminium foil vapour barrier
   Trapezoidal profile sheeting
4 Glass louvres
5 Column, IPB 100
6 Column, 139.7 dia. x 5.6 mm
   circular hollow section
7 Cast end fitting
8 22 mm dia. round section
9 130 long x 70 mm round section
10 90 x 439 x 10 mm flat
11 70 x 70 x 10 mm flat
12 Facade post:
   2 No. 51 dia. x 10 mm steel tubes
   152 x 169 x 12 mm connecting plates
13 30 mm dia. rail
14 60 x 180 mm connecting plate (tube clamp
   and other fittings in stainless steel)
15 Permanently elastic seal
16 Double glazing, 12/16/6 mm

Example 5

Protestant church, Nürnberg-Langwasser

1986

Architects:
Eberhard Schunck and Dieter Ullrich, Munich
Project team:
N. Krausen, D. Blocher, K. Greilich, F. Hacker
Structural engineers:
Fritz Sailer and Kurt Stepan, Munich

With its unadorned reconstituted-stone facades and zinc sheet roofs, the ecumenical church centre in Nürnberg-Langwasser creates a tranquil focus in the heterogeneity of this suburb of Nürnberg. The 10 buildings of this complex are laid out on both sides of a north-south axis which serves as the principal circulation zone. This crosses a less significant east-west axis to form a central plaza where the Protestant and Catholic churches face each other diagonally. The former, also used for communal activities between religious services, has an open, bright character. The south-facing room is lit via the rooflight and via the front facade, which permits users to have a view of the outside. The exposed structure to the monopitch roof consists of delicate, striking steel sections: trussed beams hinged at the columns support the roof construction. The roof beams carry purlins spaced at 2.30 m centres, reflecting the grid of the building. The pitch of the roof places the purlins in biaxial bending so HEA sections are employed. To guarantee the stiffness it was necessary to design the roof as a plate and so develop an appropriate force transfer detail between roof plate, walls and central concrete aisle. At the gables the purlins are supported directly on columns. The trussed beams consist of pairs of angles with I-sections welded between as struts; the bottom chords are formed by two round bars. The struts are stabilized by means of tie bars fixed to the purlins in the end bays.

References: [58], [67], [132], [148], [161], [477]

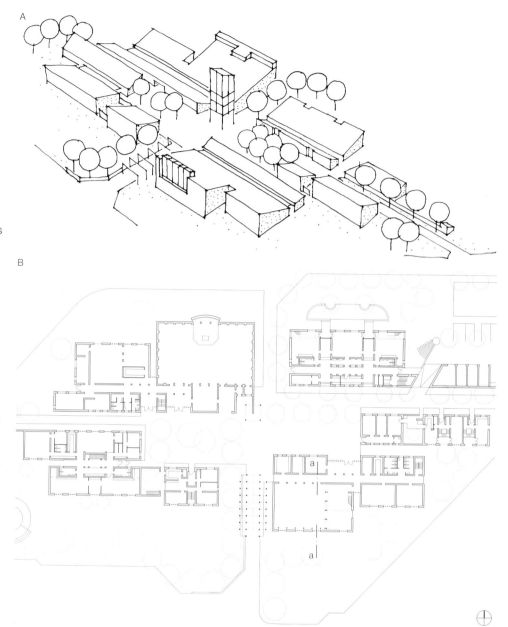

A Isometric sketch of community centre
B Plan
   scale 1:1000
C Details of roof structure
   scale 1:20
D Section
   scale 1:100

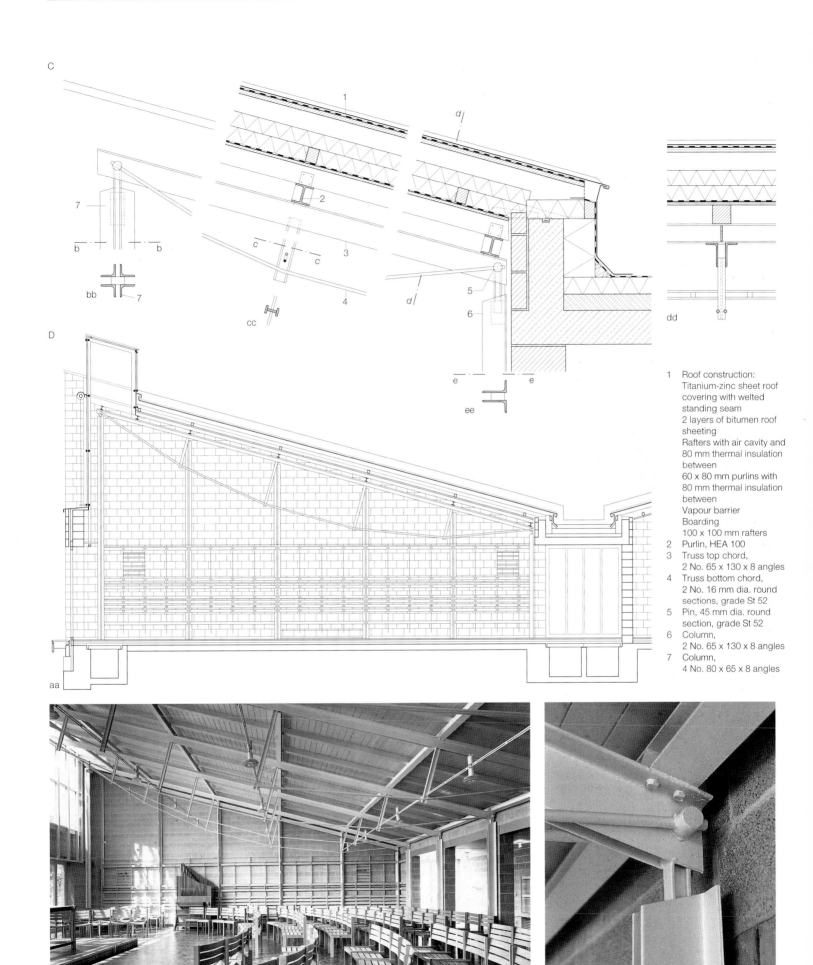

C

D

1 Roof construction:
  Titanium-zinc sheet roof
  covering with welted
  standing seam
  2 layers of bitumen roof
  sheeting
  Rafters with air cavity and
  80 mm thermal insulation
  between
  60 x 80 mm purlins with
  80 mm thermal insulation
  between
  Vapour barrier
  Boarding
  100 x 100 mm rafters
2 Purlin, HEA 100
3 Truss top chord,
  2 No. 65 x 130 x 8 angles
4 Truss bottom chord,
  2 No. 16 mm dia. round
  sections, grade St 52
5 Pin, 45 mm dia. round
  section, grade St 52
6 Column,
  2 No. 65 x 130 x 8 angles
7 Column,
  4 No. 80 x 65 x 8 angles

Example 6

Local authority offices, Langenthal, Switzerland

1992

Architect: Frank Geiser, Bern
Project team: H. Briner, A. Hagen,
I. Christeler-Schärer
Structural engineers:
Duppenthaler + Wälchli, Langenthal

Spacious parkland opposite a theatre is the setting for the building shared by regional and local government – a transparent and functional structure. The external appearance of the building reflects the internal form and steel is evident as the loadbearing material.

The basement storeys employ reinforced concrete for the loadbearing walls and masonry for the non-loadbearing partitions. The loadbearing system of the superstructure makes use of prefabricated methods with the outer columns placed well in front of the facade and cellular beams carrying the precast concrete ribbed floor planks.

The circular internal columns are placed in the corridors, outside the offices, so that the areas can be partitioned irrespective of the column spacing. A 1.06 m module forms the basis of the dimensional coordination for the building. Three reinforced concrete shafts in the middle of the building resist the horizontal loads.

The compact structure is almost totally glazed. The facade consists of several layers: each storey has a maintenance walkway on the longitudinal side, serving as weather protection and sunshading simultaneously. Where exposed, the facade elements are provided with non-coloured double glazing. In the solid spandrel and wall areas the facade elements are filled with ventilated sandwich panels.

The point where the horizontal steel floor beam penetrates the facade was investigated with the help of a full-size laboratory mock-up and a comprehensive programme of measurements. The energy loss via the 76 beams is roughly equal to 0.03% of the heating energy requirement and is hence negligible.

The internal partitions are prefabricated units made from steel tubes with coated wood-fibre boards and glass infills.

References: [11], [48], [62], [146], [166], [199], [406], [481]

A

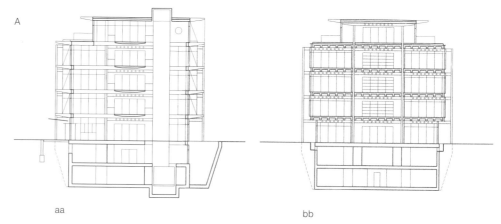

aa   bb

A   Sections, plan
    scale 1:500

242

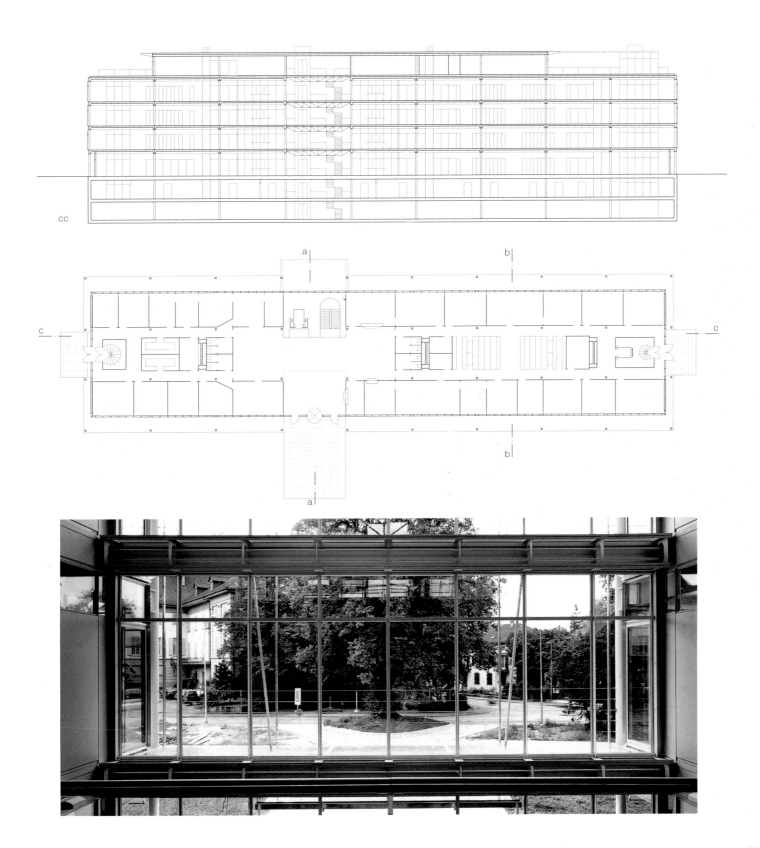

cc

a

b

c

c

b

a

Example 6

A

B

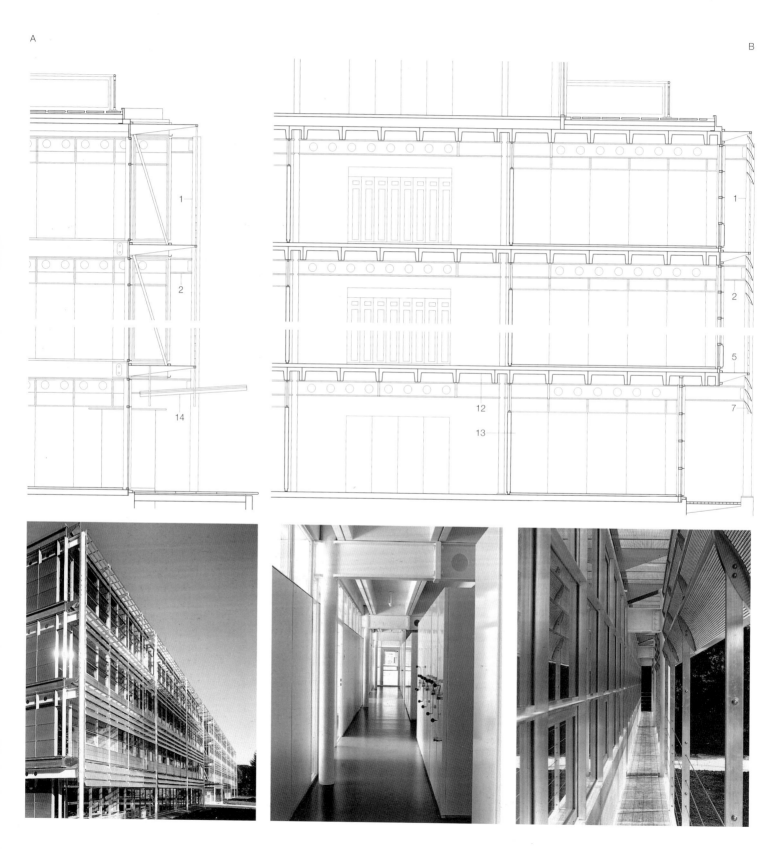

A Section through
  facade,
  entrance zone
B Section through west
  facade
Scale 1:100

C Details of facade,
  scale 1:20

1 Column, 177.8 mm dia. tube
2 Beam, IPE 400
3 2 No. 60 x 10 mm aluminium flats
4 Steel cable
5 Maintenance walkway / Sunshading,
   aluminium bracket with perforated metal sheet
6 Intermediate support, 40 x 40 x 4 channel
7 Louvre as sunshade
8 Double glazing
9 Steel frame element
10 Leaf of window
11 Radiator
12 Precast concrete flooring units
13 Modular partition with high-level glazing
14 Canopy

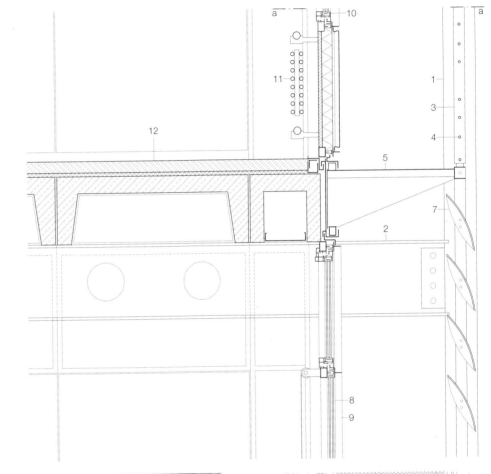

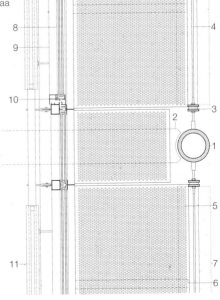

Example 7

Exhibition hall and offices, Paris

1993

Architects: Jean Nouvel,
Emmanuel Cattani & Associés, Paris
Project Manager: Didier Brault
Structural engineers:
Ove Arup & Partners, London

In the light of its inner-city location and the
valuable stock of mature trees, a compact
building of glass and steel was chosen consisting of eight storeys above and eight storeys
below ground. The basement storeys accommodate parking bays as well as archives and
plant rooms; ground floor and 1st basement
level are reserved for exhibitions and the other
storeys contain offices.
The building has been set back on its plot in
order to preserve the trees. But the building
line established in the 19th century is maintained by the glass screens in front of the
building itself. This and the transparent
facades, which extend beyond the building,
form the "backdrop" to the natural setting.
The building consists of an internal steel frame
with castellated floor beams that permit the
installation of services thanks to their hexagonal openings and curious shape at the junction
with the columns. The beams span approx.
17 m without intermediate columns and hence
provide a large, flexible, unobstructed area at
ground floor ideal for exhibitions.
The building is braced by the floor plates as
well as cross-bracing transversely and storey-
height frames longitudinally.

References: [74], [142], [194], [300], [386]

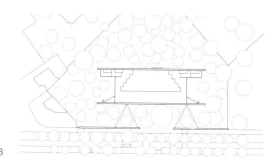

B

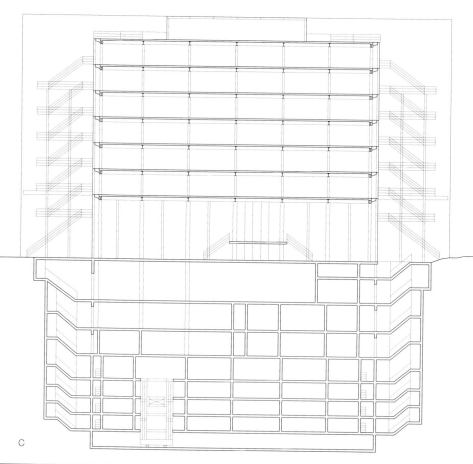

C

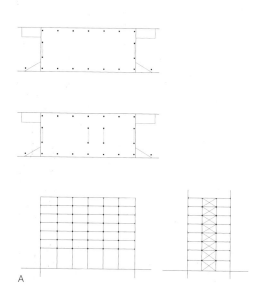

A

A   Structural system
B   Site plan,
    scale 1:2000
C   Sections,
    scale 1:500
D   Details of facade,
    scale 1:20

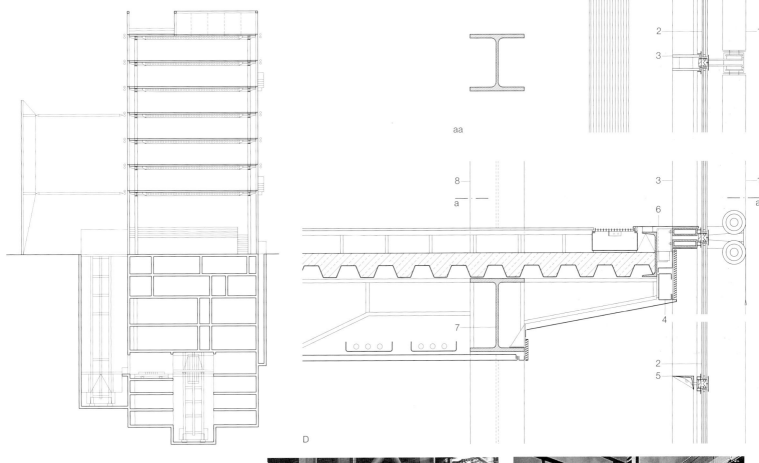

aa

D

1   Computer-controlled fabric sunshade
2   Double glazing: outer pane – non-reflective lami-
    nated safety glass, inner pane – normal glass for
    windows, toughened safety glass for spandrel
    panels
    Frame: aluminium with stainless steel glazing
    bars externally
3   Suspended glass fin (toughened safety glass)
4   Ventilation duct
5   Cast aluminium rail
6   Steel plate, painted
7   Beam, HEA 400
8   Column, 310 x 310 H-section

Example 8

Bookshop, conversion and extension, Constance

1991

Architect:
Herbert Schaudt, Constance
Project Architect: Martin Cleffmann
Assistant: T. Gabele
Structural engineer: Karl Fischer, Constance

The plan to extend the current premises resulted in a 40-m-long retail space on a narrow plot in the centre of the old quarter of the city. The aim was to achieve a transparent space flooded with light which would dispel the gloomy "backyard" atmosphere. The very confined site allowed no room for a crane nor for storage and site facilities. Therefore, prefabricated steelwork was chosen because it could be erected in situ relatively quickly. A helicopter was used twice (90 min each time) to help erect the upper floors.

The structure, based on a square grid, is stiffened by the masonry walls parallel with the adjacent buildings, wind bracing in the south facade and the floor and roof plates.

The floors comprise overlapping main and secondary beams, and the single-span main beams have a hinged joint where they connect to the columns. This connection is exposed by leaving a circular opening in the floor at this point. The lattice girders to stairs and walkways at the same time constitute the necessary balustrading. Passive fire protection was not incorporated; instead, the whole building relies on a sprinkler system.

The appearance of the new extension is characterized by generous expanses of glazed steelwork and exposed services. The design makes use of galleries instead of solid floors in order to allow light from above to penetrate to the lower floors.

References: [3], [41], [65], [226]

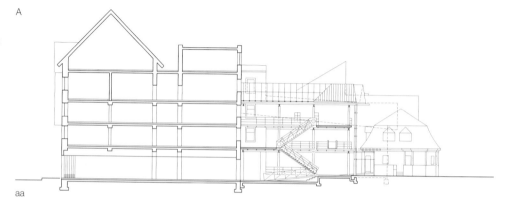

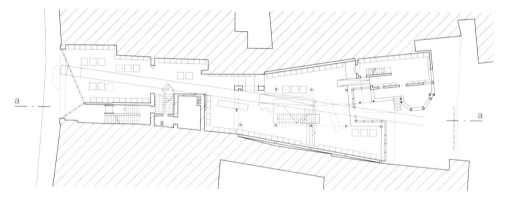

B

C

cc

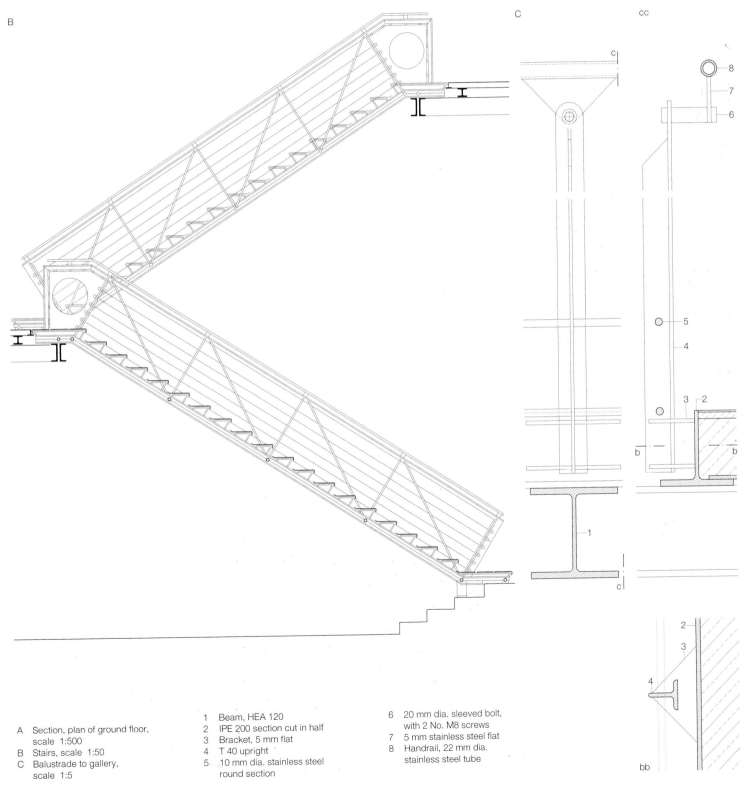

A Section, plan of ground floor,
   scale 1:500
B Stairs, scale 1:50
C Balustrade to gallery,
   scale 1:5

1 Beam, HEA 120
2 IPE 200 section cut in half
3 Bracket, 5 mm flat
4 T 40 upright
5 10 mm dia. stainless steel
   round section

6 20 mm dia. sleeved bolt,
   with 2 No. M8 screws
7 5 mm stainless steel flat
8 Handrail, 22 mm dia.
   stainless steel tube

bb

Example 8

C

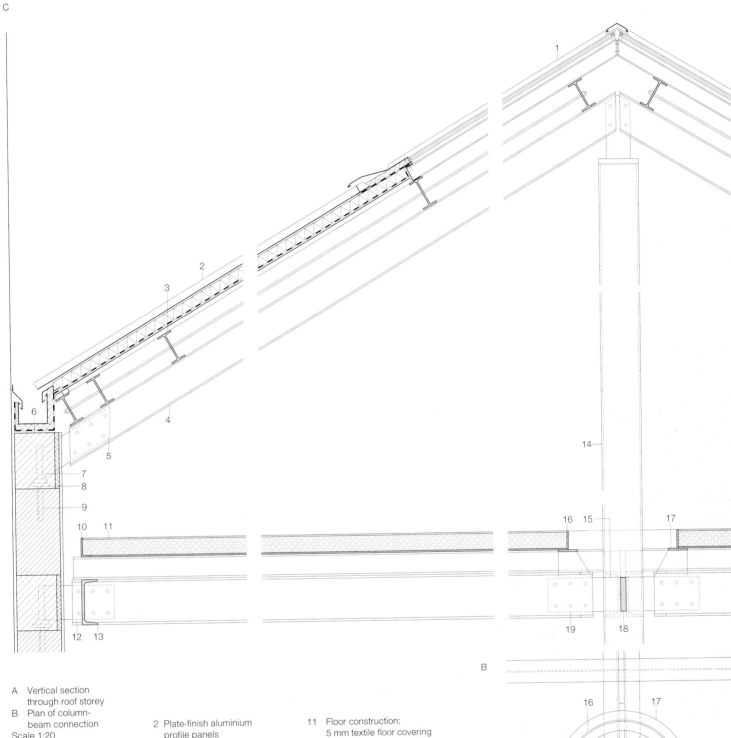

A Vertical section
   through roof storey
B Plan of column-
   beam connection
Scale 1:20

1 Rooflight strip with
   patent double glazing
   (6 mm float glass,
   10 mm cavity, 8 mm
   laminated safety glass
   inner pane), hot-dip galvanized IPE 80 transoms
   with plate-finish aluminium glazing bars

2 Plate-finish aluminium
   profile panels
   100 mm thermal insulation
   Vapour barrier
   40 mm perforated aluminium trapezoidal profile
   sheeting
3 Purlin, IPE 160
4 2 No. U 180 channels
5 428 x 140 x 30 mm flat
6 Reinforced concrete ring
   beam
7 300 x 100 x 20 mm flat
8 300 x 100 x 20 mm flat
9 Masonry anchor,
   2 No. 50 x 5 angles
10 Edge trimmer,
   100 x 50 x 8 angle

11 Floor construction:
   5 mm textile floor covering
   80 mm reinforced concrete
   5 mm steel plate rein-
   forced by T 50 sections at
   120 mm centres
   HEA 120
   2 No. U 140 channels
12 390 x 180 x 30 mm flat
13 240 mm channel
14 Column, 219.1 dia. x
   12.5 mm steel tube
15 Column splice
16 Edge trimmer, 90 x 6 mm
   flat bent to suit
17 8 mm annulus
18 860 x 180 x 30 mm flat
19 415 x 180 x 30 mm flat

Example 9

Library, Ingolstadt

1989

Architect: Wilhelm Kücker, Munich
Project team: K. Freudenfeld (Project and
Site Manager), C. Persch, M. Schneider,
H. Bouterwek, N. Hein
Structural engineers: Martinka + Grad, Eichstätt

The library of the Faculty of Economic Science
at the Eichstätt Catholic University is housed in
an exposed steel frame integrated within an
existing church.
This free-standing structure consists of storey-
high concrete-filled circular hollow section
columns and beams fabricated from steel
plates. Steel trapezoidal profile sheeting, acting as permanent formwork, in conjunction with
loadbearing concrete forms the floors. The
floors act as stiffening plates for the steel frame
and are joined to the concrete floor of the
ancillary room, the floor of which, together with
the wall plates, transfers the loads to the
ground.
Intermediate columns could not be added
along the length of the bookshelves but the
depth of the floors still had to be kept to a minimum because of the restricted height. This was
accomplished by using a made-up, welded
T-section beam, whose top flange lies within
the reinforced concrete slab, with two additional channels welded on underneath. The
balustrades consist of mesh suspended
between steel sections. Access to the individual levels is by way of a steel stair attached to
the structure or a lift housed in a glazed shaft.

References: [64], [69], [130], [158], [270]

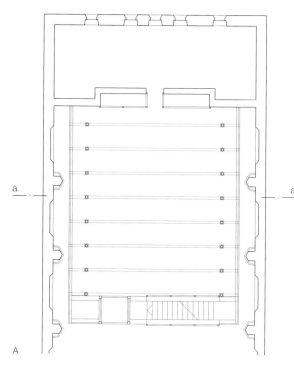

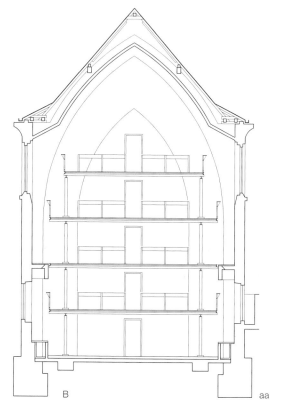

Book stacks with reading facilities
A   Plan
B   Section
    scale 1:200
C   Horizontal sections through
    top and base of column,
    section through floor beam
D   Section with elevation on column
Scale 1:10

1 Steel flat
2 Balustrade upright,
   50 x 25 x 4 rectangular
   hollow section
3 Mesh screen
4 Edge trimmer,
   100 x 50 channel
5 40 x 40 x 4 angle
6 Bottom flange of beam,
   2 No. 100 x 50 channels
7 Trapezoidal profile
   sheeting
8 Reinforced concrete,
   max. 95 mm thk

9   Top flange,
    200 x 25 mm
10 Web, 160 x 25 mm
11 8.5 mm plate
12 127 x 127 x 8.5 mm
    plate
13 132 dia. x 8.5 mm
    plate
14 Column, 127 dia. x
    4 mm concrete-filled
    circular hollow section
15 Base plate,
    200 x 200 x 15 mm

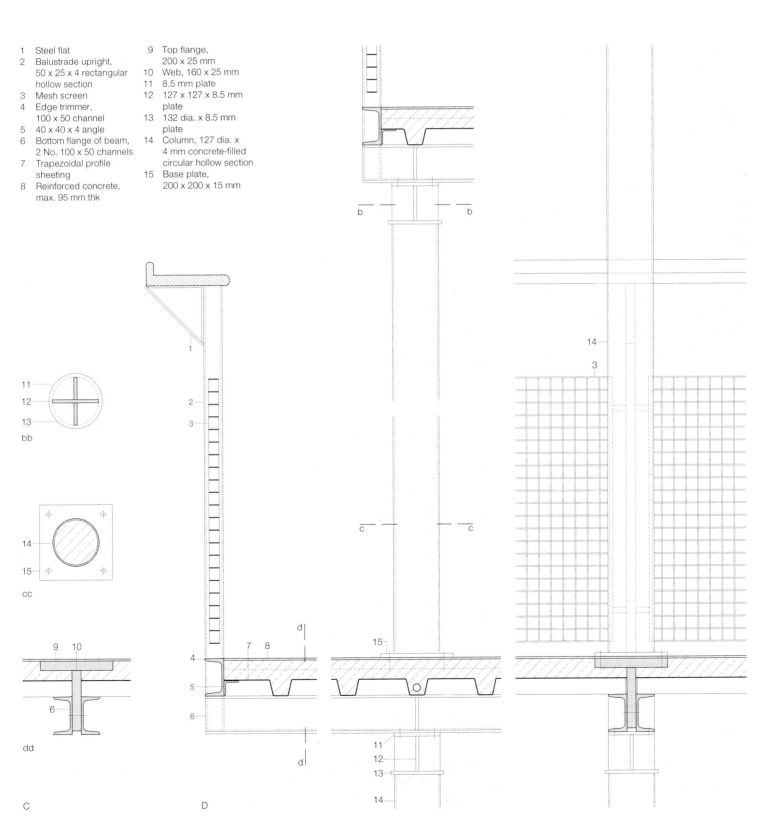

Example 10

Museum, refurbishment and conversion, London

1991

Architects:
Foster and Partners, London
Structural engineers:
Anthony Hunt Associates, London

The conversion of the Royal Academy involved both the refurbishment of galleries under the roof of the main building, Burlington House, and the improvement of the poor access to the whole complex. The narrow (less than 5 m wide) lightwell between the existing buildings was roofed over to create a new interior space which was then provided with a steel structure whose load is carried on five steel columns. The construction supports the access links between the two buildings and the glass stair as well as serving as a shaft for the hydraulic lift. The linking levels at the 1st and 2nd floors are each attached to the masonry of one adjoining building via a hinge, while a glazed transition is formed at the facade of the other building.
The roof construction employs a three-hinged frame with separate glass facade.

References: [22], [133], [328], [386]

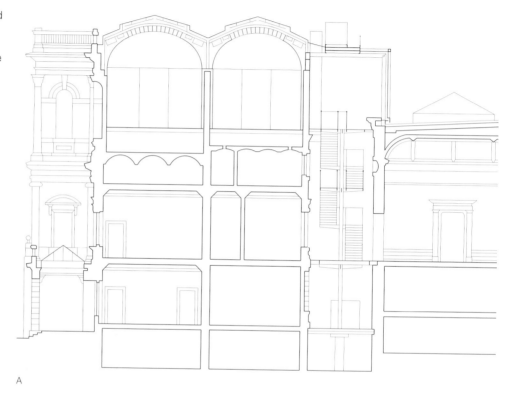

A

A Sections
scale 1:200

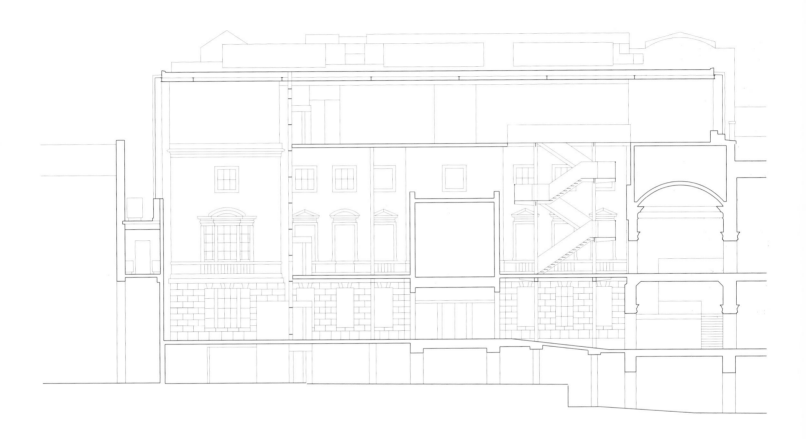

Example 10

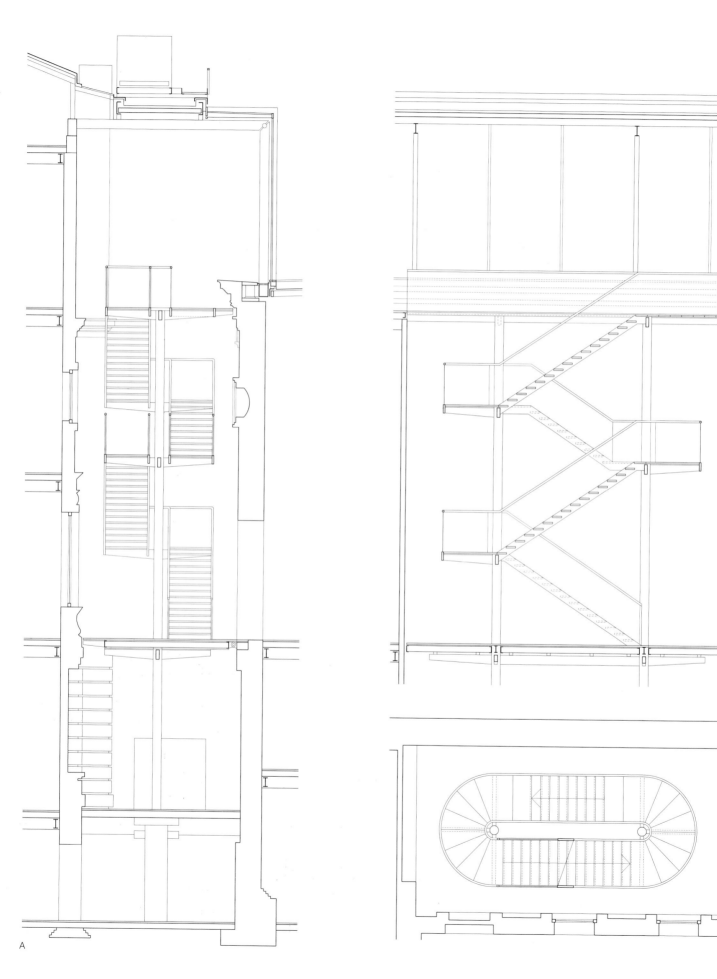

A

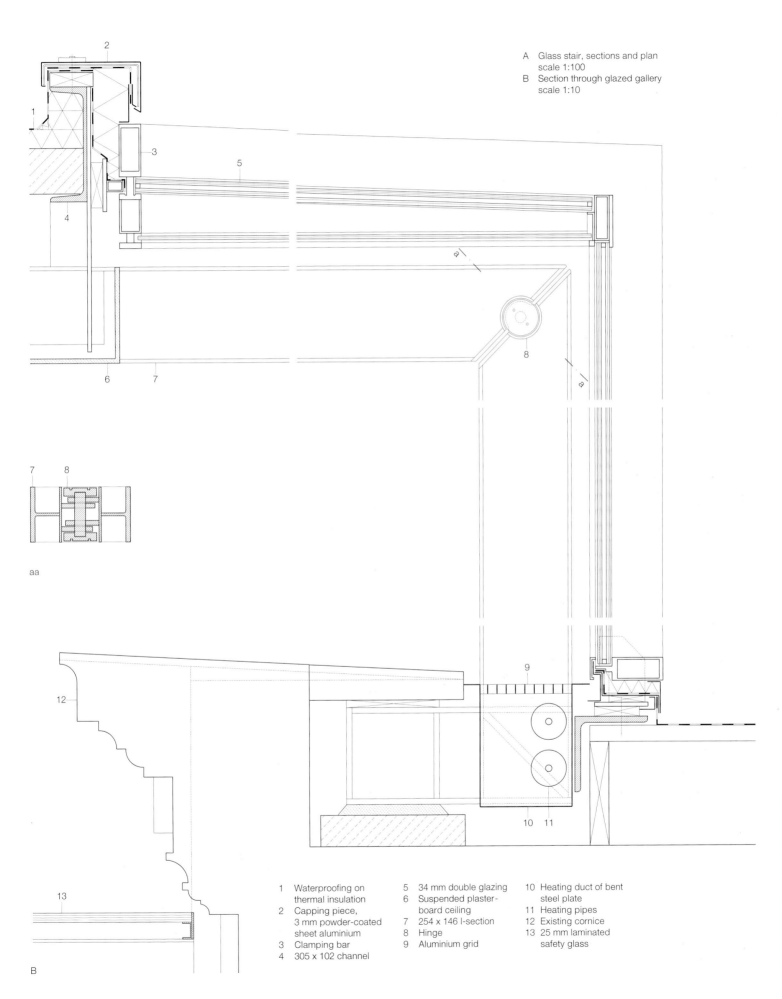

A Glass stair, sections and plan
   scale 1:100
B Section through glazed gallery
   scale 1:10

aa

B

1 Waterproofing on
   thermal insulation
2 Capping piece,
   3 mm powder-coated
   sheet aluminium
3 Clamping bar
4 305 x 102 channel

5 34 mm double glazing
6 Suspended plaster-
   board ceiling
7 254 x 146 I-section
8 Hinge
9 Aluminium grid

10 Heating duct of bent
    steel plate
11 Heating pipes
12 Existing cornice
13 25 mm laminated
    safety glass

Example 11

Fire station, Espoo, Finland

1991

Architects:
Gullichsen, Kairamo, Vormala, Helsinki
Project Architects: E. Kairamo, T. Saarelainen
Project team: A. Jylhä, T. Patomo
Structural engineer:
Raimo Sormunen, Helsinki

The remarkable feature of this fire station is its tower, used for training and practice purposes. Its distinctive architecture quite clearly announces the function of the adjacent facility. Three angles and one I-section form the corner columns of the 1 x 1 m square tower. Horizontal channel sections on all four sides link the columns at regular intervals, and between these channels the tower is braced by seven sets of diagonal ties welded to the columns via gusset plates. Gusset plates are also used at the intersections of these ties. Stability is provided by a diagonal steel tube to one side and by fixing the tower back to the main building by means of T-sections. A spiral staircase provides access to the platforms cantilevering out from the tower at various levels. The stair treads lead directly to each platform without any intermediate landings. Open-grid flooring on frames of channel sections comprise the platforms. A long, narrow panel of sheet steel and square hollow sections forms a support for ladders. At the top of the tower there is a tube on which measuring instruments are mounted.

Reference: [139]

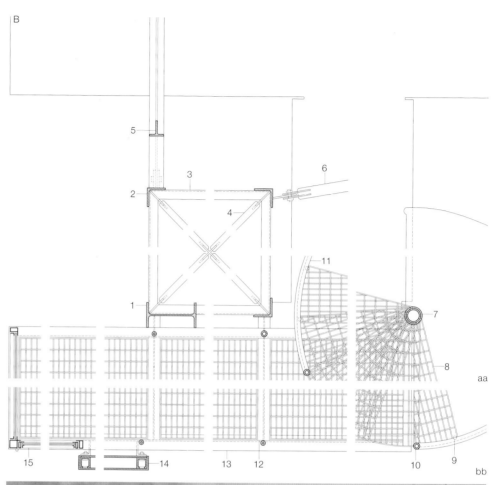

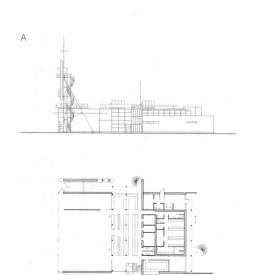

C

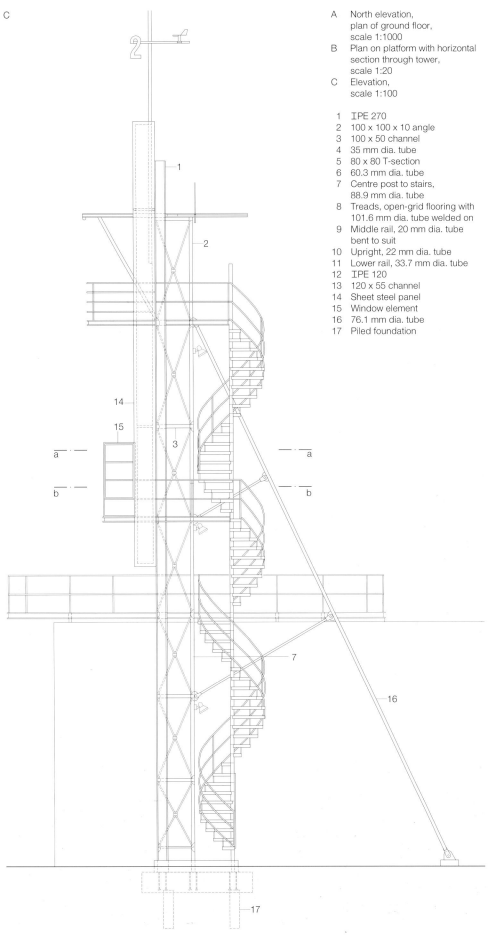

A   North elevation,
     plan of ground floor,
     scale 1:1000
B   Plan on platform with horizontal
     section through tower,
     scale 1:20
C   Elevation,
     scale 1:100

 1   IPE 270
 2   100 x 100 x 10 angle
 3   100 x 50 channel
 4   35 mm dia. tube
 5   80 x 80 T-section
 6   60.3 mm dia. tube
 7   Centre post to stairs,
     88.9 mm dia. tube
 8   Treads, open-grid flooring with
     101.6 mm dia. tube welded on
 9   Middle rail, 20 mm dia. tube
     bent to suit
10   Upright, 22 mm dia. tube
11   Lower rail, 33.7 mm dia. tube
12   IPE 120
13   120 x 55 channel
14   Sheet steel panel
15   Window element
16   76.1 mm dia. tube
17   Piled foundation

Example 12

Houses, Gaienhofen-Horn

1993

Architect:
Ingo Bucher-Beholz, Gaienhofen
Project team:
E. Baumann, B. von Sondern, T. Klettner
Structural engineer:
Helmut Fischer, Bad Endorf

These two detached houses were built to a simple design employing steel, timber and glass. The loadbearing structure consists of two-storey steel frames founded on a concrete basement. These frames span more than 6 m and are spaced every 2.25 m along the length of the 15.75 m building. Transverse stability is provided by the steel frames themselves while cross-bracing provides longitudinal rigidity. Tubes link the frames at floor level and eaves. This method of construction proved an inexpensive means of keeping the interior clear of columns and loadbearing walls. The structural steelwork has been left exposed along the sides of the buildings. The thermal bridges that ensue – and the associated build-up of condensation on the steel internally – with such a feature is a problem that needs to be considered very carefully. However, this form of construction with its open-plan interior guarantees a good circulation of air to combat the problem. As such, the thermal bridges were not seen to be a major concern and this small deficiency simply accepted.

Reference: [140]

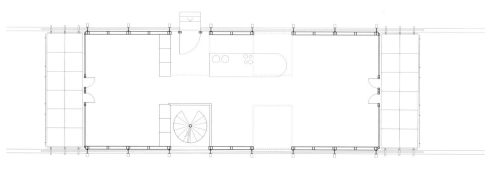

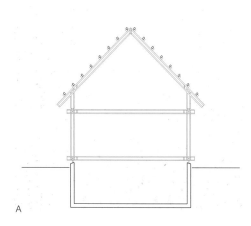

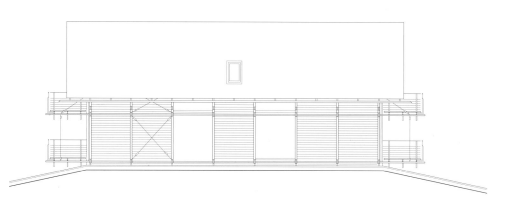

A

A   Section through load-
    bearing construction,
    plan of ground floor,
    side elevation,
    scale 1:200
B   Sections through gable
    wall and side wall
C   Horizontal section
Scale 1:20

1   Steel frame, IPE 200
2   Longitudinal strut, 60.3 dia. x 5 mm,
    contributes to stability
3   Wall construction:
    20 mm horizontal weatherboarding
    Backing sheet permitting diffusion of
    water vapour
    140 mm mineral-fibre insulation
    between 60 x 140 mm timber studding

    Vapour barrier
    19 mm chipboard
4   Floor construction:
    Linoleum floor covering
    19 mm chipboard
    5 mm impact-sound insulation
    20 x 140 mm timber boards with
    20 mm timber soft-boards between
    50 mm tongue-and-groove boards
    IPE 200 beam

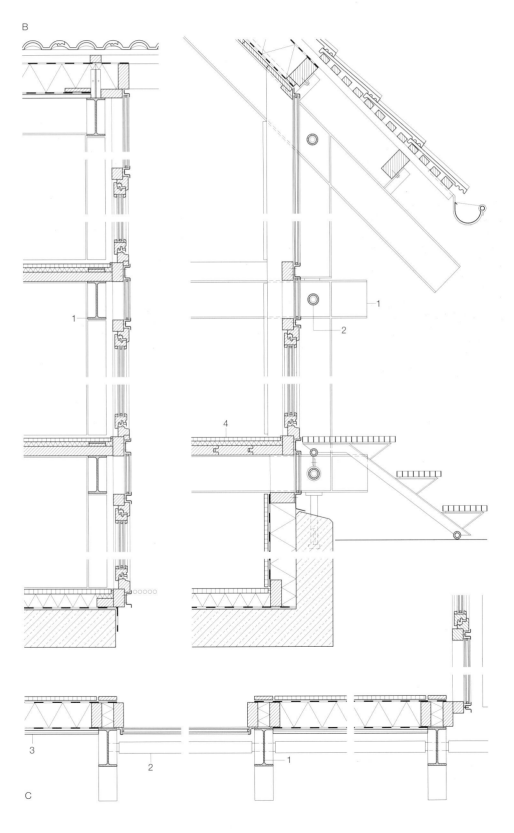

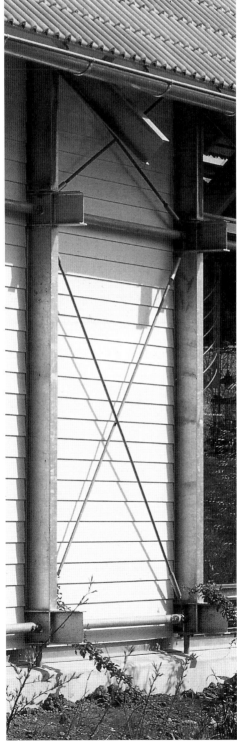

Example 13

**Detached house, Northern Territory,
Australia**

1993

Architects:
Glenn Murcutt and Associates, Mosman
Structural engineers:
James Taylor and Associates, Mosman

The design of the house takes into account the hot, tropical climate of Australia's Northern Territory. Owing to the natural conditions prevailing at the site, pad foundations are used and the house is raised clear of the ground. Erection of the house made from prefabricated elements took two operatives no more than a few weeks.

The external walls – depending on compass direction and internal function – consist of wide plywood panels or wooden louvres which can let the air through. Natural ventilation is guaranteed. The panels hinge outwards and upwards during the day – opening up the house in almost all directions depending on requirements and weather conditions – and are closed at night – thus ensuring night-time privacy for the occupants. The functional and simply organized layout is arranged on an east-west axis with the generously sized living accommodation turned a little to the south. There are four small bedrooms and a single large one. Internal plywood partitions are 2 m high; slats above ensure even cross-ventilation. Transverse timber beams and boards form the floor.

Hot air is carried away above the roof via aerodynamic "Venturi tubes". The structural steelwork is designed to withstand wind speeds of up to 63 m/s and the sizes of columns and transverse members comply with the requirements for regions at risk of tornadoes. The prefabricated columns are supported on small reinforced concrete pad foundations. The roof frames, extending well beyond the walls, are rigidly connected to the columns via generously sized plates. Wind bracing in the roof provides the necessary longitudinal stability.

Reference: [210]

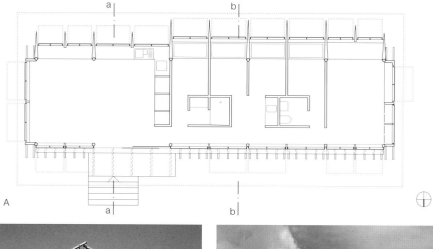

A

A Plan
B Section through gable,
   section through house
Scale 1:200
C Section through facade
Scale 1:20

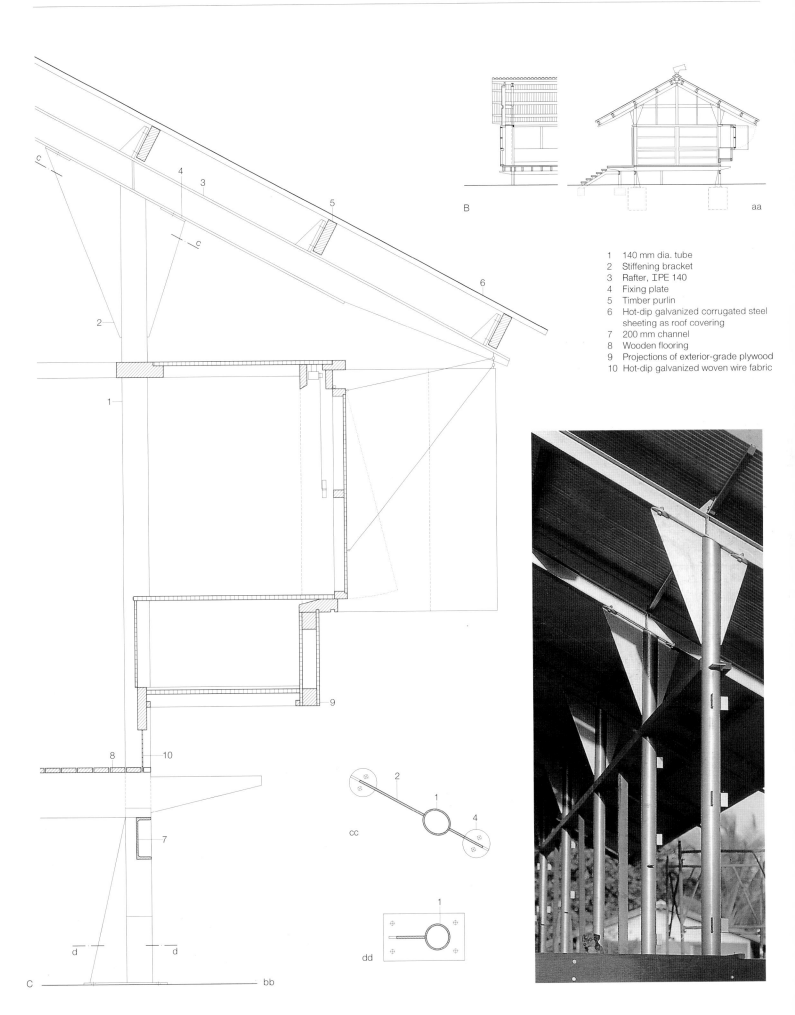

1   140 mm dia. tube
2   Stiffening bracket
3   Rafter, IPE 140
4   Fixing plate
5   Timber purlin
6   Hot-dip galvanized corrugated steel
    sheeting as roof covering
7   200 mm channel
8   Wooden flooring
9   Projections of exterior-grade plywood
10 Hot-dip galvanized woven wire fabric

263

Example 14

House, Osaka, Japan

1987

Architects:
Waro Kishi and K. Associates, Kyoto
Structural engineers:
Urban Design Institute, Osaka

This two-storey house in Osaka was erected on a narrow plot between traditional terraced houses. The one-bay wide and three-bays long building occupies the complete area of the plot, with the rooms facing onto the yard in the middle bay. A steel stair in the yard provides access to the rooms on the 1st floor, which are linked by a bridge over the yard.
The construction comprises four two-storey-high steel frames evenly spaced along the ground slab. Columns and beams – all I-sections – are rigidly connected. Vertical cross-bracing in the middle bay provides longitudinal stability; there is also horizontal bracing at roof and 1st floor levels.
Both roof sections are covered with corrugated sheeting and external walls are clad with suspended concrete panels. Aluminium window elements separate the rooms from the central yard. The exposed steel members in the facade require supplementary measures to overcome the thermal bridge problems.

Reference: [195]

B

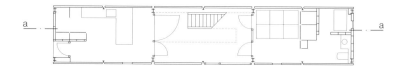

a · · · · · · · · · · · · · a

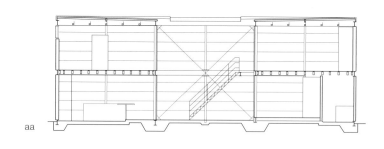

aa

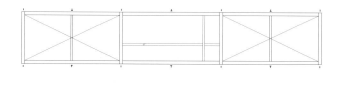

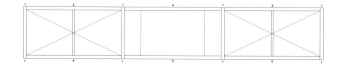

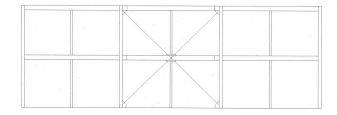

A

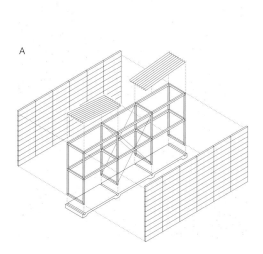

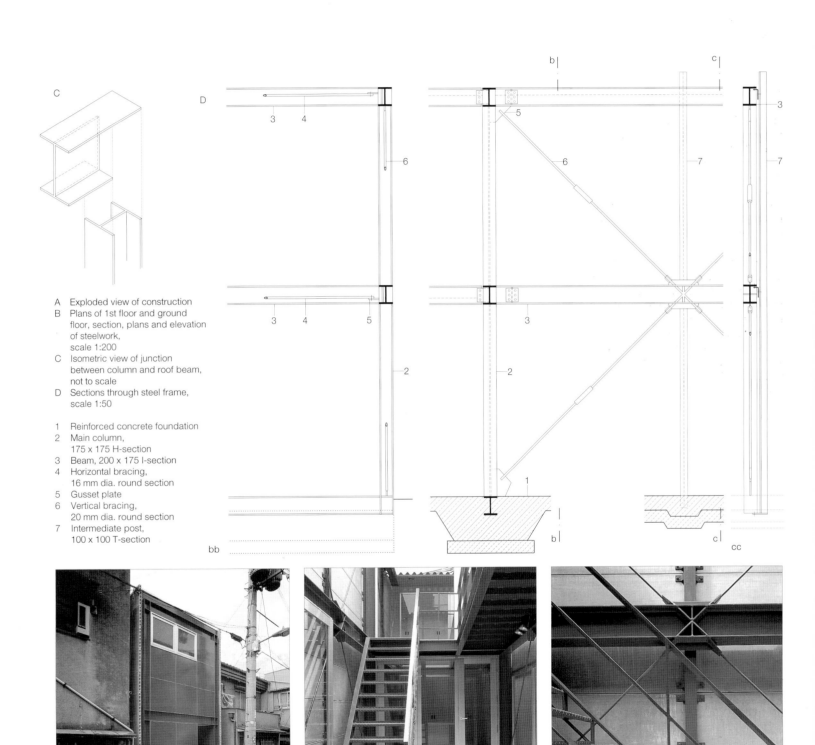

C

D

A Exploded view of construction
B Plans of 1st floor and ground
  floor, section, plans and elevation
  of steelwork,
  scale 1:200
C Isometric view of junction
  between column and roof beam,
  not to scale
D Sections through steel frame,
  scale 1:50

1 Reinforced concrete foundation
2 Main column,
  175 x 175 H-section
3 Beam, 200 x 175 I-section
4 Horizontal bracing,
  16 mm dia. round section
5 Gusset plate
6 Vertical bracing,
  20 mm dia. round section
7 Intermediate post,
  100 x 100 T-section

bb

cc

Example 15

Service building, Magdeburg

1990

Architects:
Schulitz + Partner, Braunschweig
H. C. Schulitz, J. Schüsseler
Structural engineer:
Michael Sprysch, Vechelde

A new civil engineering and landscaping company founded after German reunification required a service building to accommodate offices and staff facilities as well as a vehicle depot. The client wished to cooperate with a local former engineering cooperative which was looking to move into industrial buildings. This led to the development of a building system for industrial uses, but which could also be applied to other projects.

The construction consists of frames clad with trapezoidal profile sheeting whose thickness varies depending on the span. The cross-member of the frame is in the form of a lattice girder with T-sections as top and bottom chords, and pairs of angles for diagonals and posts.

Stability in the transverse direction is provided by the frames themselves, in the longitudinal direction by bracing in the facades, which are positioned directly in front of the columns. The cantilever brackets for the canopy are attached in such a way that the roof can be drained at the column connection along the beam axis.

Reference: [398]

B

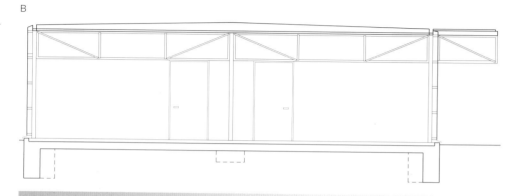

A

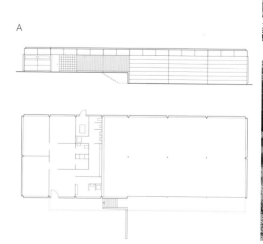

1 Facade upright, T 50
2 Cover strip, 50 x 25 channel
3 Girder end post, TB 45
4 Column, HEA 100
5 Z-section, Z 80
6 Channel, U 150
7 Rainwater downpipe
8 Bottom chord, T 70
9 Transom, 75 x 50 x 7 angle
10 Cover strip, 50 x 30 x 5 angle
11 Bottom chord of cantilever bracket, T 60
12 Top chord of girder, T 90
13 Bracket end post, TB 45
14 Diagonals, 2 No. 30 x 5 angles
15 Top chord of cantilever bracket, T 90
16 Cantilever bracket end post, TB 30
17 Wall construction:
  Plasterboard
  Vapour barrier
  Insulation, timber studding
  Airtight foil
  Corrugated aluminium sheeting
18 Base plate, 225 x 280 x 20 mm
19 Internal column, HEA 120

A Plan and elevation, scale 1:500
B Section through offices, scale 1:100
C Isometric view of column-girder connection,
  not to scale
D Horizontal and vertical sections through facade
E Detail of base of plain facade
F Detail of outer column base
G Detail of inner column base
Scale 1:10

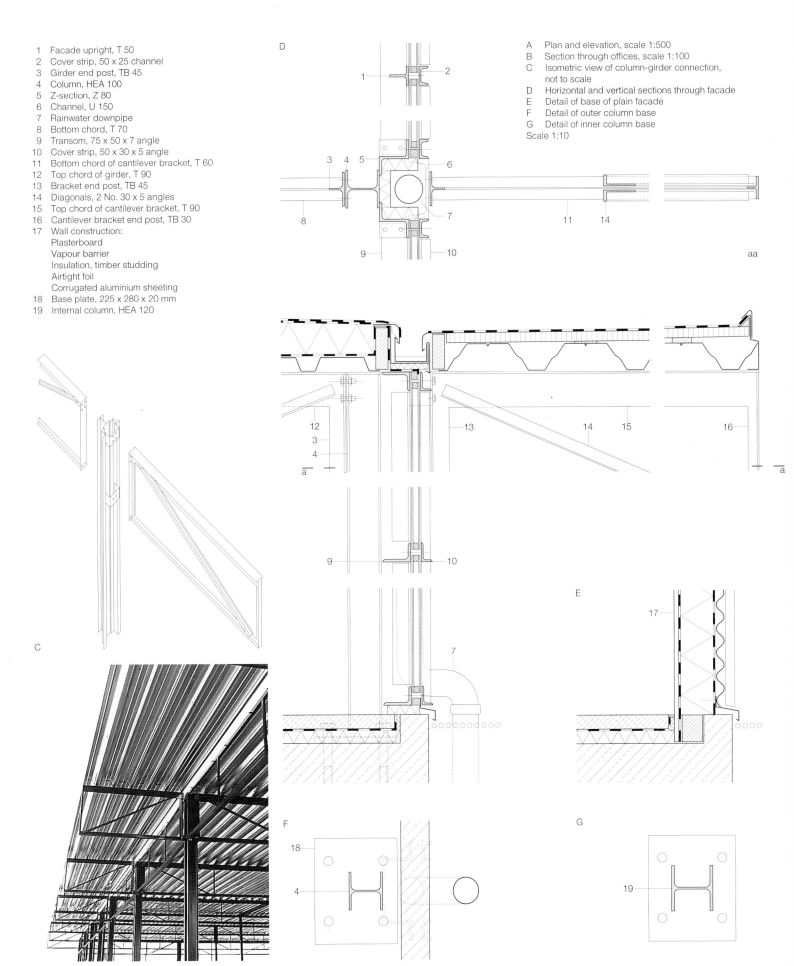

267

Example 16

Production plant, Münsingen, Switzerland

1962-94

Architect:
Fritz Haller, Solothurn
Structural engineers:
Emch + Berger, Bern

In 1960-62 Fritz Haller developed a steelwork system for the production plant of a furniture manufacturer. And the same system is still being used today. The original building completed in 1962 was extended several times between 1971 and 1994. The basic element of the construction is a 14.40 x 14.40 m bay spanned by a 1200-mm-deep grid of welded lattice girders. Aerated concrete planks, 4.80 m long, form the roof covering and act as a plate to provide horizontal stability. The modular system of single-storey elements enables the building to be readily extended in any direction at a later date. Ventilation ducts and other services are routed within the depth of the girders.

In developing the details, fabrication and erection aspects took priority over structural optimization. This resulted in identical columns throughout the building – made from 4 No. 130 x 130 x 15 angles; the structural interaction between the individual angles is ensured by way of plates welded in between. This column design guarantees the connection of facade elements at the outer columns, as well as the attachment of further girders if the building is extended. The columns also house vertical service runs.

Columns are restrained at their bases and hinged at the top where the girders are supported. The bottom chord of each girder is only continued as far as the column in order to gain lateral stability. Transfer of forces is prevented by providing a sleeve.

The entire system has hardly been altered since its inception in 1960, although a few parts were adapted to match developments in building technology. For instance, today steel trapezoidal profile sheeting is used instead of aerated concrete planks. Enhanced building science parameters were also taken into account by improving the insulation.

References: [7], [238], [396], [452], [479]

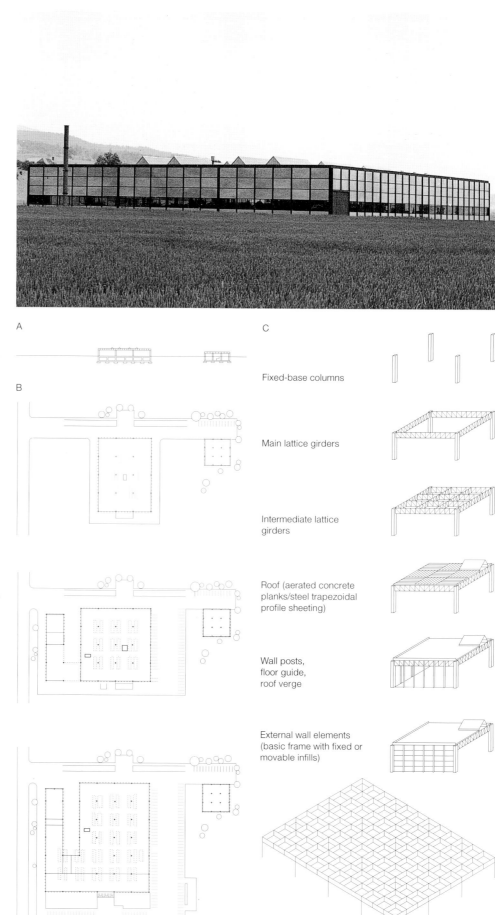

A

C

Fixed-base columns

B

Main lattice girders

Intermediate lattice girders

Roof (aerated concrete planks/steel trapezoidal profile sheeting)

Wall posts, floor guide, roof verge

External wall elements (basic frame with fixed or movable infills)

Complete roof structure

A Section
B Stages of development
   Scale 1:3000
C Isometric views of construction elements, not to scale

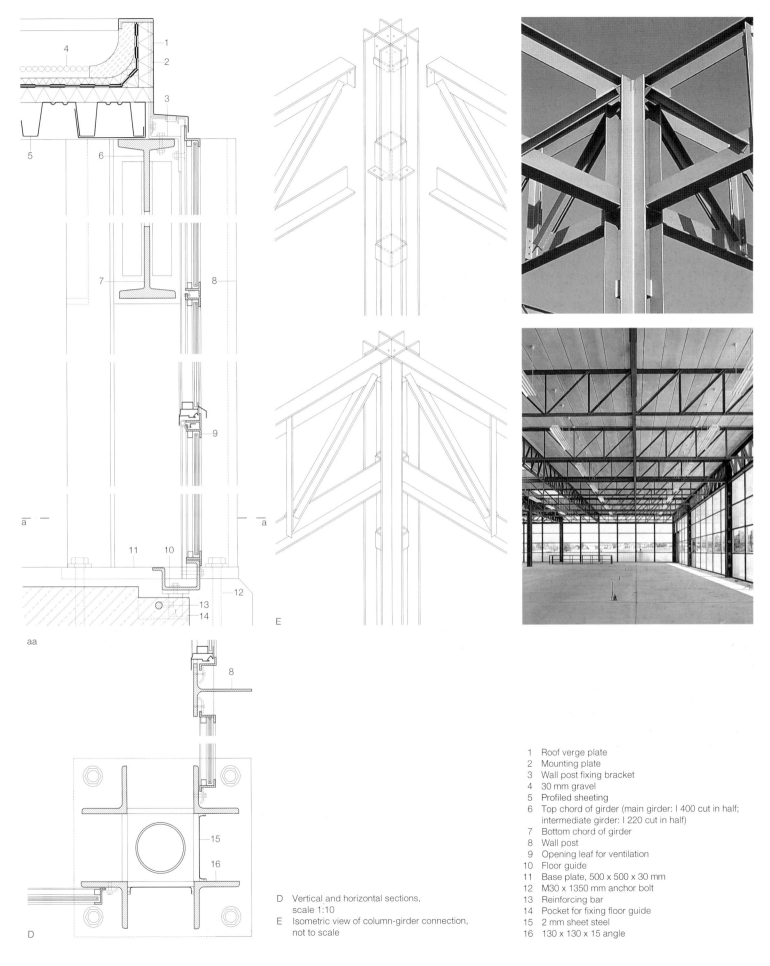

aa

D

E

1   Roof verge plate
2   Mounting plate
3   Wall post fixing bracket
4   30 mm gravel
5   Profiled sheeting
6   Top chord of girder (main girder: I 400 cut in half;
    intermediate girder: I 220 cut in half)
7   Bottom chord of girder
8   Wall post
9   Opening leaf for ventilation
10 Floor guide
11 Base plate, 500 x 500 x 30 mm
12 M30 x 1350 mm anchor bolt
13 Reinforcing bar
14 Pocket for fixing floor guide
15 2 mm sheet steel
16 130 x 130 x 15 angle

D   Vertical and horizontal sections,
    scale 1:10
E   Isometric view of column-girder connection,
    not to scale

Example 17

Industrial building, Opmeer, Netherlands

1988

Architects: Benthem Crouwel, Amsterdam
Jan Benthem, Mels Crouwel, Ton Liemburg,
Structural engineers: Ingenieurbüro Starmans,
Cees van Eden, Groningen

This building on a typical suburban industrial
estate was realized using simple means but a
high standard of architecture.
The client, a manufacturer of prefabricated wall
and roof elements, required storage and showroom space as well as offices. The rectangular
building employs the same construction
throughout but clearly demarcates the different
functions by way of a change from building
envelope placed inside to building envelope
placed outside the frame, and the glazed and
solid facades respectively. Toilets and kitchen
are situated at the transition of the two styles.
Ten frames of triangular lattice girders spaced
at 5.4 m centres and spanning 21.6 m create
an unobstructed interior. A mezzanine floor on
additional columns – separate from the main
structure – was included for the offices section.
Each frame consists of three welded, prefabricated triangular lattice girders. At the corners
they are rigidly bolted together via triangular
gusset plates with bearing plates welded to
these. The individual girder frames are linked
together by way of a tube at eaves level connected to the same junction. Longitudinal stability is provided by cross-bracing at the transition between the two parts of the building.

References: [84], [149], [223], [396]

A

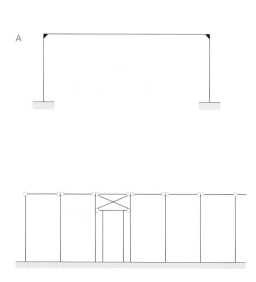

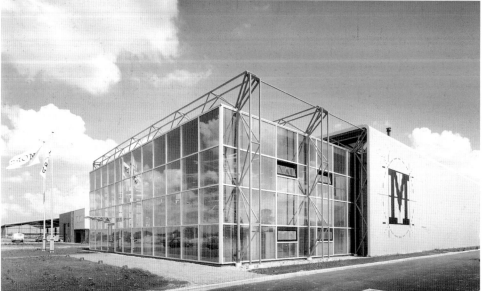

B

A Structural system,
   transverse and longitudinal
B South-west and north-west elevations,
   longitudinal section, plan,
   scale 1:500
C Sketch of principle of building components,
   not to scale

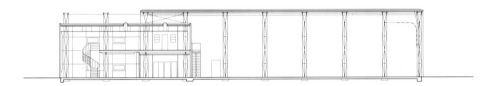

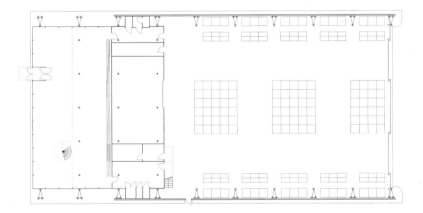

C

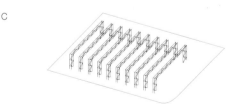

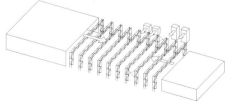

Example 17

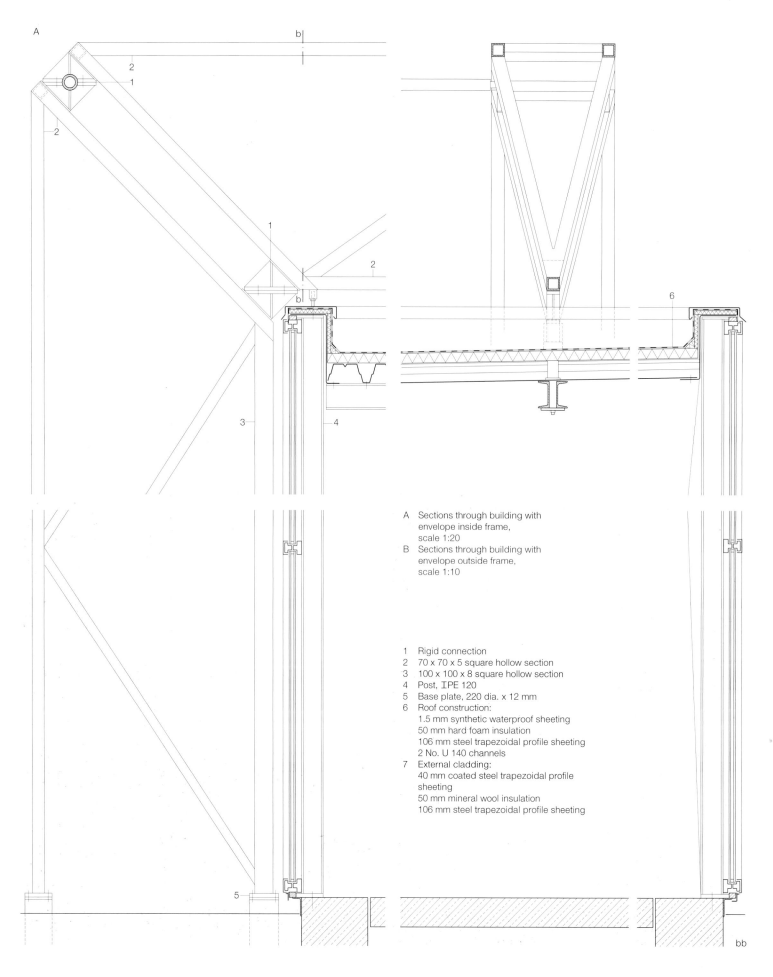

A Sections through building with
   envelope inside frame,
   scale 1:20
B Sections through building with
   envelope outside frame,
   scale 1:10

1 Rigid connection
2 70 x 70 x 5 square hollow section
3 100 x 100 x 8 square hollow section
4 Post, IPE 120
5 Base plate, 220 dia. x 12 mm
6 Roof construction:
   1.5 mm synthetic waterproof sheeting
   50 mm hard foam insulation
   106 mm steel trapezoidal profile sheeting
   2 No. U 140 channels
7 External cladding:
   40 mm coated steel trapezoidal profile
   sheeting
   50 mm mineral wool insulation
   106 mm steel trapezoidal profile sheeting

bb

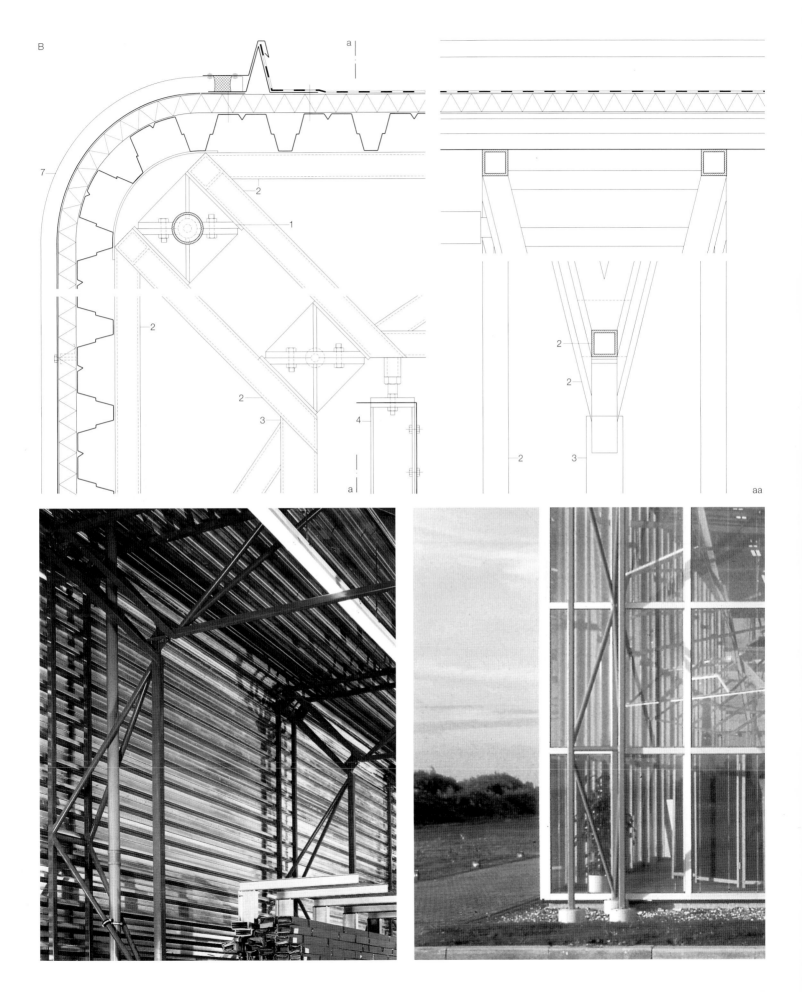

Example 18

School of Art, Limoges, France

1994
Architects:
Finn Geipel, Nicholas Michelin, LAB FAC, Paris
Project Manager: Michel Delplace
Project team: C. Balay, N. Boudier, A. Johnson,
K. Labbay, E. Laurent, P. Marguc,
N. Papadede, C. Tretout, M. Wacheux, L. Wong
Structural engineers: Werner Sobek Inge-
nieure, Stuttgart, with Andrew Sedgwick,
Ove Arup & Partners, Cetec Limoges

The School of Art is located in a suburb on the edge of the campus. The building, positioned between forest and main road, acts as an inter-face between town and country, with a glazed facade on one side and a solid one on the other. The various functions are arranged along a main access corridor within the 145 x 37 m overall plan size, .

Offices, library and the massive in-situ con-crete cube of the auditorium face the entrance. Four large, full-height workshops, independent of the main structure, face onto the forest; these can be subdivided as required by means of movable partitions.

The climatic concept provides for heating merely the innermost areas of the building. The large rooms, as buffer zones, allow the chang-ing seasons to be experienced. Large expanses of roof glazing and projecting louvre boxes guarantee natural anti-glare protection.

The loadbearing structure of the outer skin consists of lattice girders made from box sec-tions. An intermediate column divides them into two segments, with pinned and Vierendeel frame actions. The girders are placed at 5 m centres and rigidly connected to the columns and the concrete wall.

Secondary beams are constructed as Vieren-deel elements and span 5 m. These provide lateral support for the main girders. They are the same depth as the main girders and are connected to them via web plates.

Diagonal wind bracing stiffens both the roof as well as the whole building in the longitudinal direction. The solid and glazed roof elements are secured by means of individual fixings which also permit roof structures to be attached.

References: [3], [15], [34], [75], [215]

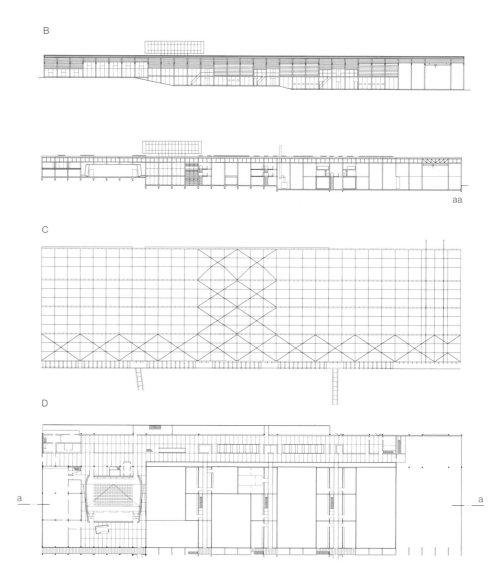

A   Structural scheme
B   West elevation, longitudinal section
C   Wind bracing at roof level
D   Plan
Scale 1:1250
E   Sections
Scale 1:250

E

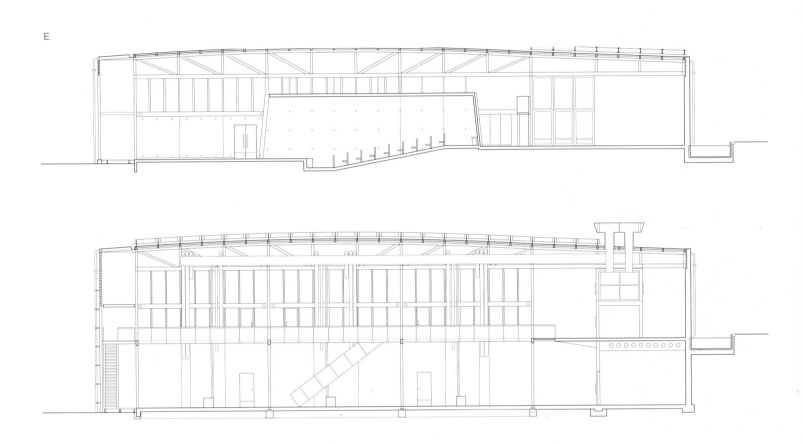

Example 18

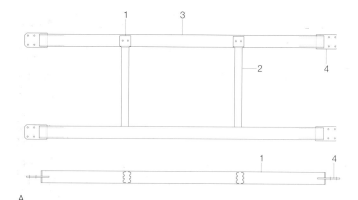

A Vierendeel (secondary) girder,
   elevation and horizontal section
B Section through roof
Scale 1:50

1 18 mm connecting plate
2 150 x 100 x 3 rectangular
   hollow section
3 160 x 160 x 3.6 square hollow section
4 360 x 180 x 12 mm connecting plate
5 Rooflight
6 Sunshading
7 Main lattice girder

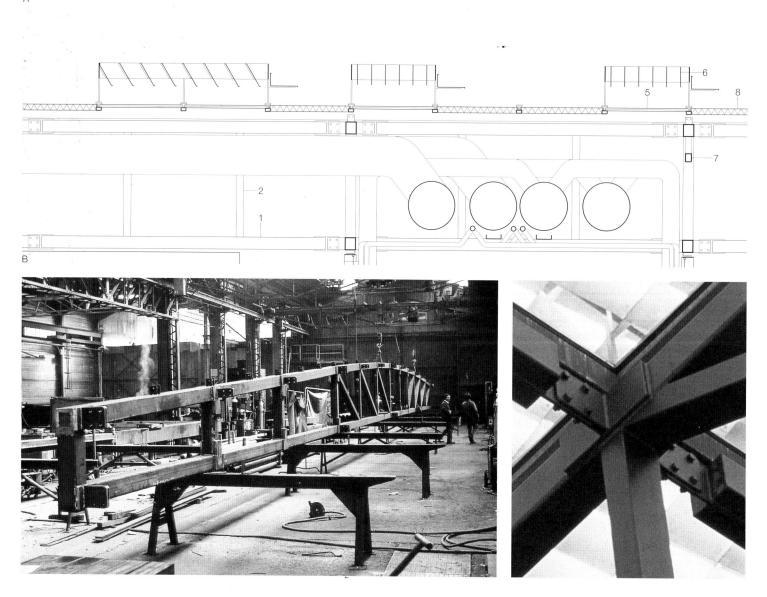

Individual fixings
C   Roof panel
D   Glazing
Scale 1:5

8   Construction of roof panel:
    1 mm sheet aluminium
    80 mm insulation
    1 mm coated sheet steel
9   150 x 40 x 3 rectangular
    hollow section
10 8 mm flat
11 Girder
12 Double glazing
13 60 x 40 x 3 rectangular
    hollow section

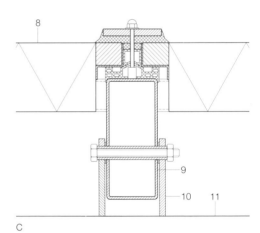

C

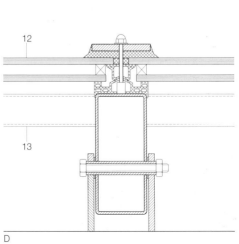

D

Example 19

British Pavilion, EXPO 92, Seville, Spain

1992

Architects:
Nicholas Grimshaw and Partners, London
N. Grimshaw, E. Billings, P. Cook, M. Fisher,
D. Jackson, A. Hall, R. Latter, J. Martin, C. Nash,
J. Scanlan, R. Watson
Structural engineers: Ove Arup & Partners,
London

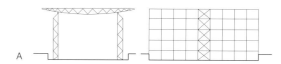

The appearance of the pavilion is dominated by technical measures, a response to the hot climate of Andalusia. The roof surface is shaded by fabric panels and photovoltaic panels visible from afar. The latter supply the power for the pumps of the water cooling system for the 18-m-high east elevation: water from a reservoir at the base of the facade is pumped to the 1400 nozzles at the top from where it flows back down the facade. The south facade is shaded by PVC-coated polyester panels fixed to nine pretensioned, curved steel masts. A wall of stacked, water-filled steel freight containers on the solid west side serves as heating/cooling mass storage in a day/night cycle.

Inside, the single volume is divided up by the three exhibition decks, structurally independent of the steelwork of the building envelope. These decks are reached via an exciting, predefined route. Two enclosed "pods" on the upper deck serve for multimedia presentations. The 22-m-high fixed-base lattice columns at 7.20 m centres brace the building in the transverse direction and support, via a pinned joint, the fish-belly roof girders spanning 32 m. To accommodate torsion, caused by the shading and photovoltaic panels fixed to the roof, the girders are braced by diagonal ties, with struts in the end bays. Stability is provided in the longitudinal direction by cross-bracing in the centre bay.

The design of the structure was chiefly determined by fabrication, transport and erection aspects. All the components were produced in England and conceived as shallow as possible for transport on low-loaders. It proved cheaper to ship prefabricated pieces up to 24 m long and weighing up to 7.5 t to the large port at Santander in northern Spain and then take them by road over a long and arduous route to Seville than ship smaller pieces, which would be complicated to erect, directly to Cadiz.

References: [23], [40], [123], [135], [444], [478]

A Structural system, transverse and longitudinal
B Part elevation, part longitudinal section,
   transverse section, scale 1:500

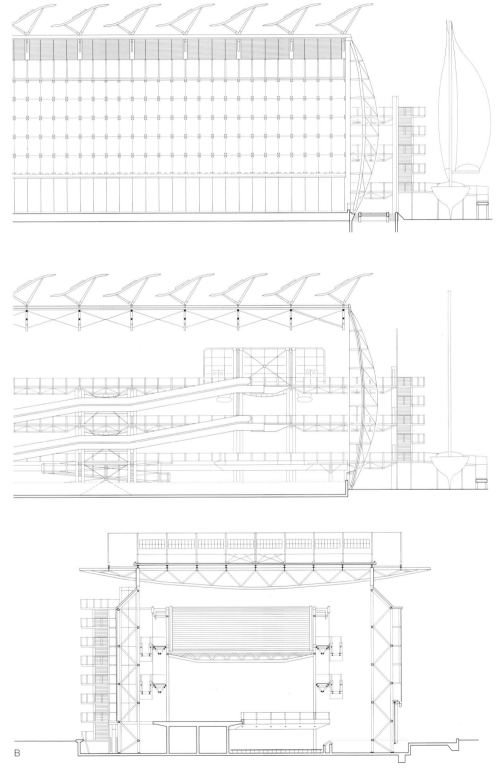

B

Example 19

Sections, scale 1:100
A   South facade
B   East facade
Details, scale 1:20

1   Frame of
    152 x 89 channels
2   Fabric shades
3   Solar panels
4   Roof construction:
    Polyester membrane
    Thermal insulation
    Profiled steel sheeting

5   Purlins,
    203 x 203 H-sections
6   Tubular roof girders
7   Tubular mast,
    324 mm dia.
8   Tapered spreader,
    pressed steel
9   Stainless steel rod,
    36 mm dia.
10 Stainless steel rod,
    12 mm dia.
11 12 mm toughened
    safety glass

A

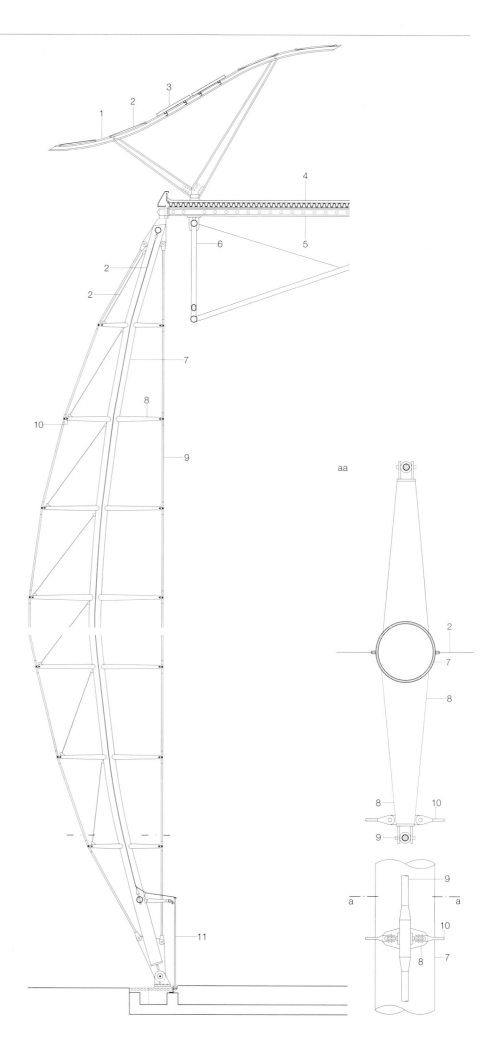

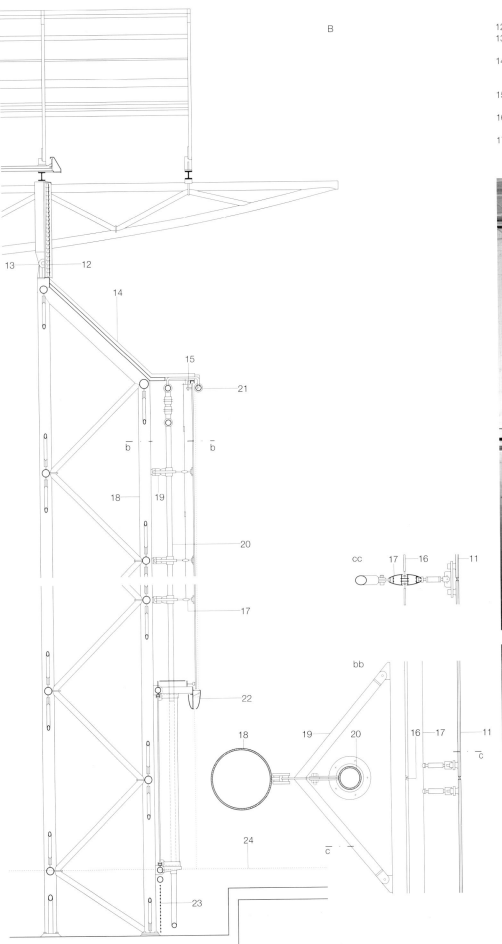

B

12 Polycarbonate louvres
13 Pinned joint between
column and roof girder
14 Insulation, laminated
both sides with GRP
panels
15 Glazing suspension
assembly
16 Stainless steel rod with
turnbuckles
17 Extruded aluminium
section

18 Circular hollow sec-
tion, 327 mm dia.
19 Tubular brace,
48.3 mm dia.
20 Water supply pipe,
180 mm dia.
21 Water pipe with outlets
22 Stainless steel gutter
23 Mesh screen
24 Water reservoir

Example 20

Trade fair hall, Hannover

1996

Architects:
von Gerkan · Marg + Partner, Hamburg
Draft design: Volkwin Marg with Jörg Schlaich
Structural engineers:
Schlaich, Bergermann + Partner, Stuttgart

The design for Hall 4 at Hannover's trade fair grounds was determined by its position among a series of existing halls and by the planned access route to the grounds which was to bridge the adjoining dual carriageway and pass through the hall at the same level.
The solid side walls facing the adjoining halls give the building an orientation towards the central trade fair plaza and the dual carriageway. The necessary unobstructed floor space is achieved by using long-span fish-belly girders pin-jointed to concrete "abutments". Together, the concrete abutments form a sort of bulkhead along each long side, with two-storey service blocks located between them. In order to avoid restraint stresses caused by expansion, the girders are mounted on sliding bearings. Beneath the supports, the horizontal forces are transferred into the concrete abutment via a fork. The hall is illuminated via rooflights adjacent the girders and the two fully glazed elevations.
The roof covering, originally planned as a two-skin PTFE foil, was replaced with conventional metal trapezoidal profile sheeting during the course of the planning.
The ventilation ducts are located beneath the solid roof surfaces and are concealed by a suspended metal ceiling.

References: [77], [301]

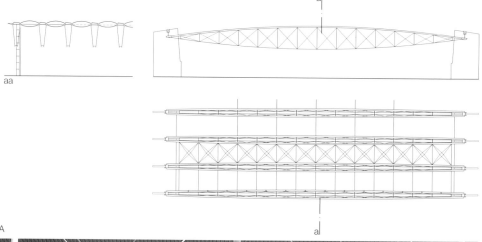

A Structural system: part longitudinal section, transverse section, plan, scale 1:500
B Details of girder and support (side elevation and plan)
C Section through girder
Scale 1:50

1 Top chord, 508 dia. x 17.5 mm
2 Circular hollow section, 219.1 mm dia.
3 Circular hollow section, 318 mm dia.
4 Circular hollow section, 133 mm dia.
5 Cable clamp, grade St 52
6 8 mm shaped cleat
7 Tie, grade St 52, 42 mm dia. in end bay,
 otherwise 36 mm dia.
8 Bottom chord, 75 mm dia. steel cable, grade VVS
9 64 mm dia. round section
10 2 No. 24 mm dia. anchor bars
11 Bearing plate
12 Frame with stiffeners and shear cleat with 2 x 6 holes
13 Horizontal plates set into top chord and
 horizontal tube
14 Fork made from 30 mm flat

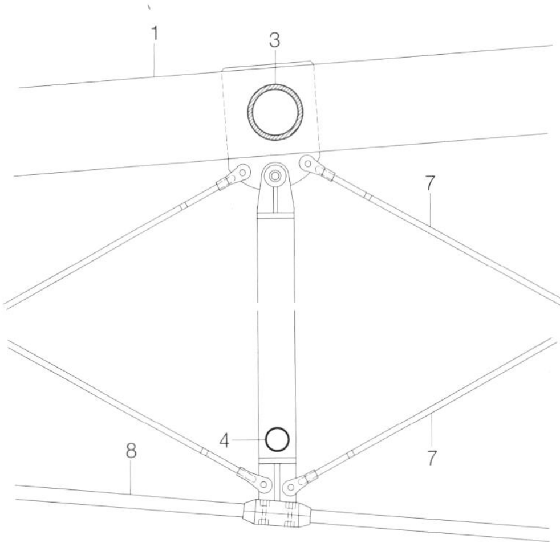

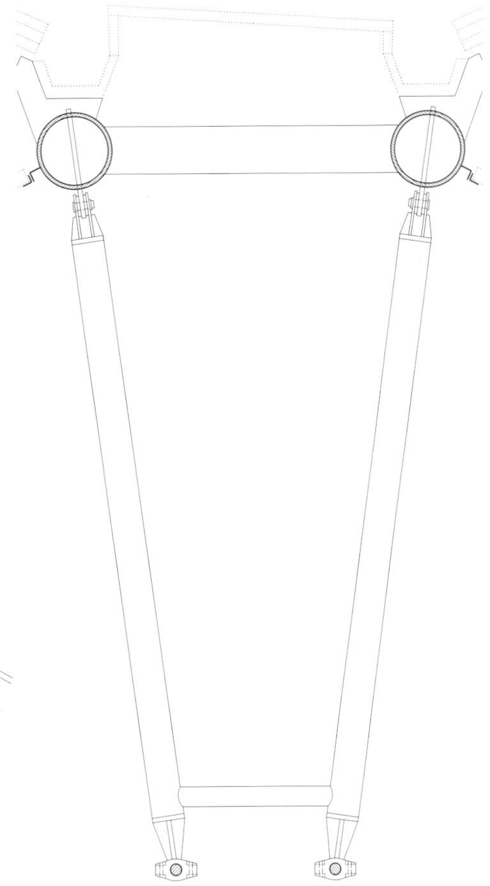

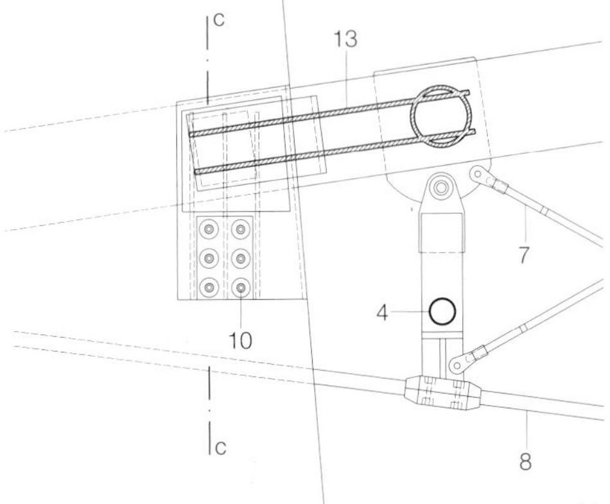

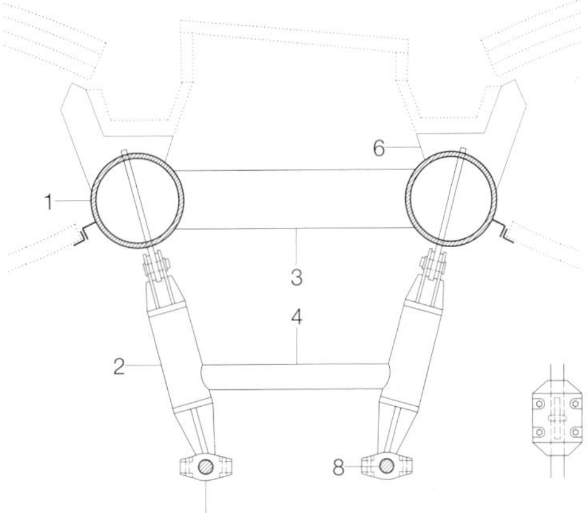

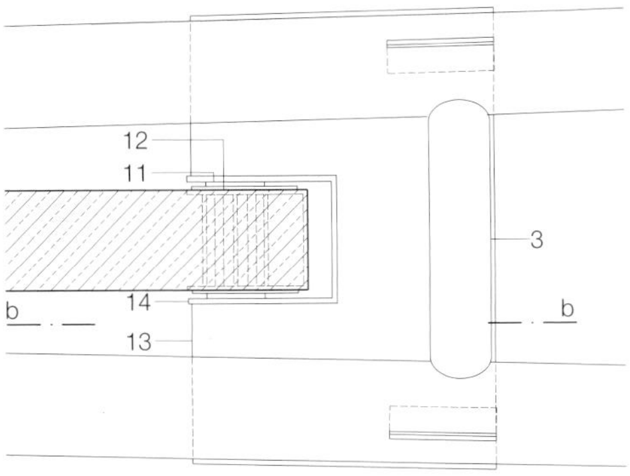

B

bb

dd

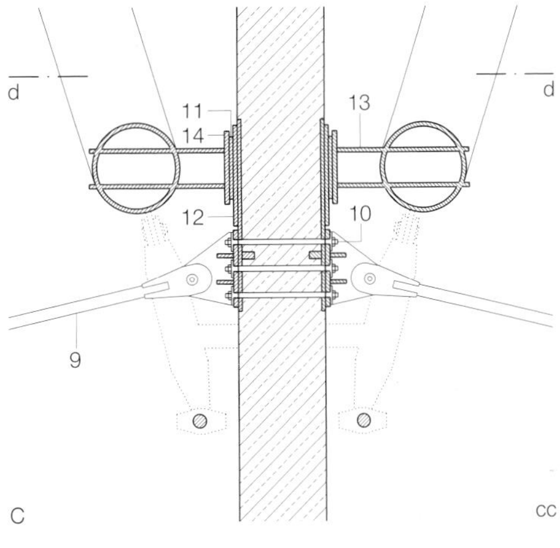

C

cc

Example 21

CIM Institute, Braunschweig

1992

Architects:
Schulitz + Partner, Braunschweig
H. C. Schulitz, S. Worbes, B. Möller
Structural engineers:
Motzkus & Völker, Wolfenbüttel
Michael Sprysch, Vechelde

As an analogy to the link between development and production, the machine shop was intended to merge with the laboratories and offices to form one homogeneous unit. Despite the differing requirements of an 11-m-high machine shop and a laboratory just 3.75 m high, the building was to comprise just a single cube but at the same time render the height and width of the shop and the laboratory floor legible externally. The structure complies with the various requirements for preventive fire protection: the upper floor is protected by an F 30 coating, while basement, ground floor and 1st floor are protected by requirements ranging from F 60 to F 90 in reinforced concrete, composite floors (ribbed steel sheeting with a concrete topping) and steel beams with concrete infills. A frame system spanning 22.5 m forms the loadbearing framework to the machine shop with the crane rails forming an integral part of the construction. Here, the loadbearing structure and the crane rails are clearly visible and are further emphasized by the interruption in the necessary longitudinal stiffening. In the case of the twin-leg column, the I-section below the crane rail was incorporated with its major axis lengthwise. The concept of flexibility is also apparent internally: exposed services provide easy access for maintenance and modifications. There is generous clear headroom in the laboratory and the dovetail slots beneath the composite floor slabs enable further services to be readily attached.

References: [29], [157], [170], [398]

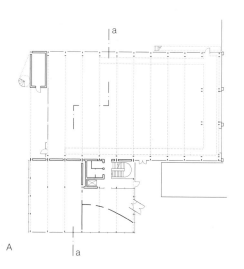

A

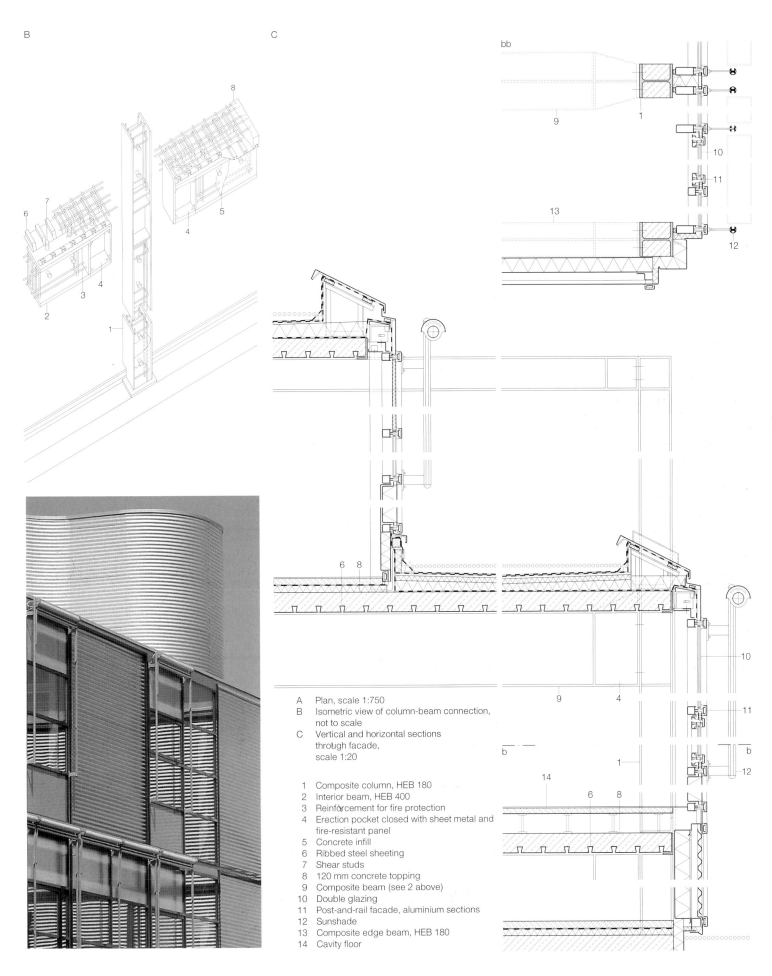

B

C

bb

b   b

A   Plan, scale 1:750
B   Isometric view of column-beam connection,
     not to scale
C   Vertical and horizontal sections
     through facade,
     scale 1:20

1   Composite column, HEB 180
2   Interior beam, HEB 400
3   Reinforcement for fire protection
4   Erection pocket closed with sheet metal and
     fire-resistant panel
5   Concrete infill
6   Ribbed steel sheeting
7   Shear studs
8   120 mm concrete topping
9   Composite beam (see 2 above)
10   Double glazing
11   Post-and-rail facade, aluminium sections
12   Sunshade
13   Composite edge beam, HEB 180
14   Cavity floor

Example 21

A

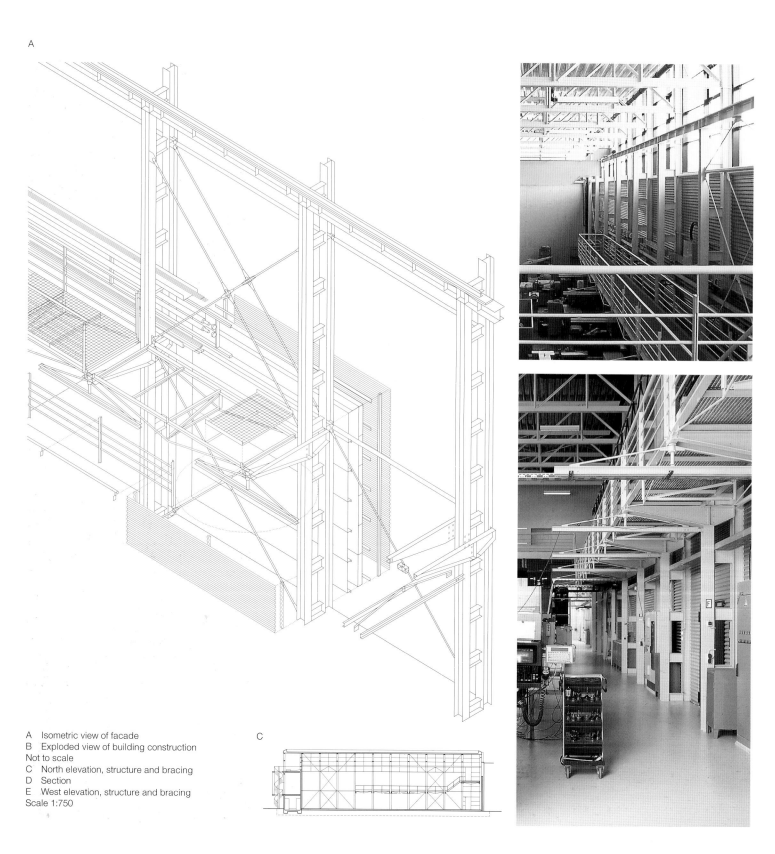

A Isometric view of facade
B Exploded view of building construction
Not to scale
C North elevation, structure and bracing
D Section
E West elevation, structure and bracing
Scale 1:750

C

B

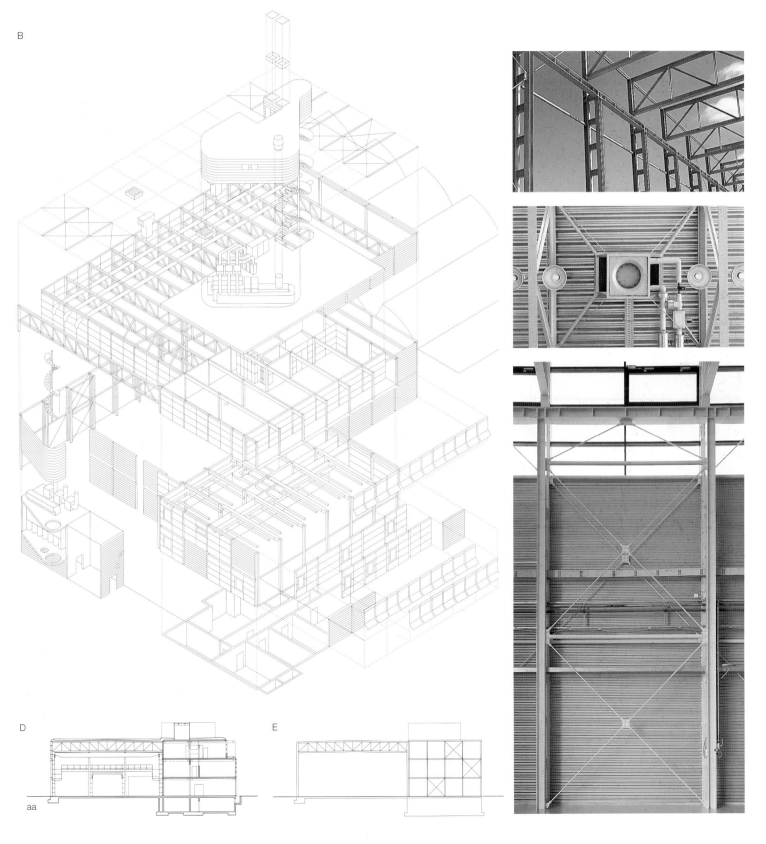

D

aa

E

Example 22

Information centre, Berlin

1995

Architects: Schneider + Schumacher, Frankfurt
am Main
M. Schumacher (Project Architect), K. Dirschl,
C. Simons, T. Zürcher, S. Widmer, P. Pfeiffer,
P. Schiffer, P. Begon,
Structural engineers:
Bollinger + Grohmann, Frankfurt am Main

Berlin's so-called "Info-Box" lies in the midst of
the many building sites around Leipziger Platz.
The exhibition inside, which runs until 2002,
provides information on all the projects of private investors and public bodies. The brief
called for an easily dismantled building to be
erected within a period of just three months.
The result is a box 62 m long x 15 m wide x
13 m high and raised 7 m clear of the ground.
Facades clad with rectangular steel panels
painted bright red and two escape stairs positioned clear of the building give the building its
distinctive appearance.
The tight construction schedule led to the use
of a prefabricated steel and reinforced concrete composite design. Supported on 14 concrete-filled steel tubes resting on tubular piles
founded 15 m below ground, the box itself was
fabricated entirely from bolted rolled sections.
With their concrete infilling between the
flanges, the main beams and columns achieve
the F 90 fire resistance class. The secondary
beams at 1.5 m centres span as continuous
beams over two bays each measuring 7.5 m
and are protected by an F 30 paint system.
Along the column axes the beams are
designed compositely, with concrete infills.

References: [65], [76], [159], [172], [173]

A

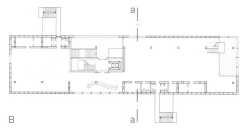

B   a

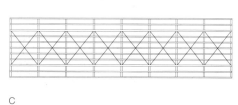

C

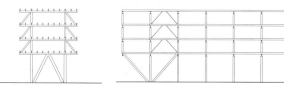

A Perspective view of structural
   steelwork
B Plan
C Schematic view of bracing
   and beams, sections
Scale 1:1000
D Section, scale 1:200
E Section through facade,
   scale 1:20
F Detail of connection,
   scale 1:20
G Isometric view of node

1 Main beam, HEB 500
2 Beams, IPE 300
3 Composite beam, HEB 300
4 Wall construction:
 2 layers of plasterboard with joints filled
 Latex paint
 Sandwich panel 100 mm
 Sheet steel with stove-enamelled finish
5 Waterproof sheeting with thermal insulation
6 Floor construction (F 90 fire protection class):
 5 mm linoleum
 cement-bound timber-derivative boards,
 2 No. 10 mm + 15 mm, with 18 mm rubber mat between
 Anodised trapezoidal profile sheeting, 40 x 183 x 0.88 mm
7 Casing of cement-bound silicate fire protection panels
8 Ventilation outlet
9 Stilts, 450 dia. x 13 mm circular hollow sections welded to anchor plates, filled with concrete and painted
10 Fixing plate for raking stilts, made from welded flats

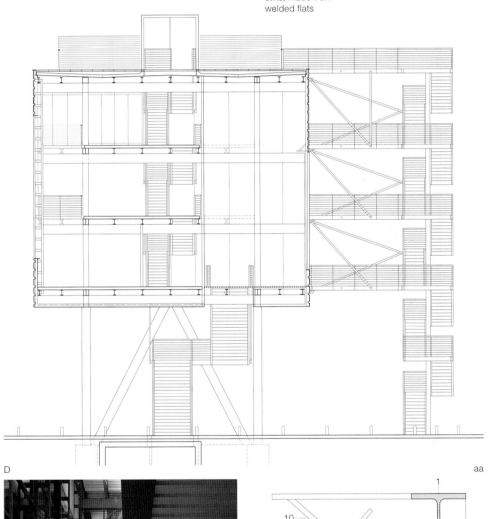

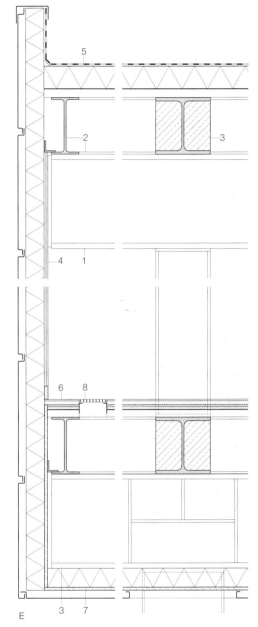

D

aa

E

F

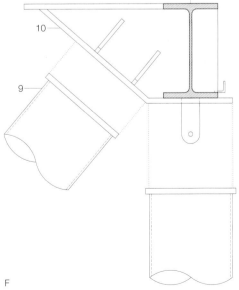

G

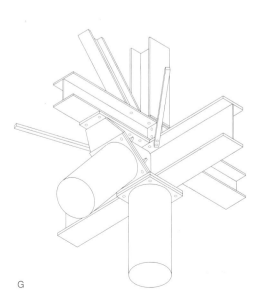

Example 23

Editorial offices, Berlin

1991

Architect:
Gerhard Spangenberg, Berlin,
with Brigitte Steinkilberg
Structural engineers:
GSE-Ingenieurgesellschaft, Berlin

This extension to the offices of a newspaper publisher adjoins a sandstone building from the boom years of the late 19th century and acts as a link between two different building lines.
The design of the facade and the storey heights are related to the arrangement of the neighbouring building but the choice of materials has led to the creation of a lightweight and open building with an industrial appearance. This character is underscored by the interior design.
The entire loadbearing structure consists of rolled sections with concrete infilling between the flanges, which gives the construction the necessary fire protection. The composite beams (spanning 8 m) are connected to the composite columns by way of welded cleats. Stability is provided by the floor plates as well as by the party wall adjacent the old building and by the stair shaft. Composite construction is also employed for the floor slabs; the underside of the steel sheeting has been left exposed and the dovetail slots of this serve to attach service installations.

References: [35], [59]

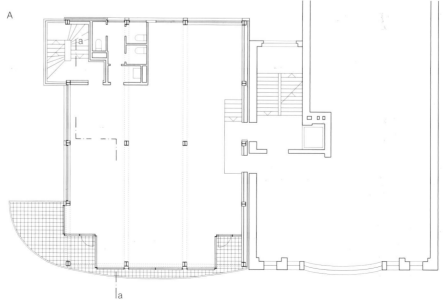

A   Plan and section
Scale 1:250
B   Details of facade
Scale 1:20

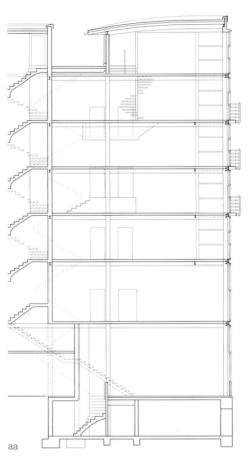

aa

B

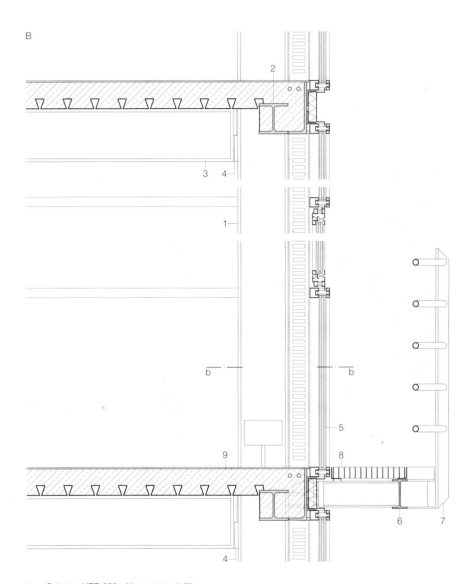

1   Column, HEB 280 with concrete infills
     between flanges
2   Beam, HEB 160 with concrete infills
     between flanges
3   Beam, HEB 280 with concrete infills
     between flanges
4   Welded cleat
5   Window element with double glazing
6   Beam, IPE 160, with sprayed
     zinc finish
7   Upright, 70 x 70 x 8 T-section,
     hot-dip galvanized
8   Open grid flooring
9   140 mm in-situ concrete topping
     (ribs of steel sheeting act as
     reinforcement)
10   Sound-insulated permanent ventilation
11   Slotted sheet metal cover
12   Bent titanium-zinc sheet

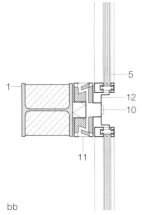

bb

Example 24

Office buildings, Bedfont Lakes, UK

1992

Architects:
Michael Hopkins and Partners, London
Sir Michael Hopkins, I. Sharratt, P. Romaniuk,
P. Bate, P. Cartwright, B. Phelan
Structural engineers: Buro Happold, Bath
M. Dixon, M. Cook, M. Shaw

A former landfill site near London's Heathrow Airport was chosen as the location for the UK headquarters of several international groups. The architect was appointed to draw up a master plan and also to design the premises for a computer multinational, which turned out to be half of the final development.

Situated in a park-like setting, the trio of office buildings is grouped symmetrically around a central plaza with parking. The client uses the main building and the two side wings for marketing, research and exhibition purposes.

The three-storey braced steel frame is left exposed, both internally and externally. Corresponding to the loads, the column size increases towards ground floor. Specially developed cast node pieces link the different column sizes and function as a hinged joint for the incoming beams. Aluminium frames with aluminium panels and glazing units form the building envelope. These are installed as modules and compensate for the differing clear widths between columns caused by the changing column sizes. Lattice girders – maximum transverse span 18 m – span across the atrium of the main building. These carry the supporting construction for the large expanse of glazing (Planar® system). Sunshading is provided by panels provided in the plane of the structure.

The galleries in the atrium are linked by bridges. Their minimalist construction comprising slender solid-web beams is rendered possible by the use of ties and central spans supported on cantilever end spans.

References: [25], [124]

A Section, scale 1:500
B Detail of floor slab, scale 1:20
C Axonometric view of corner of building
D Elevation on column, scale 1:50

1 Column, I-section
2 Beam, 305 x 305 H-section with web stiffeners, external flanges trimmed
3 150 x 65 channel
4 Hollow-core prestressed concrete floor planks
5 Beam, 203 x 203 H-section with shear studs

6 Plate welded to bottom flange
7 Concrete topping
8 Aluminium panel painted grey
9 Glazing
10 Fixed sunshading
11 Cast steel node piece

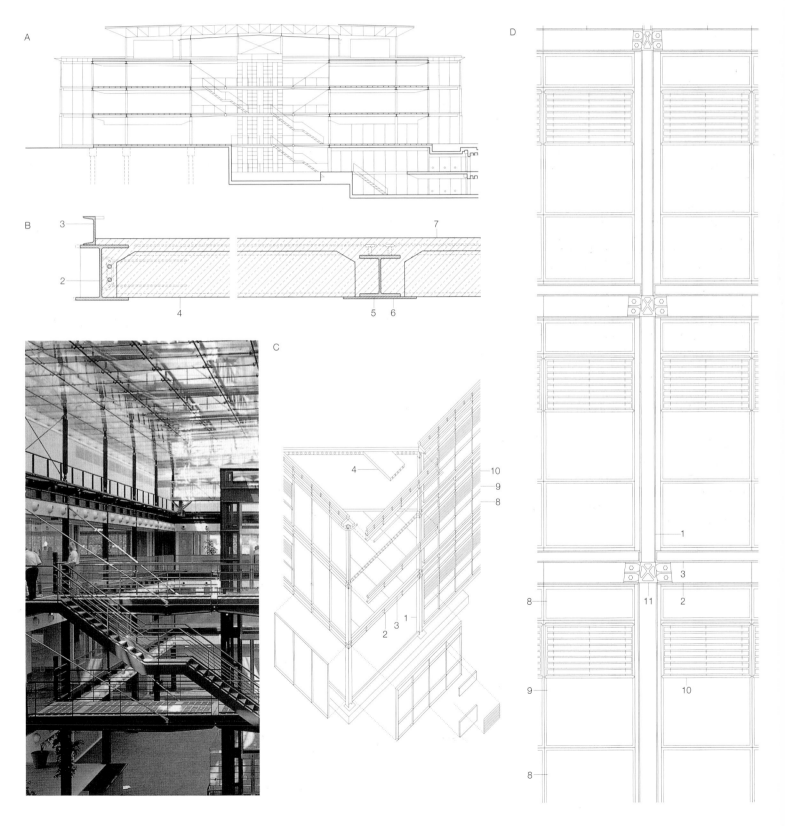

Example 25

Circular hall, Berlin

1986

Architects: Gerd Fesel, Peter Bayerer,
Hans-Dieter Hecker, Roland Ostertag, Berlin
Project team: J. Reiter, W. Schuster,
R. Heidenreich, H. Schneider, H. Vetter,
E. Zickgraf, B. Müller, K. Fischer et al.
Structural engineers: Stefan Polónyi,
Herbert Fink, Peter Koch, Berlin
Assistant: J. Böckl

This belongs to the complex of buildings forming Berlin Technical University. The design is
intended to offer a solution to one problem of
university planning, i.e. that of combining
smaller spaces, e.g. for administration purposes, with a large-volume structure for production
and research work. This problem was overcome by the multistorey ring of individual
rooms around the central hall.
The roof construction of the hall is made up of
14 trusses and 13 IPE beams placed alternately in a radial arrangement. In the middle the
trusses are connected to a central hub, a steel
tube 812.8 dia. x 16 mm and nearly 4 m tall. At
the top there is a compression ring and at the
bottom a tension ring, both fabricated from
welded steel plates. The top and bottom
chords of the trusses are bolted onto plates on
the rings. However, the IPE 600 sections positioned between the trusses do not span to the
hub but are instead supported on a ring of
purlins spanning from truss to truss at a radius
of 12 m from the centre of the roof. The secondary beams are arranged in rings supported
on the trusses and beams. All beams and
trusses have hinged supports at the composite
columns of the facade. Two overhead travelling cranes are suspended from the central
hub and run on a rail fixed to an IPE 500 section supported on steel corbels on the
columns.
The hall is stabilized by cross-bracing in roof
and facade. The bracing right around the
perimeter in the outermost bay of the roof and
three sets of bracing, in each case spanning
between a pair of girders, ensure that the roof
acts like a plate.
A conical rooflight was erected in the centre to
improve daylight levels in the interior and to act
as smoke and heat vent. It marks the focus of
the complex and the most interesting part of
the construction.

References: [66], [129], [429]

A

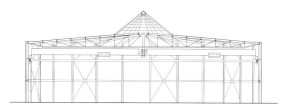

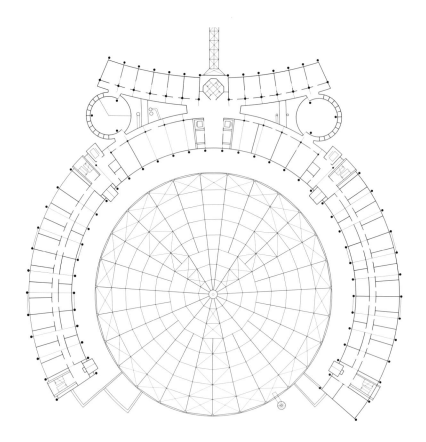

A Plan and section,
  scale 1:1000
B Details of column and
  central hub, scale 1:50
1 Composite column
2 Crane rail
3 Perimeter purlin,
  HEB 260
4 Top chord, HEB 320
5 Bottom chord, HEA 300
6 Strut, HEA 100
7 Diagonals,
  2 No. 80 x 40 x 8 angles
8 812.8 dia. x 16 mm tube
9 Cover plate
10 Steel annulus
11 Steel ring,
   2780 dia. x 20 mm
12 Steel flat ribs, 30 mm
13 Steel annulus with connecting plates
14 Steel plate,
   1004 dia. x 50 mm

B

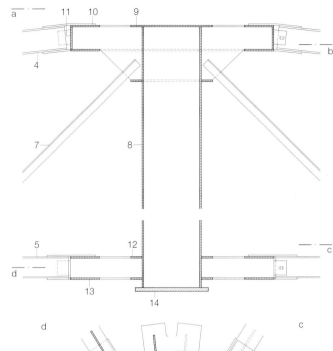
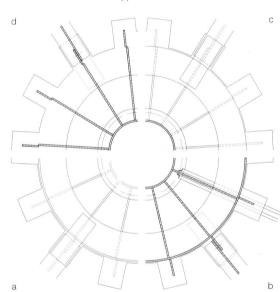

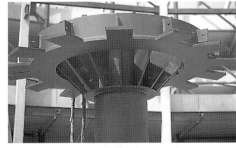

Example 26

Production plant,
Saint-Quentin-en-Yvelines, France

1991

Architects: Renzo Piano Building
Workshop, Paris
P. Vincent, A. Gallissian, D. Rat, M. Henry,
L. Le Voyer, A.H. Temenides, A. El Jerari,
A. O´Carroll
Structural engineers:
Ove Arup & Partners, London

Governing design factors for the production
plant of a developer and manufacturer of high-
precision optical instruments were: flexible
extension options for individual production
areas, provision of daylight without glare at
workstations, and an extremely tight timetable.
Starting from a curved service wall marking the
eastern boundary of the site, numerous single-
storey sheds, each 14.4 m wide but with differing lengths, stretch out in a westerly direction.
Access corridors, 3.6 m wide, with high-level
service ducts are located between each shed.
Both the 10-m-high sheds and the access corridors are made up of 7.2-m-wide modules
placed in rows.
The production area modules are spanned by
curved IPE 180 beams, each pair being
trussed together to form a three-dimensional
loadbearing system. On one side these systems are supported directly on the access corridors and on the other (northern) side on a
group of four raking steel tubes at a higher
level in such a way that a type of northlight roof
is formed – guaranteeing natural interior illumination. Whereas the two steel tubes directly
in front of the glazing only act as struts, the two
outer ones must serve as both struts and ties.
The individual modules of the production areas
are joined by a stable roof shell of trapezoidal
profile sheeting on the underside, insulation
and, as the outer skin, another layer of trapezoidal profile sheeting, but at right-angles to the
first layer.
Bracing at roof level in certain bays provides
the necessary stability for the production area
modules. In addition there are longitudinal
braces between the frame construction of the
access corridor and, transversely, two struts
per column in front of the facade.

References: [39], [71], [135], [482],

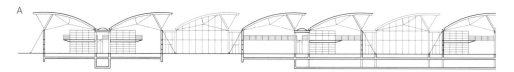

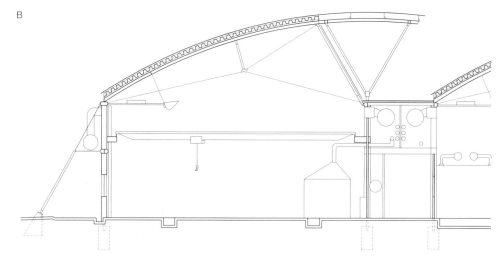

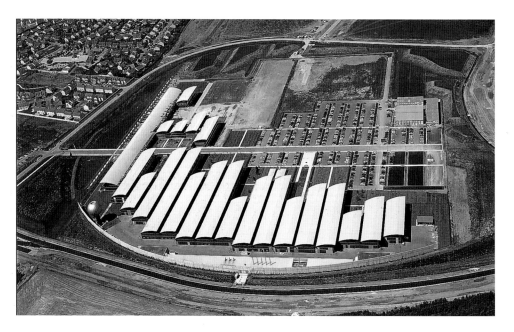

A   Section,
    scale 1:1000
B   Part section,
    scale 1:200

C

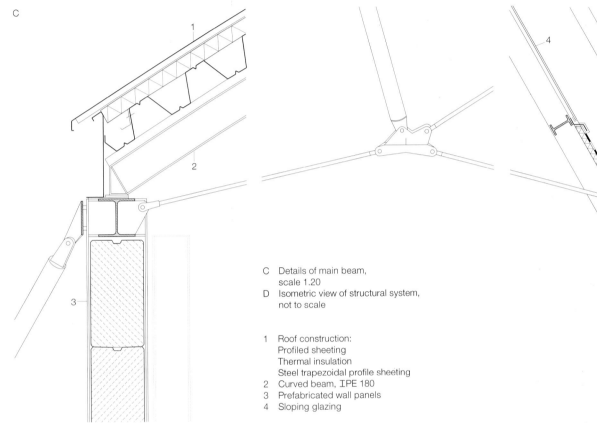

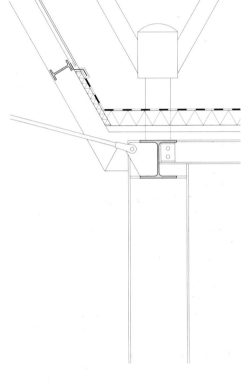

C   Details of main beam,
     scale 1.20
D   Isometric view of structural system,
     not to scale

1   Roof construction:
     Profiled sheeting
     Thermal insulation
     Steel trapezoidal profile sheeting
2   Curved beam, IPE 180
3   Prefabricated wall panels
4   Sloping glazing

D

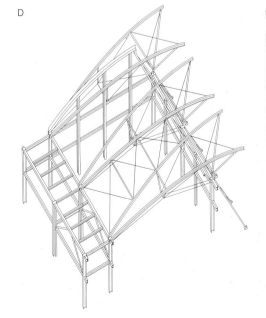

Example 27

Design offices, Gundelfingen

A

1991

Architects:
Kurt Ackermann + Partner, Jürgen Feit,
Munich
Structural engineers:
Behringer + Müller, Munich

The desire for naturally and evenly lit teamwork stations played a key role in the design for this long, low-rise building. There are two wings, 42 x 21 m and two storeys high, linked by a glazed entrance block. A row of rooflights, 5 m wide, runs the full length of the ridge, hence guaranteeing the desired level of illumination in the interior. Large openings have been left in the first floor so that ample daylight can penetrate to the ground floor. The roofs slope inwards and thus enlarge the area of the facade, which results in more daylight entering the interior.

The steel-concrete composite construction is made up of steel columns and a composite floor acting as a plate to provide both longitudinal and transverse stability. The main frames at 6.80 m centres consist of tubular posts and welded rolled-section cantilever arms. Frame action between concrete and steel is achieved by welding the reinforcement to the steel columns. The floor beams and cantilever roof beams are tied to rectangular posts in the facade. This backstay-type arrangement prevents having to join the roof beams below the rooflights, and thus achieves a clear demarcation between the opaque and transparent sections of the roof.

The rooflight frame consists of rectangular hollow sections connected to a trussed ridge member, which is itself supported by trussed constructions on the axes of the cantilever roof beams.

References: [135], [155], [168], [347], [394]

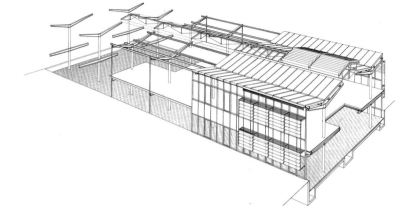

B

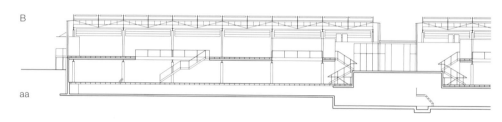

aa

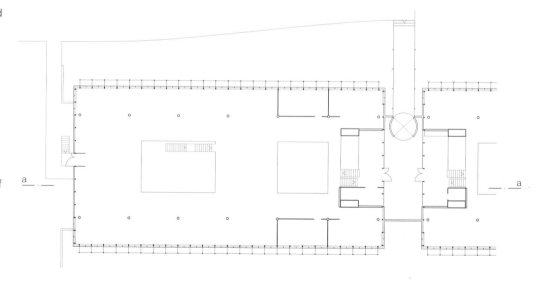

a

a

A   Isometric view of construction
B   Part section and part plan,
    scale 1:500
C   Section, scale 1:50

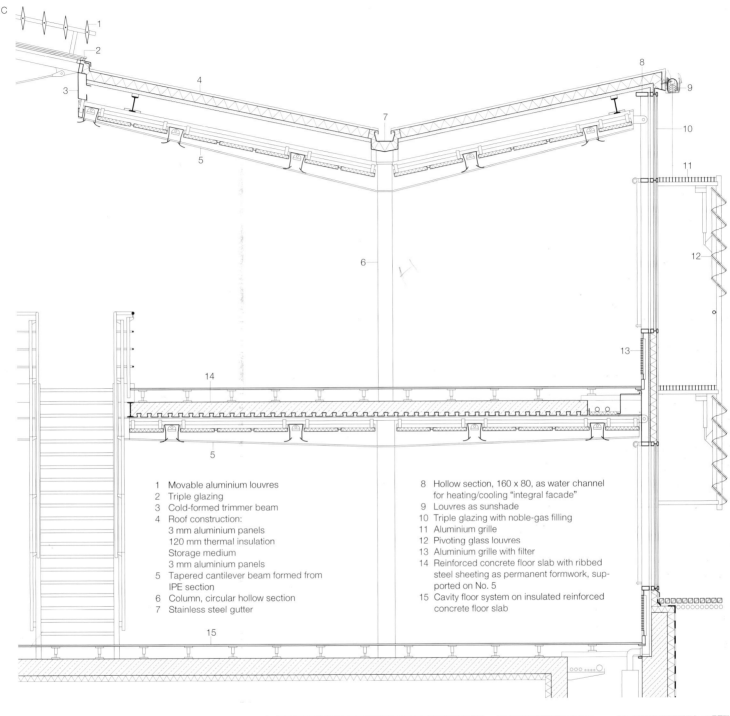

1 Movable aluminium louvres
2 Triple glazing
3 Cold-formed trimmer beam
4 Roof construction:
   3 mm aluminium panels
   120 mm thermal insulation
   Storage medium
   3 mm aluminium panels
5 Tapered cantilever beam formed from
   IPE section
6 Column, circular hollow section
7 Stainless steel gutter
8 Hollow section, 160 x 80, as water channel
   for heating/cooling "integral facade"
9 Louvres as sunshade
10 Triple glazing with noble-gas filling
11 Aluminium grille
12 Pivoting glass louvres
13 Aluminium grille with filter
14 Reinforced concrete floor slab with ribbed
   steel sheeting as permanent formwork, supported on No. 5
15 Cavity floor system on insulated reinforced
   concrete floor slab

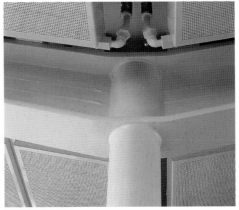

Example 28

Sports hall, Lorch a. d. Rems

1975

Architects:
Behnisch & Partner, Stuttgart
Project team:
H. Hübner, P. Kaltschmidt, H. Peltz
Structural engineer:
Julius Natterer, Munich

The sports hall is sited on a hill overlooking the town of Lorch and the Rems valley, positioned alongside two new schools. In order to prevent the hall from having an overpowering effect in its modest surroundings, it was sunk 3 m into the ground, the perimeter of the roof lowered considerably and the roof surfaces and external walls clearly defined. Therefore, the building blends in well with the undulating landscape. The span of the main loadbearing structure is shortened optically on both sides by the cantilever beams with backstays, which are left exposed externally in front of the longitudinal facades. The cantilever beams (in a dark colour) are spaced at 5.75 m and consist of welded rolled sections with rigid connections at the columns; those on the spectators' side have fixed bases, those on the other side pinned bases. However, the tie on the seating side must also cope with compression in the most unfavourable loading case. Inside the hall, secondary beams are supported at the ends of the heavily stayed cantilever arms. These beams form the supports for the delicate 19.20-m-span roof trusses placed at 2.875 m centres, i.e. half the construction grid. The centre bay of the truss has cross-bracing in order to be able to withstand asymmetric vertical loads as well. The struts are stabilized by a cable in the longitudinal direction and the horizontal stiffening in the transverse direction is achieved by means of the frame action of the stayed cantilevers, in the longitudinal direction by vertical bracing along the column axes and inclined props at the gables. Bracing in the flat and pitched areas of the roof also contributes to the overall stability.

References: [127], [428]

B

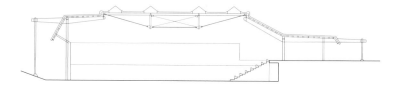

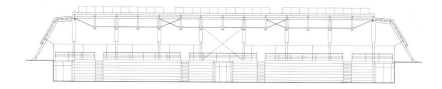

C

A

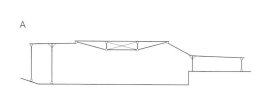

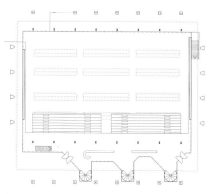

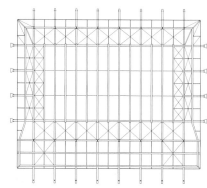

D

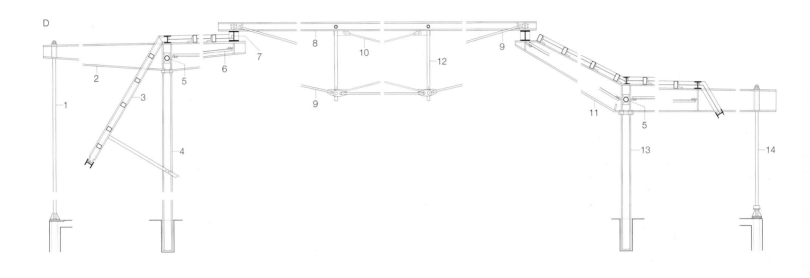

A Structural system
B Sections, scale 1:500
C Plan of entrance level, beam layout, scale 1:1000
D Section through structural steelwork, scale 1:100
E Details, scale 1:20

1 Backstay, 2 No. 45 dia. round sections
2 Tapered cantilever beam made from HEB 600,
  400-700 mm deep
3 2 No. U 180 channels
4 Column, HEA 260
5 60.3 dia. x 5 mm circular hollow section
6 Roof bracing, 55 x 6 angle
7 Longitudinal beam, HEB 260
8 Trussed roof beam, HEA 220
9 Tie, 2 No. 42 dia.
10 Bottom chord, 30 mm dia.
11 Cantilever arm made from welded plates,
   400-700 mm deep
12 127 dia. x 5 mm circular hollow section
13 Column, HEB 260
14 Backstay, 60.3 dia. x 8.8 mm circular hollow section

E

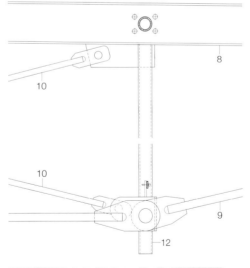
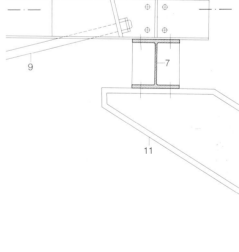

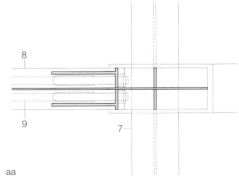

aa

Example 29

"Georges Pompidou" arts centre, Paris

1977

Architects:
Renzo Piano, Richard Rogers, London
R. Piano, R. Rogers, G. F. Franchini
Structural engineers:
Ove Arup & Partners, Paris

The various facilities of this arts centre include a museum, a library and the various galleries. The idea of unconstrained accommodation for diverse functions in a generous open-plan lay-out led to means of access and many services being repositioned outside the envelope, where they remain exposed. This resulted in unobstructed floor areas of 166.4 x 44.8 m internally, with storey heights of 7 or 10.5 m. The primary structure of the braced steel frame consists of lattice girders supported on hinged bearings at the columns, large cast arms, so-called "Gerberettes". The girders, with cast nodes, span 48 m and are placed at 12.8 m centres. The cast steel Gerberettes, almost 8 m long and weighing 10 t, and their associated backstays achieve a continuous effect. They are hinged at the columns, cantilever 1.6 m inwards, where the lattice girders are supported, and 6 m outwards, where the back-stays are attached. The continuous columns of spun-cast tubes, with diminishing wall thick-ness as they rise higher, are mounted on ball joints. The secondary structure, carrying 110 mm reinforced concrete slabs 3.2 x 6.4 m, consists of pairs of IPE 500 sections placed at 6.4 m centres on the girders.
Longitudinal stability to the building is by means of diagonals, not in the plane of the columns but in that of the external backstays. This necessitates horizontal K-bracing to link the vertical longitudinal bracing with the floor slabs. Transverse bracing is placed in the gable bays, where the standard beams are joined to additional diagonals to form a five-storey truss. At ground floor level, the trans-verse bracing is positioned outside in front of the columns.
For reasons of fire protection, the lattice gir-ders were clad with mineral wool, sprayed plaster and a cladding of stainless steel. The columns were filled with water. Sprinkler and inert-gas systems as well as monitoring by sensors throughout provide active fire protec-tion.

References: [103], [184], [244], [339], [362], [427], [450]

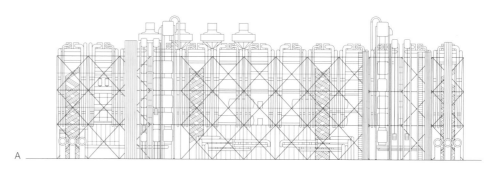

A

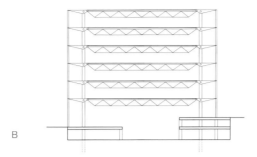

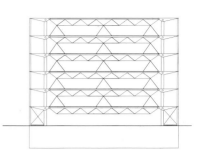

B

A   Rear elevation
B   Column-and-girder structural system,
    standard axis, gable axis
C   Wind bracing to plaza elevation
D   Plan of structural system
E   Plan of standard floor
Scale 1:500

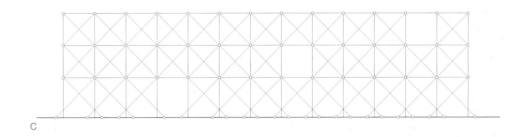

C

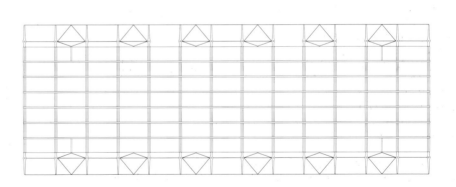

D

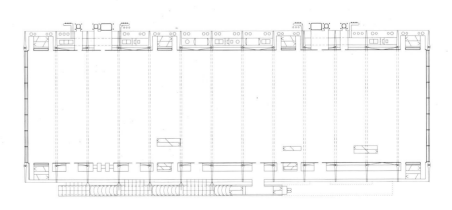

E

Example 29

A Lattice girder: plan, section, elevation,
   view from below, scale 1:200
B Isometric view of Gerberette node
C Plan on bay between Gerberettes, scale 1:200
D Gerberette, scale 1:50

1-4 Top chord of girder, 2 No.:
1 419 dia. x 50 mm
2 419 dia. x 47 mm
3 419 dia. x 31 mm
4 409 dia. x 22 mm
5 Tie, round section/tube
6 Tubular strut

7-9 Bottom chord of girder, 2 No. round sections:
7 160 mm dia.
8 200 mm dia.
9 225 mm dia.
10 Secondary beam, 2 No. I-sections
11 Cast steel Gerberette
12-14 Bracing, connecting vertical bracing with floor
   slabs:
12 323.9 dia. x 7.1 mm circular hollow section
13 273 dia. x 9.5 mm circular hollow section
14 193.7 dia. x 5.4 mm circular hollow section
15 Front edge of facade
16 Front edge of structural slab

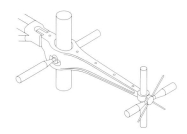

B

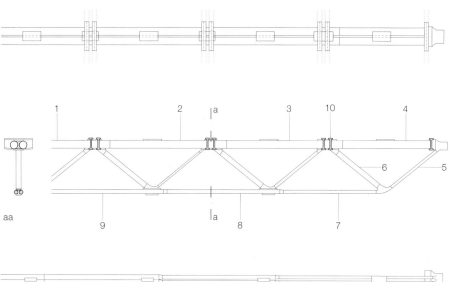
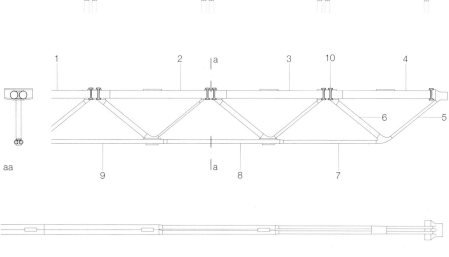

aa

A

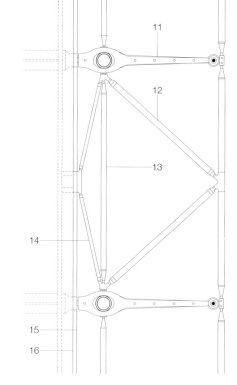

C

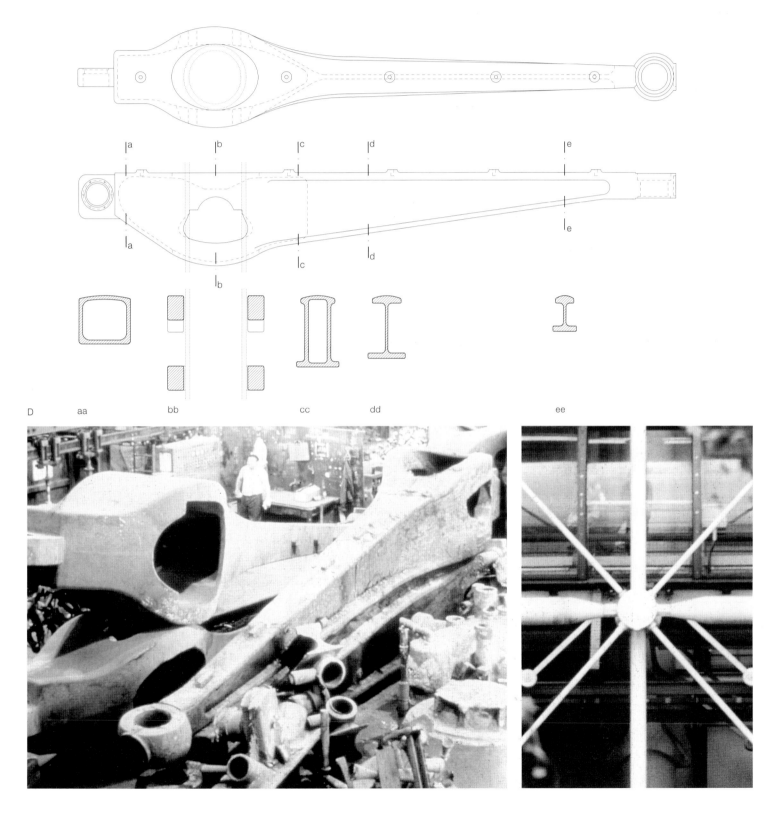

D   aa   bb   cc   dd   ee

Example 30

Exhibition centre, Sydney, Australia

1988

Architects:
Cox, Richardson, Taylor & Partners, Sydney
Project Architects: R. Lee, S. Buzacott,
T. Armitage
Structural engineers:
Ove Arup & Partners, London

Philip Cox was awarded the contract to design an exhibition centre to mark Australia's 200th anniversary.
This project was intended as a sensible urban redevelopment of a former dockyard area. One of the new buildings was this exhibition centre consisting of five individual halls each of 5000 m^2.
The architect opted for a stayed structure to conjure up ideas of a ship's rigging and hence reflect the history of the surroundings in the architectural language. At the same time, this type of construction left the interior unencumbered by columns and so provided for a flexible hall layout.
Each hall is an independent structure consisting of four pylons from which the main beams are suspended. This arrangement produces unobstructed internal spaces measuring 83 x 54 m. The main beams consist of triangular pin-jointed girders split into three segments. Secondary beams, likewise triangular pin-jointed girders, span between the main girders. The external, horizontal struts are in each case hinged at the pylons, secured horizontally by pairs of ties, and provided with backstays at the outer end. Cross-bracing at roof level ensures stability.

References: [41], [339]

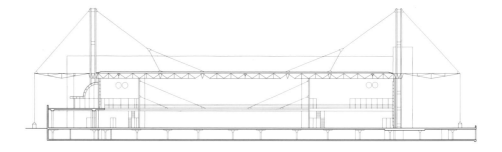

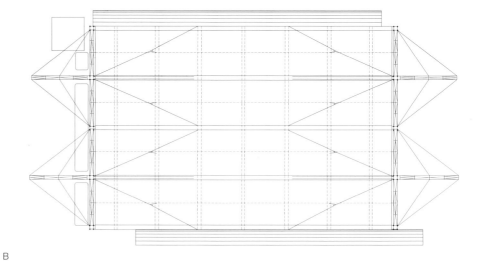

B

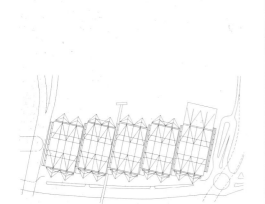

A

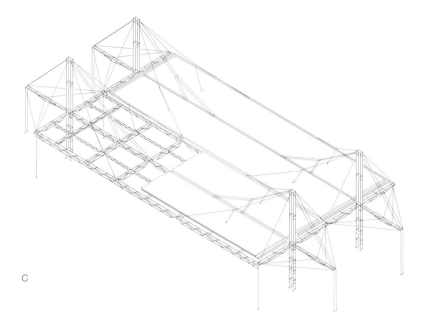

C

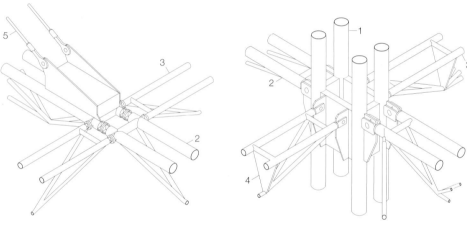

D

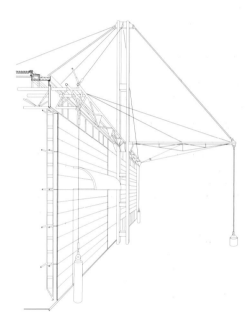

E

A   Site plan,
    not to scale
B   Roof plan and section,
    scale 1:1000

C   Isometric view of structural system
D   Connections: main-secondary girders, girder-pylon
E   Isometric view of facade
Not to scale

1   Pylon, 406 mm dia. circular hollow sections
2   Triangular main girder, 273 mm dia. circular hollow
    sections
3   Triangular secondary girder, 168 mm dia. circular
    hollow sections
4   10 mm plate
5   Tie, 2 No. 60 mm dia.

Example 31

Factory, Newport, UK

1982

Architects:
Richard Rogers Partnership, London
Structural engineers:
Anthony Hunt Associates, London

This semiconductor factory produces microchips, and besides the production centre it includes offices, a works canteen and ancillary facilities. Chip production is extremely sensitive to dust and so air-conditioning and cleanliness play a crucial role. Key design parameters were maximum flexibility, ease of extension, and a short design and construction schedule. At the time of its design the site for the building had not been fixed.

A central circulation and services corridor forms a focal point for the structure. The dust-sensitive production areas are on the north side and the offices, canteen and an internal courtyard on the south side.

The design is based on a stayed construction comprising space and plane trusses and columns. The structure above the central corridor spans 38 m without intermediate columns across the production and administration areas, with the trusses suspended at third-points from 25-m-high pylons. The roof structure is in the form of a grid of rectangular hollow sections, suspended from the main and secondary girders. Steel trapezoidal profile sheeting with thermal insulation and sealing gaskets forms the roof covering.

The entire primary loadbearing structure is conceived as a modular system with quickly erected, mostly prefabricated individual components, and hence allows the building to be built bay by bay. Eight of the planned 20 bays were erected in the first construction phase. The external walls are based on a standardized post-and-rail system which can accept various types of infills, e.g. double glazing or fixed, insulated sandwich panels.

References: [6], [7], [16], [18], [101], [122], [128], [339], [362], [394], [450]

A   Section,
    north-west elevation,
    plan on girder layout,
    scale 1:750

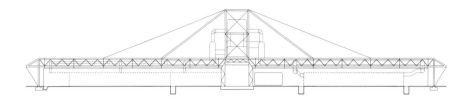

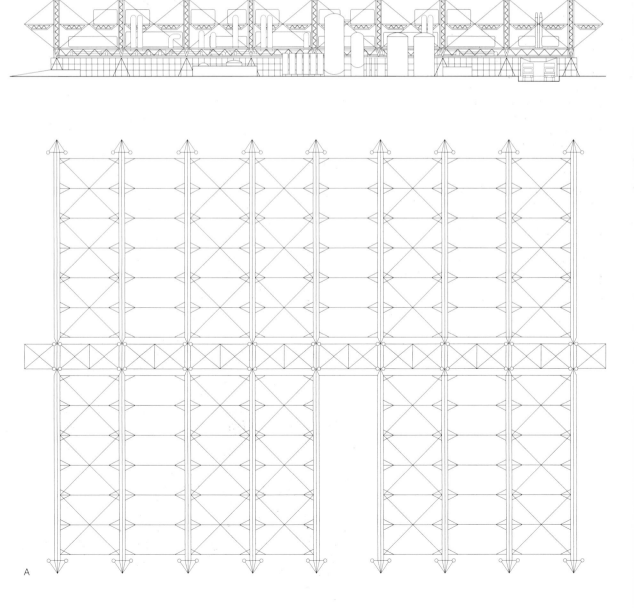

A

Example 31

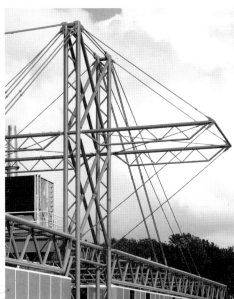

A   Isometric view of basic structural elements
B   Exploded view of secondary girder connection
C   Exploded view of top of pylon
D   Exploded view of main girder connection
E   Horizontal and vertical sections through column-main girder
     portal frame
Not to scale

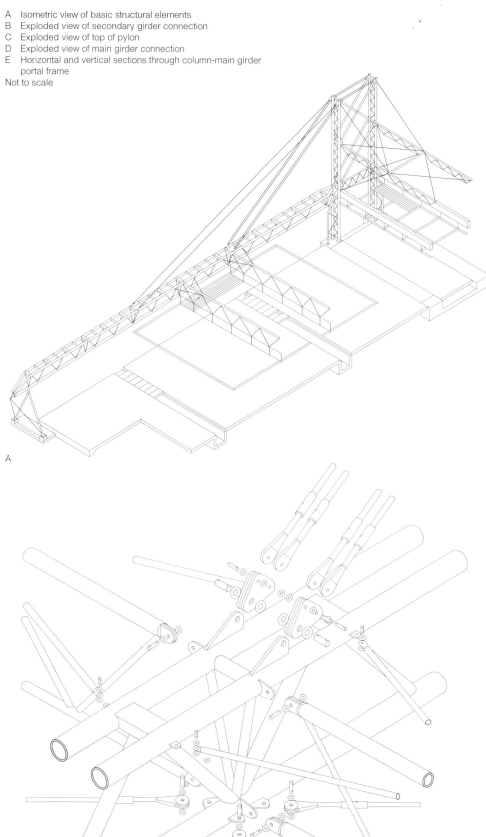

A

B

1 Main lattice girder, welded tubes
2 Lattice column, welded tubes
3 Lattice girder, welded tubes
4 Beam, IPE section
5 Lattice portal frame, welded tubes
6 Ties

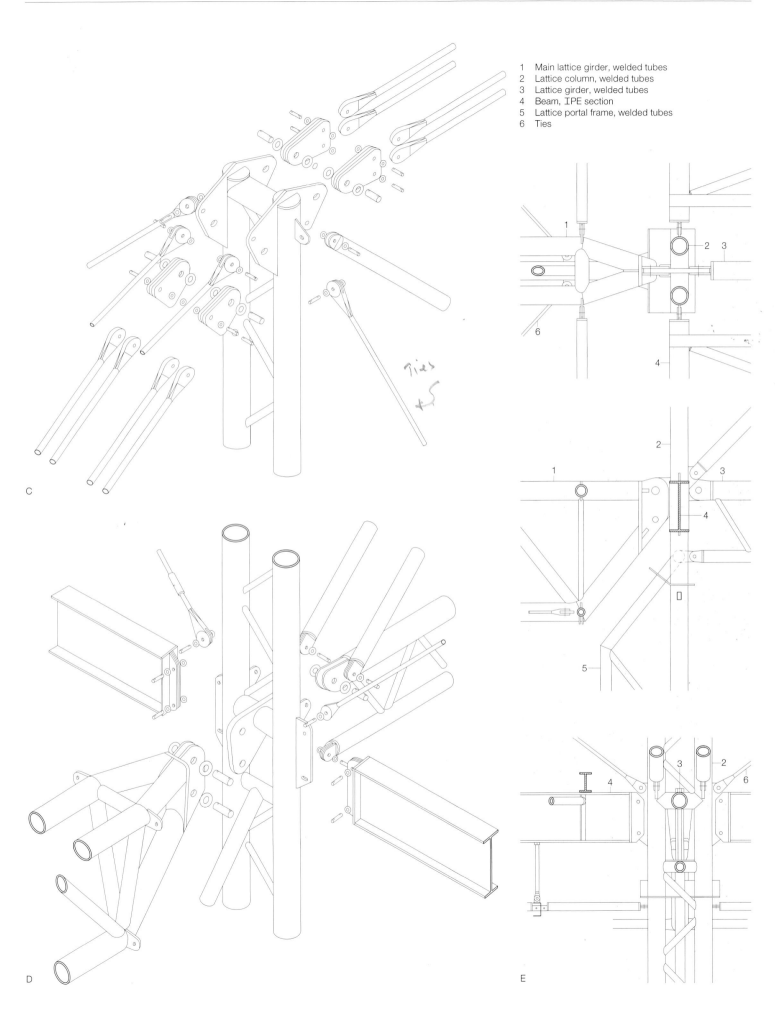

C

D

E

Example 32

Factory, Quimper, France

1981

Architects:
Richard Rogers Partnership, London
Project team: R. Ahronov, I. Davidson,
M. Goldschmid, K. Hayashi, A. Kalsi,
S. McMillan, R. Rogers, R. Soundy, J. Young
Structural engineers:
Ove Arup & Partners, London

For the client, a manufacturer of air, petrol and
oil filters, it was important to have a prestigious
and eye-catching building which guaranteed
flexibility of use and easy extension at a later
date. The building houses a production centre,
storage space and offices (in a two-storey section).
The columns positioned on an 18 x 18 m grid
and the hangers determine the appearance of
the factory and ensure a moderate construction
depth for the two-way spanning main beam layout. The one-way spanning secondary beam
layout is at the same level as the main beams.
Therefore, services can be arranged as desired below beam level. While the roof of trapezoidal profile sheeting is supported on main
and secondary beams, the walls are separated
from the structure and placed inside the outer
columns.
The three-dimensional suspension arrangement
to the roof structure between the concrete-filled
columns has three functions: transferring vertical loads into the columns, counteracting the
uplift forces of wind suction (in the form of
arched framing to the main beams), and also
acting as wind bracing. Bracing has been
included on the north and west sides to provide horizontal stability, together with the internal structure of the northern offices section;
therefore, this favours a later extension to the
east.

References: [6], [17], [101], [122], [362], [394]

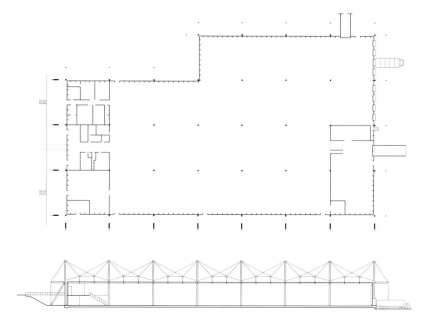

A

A Plan and section,
    scale 1:1500
B Part section,
    scale 1:200

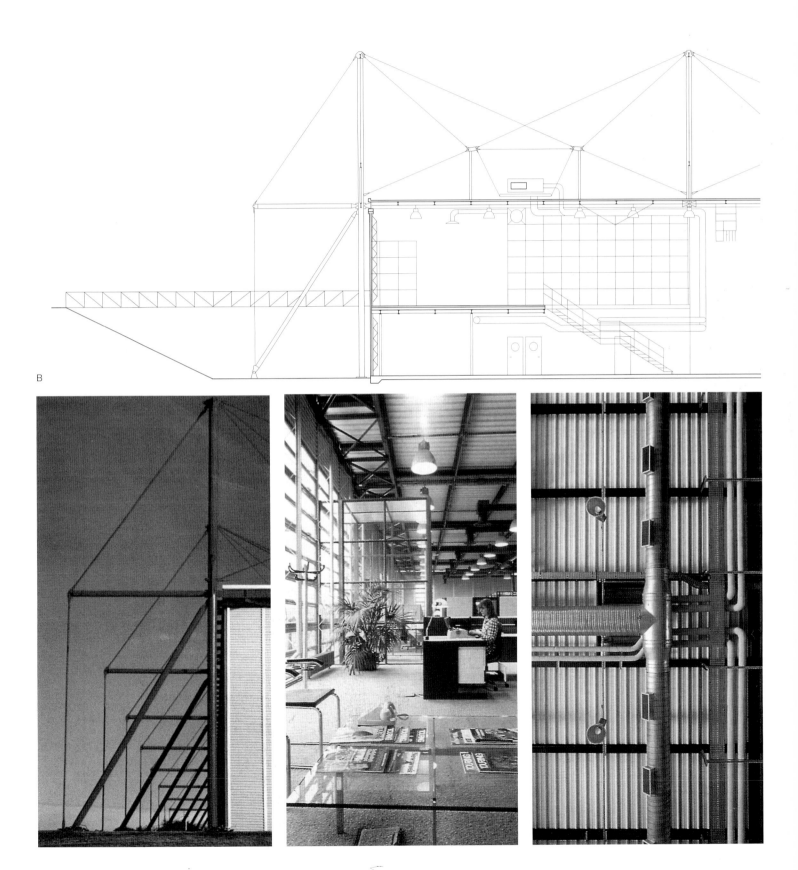

B

Example 32

A Exploded views of column connections, not to scale
B Vertical section,
  scale 1:20

1 Tubular hanger (also resists uplift)
2 Main beam, IPE 330
3 Horizontal wind bracing
4 Vertical wind bracing to the wall
5 Concrete-filled steel column, 355 mm dia.
6 Diagonal member to vertical wind bracing, subjected
  to tension and compression

7 Tie with clevis
8 Column head
9 Base plate, 20 mm plate
10 Foundation for backstay and diagonal strut of wind
   bracing
11 Turnbuckle

A

314

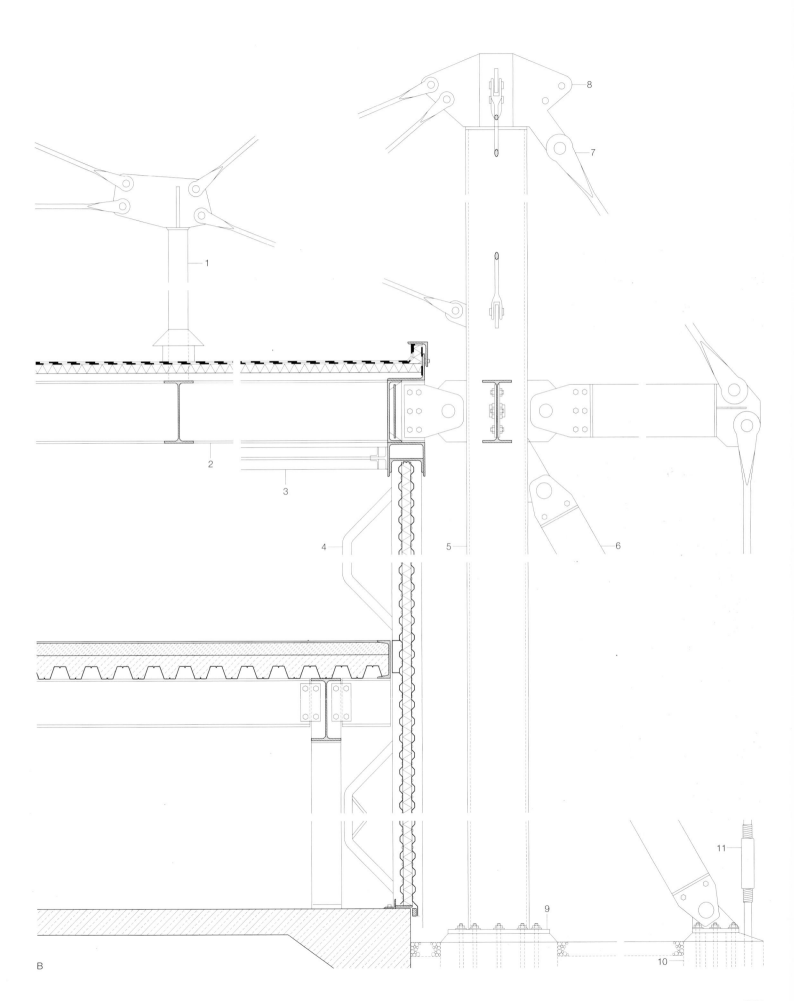

B

Example 33

Production building and offices, Cologne

1992

Architects:
Nicholas Grimshaw + Partners, London
Structural engineers:
Whitby + Bird, London

For this production plant the client required flexible production units which could be extended as necessary. This resulted in a facility with, initially, four units each with a central courtyard containing a pylon from which the roofs are suspended. These internal open spaces serve to admit daylight and provide rest zones for the personnel.

The pylons are lattice masts with a circular cross-section; they taper from points at top and bottom to a maximum of 2.5 m diameter in the centre. The individual members are circular hollow sections. Ties are connected to the top of the pylon which carry the roof via four points in each unit. The roof construction consists of steel beams arranged on an 11.25 m grid. External and courtyard facades include additional supports. A smaller, diagonal grid is superimposed on the square grid. Each bay has a GRP dome containing a glazed section facing north.

References: [136], [165], [361]

A Elevation, section, plan,
   scale 1:1500
B Axonometric view of facade construction,
   not to scale

A

B

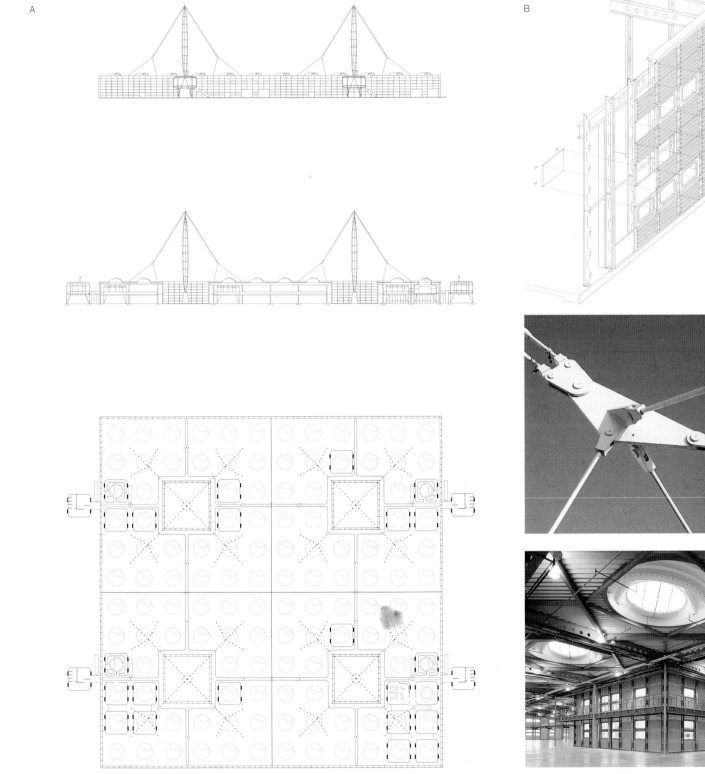

Example 34

**Plenary chamber & presidential annex,
German Bundestag, Bonn**

1992
Architects: Behnisch + Partner, Stuttgart
Gerald Staib (partner responsible), H. Eilers,
M. Burkart, E. Pritzer, A. von Salmuth,
E. U. Tillmanns
Assistant: Christian Kandzia
Structural engineers:
Schlaich, Bergermann + Partner, Stuttgart

The roof structure to the plenary chamber consists of two 1700-mm-deep box girders supported on four steel columns. At right-angles to
these there are six fish-belly plate girders.
Above this primary structure, and arranged
diagonally to the square plan, there are
movable sunshading louvres made from light-
diffusing acrylic glass elements. The actual
roof structure is situated underneath. This consists of a beam grid suspended from the fish-
belly girders and spanning between
6 and 12 m. This supports the daylighting roof
made from steel trusses and laminated safety
glass.
The vertical roof loads are transmitted to the
basement via welded steel columns, filled with
concrete for fire protection purposes. Prestressed stainless steel cables stiffen the roof
horizontally.

References: [26], [61], [135], [141], [386], [431], [480]

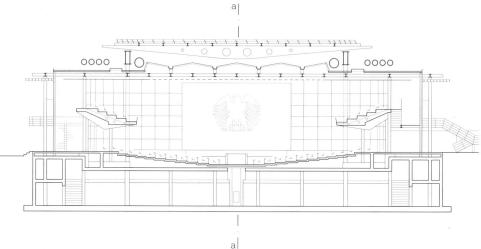

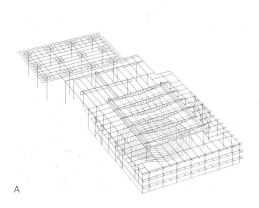

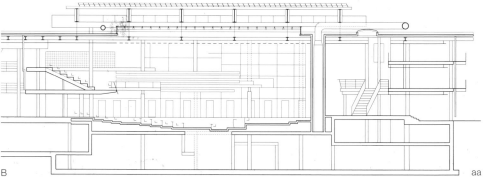

A

B

aa

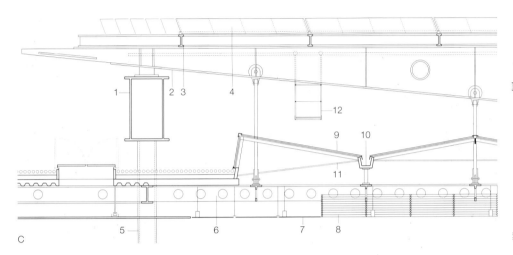

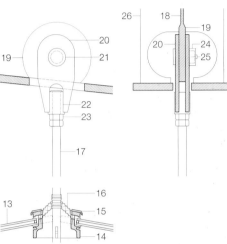

C

D

A	Isometric view of structural steelwork, not to scale		
B	Sections, scale 1:500		
C	Roof construction, scale 1:100		
D	Suspension arrangement, scale 1:5		

1 Main beam, 1200 x 1700 mm welded box girder
2 Fish-belly plate girder, flanges 550 mm wide
3 Beam of welded plates, 110 x 300 mm, laid diagonally, supporting No. 4
4 Movable sunshading louvres made from light-diffusing acrylic glass elements
5 Main column to

daylighting roof, 508 dia. x 40 mm tube
6 Beam grid of HEB 450 cellular sections
7 Aluminium panel
8 Grid ceiling of reflective metal and prism-shaped cast glass (Fresnel lenses)
9 Daylighting roof on IPE 80 beam sections
10 Stainless steel valley gutter
11 Ties, 16 mm dia.

12 Inspection cradle
13 Double glazing, 33 mm laminated safety glass
14 2-part cast aluminium ring
15 Aluminium sealing ring
16 Sealing collar packed with mineral wool
17 Beam hanger, 45 mm dia. round section
18 15 mm plate
19 30 mm plate

20 2 No. 20 mm eye plates
21 65 mm dia. pin with head
22 88.9 mm dia. x 25 thk tube
23 Hexagonal nut with fine-pitch thread
24 Sleeve, 76.1 mm dia. x 4 mm
25 M8 hexagon-head screw
26 15 mm stiffener

Example 35

Regional parliament building, Dresden

1994

Architect: Peter Kulka, Dresden
Project team: N. Cravo-Cacoilo, K. Radau,
K. Wimmer, C. Anderhalten, M.Beckmann,
H. Braunisch, U. Friedemann, J. Kastner,
U. Königs, S. Liese, K. Messerschmidt,
S. Mosert, K. Pfeiffer, K. Pilcher
Structural engineers:
Varwik-Horz-Ladewig, Cologne

Together with the existing L-shaped building,
the flat-roofed new structures create an inner
courtyard. While the two narrow wings exhibit a
one-way spanning layout, the main structure of
the plenary chamber consists of a two-way
spanning beam grid. This is supported on four
fixed-base columns with modified-cruciform
cross-section.

The beam grid spans over 30 m between the
columns and cantilevers 6.8 m on all sides. It
consists of 1300-mm-deep plate girders
arranged on a 5 x 5 m grid. Another beam grid
of HEA 140 sections forms the secondary
beam level, the ceiling of the chamber, suspended 1.2 m below the main structure. The
hangers are made from profiled plates which
are thicker in the region of structural bracing.
The thermal insulation, laminated with aluminium both sides, is placed on these secondary
beams. The actual ceiling is suspended below
the secondary beam grid. The space between
the thermal insulation units and the outer primary structure is closed off with anti-bird netting and snow guards.

Only one of the four main columns is inside the
building. For this one a special head detail was
necessary to ensure a good building science
detail. At the point where the column penetrates the insulation an opening was left in the
internal ceiling and the main beam grid and
supports exposed, all accentuated by a rooflight. Heating to the beams as well as insulation help to prevent condensation problems.

References: [70], [72], [141], [153], [167], [169], [292]

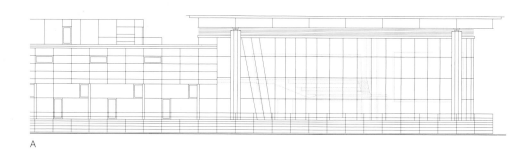

A

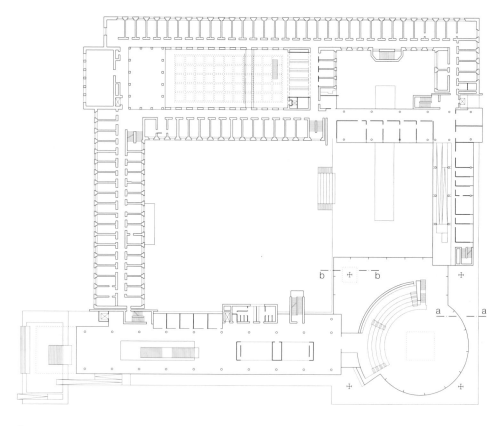

B

A   Part elevation of plenary chamber,
    scale 1:500
B   Plan, scale 1:1000
C   Section through facade
    with external column
D   Detail of rooflight over internal column
Scale 1:100

1 Roof construction:
   Gravel
   3 layers of waterproof sheeting
   Wedge-shaped insulation (to provide falls)
2 Open grid flooring for maintenance purposes
3 Trapezoidal profile sheeting
4 Beam, HEA 140
5 Beam grid, 1300 mm deep
6 125 mm aluminium insulation panel
7 Perforated aluminium sheeting
8 Ceiling of perforated metal sheeting
9 Aluminium snow guard
10 Bent aluminium plate
11 Column: 4 No. 550 x 60 mm flange plates,
   1 No. 1180 x 20 mm and
   2 No. 580 x 20 mm web plates
12 Post, IPE 240
13 120 x 40 mm flat
14 Perforated aluminium screen
15 Steel post-and-rail facade, 60 x 60 mm, heated,
   double glazing with thermal break and low-e coating, iron-grey anodised aluminium cover strips
16 Base plate, 1620 x 1620 x 60 mm
17 Sunshading
18 Casing to main beam

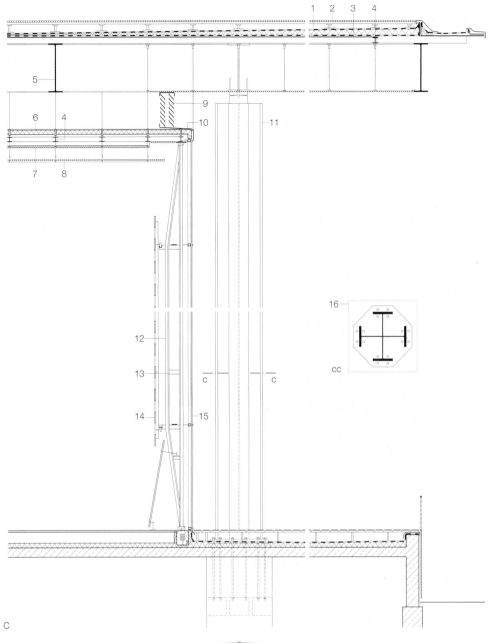

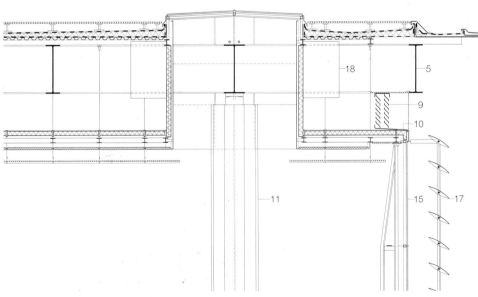

Example 36

Bus terminal, Delmenhorst

1996

Architects:
Schomers, Schürmann, Stridde, Bremen
Project team: Leiermann, Ravens
Structural engineers:
Sobek and Rieger, Stuttgart

Following the reorganization of bus services in Delmenhorst, this terminal is intended to illustrate the importance of local public transport. This structure covers a passenger island of 133 x 11 m which can accommodate up to 12 buses. The steel-and-glass canopy fully covers the island and is supported on pairs of fixed-based columns spaced at 6.75 m centres.
The canopy structure consists of T-beams cantilevering out on both sides. These are joined via hinges and welded to longitudinal tubes butted on the column axes and pin-jointed to the columns via steel plates. Stability is provided by the restrained columns and the pairs of columns, which are linked to form rigid frames.

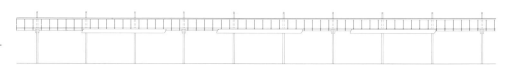

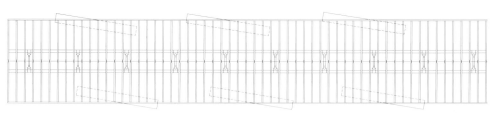

A

A Elevation and plan,
   scale 1:500
B Section and plan,
   scale 1:100
C Connection: hanger-rain guard,
   scale 1:10
D Section through rain guard,
   scale 1:20

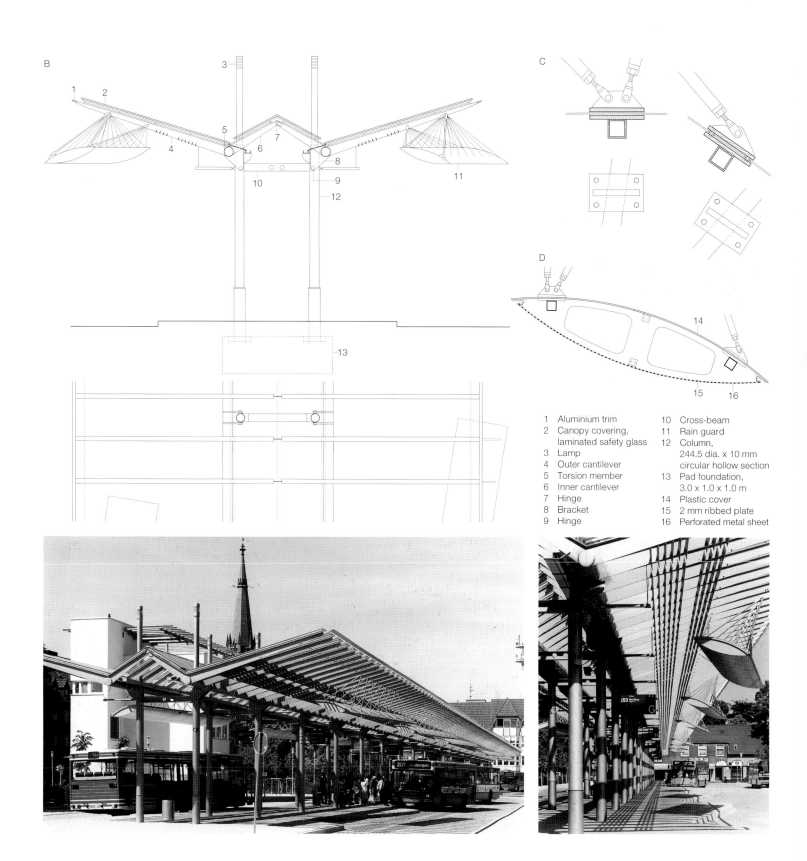

B

1 Aluminium trim
2 Canopy covering,
   laminated safety glass
3 Lamp
4 Outer cantilever
5 Torsion member
6 Inner cantilever
7 Hinge
8 Bracket
9 Hinge
10 Cross-beam
11 Rain guard
12 Column,
   244.5 dia. x 10 mm
   circular hollow section
13 Pad foundation,
   3.0 x 1.0 x 1.0 m
14 Plastic cover
15 2 mm ribbed plate
16 Perforated metal sheet

Example 36

A Column, roof, sections,
  scale 1:20
B Details of column,
  scale 1:10

A

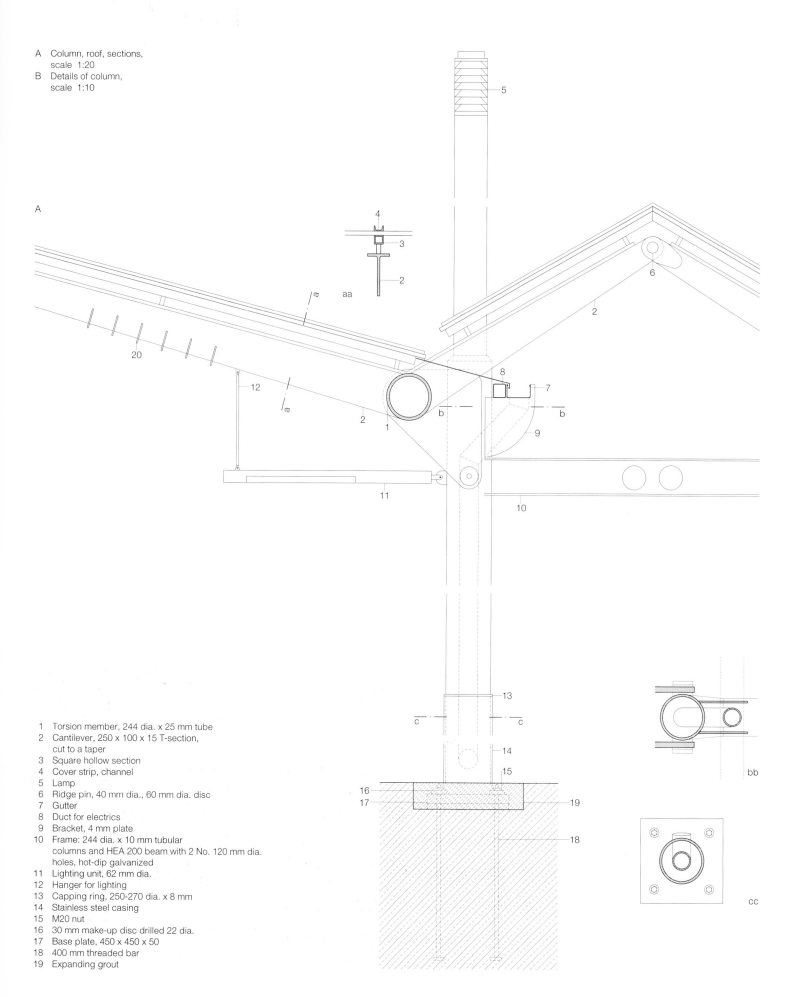

1 Torsion member, 244 dia. x 25 mm tube
2 Cantilever, 250 x 100 x 15 T-section,
  cut to a taper
3 Square hollow section
4 Cover strip, channel
5 Lamp
6 Ridge pin, 40 mm dia., 60 mm dia. disc
7 Gutter
8 Duct for electrics
9 Bracket, 4 mm plate
10 Frame: 244 dia. x 10 mm tubular
   columns and HEA 200 beam with 2 No. 120 mm dia.
   holes, hot-dip galvanized
11 Lighting unit, 62 mm dia.
12 Hanger for lighting
13 Capping ring, 250-270 dia. x 8 mm
14 Stainless steel casing
15 M20 nut
16 30 mm make-up disc drilled 22 dia.
17 Base plate, 450 x 450 x 50
18 400 mm threaded bar
19 Expanding grout

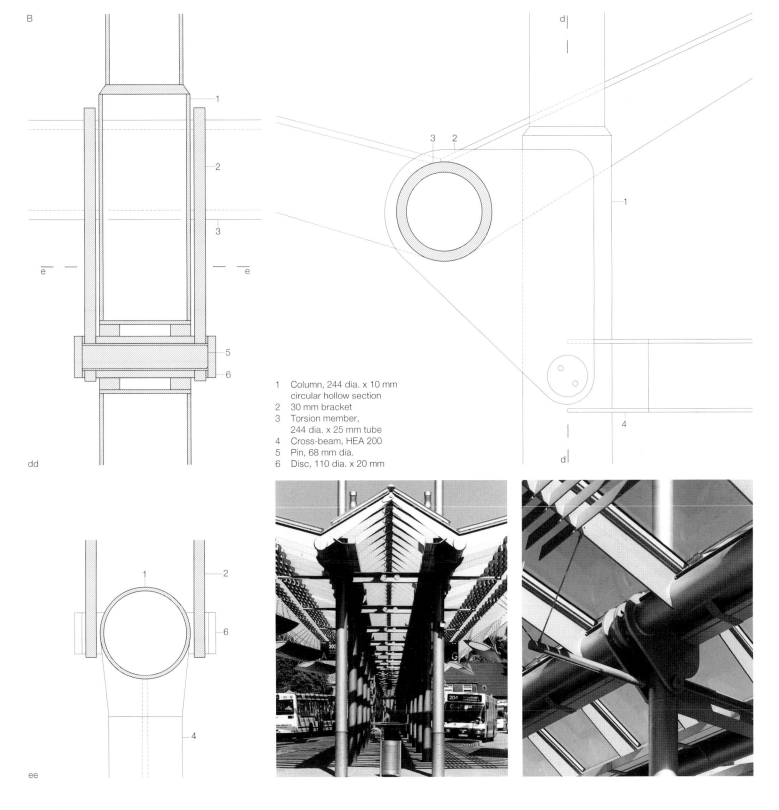

B

dd

e——e

1 Column, 244 dia. x 10 mm
  circular hollow section
2 30 mm bracket
3 Torsion member,
  244 dia. x 25 mm tube
4 Cross-beam, HEA 200
5 Pin, 68 mm dia.
6 Disc, 110 dia. x 20 mm

ee

Example 37

Airport terminal, Stuttgart

1990

Architects:
von Gerkan · Marg + Partner, Hamburg
Draft design: Meinhard von Gerkan,
Karsten Brauer
Partner responsible: Klaus Staratzke
Structural engineers:
Weidleplan Consulting, Stuttgart

Besides fulfilling the functional demands placed on an airport, such as ease of orientation and the smooth flow of passengers, staff and baggage, it was important to create a distinctive facility in the no man's land on the outskirts of Stuttgart.

In this design the terminal separates landside from airside. It is composed of two structures: an elongated block with truncated triangular cross-section, and a rectangular hall with a monopitch roof rising towards the airside.

The appearance of the airport is characterized by the remarkable supporting structure to the roof of the hall. The structure comprises 12 umbel columns supporting a beam grid at roof level. These umbel columns have the advantage of providing closely spaced supports at roof level while achieving an unobstructed usable area of 21.6 x 32.4 m between the columns at floor level. The connections between beam grid and column members are pin-jointed. The various "branches" of the columns are fabricated from circular hollow sections and transfer forces essentially axially via cast steel nodes down to the foundations, where the "trunks" are restrained. Additional bracing in facade and floor planes also helps to stabilize the building.

As no requirements were stipulated regarding preventive fire protection, no cladding was necessary for the steel umbel columns.

References: [32], [68], [162], [218], [224], [430], [437], [455]

A   Plan and sections,
    scale 1:1000
B   View of underside of roof structure,
    scale 1:250

A

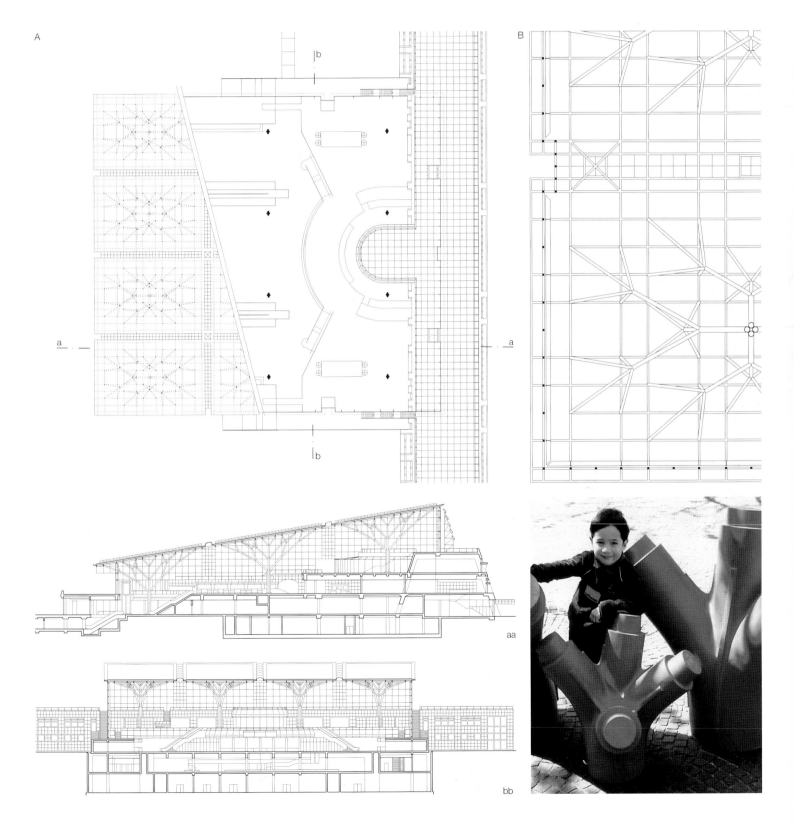

aa

bb

Example 37

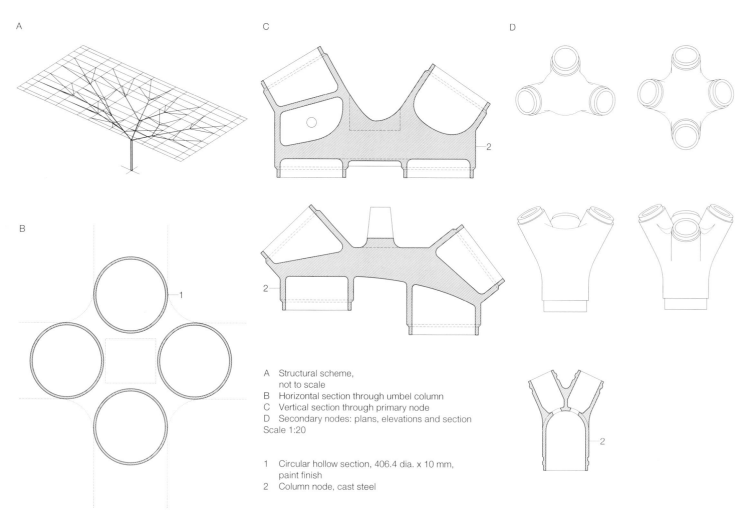

A Structural scheme,
  not to scale
B Horizontal section through umbel column
C Vertical section through primary node
D Secondary nodes: plans, elevations and section
Scale 1:20

1 Circular hollow section, 406.4 dia. x 10 mm,
  paint finish
2 Column node, cast steel

E   Beam grid junction, section
    and view of underside, scale 1:20
F   Beam grid junction, elevation, section and view of
    underside, scale 1:20,
    (isometric view not to scale)

1   Box section, 340 x 150 mm
2   Connecting piece, cast steel
3   HSFG bolts
4   Supporting "branch", 159 mm dia. tube
5   Assembly opening with cover plate

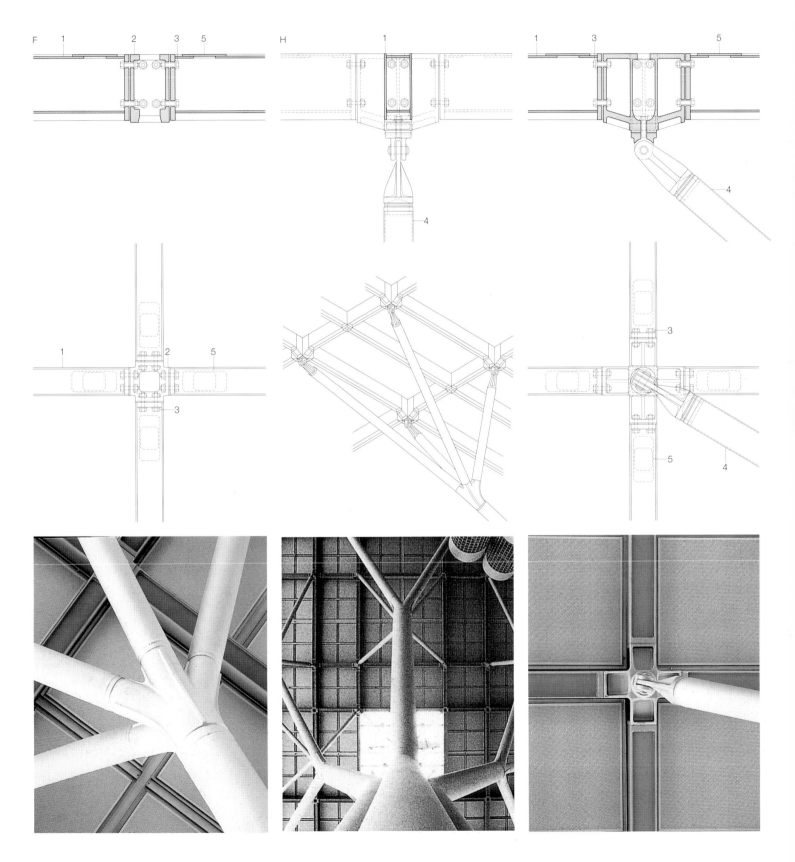

Example 38

**Access pavilion to underground car park,
Biberach**

1989

Architects:
Kaag + Schwarz, Stuttgart
Structural engineers:
Schlumbohm, Stuttgart,
A. Furche

Two steel pavilions with glass roofs provide
access to this underground car park in Biberach. The governing criterion of the design brief
was to achieve a means of access which did
not appear intimidating in any way. Therefore,
a steel-and-glass construction was favoured:
glazed roof and walls are complemented by
sand-blasted glass treads to the stairs. One of
the pavilions includes a glazed hydraulic lift in
the centre of the stairwell. This extensive use of
glass enables daylight to penetrate right to the
base of the access shaft and so creates a
pleasant atmosphere for users.

The pavilion is composed of a tubular frame,
stairs and roof structure. The primary structure,
the frame, consists of four tubular columns,
one in each corner of the stairwell, which are
rigidly connected at each floor level. Cantilever
beams transfer the loads from the stair
stringers back to the frame. The column bases
are designed as fully restrained and the steel
construction is free-standing within the shaft.
A four-legged trestle sits on the top of the
columns and the outer corners of the roof
structure are suspended from the top of this
trestle. The roof structure comprises two tubular frames pin-jointed to the main frame via
diagonal members. The longer perimeter
beams of the roof have an underslung framing.
The roof slopes inwards and is covered with
laminated safety glass on steel sections supported directly on the roof frame. Drainage is
by way of stainless steel gutters, which are
heated to guarantee their function in cold
weather.

References: [131], [222], [476]

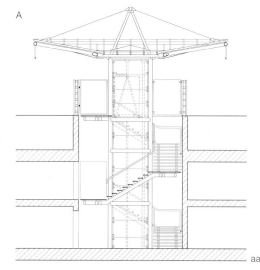

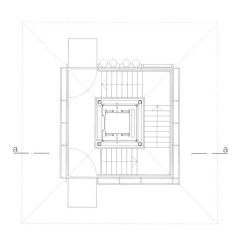

A Section and plan of pavilion A,
    scale 1:200
B Details of roof construction,
    section and plan,
    scale 1:20
C Details of stair treads,
    scale 1:20
D Section,
    scale 1:5

1 219 mm dia. tube
2 133 mm dia. tube
3 159 mm dia. tube
4 Roof hanger, round-section tie
5 Glazing bar, 90 x 50 x 5 rectangular hollow section,
    with cover strip
6 11mm laminated safety glass
7 Stainless steel gutter
8 Point support to end, one-piece glass section

B

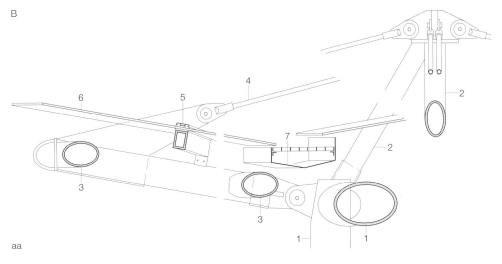

aa

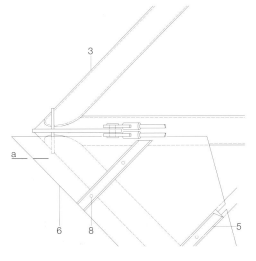
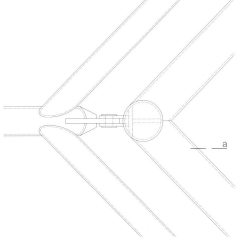

C   D

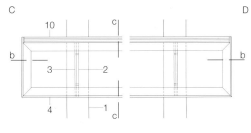
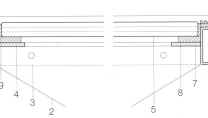
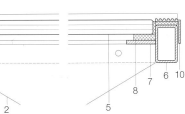

cc

1 Stringer, 200 x 100
    rectangular hollow
    section
2 10 mm flat, welded to 1
3 Stainless steel, 26 x 6 mm
4 Tread frame,
    40 x 40 x 5 SS angle
5 19 mm laminated safety
    glass, sand-blasted

6 Stainless steel nosing,
    50 x 30 x 3 rectangular
    hollow section
7 Stainless steel,
    50 x 5 mm
8 Bearing, 30 x 8 mm
9 3 mm peripheral
    silicone joint
10 Non-slip nosing

bb

Example 39

Airport terminal, Stansted, UK

1991

Architects:
Foster & Partners, London
Structural engineers:
Ove Arup & Partners, London

The underlying concept of this airport terminal at Stansted near London was to ensure that circulation within the building remained as simple and direct as possible. Terminal facilities from the early days of aviation served as a model; passengers should be able to find their way with ease. One of the consequences of this approach was the location of all infrastructure facilities, e.g. vehicular access, on one level. In contrast, all ancillary installations, from baggage transport to building services, are positioned underneath the circulation level.
The railway station is also located in the basement and is linked to the passenger concourse via ramps and lifts.
The roof construction, a two-way spanning system, consists of modular bays.
There are 36 open, flared-head column structures. The roof measures 198 x 198 m but the hall is only 162 m wide, thus allowing generous canopies north and south (airside and landside respectively).
The 36 column structures support a roof of 121 square, vaulted lattice domes, 18 x 18 m; four triangular rooflights are located centrally in each. Together, the domes form a stiff roof plate and thus stabilize the column structures, which have little torsional strength.
The columns, which define the scale of the space, are positioned on a 36 x 36 m grid and are 20 m high. They are made up of four circular hollow sections (457 dia.) and rigidly connected at three levels by horizontal tubes (344 dia.).

References: [21], [37], [57], [134], [225], [426]

A   System sketches
B   Section and plan,
     scale 1:2000
C   Axonometric view of roof elements
     and column
D   Part section,
     scale 1:500

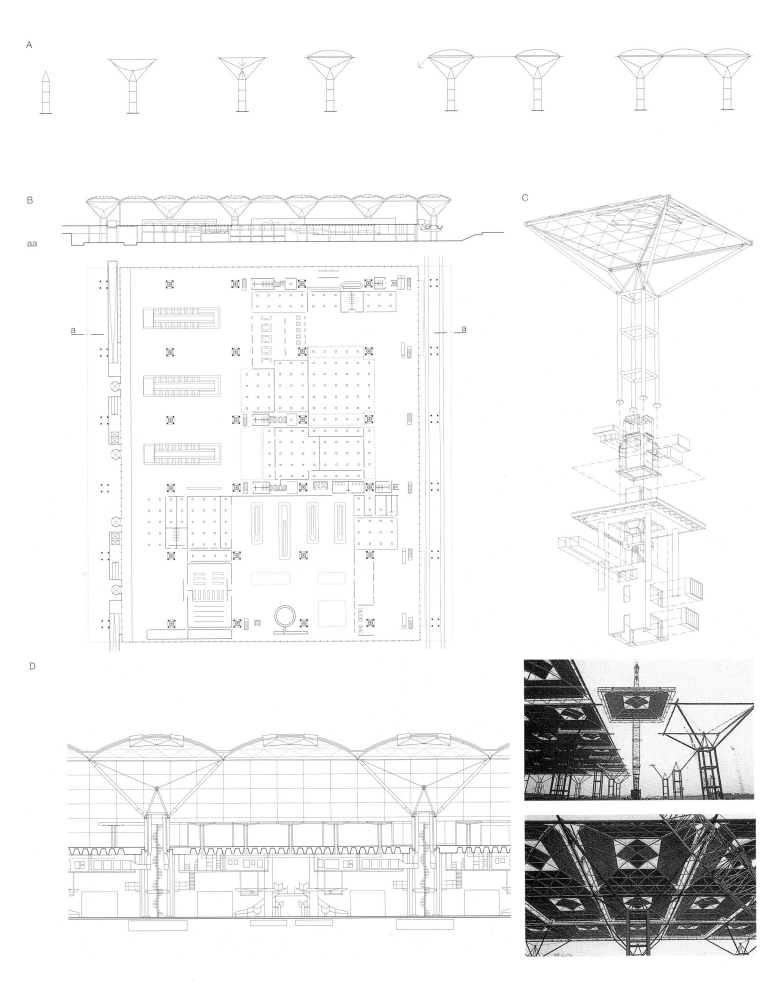

A

B

aa

a   a

C

D

Example 39

A

B

11

12

10

9

8

7

6

1

5

4

2

3

1

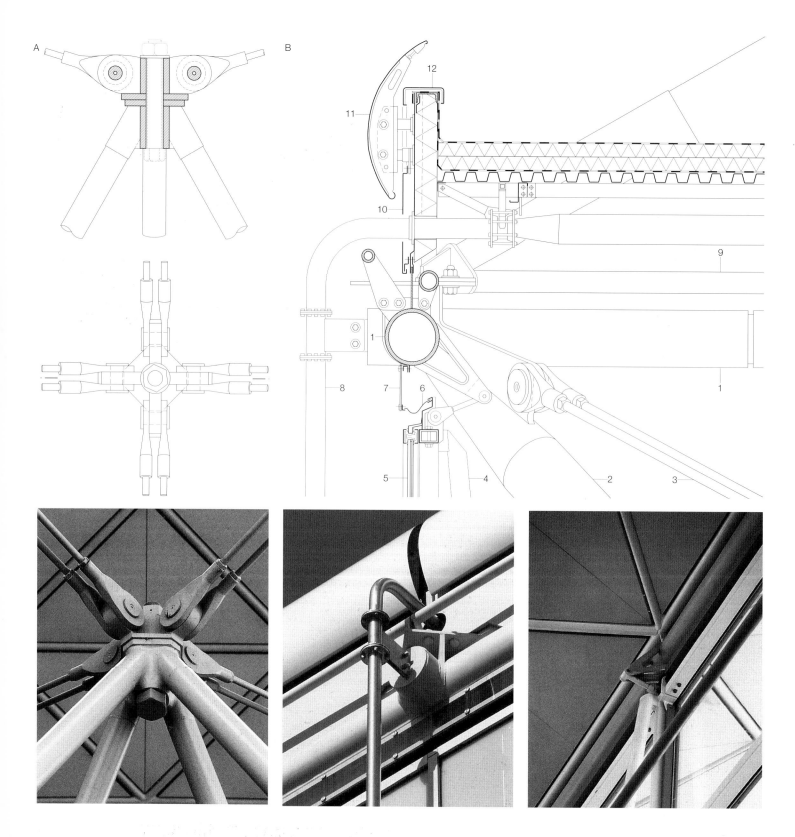

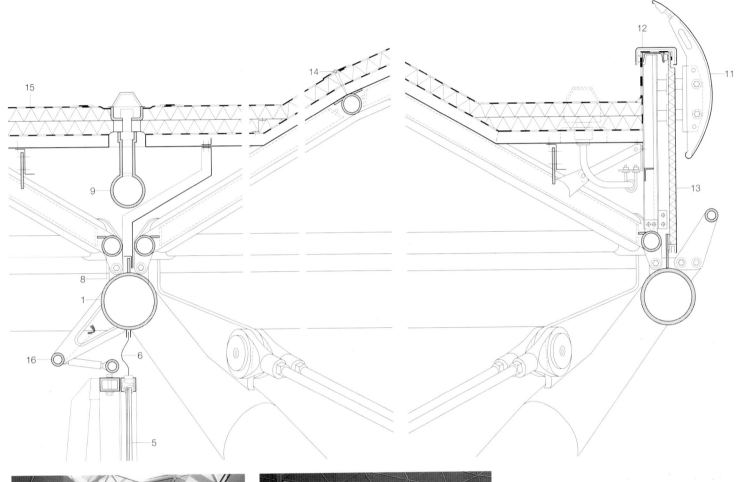

A Node: elevation and plan,
  scale 1:20
B Roof details, scale 1:20

1 323 mm dia. tube linking tops of raking column
   members
2 Raking member, 355 mm dia. tube
3 Tie to centre of column trestle
4 Facade post
5 Double glazing in aluminium frame
6 Flexible plastic foil
7 12 mm toughened safety glass
8 Roof framing, 114 mm dia. tube
9 Stainless steel connecting tube
10 Fascia cladding, powder-coated aluminium plate
11 Wind deflector, aluminium
12 Capping piece
13 Aluminium panel with mineral wool filling
14 Expansion joint
15 Roof construction:
   Synthetic waterproofing layer
   150 mm mineral wool
   Vapour barrier
   Aluminium trapezoidal profile sheeting
16 Tubular facade bracing

Example 40

Pedestrian walkway, trade fair grounds, Hannover

1998

Architects:
Schulitz + Partner, Braunschweig
Helmut C. Schulitz, S. Worbs, J. König,
J. Jaspers, M. Rötzel
Structural engineers: RFR, Paris

The 332-m-long "Skywalk" connects Laatzen station with Hannover's trade fair grounds. This elevated pedestrian walkway, which houses two travelators in the middle and two walkways either side, is distinguished by its cross-section of two intersecting circles. The structure consists of suspended lattice girders spanning 20, 24 and 28 m. Horizontal forces induced by the suspension arrangement are carried by roof beams in each bay, thus forming a closed loadbearing system. The passenger conveyors are supported on transverse beams spanning between the main girders and the walkways cantilever as horizontal girders from the main girders. The resulting torsion moments are transferred via rigidly connected beams into the two main girders and then conveyed as bending moments to the columns.
Expansion joints divide the structure into three segments. The columns of the end segments are pin-jointed to cantilevering tubular plinths rigidly fixed to the foundation. Longitudinal stability is provided by restrained columns in the middle segment as well as by diagonal members alongside the stairs at the two ends. In the transverse direction there is bracing between each pair of columns. The facades are made from curved laminated safety glass fastened to the solid steel facade sections by means of individual fixings.

1	45 mm gusset plate
2	8 mm eye plate
3	HEB 100
4	HEB 240
5	IPE 240
6	244.5 dia. x 20 mm tube
7	244.5 dia. x 10 mm tube

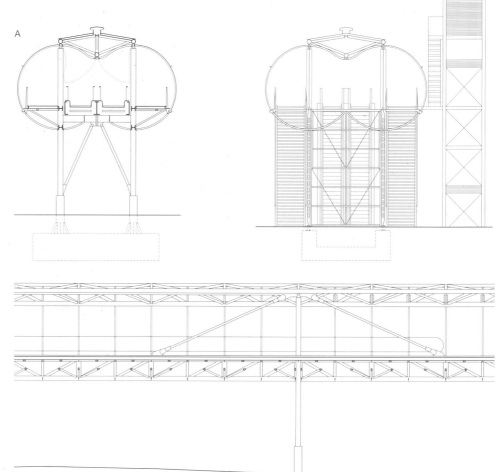

A Section, elevation, longitudinal section, scale 1:200

B Isometric view of construction

C Detail of hanger bottom connection, scale 1:20

D Detail of hanger top connection, scale 1:50

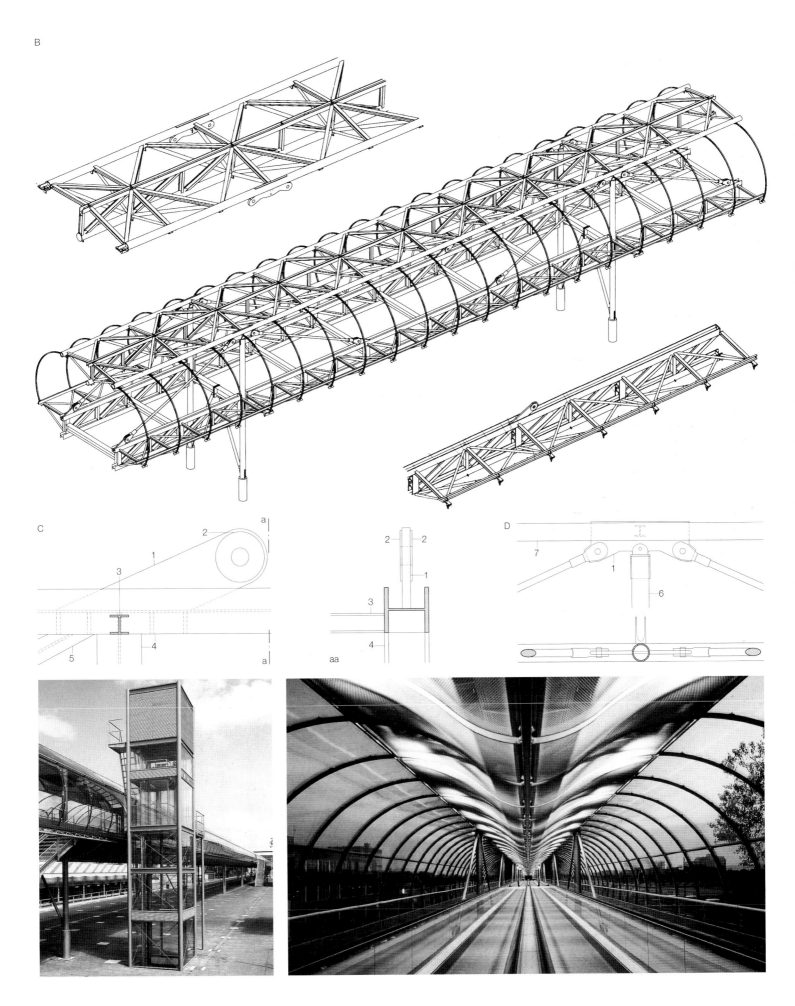

B

C

2
1
3
a
4
5
a

2   2
1
3
4
aa

D
7
1
6

Example 40

A

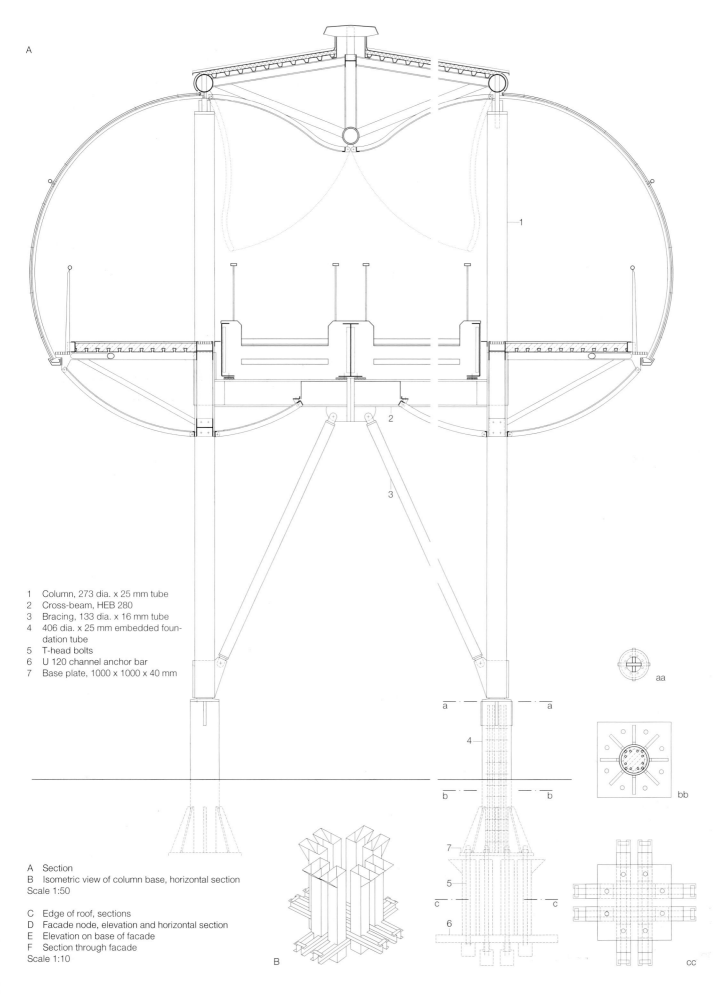

1   Column, 273 dia. x 25 mm tube
2   Cross-beam, HEB 280
3   Bracing, 133 dia. x 16 mm tube
4   406 dia. x 25 mm embedded foun-
    dation tube
5   T-head bolts
6   U 120 channel anchor bar
7   Base plate, 1000 x 1000 x 40 mm

A   Section
B   Isometric view of column base, horizontal section
Scale 1:50

C   Edge of roof, sections
D   Facade node, elevation and horizontal section
E   Elevation on base of facade
F   Section through facade
Scale 1:10

1   244.5 dia. x 10 mm tube
2   Beam, HEA 120
3   76.1 dia. x 4 mm tube
4   40 mm trapezoidal profile sheeting
5   Mineral wool insulation, 50/40 mm
6   Metal roof finish with standing seams, 65 x 400 mm
7   Frame, 60 x 30 x 5 angles with expanded metal
8   Column, 273 dia. x 25 mm
9   Facade profile, 50 x 40 mm square section, curved
10 Clamping profile, aluminium, with foil seal
11 2 mm sheet metal cladding
12 Clamping plate, 70 mm dia.
13 Glass support, factory-welded to facade profile
14 Glazing, 2 panes of 6 mm laminated
    safety glass, curved
15 Snow guard, 48.3 dia. x 2.6 mm tube
16 Angle glass support
17 Sealing gasket and silicone joint
18 Gutter, 1 mm zinc sheet
19 Beam, HEB 100
20 Floor trimmer, U140 channel
21 Bracing, 70 dia. x 6.3 mm tube
22 Concrete on "Holorib" steel sheeting
23 Open-grid flooring, 30 x 30 mm, galvanized
24 Handrail upright, 2 No. 12 x 25-60 mm
25 Expanded metal screen in angle frame,
    25 x 25 x 4 mm
26 Wooden handrail, 50 mm dia.
27 4 mm stainless steel cable

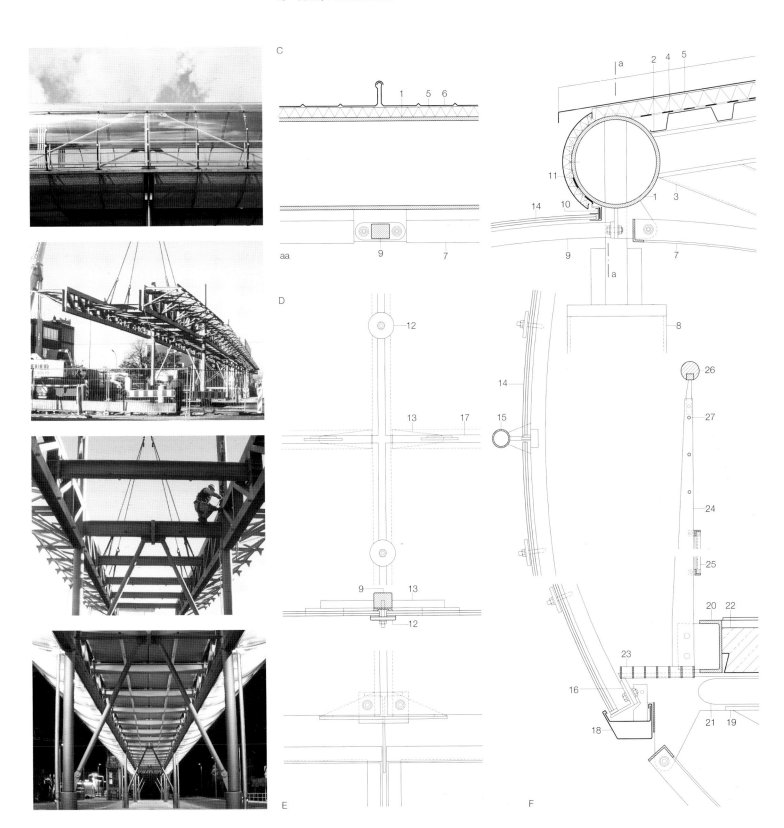

Example 41

Station for light rail network, Genoa, Italy

1994

Architects: Renzo Piano Building Workshop,
Genoa
Project team: S. Ishida, F. Marano, M. Varatta,
D. Defilla
Structural engineers:
L. Mascia, D. Mascia, Genoa

A standardized but variable building system, which could be adapted to suit each location, was developed for the stations of the city's light rail network. The majority of the individual parts were prefabricated and, owing to the salt-laden air of Genoa, carefully protected against corrosion.

Brin station, whose design is typical of the basic form, marks the point where the network switches from underground tunnel to elevated system. As a result, the station has two main sections. At road level there is an entrance zone and plant rooms, confined to the area directly beneath the elevated track.

Rigid, fixed-base frames placed at 17.5 m centres span over a width of 9.5 m. These frames consist of bolted and welded box sections. The track bed comprises suspended secondary beams (IPE 1000) at right-angles to the frames and acting compositely with reinforced concrete panels.

Two more box-section beams are supported on the frames and form the platforms. Services are routed inside these sections. This heavy-weight substructure contrasts with the 90-m-long lightweight roof. Every 2.5 m, two-hinged arches comprising curved, cellular IPE 300 sections span 13 m over platforms and tracks. The arches, welded together from three separate pieces, carry the roof covering of solar-control glass – flat panes arranged like roof tiles to follow the contour.

Stainless steel diagonal bracing provides stability.

References: [2], [104], [137], [268], [356]

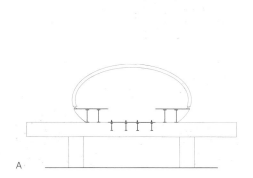

A

A   Structural system, not to scale
B   Details of envelope:
    sections
    Details of bracing:
    front and side elevations of connection
Scale 1:10
C   Section
Scale 1:200

1   Laminated safety glass with internal coating
2   T-section with cover strip
3   Extruded aluminium glazing bar
4   Stainless steel tie, 20 mm dia.
5   Stainless steel fixing
6   Cellular arch beam, IPE 300
7   Stainless steel tube, 100 mm dia.

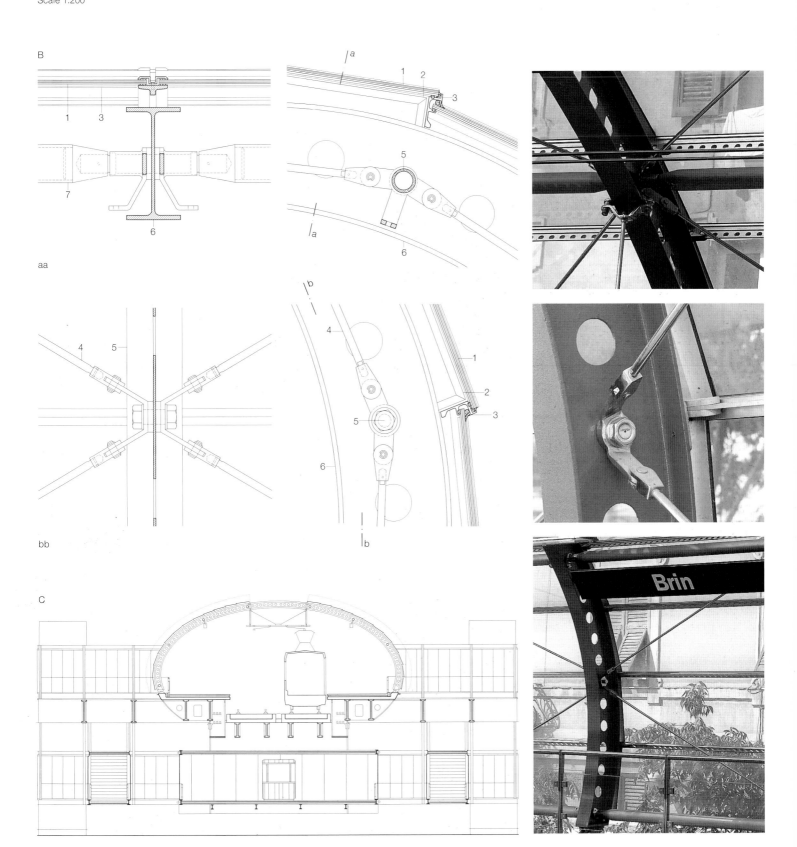

B

aa

bb

C

Example 42

Exhibition & congress centre, Linz, Austria

1993

Architects: Herzog + Partner, Munich
Thomas Herzog with Hanns Jörg Schrade
Project management: Heinz Stögmüller, Linz
Project team: R. Schneider, A. Schankula,
K. Beslmüller, A. Heigl, O. Mehl,
Structural engineers: Sailer + Stepan, Munich

The Design-Center is a large-scale multi-purpose facility. Its unobstructed interior offers space for exhibitions, congresses, cultural events and festivals under a glazed skin, in a sort of controlled climate.

The building has an affinity with the naturally lit, steel-and-glass sheds of the 19th century. Here, however, the ingress of light is much improved and the greenhouse effect reduced by way of a reflective grid, achieving an economic energy profile with insulating glass having a low U-value.

The arched cross-sectional form leads to optimum use of space, through the interplay of high and low headroom, as well as a reduction in the volume of air to be heated.

Founded on a basement of masonry and reinforced concrete, the lightweight steel construction rises as a shallow arch spanning 73 m without intermediate columns. The arches are spaced at 7.20 m centres, or 2.40 m adjacent stairs and ancillary rooms.

The structural system consists of a tied two-hinged arch. Each arch is formed by a pair of IPE beams laid with their major axes horizontal and their flanges joined by plates to form a welded box section measuring 900 x 371 mm. Four segments, steel grade St 510 C, make up each arch. Bolted end plates are used at the splices.

The base of the arch is fixed to the basement roof slab by way of threaded anchor bars and plates. The prestressed cables for accommodating the arch thrust forces are also located at this level: two cables per standard arch, prestressing force 1000-1200 kN per cable.

The forces are diverted via the floor slab where the lecture hall interrupts the standard situation. The secondary beams of welded T-sections and flats are spaced at 2.70 m centres and form a simple trussed arrangement. They are connected to the sides of the arch members via end plates. Web plates transfer the forces to the inside of the box. Diagonal bracing (round sections) placed at regular intervals stiffen the structure in the longitudinal direction. Five expansion joints are arranged along the length of the building.

References: [29], [63], [73], [138], [152], [154], [255], [256], [386]

A

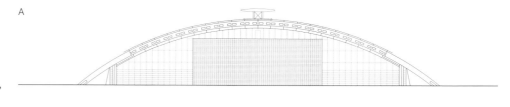

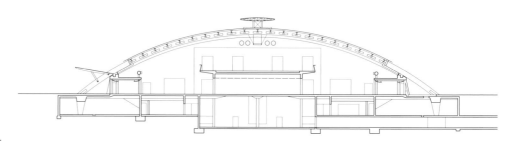

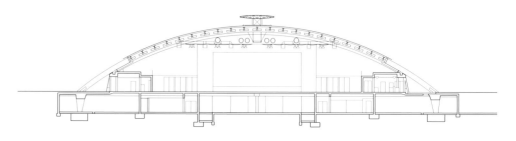

A   North-west gable, sections,
    scale 1:750
B   Isometric views,
    not to scale

B

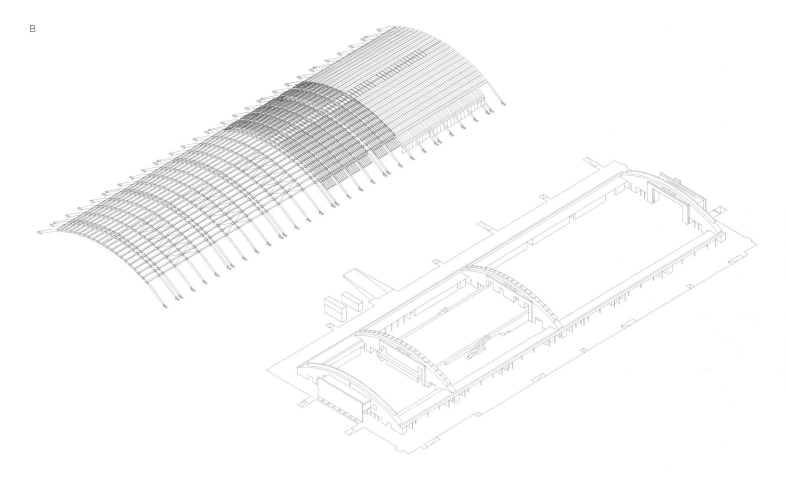

Example 42

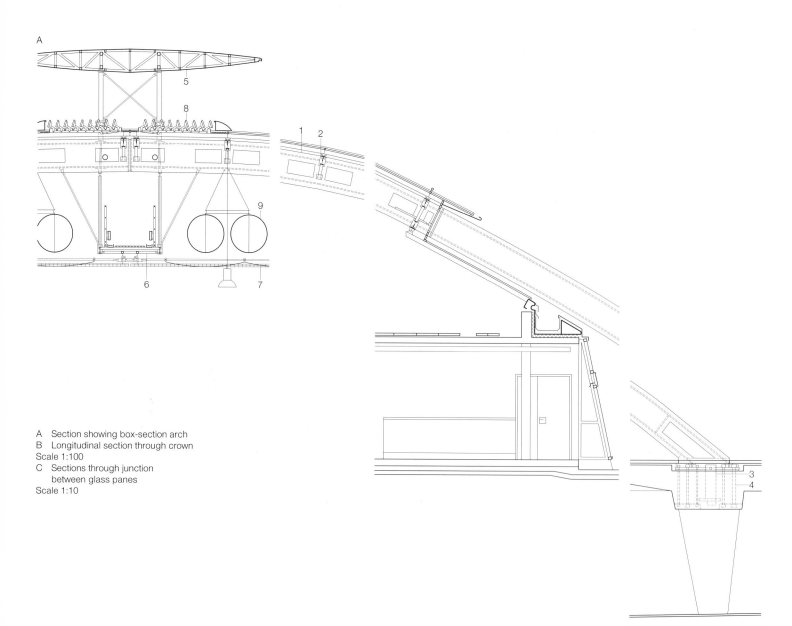

A   Section showing box-section arch
B   Longitudinal section through crown
Scale 1:100
C   Sections through junction
    between glass panes
Scale 1:10

B

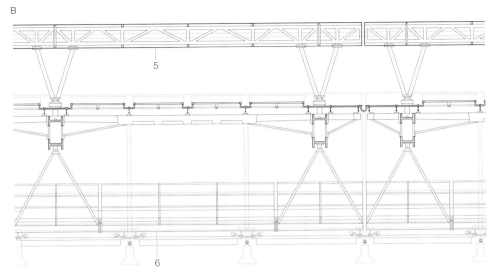

5

6

C

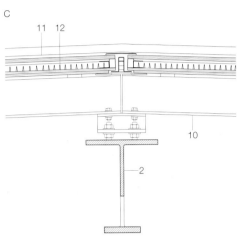

11 12

10

2

11 12

10

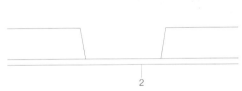

2

1   Arch, 900 x 370 box section, grade St 510 C
2   Secondary beam
3   Shear connector, 60 mm plate
4   16 No. 40 dia. x 1200 mm long threaded anchor bars
5   Crown spoiler to assist the natural ventilation
6   Suspended maintenance walkway
7   Movable panels to improve the internal acoustics

8   Louvres for natural ventilation
9   Ducts for mechanical ventilation
10 Glazing support, IPE 100
11 Insulating glass
12 Retro-reflecting grid, 16 mm high, coated with very high grade aluminium

Example 43

Rail and bus terminal, Chur, Switzerland

1993

Architects: Richard Brosi + Partner, Chur
Robert Obrist + Partner, St Moritz
Structural engineers:
Ove Arup & Partners, London,
with Peter Rice, Alastair Hughes
Project Engineer: E. Toscano, Zürich

The bus terminal, situated above the tracks of
Chur station, is covered by a single-span glass
roof, a tubular structure forming an arc. The
main members are suspended in pairs from
restrained two-legged columns. Each arch
consists of two steel tubes rising in an arc
towards the crown but at the same time veer-
ing away from each other to present the great-
est spacing at the crown, actually closer to the
member of the next arch. Radial spokes meeting at a cast steel node stabilize the arches.
The ties required to counteract the arch thrust
at the base are also connected to this node.
Secondary beams, also steel tubes, are rigidly
connected in the plane of the main beams.
This arrangement, together with the inclination
of the trusses results in an optimum three-
dimensional loadbearing behaviour; supplementary wind bracing is not required. The steel
tubes of the two outermost arches have thicker
walls to take account of the higher wind loads
in the end zones.
The covering of laminated safety glass is
raised clear of the loadbearing structure. The
panes are supported on steel sections in the
direction of the main beams.

References: [9], [29], [73], [227], [268], [407], [483],

A

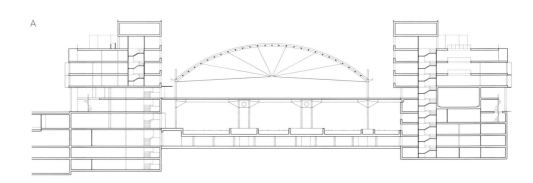

A Sections,
  scale 1:1000
B Node for spokes,
  elevation and plan,
  scale 1:20
C Eaves detail, side and
  front elevations,
  scale 1:20

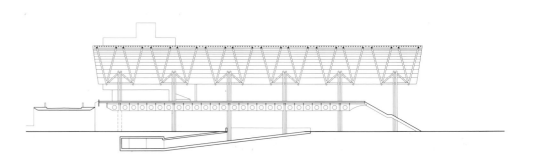

1 Column, 406.4 dia. x 16 mm tube
2 Inclined hanger,
  244.5 dia. x 20 mm tube
3 Horizontal brace, 244.5 dia. x 20 mm tube
4 Purlin, 193.7 dia. x 5 (8) mm tube
5 Main arch member, 323.9 dia. x 12.5-20 mm tube
6 Fork, 2 No. 40 mm flats
7 Arch hanger bracket, 60 mm flat, 95 mm dia. pin
8 Connecting plate, 50 mm flat

9 Forks to permit horizontal and vertical movement
10 Tie bars, 2 No. 56 dia.
11 Gutter bracket, 8 mm flat
12 Gutter support, 10 mm flat
13 Laminated safety glass
14 EPDM gasket with aluminium cover strip
15 Stainless steel glazing bar
16 Glazing support, 50 x 5 angle made
   from welded flats
17 Gutter, 3 mm stainless steel sheet

B

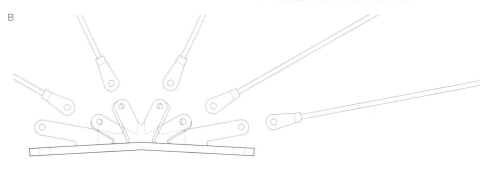

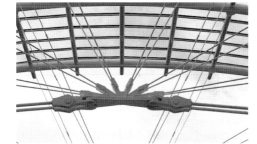

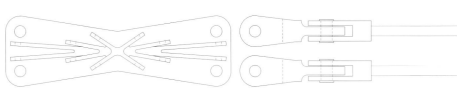

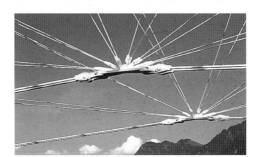

C

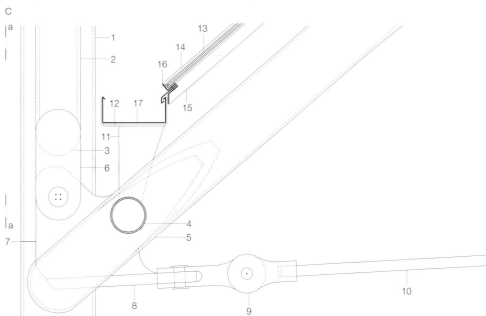

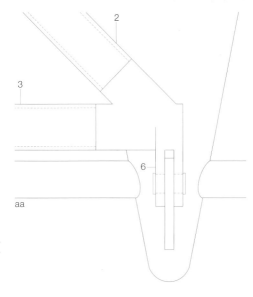

Example 44

Central entrance hall, new trade fair grounds, Leipzig

1996

Architects: von Gerkan • Marg + Partner, Hamburg
Draft design: Volkwin Marg
Partner responsible: Hubert Nienhoff
Structural engineers: Polónyi + Partner, Cologne
Schlaich, Bergermann + Partner, Stuttgart

Within the concept of Leipzig's new trade fair grounds, the 250 x 80 m central entrance hall takes on the function of providing a covered circulation zone between the individual exhibition halls. It accommodates ticket booths, admission gates, information counters and general service facilities. Its structure consists of a tubular lattice shell stiffened by arch trusses every 25 m. The glazing – frameless individual panes each approx. 1.5 x 3.0 m – is suspended inside the lattice shell.

The gables consist of curved lattice girders interconnected via slender bars. This keeps barrel vault and gables separate. An elastic joint separates the two.

Bolted individual elements make up the barrel vault. Simple end-plate connections with one central HSFG bolt were chosen. To ensure that the bolts are not loaded in shear, the end plates have interlocking connections.

One special feature of the arch trusses is the splayed diagonals, which are supported on transverse members abutting the bottom chord, to which the outriggers linking barrel vault and trusses are connected. The junction between transverse member and outrigger is formed by a cast elbow.

References: [54], [228], [336], [386], [432], [484]

A

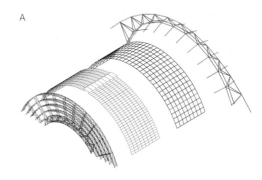

A Structural scheme
B Section and plan,
   scale 1:2000

B

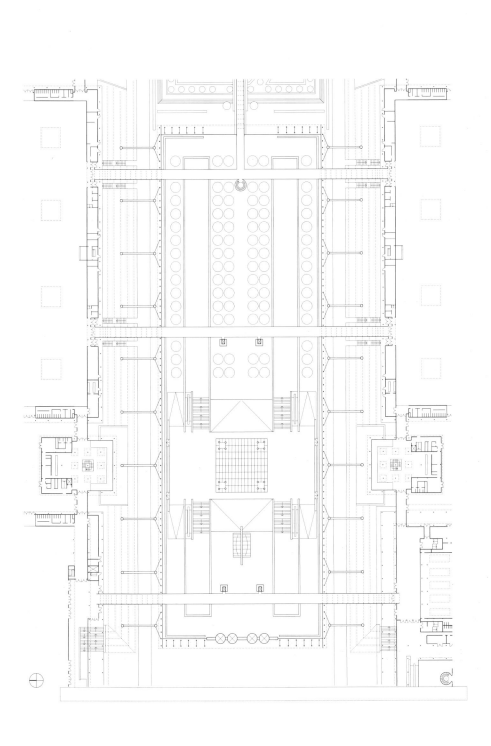

Example 44

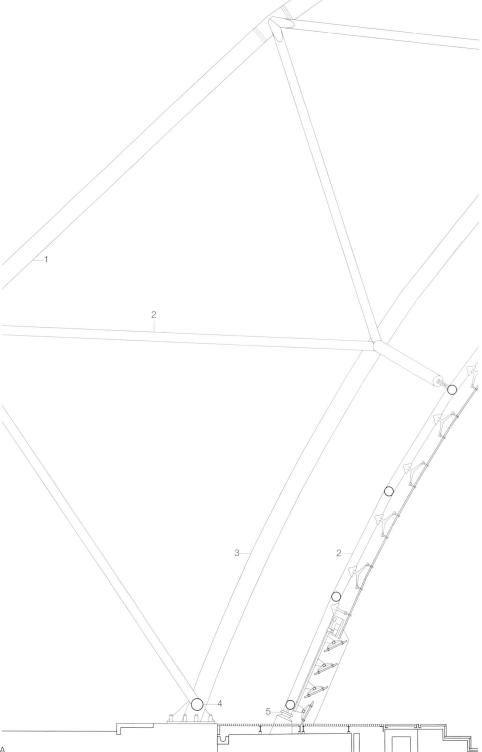

A

Arch truss

A Base
B Crown
C Section
D Elevation on
   lattice shell

Scale 1:100

Barrel vault

E Glazing fixing detail
F Junction between
   transverse member
   and outrigger
G Tube splice
H Intersection

Scale 1:20

1 Top chord,
  406 mm dia. tube
2 Lattice member,
  244.5 dia. x 8 mm tube
3 Bottom chord,
  473 dia. x 16 mm tube
4 Longitudinal member,
  318 dia. x 12.5 mm
  tube

5 Sliding bearing
6 Truss diagonal,
  159 dia. x 6.3 mm tube
7 Outrigger,
  273 dia. x 8 mm tube
8 Transverse member,
  323.9 dia. x 12.5 mm
  tube

9 End plate,
  244.5 dia. x 33 mm
10 Assembly access hole
11 Cast glazing fixing arm
12 Individual bolted fixing
13 Laminated safety glass,
  2 No. 8 mm panes
14 Cast elbow
15 HSFG bolt

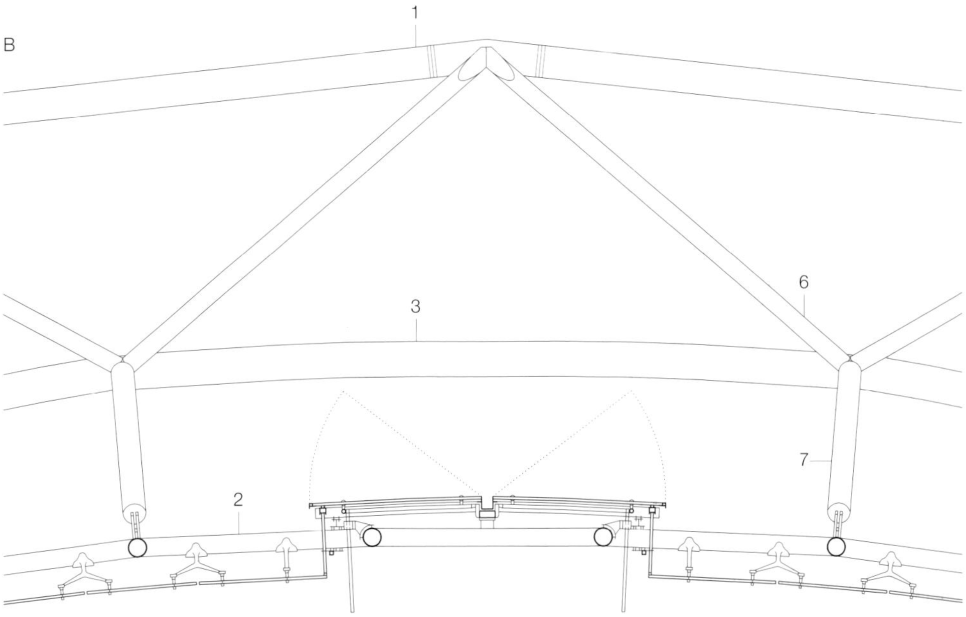

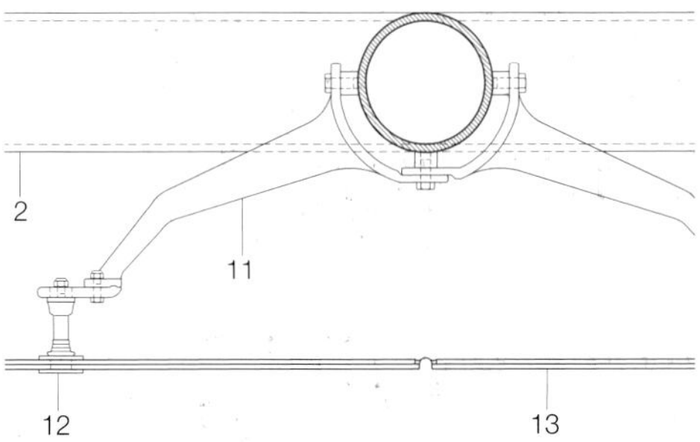

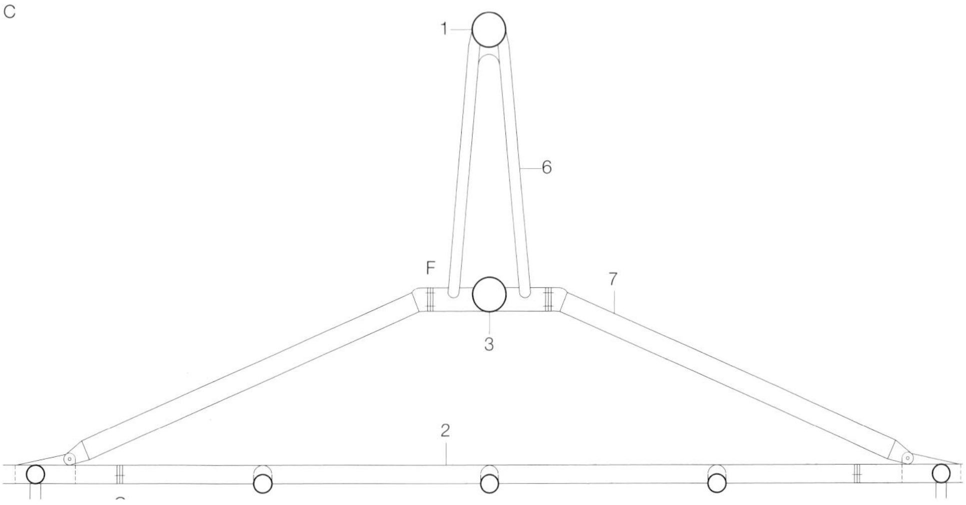

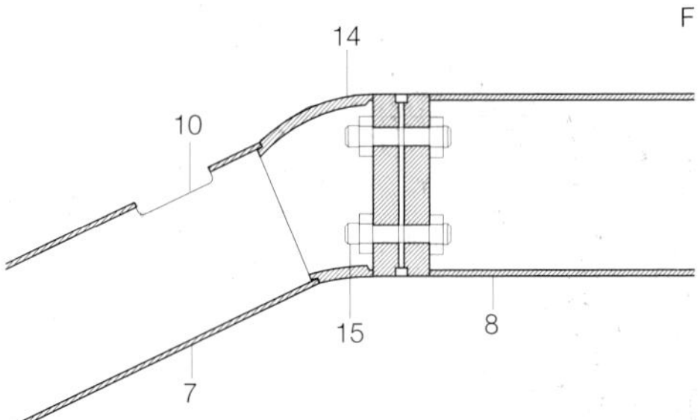

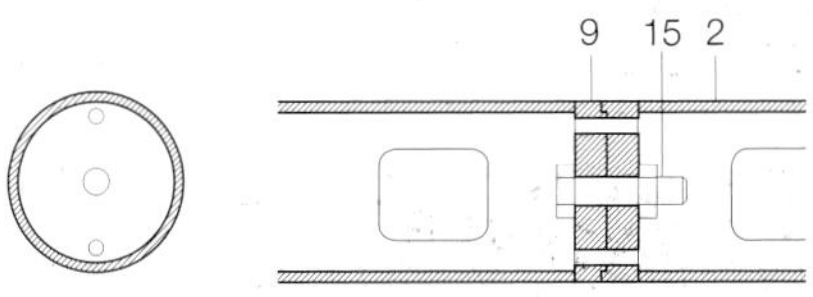

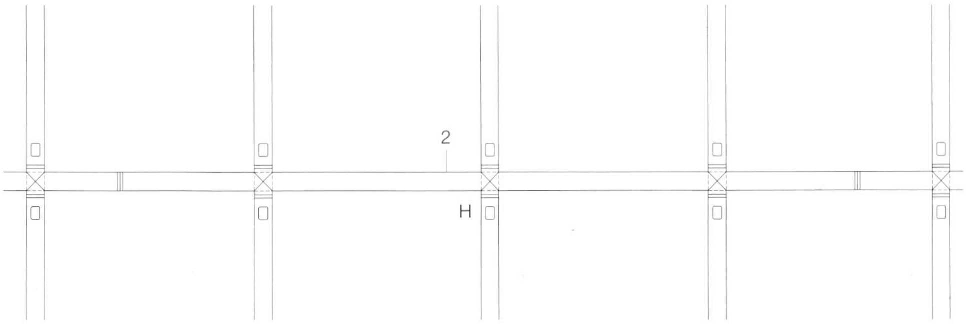

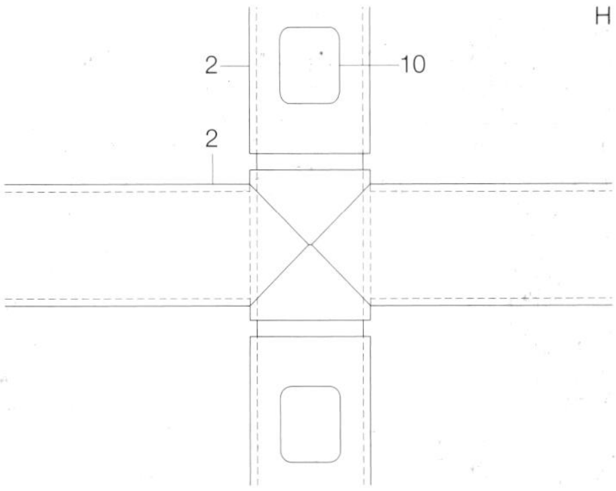

Example 45

Airport terminal, Hamburg

1993

Architects:
von Gerkan • Marg + Partner, Hamburg
Meinhard von Gerkan, Karsten Brauer
Structural engineers:
Weber, Poll + Kockjoy, Hamburg

The cross-sectional shape of the roof to this terminal was based on an aircraft wing. Seven triangular lattice girders, spaced at 10.8 m centres, span a clear width of 62.4 m and cantilever 18.7 m at the ends. They were transported in five segments per girder and welded together with the help of a jig. The nodes of these triangular girders were shifted slightly, which resulted in a minor structural disadvantage due to the displaced line of action of the diagonals but improved the welding details and produced neater penetration points. The girders are supported on pairs of raking columns which transfer the roof loads to 12 column heads of reinforced concrete. Each of the upper bearings can slide in the direction of the span. Support nodes, bearing shells to bottom chord and raking columns are all made from cast steel, thus enabling slender components and optimum fit. The raking columns – max. 11 m long – are fabricated from individual pieces; the hollow central section consisting of two butt-welded halves is connected to the forks by means of pins and tension bolts. Owing to the lateral instability of the lattice girders in the chord bearing shells, the roof purlins provide the transverse stiffness and are correspondingly large. On site pairs of girders were joined by the purlins, which were slid on rails over the final position and affixed to the next pair. The butt-jointed purlins act as continuous beams with a clear span of 9.62 m. As the girders at the ends are only supported on one side, the horizontal forces are diverted via ties to the next support and from there to the substructure.

The inner layer of the roof structure consists of insulated trapezoidal profile sheeting, spanning 3.20 m. On top of this there is a standing seam aluminium roof. Trussed posts stabilize the glass curtain walls to front and rear facades, which are joined to the roof by flexible make-up pieces and fixings. The facade posts are offset, passing either side of the primary structure, which is fitted with a flexible collar where it penetrates the glass.

References: [36], [73], [139], [150], [168], [218], [219], [220], [227], [436]

A

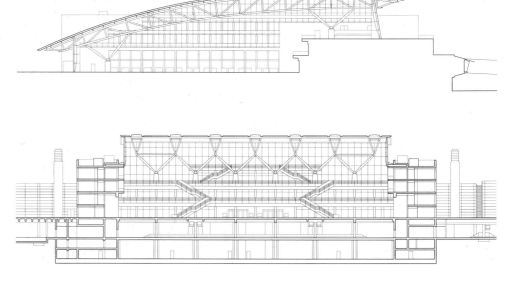

A Sections,
   scale 1:1000
B Section through facade,
   scale 1:100
C Detail of facade-roof junction,
   scale 1:50

B   C

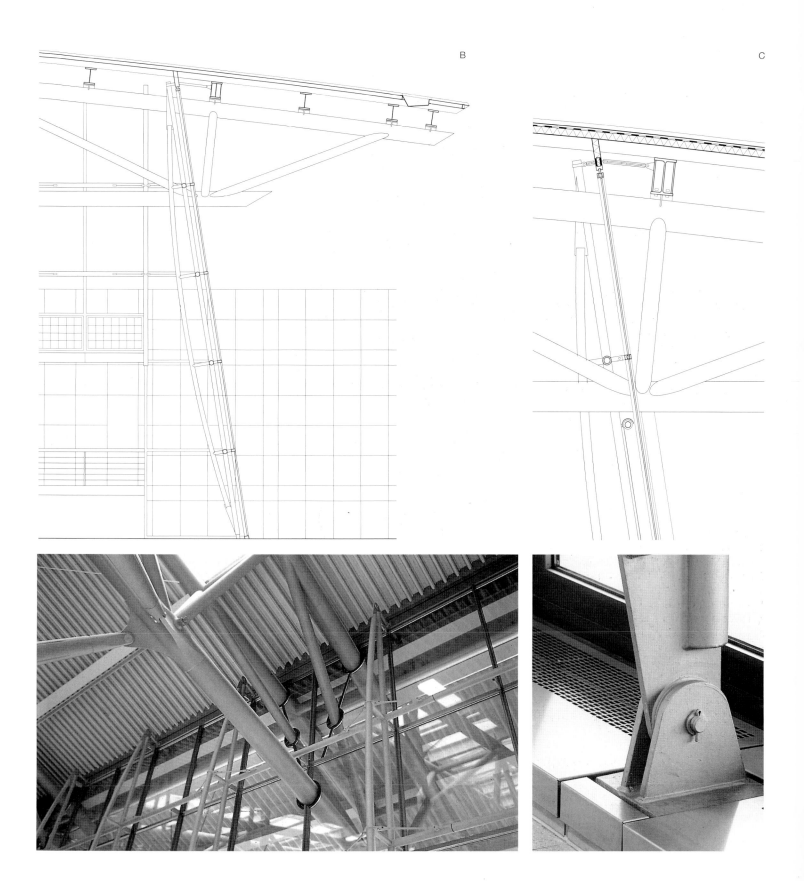

Example 45

1 Roof construction:
  Standing seam aluminium roofing
  Polymer-bitumen sheeting
  Closed-cell foamed glass
  Bituminous primer
  Galvanized steel sheeting
  Steel trapezoidal profile sheeting, perforated

2 Purlin, HEA 450
3 Top chord, 406 dia. x 12.5 mm tube
4 Tie between top chords, 219 dia. x 10 mm tube
5 Diagonals, 219 dia. x 6.3 mm tube

6 Bottom chord, 406 dia. x 12.5 mm
7 Cast bearing shell to bottom chord, grade St 52.3
8 Connecting pins, 110 mm dia., grade St 460
9 Raking column, max. 500 dia. x 25 mm tube

A

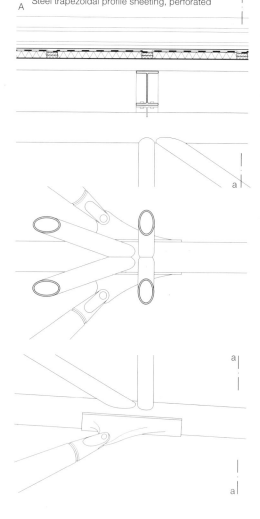

B

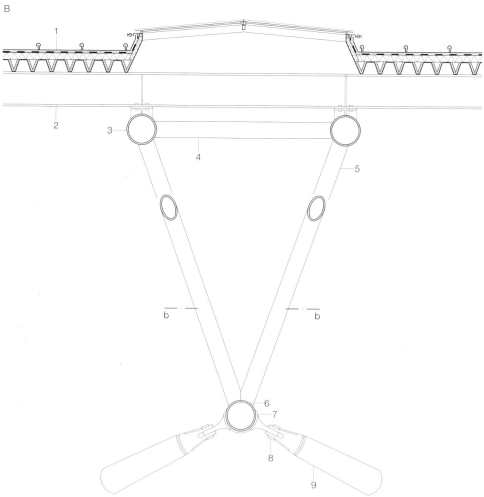

bb

aa

A   Section through roof
B   Section through main girder
Scale 1:50
C   Bending moment diagram for purlin
D   Isometric view of structural system
E   Section through structural system
Not to scale
F   Detail of fork
G   Detail of support
Scale 1:20

F

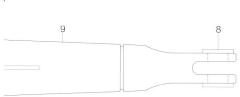

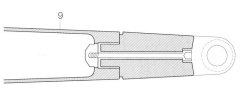

G

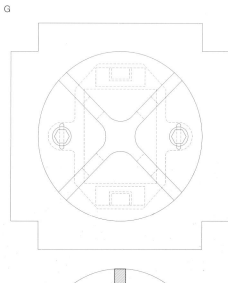

C

D

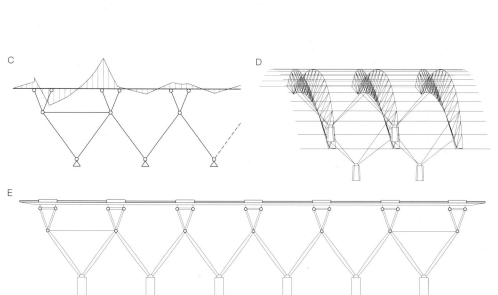

E

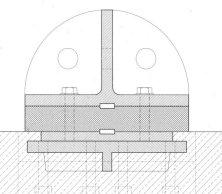

Example 46

Airport terminal, Osaka, Japan

1994

Architect:
Renzo Piano Building Workshop, Paris,
with Noriaki Okabe
Structural engineers:
Ove Arup & Partners, London

A man-made island was created in Osaka-wan
Bay to provide a home for this new airport. The
wave-shaped geometry of the terminal roof
was generated by computer and is divided into
two sections: a compact passenger hall measuring approx. 315 x 100 m on plan and up to
30 m high, where various airport facilities are
housed on several mezzanine floors along a
continuous passenger concourse, and the
adjoining 1.7-km-long arrivals and departures
wing, with space for over 40 aircraft simultaneously.
The structure must be able to withstand earthquakes, extremely high wind loads and the
settlement patterns of the seabed. Expansion
joints divide the structure into 200 segments
and further transverse construction joints permit tolerances of up to 500 mm. In addition, the
heights of the 900 column foundations can be
regulated by means of computer-controlled
hydraulics.
The loadbearing structure to the main hall rises
above the storeys of the airport facilities and
consists of a row of triangular lattice girders
supported by pairs of raking columns. These
asymmetric girders span 82.5 m and the
longest struts are 4 m long. In the side wing
the construction is reduced to just one chord
stabilized by chordal ties. The secondary
beams (I-sections) at 4 m centres run at right-
angles to the main girders.
Diagonal bracing provides longitudinal stiffening to the building and as a result, in contrast
to the conventional system of the hall, the
arrivals and departures wing exhibits a spiral-
type loadbearing behaviour.
Insulated trapezoidal profile sheeting forms the
underside of the roof construction. On top of
this a ventilated structure carries the outer skin
of 90 000 identical stainless steel panels. The
large expanses of glazing in the gables are
made possible by the posts spaced at 4 m
centres and trussed on both sides. In order to
continue the glass facade right up to the roof,
the triangular lattice girders at the ends of the
building were each split into two symmetrical
parts to allow the facade to pass between.

References: [12], [30], [103], [156], [160], [356]

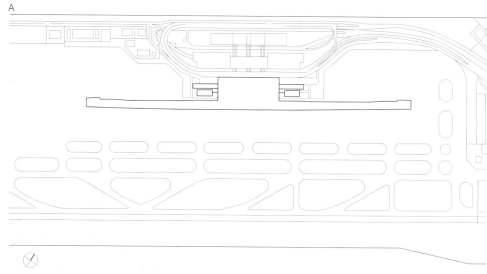

A

A Site plan,
   scale 1:20 000
B Section,
   scale 1:1250
C Plans,
   scale 1:10 000

B

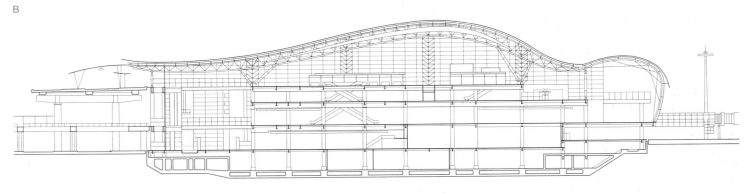

C

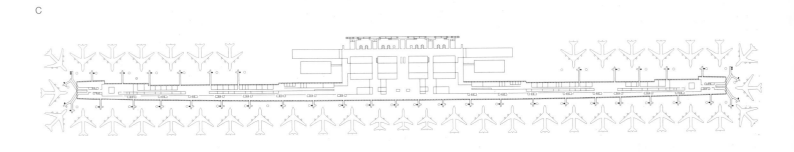

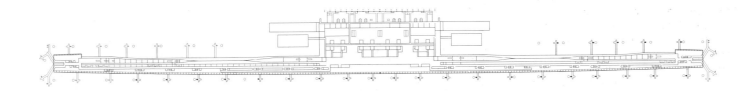

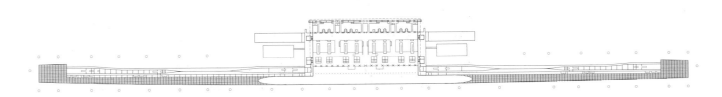

Example 46

A

C

D

B

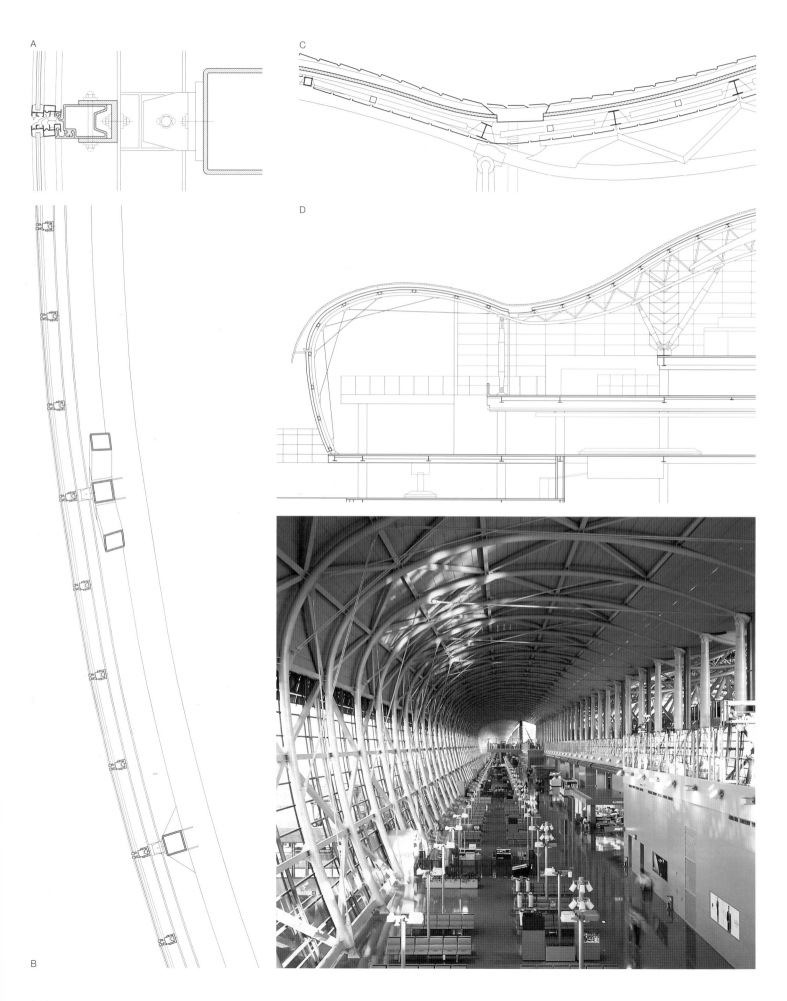

Details of arrivals and departures zone:
A Vertical section through glazing,
    scale 1:10
B Vertical section through facade,
    scale 1:50
C Section through transition from hall roof to side wing,
    scale 1:100
D Part section,
    scale 1:500

Details of gables:
E Stiffening to node point: axonometric view, horizontal
    and vertical sections
F Base of facade post
Scale 1:10

E

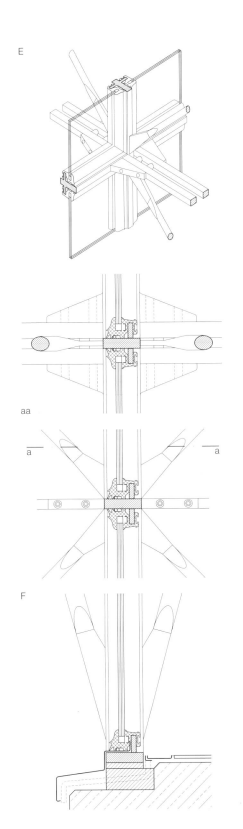

aa

a   a

F

Example 47

Waterloo International Terminal, London

1993

Architect:
Nicholas Grimshaw and Partners, London
N. Grimshaw, N. Sidor,
D. Kirkland, U. Heinemann
Structural engineers:
Anthony Hunt Associates, Cirencester
A. Hunt, A. Jones, M. Otlet, D. Dexter

This railway station serves as the terminus for the new Channel Tunnel line. While it remains true to the tradition of older railway stations, it also symbolizes a new age of train travel. The confined inner-city site adjacent the existing Waterloo station meant that the 400-m-long structure had to follow the curving line of the tracks. The platforms are reached from below, where the passport and customs controls are carried out. The lower levels, illuminated by daylight via the glazed west facade, also contain waiting areas, shops and offices.
The span of the roof structure varies from 32 to 48 m; there are no intermediate supports. It is designed as a three-hinged arch and consists of two distinct segments, both of which are constructed as triangular trusses. On the western side the structure is placed outside, in front of the glazing in order to ensure sufficient headroom for the trains. On the longer-span eastern side, the structure is placed internally. All three hinges are comprised of stainless steel pins fitted in cast steel elements.
The cross-section of the compression chords of each truss corresponds to the forces diagram. The complicated three-dimensional nodes are produced from standardized castings. Despite the organic form of the building arising from the curvature of the platforms and the tapering width of the structure, the strips of overlapping roof glazing are composed of standard panes, all one size and with 90° corners! The glazing bars are attached to articulated stainless steel fixings which allow the roof structure to move. At the sides the laminated glass panes are held by neoprene gaskets which adapt to the different clearances and accommodate movement.

References: [27], [144], [145], [386], [444]

B

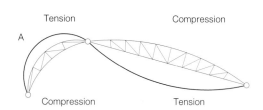

A

Tension   Compression

Compression   Tension

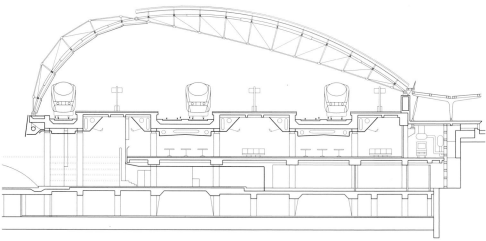

C

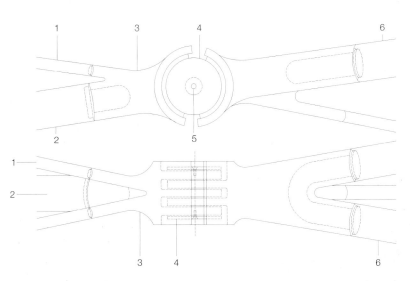

A Bending moments in
  three-hinged arch
B Section,
  scale 1:500
C Roof hinge: elevation
  and plan,
  scale 1:20
D Part plan of roof,
  not to scale

1 75 mm dia. round
  section
2 228 mm dia. tube
3 Cast steel hinge
4 Stainless steel cover
  plate
5 100 mm dia. stainless
  steel pin
6 219 mm dia. tube

D

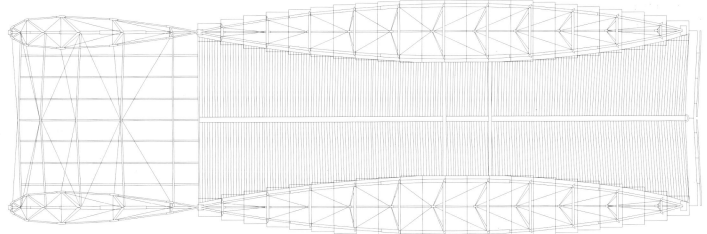

Example 47

A

B

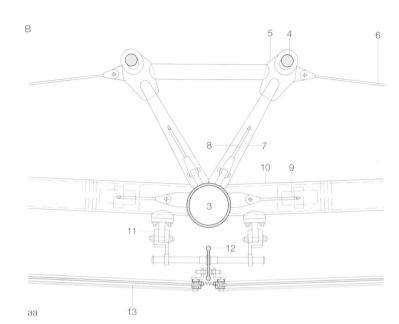

aa   13

A   Axonometric view, not to scale
B   Details of facade:
     horizontal and vertical sections, base,
     scale 1:20

1   Base plate, 50-58 mm
2   Base hinge, cast steel
3   228 mm dia. tube
4   75 mm dia. round section
5   Cast steel node

6   30 mm dia. round section
7   Tapering tube
8   Diagonal, 30 mm dia. round section
9   Bracing, round section
10   168 mm dia. tube
11   Stainless steel hinge
12   Extruded aluminium section, slotted
13   10 mm toughened safety glass
14   Aluminium glazing bar
15   EPDM gasket

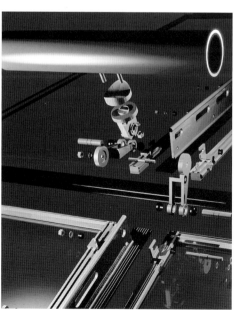

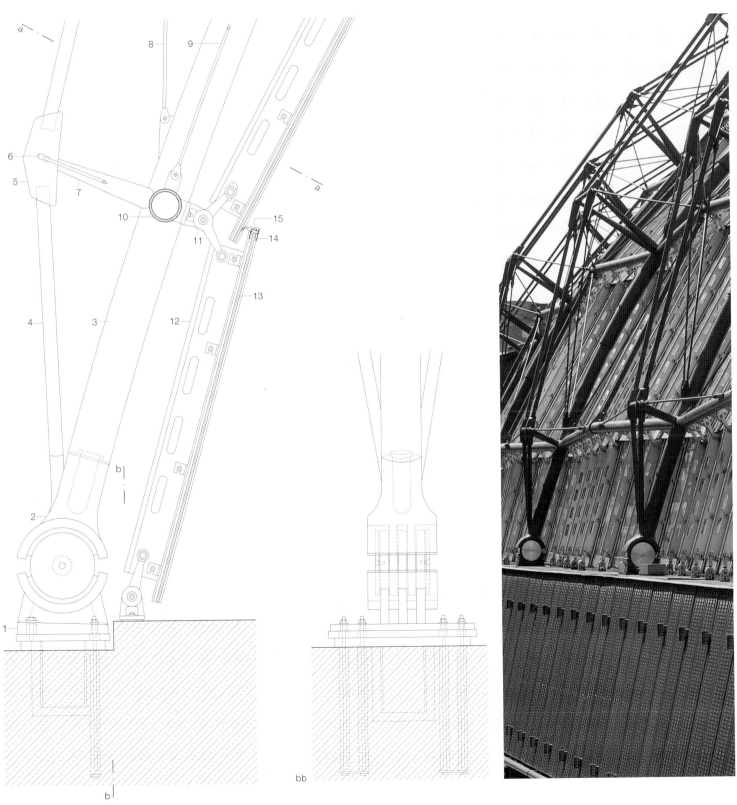

Example 48

Multi-purpose hall, Nottingham, UK

1995

Architects:
Michael Hopkins and Partners, London
Sir Michael Hopkins, W. Taylor, I. Sharratt,
P. Romaniuk, P. Bate, B. Phelan
Structural engineers:
Ove Arup & Partners, London

A former industrial site on the edge of Nottingham city centre was chosen as the location for the offices of the tax authorities.
The focus of this complex is formed by a building housing common facilities such as kindergarten, restaurant and a hall for sports and other purposes. The building is spanned by a textile membrane and consists of a pair of two-storey blocks which frame the hall. The main roof comprises five suspended arched trusses which are glazed to provide internal illumination. Translucent membranes are stretched between the trusses, the loads being transferred to the reinforced concrete columns of the blocks via additional struts. Between the main and side membranes there are areas of glass, fixed by means of struts to two curved tubes. The side membranes are suspended from the lower tube and the building envelope between upper tube and main membrane is formed by an extra strip of fabric.
The steelwork supporting the membrane is supported around the edges by a cantilevering reinforced concrete slab carried by reinforced concrete columns. The separation of the main and edge membranes creates a flat edge to the roof which enables further daylight to be admitted.

References: [31], [124], [144]

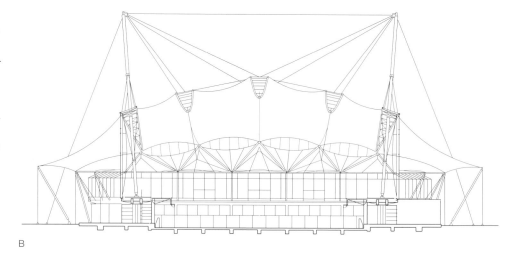

B

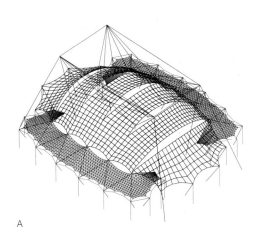

A

A   Isometric view of roof
B   Sections and roof plan,
    scale 1:500

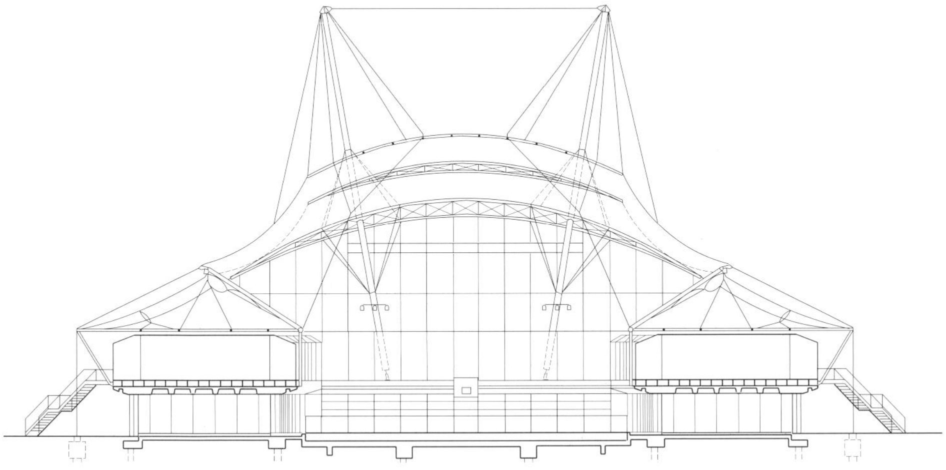

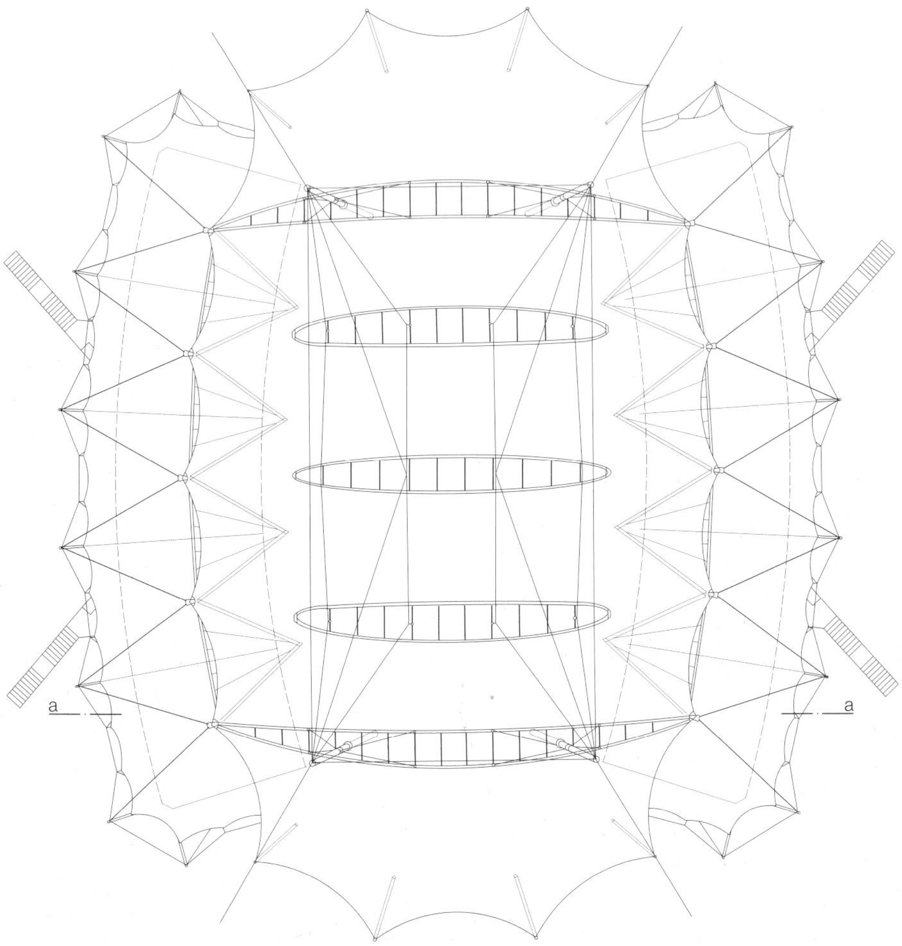

Example 48

A   Section through block
B   Plan on junction between main and
    side membranes showing struts
Scale 1:100

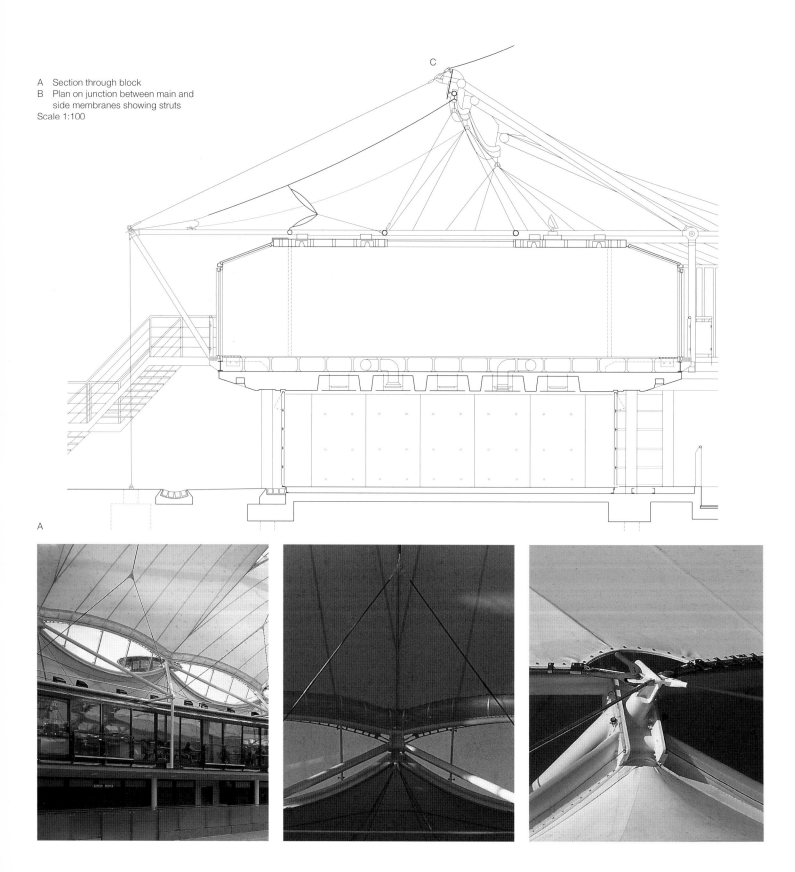

A

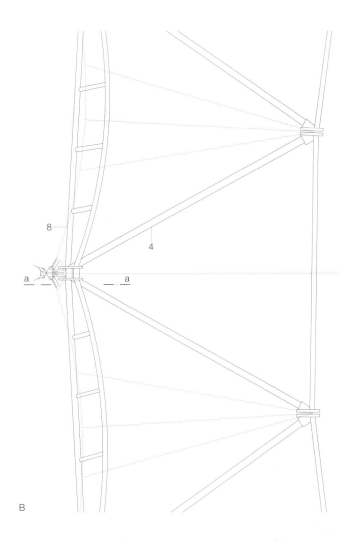

B

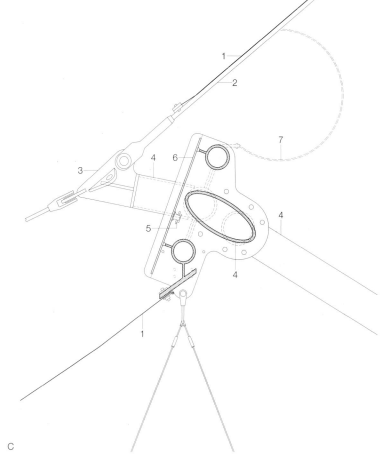

C

Junction between main and side
membranes
C   Section
D   Plan
Scale 1:20

1   Membrane
2   Cable, 25 mm dia.
3   Connecting plate, 16 mm
4   193.7 mm dia. tube
5   Screwed glass fixing
6   Laminated safety glass
7   Strip of fabric
8   Tension cable, 22 mm dia.
9   Cable clamp
10   Clamping plate
11   Turnbuckle

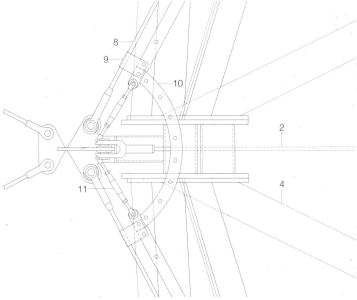

D

Example 49

Tennis stadium, Hamburg

1997

Architects: Schweger + Partner, Hamburg
Peter P. Schweger, Hartmut H. Reifenstein,
Bernhard Kohl, Wolfgang Schneider,
Wilhelm Meyer
Draft design of roof structure and structural
engineering:
Sobek and Rieger, Stuttgart

The roof to this tennis stadium is made up of
two sections: the outer membrane forms a
fixed ring over the grandstand, while the inner,
folding membrane can be opened. When
open, the folds of material are stowed around
an off-centre hub.
The loads of the opening roof section are transferred via the "mid-air struts" to the outer compression ring and outer columns. Together with
the compression ring and the ties, the tension
ring forms a self-stabilizing system comparable
to a spoked wheel. Therefore, the individual
members of the compression ring can be pin-
jointed.
The peaks of the grandstand roof section are
suspended from the tops of the mid-air struts.
The inner membrane roof can be opened and
closed by means of a motorized cable mechanism which drives the motors at different
speeds to allow for the asymmetric arrangement. The design called for a pitched roof so a
gutter is attached below the mid-air struts; rainwater is pumped out and drained to the outside.

A

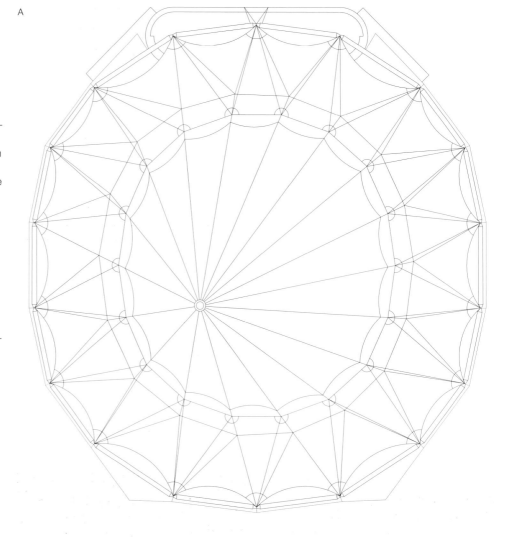

A   Roof plan and section,
    scale 1:800

Compression ring, columns:
B   Elevation and plan
C   Section
Scale 1:200

D   Spherical bearing,
    section and elevation,
    scale 1:100

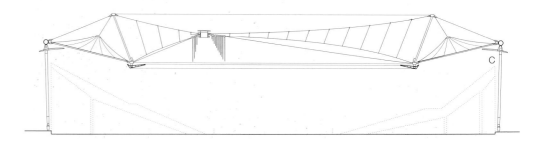

C

B

C

D

D

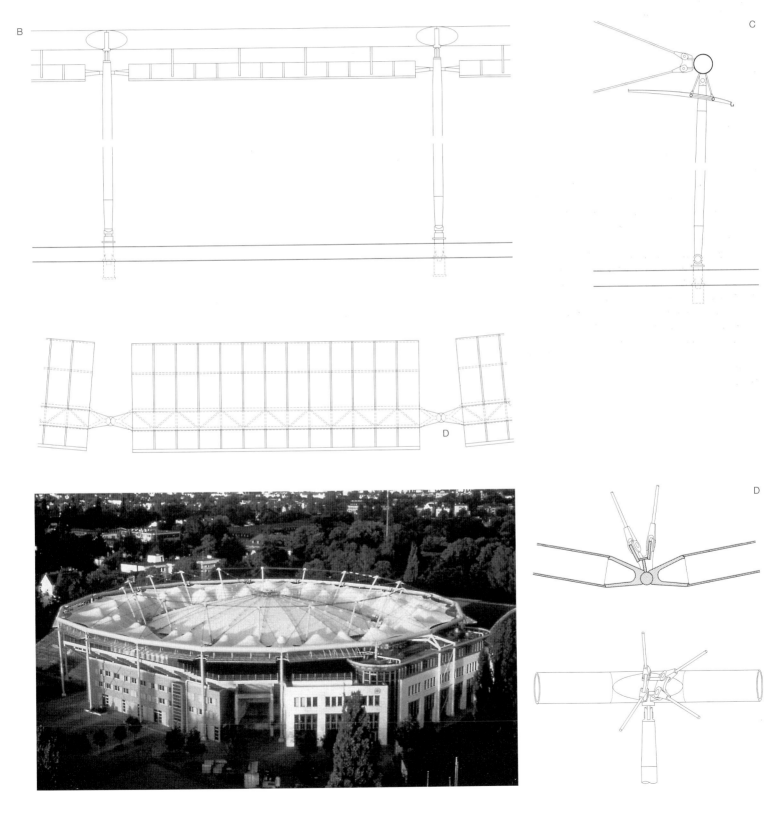

Example 49

A Mid-air strut with gutter,
   scale 1:100
B Isometric view of upper node
C Section through lower node
Scale 1:50

1 Cable, 87 mm dia., grade VVS-3
2 Perimeter cables, 58 mm dia., grade VVS-3
3 Pulley

4 Top chord of cable truss, 70 mm dia. cable
5 Mid-air strut, 323.9 dia. x 17.5 mm
6 Cable, 16 mm dia., grade OSS
7 Cable, 79 mm dia., grade VVS-3
8 Gutter
9 Perimeter cables, 4 No. 79 mm dia., grade VVS-3
10 Cable, 9 mm dia.
11 Bottom chord of cable truss, 2 No. 37 mm dia.
   cables, grade VVS-2
12 Drive mechanism

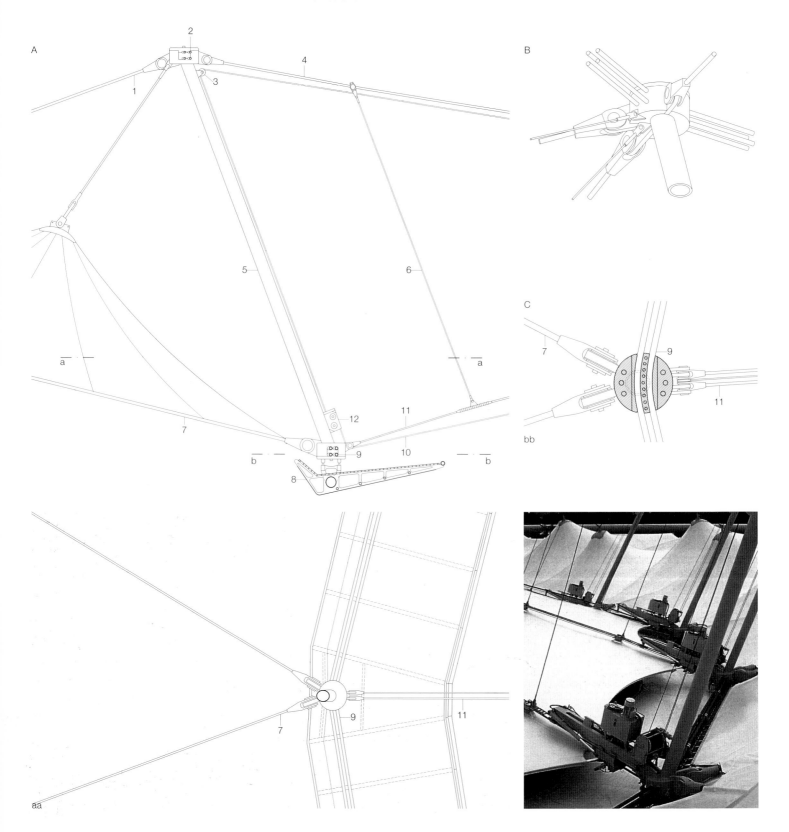

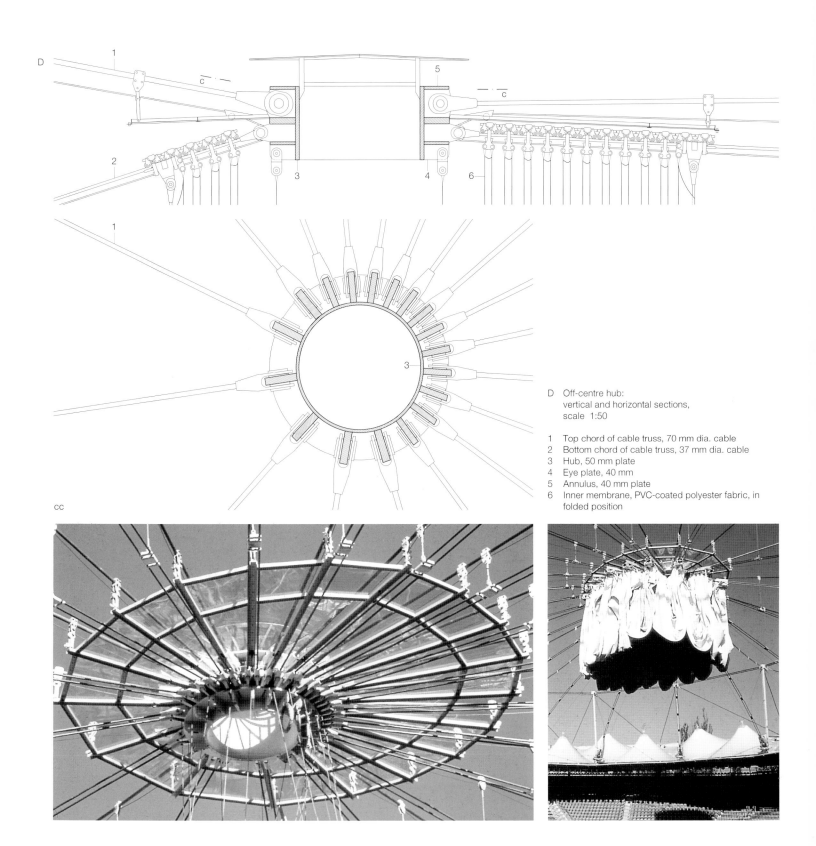

D   Off-centre hub:
    vertical and horizontal sections,
    scale 1:50

1   Top chord of cable truss, 70 mm dia. cable
2   Bottom chord of cable truss, 37 mm dia. cable
3   Hub, 50 mm plate
4   Eye plate, 40 mm
5   Annulus, 40 mm plate
6   Inner membrane, PVC-coated polyester fabric, in
    folded position

Example 50

Telecommunications tower, Barcelona, Spain

1992

Architects:
Foster and Partners, London
Structural engineers:
Ove Arup & Partners, London
Julio Martinez Calzon

The 288 m tower is located on a chain of hills overlooking the city of Barcelona. This striking structure was erected to handle the television broadcasts of the 1992 Olympic Games. In addition, the tower houses the technical installations of several telephone companies.
The stayed arrangement means that the footprint of the tower is minimal – a significant factor here in the Collserola nature conservation area – and the structure presents a filigree engineering landmark above the capital of Catalonia.
The "spine" of the tower consists of a reinforced concrete shaft 4.50 m O.D. x 190 m high; the thickness of the shaft wall varies from 760 mm at the base to 300 mm at the top. The shaft is anchored to an underground building which houses the operational facilities. Stability for the shaft is provided by an interactive system consisting of four main platforms, diagonal struts and three-dimensional stays. The nine intermediate platforms are suspended within the primary structure. The stays are connected to the ends of the platform block, whose plan shape is that of an equilateral triangle with rounded sides. This shape is beneficial to the wind flows around the tower.
The entire platform block was built at ground level and subsequently raised into position using hydraulic jacks, which proved to be economical and safe. The forces from the radiating steel struts are accommodated inside the concrete shaft; services, stairs and lift are positioned outside. Finally, the main aerial was installed and, like a telescope, extended to its full height of 80 m.
To rule out transmission interference and a rise in temperature caused by induction currents, non-conductive polyamide fibres were chosen for the three upper cable stays.

References: [2], [6], [20], [21], [29], [38], [164], [197], [435]

A

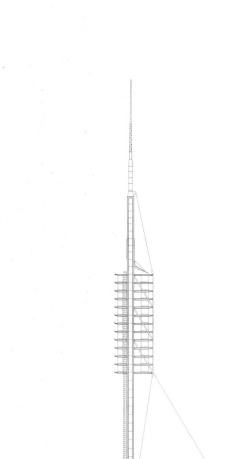

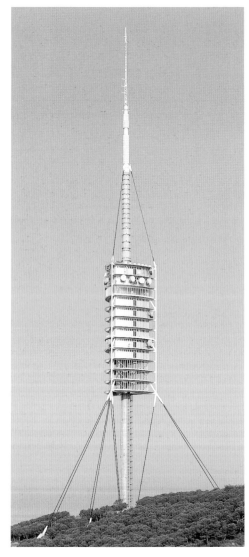

B

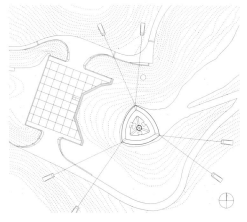

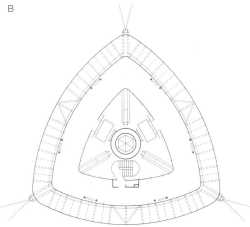

A Section and site plan, scale 1:2500
B Plan of standard platform, scale 1:500
C Erection phases 1-9
D Isometric view of primary structure, not to scale
Details of main platform beams, scale 1:100
E During raising
F After raising

C

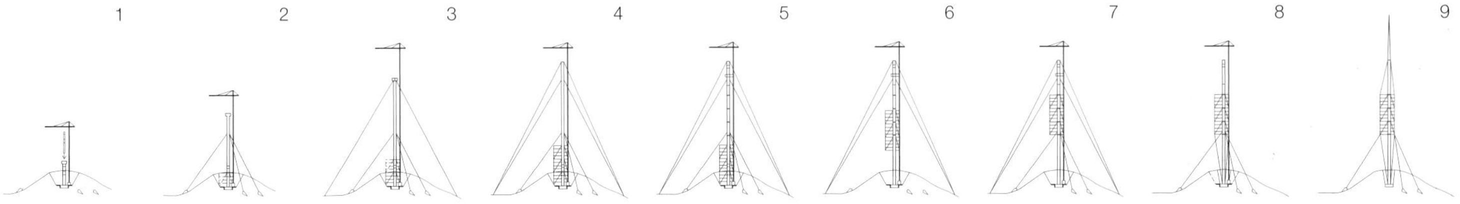

1   2   3   4   5   6   7   8   9

D

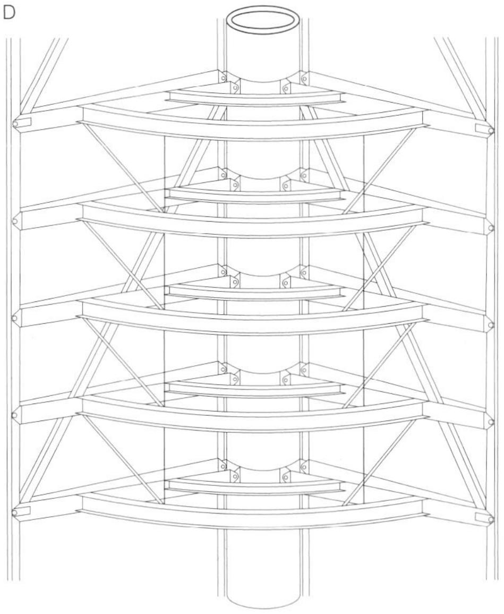

1   Main platform beam
2   Bracket with hinge
3   Connecting pin

E

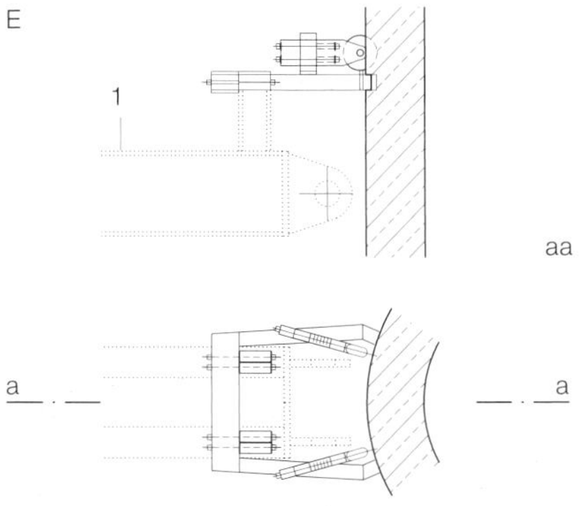

1

aa

a   a

F

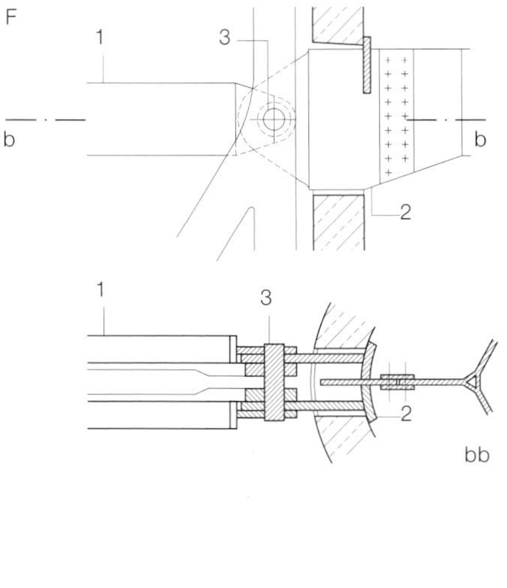

1   3

b   b

2

1   3

2

bb

Example 51

State of Illinois Center, Chicago, USA

1985

Architects:
Murphy/Jahn and
Lester B. Knight & Associates, Chicago
Structural engineers:
Murphy/ Jahn, Chicago, Lou Moro

The headquarters of the Illinois state authorities occupies a complete inner city block. However, the south-east corner of the 17-storey building is curved in order to allow space for a public forecourt. From here the facade slopes back into the building. The facade itself is supported by five-storey-high inclined trusses which are in turn supported by the primary structure of the office levels. This construction results in a vast atrium underneath. At the transition from forecourt to central hall, the supporting office structure is omitted and its structural function replaced by large horizontal girders. The central circular atrium reaching right up to the roof serves as a circulation zone and enables daylight to penetrate to all levels. The top of this open internal space – about 50 m in diameter – is terminated by a truncated glass cylinder. The two-way spanning structure of this cylinder is formed by steel tubes with the complicated nodes being solved in a very simple manner. The construction of the edge detail illustrates the special but necessary precautions required for draining the rainwater at this exposed point.

References: [275], [267], [364]

A   Section and plan,
scale 1:1000

A

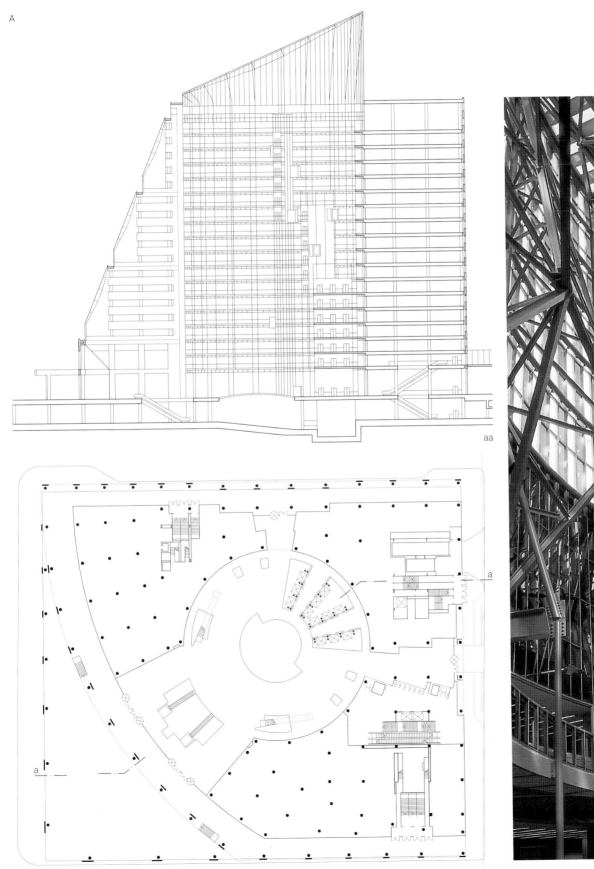

aa

Example 51

A Section through
   facade, scale 1:200
B Detail of facade,
   scale 1:50
C Plan on glass roof,
   scale 1:400
Sections aa, bb, cc and dd,
scale 1:50

1 Steel panel
2 Insulation
3 Metal cladding
4 Alternately clear and
   coated glass, both with
   internal sunshades
5 Suspended ceiling
6 Free-standing granite
   arcade wall
7 Plastered columns
8 Aluminium cladding to
   columns

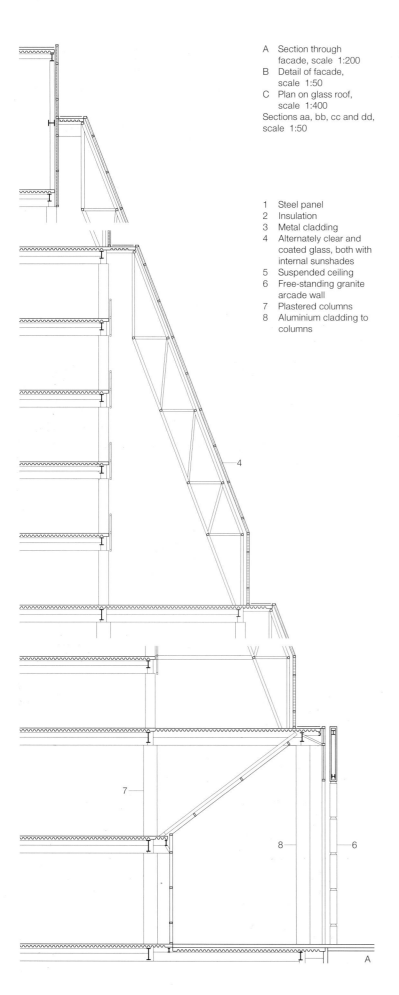

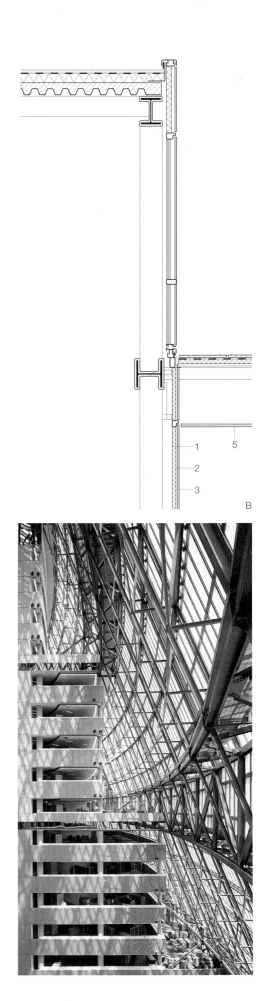

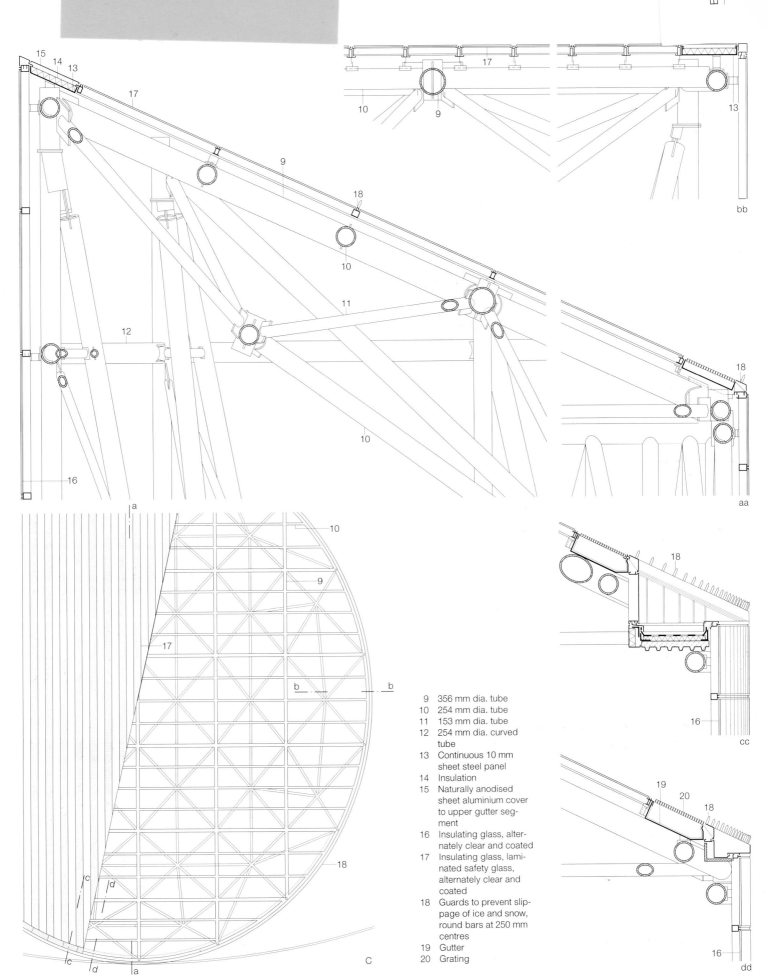

bb

aa

cc

dd

C

9   356 mm dia. tube
10   254 mm dia. tube
11   153 mm dia. tube
12   254 mm dia. curved
    tube
13   Continuous 10 mm
    sheet steel panel
14   Insulation
15   Naturally anodised
    sheet aluminium cover
    to upper gutter seg-
    ment
16   Insulating glass, alter-
    nately clear and coated
17   Insulating glass, lami-
    nated safety glass,
    alternately clear and
    coated
18   Guards to prevent slip-
    page of ice and snow,
    round bars at 250 mm
    centres
19   Gutter
20   Grating

Business premises, Tokyo, Japan

1993

Architects:
Richard Rogers Partnership, London
Architect 5 Partnership
Structural engineers:
Umezawa Design Office, Tokyo

This building is situated on a narrow street in an old quarter of the city centre. To comply with local building regulations, the tallest part of the structure was erected at the rear boundary of the plot. This created a forecourt under which there are two basement levels provided with daylight via a sloping glazed roof.
A bridge at ground floor level provides access to the 10-storey main tower, which has a concrete-cased steel frame. Four columns each 560 x 560 mm with 40 mm walls are cased in an insulated 120 mm layer of concrete. The columns are 8 m apart and are connected by beams. This construction is earthquake-resistant and is considerably slimmer than an equivalent version in reinforced concrete.
The loadbearing system of the glass roof is very light in order to admit as much daylight as possible into the public zone underground, with bars and restaurants. A computer was used to calculate the smallest possible cross-sections and provide an efficient structure, which was implemented in stainless steel. Yacht rigging served as an archetype.
The lift shaft is placed outside the main system together with the ancillary rooms in add-on boxes. Services and escape stairs too, whose prestressed construction is suspended from the lift shaft on damped mountings to eliminate vibrations.

References: [1], [28], [62], [142], [361], [450]

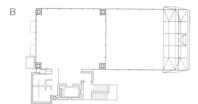
B

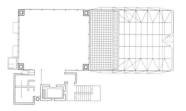

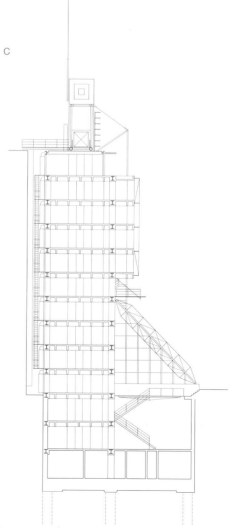
C

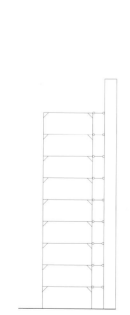
A

D

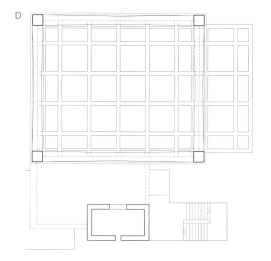

A Structural system, sketch of principle
B Plans of 2nd and 5th floors
C Section
Scale 1:500

D Plan of floor layout, scale 1:200
E Details of steel beam and composite steel
   beam, scale 1:50 and 1:20

1 Box column, 560 x 560 x 40 mm
2 450 mm deep frame beam,
   flange = 380-560 x 32 mm,
   web = 386 x 19 mm
3 Connecting plate with reinforcing bars welded on for
   concrete waffle floor slab
4 Reinforcing bars welded to connecting plate
5 Assembly plates for column splice

E

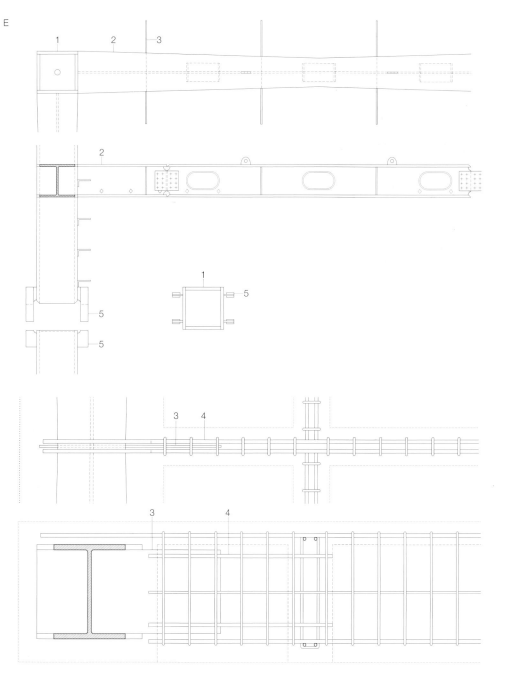

Example 53

Bank headquarters, Frankfurt a. M.

1994

Architects:
Foster and Partners, London
Project Manager:
S. deGrey, U. Nienstedt, S. Ollmann
Structural engineers:
Ove Arup & Partners, London
Krebs & Kiefer, Darmstadt

This bank headquarters is the first high-rise building of this order of magnitude in Germany to employ pure steel-and-reinforced-concrete composite construction. Instead of the conventional internal core, the loadbearing structure consists of a total of three cores located in the rounded corners of the triangular tower. This permits a central atrium to be incorporated over the full height of the building. Eight-storey blocks of offices alternating with four-storey "skygardens" span between the "corner cores". The upper sections of the set-back facades to the gardens may be opened. As sufficient air and light penetrates the atrium, there are offices adjacent the atrium as well. The rounded equilateral triangle plan shape has side lengths of approx. 60 m. The primary structure in each core consists of two composite columns (megacolumns) which, together with the link frames and the eight-storey Vierendeel frames to the office sections, form a rigid frame. The whole system is restrained at the base of each core.

The three-story basement box of in-situ reinforced concrete acts here as a stiff connection for the framework. The tower is founded on 111 large-diameter, bored, cast-in-situ concrete piles. During the construction phase the megacolumns, designed as multistorey composite frame members, were solely responsible for the stability. The eight-storey Vierendeel frames are positioned directly behind the facade and span 36 m between the megacolumns. The horizontal forces generated by the curvature of the Vierendeel frames are transferred via additional struts to the floor beams and from there to the floors – acting as stiffening diaphragms – by way of shear studs. The triangular atrium columns are composite members with inner and outer plates. Long-span floor beams span from the atrium edge beams to the Vierendeel frames. The composite floors supported by the beams function as horizontal diaphragms, transmitting local loads to the main structure and guaranteeing its stability. Above the final office block, the west core continues for a further 10 storeys in composite construction and supports a tubular steel aerial structure.

References: [115], [147]

A

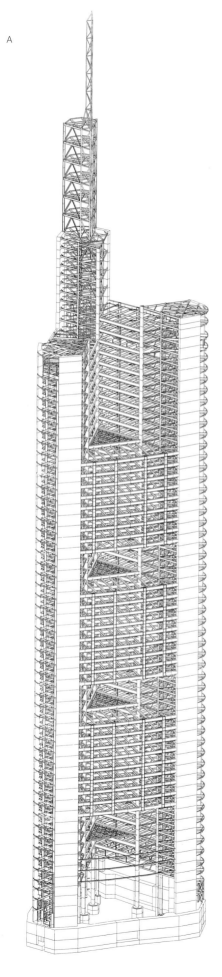

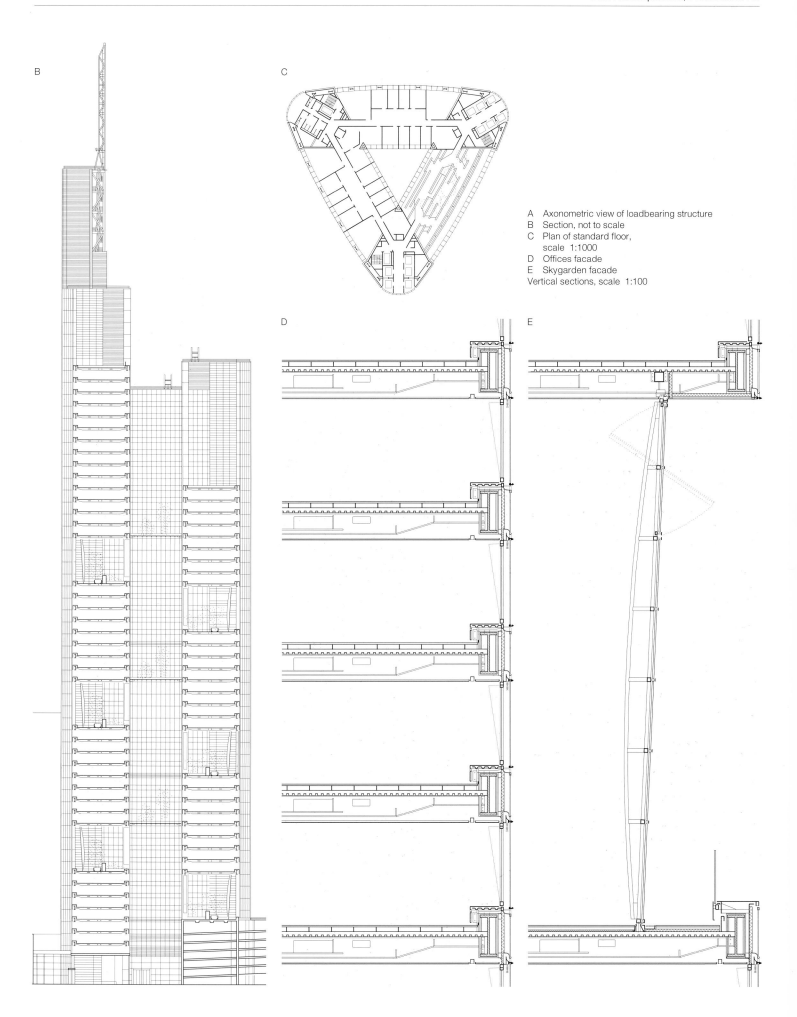

B

C

A   Axonometric view of loadbearing structure
B   Section, not to scale
C   Plan of standard floor,
    scale 1:1000
D   Offices facade
E   Skygarden facade
Vertical sections, scale 1:100

D

E

Example 53

A   Axonometric view of composite con-
    struction, not to scale
B   Section through megacolumn showing
    link frame and curved facade
C   Floor beam
D   Vierendeel frame
E   Section through atrium column
Scale 1:50

1   Megacolumn
2   Beam of link frame, 1100 x 300 mm welded I-section
3   Internal core column, 539 x 409 x 70-130 mm I-section
4   Core edge beam, 270 x 200 mm I-section
5   Floor beam, 556 x 210 mm I-section
6   Vierendeel frame, 1100 x 475 mm I-section
7   Triangular internal column, 600-900 mm side length,
    20-55 mm thk
8   Atrium column: outer plate 1400 mm side length,
    10-40 mm thk; inner plate 850 mm side length, 25-80 mm thk
9   Atrium edge beam, 1100 x 475 mm I-section

10 Roof over skygarden
11 Beam, normally 300 x 300 mm, welded H-section
12 Shear studs
13 Column, 1000 x 475 mm, welded I-section
14 Column, 900 x 300 mm, welded I-section
15 Column, 1146 x 300 mm, welded I-section
16 Concrete, grade B 65
17 200 x 16 angle
18 150 x 150 x 10 square hollow section
19 120 x 240 rectangular hollow section
20 Link frame column, 1000 x 300 mm, welded I-section

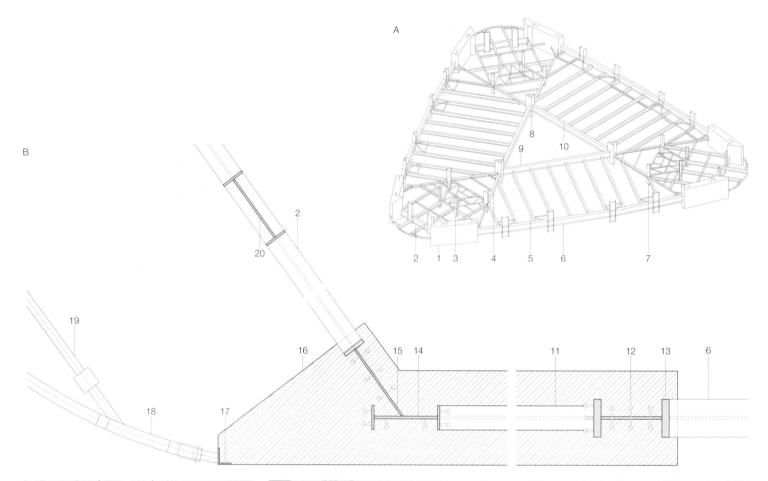

1 Vierendeel frame (or atrium beam), 1100 x 475 mm, welded I-section
2 Stiffener, 10 mm plate
3 Vertical stiffener, 60 x 370 x 10 mm
4 Horizontal stiffener, 100 x 1750 x 18 mm
5 Opening for services, 470 x 180 mm to 1050 x 320 mm or d = 250 mm
6 Edge support for composite floor slab, 80 x 25 mm
7 Shear studs

8 Vertical stiffener, 220 x 970 x 35 mm
9 Connecting plate, 138 x 590 x 30 mm, bolted
10 Megacolumn
11 Frame beam, 1000 x 475 mm, welded I-section
12 Frame column, 1000 x 475 mm, welded I-section
13 Bolted splice
14 Edge support for composite floor slab
15 Vertical stiffener
16 Welded beam splice (using plates)

17 Outer plate, 1400 x 10-40 mm
18 Inner plate, 850 x 25-80 mm
19 Concrete filling, grade B 65
20 Connecting plate, 55 mm
21 Collar plate, 80 x 10 mm
22 Floor edge beam, 350 x 184 mm, welded I-section
23 Atrium beam, 1100 x 475 mm, welded I-section
24 Connecting plate, 25 mm

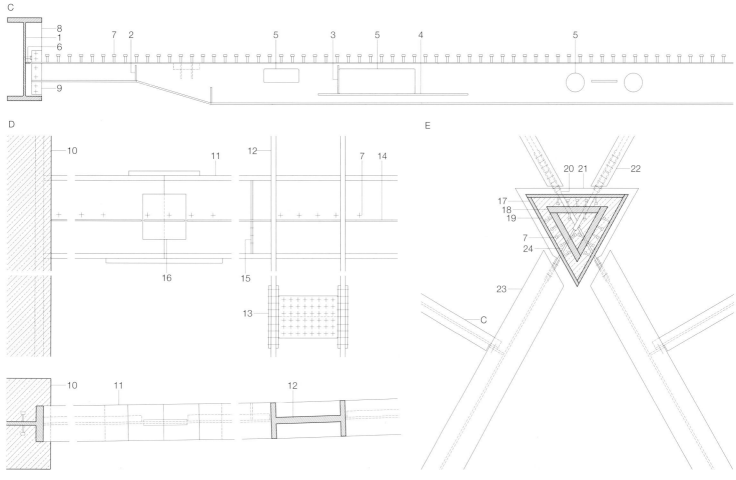

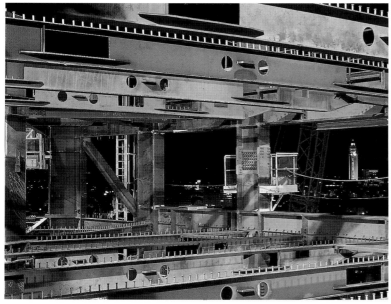

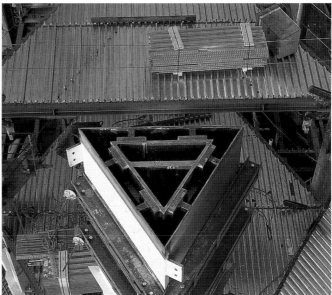

Example 54

Bank headquarters, Hong Kong

1986

Architects:
Foster and Partners, Hong Kong/London
Structural engineers:
Ove Arup & Partners, London

The structure of this 47-storey office block is exposed on the outside, thus giving the building its distinctive appearance. The ground floor serves as a public plaza from where escalators lead to a 10-storey atrium. Above this there are open-plan offices interrupted by the two-storey-high suspension trusses. Express lifts speed staff and visitors to these levels, from where escalators lead to the intermediate floors.

The primary structure of suspended structural steelwork consists of four successive construction layers. The vertical loads of the floor blocks are transferred via the suspension trusses to the external masts and the horizontal loads resulting from the suspension "neutralized" by compression members, apart from the topmost floor block. In this way, the envisaged bending moments in the masts remain small. Each mast comprises four tubular columns rigidly connected at every floor so that they act like vertical Vierendeel frames. The ratio of diameter to wall thickness of these columns varies from 1400:100 mm at ground floor to 800:25 mm at the top. Horizontal cross-bracing copes with the torsion.

The suspension trusses span 33.6 m and cantilever 10.8 m to both sides. Whereas the inner trusses incorporate an upper compression boom, this is omitted from the facades for aesthetic reasons. The suspended prefabricated service modules and escape stairs relieve the inner bay of the truss. Bracing in the transverse direction is by way of diagonals at the level of the suspension trusses and supplementary cross-bracing extending over three storeys in the atrium. The interaction of trusses and masts acting as a stiff frame provides stability in the longitudinal direction. All components were supplied prefabricated and then assembled on site.

Anti-corrosion measures consist of a 12 mm layer of a polymer-cement-sand mixture with stainless steel fibres. Fire protection is provided by a ceramic-fibre blanket on a stainless steel mesh. The loadbearing structure and the curtain walls are clad in aluminium profiles.

References: [19], [56], [114], [122], [129], [207], [260]

A

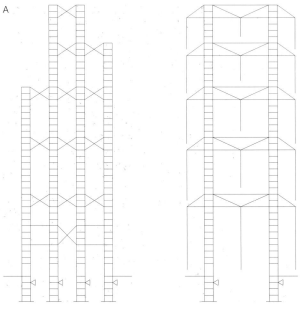
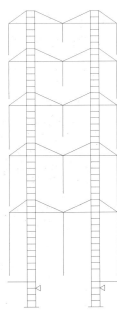

B

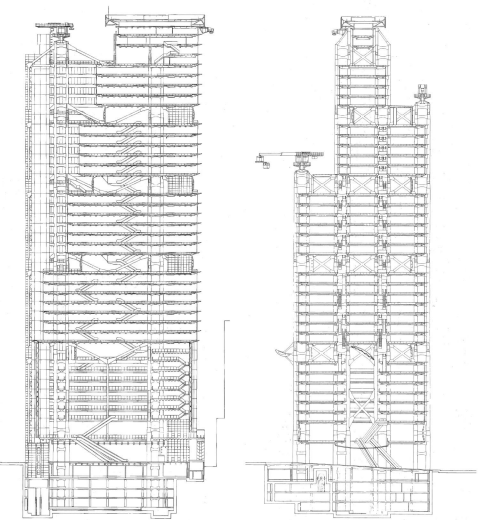

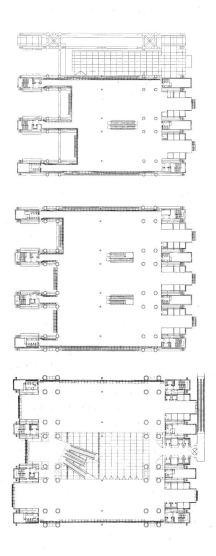

A   Structural system: transverse,
     longitudinal inside,
     longitudinal outside
B   East-west and north-south sections,
     plans of 31st-34th,
     22nd-27th and atrium floors,
     Scale 1:1500

Example 54

A Part isometric view of mast with suspension truss
B Part section through floor, scale 1:100
C Part isometric view of floor slabs
D Erecting the service modules
E Isometric view of service module

A

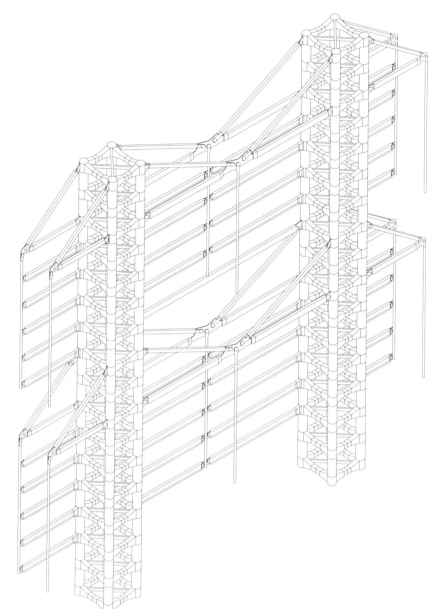

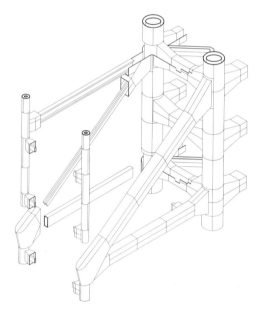

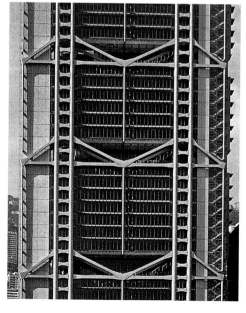

B

C

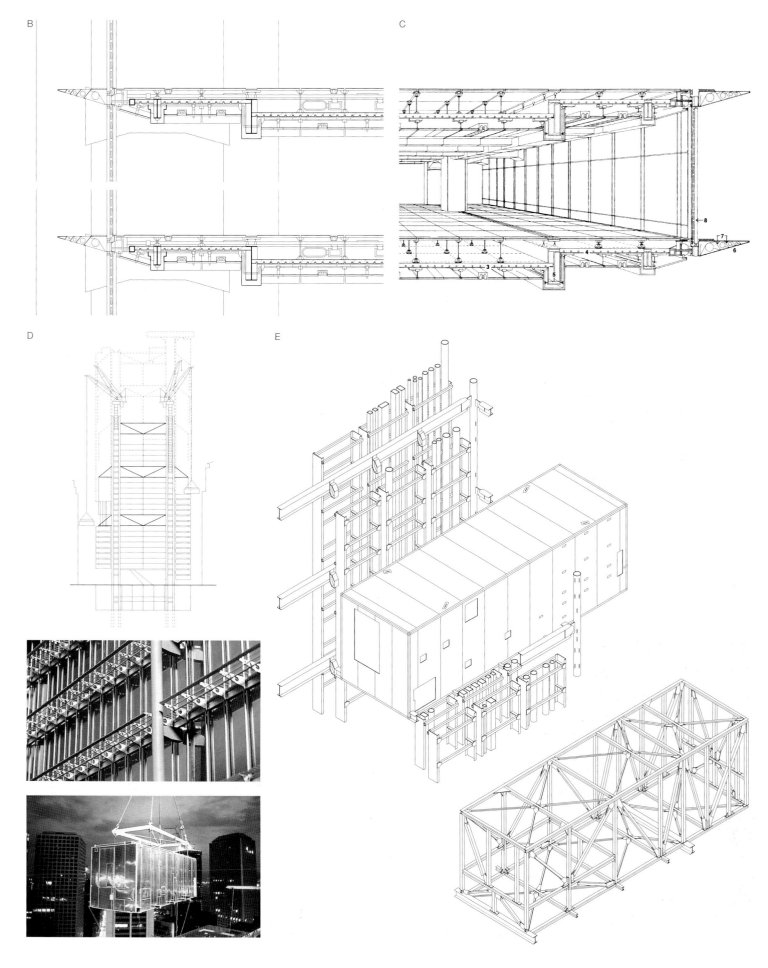

D

E

References

[1] A + U 12/1988
[2] A + U 7/1992
[3] Acier pour construire, No. 95, s/1996
[4] Acier, Stahl, Steel, 7–8 1973
[5] Ackermann, Kurt, Grundlagen für das Entwerfen und Konstruieren, Stuttgart 1983
[6] Ackermann, Kurt, Industriebau, Stuttgart 1984
[7] Ackermann, Kurt, Tragwerke in der konstruktiven Architektur, Stuttgart 1988
[8] Adams, John; Elkin, Paul, Isambard Kingdom Brunel, Norwich 1988
[9] Addis, Bill, The Art of the Structural Engineer, London 1994
[10] Adler, L., Wasmuths Lexikon der Baukunst, Berlin 1930
[11] AIT 4/1993
[12] AIT 7+8/1994
[13] Amery, Colin, Architektur, Industrie, Innovation. Nicholas Grimshaw & Partners. Bauten und Projekte, Berlin 1996
[14] Ammann, Walter; Bachmann, Hugo, Schwingungsprobleme bei Bauwerken, Structural Engineering Documents 3d, Durch Menschen und Maschinen induzierte Schwingungen, Zürich 1987
[15] Archis 4/1995
[16] Architectural Design, British Architecture, 1982
[17] Architectural Review 2/1982
[18] Architectural Review 12/1982
[19] Architectural Review 4/1986
[20] Architectural Review 7/1988
[21] Architectural Review 5/1991
[22] Architectural Review 12/1991
[23] Architectural Review 6/1992
[24] Architectural Review 8/1992
[25] Architectural Review 10/1992
[26] Architectural Review 3/1993
[27] Architectural Review 9/1993
[28] Architectural Review 11/1993
[29] Architectural Review 5/1994
[30] Architectural Review 11/1994
[31] Architectural Review 5/1995
[32] Architecture d'aujourd'hui 4/1987
[33] Architecture d'aujourd'hui 11/1988
[34] Architecture d'aujourd'hui 2/1995
[35] Architektur in Berlin: Yearbook 1992, pub. by Architektenkammer Berlin, Hamburg 1992
[36] Architektur in Hamburg, Yearbook 1994, Hamburg 1994
[37] Arup Journal Spring 1990
[38] Arup Journal Spring 1992
[39] Arup Journal Summer 1992
[40] Arup Journal Autumn 1992
[41] Australian Building, Construction and Housing, April 1990
[42] Bach, Klaus; Burkhardt, Berthold; Graefe, Rainer et al., IL 8 – Netze ... Technik, 2nd Interdisciplinary Colloquium on "Biology and Building", Institute for Lightweight Structures, Stuttgart 1975
[43] Badger, Daniel D., Badger's Illustrated Catalogue of Cast-Iron Architecture, New York 1865
[44] Barkhausen, Georg, Konstruktions-Elemente in Eisen, Darmstadt 1891
[45] Barthel, Rainer, Die Münchner Schrannenhalle, Munich 1998
[46] Barthes, Roland; Martin, André, Der Eiffelturm, Munich 1970
[47] Über den Bau eiserner Häuser, Vienna 1845
[48] Bauen in Stahl 16/1994
[49] Bauen in Stahl, pub. by Schweizer Stahlbauverband, Zürich 1956
[50] Bauen in Stahl 2, pub. by Schweizer Stahlbauverband, Zürich 1962
[51] Bauer, Manfred, Luftschiffhallen in Friedrichshafen, Friedrichshafen 1985
[52] Bauernfeind, Carl Maximilian, Vorlegeblätter zur Brückenbaukunde, Munich 1854
[53] Bauingenieur 1972
[54] Bauingenieur vol. 71, 1996

[55] Baukultur 6/1996
[56] Baumeister 11/1986
[57] Baumeister 7/1991
[58] Baumeister 8/1991
[59] Baumeister 5/1992
[60] Baumeister 6/1992
[61] Baumeister 12/1992
[62] Baumeister 11/1993
[63] Baumeister spec. issue 4/1994
[64] Baumeister 1/1995, supplement Exkursion
[65] Baumeister 12/1995
[66] Bauwelt 44/1986
[67] Bauwelt 45/1987
[68] Bauwelt 12/1989
[69] Bauwelt 11/1990
[70] Bauwelt 6/1991
[71] Bauwelt 44/1992
[72] Bauwelt 3/1994
[73] Bauwelt 23/1994
[74] Bauwelt 26/1994
[75] Bauwelt 4/1995
[76] Bauwelt 4/1996
[77] Bauwelt 3/1997
[78] Bayerisches Landesamt für Denkmalpflege (ed.), Das Kurhaustheater in Augsburg – Göggingen, Munich 1982
[79] Behfar et al., Stahl im Hochbau, Düsseldorf 1995
[80] Behne, Adolf, Architekturkritik in der Zeit und über die Zeit hinaus, Texte 1913–1946, pub. by Haila Ochs, Basel 1994
[81] Behnisch, Günter, Konstruktion und Gestalt, Stuttgart 1978
[82] Behnisch, Günter; Hartung, Giselher, Eisenkonstruktionen des 19. Jahrhunderts, Munich 1983
[83] Beitz, Wolfgang; Grote, Karl-Heinrich (ed.), Taschenbuch für den Maschinenbau, 19th fully revised edition, Berlin/Heidelberg/New York 1997
[84] Benthem + Crouwel: Architecten, Monografieen van Nederlandse architecten 7, Rotterdam 1992
[85] Berger, Manfred (ed.), Atlas Deutsche Profanbauten 1852–1912, Düsseldorf 1987
[86] Berlage, Hendrik Petrus, Über Architektur und Stil, Aufsätze und Vorträge 1894–1928, Basel 1991
[87] Betschart, Anton-Peter, Neue Gußkonstruktionen in der Architektur, Stuttgart 1985
[88] Beutler, Christian, Französische Eisenkonstruktionen des 19. Jahrhunderts, Munich 1971
[89] Bird, Anthony, Paxtons Palace, London 1976
[90] Birkmire, William H., Skeleton Construction in Buildings, New York 1907
[91] Blanc, Alan; McEvoy, Michael; Plank, Roger (eds.), Architecture and Construction in Steel, London 1992
[92] Blecken, Das deutsche Stahlhaus, Berlin 1928
[93] Bohle-Heintzenberg, Sabine, Berlins Weg vom Eisen zum Stahl – Die Anfänge des Stahlbaus in Berlin, Wiesbaden 1992
[94] Böhme, D.; Herrmann, F.-D., Handbuch der Schweißverfahren, Part 2, Düsseldorf 1992
[95] Borsi, Franco; Portogesi, Paolo, Victor Horta, Stuttgart 1991
[96] Bourrier, Pierre et al., Construire en Acier, Paris 1993
[97] Boyken, Immo, Zum Versand vorgefertigte Aussichtstürme aus Dresden, Stuttgart 1991
[98] Brandt, E., Lehrbuch der Eisenkonstruktionen, Berlin 1876
[99] Breymann, G. A., Allgemeine Baukonstruktionslehre. Die Konstruktionen in Eisen, Leipzig 1902
[100] Briggs, Asa, Iron Bridge to Crystal Palace, London 1979
[101] Brooks, Alan J., Concepts in cladding: case studies of jointing for architects and engineers, London 1985
[102] Brooks, Alan J.; Grech, Chris, Das Detail in der High-Tech-Architektur, Basel 1991
[103] Buchanan, Peter, Renzo Piano Building Workshop, Sämtliche Projekte, vol. 1, Stuttgart 1994
[104] Buchanan, Peter, Renzo Piano Building Workshop, Sämtliche Projekte, vol. 2, Stuttgart 1995

[105] Burkhardt, Berthold, Gitter und Netze, Berlin 1988
[106] Burkhardt, Berthold, Eiserne Rohrkonstruktionen im 19. Jahrhundert, Stuttgart 1991
[107] Busch, Wilhelm, F. Schupp, M. Kremmer Bergbauarchitektur 1919–1974, Cologne 1980
[108] Buschmann, Walter, Denkmalpflegerische Probleme bei der Erhaltung historischer Eisenund Stahlkonstruktionen, Stuttgart 1991
[109] Büttner, Oskar; Stenker, Horst, Metalleichtbauten, vol. 1 Ebene Raumstabwerke, Stuttgart 1971
[110] Büttner, Oskar; Stenker, Horst, Stahlhallen Entwurf und Konstruktion, Berlin 1986
[111] Calatrava, Santiago, Ingenieur – Architektur, Basel/Boston/Berlin 1990
[112] Cartier, Claudine; Jantzen, Hélène; Valentin, Marc, Noisiel, La Chocolaterie Menier Seine-et-Marne, Paris 1994
[113] Chaley, M., Pont Suspendu de Fribourg, Fribourg 1839
[114] Chaslin, François et al., Norman Foster – Beispielhafte Bauten eines spätmodernen Architekten, Stuttgart 1987
[115] Commerzbank Tower, pub. by DSD Dillinger Stahlbau GmbH 1996
[116] Condit, Carl W., American Building Art The Nineteenth Century, New York 1960
[117] Condit, Carl W., Die Tradition der Architektur in Chicago, Munich 1972
[118] Cornelius, W., Die statische Berechnung eines seilverspannten Daches (US-Pavilion Brussels 1958), Düsseldorf 1958
[119] Courtrivron + Bouchu, Abhandlung von den Eisenhammern und hohen Oefen, Berlin 1763
[120] Cruickshank, Dan, House of iron, London 1991
[121] Daly, Cesar M., Revue generale de l'Architecture et de Travaux Publics, Paris 1856
[122] Davies, Colin, High-Tech-Architecture, Stuttgart 1988
[123] Davis, Collin, British Pavilion, Seville, in: Architecture in Detail 1992
[124] Davies, Colin, Michael Hopkins and Partners, Bauten und Projekte, Berlin 1993
[125] Dengler, Anton, Der deutsche Stahlhochbau, Dortmund 1930
[126] Deswarte, Sylvie; Lemoine, Bertrand, L'architecture et les ingénieurs. Deux siècles de réalisation, Paris 1997
[127] Detail 1/1977
[128] Detail 5/1983
[129] Detail 4/1986
[130] Detail 5/1990
[131] Detail 1/1991
[132] Detail 3/1991
[133] Detail 6/1991
[134] Detail 3/1992
[135] Detail 6/1992
[136] Detail 3/1993
[137] Detail 4/1993
[138] Detail 6/1993
[139] Detail 2/1994
[140] Detail 3/1994
[141] Detail 4/1994
[142] Detail 1/1995
[143] Detail 3/1995
[144] Detail 4/1995
[145] Detail 5/1995
[146] Detail 2/1996
[147] Detail 3/1997
[148] Deutsche Bauzeitschrift 9/1988
[149] Deutsche Bauzeitschrift 3/1989
[150] Deutsche Bauzeitschrift 9/1991
[151] Deutsche Bauzeitschrift 6/1992
[152] Deutsche Bauzeitschrift 9/1992
[153] Deutsche Bauzeitschrift 8/1994
[154] Deutsche Bauzeitschrift 9/1994
[155] Deutsche Bauzeitschrift 10/1994
[156] Deutsche Bauzeitschrift 1/1995
[157] Deutsche Bauzeitschrift 5/1995
[158] Deutsche Bauzeitschrift 6/1995
[159] Deutsche Bauzeitschrift 1/1996

[160] Deutsche Bauzeitschrift 5/1996
[161] Deutsche Bauzeitung 4/1990
[162] Deutsche Bauzeitung 11/1990
[163] Deutsche Bauzeitung 5/1991
[164] Deutsche Bauzeitung 10/1992
[165] Deutsche Bauzeitung 1/1993
[166] Deutsche Bauzeitung 10/1993
[167] Deutsche Bauzeitung 2/1994
[168] Deutsche Bauzeitung 5/1994
[169] Deutsche Bauzeitung 9/1994
[170] Deutsche Bauzeitung 4/1995
[171] Deutsche Bauzeitung 7/1995
[172] Deutsche Bauzeitung 12/1995
[173] Deutsche Bauzeitung spec. issue 6/1996
[174] Deutsche Bauzeitung 12/1997
[175] Deutscher Stahlbauverband (ed.), Stahlbauten, Berlin 1929
[176] Deutscher Stahlbauverband (ed.), Denkschrift zum 25jährigen bestehen des Deutschen Stahlbau-Verbandes 1904–1929, Berlin 1929
[177] Deutscher Stahlbauverband (ed.), Berliner Stahl-hochbauten, Berlin 1936
[178] Deutscher Stahlbauverband (ed.), Deutscher Stahlbau, Berlin 1937
[179] Deutscher Stahlbauverband (ed.), Neuzeitliche Stahlhallenbauten, Berlin 1938
[180] Deutscher Stahlbauverband (ed.), Vom Werde-gang der Stahlbauwerke vol. 1, Berlin 1939
[181] Deutscher Stahlbauverband (ed.), Deutscher Stahlbau, Cologne 1953
[182] Deutscher Stahlbauverband (ed.), Stahlbauten in Berlin, Cologne 1970
[183] Dietz, Albert G.H., Large enclosures and Solar energy, London 1970
[184] Dini, Massimo, Renzo Piano, Milan 1983
[185] Downes, Charles, The Building erected in Hyde Park for the Great Exhibition of the Works of all Nations 1851, London 1852
[186] Durant, Stuart, Palais de Machines Ferdinand Dutert, London 1994
[187] Ebe, G., Entwickelung der Baukunst, Leipzig 1896
[188] Eder, G., Breitflanschige I-Träger (System Grey), Munich 1903
[189] Eekhout, Mick, Buisconstructies in de Architectuur, Delft 1996
[190] Eggen, Arne Petter; Sandaker, Bjørn Normann, Stahl in der Architektur, Stuttgart 1996
[191] Eiffel, Gustave, L'Architecture métallique, Paris 1888
[192] Eiffel, Gustave, La Tour de 300 Mètres, Paris 1900
[193] Eisenbiegler, Günter, Tragwerke transparenter Bauten unter-, ab-, überspannte Tragstrukturen, Düsseldorf 1990
[194] EL Croquis, 1994/II, 65/66: Jean Nouvel 1987–1994
[195] EL Croquis, 1996/I, 77 II: Waro Kishi 1987–1996
[196] Endell, August, Vom Sehen: Texte 1896–1925 über Architektur, Formkunst und "Die Schönheit der großen Stadt", Basel 1995
[197] Engineering News Record 11/1991
[198] Ersch + Gruber, Allgemeine Enzyklopädie der Wissenschaften und Künste, 1838
[199] Europäischer Stahlbaupreis 1995, Bauen mit Stahl No. 80, Informationszentrum Bauen mit Stahl, Düsseldorf 1995
[200] Europäisches Stahlbau-Lehrprogramm, pub. by Stahlinformationszentrum, Düsseldorf 1996
[201] Fairbairn, William, On the Application of Cast and Wrought Iron to Building Purposes, London 1854
[202] Faulwasser, J., Technik des Bauwesens, Leipzig 1896
[203] Fedorow, Sergei G., Sprengwerkdächer des Winterpalastes in St. Petersburg: 1838–1842, Stuttgart 1991
[204] Fischer, Wend, Die andere Tradition, Munich 1981
[205] Fischmann, Die Ausstellung des Stahlwerks-Verbandes in Leipzig 1913, Düsseldorf 1913

[206] Foerster, Max, Die Eisenkonstruktionen der Ingenieur-Hochbauten, Leipzig 1909
[207] Foster, Norman, Buildings and Projects of Foster Associates, vol. 3, Berlin 1989
[208] Frampton, Kenneth, Modern Architecture 1851–1919, Tokyo 1981
[209] Frampton, Kenneth, Modern Architecture 1920–1945, Tokyo 1983
[210] Fromonot, Françoise, Glenn Murcutt, Bauten und Projekte, Berlin 1994
[211] Fuchtmann, Engelbert, Stahlbrückenbau: Bogenbrücke, Balkenbrücke, Fachwerkbrücke, Hängebrücke, Munich 1996
[212] Garnham, Trevor, Oxford Museum Deane and Woodward, London 1992
[213] Gatz, Konrad; Hart, Franz, Stahlkonstruktionen im Hochbau, Munich 1966
[214] Gayle, Margot; Gillon, Edmund V., Cast-Iron Architecture in New York, New York 1974
[215] Geipel, Finn; Michelin, Nicholas, Ecole Nationale d'Art Decoratif, Limoges, Büropublikation, Paris 1994
[216] Geist, Johann Friedrich, Passagen. Ein Bautyp des 19. Jahrhunderts, Munich 1982
[217] Georg, W.; Wanderley, G., Der Metallbau, Halle 1873
[218] Gerkan, M. von, Von Gerkan, Marg und Partner 3, Architektur 1988–1991, Basel/Boston 1991
[219] Gerkan, M. von, Idea and Model, Berlin 1994
[220] Gerkan, M. von, Von Gerkan, Marg und Partner 4, Architektur 1991–1995, Basel/Boston 1995
[221] Giedion, Sigfried, Bauen in Frankreich. Bauen in Eisen. Bauen in Eisenbeton, Leipzig/Berlin 1928
[222] Glasforum 2/1990
[223] Glasforum 4/1990
[224] Glasforum 3/1991
[225] Glasforum 5/1991
[226] Glasforum 6/1991
[227] Glasforum 3/1994
[228] Glasforum 5/1995
[229] Gloag, John (Intro.), The Crystal Palace Exhibition Illustrated Catalogue London 1851, New York 1970
[230] Gottgetreu, Rudolph, Lehrbuch der Hochbaukon-struktionen, 3.Teil Eisenkonstruktionen, Berlin 1885
[231] Götz, Jürgen, Das Stahlhaus in Dessau-Törten, Wiesbaden 1997
[232] Graefe, Rainer; Gappoev, Murat; Pertschi, Ottmar, V.G. Šuchov 1853–1939. Kunst der Konstruktion, Stuttgart 1990
[233] Gregor, Alfred, Der praktische Eisenhochbau, Berlin 1930
[234] Grimshaw, Nicholas, Nicholas Grimshaw & Partners, Book 1 Product, Book 2 Process, London 1988
[235] Grimshaw, Nicholas, When structure becomes architecture, Stuttgart 1988
[236] Grube, Oswald W., Industriebauten – international, Stuttgart 1971
[237] Grüning, Michael, Der Architekt Konrad Wachs-mann, Vienna 1986
[238] Haller, Fritz, Bauen und Forschen, Dokumentation der Ausstellung im Kunstverein Solothurn, Solothurn 1988
[239] Haller, Fritz, Fritz Haller, Zürich 1992
[240] Hammerwerke von Fourchambault, Leipzig 1849
[241] Harris, James B.; Pui-K Li, Kevin, Masted Struc-tures in Architecture, Oxford 1996
[242] Harris, Joseph, The tallest tower – Eiffel and the Belle Epoque, Boston 1975
[243] Hart, Franz, Meilensteine in der Geschichte des Brückenbaus, Zürich 1979
[244] Hart, Franz; Henn, Walter; Sontag, Hansjürgen, Stahlbauatlas. Geschoßbauten, Munich 1982
[245] Hartmann, Carl, Praktisches Handbuch der Stahl-fabrikation, Weimar 1861
[246] Hartmann, Friedrich, Ästhetik im Brückenbau unter besonderer Berücksichtigung der Eisenbrücken, Leipzig/Vienna 1928
[247] Hartmann, Kristiana; Bollerey, Franziska, 200 Jahre Architektur. Bilder und Dokumente zur neueren Architekturgeschichte, Delft 1987

[248] Hauenschlild, Hans, Eisen und Stahl, Darmstadt 1883
[249] Haward, Birkin; Charles, Martin, Oxford University Museum. Its architecture and art, Oxford 1991
[250] Hawranek, Alfred, Der Stahlskelettbau, Berlin & Vienna 1931
[251] Heinzerling, F., Die Brücken der Gegenwart. Eiserne Brücken, Aachen 1880
[252] Hennig-Schefold, Monica; Schaefer, Inge, Struktur und Dekoration. Architekturtendenzen in Paris und Brüssel im späten 19. Jh., Basel 1968
[253] Hennig-Schefold, Monica; Schmidt-Thomsen, Helga, Transparenz und Masse, Cologne 1972
[254] Herzog, Max, Die Tragwirkung der Brooklyn-Brücke in New York, 1997
[255] Herzog, Thomas, Thomas Herzog – Bauten 1978–1992, Stuttgart 1992
[256] Herzog, Thomas, Design Center Linz, Stuttgart 1994
[257] Heyen, J.; Körprich, E.; Pohle, K., Fachkenntnisse Karosserie- und Fahrzeugbauer, Hamburg, Hand-werk und Technik, 1985
[258] Hitchcock, Henry-Russel, Early Victorian Architec-ture in Britain, New Haven 1954
[259] Holgate, Alan, The Art of Structural Engineering, The Work of Jörg Schlaich and his Team, Stutt-gart/London 1997
[260] Hongkong Architektur, Die Ästhetik der Dichte, Munich 1994
[261] Hütsch, Volker, Der Münchner Glaspalast 1854–1931. Geschichte und Bedeutung, Munich 1981
[262] ICOMOS, Eisen Architektur. Die Rolle des Eisens in der historischen Architektur der ersten Hälfte des 19. Jahrhunderts, Hannover 1979
[263] ICOMOS, Eisen Architektur. Die Rolle des Eisens in der historischen Architektur der ersten Hälfte des 19. Jahrhunderts, Part 2, Hannover 1979
[264] ICOMOS, Eisen Architektur. Die Rolle des Eisens in der historischen Architektur der zweiten Hälfte des 19. Jahrhunderts, Hannover 1982
[265] ICOMOS, Eisen Architektur. Die Rolle des Eisens in der historischen Architektur der zweiten Hälfte des 19. Jahrhunderts, Part 2 , Hannover 1982
[266] ICOMOS, Eisen Architektur. Die Rolle des Eisens in der historischen Architektur der ersten Hälfte des 20. Jahrhunderts, Hannover 1985
[267] Inland Architect Mar/Apr 1987
[268] Innovations in Steel, pub. by International Iron and Steel Institute, 1994
[269] Jackson, Neil, The Modern Steel House, London 1996
[270] Jahrbuch für Licht + Architektur 1993, Berlin 1994, p. 119f.
[271] Jesberg, Paulgerd, Die Geschichte der Ingenieur-baukunst aus dem Geist des Humanismus, Stuttgart 1996
[272] Jodice, Romano, l'architettura del ferro gli stati uniti 1776–1876, Rome 1988
[273] Jodice, Romano, l'architettura del ferro gli stati uniti 1893–1914, Rome 1988
[274] Jodice, Romano, l'architettura del ferro l'itatia 1796–1914, Rome 1985
[275] Joedicke, Joachim Andreas, Design einer neuen Architektur, Stuttgart 1986
[276] Johannssen, Otto, Geschichte des Eisens, Düsseldorf 1925
[277] Jones, Edgar, Industrial Architecture in Britain 1750–1939, London 1985
[278] Jordan, H.; Michel, E., Die künstlerische Gestal-tung von Eisenkonstruktionen, Berlin 1913
[279] Junghanns, Das Haus für Alle. Zur Geschichte der Vorfertigung in Deutschland, Berlin 1994
[280] Junk, C., Metallkonstruktionen des Aufbaus in Baukunde des Architekten, vol. 1, Berlin 1893
[281] Kallen, Hans, Der Werkstoff Stahl in der techni-schen Entwicklung der letzten hundert Jahre, Essen 1960
[282] Killing, R., Handbuch der Schweißverfahren, Part 1, Düsseldorf 1984

[283] Knauer, Roland, Qualitätsstahl aus dem Lehmofen, Hamburg 1995
[284] Knight, Edward H., Practical Dictionary of Mechanics, Boston/London 1876
[285] Kohlmaier, Georg Sartory von, Barna, Das Glashaus, Munich 1981
[286] Kollmann, J.; Kayser, H. et al., Eisen- und Eisenbetonbau, Stuttgart 1912
[287] König, Felix von, Das praktische Windenergie-Lexikon, 1700 Stichwörter, Karlsruhe 1982
[288] Krausse, Joachim, Buckminster Fuller und die Ephemerisierung der Architektur, Aachen 1992
[289] Krausse, Joachim, Bauen von Weltbildern: Die Dymaxion Weltkarte von Buckminster Fuller, Aachen 1993
[290] Krünitz, Johann Georg, Oeconomische Enzyklopädie, 1785
[291] Kühne, Helmut R. W., Über die Beziehung Sempers zum Baumaterial, Zürich 1974
[292] Kulka, Peter, Bauten und Projekte 1990–1995, Cologne 1996
[293] Kurrer, Karl-Eugen, Konstruktiver Ingenieurbau, Berlin 1987
[294] Lambot, Ian, Norman Foster, Berlin 1989
[295] Lampugnani, Vittorio Magnago, Renzo Piano – Bauten und Projekte, 1st ed., Stuttgart/Milan 1994/1995
[296] Landsberg, T., Die Kornhausbrücke in Bern, Berlin 1898
[297] Larson, Gerald R., Der Eisenskelettbau: Entwicklungen in Europa und den Verreinigten Staaten, Munich 1987
[298] Lemoine, Bertrand, Gustav Eiffel, Basel 1988
[299] Lemoine, Bertrand, La lumière venue des toits; toits de verre, Paris 1994
[300] Leonardo 3/1994
[301] Leonardo 2/1997
[302] Lewenton, Georg, Stahlkonstruktion und Stahlarchitektur, Munich 1966
[303] Liesenberg, O., Stahlguß- und Gußeisenlegierungen, Stuttgart 1992
[304] Linters, Adriaan, Industria Architecture industrielle en Belgique, Brussels 1986
[305] Lixante, Auguste, Der Straßen-, Eisenbahn- Canal-, Brücken-, Küstendamm-, Deich- und Hafenbau, Weimar 1851
[306] Lohse, Wolfgang; Thiele, Albrecht: Stahlbau 1, 22nd ed., Stuttgart 1993
[307] Lohse, Wolfram; Thiele, Albrecht, Stahlbau – Part 1, 23rd revised & enlarged ed., Stuttgart 1997
[308] Lohse, Wolfram; Thiele, Albrecht, Stahlbau Part 2, 18th revised & enlarged ed., Stuttgart 1997
[309] Lorenz, Werner, Die Entwicklung des Dreigelenksystems im 19. Jahrhundert, Berlin 1990
[310] Lorenz, Werner, "Architectur ist Construction" Schinkel und Borsig als Baukonstrukteure, Berlin 1994
[311] Lorenz, Werner, Konstruktion als Kunstwerk. Bauen mit Eisen in Berlin und Potsdam 1797–1850, Berlin 1995
[312] Lorenz, Werner, Galerie des machines, Munich 1996
[313] Louis, Jean; Wohlmuth, Christine, Ingenieurbaukunst in Königreich Bayern, Munich 1988
[314] Luckenbacher, Roth, Zöllner, Das Eisen und die Eisenindustrie im Buch der Erfindungen, Gewerbe und Industrien, Leipzig & Berlin 1877
[315] Mackay, Sheila, The Forth Bridge, Edinburgh 1993
[316] Makowski, Z.S., Räumliche Tragwerke aus Stahl, Düsseldorf 1963
[317] Mangiarotti, Anna, Le Techniche dell'Architettura Contemporeana, Milan 1995
[318] Marrey, Bernard, Le Fer à Paris Architectures, Paris 1989
[319] Mäurer, Eduard, Die Maß- und Gewichtsverhältnisse der Roh- und Zwischenprodukte bei der Darstellung des Schmiedeeisens, Stuttgart 1861
[320] McGrath, Raymond; Frost, A.C., Glass in Architecture and Decoration, London 1961
[321] McKean, John, Crystal Palace Joseph Paxton and Charles Fox, London 1994

[322] Melan, J.; Landsberg, T. Eiserne Bogenbrücken und Hängebrücken, Leipzig 1906
[323] Mengeringhausen, Max, Komposition im Raum, Würzburg 1962
[324] Meyer, Alfred Gotthold, Eisenbauten Ihre Geschichte und Aesthetik, Esslingen 1907
[325] Mignot, Claude, L'architecture au XIXe siècle, Fribourg 1983
[326] Modern Steel Construction in Europe, pub. by Bouwcentrum Rotterdam, Amsterdam 1963
[327] Modern Steelwork, pub. by British Steelwork Association, London 1933
[328] Moore, Rowan, Sackler Galleries, Royal Academy London, Architects Foster Associates, Blueprint Extra 04, London 1992
[329] Morel, A. (ed.), Gazette des Architectes et du Batiment, Paris 1867/1877
[330] Moritz, Felix, Schlachthöfe und Viehmärkte, Leipzig 1909
[331] Müller, F.P.; Keintzel, E., Erdbebensicherung von Hochbauten, Veröffentlichung der Forschungsgemeinschaft Bauen und Wohnen Stuttgart, Issue 112, Berlin/Munich/Düsseldorf 1978
[332] Müller, Klaus-Peter, Praktische Oberflächentechnik, Vorbehandeln, Beschichten, Prüfen, 2nd ed., Braunschweig/Wiesbaden 1996
[333] Nakamura, Toshio (ed.), Richard Rogers 1978–1988, Tokyo 1988
[334] Narjoux, Félix, Histoire d'un pont, Paris 1884
[335] Nerdinger, Winfried (ed.), Zwischen Glaspalast und Maximilianeum, Munich 1997
[336] Neue Messe Leipzig, Zentrale Eingangshalle, Firmenbroschüre Glasbau Seele, Gersthofen
[337] Notizen über den Bau gußeiserner Brücken, mit besonderer Rücksicht auf den Guß ihrer Bestandtheile, Vienna 1860
[338] Odenhausen, Helmuth, Einfamilienhäuser in Stahlbauweise, Düsseldorf 1961
[339] Ogg, Alan, Architecture in Steel: The Austalian Context, pub. by The Royal Australian Institute of Architects, 1987
[340] Oosterhoff, J. et al., Bowtechniek in Nederland Constructies van ijzeren en beton Gebouwen 1800–1940, Delft 1988
[341] Otto, Frei; Schleyer, Friedrich-Karl, Zugbeanspruchte Konstruktionen, vol. 2, Berlin 1966
[342] Otto, Frei; Barthel, Reiner; Burkhardt, Berthold et al., Natürliche Konstruktionen, Formen und Strukturen in Natur und Technik, 2nd ed., Stuttgart 1985
[343] Paul, Bruno, Stahlbau und Architektur, Berlin 1931
[344] Pawley, Martin, Buckminster Fuller, London 1990
[345] Pawley, Martin, Theory and design in the second machine age, Oxford 1990
[346] Pélissier, Alain, Reichen & Robert Transforming Space, Basel 1994
[347] Peters, Paulhans, Konstruktionsbüro Gartner, Stuttgart 1994
[348] Peters, Tom F., Building the Nineteenth Century, Cambridge, Mass. 1996
[349] Peters, Tom F., Time is Money. Die Entwicklung des modernen Bauwesens, Stuttgart 1981
[350] Petersen, Christian, Stahlbau, Grundlagen der Berechnung und baulichen Ausbildung von Stahlbauten, 3rd revised & enlarged ed. 1993, reprint with corrections 1994, Braunschweig/Wiesbaden 1993
[351] Pevsner, Nikolaus, Wegbereiter moderner Formgebung: von Morris bis Gropius, Reinbek 1957
[352] Pevsner, Nikolaus, Der Beginn der modernen Architektur und des Designs, Cologne 1971
[353] Pfammatter, Ulrich, 1795: Geburtsstunde der modernen Architekten- und Ingenieurausbildung, Zürich 1995
[354] Pfammatter, Ulrich, Die Erfindung des modernen Architekten, Basel 1997
[355] Pfitzner, C., Die Gießereihalle der ehemaligen Eisenhütte zu Sayn, 1936
[356] Piano, Renzo, Bauten und Projekte, Renzo Piano, Stuttgart 1995
[357] Picon, Antoine, L'Art de l'ingenieur, Paris 1997

[358] Piessat, Louis, Tony Garnier 1869–1948, Lyon 1988
[359] Polónyi, Stefan, Leitlinien zum Entwerfen von Stahl-Dachkonstruktionen, Cologne 1990
[360] Posener, Julius, Die Architektur und das Eisen: Labrouste, Semper, Gurlitt, Gropius, Aachen 1983
[361] Powell, Kenneth; Moore, Rowan, Nicholas Grimshaw und Partner, Bauten und Projekte, Berlin 1993
[362] Powell, Kenneth, Richard Rogers, London 1994
[363] Prechtl, Johann Joseph, Technologische Enzyklopädie, Stuttgart 1837
[364] Progressive Architecture Dec/1985
[365] Pruschka, Carl, Das Semper-Depot, Munich 1997
[366] Pudor, Heinrich, Erziehung zur Eisen-Architektur, Munich 1903
[367] Ragon, Michel, Histoire de l'architecture et de l'urbanisme modernes 1. Idéologies et pionniers 1800–1910, Paris 1986
[368] Rankine, William John Macquorn, Handbuch der Bauingenieurkunst, Vienna 1880
[369] Reconstruction du Pont des Arts, Paris 1983
[370] Rice, Peter, An Engineer Imagines, 1st ed., London/Zürich/Munich, 1994
[371] Ricken, Herbert, Der Bauingenieur Geschichte eines Berufes, Berlin 1994
[372] Rödel, Volker, Ingenieurbaukunst in Frankfurt am Main 1806–1914, Frankfurt 1983
[373] Roisecco, Giulio, l'architettura del ferro gli stati uniti 1876–1893, Rome 1982
[374] Roisecco, Giulio, l'architettura del ferro l'ingliterra 1688–1914, Rome 1972
[375] Rondelet, Jean-Baptiste, Traité théorique et pratique de l'art de bâtir, Paris 1802
[376] Rühle, Herrmann et al., Räumliche Dachtragwerke. Konstruktion und Ausführung, vol. 2, Cologne 1970
[377] Saulnier, Jules, Usine Menier à Noisiel, Paris 1877
[378] Schädlich, Christian, Das Eisen in der Architektur des 19. Jahrhunderts. Beitrag zur Geschichte eines neuen Baustoffs, Weimar 1967
[379] Schädlich, Christian, Der Baustoff Eisen als Grundlage für die Herausbildung qualitativ neuer Baukonstruktionen im 19. Jahrhundert, Stuttgart 1989
[380] Schädlich, Christian, Der eiserne Brückenbau von den Anfängen bis in die Mitte des 19. Jahrhunderts, Stuttgart 1991
[381] Schädlich, Christian, Vom Holz zum Eisen: Die Entwicklung des weitgespannten Fachwerkträgers 1820–1850, Stuttgart 1991
[382] Scharabi, M., Architekturgeschichte des 19. Jahrhunderts, Tübingen 1995
[383] Scharowsky, C., Musterbuch für Eisenkonstruktionen, Berlin 1888
[384] Scheer, Leopold, Was ist Stahl?, 14th ed., Berlin/Heidelberg/New York 1974
[385] Schild, Erich, Zwischen Glaspalast und Palais des Illusions Form und Konstruktion im 19. Jahrhundert, Berlin 1967
[386] Schittich, Christian et al., Glasbauatlas, Munich 1998
[387] Schmitt, Eduard, Markthallen, Leipzig 1909
[388] Schmitt, Eduard, Empfangsgebäude der Bahnhöfe und Bahnsteigüberdachungen, Leipzig 1911
[389] Schödter + Beumer, Stahl und Eisen, Düsseldorf 1889
[390] Schödter + Beumer, Stahl und Eisen, Düsseldorf 1895
[391] Schöler, R., Die Eisenkonstruktionen des Hochbaus, Leipzig 1901
[392] Schüler, Edmund, Neue Amerikanische Baukunst, Munich 1926
[393] Schulitz, Helmut C., Ein Haus – ein Stahlskelett – ein offenes System, Stuttgart 1976
[394] Schulitz, Helmut C., Constructa-Preis 1986, Industriearchitektur in Europa, Braunschweig 1986
[395] Schulitz, Helmut C., Industriebau – Zukunft der Tradition, Hannover 1986
[396] Schulitz, Helmut C., Constructa-Preis 1990, Industriearchitektur in Europa, Hannover 1990
[397] Schulitz, Helmut C., Wohnen in Stahl und Glas, Düsseldorf 1990

[398] Schulitz und Partner, Bauten und Projekte, Berlin 1996

[399] Schulitz, Helmut C., Die unvollendete Moderne, Berlin 1997

[400] Schulze, Konrad Werner, Der Stahlskelettbau Geschäfts- und Hochhäuser, Stuttgart 1928

[401] Schumacher, Fritz, Das bauliche Gestalten, Hamburg 1926

[402] Schupp, Fritz; Kremmer, Martin, Architekt gegen oder und Ingenieur, Berlin 1929

[403] Schwatlo, C., Eisen-Konstruktion, Berlin 1870

[404] Schwedler, Wilhelm Theodor, Theorie der Brücken-balkensysteme, Berlin 1851

[405] Schweiger-Lerchenfeld, Armand Freiherr von, Im Reiche der Cyclopen – Eine populäre Darstellung der Eisen- und Stahltechnik, Vienna 1900

[406] Schweizer Ingenieur und Architekt, No. 42, 12 Oct 1995, p. 965 V

[407] Schweizerische Zentralstelle für Stahlbau: Bauen in Stahl 12+13/1993

[408] Sealey, Antony, Bridges and Aqueducts, London 1976

[409] Sedlacek, Flachdecken in Stahlbauweise, Aachen 1994

[410] Sembach, Klaus-Jürgen, Das Jahr 1851 – Fixpunkt eines Wandels, Munich 1971

[411] Sembach, Klaus-Jürgen; Hütsch, Volker, Industrie-denkmäler des 19. Jahrhunderts im Königreich Bayern, Munich 1990

[412] Seward, H.F., Early Cast Iron in England, Charlottesville 1956

[413] SFB 230, Vom Holz zum Eisen: Weitgespannte Konstruktionen des 18. und 19. Jahrhunderts, Stuttgart 1991

[414] Simiu, Emil; Scanlan, Robert, H., Wind Effects On Structures, Fundamentals and Applications to Design, 3rd ed., New York/Chichester/Brisbane/Toronto/Singapore 1996

[415] Simmer, Konrad; Schulze, Walter E., Grundbau, 14th enlarged ed., Stuttgart 1967

[416] Simon, Harald; Thoma, Martin, Angewandte Ober-flächentechnik für metallische Werkstoffe, Eignung – Verfahren – Prüfung, 1st ed., Munich/Vienna 1985

[417] Sobek, Werner, Fazlur Khan 1930–1982 I, Munich 1998

[418] Sobek, Werner, Fazlur Khan 1930–1982 II, Munich 1998

[419] Sobek, Werner; Eckert, Anja, Trapezkunst und Wellenspiel, Stuttgart 1995

[420] Sockel, Helmut, Aerodynamik der Bauwerke, Braunschweig/Wiesbaden 1984

[421] Spiegel, Hans, Der Stahlhausbau 1. Wohnbauten aus Stahl, Leipzig 1928

[422] Spiegel, Hans, Der Stahlhausbau 2. Grundlagen zum Bauen mit Stahl, Berlin 1930

[423] Spiegel, Hans, Die Auflösung der Gebäudekon-struktion durch den Skelettbau, Berlin 1930

[424] Spur, G.; Stöferle, T., Handbuch der Fertigungs-technik, vol. 5: Fügen, Handhaben, Montieren, Munich 1986

[425] Stadelmann, Werner, Die Brooklyn-Brücke Kampf, Leiden, Triumph, Zürich 1984

[426] Stadtbauwelt 12/1989

[427] Stahl und Form, Centre Georges Pompidou, pub. by Stahl-Informations-Zentrum, Düsseldorf 1972

[428] Stahl und Form, Acht Sporthallen Entwicklung und Vergleich, Architekten Behnisch und Partner 1957–1982, pub. by Stahl-Informations-Zentrum, Düsseldorf 1984

[429] Stahl und Form, Zentrum für Produktionstechnik, pub. by Stahl-Informations-Zentrum, Düsseldorf 1986

[430] Stahl und Form, Flughafen Stuttgart, pub. by Stahl-Informations-Zentrum, Düsseldorf 1991

[431] Stahl und Form, Plenarbereich des Deutscher Bundestags, pub. by Stahl-Informations-Zentrum, Düsseldorf 1993

[432] Stahl und Form, Neue Messe Leipzig, Architekten von Gerkan, Marg + Partner, pub. by Stahl-Informations-Zentrum, Düsseldorf 1997

[433] Stahl-Informations-Zentrum, Dokumentation 532 Wohnbauten in Stahl, pp. 24-25

[434] Stahlbau 5/1969

[435] Stahlbau 4/1993

[436] Stahlbau 11/1993

[437] Stahlbau Aktuell No. 73: Bauen mit Stahl, 1992

[438] Stahlbau. Organisationen, Formeln, Vorschriften, Profile, Cologne 1998

[439] Stahlbau Arbeitshilfen für Architekten und Ingenieure, Cologne 1995

[440] Stahlbau Handbuch, vol. 1, Cologne 1982

[441] Stahlbau Handbuch, vol. 2, für Studium und Praxis, 2nd revised ed., Cologne 1985

[442] Strike, James, Construction into design. The Influence of new methods of construction on architectural design 1690-1990, Oxford 1991

[443] Strukel, M., Die Forth-Brücke bei Queensferry, Queensferry 1890

[444] Struktur Raum und Haut, N. Grimshaw und Partner, Bauten und Projekte, Berlin 1993

[445] Suckle, Abby, By their own design, New York 1980

[446] Sugden, Derek, Der Skelettbau von Arkwright bis Arup, Cologne 1986

[447] Sudgen, Derek, Ein Rückblick über tranparentes Bauen in Großbritannien, Düsseldorf 1990

[448] Sudjic, Deyan, Norman Foster, London 1986

[449] Sudjic, Deyan, Norman Foster, Richard Rogers, James Stirling. New directions in British architec-ture, London 1986

[450] Sudjic, Deyan, The architecture of Richard Rogers, London 1994

[451] Sulzer, Peter, Jean Prouvé: Meister der Metall-umformung, Cologne 1991

[452] Systemordner der Firma USM, Münsingen

[453] Taranath, Bungale S., Steel, concrete and com-posite design of tall buildings, New York 1998

[454] Technique and Aesthetics in the Design of Tall Buildings, Bethlehem, PA., USA 1986

[455] Techniques & Architecture Nov/1991

[456] Thiersch von, Friedrich, Die Eisenkonstruktion der Ausstellungs- und Festhalle zu Frankfurt am Main, Frankfurt 1909

[457] Thorne, Robert, Crystal exemplar, London 1984

[458] Thorne, Robert, The Iron Revolution Architects, Engineers and Structural Innovation 1780–1880, London 1990

[459] Trautz, Martin, Entwicklung der eisernen Fach-werkbrücken in Deutschland in der Mitte des 19. Jahrhunderts, Stuttgart 1991

[460] Valentin, Marc; Cartier, Claudine; Jantzen, Hélène, La Chocolaterie Menier, Saint-Herblain 1994

[461] Vierendeel, Esquisse d´une histoire de la tech-nique, Brussels/Paris 1921

[462] Viollet-le-Duc, E.-E. et al. (ed.), Gazette des Archi-tectes et du Batiment Encyclopédie d'Architecture, Paris 1863

[463] Viollet-le-Duc, Eugène-Emmanuel, Lectures on Architecture, London 1877

[464] Vollaard, Piet, Cepezed architecten – architects Jan Pesman & Michiel Cohen, Rotterdam 1993

[465] Wachsmann, Konrad, Bauen in unserer Zeit, Munich 1958

[466] Wachsmann, Konrad, Wendepunkt im Bauen, Wiesbaden 1959

[467] Wagner, Peter (coordinator), Hallen großer Spann-weite, Berlin 1992

[468] Wagner, Rosemarie, Die ersten Drahtkabel-brücken, Stuttgart 1991

[469] Waissenberger, Robert, Beispiele früher Ingenieurbauten in Wien – Eisenkonstruktionen, Vienna 1975

[470] Waite, John G., Iron Architecture in New York City – Two Studies in Industrial Archeology, New York 1972

[471] Walker, Derek, Architecture of Glasgow, London 1987

[472] Wangenheim, Ernst, Der Bessemerprozeß zur einfachsten und billigsten Erzeugung von Guß-stahl, Weimar 1863

[473] Wegele, H.; Eggert, H., Die Hauptbahnhofs-anlagen in Frankfurt a.M. und das Empfangs-gebäude des Hauptbahnhofs, Berlin 1892

[474] Weitgespannte Flächentragwerke, 2nd Inter-national Symposium, Stuttgart 1979, Proceedings 2, Stuttgart 1979

[475] Wendehorst, Reinhard; Achten, Hubert, Bautechnische Zahlentafeln, mit 245 Beispielen, 27th revised & enlarged ed., Stuttgart/Cologne 1996

[476] Werk, Bauen + Wohnen 4/1990

[477] Werk, Bauen + Wohnen 5/1991

[478] Werk, Bauen + Wohnen 6/1992

[479] Werk, Bauen + Wohnen 7/1992

[480] Werk, Bauen + Wohnen 12/1992

[481] Werk, Bauen + Wohnen 6/1993

[482] Werk, Bauen + Wohnen 7/1993

[483] Werk, Bauen + Wohnen 11/1993

[484] Werk, Bauen + Wohnen 3/1997

[485] Wiedemann, Johannes, Leichtbau, vol. 2, Elemente, 1st ed., Berlin/Heidelberg/New York/Tokyo 1986

[486] Wiedemann, Johannes, Leichtbau, vol. 1, Konstruktion, 1st ed., Berlin/Heidelberg/New York/Tokyo 1989

[487] Zuranski, Jerzy Antoni, Windeinflüsse auf Bau-konstruktionen, 2nd enlarged & revised ed., Cologne-Braunsfeld 1978

Directives and standards for structural steelwork

The following pages contain the designations and titles of directives and standards relevant to structural steelwork. DIN publications can be obtained from Beuth-Verlag, Burggrafenstr. 6, 10787 Berlin; DASt directives from Stahlbau-Verlagsgesellschaft mbH, Postfach 100945, 50449 Cologne; railway directives from Bundesbahn-direktion Karlsruhe, Drucksachenzentrale der Deutschen Bundesbahn, Stuttgarter Str. 61a, 76137 Karlsruhe, foreign directives and standards from Deutscher Normenausschuss, Auslandsarchiv, Burggrafenstr. 4-7, 10787 Berlin, tel. +49 30 2601-231.

I. Materials standards

DIN 1627	Hot-finished structural hollow sections for structural steelwork Pt 1: General requirements, properties (St37-2, St44-2, St52-3) Pt 2: Square and rectangular sections Pt 3: Circular sections
DIN 1681	Cast steels for general engineering purposes, technical delivery conditions (Jun 1985)
DIN 1691	Flake graphite cast iron (grey cast iron), properties (May 1985)
DIN 17111	Low-carbon unalloyed steels for bolts, nuts and rivets, technical delivery conditions
DIN 17172	Steel pipes for long-distance pipelines for combustible liquids and gases
DIN 17173	Seamless steel tubes made from steels with low-temperature toughness, technical delivery conditions
DIN 17174	Welded circular tubes made from steels with low-temperature toughness, technical delivery conditions
DIN 17175	Seamless tubes of heat-resistant steels, technical delivery conditions
DIN 17177	Electric pressure-welded steel tubes for elevated temperatures
DIN 17182	General purpose steel castings with enhanced weldability and higher toughness
DIN 17210	Case-hardening steels, technical delivery conditions
DIN 17243	Forgings and hot-rolled or forged bars of weldable steels for elevated temperatures, technical delivery conditions
DIN 17445	Corrosion-resistant steel castings
DIN 17455	Welded circular stainless steel tubes with general quality requirements, technical delivery conditions
DIN 17456	Seamless circular stainless steel tubes with general quality requirements, technical delivery conditions
DIN 17457	Welded circular austenitic stainless steel tubes subject to special requirements
DIN 17458	Seamless circular austenitic stainless steel tubes subject to special requirements
DIN 17465	Heat-resisting steel castings, technical delivery conditions
DIN 50125	Test pieces for the tensile testing of metallic materials
DIN 50190	Hardness depth of heat-treated parts
DIN 50601	Metallographic examination, determination of the ferric or austenitic grain size of steel and ferrous materials
DIN 50900	Corrosion of metals, terminology Pt 1: General concepts Pt 2: Electrochemical terms Pt 3: Corrosion testing
DIN EN 895	Destructive tests on welds in metallic materials, transverse tensile test
DIN EN 910	Destructive tests on welds in metallic materials, bend tests

DIN EN 1043	Destructive tests on welds in metallic materials, hardness testing Pt 1: Hardness test on arc-welded joints Pt 2: Microhardness testing on welded joints
DIN EN 10002	Tensile testing of metallic materials
DIN EN 10021	General technical delivery requirements for steel and iron products (Oct 1993)
DIN EN 10025	Hot-rolled products of non-alloy structural steels, technical delivery conditions (Mar 1994)
DIN EN 10027	Designation systems for steels (Sept 1992) Pt 1: Steel names and principal symbols Pt 2: Numerical system
DIN EN 10028	Flat products made from steel for pressure purposes Pt 1: General requirements Pt 2: Non-alloy and alloy steels with specified elevated temperature properties Pt 3: Weldable fine-grain steels, normalized Pt 4: Nickel-alloyed steels with specified low-temperature properties Pt 5: Weldable fine-grain steels, thermomechanically rolled Pt 6: Weldable fine-grain steels, quenched and tempered Pt 7: Stainless steels
DIN EN 10045	Charpy impact test on metallic materials
DIN EN 10083	Quenched and tempered steels Pt 1: Technical delivery conditions Pt 2: Technical delivery conditions for unalloyed quality steels Pt 3: Technical delivery conditions for boron steels
DIN EN 10113	Hot-rolled products in weldable fine-grain steels (Apr 1993) Pt 1: General delivery conditions Pt 2: Delivery conditions for normalized and normalized-rolled steels Pt 3: Delivery conditions for thermomechanically rolled steels
DIN EN 10204	Metallic products, types of inspection documents (Aug 1994)
DIN EN 10210	Hot-finished structural hollow sections of non-alloy and fine-grain structural steels
DIN EN 10219	Cold-formed welded structural hollow sections of non-alloy and fine-grain structural steels
DIN EN 22063	Metallic and other inorganic coatings, thermal spraying, zinc, aluminium and their alloys
DASt-Ri.007	Weathering structural steels (May 1993)
DASt-Ri.009	Recommendations for the selection of steel grade groups for welded structural steelwork (under review)
DASt-Ri.014	Recommendations for the avoidance of lamellar tearing in welded structural steelwork (Jan 1981)
SEW 410	Stainless cast steel, quality regulations
SEW 510	Heat-treatable steel casting for forgings with wall thickness up to 100 mm
SEW 515	Heat-treatable steel casting for forgings with wall thickness more than 100 mm
SEW 685	Low-temperature cast steel

II. General standards for the design and construction of steel structures

DIN 824	Technical drawings, folding to filing size (Mar 1981)
DIN 1080	Terms, symbols and units used in civil engineering Pt 1: Principles (Jun 1976) Pt 2: Statics (Mar 1980) Pt 3: Concrete construction and reinforced concrete construction, prestressed concrete construction, masonry construction (Mar 1980) Pt 4: Concrete construction, composite steel construction and steel girders in concrete (Mar 1980) Pt 5: Timber construction (Mar 1980) Pt 6: Soil mechanics and foundation engineering (Mar 1980) Pt 7: Water engineering (Mar 1979) Pt 9: Railway construction (Feb 1981)
DIN 1353	Pt 2: Abbreviations of denominations for half-finished products (Apr 1971)
DIN 1356	Building and civil engineering drawings (Oct 1988)
DIN 2310	Thermal cutting (Nov. 1987) Pt 1: Terminology and nomenclature Pt 2: Determination of quality of cut faces Pt 3: Oxygen cutting, process principles, quality dimensional tolerances
DIN 6771	Pt 1: Title blocks for drawings, plans and lists (Dec 1970)
DIN 8563	Quality assurance of welded structures
DIN 8567	Pretreatment of metallic surfaces for thermal spraying
DIN 8580	Manufacturing methods, classification
DIN 8582	Manufacturing processes, forming, classification, subdivision, alphabetical index
DIN 8583	Manufacturing processes, forming under compressive conditions Pt 1: Classification, subdivision, definitions Pt 2: Rolling, subdivision, definitions Pt 3: Free-forming, subdivision, definitions Pt 4: Die-forming, subdivision, definitions Pt 5: Indentation-forming, subdivision, definitions Pt 6: Manufacturing processes, forming by forcing through an orifice (extrusion), subdivision, definitions
DIN 8584	Manufacturing processes, forming under combination of tensile and compressive conditions Pt 1: Classification, subdivision, definitions Pt 2: Drawing through constricted tool orifices, subdivision, definitions Pt 3: Deep-drawing, subdivision, definitions Pt 4: Spinning, subdivision, definitions Pt 5: Forming by raising, definition Pt 6: Upset-bulging, definition
DIN 8585	Manufacturing processes, forming under tensile conditions Pt 1: Classification, subdivision, definitions Pt 2: Manufacturing processes, tensile-shaping, stretch-reducing, subdivision, definitions Pt 3: Manufacturing processes, tensile-shaping, bulge-forming, subdivision, definitions Pt 4: Manufacturing processes, tensile-shaping, stretch-forming, subdivision, definitions
DIN 8586	Manufacturing processes, forming by bending, classification, subdivision, definitions
DIN 8587	Manufacturing processes, forming under shearing conditions, classification, subdivision, definitions
DIN 8588	Manufacturing production processes, severing, classification, subdivision, definitions

DIN 8589   Pt 0: Manufacturing processes, cutting, classification, subdivision, definitions
Pt 1: Manufacturing processes by chip removal, turning, classification, subdivision, definitions
Pt 2: Manufacturing processes by chip removal, drilling, countersinking and counterboring, reaming, classification, subdivision, definitions
Pt 3: Manufacturing processes by chip removal, milling, classification, subdivision, definitions
Pt 4: Manufacturing processes by chip removal, planing, shaping, classification, subdivision, definitions
Pt 5: Manufacturing processes by chip removal, broaching, classification, subdivision, definitions
Pt 6: Manufacturing processes by chip removal, sawing, classification, subdivision, definitions
Pt 7: Manufacturing processes by chip removal, filing, rasping, classification, subdivision, definitions
Pt 8: Manufacturing processes by chip removal, machining with brush-like tools, classification, subdivision, definitions
Pt 9: Manufacturing processes by chip removal, scraping, chiselling, classification, subdivision, definitions

DIN 17162   Flat steel products, hot-dip zinc-coated strip and sheet of mild alloyed steels, technical delivery conditions

DIN 18335   Contract procedures for building works; Pt C: Steel construction works (Sept 1988)

DIN 18364   Contract procedures for building works; Pt C: Corrosion protection of steel and aluminium structures (Sept 1988)

DIN 18800   Pt 1: Steel structures, design and construction (Mar 1981)

DIN 18800   Structural steelwork
Pt 1: Design and construction (Nov 1990)
Pt 2: Analysis of safety against buckling of linear members and frames (Nov 1990)
Pt 3: Analysis of safety against buckling of plates (Nov 1990)
Pt 4: Analysis of safety against buckling of shells (Nov 1990)
Pt 7: Steel structures, fabrication, verification of suitability for welding (May 1983)

DIN 50902   Coatings for corrosion protection of metals, vocabulary, processes and surface preparation (Jul 1994)

DIN 50959   Electrodeposited coatings, corrosive resistance of electrodeposited coatings on iron and steel under different climatic conditions

DIN 50960   Electroplated and chemical coatings

DIN 50976   Corrosion protection, hot-dip batch galvanizing, requirements and testing (May 1989)

DIN 54150   Non-destructive testing, impression methods for surface examination (Replica technique)

DIN 55928   Corrosion protection of steel structures by the application of organic or metallic coatings
Pt 1: General (May 1991)
Pt 2: Designing for the prevention of corrosion (May 1991)
Pt 3: Planning of corrosion protective work (May 1991)
Pt 4: Preparation and testing of surfaces (May 1991)
Pt 5: Coating materials and protective systems (May 1991)
Pt 6: Execution and inspection of corrosion protection work (May 1991)
Pt 7: Reference areas (May 1991)
Pt 8: Protection of thin-walled building components from corrosion (Jul 1994)

DIN ISO 5261   Technical drawings, simplified representation of bars and profile sections (1981)

DIN ISO 6410   Pt 1-3: Technical drawings, screw threads and threaded parts (May 1993)

DIN ISO 6433   Technical drawings, item references (Sept 1982)

DASt-Ri.006   Build-up welding of finish coatings in structural steelwork (Jan 1980)

DASt-Ri 012   Buckling analysis for plates (Oct 1978)[1]

DASt-Ri 013   Buckling analysis for shells (Jul 1980)[1]
[1] Only for use in conjunction with DIN 18800 Pt 1 (Mar 1981)

DASt-Ri 015   Beams with slender webs (1990)

DASt-Ri 016   Design and detailing of loadbearing structures of thin-walled cold-formed components (1992)

DASt-Ri 017   Draft buckling analysis for shells, special cases (1992)
Guidelines for the design and construction of composite steel beams (Mar 1981)

III. Standards for buildings and cranes

DIN 1055   Design loads for buildings
Pt 1: Stored materials, building materials and structural members, dead load and angle of friction (Jul 1978)
Pt 2: Soil characteristics, specific weight, angle of friction, cohesion, angle of wall friction (Feb 1976)
Pt 3: Live loads (Jun 1971)
Pt 4: Imposed loads, wind loads on buildings not susceptible to vibration (Aug 1986)
Pt 5: Live loads, snow load and ice load (Jun 1975)
Pt 6: Loads in silo bins (May 1987)

DIN 4102   Fire behaviour of building materials and building components
Pt 1: Building materials, concepts, requirements and tests (May 1981)
Pt 2: Building components, definitions, requirements and tests (Sept 1977)
Pt 3: Fire walls and non-loadbearing external walls, definitions, requirements and tests (Sept 1977)
Pt 4: Synopsis and application of classified building materials, components and special components (Mar 1994)

DIN 4108   Pt 1-5: Thermal insulation in buildings (Pt 1-3 and 5: Aug 1981; Pt 4: Nov 1991)

DIN 4109   Sound insulation in buildings (Nov 1989); Supp. 1 (Nov 1989)

DIN 4112   Temporary structures, code of practice for design and construction (Feb 1983)

DIN 4113   Pt 1: Aluminium constructions under predominantly static loading, static analysis and structural design (May 1980)

DIN 4118   Head frames and winding towers for mines, design loads, calculation principles and design principles (Jun 1981)

DIN 4119   Above-ground cylindrical flat-bottomed tank installations of metallic materials
Pt 1: Fundamentals, design, tests (Jun 1979)
Pt 2: Calculation (Feb 1980)

DIN 4131   Steel radio towers and masts (Nov 1991)

DIN 4132   Craneways, steel structures, principles for calculation, design and construction (Feb 1981)

DIN 4133   Steel stacks (Nov 1991)

DIN 4149   Pt 1: Buildings in German earthquake zones, design loads, dimensioning, design and construction of conventional buildings (Apr 1981)

DIN 4172   Modular coordination in building construction (Jul 1955)

DIN 4420   Service and working scaffolds (Dec 1990)
Pt 1: General rules, safety requirements, tests
Pt 2: Ladder scaffolds, safety requirements

DIN 15018   Cranes, steel structures (Nov 1984)
Pt 1: Verification and analysis
Pt 2: Principles of design and construction

DIN 15019   Pt 1: Cranes, stability for all cranes except non-rail-mounted mobile cranes and except floating cranes (Sept 1979)

DIN 15020   Lifting appliances, principles relating to rope drives
Pt 1: Calculation and construction (Feb 1974)
Pt 2: Supervision during operation (Apr 1974)

DIN 18230   Structural fire protection in industrial buildings (see section on structural fire protection) Pt 1: Analytically required fire-resistance time (draft: Sept 1987)
Supp. to DIN V 18230: Combustion factors (Nov 1989)
Pt 2: Determination of the combustion factor (Sept 1987)

DIN 18801   Structural steel in building, design and construction (Sept 1983)

DIN 18806   Pt 1: Composite steel and concrete structures, composite columns (Mar 1984)

DIN 18807   Trapezoidal sheeting in building, trapezoidal steel sheeting (Jun 1987)
Pt 1: General requirements and determination of loadbearing capacity by calculation
Pt 2: General requirements and determination of loadbearing capacity by testing
Pt 3: Structural analysis and design

DIN 18808   Steel structures, structures made from hollow sections subjected to predominantly static loading (Oct 1984)

DIN 19700   Pt 10: Dam plants, general specifications (Jan 1986)
Pt 13: Dam plants, weirs (Jan 1986)

DIN 19702   Stability of solid structures in water engineering (Oct 1992)

DIN 19704   Hydraulic steel structures, criteria for design and calculation (Sept 1976)

DIN 19705   Hydraulic steel structures, recommendations for design, construction and erection (Sept 1976)

IV. Standards for road bridges

DIN 1072   Road bridges and footbridges, design loads (Dec 1985)

DIN 1076   Engineering structures connected with roads and tracks, observation and inspection (Mar 1983)

DIN 18809   Steel road bridges and footbridges, design and construction (Sept 1987)

V. Railway directives

DS 804   Directive for railway bridges and other engineering works (VEI) (Jun 1993)

DS 805   Existing railway bridges, evaluation of structural safety and constructional advice (Mar 1991)

DS 80002   Directive for the design of railway facilities, new routes (Jul 1991)

Technical supply conditions No. 91802: Structural steels for general use, cold-rolled sections and cold-finished welded hollow sections (Oct 1984)

Technical supply conditions No. 918164: Steel masts for overhead power lines and 110 kV power lines (Sept 1968)

Technical supply conditions No. 918300 sht 85: For coating materials with alkali-silicate substrate (Jan 1990)

VI. Standards for rolled products

DIN 536   Crane rails
Pt 1: Dimensions, sectional properties, steel grades for crane rails with flat foot flange, form A (Sept 1991)
Pt 2: Type F (flat), dimensions, static values, steel grades (Dec 1974)

DIN 997   Tracing dimensions for bars and rolled steel sections (Oct 1970)

DIN 998   Hole pitches in unequal angle steels (Oct 1970)

DIN 999   Hole pitches in equal angle steels (Oct 1970)

DIN 1013   Steel bars (Nov 1976)
Pt 1: Hot-rolled round steel for general purposes, dimensions, permissible variations for dimensions and form
Pt 2: Hot-rolled round steel for special purposes, dimensions, permissible variations for dimensions and form

DIN 1017   Steel bars
Pt 1: Hot-rolled flat steel for general purposes, dimensions, weights, permissible variations (Apr 1967)
Pt 2: Hot-rolled flat steel for special purposes (in bar-drawing mills, bolt and screw factories, etc.), dimensions, weights, permissible variations (Mar 1964)

DIN 1018   Steel bars, hot-rolled half-round steel and half-oval steel, dimensions, weights, permissible variations (Oct 1963)

DIN 1022   Steel bars, hot-rolled equal angle squared-edge steel (LS steel), dimensions, weights, permissible variations (Oct 1963)

DIN 1024   Steel bars, hot-rolled round-edged T-bars, dimensions, weights, permissible deviations, static values (Mar 1982)

DIN 1025   Hot-rolled I-beams
Pt 1: Narrow-flange I-beams, I-series, dimensions, masses, sectional properties (Oct 1963)
Pt 2: Wide-flange I-beams, IPB series, dimensions, masses, sectional properties (Mar 1994)
Pt 5: Medium-flange I-beams, IPE series, dimensions, masses, sectional properties (Mar 1994)

DIN 1026   Round-edge channels (Oct 1963)
DIN 1026   I-Stahl (Ausgabe 10.63.)
DIN 1027   Steel bars, hot-rolled round-edge zeds, dimensions, weights, permissible variations, static values (Oct 1963)

DIN 1028   Hot-rolled equal-leg angles with round edges, dimensions, masses, sectional properties (Mar 1994)

DIN 1029   Hot-rolled unequal-leg angles with round edges, dimensions, masses, sectional properties (Mar 1994)

DIN 1544   Flat steel products, cold-rolled steel strip, dimensions, permissible variations for dimensions and form (Aug 1975)

DIN 1626   Welded circular unalloyed steel tubes subject to special requirements, technical delivery conditions (Oct 1984)

DIN 1628   High-performance welded circular unalloyed steel tubes, technical delivery conditions (Oct 1984)

DIN 1629   Seamless circular unalloyed steel tubes subject to special requirements, technical delivery conditions (Oct 1984)

DIN 1630   High-performance seamless circular unalloyed steel tubes, technical delivery conditions (Oct 1984)

DIN 2448   Seamless steel pipes and tubes, dimensions, conventional masses per unit length (Feb 1981)

DIN 2458   Welded steel pipes and tubes, dimensions, conventional masses per unit length (Feb 1981)

DIN 17121   Seamless circular steel tubes for structural steelwork, technical delivery conditions (Jun 1984)

DIN 59 051   Steel bars, hot-rolled sharp-edged T-bars, dimensions, weights, permissible deviations (Aug 1981)

DIN 59200   Flat steel products, hot-rolled wide flats, dimensions, permissible deviations on dimensions, form and weight (Oct 1975)

DIN EN 10130   Cold-rolled steel flat products for cold-forming, technical delivery conditions (Oct 1991)

DIN EN 10210   Pt 2: Hot-finished structural hollow sections of non-alloy and fine-grain structural steels, tolerances, dimensions and sectional properties (1996)

DIN EN 10219   Pt 2: Cold-formed welded structural hollow sections of non-alloy and fine-grain structural steels, tolerances, dimensions and sectional properties (1996)

VII. Standards for fasteners

DIN 101   Rivets, technical specifications (May 1993)
DIN 124   Steel round-head rivets with nominal diameters from 10 to 36 mm (May 1993)
DIN 267   Fasteners, technical delivery conditions
Pt 1: General requirements
Pt 2: Design and dimensional accuracy (Nov 1984)

DIN 302   Countersunk-head rivets, nominal diameters from 10 to 36 mm (May 1993)

DIN 1732   Filler metals for welding aluminium and aluminium alloys

DIN 1733   Filler metals for welding copper and copper alloys

DIN 1736   Welding filler metals for welding nickel and nickel alloys

DIN 1910   Welding
Pt 1: Concepts, classification of welding processes (Jul 1983)
Pt 2: Welding of metals, processes (Aug 1977)
Pt 4: Terminology associated with gas-shielded arc welding processes (Apr 1991)
Pt 5: Welding of metals, resistance welding, classification of processes (Dec 1986)

DIN 1912   Graphical representation of welded, soldered and brazed joints
Pt 1: Definitions and terms for welding joints, edges and welds (Jun 1976)
Pt 2: Working positions, slope rotation (Sept 1977)

DIN 1913   Pt 1: Covered electrodes for the joint welding of unalloyed and low-alloy steel, classification, designation, technical delivery conditions (Jun 1984) (Supp. May 1991)

DIN 6914   High-strength hexagon-head bolts with large widths across flats for structural steel bolting (Oct 1989)

DIN 6915   High-strength hexagonal nuts with large widths across flats for structural steel bolting (Oct 1989)

DIN 6916   Round washers for high-strength structural steel bolting (Oct 1989)

DIN 6917   Square taper washers for high-strength structural steel bolting of steel I-sections (Oct 1989)

DIN 6918   Square taper washers for high-strength structural steel bolting of steel channel sections (Apr 1990)

DIN 7513   Thread-cutting screws, hexagonal screws and slotted-head screws, dimensions, requirements, testing

DIN 7968   Hexagon-fit bolts for structural steel bolting for supply with or without nut (Oct 1989)

DIN 7969   Slotted countersunk-head screws for structural steel bolting for supply with or without nut (Oct 1989)

DIN 7989   Plain washers (Jul 1974)
DIN 7990   Hexagon-head bolts for structural steel bolting for supply with nut (Oct 1989)

DIN 7999   High-strength hexagon-fit bolts with large widths across flats for structural steel bolting (Dec 1983)

DIN 8522   Production processes of autogenous engineering, survey

DIN 8524   Defects in metallic welded joints
DIN 8528.   Pt 1: Weldability, metallic materials, definitions (Jun 1973)

DIN 8551   Pt 4: Edge preparation for welding, edge forms on steel, submerged arc welding (Nov 1976)

DIN 8558   Pt 1: Directions for welded assemblies for boilers, vessels and piping in unalloyed and alloy steels, examples of fabrication (May 1967) (Supp. Dec 1987)

DIN 8562   Welding of vessels, vessels of metallic materials, principles for welding (Jan 1975)

DIN 50121   Testing of metallic materials; technological bending test on welded joints and weld platings; fusion-welded platings

DIN 53281   Testing of metallic materials, technological bending test on welded joints and weld platings, fusion-welded platings

DIN 53281   Testing of adhesives for metals and adhesively bonded metal joints, test specimens
Pt 1: Surface preparation (draft: Mar 1978)
Pt 2: Manufacturing

DIN 53282   Testing of adhesives for metals and adhesively bonded metal joints, T-peel test

DIN 53284   Testing of adhesives for metals and adhesively bonded metal joints, creep test on single-lap joints

DIN 53286   Testing of adhesives for metals and adhesively bonded metal joints, conditions for testing at different temperatures

DIN 53287   Testing of adhesives for metals and adhesively bonded metal joints, determination of the resistance to liquids

DIN 53288   Testing of adhesives for metals and adhesively bonded metal joints, tensile test

DIN 53 290– DIN 53 297   Testing of sandwiches

DIN 65118   Aerospace, welded metallic component parts
Pt 1: Indications on drawings
Pt 2: Directives for design
Pt 3: Acceptance test for jigs and auxiliary equipment for fusion welding, accuracy of guiding and movement

DIN EN 760   Powder for submerged welding
DIN EN 439   Welding consumables, shielding gases for arc welding and cutting

DIN EN 440   Welding consumables, wire electrodes and deposits for gas-shielded metal-arc welding of non-alloy and fine-grain steels, classification

DIN EN 719   Welding coordination, tasks and responsibilities

DIN EN 756   Welding consumables, wire electrodes and wire-flux combinations for submerged arc welding of non-alloy and fine-grain steels, classification

DIN EN 758   Welding consumables, tubular cored electrodes for metal-arc welding with and without a gas shield of non-alloy and fine-grain steels, classification

DIN EN 759   Welding consumables, technical delivery conditions for welding filler metals, type of product, dimensions, tolerances and marking

DIN EN 895   Destructive tests on welds in metallic materials, transverse tensile test

DIN EN 910   Destructive tests on welds in metallic materials, bend tests

DIN EN 1599 Welding consumables, covered electrodes for manual metal-arc welding of
creep-resisting steels, classification

DIN EN 1600 Welding consumables, covered electrodes for manual metal-arc welding of
stainless and heat-resisting steels, classification

DIN EN 1668 Welding consumables, rods, wires and
deposits for tungsten inert-gas welding of
non-alloy and fine-grain steels, classification

DIN ISO
8992   Fasteners, general requirements for bolts,
screws, studs and nuts

EN 1464   Adhesives, determination of peel resistance of high-strength adhesive bonds,
floating roller method

EN 1465   Adhesives, determination of tensile lap-
shear strength of rigid-to-rigid bonded
assemblies

VIII. Euronorms

19 IPE beams, I-beams with parallel flange facings
(Apr 1957)
24 Normal I-beams, U-beams, permissible deviations
(May 1962)
44 Hot-rolled medium-broad-flanged I-beams, IPE
series, permissible deviations (Sept 1963)
53 Hot-rolled broad-flanged I-beams with parallel flange
facings (Jul 1962)
54 Hot-rolled small U-beams (May 1980)
55 Hot-rolled round-edge equal angle T-beams
(May 1980)
56 Hot-rolled round-edge equal angle steel (May 1977)
57 Hot-rolled round-edge unequal angle steel
(May 1978)
58 Hot-rolled flat steel for general use (Nov 1978)
59 Hot-rolled square steel for general use (Nov 1978)
60 Hot-rolled round steel for general use (May 1977)

Eurocode series

The following Eurocodes for structural engineering applications are currently being drafted. Each Eurocode
usually consists of several parts.

EN 1991
Eurocode 1 Basis of design and actions on structures
EN 1992
Eurocode 2 Design of concrete structures
EN 1993
Eurocode 3 Design of steel structures
EN 1994
Eurocode 4 Design of composite steel and concrete
structures
EN 1995
Eurocode 5 Design of timber structures
EN 1996
Eurocode 6 Design of masonry structures
EN 1997
Eurocode 7 Geotechnical design
EN 1998
Eurocode 8 Design provisions for earthquake resistance
of structures
Furthermore, the series may be supplemented by:
EN 1999
Eurocode 9 Design of aluminium structures

National Application Documents (NAD):
Guidelines on the application of Eurocode 1 (Jun 1995)
DASt-Ri.103 Guidelines on the application of Eurocode
3 (Nov 1993)
DASt-Ri.104 Guidelines on the application of Eurocode
4 (Feb 1994)
Guidelines on the application of Eurocode 5 (Feb 1995)

Belgium

NBNB 51-001 Charpentes en acier (1977) Calcul par
la méthode des contraintes admissibles
(5ème édition)
NBNB 03-001 Principes généraux de détermination
de la sécurité et de l'aptitude au service
des structures 2e éd., décembre 1988
NBNB 51-002 Charpentes en acier. Calcul par la
méthode des états-limites le éd.,
août 1988
NBN 1.01   Conditions générales applicables aux
charpentes métalliques (1ère édition
1968)
NBN 1.50   Charpentes en alliage d'aluminium
(1968)
NBN B 52001 Ponts métalliques (4ème édition. 1969)
in preparation
NBN E 52-001 Engins de levage - Disposition géné-
rales (1974)
NBN E 52-002 Engins de levage Sollicitations et com-
binaisons de sollicitations (1980)
NBN E 52-003 Engins de levage - Charpente
métallique (1 éd.) (avec erratum).
NBN E 52-004 Engins de levage - Equipement méca-
nique (1 éd.)(avec erratum).
NBN E 52.004. 1 Addendum à NBN E 52-004 (1980).
NBN E 52-005 Engins de levage - Equipements
électriques (1977)
NBN E 52-006 Engins de levage - Stabilité (1997)
NBN E 52-006. 1 Addendum à NBN E 52-006.
NBN E 52-006. 2 Addendum2 à NBN E 52-006.
NBN E 52-007 Engins de levage- Exigences construc-
tives en rapport avec al sécurité (1974)
NBN E 52-008 Engins de levage - Documents, mise en
service, exploitation et entretien (1974)
NBN E 52-009 Gestes de commandement pour engins
de levage (1 éd.)
NBN E 52-010 Engins de levage - Appareillage de limi-
tation automatique (3 éd.)
NBN E 52-010Q Addendum à NBN E 52-010 (1982).
NBN E 27-071 Boulons à haute résistance, à larges
surplats, pour constructions en acier.
Conception et calcul des assemblages,
1e éd., avril 1987
NBN E 27-072 Boulons à haute résistance, à larges
surplats, pour constructions enacier.
Exécution des assemblages, 1e éd.,
juin 1987
NBN E 27-073 Boulons à haute résistance, à larges
surplats, pour constructions enacier.
Réception-Livraison, 1e éd., novembre
1988

France

Uniform Technical Regulations (Documents Techniques
Unifiés - DTU)

DTU P 22-701 Règles de calcul des constructions en
acier, encore appelés »règles CM66«
(déc. 1966) Règles de calcul des constructions en acier, additif 80 (mars 1981)
DTU P 06-002 Règles définissant les effets de la neige
et du vent sur constructions et annexes
(nov. 1965, révisées 1967, 1970, 1974,
1975 et. 1976, 1994)
DTU P 06-006 Règles N 84 - modifier 95, Actions de
la neige sur les constructions (1996)
P 92-702   Règles de calcul. Méthode de prévision
par le calcul du comportement au feu
des structures en acier et annexe
(Méthodologie de caractérisation de
produits de protection (1993)
DTU P 22-703 Règles de calcul des constructions ou
éléments à parois minces en acier
(déc. 1978)
DTU 40.35   Couvertures en plaques nervurées issues
de tôle d'acier galvanisés prelaqués ou
de tôles d'acier gravanisés. CSTB. (1983)

DTU P 22-201 Construction métallique -Charpente en
acier (1964) DTU 32.1
DTU P 92-704 Règles FPM 88 - Méthodes de prévision
par le calcul du comportement au feu
des poteaux mixtes (acier + béton)
(1988)

Standards

NF P 22-202-1 Travaux de bâtiments - Construction
métallique - charpentes en alliages
d'aluminium - Partie 1; cahier des
clauses techniques (1993).
NF P 22-202-2 Traveaux de bâtiments - Marchés privés
- Construction métallique - Charpentes
en alliages d'aluminium - Partie 2;
cahier des clauses spéciales (1993)
NE P 22-250 Assemblages soudés de profils creux
circulaires avec découpes d'intersection - Conception et vérification des
assemblages (1978).
NF P 22-251 Assemblages spudés de profils creux
circulaires avec découpes d'intersection - Dispositions constructives (1978).
NF P 22-252 Assemblages soudés de profils creux
circulaires avec découpes d'intersection - Compléments aux normes NF P
22-250/251 (1978).
NF P 22-255 Assemblages soudés de profils creux,
ronds ou rectangulaires sur profils de
types 1 et H - Conception et vérification
(1979).
NF P 22-258 Assemblages soudés de profils creux
sur profils creux rectangulaires soumis
à un chargement statique - Conception
et vérification (1982)
P 22-311   Eurocode 3 »Calcul de structures en
acier« et Document d'Application Nationale - Partie 1.1; Règles générales et
règles pour les bâtiments (1992).
NF PO6-013   Règles de constructions parasismique
décembre 1995 Règles P5 applicables
aux bâtiments, dites Règles PS92
NFP 84.206-1 Travaux de bâtiment. Mise en oeuvre
des toitures en toles d'acier
DTU 43.3   Nervuvées avec revêtement
d'etancheité - Partie 1; cahier des
clauses juin 1995 techniques
NF P 84-206.2 Travaux de bâtiments
DTU 43.3
Partie 2; Cahier des clauses speciales
Juin 1995
P 22-391
Eurocode 4   Conception et dimensionnement des structures mixtes acier-béton« et Document
d'Application Nationale; Partie 1.1; Règles
générales et règles pour les bâtiments (1994).
NF P 22-410 Assemblages rivés - Dispositions constructives - Calcul des rivets (1982)
NF P 22-411 Assemblages rivés - Exécution des
assemblages (1978)
NF P 22-430 Assemblages par boulons non précon-
traints - Disposition constructives et calculs
des boulons (1982)
NF P 22-431 Assemblages par boulons non précon-
traints - Exécution des assemblages (1978)
NF P 22-460 Assemblages par boulons à serrage con-
trôlé - Dispositions constructives et vérification des assemblages(1979)
NF P 22-461 Assemblages par boulons à serrage con-
trôlé - Détermination du coefficient conven-
tionnel de frottement (1979)
NF P 22-462 Assemblages par boulons à serrage con-
trôlé - Usinage et préparation des
pièces (1978)
NF P 22-463 Assemblages par boulons à serrage con-
trôlé - Exécution des assemblages (1978)
NF P 22-464 Assemblages par boulons à serrage con-
trôlé - Programme de pose des boulons
(1991)

NF P 22-466 Assemblages par boulons à serrage con-
trôlé - Méthodes de serrage et de contrôle
de boulons (1979)

NF P 22-468 Assemblages par boulons à serrage con-
trôlé - Serrage par rotation contrôlée de
l'ecrou - Détermination de l'angle de rotation (1987)

NF P 22-469 Assemblages par boulons à serrage con-
trôlé - Etalonnage des clés dynamo-
métriques (1978)

NF P 22-470 Assemblages spudés. Dispositions constructives et justification des soudures (1989)

NF P 22-471 Assemblages soudés - Fabrication (1984)

NF P 22-472 Consruction métallique - Assemblages soudés - Qualification des modes opératoires
de soudage (1994)

NF P 22-473 Assemblages soudés - Etendue des con-
trôles non destructifs (1986)

NF P 22-615 Poutres de roulement de ponts roulants -
Déformation en service et tolérances (1978)

P 22-630 Silos en acier - Calcul des actions dans les
cellules (1992)

NF P 22-800 Préparation des pièces en atelier (1981)

P 22-810 Ouvrages d'art - Tolérances dimension-
nelles (1994)

P 22-474 Assemblages soudés - Guide de choix de
la classe de qualité

NF P 06-014 Règles de Construction parasismique. Construction parasimique des maisons individu-
elles et des bâtiments assimiles. Règles PS-
Mi 89 reviséas 1992 - Domaine d'applica-
tion-conception - Exécution.c

Recommendations

Planchers mixtes acier-béton (CTICM, Construction
métallique, no. 3, 1965).

Calcul et exécution des chemins de roulement de ponts
roulants (CTICM, Construction Métallique, no. 3, 1967;
no.4, 1970 et no.1, 1973.)

Calcul des âmes de poutres (CTICM, Construction
Mètallique, no.1 et no.3, 1969).

United Kingdom

DD ENV 1993;
Eurocode 3 Design of steel structures.
DD ENV
1993-1-1; General rules and rules for buildings
(together with United Kingdom National
Application Document)

DD ENV 1994;
Eurocode 4 Design of composite steel and concrete
structures.

DD ENV
1994-1-1; 1994; General rules and rules for buildings
(together with United Kingdom National
Application Document)

CP3; Code of basic data for the design of buildings Chapter V Part 2; 1972; Wind loads.
(replaced by BS 6399; Part 2; 1995, but
remains current so as to allow an overlap
period)

BS 4 Part 1;1993; Structural steel sections.
Specification for hot-rolled sections

BS 449; Specification for the use of structural steel
in building. Part 2; 1969; Metric units

BS 499; Welding terms and symbols Part 1; 1991;
Glossary for welding, brazing and thermal
cutting

BS 709;
1983; Methods of destructive testing fusion
welded joints and weld metal in steel

BS 729;
1986 (1994); Specification for hot dip galvanized
coatings on iron and steel articles

BS 3692;
1967 (Obsolescent) Specification for ISO metric
precision hexagon bolts, screws and nuts.
Metric units

BS 4165;
1984; Specification for electrode wires and fluxes
for the submerged are welding of carbon
steel and medium-tensile steel

BS 4190;
1967; (Obsolescent) Specification for ISO metric
black hexagon bolts, screws and nuts

BS 4360; Specification for weldable structural steels.
(Withdrawn, replaced by BS 7613);
1994, BS 7668; 1994, BS EN 10029; 1991, Parts 1-3 of
BS EN 10113; 1993, BS EN 10137; 1996, BS EN 10155;
1993 and BS EN 10210-1; 1994)

BS 4395; Specification for high strength friction grip
bolts and associated nuts and washers for
structural engineering.
Part 1; 1969 General grade
Part 2; 1969 Higher grade bolts and nuts
and general grade washers

BS 4604; Specification for the use of high strength
friction grip bolts in structural steelwork.
Metric series.
Part 1; 1970; General grade
Part 2; 1970 Higher grade (parallel shank)

BS 4848; Hot rolled structural steel sections.
Part 2; 1991; Specification for hot finished
hollow sections
Part 4; 1972 (1986); Equal and unequal
angles
Part 5; 1980; Bulb flats

BS 4872; Specification for approval testing of welders
when welding procedure approval is not
required. Part 1; 1982 (1995); Fusion welding of steel

BS 5135;
1984; Specification for arc welding of carbon and
carbon manganese steels

BS 5400; Steel concrete and composite bridges.
Part 1; 1988; General statement
Part 2; 1978; Specification for loads
Part 3; 1982; Code of practice for design of
steel bridges
Part 5; 1979; Code of practice for design of
composite bridges
Part 6; 1980; Specification for materials and
workmanship, steel
Part 9; 1983; Bridge bearings
Part 10; 1980; Code of practice for fatigue.

BS 5493; 1977; Code of practice for protective
coating of iron and steel structures against
corrosion

BS 5531;
1988; Code of practice for safety in erecting structural frames

BS 5950; Structural use of steelwork in building
Part 1; 1990; Code of practice for design in
simple and continuous construction; hot
rolled sections
Part 2; 1992; Specification for materials,
fabrication and erection; hot rolled sections
Part 3; Section 3.1; 1990; Design of simple
and continuous composite beams
Part 4; 1994; Code of practice for design of
floors with profiled steel sheeting
Part 5; 1987; Code of practice for design of
cold-formed sections
Part 6; 1995; Code of practice for design of
light gauge profiled steel sheeting
Part 7; 1992; Specification for materials and
workmanship; cold formed sections
Part 8; 1990; Code of practice for fire
resistant design
Part 9; 1994; Code of practice for stressed
skin design

BS 6363
1983; Welded cold formed steel structural sections

BS 6399; Loading for buildings
Part 1; 1996; Code of practice for dead and
imposed loads
Part 2; 1895; Code of practice for wind loads
Part 3; 1988; Code of practice for imposed
roof loads

BS 8202; Coatings for fire protection of building elements
Part 1; 1985; Code of practice for the
selection and installation of sprayed mineral
coatings
Part 2; 1992; Code of practice for the use of
intumenscent coating systems to metallic
substrates for providing fire resistance

BS EN 287; Approval testing of welders for fusion
welding.

BS EN 287-1; 1992;
Steels

BS EN 288; Specification and approval of welding procedures for metallic materials

BS EN 288-3; 1992;
Welding procedures specification for arc
welding

BS EN 729; Quality requirements for welding. Fusion
welding of metallic materials

BS EN 729-1; 1995;
Guidelines for selection and use

BS EN 729-2; 1995;
Comprehensive quality requirements

BS EN 729-3; 1995;
Standard quality requirements

BS EN 729-4; 1995;
Elementary quality requirements

BS EN 10024; 1995;
Hot rolled taper flange I sections -
Tolerances on shape and dimensions

BS EN 10025; 1993;
Hot-rolled products for non-alloy structural
steels - Technical delivery conditions

BS EN 10034; 1993;
Structural steel I and H sections -
Tolerances on shape and dimensions.

BS EN 10113;
Hot-rolled products in weldable fine grain
structural steels

BS EN 10113-1; 1993;
General delivery conditions

BS EN 10113-2; 1993;
Delivery conditions for normalized/
normalized rolled steels

BS EN 10113-3; 1993;
Delivery conditions for thermomechanical
rolled steels

BS EN 10155; 1993;
Structural steels with improved atmospheric
corrosion resistance. Technical delivery
conditions

BS EN 10163;
Specification for delivery requirements for
surface conditions of hot rolled steel plates,
wide flats and sections

BS EN 10163-1; 1991;
General requirements

BS EN 10163-2; 1991;
Plates and wide flats

BS EN 10163-3; 1991;
Sections

BS EN 10210-1; 1994;
Hot finished structural hollow sections of
non-alloy and fine grain structural steels.
Technical delivery requirements.

BS EN 24014; 1992;
Hexagon head bolts -
Product grades A and B

BS EN 24016; 1992;
Hexagon head bolts -
Product grade C

BS EN 24017; 1992;
Hexagon head screws -
Product grades A and B

BS EN 24018; 1992;
Hexagon head screws -
Product grade C

BS EN 24032; 1992;
Hexagon nuts, style 1 -
Products grades A and B

BS EN 24033; 1992;
Hexagon nuts, style 2 -
Products grade A and B
BS EN 24034; 1992;
Hexagon nuts - Product grade C
BS EN ISO 9000;
Quality management and quality
assurance standards (See also BS 5750)
BS EN ISO 9001; 1994;
Quality systems. Model for quality
assurance in design, development, pro-
duction, installation and servicing.
BS EN ISO 9002; 1994;
Quality systems. Model for quality
assurance in production, installation and
servicing.
BS EN ISO 9003; 1994;
Quality systems. Model for quality assu-
rance in final inspection and test.
BS EN ISO 9004;
Quality management and quality assu-
rance standards (See also BS 5750)
BS EN ISO 9004-1; 1994;
Guidelines

Netherlands

NEN-ENV 109-1 Het vervaardigen van staalconstructies
Deel 1; Algemene regels en regels voor
gebouwen (1997)
NVN-ENV 109-3 Vervaardigen van staalconstrucies
Deel 3; Aanvullende regels voor staal-
soorten met een hoge treksterkte (1997)
NEN 2008   Voorschriften voor het vervaardigen van
stalen bruggen VVSB 1977 (1;1979)
NEN 6072   Rekenkundige bepaling van de brand-
werendheid van bouwdelen Staalconstructies (1991/A 1;1997)
NEN 6770   TGB 1990 Staalconstructies Basiseisen
en basis rekenregels voor overwegend
statisch belaste constructies (1997)
NEN 6771   TGB 1990 Staalconstructies Stabiliteit
(1991/A 1;1997)
NEN 6772   Staalconstructies TGB 1990 Verbindin-
gen (1991/A 1;1997)
NEN 6773   Technische grondslagen voor bouw-
constructies TGB 1990
Staalconstructies Basiseisen, rekenregels en beproevingen voor overwegend statisch belaste dunwandige
koudgevormde stalen profielen en
geprofileerde platen (1997 Ontw.)
NEN 6774   Technische grondslagen voor bouw-
constructies TB 1990
Staalconstructies Eisen voor de staal-
soorten volgens NEN-EN 100215 en
NEN-EN 10113 in relatie tot het brosse-
breukgedrag, voor overwegend statisch
belaste constructies (1996 Ontw.)
NEN 6786   Voorschriften voor het ontwerpen van
beweegbare bruggen - VOBB -. (1995
Ontw.)
NEN 6788   Het ontwerpen van stalen bruggen
Basiseisen en eenvoudige rekenregels
VOSB 1995
NVN-ENV 1991-1
Eurocode 1   Ontwerpgrondslagen en belastingen op
constructies
Deel 1; Ontwerpgrondslagen (1995)
NVN-ENV 1991-2-1
Eurocode 1   Ontwerpsgrondslagen en belastingen op
constructies
Deel 2-1; Belastingen op constructies
Dichtheden, eigengewicht en opger-
legde belastingen (1995)
NVN-ENV 1991-2-2
Eurocode 1   Ontwerpgrondslagen en belastingen op
constructies
Deel 2-2; Belastingen op aan brand
bloodgestelde constructies (1995)

NVN-ENV 1991-2-3
Eurocode 1   Ontwerpgrondslagen en belastingen op
constructies
Deel 2-3; Sneeuwbelastingen (1995)
NVN-ENV 1991-2-4
Eurocode 1   Ontwerpgrondlagen en belastingen op
constructies
Deel 2-4; Belastingen op constructies
Windbelastingen (1995)
NVN-EV 1991-2-5
Eurocode 1   Ontwerpgrondslagen en belastingen op
constructies
Deel 2-5; Thermische belastingen (1997)
NVN-ENV 1991-2-6
Eurocode 1   Ontwerpgrondslagen en belastingen op
constructies
Deel 2-6; Belastingen op constructies
Belastingen in de bouwfase (1997)
NVN-ENV 1991-3
Eurocode 1   Ontwerpgrondslagen en belastingen op
constructies
Deel 3; Verkeersbelastingen op bruggen
(1995)
NVN-ENV 1991-4
Eurocode 1   Ontwerpgrondslagen en belastingen op
constructies
Deel 4; Belastingen in silo's en opslag-
tanks (1995)
NVN-ENV 1993-1-1
Eurocode 3   Ontwerp en berekening van staal-
constructies
Deel 1-1; Algemene regels en regels
voor gebouwen (1995/A 1; 1995)
NVN-ENV 1993-1-1-NAD Richtlijnen voor het gebruik van
NVN-ENV 1993-1-1 Eurocode 3 Ontwerp en berekening
van staalconstructies
Deel 1-1; Algemene regels en regels
voor bebouwen NAD STAAL (1995)
NVN-ENV 1993-1-2
Eurocode 3   Ontwerp en berekening van staal-
constructies
Deel 1-2; Algemene regels
Constructieve brandveiligheid (1995)
NVN-EN 1993-1-3
Eurocode 3   Ontwerp en berekening van
staalcostructies
Deel 1-3; Algemene regels
Aanvullende regels voor koudgevormde
dunwandige profielen en platen (1996)
NVN-ENV 1993-1-4
Eurocode 3   Ontwerp en berekening van staal-
constructies
Deel 1-4; Algemene regels
Aanvullende regels voor corrosievaste
staalsorten (1997)
NVN-ENV 1994-1-1
Eurocode 4   Ontwerp en berekening van staal beton-
constructies
Deel 1-1; Algemene regels en regels
voor gebouwen (1995)
NVN-ENV 1994-1-1 NAD Richtlijnen voor het gebruik van
NVN-ENV 1994-1-1
Eurocode 4   Ontwerp en berekening van staal-beton-
constructies
Deel 1-1; Algemene regels en regels
voor gebouwen NAD STAAL-BETON
(1995)
NVN-ENV 1994-1-2
Eurocode 4   Ontwerp en berekening van staal-beton-
constructies, Deel 1-2; Algemene regels
Constructieve brandbeveiliging
(1995/C1;1997)
NVN-ENV 1994-1-2
NVN-ENV 1994-2
Eurocode 4;   Ontwero en berekening van staal-beton-
constructies
Deel 2; Staal-betonbruggen (1997 Ontw.)
(C1 = eerste correctieblad, A1 = eerste
aanvullinsblad)

Italy

CNR-10011/86 »Costruzioni di acciaio. Istruzioni per il
calcolo, l'esecuzione, il collaudo e la
manutenzione« (n. 164, 1992)
CNR-10012/85 »Istruzioni per la valutazione delle;
Azioni sulle costruzioni«
(n. 117-27 maggio 1986)
CNR-10016/85 »Travi composte di acciaio e calcestruz-
zo. Istruzioni per l'impiego nelle costruzioni« (4.1985)
CNR-10021/85 »Strutture di acciaio per apparecchi di
sollevamento. Isruzioni per il calcolo,
l'esecuzione, il collaudo e la manutenzione« (n. 127-18 maggio 1988)
CNR-10022/84 »Profili formati e freddo. Istruzioni per
l'impiego nelle costruzioni« (n. 126-3
maggio 1988)
CNR 10026/85 »Piattaforme di lavoro elevabili. Istruzioni
per il calcolo e la manutenzione«
(n. 115-23 aprile 1986)
CNR-10027/85 »Strutture di acciaio per opere prov-
visionali. Istruzioni per il calcolo, l'esecuzione, il collaudo e la manutenzione« (n.
116-26 aprile 1986)
CNR-10028/85 »Strutture in leghe di alluminio per appa-
rechi di sollevamento, Istruzioni per il calcolo, l'esecuzione, il collaudo e la manutenzione« (4.1986)
CNR-10030/87 »Anime irrigidite di travi e parete piena«
(n. 163, 1992)
CNR-10029/87 »Costruzione di acciaio ad elevata resi-
stenza. Istruzioni per il calcolo, l'esecuzione, il collaudo e la manutenzione
(n° 162, 1992)
CNR-10018/87 »Apparecchi d'apoggio in comma e
PTFE nelle costruzioni. Istruzioni per il
calcolo e l'impiego (n° 161/1992)
CNR-10024/86 »Analisi di strutture mediante elaborato-
re; impostazione e redazione delle rela-
zioni di calcolo« (n° 160, 1992)

Austria

ÖNORM No.
A 6230   Technical drawings for steel construction
(Dec 1987)
B 3800   Behaviour of building materials and
components in fire
Pt 1: Building materials; requirements and
tests (draft: Dec 1988)
Pt 2: Components; definitions, require-
ments, tests (Mar 1997)
Pt 3: Special components; definitions,
requirements, tests (Dec 1995)
Pt 4: Components; assignment to the
classes of fire resistance (Mar 1990)
B 4001   Design loads in building; general basic
data for calculation in building construction
(Oct 1981)
B 4002   Highway bridges; general rules for con-
struction
B 4003   Bridges for railroads and trams; general
principles for design and construction
B 4004   Cranes and runways
Pt 1: Calculation of structures; general prin-
ciples (Apr 1985)
Pt 2: Calculation of stability (May 1985)
Pt 3: Wind forces (May 1981)
Pt 4: Calculation of structures of runways;
fatigue proof; loading conditions and group
classification (Dec 1985)
B 4007   Scaffolds; general requirements; use, type
and loading (Jul 1988)
B 4010   Design loads in building; dead loads of
building materials and components
(May 1982)
B 4011   Design loads in building; stored materials
Pt 1: Load effect and angle of internal
friction of bulk materials as well as pressure
of liquids (May 1982)

Pt 2: Load effect of stacked materials (May 1982)

Pt 3: Load effect of filling material in silos (May 1987)

B 4012 Design loads in building; variable actions; imposed loads (Apr 1997)

B 4013 Design loads in building; snow and ice loads (Dec 1983)

B 4014 Design loads on structures
Pt 1: Static wind loads (non-sway loads) (May 1993)
Pt 2: Dynamic wind loads (sway structures) (Apr 1994)

B 4015 Pt 1: Design loads in building; accidental actions; seismic actions; general principles (Oct 1997)

B 4016 Design loads in building; accidental actions; horizontal impacts from vehicles (Nov 1988)

B 4020 Units preferred in structural engineering (Mar 1979)

B 4300 Steel structures
Pt 1: Design and construction; limit states (Mar 1994)
Pt 2: Buckling of bars and skeletal structures (Apr 1994)
Pt 3: Buckling of plates (Apr 1994)
Pt 5: Fatigue strength (Apr 1994)
Pt 7: Workmanship (Apr 1994)

B 4303 Steel structures; railway bridges (Mar 1994)

B 4500 Composite structures of steel and concrete
Pt 1: Dimension and identification letters, key to equations (Aug 1972)
Pt 2: Design and construction of loadbearing structures (May 1974)

B 4502 Composite structures of steel and concrete; road bridges; design and construction (May 1981)

B 4600 Steel structures
Pt 2: Design and calculation (Aug 1978)
Pt 3: Calculation of fatigue strength (Jun 1979)
Pt 4: Calculation of stability; basic problems (Oct 1978)
Pt 7: Specifications for erection and workmanship (Aug 1975)
Pt 11: Bolted connections (Jun 1982)

B 4601 Steel structures; loadbearing structures for buildings; calculation and execution (Nov 1969)

B 4602 Steel constructions; road bridges (Aug 1975)

B 4604 Steel constructions; structures of cranes (Jan 1974)
Pt 1: Calculation and workmanship
Pt 2: Requirements for welded joints

B 4605 Steel structures; towers; analysis, erection and workmanship (Jul 1984)

B 4650 Steel structures
Pt 1: Tables for the calculation of stability (Jun 1979)
Pt 3: 2nd order theory (Dec 1976)
Pt 4: Buckling of circular cylindrical shells (Nov 1977)
Pt 5: Buckling of circular cylindrical shells with gradually varying thickness (Aug 1980)
Pt 7: Buckling of spherical shells (Dec 1980)

B 8110 Pt 1: Thermal protection in building construction; requirements for the thermal insulation and reference method (Jun 1998)

B 8115 Sound insulation and room acoustics in building construction
Pt 1: Concepts and units (Oct 1998)
Pt 2: Requirements for sound insulation (Oct 1998)
Pt 3: Architectural acoustics (Apr 1996)

C 2125 Pt 1: Above-ground cylindrical flat-bottom tanks of metallic materials; basic rules, constructions, tests (Nov 1992)

Pt 2: Above-ground cylindrical flat-bottom tanks of metallic materials; design (Nov 1992)

Pt 3: Above-ground vertical tanks made of metallic materials; single-walled, with flat bottom and fixed roof (Apr 1985)

C 2540 Protection of iron materials against corrosion; by thermal spraying of zinc or aluminium (Dec 1981)

E 4015 Hot-dip zinc coating of structural parts fabricated from steel and other ferrous materials (Oct 1982)

M 7800 Symbols for welded joints; fusion welding (Apr 1981)
Amendment 1: Symbols for welded joints; structural steelwork; fusion welding (Nov 1981)

M 7805 Staff for welding; classification and requirements (Aug 1993)

M 7812 Quality assurance of welding (Jan 1996)
Pt 1: Requirements for plants, performing welding operations according to quality classes
Pt 2: Quality classes

M 7813 Welder's certificate (Jan 1978)

The German standard DIN 55928 is valid as the Austrian standard for the corrosion protection of steel structures.

Directives and information sheets published by Österreichischer Stahlverband.

Austrian standards and directives can be obtained from Österreichischer Stahlverband, Eschenbachgasse 9/3, 1010 Vienna, tel. +43 1 585 2774, fax +43 1 585 2865.

DIRECTIVE for determining the extent of anti-corrosive treatments, 2nd ed., Dec 1984

DIRECTIVE for the production, recording and checking of structural calculations, 1st ed., Jul 1982

DIRECTIVE for the quality assessment of the strength properties of cold-rolled sections and hollow sections whose work-hardening is exploited when designing a section, 1st ed., 1975

DIRECTIVE for the calculation and execution of light-weight steel structures, 2nd ed., 1984

DIRECTIVE for determining the permissible stresses of non-standard steels, 2nd ed., May 1981

MEMO for the execution of connections with HSFG bolts, 3rd ed., Jul 1976; partly superseded by ÖNORM B 4600 Pt 11 (see above)

DIRECTIVE for the use of abrasion-resistant paints for the contact faces of HSFG and HVP connections, 1st ed., Aug 1976

DIRECTIVE for the forming and calculation of profiled steel sheet floors with and without composite action, 1st ed., Jan 1980

DIRECTIVE for the design of aluminium constructions, 2nd ed., June 1980

DIRECTIVE for corrosion protection by means of coatings (paints), 4th ed., Sept 1991

DIRECTIVE for corrosion protection by means of hot-dip galvanizing, 4th ed., Jul 1987

DIRECTIVE for the production and checking of drawings for steelwork, 1st ed., Jul 1984

DIRECTIVE for composite construction in buildings, 2nd ed., Sept 1988

MEMO for the introduction of CAD/CAM, 1st ed., Aug 1988

DIRECTIVE for the calculation of steel constructions subject to fatigue, 1st ed., Nov 1988

DIRECTIVE for verifying the fire resistance of steel constructions by way of calculation, 1st ed., Dec 1989

RECOMMENDATIONS for the fracture-mechanics evaluation of faults in constructions made from metallic materials, 2nd ed., Jun 1992

DIRECTIVE for the calculation and execution of loadbearing structures of rustproof, austenitic steels, 1st ed., Oct 1991.

DIRECTIVE for verifying the fire resistance of composite floors, 1st ed., May 1993

DIRECTIVE for building biology and building ecology in steel buildings, 1st ed., Apr 1995

DIRECTIVE for sound insulation in steel buildings, 1st ed., Apr 1996

MEMO for determining stress values of steel grades S 460 and S 420, to ÖNORM ENV 1993-1-1/A, 1st ed., Dec 1996

Switzerland

Norm SIA 118 General conditions for building works (1977/1991)

Norm SIA 160 Actions on loadbearing structures (1989)

Norm SIA 161 Steel structures; communication; principles for project management and execution, calculation, design and verification, design of components, materials, manufacture and assembly, duties of specialists involved (1990)

Norm SIA 161/1 Steel structures; quality management, company IDs, tests, materials (1990/1995)

Norm SIA 230 Steel structures; performance and supply (1979)

Publications of the Technical Committee of the Schweizerische Zentralstelle für Stahlbau.

- Structural steelwork tables (1997)
- Construction details for structural steelwork
  Design rules for structural steelwork, catalogue of types (1996)
- Design tables for structural steelwork (1995)
- Composite beams in buildings
  Theoretical basis, examples, design tables (1982) with supplement (1993)
- Steelwork in practice 1 (1983)
  End-plate connections with high-strength bolts
  Beam junctions with double angles
  Non-stiffened beam supports
- Fire resistance of steel components
  Classification by means of calculation (SIA 82, 1985)
- Fire resistance of steel components (summary, 1991)
- Composite columns of square and rectangular hollow sections (1993)
- Surface protection of steel constructions (1990/1993)
- Steel buildings, weights (1965)
- Guidelines for the fixing of profiled steel sheeting (1993)
- Building with steel for everyman (introduction to steelwork, 1988)
- Steelwork drawings – guidelines for structural steelwork drawings (1996)
- Fire-resistant steel and concrete composite loadbearing structures (1997)
- Model apprenticeship for steelwork draughtsmen – programme and content of training scheme (1995)

Index of names

Picture credits

The authors and publishers would like to express their sincere thanks to all those who provided visual material, gave us permission to reproduce details or provided information and so contributed to the production of this book. All the drawings and diagrams were specially commissioned. Photographs not specifically acknowledged were supplied by the architects named in the "Index of Names" or from the archives of the journal *DETAIL*. The numbers refer to the figures in part 1 of the book. All the photographs in parts 2-5 were kindly provided by the Institute for Lightweight Structures, Stuttgart University.

From photographers and picture archives
Architekturmuseum, Munich: 1.104
Archiv der Luftschiffbau Zeppelin GmbH: 1.123, 1.124
Art Institute of Chicago, Chicago: 1.139, 1.140
Bartenbach, Peter, Munich: p. 345 right
Bayerische Staatsbibliothek, Munich: 1.36, 1.38, 1.79, 1.80
Bednorz, Achim, Cologne: 1.120
Berengo Gardin, G., Genua: p. 305 bottom right
Betschart, Anton-Peter, Bad Boll: p. 329 bottom left
Bibliothèque Nationale de France, Paris: 1.81
Bingham Hall, Patrick, Sidney: p. 306, 307 centre
Blunck, Reiner, Tübingen: p. 228, 229 right, 248–250, 262, 263
Brohm, Joachim, Essen: 1.146
Bryant, Richard/Arcaid, Kingston on Thames: 1.91, 1.92, p. 308 bottom, 310 top & centre
Busam, Friedrich, Düsseldorf: p. 288
Callahan, Harry, Chicago: 1.197
Charles, Martin, Isleworth: 1.39, 1.40
Chicago Historical Society, Chicago, Taylor, J.W.: 1.138; Collection Hedrich Blessing 1.155
Chicago Sun Times, Chicago: 1.141
Collection Centre Canadien d'Architecture/Canadian Centre for Architecture, Montréal, Fonds Phyllis Lambert: 1.151
Connor, Jay, Santa Monica, California: 1.184
Cook, Peter, London: p. 332 bottom
Couturier, Stéphane/Archipress, Paris: p. 302
Davies, Richard, London: 1.70, p. 333, 335 left, 387 top
Demonfaucon, Christophe, Chateaufort: p. 276
Denancé, Michel/Archipress, Paris: p. 296, 297, 341
Deutsches Museum, Munich: 1.53, 1.106, 1.107, 1.108, 1.127
Dudley-Smith, Richard, London: p. 255 left
Esch, Hans Georg, Cologne: p. 348
Eustache, Franck/Archipress, Paris: p. 303
Fessy, Georges, Paris: p. 274, 275, 277 bottom
Fondation Le Corbusier/VG Bild-Kunst, Bonn: 1.57
Fortin, Philippe, Paris: 1.105
Foster, Norman and Partners, London: 1.64
Foto Marburg, Marburg: 1.145, p. 43
Frahm, Klaus, Hamburg: p. 282 bottom, 283 top & bottom, 350 top, 352, 355
Gartner, Gundelfingen: p. 298, 299
Gericke, Wolf Dieter, Stuttgart: p. 328, 329 right
Gilbert, Dennis, London: p. 254, 255 centre & right, 356, 358
Görner, Reinhard/Contur, Berlin: p. 294
Graefe, Rainer, Innsbruck: 1.84
Grimmenstein, Bernadette, Hamburg: p. 353 right, 354 right
Habermann, Karl J., Munich: 1.41, 1.42, 1.43, 1.47, 1.48, 1.93, 1.152, 1.193, 1.194, 1.195, 1.199, 1.200, p. 9, 20, 29, 37, 63, 241 right, 365, 366 centre & right
Hadden, David: p. 279
Hamilton Knight, Martine, West Bridgford: p. 364, 366 left
Harmer, Paul, London: p. 293
Haut, Wolfgang, Frankfurter Allgemeine Zeitung: 1.22
Hempel, Jörg, Aachen: p. 289
Herzog-Loibl, Verena, Munich: p. 344 centre
Hinrichs, Dieter, Munich: p. 252
Hirayuki, Hirai, Tokyo: p. 265

Holzmann AG, Philipp, Düsseldorf: p. 319 left
Institut für Leichte Flächentragwerke, Stuttgart: 1.60, 1.61
Ishida, Shunji, Genua: p. 359 top left & bottom left
Johnson, Ben, London: p. 372, 373 top & bottom right
Kandzia, Christian, Esslingen: p. 301, 318, 319 centre & bottom
Kenny, Simon, Sydney: p. 307 right
Kinumaki, Yutaka, Osaka: p. 357
Kirkwood, Ken, London: 1.130, p. 310 bottom, 313, 314
Kitajima, Toshihara: p. 359 right
Kolar, Walter, Linz: p. 345 left
Lamb, René, Radolfzell: p. 260, 261
Lambot, Ian, Wiltshire: 332 top, 334 centre, 381–385, 387 bottom
Leistner, Dieter/Architekton, Mainz: p. 342, 343, 380
Lemoine, Bertrand, Paris: 1.96
Lenz, A., Mastrils: p. 347 top right, 347 centre right
Linden, John Edward, Marina del Rey: p. 281 bottom
Meschede, Michael, Kaufungen: p. 349
Minetti, E.: p. 340 top
Neubert, Sigrid, Munich: 1.125, 1.126
Neulinger, Walter, Linz: p. 344 right
Nye, John: p. 386 right
Ortmeyer, Klemens, Dortmund: p. 286 bottom, 287 bottom centre
Ove Arup & Partners, London: 1.72
Photothèque des Musées de la Ville de Paris, Cliché: Ladet: 1.21
Prugger, Max, Munich: 1.69
Reid, Jo & Peck, John, Newport: p. 278, 280, 281 top, 316, 317 top, 360
Rista, Simo, Helsinki: p. 258, 259
Roger-Viollet, Documentation Photographique, Paris: 1.19, 1.35
Ruault, Philippe, Nantes: p. 246, 247 top
Schittich, Christian, Munich: p. 334 left & right, 335 right, 340 bottom, 361 top, 363
Schmidt, Jürgen, Cologne: p. 282 top, 283 centre
Schöner, Jörg, Dresden: p. 320
Schulitz, Helmut C., Braunschweig: 69, 225, 232, 233, 234, 235, 266, 267, 284, 285, 286 top, 287, 325 right, 336, 337, 339, p. 344 bottom left, 353 bottom left, 375, 386 left
Sekiya, Masaaki: p. 378, 379
Shulman, Julius, Los Angeles: 1.183
Siskind, Aaron, Institute of Design Chicago: 1.198
Soar, Timothy, London: p. 292
Springer, Frank, Düsseldorf: p. 236, 237
Skidmore, Owings & Merrill LLP, Chicago:1.132, 1.156
Stadtmuseum, Munich: 1.99; 1.168 (Josef Albert)
Sugden, Derek, Arup Associates, London: 1.23
Suzuki, Hisao, Barcelona: p. 247 bottom
Tuchschmid AG, Frauenfeld: p. 347 bottom left & centre
Urbanietz, Henryk, Aachen: p. 321
Valentin, Christophe, Paris: 1.73
Valentin, Emmanuel, Paris: 1.74
van der Vlugt, Ger, Amsterdam: p. 230
Versnel, Jan & Fridjof, Amsterdam: p. 270 bottom, 271, 272 left
Vincent, B., Genoa: p. 305 bottom left
WESTOK Structural Services Ltd., Wakefield, UK: 1.12
Willebrand, Jens, Cologne: p. 317 left
Wise, Chris, London: p. 373 bottom left
Wortmann, Michael, Hamburg: p. 323, 325

From books and journals
Allgemeine Bauzeitung, 8/1843, plate DXIV: 1.20
Allgemeine Bauzeitung, Vienna 1845, p. 111: 1.2
Allgemeine Bauzeitung, 1856, sht 10: 1.98; sht 9: 1.100
Badger, D. D., Illustrations of Iron Architecture made by the Architectural Iron Works of the City of New York, New York 1865, p. 154: 1.101
Barnes, G. W. and Stevens, Thomas, The History of Clifton Suspension Bridge, 19th Edition 1977, p. 2:1.46
Barthes, Roland, Der Eiffelturm, Munich 1970: 1.114
Bauen in Stahl 2, Schweizer Stahlbauverband, Zürich 1962, p. 310: 1.153
Birkmire, William H., Skeleton Construction in Buildings, 4th Edition, New York/London 1907, p. 184: 1.134; p. 196: 1.135; p. 199: 1.136; p. 202: 1.137

Brandt, E., Lehrbuch Der Eisen-Constructionen, Berlin 1876, p. 389, Fig. 707: 1.78; p. 474, Fig. 951: 1.103
Buch der Erfindungen, Gewerbe und Industrien I, Leipzig 1896, p. 386, plate 296: 1.169, 1.170
Casabella, No. 548, vol. 52, Jul./Aug. 1988, Milan, p. 47: 1.147, 1.148
Crystal Palace Exhibition, Illustrated Catalogue, London 1851, New York 1979, p. 19: 1.167
Dietrich, Richard J., Faszination Brücken, Munich 1998: 1.116
Durm, Jospeh, Handbuch der Architektur, 1905: 1.1
Engineering (May 3, 1889): 1.109, 1.110, 1.111
Gottgetreu, Rudolph, Lehrbuch der Hochbaukonstruktionen, 3. Teil, Eisenkonstruktionen, Berlin 1885, plate I: 1.13; Dachkonstruktionen aus Holz und Eisen: 1.77
Graefe, Rainer et al., V.G. Šuchov 1853–1939, Kunst der Konstruktion, Stuttgart 1990, p. 95, Fig. 178: 1.131; p. 32, Fig. 36: 1.55, Fig. 37: 1.54; p. 33, Fig. 43: 1.56; p. 55, Fig. 93: 1.86
Grube, Oswald W., Industriebauten – international, Stuttgart 1971, p. 90: 1.129; p. 195: 1.190, 1.191, 1.192
Handbuch der Ingenieurswissenschaften in 5 Bänden, vol. 2, Der Brückenbau, pub. by T. Landsberg, Leipzig 1906, section 5, plate V: 1.45; plate IV: 1.51, 1.52
Hauptbahnhofsanlagen in Frankfurt a. M., offprint from Zeitschrift für Bauwesen, Berlin 1892: 1.117, 1.118, 1.119
Jesberg, Paulgerd, Die Geschichte der Ingenieurbaukunst, Stuttgart 1996, p. 130: 1.18, 1.44; p. 200: 1.133
Lemoine, Bertrand, L'Architecture Du Fer, France: XIXe Siècle, Seyssel 1986, p. 33: 1.24; p. 110: 1.113
Lemoine, Bertrand, Gustave Eiffel, Basel/Boston 1988, p. 81: 1.115
Luckenbacher, Roth, Zöllner, Buch der Erfindungen, Gewerbe und Industrien, vol. 4, 7th ed., Leipzig und Berlin 1877: 1.5 , 1.6, 1.7, 1.8, 1.9
McKean, John, Crystal Palace, Joseph Paxton and Charles Fox, Architecture in *DETAIL*, London 1994, p. 52–55: 1.161, 1.162, 1.163, 1.164, 1.165; p. 22: 1.166
Meyer, Alfred Gotthold, Eisenbauten, Ihre Geschichte und Ästhetik, Gebr. Mann Verlag, Berlin 1997, plate XXIII: 1.121
Mittag, Martin, Thyssenhaus, Essen/Detmold 1962, p. 35: 1.154
Modern Steelwork, The British Steelwork Association, 1933, p. 37: 1.157
Nouvelles Annales de la Construction. T 15, 1869, pl. 21: 1.37
Ogg, Alan, Architecture in Steel, The Australian Context, pub. by The Royal Australian Institute of Architects, 1989, p. 60, Fig. 3: 1.94; 1.178
Peters, Tom Frank, Time is Money. Die Entwicklung des modernen Bauwesens, Stuttgart 1981, p. 110: 1.49; p. 107: 1.50
Picton, Antoine, L'Art de l'ingénieur, Editions du Centre Pompidou, Paris 1997, p. 175: 1.95
Prouvé, Jean, Meister der Metallformung. Das Neue Blech 15, Arcus, Cologne 1991, p. 28: 1.176, 1.177
Renaissance der Bahnhöfe, Wiesbaden 1996, p. 266: 1.112
Roisecco, Giulio, l'architettura del ferro, l'inghliterra 1688–1914, Rome 1972, p. 19, Fig. 172: 1.97; p. 118: 1.16; p. 119: 1.17
Schulitz + Partner, Bauten und Projekte, Berlin 1996, p. 24: 1.187
Spiegel, Hans, Der Stahlhausbau, 1 Wohnbauten aus Stahl, Leipzig 1928, p. 93: 1.171; p. 139: 1.172; p. 138: 1.173, 133: 1.174, 1.175
Sugden, Derek, Ein Rückblick über transparentes Bauen in Großbritannien, Düsseldorf 1990: 1.25
Thiersch, Friedrich von, Die Eisenkonstruktion der Ausstellungs- und Festhalle zu Frankfurt am Main, Frankfurt a.M. 1909: 1.142, 1.143, 1.144
Viollet-le-Duc, Eugène-Emmanuel, Lectures on Architecture, London 1877–81, New York 1987, vol. II, p. 63: 1.15
Waite, John G., Iron Architecture in New York City – Two Studies in Industrial Archeology, New York 1972: 1.26, 1.27, 1.28, 1.29, 1.30, 1.31, 1.32, 1.33, 1.34
Wilkinson, Chris, Supersheds, Oxford 1991, p. 48: 1.128